THE DEVELOPMENT OF THE SOVIET BUDGETARY SYSTEM

By R. W. Davies

With a Foreword by
Professor Alexander Baykov

The nature of the Soviet system, and Soviet economic policy in particular, are well known: but within this general framework are the budgetary arrangements efficient, and do they seem appropriate? It is this question which Dr Davies sets himself to answer. He believes that the most useful way to investigate the pattern of Soviet planning is to study its historical development; this book traces the emergence and growth of the budgetary system from the 1917 Revolution to the German invasion of 1941. This was the period of large-scale industrialization, the planning of which naturally occupied an important place in the Soviet budget.

Dr Davies begins with a consideration of the budget under War Communism (1917–20); the next section deals with the Mixed Economy (1921–9); and a careful discussion and analysis of the period of Planned Industrialization (1930–41) follows. In a final chapter, Dr Davies examines the pre-war budgetary system in the light of recent changes; he discusses the extent to which the old system is likely to be continued in the future, and considers how far the investigation is relevant to other societies in which State planning is being introduced.

His book has a particular importance for those concerned with the study of Soviet policy and finance. It will also promote a more general understanding of how the budget can function in a State-controlled economic system, and will therefore interest economists, historians, and students of public affairs.

THE
DEVELOPMENT OF THE
SOVIET BUDGETARY
SYSTEM

THE
DEVELOPMENT OF THE SOVIET BUDGETARY SYSTEM

BY

R. W. DAVIES

*Research Fellow in the Department of Economics
and Institutions of the U.S.S.R.,
Faculty of Commerce and Social Science,
University of Birmingham*

WITH A FOREWORD BY

ALEXANDER BAYKOV

CAMBRIDGE
AT THE UNIVERSITY PRESS
1958

PUBLISHED BY
THE SYNDICS OF THE CAMBRIDGE UNIVERSITY PRESS

Bentley House, 200 Euston Road, London, N.W.1
American Branch: 32 East 57th Street, New York 22, N.Y.

©

CAMBRIDGE UNIVERSITY PRESS
1958

Printed in Great Britain at the University Press, Cambridge
(*Brooke Crutchley, University Printer*)

CONTENTS

Foreword	*page* ix
Preface	xiii
List of Tables	xv
List of Figures	xvii
Explanatory Notes	xviii
Abbreviations	xix
People's Commissars of Finance, 1917–41	xxi

PART I. REVOLUTION AND CIVIL WAR, 1917–20

Chapter I THE BACKGROUND AND THE POLICY 3
    1. The economic and financial background to 1917 3
    2. Finance and the war 7
    3. Provisional government 9
    4. The policy of the Bolsheviks 10

Chapter II FIRST STEPS, OCTOBER 1917–OCTOBER 1918 14

Chapter III TOWARDS A BUDGET IN KIND, 1918–20 26
    1. The decline of the money economy 26
    2. The growth of the scope of the budget 30
        (*a*) Industry and the budget 30
        (*b*) Local finance 33
    3. Control of budget expenditure 35
    4. The moneyless economy and the material budget 38

Part II. The Mixed Economy, 1921–9

Chapter IV THE EMERGENCE OF A NEW BUDGETARY SYSTEM, 1921–4 *page* 49
    1. The New Economic Policy, 1921   49
    2. The inflation of 1921–2   51
    3. The restoration of the budget, 1921–2   54
    4. The abolition of the budget deficit, 1923–24   58
    5. Pre-war features in the N.E.P. system   64
    6. Innovations   67
        (*a*) Budgetary revenue   67
        (*b*) Budgetary expenditure   70
    7. The budget and the economy   70
    8. The system of local budgets   74
    9. The system of republican budgets   78

Chapter V THE BEGINNINGS OF CAPITAL INVESTMENT AND THE PLANNED ECONOMY, 1925–9   85
    1. The decision to industrialise   85
    2. The suppressed inflation of 1925–9   87
    3. The policy of price reduction   93
    4. The policy of industrialisation and the growth of direct planning   94
    5. The beginnings of financial planning   97
    6. The problem of accumulation   100
    7. Internal industrial accumulation   104
    8. The budget and accumulation   106
    9. Budgetary accumulation and the private sector   109
        (*a*) Taxation of the private sector in the towns   109
        (*b*) Taxation of the private sector in the countryside   113
    10. Accumulation from the state sector   117
        (*a*) Deductions from profits, and income tax   119
        (*b*) Promtax   121
        (*c*) Excises   121
    11. State loans   124
    12. Budget expenditure   128

Part III. The Planned Economy, 1930–41

Chapter VI   FINANCIAL PLANNING AND THE BUDGET   *page* 139

    1. Economic planning in the U.S.S.R.   139
    2. Money and direct planning   141
    3. Accumulation and investment   144
    4. Accumulation through profits and the budget   147
    5. The unified financial plan and the budget   152
    6. Refinements of the simplified system   157
        (*a*) Industry   157
        (*b*) Relations with the non-state sector   167
        (*c*) Modifications in the revenue system   174
        (*d*) Balancing the retail market   176
    7. The financial planning system as a whole   177
    8. How financial plans and the budget are compiled   182
    9. The budget and the national economic plan   186
   10. Balancing the budget   191

Chapter VII   THE BREAKDOWN OF THE OLD BUDGETARY SYSTEM, 1928–30   194

    1. Failure of the accumulation plans   194
    2. The system of budgetary revenue   199
    3. Control of expenditure   203

Chapter VIII   THE EMERGENCE OF A NEW BUDGETARY SYSTEM, 1930–4   211

    1. Reform of the revenue system   211
    2. Turnover tax   213
    3. Profits tax (deductions from profits)   220
    4. Taxes on agriculture   222
    5. Other sources of revenue   224
    6. Budgetary expenditure   226
    7. Expenditure on agriculture and transport   239
    8. Other budgetary expenditures   240

Chapter IX IMPROVEMENTS AND MODIFICATIONS IN THE BUDGETARY SYSTEM AFTER THE ABOLITION OF RATIONING, 1935–41 *page* 244

1. The administration of budgetary expenditure after the abolition of rationing   255
   - (*a*) Capital investment   255
   - (*b*) Non-investment allocations to the economy   262
   - (*c*) The financing of institutions maintained by the budget   264
2. The financial control of industry after the abolition of rationing   272
3. Changes in the revenue system after the abolition of rationing   280
   - (*a*) Revenue directly from the population   280
   - (*b*) Method of payment of turnover tax   283
   - (*c*) Rates of turnover tax   284

Chapter X THE SYSTEM OF LOCAL AND REPUBLICAN BUDGETS   297

Chapter XI THE BUDGETARY SYSTEM IN PERSPECTIVE   314

1. The war years, 1941–5   314
2. Post-war changes   316
3. Limitations of the system   322
4. Possible changes in the system   329
   - (*a*) Decentralisation   329
   - (*b*) Innovation and investment at the level of the enterprise   332
   - (*c*) Consumer demand   335
5. The pre-war budgetary system in perspective   337

Bibliography   344

Index   353

FOREWORD

OVER ten years ago, in the preface to my book *The Development of the Soviet Economic System*, I expressed the hope that it would arouse further interest in problems which I had only touched upon, stressing my awareness of the shortcomings of my work, which were partly due to the fact that 'in my approach and method of treatment, "I was thinking alone"'. Since then, several serious studies have been published on different aspects of Soviet economic development and on some aspects of the functioning of the Soviet economic system. A number of major fields of study, however, have not yet been subjected to sufficiently close analysis by scholars. Such has been the case with the role played by finance in the Soviet economic system. Both actual financial developments in the U.S.S.R. and the working principles of the Soviet financial system have so far remained almost untouched as subjects of serious and comprehensive study. The gap has now, to a large extent, been closed in this systematic survey of the subject by Dr Davies.

Despite the fact that he is concerned mainly with the development of the Soviet budgetary system, he has not only studied it in its relations with other aspects of the Soviet financial system, but has analysed it in the light of the application of the general economic policies of the Soviet government to the development of the national economy during the whole past period. He has applied a method of historical approach to his study of the financial system somewhat similar to that which I tried to apply in my very general introductory work to the study of the development of the Soviet economic system as a whole.

This method has enabled him to distinguish to what degree some of the features of the Soviet financial system have been, on the one hand, the products of specifically Russian environment, a heritage having its roots in pre-revolutionary conditions, in the circumstances of the initial stages of building the system during the N.E.P. period, or in particular policies of the Soviet government; or, on the other hand, have been the products of *any* system of *direct* economic planning in which the financial system, as such, plays a part of but secondary importance, that of facilitating the carrying out of the main economic decisions of the government.

In a historically short period, the U.S.S.R. has been converted from a comparatively backward agricultural country into a highly industrial one. It has been possible to achieve this only by the concentration of effort in allocating the material and human resources of the country for carrying out the economic policy pursued by the government. What roles have the budgetary system and the financial system as a whole played in the allocation of resources between competing ends? In an attempt to answer this question, it has been necessary, first of all, to make a detailed study of the actual developments in Soviet finance in the light of the application of economic policies. But, in order to appreciate the functioning of the financial system, to elucidate its working principles, it has been necessary to go further and to try to answer the question not only as to *what* role it has played, but *how* it has played it. How is the accumulation of financial resources for investment carried on in an all-embracing nationalised economy? What kind of problems arise in seeking to promote efficiency in the use of financial resources for capital investment and current production and in controlling their use? What part is finance playing in promoting efficient management, in ensuring technical and economic progress, in costing and pricing, in balancing supply and consumers' demand, in the organisation of collective and individual saving and their application to the productive and cultural activities of society? To what extent have the problems been solved in the Soviet financial system of reconciling the rigidity of centralised planning with the flexibility of administrative decision, of encouraging experimentation, and of ensuring the introduction of useful innovations by executive units?

The value of this work of Dr Davies is that in it he shows that he is constantly aware of these problems. It is for this reason that I consider that this work is of great value, not only to economists who are interested in financial and economic development in the Soviet Union, but to all economists who give some thought to macro-economic problems, to the problems of the functioning of an economic system as a whole.

One of the main economic problems of our time is that of investment, the problem of the efficient allocation of the material and human resources of society as a whole between competing ends. In a capitalist economic system the financial processes play a decisive role in this socially vital function. In the Soviet economic system, finance is subordinate to the direct planning of production and distribution. Despite this subordinate role, however, financial operations are still of paramount importance in determining the success or failure in practice of the plans of economic development drawn up. Dr Davies's work throws much light on Soviet approaches in this field and poses many problems deserving serious examination by economists.

ALEXANDER BAYKOV

UNIVERSITY OF BIRMINGHAM
FEBRUARY, 1956

PREFACE

THIS essay attempts to trace the development of the Soviet budgetary system before the second world war through three main periods—War Communism (1918–20), the Mixed Economy of the New Economic Policy (1921–9), and the Planned Economy (1930–41). In the light of wartime and post-war experience, a final chapter ventures some suggestions on how far the pre-war budgetary system was a purely historical phenomenon resulting from the special conditions of Soviet industrialisation, and how far it is likely to be permanently appropriate to directly planned economies in the U.S.S.R. and elsewhere.

In dealing with so large a theme over so long a period I have necessarily had to concentrate my attention on those aspects of the Soviet budgetary system which appear to be most important for a general assessment of its main characteristics, and which most distinguish it from the systems of other countries. The technical problems of the organisation and administration of the assessment, collection and disbursement of budgetary funds are therefore treated in summary fashion, although reference is made to sources in which these matters may be pursued further. Similarly the annual budget figures and data on their fulfilment are not analysed in detail, but are adduced only to illustrate the main features of the evolution of the system. Particular attention is given to the part played by general economic policy and development in shaping the main features of the budgetary system in each period; but in this treatment the economic policy of the Soviet government is taken as given—no attempt is made at a critique of this policy or at a fresh analysis of the development of the economy; my aim is rather to see how far budgetary policy was appropriate to the general policy of the government. Thus the scope of the argument is restricted.

The present book is a revised version of a Ph.D. thesis presented at the University of Birmingham in 1954, with a final chapter added. I should like to express my gratitude to the Treasury Committee in Foreign Languages and Cultures, which awarded the scholarship that enabled me to pursue studies in this field, and to the Research

Board of the Faculty of Commerce and Social Science of the University of Birmingham, which in the person of its chairman, Professor P. Sargant Florence, acted as sponsors for this studentship.

In both its original and its revised form this study was prepared under the supervision of Professor Alexander Baykov. His continuous training and guidance, and unfailing patience, were the *sine qua non* of my research; and I should like to express my warmest gratitude to him for all his assistance.

I should also like to thank those who gave me assistance and advice during the revision of the original thesis. These include Professor Cairncross, Dr Schlesinger, and Messrs E. H. Carr, M. H. Dobb, A. Mackintosh, J. Miller, and A. Nove, each of whom read part or all of the typescript and made valuable comments and suggestions. Mrs B. M. D. Smith undertook the painstaking work of preparing the index.

R. W. DAVIES

DECEMBER, 1955

TABLES

1.	State budget revenue and expenditure, 1909 and 1913	page 4
2.	Revenue and expenditure of state budget, 1914–17	8
3.	Currency circulation, 1914–17	9
4.	Currency circulation, 1917–18	24
5.	Currency circulation, 1918–21	31
6.	Budgetary revenue as proportion of expenditure, 1918–20	31
7.	Reduction of estimates, 1918–20	37
8.	Revenue of state budget, 1917–21	42
9.	Expenditure of state budget, 1917–21	42
10.	Currency circulation, 1921–4	53
11.	Variations in budget estimates, 1922–4	62
12.	Budgetary revenue and expenditure, 1913 and 1924/5	65
13.	Local budgets, 1921–4	76
14.	Revenue of state budget, 1922/3–1929/30	82
15.	Expenditure of state budget, 1922/3–1929/30	83
16.	A Soviet index of prices, 1924–9	89
17.	Financing of socialised industry, 1924/5–1928/9	103
18.	Reduction of industrial costs, 1923/4–1928/9	105
19.	National income and the budget, 1924/5–1928/9	107
20.	Direct tax on different income levels and groups, 1923–30	112
21.	Agricultural tax by income groups, 1924/5–1929/30	116
22.	Distribution of profits of state industry, 1923–9	120
23.	Revenue from excises, 1913–1927/8	123
24.	State loans and national debt, 1924/5–1928/9	126
25.	Expenditure of overall budget, 1924/5–1928/9	129
26.	The financing of agriculture, 1927/8	135
27.	National economic plan data used in compiling the state budget: example of NK of coal industry, 1941	188
28.	Rates of turnover tax on selected goods, 1930–2	218
29.	Sources of agricultural tax, 1931–5	223
30.	Some changes in price levels, 1928–41	228
31.	Wage fund, 1933–40	249

32.	Expenditure on defence and the NKVD, 1937–41	page 250
33.	Social insurance budget, 1930–41	254
34.	Allocations to foreign affairs as set out in 1917 and 1935 budgets	268
35.	Sources of capital investment, 1932–40	279
36.	Total turnover tax and profits, 1934–41	280
37.	Loans to state, 1931–41	282
38.	Turnover tax rates on selected goods, 1932–41	288
39.	Uses of turnover tax for discrimination	289
40.	Oil products: percentage rates of turnover tax	291
41.	Turnover tax by branches of the economy, 1929/30–41	292
42.	Revenue of state budget in standardised classification, 1928/9–41	295
43.	Expenditure of state budget in standardised classification, 1928/9–41	296
44.	Expenditure of Union, republican and local budgets, 1925/6–41	300
45.	Expenditure of republican budgets, 1925/6–41	301
46.	Local budget expenditure, 1924/5–39	301
47.	Expenditure of all-Union bodies by republics, 1926/7 and 1936	305
48.	Expenditure per head of local and republican budgets, by republics, 1926/7–39	307
49.	Percentage of turnover tax deducted to republics from amount collected on their territory, 1932–40	310
50.	Local revenue, 1924/5–39	312
51.	Profits, turnover tax and price reductions, 1949–55	318
52.	Reduction in industrial costs, 1949–55	319

FIGURES

1. The Soviet system of financial planning: a first approximation
 page 154
2. (*a*) The finances of an industry 166
   (*b*) Sources of the capital investment plan 167
   (*c*) The structure of budget expenditure on the national economy (industry) 168
3. (*a*) Distribution in kind of gross agricultural production of collective farm sector 169
   (*b*) Money income and expenditure of collective farms 170
   (*c*) Income and expenditure of collective farmers 170
   (*d*) Relations of budget with collective farm agriculture 173
4. The adoption of the budget and the national economic plan 183
5. Soviet financial planning *at end*

EXPLANATORY NOTES

(1) Abbreviations are given in full and Russian terms are defined when they first appear, and a list of them is appended.

(2) Sources are given in full when they are first cited; and full titles are given in the Bibliography.

(3) The official collection of laws and decrees published by the R.S.F.S.R. government (*Sobranie uzakonenii i rasporyazhenii*...) is cited as SU (this was the main collection until the formation of the U.S.S.R. government in 1924); and the *Sobranie zakonov i rasporyazhenii*... of the U.S.S.R. government is cited as SZ. In both cases the symbol is followed by number of decree, year of publication, and date of approval of the decree by the government.

The verbatim reports of sessions of TsIK (listed in the Bibliography) are referred to in the text as TsIK, followed by number of session (*sessiya*) in Arabic numerals and number of convocation (*sozyv*) in Roman numerals.

(4) Dates are given Old Style before the calendar reform of February 1918 (i.e. 13 days behind the Western calendar).

ABBREVIATIONS

A.S.S.R. Autonomous Soviet Socialist Republic (*Avtonomnaya sovetskaya sotsialisticheskaya respublika*).
A.U.C.C.T.U. All-Union Central Council of Trade Unions (*Vsesoyuznyi tsentral'nyi sovet professional'nykh soyuzov*).
C.C. Central Committee (*Tsentral'nyi komitet*) of the Communist Party.
Elektrobank (*Bank elektrifikatsii*). Bank for electrification.
E.C. Executive Committee (*Ispolnitel'nyi komitet*).
E.R.T. Extraordinary Revolutionary Tax.
Finotdel (*Finansovyi otdel*). Financial department (of local soviet).
FUBR (*Fond uluchsheniya byta rabochikh i sluzhashchikh*). Fund to improve the welfare of workers and employees (later Director's Fund; now Factory Fund).
glavk (*Glavnoe upravlenie*). Chief administration (of branch of industry—replaced temporarily by combines (*ob"edineniya*), xii. 1929–ix. 1932).
Gosplan (*Gosudarstvennaya planovaya komissiya*). State Planning Commission.
khozraschot (*khozyaistvennyi raschot*). Economic, profit-and-loss or cost accounting.
kolkhoz(-nik) (*kollektivnoe khozyaistvo*). Collective farm(-er).
MTS (*Mashino-traktornaya stantsiya*). Machine-Tractor Station.
N.E.P. New Economic Policy (*Novaya ekonomicheskaya politika*).
N.I. National Income.
NK (*Narodnyi komissar(-iat)*). People's Commissar(-iat).
NKF (*Narodnyi komissar(-iat) finansov*). People's Commissar(-iat) of Finance.
NKPP (*Narodnyi komissariat pishchevoi promyshlennosti*). People's Commissariat of the Food Industry.
NKPS (*Narodnyi komissariat putei soobshcheniya*). People's Commissariat of Transport.
NKPT (*Narodnyi komissariat pochty i telegrafa*). See NK Svyazi.
NK RKI (*Narodnyi komissariat raboche-krest'yanskoi inspektsii*). People's Commissariat of Workers' and Peasants' Inspection.
NK Snab (*Narodnyi komissariat snabzheniya*). People's Commissariat of Supply (Internal Trade), 1930–4.
NK Svyazi (*Narodnyi komissariat svyazi*). People's Commissariat of Posts and Telegraphs, 1932–.
NKVD (*Narodnyi komissariat vnutrennikh del*). People's Commissariat of Internal Affairs.
NKYu (*Narodnyi komissariat yustitsii*). People's Commissariat of Justice.
NKZ (*Narodnyi komissariat zemledeliya*). People's Commissariat of Agriculture.

OGPU (*Obshchegosudarstvennoe politicheskoe upravlenie*). General State Political Administration (=political police).
Prombank (*Bank Finansirovaniya...promyshlennosti i elektrifikatsii*). Bank for financing industry and electrification.
Promtax (*promyslovyi nalog*). Tax on crafts and industry.
RKI. See NK RKI.
RKP(b) (*Rossiiskaya kommunisticheskaya partiya (bol'shevikov)*). Russian Communist Party of Bolsheviks.
R.S.F.S.R. Russian Soviet Federative Socialist Republic (*Rossiiskaya sovetskaya federativnaya sotsialisticheskaya respublika*).
S.F.S.R. Soviet Federative Socialist Republic (*Sovetskaya federativnaya sotsialisticheskaya respublika*).
SNK (*Sovet narodnykh komissarov*). Council of People's Commissars.
S.S.R. (*Sovetskaya sotsialisticheskaya respublika*). Soviet Socialist Republic.
STO (*Sovet truda i oborony*). Council of Labour and Defence (=in practice Economic Council).
TsIK or (before 1923) VTsIK ((*Vserossiiskii) tsentral'nyi ispolnitel'nyi komitet*). (All-Russian) Central Executive Committee (of soviets).
TsSU (*Tsentral'noe statisticheskoe upravlenie*). Central Statistical Administration.
U.S.S.R. Union of Soviet Socialist Republics (*Soyuz sovetskikh sotsialisticheskikh respublik*).
VSNKh or *Vesenkha* (*Vyshii sovet narodnogo khozyaistva*). Supreme Council of National Economy (=in practice a commissariat dealing with industry as a whole, 1917–32).
VTsIK. See TsIK.
VTUZ (*Vysshee tekhnicheskoe uchebnoe zavedenie*). Higher technical education institute.
VUZ (*Vysshee uchebnoe zavedenie*). Higher educational institute.

PEOPLE'S COMMISSARS OF FINANCE 1917–41

October 1917	I. I. SKVORTSOV (STEPANOV)
October 1917–March 1918	V. P. MENZHINSKII
March 1918–August 1918	I. E. GUKOVSKII
August 1918–21	N. KRESTINSKII
1921–6	G. YA. SOKOL'NIKOV
1926–30	L. P. BRYUKHANOV
1930–7	G. F. GRIN'KO
1937	A. CHUBAR'
1937–	A. ZVEREV

PART I
REVOLUTION AND CIVIL WAR
1917–20

CHAPTER I

THE BACKGROUND AND THE POLICY

1. THE ECONOMIC AND FINANCIAL BACKGROUND TO 1917

THE establishment of a modern iron and steel industry in the south in the 1890's and the subsequent expansion of industry in the eve-of-war boom of 1909–13 marked the beginnings of industrialisation in Russia. But in 1914 the economy was still predominantly agrarian at a low technical level. Internal capital accumulation was small; industrial expansion had taken place principally through the investment of foreign capital. By West European and United States standards the economy was backward and unstable. This was reflected in the banking and credit system: efficient joint-stock banks, largely foreign-owned, worked in close association with the State Bank and served the new industries in the main industrial towns, but elsewhere the banking network was sketchy.

The financial policy of the government stood out in contrast to the unevenness and instability of the general economic background. The government strove to maintain Russia as a leading economic and military power. To this end, the currency had been put on a strict gold standard by Witte in 1897, and the budget had on paper been kept in surplus. This apparent surplus was made possible, however, only by large increases in the national debt, which appeared on the revenue side of the budget as 'extraordinary revenue'. By 1913 the debt totalled some 8–9 milliard roubles (over half the national income); a large part of it was held abroad. Repayments on the debt were a major item of budget expenditure by 1913. The attempt to maintain Russian military equality with the economically more advanced western powers meant that very large defence expenditures had to be met by the budget. The active economic policy of the government also involved considerable budgetary expenditures, and the cost of administration, which tended to be archaic and bureaucratic, was high. As a result of all these factors (for details see

Table 1. *State budget revenue and expenditure, 1903 and 1913*

	1903		1913	
	Amount	%	Amount	%

(i) Revenue of pre-war state budget (million roubles)

I. DIRECT TAXES				
Promtax	67·5	3·1	150·1	4·4
Tax on interest on capital	17·7	0·8	35·1	1·0
Miscellaneous [1]	49·8	2·3	87·2	2·5
Total	135·0	6·1	272·4	7·9
II. INDIRECT TAXES				
Sugar	75·5	3·4	149·1	4·3
Tobacco, cigarette tubes and paper	49·0	2·2	83·5	2·4
Oil	31·9	1·4	48·5	1·4
Matches	8·0	0·4	20·0	0·6
State alcohol monopoly [2]	371·6	16·9	664·3	19·4
Alcoholic drinks	34·1	1·5	53·7	1·6
Customs	241·4	11·0	352·9	10·3
Total	811·5	36·8	1,372·0	40·0
III. DUES (*poshliny*) [3]	106·0	4·8	231·0	6·7
Total from state taxes	1,052·5	47·8	1,875·4	54·7
IV. GOVERNMENT REGALIA AND OTHER INCOMES				
Gross revenue of posts and telegraphs	58·0	2·6	120·0	3·5
Gross revenue of railways	455·6 [4]	20·7	840·1 [5]	24·5
Spirits' monopoly self-balancing revenue	170·6	7·7	234·9	6·8
Forests	62·0	2·8	92·3	2·7
State factories	11·3	0·5	26·0	0·8
Other [6]	30·9	1·4	49·2	1·4
Total	788·4	35·8	1,362·4	39·7
V. OTHER [7]	190·9	8·7	179·6	5·2
Extraordinary revenue	170·9	7·8	13·8	0·4
Total revenue	2,202·7	100·0	3,431·2	100·0

(ii) Expenditure of pre-war state budget (million roubles)

I. ECONOMIC BODIES				
Ministry of Trade and Industry	40·2	1·9	64·5	1·9
Ministry of Transport [8]	32·9	1·6	53·8	1·6
Department of agriculture and land settlement	31·5	1·5	135·8	4·0
Department of state horse breeding	2·1	0·1	3·3	0·1
Total economic bodies	106·7	5·1	257·4	7·6
II. GROSS EXPENDITURE OF SELF-SUPPORTING ECONOMIC BODIES				
Railways [9]	416·3	19·8	586·8	17·4
Departments of posts and telegraphs	39·1	1·9	80·2	2·4
Spirit monopoly	170·6	8·1	234·9	6·9
Total self-supporting bodies	626·0	29·7	901·9	26·7

4

Table 1 (continued)

		1903 Amount	1903 %	1913 Amount	1913 %
III.	MINISTRY OF EDUCATION	39·4	1·9	143·0	4·2
IV.	DEFENCE BODIES				
	Ministry of War	352·4	16·7	581·1	17·2
	Ministry of Navy	113·9	5·4	244·8	7·2
	Total defence bodies [10]	466·3	22·1	825·9	24·4
V.	ADMINISTRATIVE BODIES				
	Ministry of Imperial Court	15·9	0·8	17·3	0·5
	Supreme Imperial Assemblies [11]	3·7	0·2	9·4	0·3
	Ministry of Internal Affairs [12]	61·0	2·9	105·1	3·1
	Ministry of Finance [13]	183·2	8·7	247·2	7·3
	Ministry of Justice	49·1	2·3	92·6	2·7
	Ministry of Foreign Affairs	6·1	0·3	11·5	0·3
	State Control	8·4	0·4	12·1	0·4
	Total administrative bodies	327·4	15·5	495·2	14·6
VI.	NATIONAL DEBT	288·7	13·7	424·3	12·5
VII.	OTHER EXPENDITURE [14]	28·5	1·4	45·6	1·3
	Extraordinary expenditure [15]	224·8	10·7	288·7	8·5
	Total expenditure	2,107·8	100·0	3,382·0	100·0

Sources: *Russian finance during the war* (1928); *Règlement définitif du budget de l'Empire pour l'exercice 1903* (1904); *Proekt gosudarstvennoi rospisi dokhodov i raskhodov na 1917 god...* (1916).

Notes:
(1) Includes land tax, tax on urban property, and tax on dwelling houses.
(2) Net *gain* only. Revenue which was used to cover expenditure on the alcohol monopoly system is included in section IV.
(3) Includes stamp tax, and taxes on registration of deeds, on free transfers of property, and on transport of passengers and goods.
(4) Includes 2·3 million roubles from participation in private railways.
(5) Includes 26·5 million roubles from participation in private railways.
(6) Includes revenue from mines, coinage, land and leases, and sale of state property.
(7) Includes state funds and funds from State Bank; and repayment of advances from treasury.
(8) Excludes operational expenditure on railways.
(9) Excludes construction and improvement of railways, which appears under extraordinary expenditure (133·3 million roubles in 1913).
(10) Excludes expenditure by military department for economic and strategic purposes (127·3 million roubles in 1913), which appears under extraordinary expenditure.
(11) State Council, Council of Ministers, Senate, and (in 1913) State Duma.
(12) Excluding posts and telegraphs.
(13) Excluding expenditure on alcohol monopoly.
(14) Includes Holy Synod, 28·5 million roubles in 1903 and 45·6 million in 1913.
(15) Mainly items referred to in notes (9) and (10) above.

Table 1 (ii)) the percentage of the national income passing through the budget was very high for that period, particularly for a backward country with a population mainly engaged in subsistence farming.[1]

This expenditure was financed mainly from revenue raised from the lower income groups. There was no tax on personal incomes, and the rates of tax on the rent received by landowners were not high. Taxes on business were also relatively small: the most important was the tax on industry, crafts and trade (*promyslovyi nalog*—referred to here as the Promtax), which was imposed in two parts, a graded licence-fee (*patentnyi sbor*) and a progressive tax on profits (*uravnitel'nyi sbor* or 'equalising levy'). The principal sources of budgetary revenue, as is shown in Table 1 (i), were excises and other forms of indirect taxation, mainly imposed on consumer goods, principally alcohol, sugar, kerosene, and tobacco. These excises were mainly of long standing, and had been increased to their current importance in the budget when the old direct 'soul tax' (*podushnaya podat'*) on the peasantry had been abolished in the 1880's. The remaining revenue came from various incomes from state property and other dues which are of purely historical interest.

The state budgetary system had been modernised by the financial reforms of the 1860's, associated with Tatarinov.[2] From 1863 the Ministry of Finance was given unified control of all state revenue and expenditure—all revenues had to be deposited in the pay-offices (*kassy*) of the ministry and all allocations paid from them. The budget was published for the first time and was made subject to documentary audit by the State Control Department. Forty years later, after the constitutional changes of 1905–6, the State Duma was given the right to debate and vote the budget.

However, in spite of the progress that had been made towards a modern budget subject to parliamentary control, the system remained backward in several important respects. Ultimate budgetary powers remained with the tsar, and some items of expenditure in any case were the imperial prerogative, and not subject to audit by the State Control Department. The work of the Control Department was

---

[1] According to S. N. Prokopovich (ed.), *Opyt ischisleniya narodnogo dokhoda 50 gubernii Evropeiskoi Rossii v 1900–1913gg.* (1918), p. 66, the total net national income was 16·4 milliard roubles in 1913. The net revenue of the state budget, excluding those items which were included in the budget in gross form (railways, posts and telegraphs, etc.), was about 2,500 million roubles, or 15% of national income; and of the local budgets, about 400 million roubles, or 2½% of national income.

[2] For an account of Tatarinov's reforms see *Voprosy istorii*, no. 10 (1951).

largely formal and in need of radical reform. The Ministry of Finance was bureaucratic and not very efficient, particularly in its methods of tax collection. The classification used in the budget estimates was out-of-date and confused.

Local budgets, which were largely independent of the state budget, had grown rapidly since the reforms of the 1860's, and were responsible for most education and health expenditure.[1] This expansion had mainly taken place at town and provincial (*gubernia*) level. Village and *volost'* (see p. 77, text and n. 7) financial powers were limited and the budgets were small. Local finance in the Transcaucasus and Central Asia was controlled by governors who were appointed centrally, and little effort was made through the financial system to encourage or subsidise the development of backward regions.[2]

2. FINANCE AND THE WAR

The economy proved unequal to the strain of war against a great industrial power. After an initial boom in 1914–15, a food, fuel, and transport crisis developed rapidly during 1916, and by the beginning of 1917 the economy appeared to be on the verge of collapse.[3] The relative financial stability of the pre-war period was replaced by inflation, instability, and speculation.[4]

Normal methods of raising revenue proved incapable of meeting the state expenditures entailed by the war. Excises on most goods were increased, but the introduction of prohibition at the outbreak of war resulted in a net fall in revenue from indirect taxation. The rates of Promtax were raised drastically (so that the yield from the tax trebled), and an excess profits tax was imposed. A progressive tax on personal incomes was introduced for the first time in 1916, rising to a maximum rate of 12·5%. A war tax was imposed on persons exempt from military service.[5]

But these increases in taxation were barely sufficient to cover increases in *civilian* expenditure in 1915, and provided a surplus on

---

[1] For material on local budgets in 1913 see *Vestnik finansov*, no. 12 (1924), pp. 188–90.
[2] See bibliography for detailed material on the budgetary system before 1917.
[3] See Belevsky and Voronoff, *Les organisations publiques russes et leur rôle pendant la guerre* (1917), pp. 36–260, 333; Gorky, Molotov *et al.*, *The History of the Civil War*, vol. 1 (1936), pp. 27–41; S. N. Prokopovich, *Voina i narodnoe khozyaistvo* (1918).
[4] Gindin, *Russkie kommercheskie banki* (1948), pp. 219–27.
[5] For details of all these taxes, see A. M. Michelson in *Russian Finance during the War* (1928); D. Bogolepov, *Voina i finansy* (1917), p. 15; Sokol'nikov *et al.*, *Finansovaya entsiklopedia*, cols. 264, 272–3, 844; *Rospis' obshchegosudarstvennykh dokhodov i raskhodov rossiiskoi sotsialisticheskoi federativnoi respubliki na vii.–xii. 1918 s ob"yasnitel'noi zapiskoi NKF.*

the ordinary account equal to only one-fifteenth of military expenditure on the 'extraordinary [war] account' in 1916. As Tables 2 and 3 show, the tremendous growth in military expenditure had to be met by internal and foreign loans, and by currency issue. By January 1917 the state debt (including short-term issues) had grown to over 30 milliard roubles, and currency in circulation had increased six-fold as compared with the outbreak of war.

Table 2. *Revenue and expenditure of state budget, 1914–17 (million roubles)*

	1914[a]	1915[b]	1916[c]	1917[c]
TOTAL REVENUE	4,556	11,195[1]	17,794·6	22,164·7
Of which				
Ordinary revenue	2,898	2,835	3,978·5	4,678·5
Extraordinary revenue	8	127	326·8	320·
Remains of previous estimates	55	39	40·	40·
Total 'normal' revenue	2,961	3,001	4,345·3	5,038·5
Internal loans	708	2,879	4,173·9	3,729·0
External loans	82	2,140	3,664·8	2,553·5
Short-term issues in Russia	805	3,176	5,610·6	10,843·7
Total 'war' revenue	1,595	8,195	13,449·3	17,126·2
TOTAL EXPENDITURE	4,859	11,562[1]	18,100·5	30,606·6[2]
Of which				
Total 'normal' expenditure[3]	3,204	2,839	3,151·7	4,445·9
Extraordinary war expenditure	1,655	8,621	14,572·8	25,560·7
Interest on short-term issues	—	103	376·0	600·0
Total 'war' expenditure	1,655	8,724	14,948·8	26,160·7

Sources:
(a) *Rospis'...na vii.–xii. 1918...* (1919), p. 12.
(b) *Rospis'...na i.–vi. 1919...* (1919), p. 3.
Both the above taken from the State Control accounts.
(c) *Ibid.* p. 7.
Both these years from preliminary data of the NKF.

Notes:
(1) Excludes 4,550·2 million roubles 'turnover' revenue and expenditure on short-term issues, of a purely book-keeping character.
(2) Includes 3000 million roubles war credits transferred to 1918 estimates.
(3) This includes both 'ordinary' expenditure and 'extraordinary' expenditure not for war purposes.

In 1914 all military expenditure had been transferred to an 'extraordinary budget', financed from a war fund exempt from Duma control. Criticism of the use of this fund was widespread, and in June 1916 the Duma passed a resolution complaining of extravagance in expenditure. This was a reflexion of the mounting dissatisfaction of business and liberal circles with the way in which the government and the court were managing the war and the economy.

The military situation and the growing chaos throughout the country finally led to the overthrow of the tsarist government in February 1917, and its replacement by a provisional government, supported both by industrial and commercial interests and by the St Petersburg Soviet, the newly formed council of representatives of the revolutionary sections of the population, which was under Menshevik leadership.

Table 3. *Currency circulation, 1914–17*

Date	Notes in circulation (million roubles)	Commodity prices (1. vii. 1914 = 100)
1. vii. 1914	1,530	100
1. i. 1915	2,946	115
1. i. 1916	5,617	238
1. i. 1917	9,103	702
1. iii. 1917	10,044	—
1. x. 1917	17,175	1,171

Sources: P. I. Lyaschenko, *Istoriya narodnogo khozyaistva SSSR*, vol. II (1952), p. 648, except 1. iii. 1917, which is from L. N. Yurovskii, *Denezhnaya politika sovetskoi vlasti, 1917–1927* (1928), pp. 16, 27.

3. PROVISIONAL GOVERNMENT

Serious attempts were made to overcome the economic crisis between March and October 1917, but as a result of the continuation of the war the situation progressively worsened. The political developments which took place against this background and culminated in the seizure of power by the Bolsheviks in October need not be described here.

The provisional government drastically increased direct taxation.[1] The maximum rate of income tax was raised to 30·5%,[2] an extraordinary levy on large incomes was introduced, and excess profits tax was raised from 50 to 90%. The government raised 4 milliard roubles by means of a 'liberty loan' (*zaem svobody*), but Haensel and Tugan-Baranovskii's proposals for a compulsory loan of 10 milliard roubles[3] were not put into effect, and no substantial loans were raised from the allies. The government prepared measures to increase indirect taxes, but here it met with the opposition of the left-wing

[1] For details see Michelson, *op. cit.*
[2] This tax was not, however, actually imposed in 1917.
[3] Put forward in *Vestnik finansov*, nos. 16 and 17 (1917). See also Gorky *et al.* (eds.), *The History of the Civil War in the U.S.S.R.* vol. I, p. 370.

parties, who considered that direct taxation should be further increased.

Even if all these measures had been put into effect, they would have been inadequate to cover the mounting war costs, and in fact over 60% of the military expenditure incurred in 1917 had to be met by currency issue. Total currency in circulation increased by 70% between March and October, so that it reached over ten times the pre-war level (see Table 3). It proved impossible to draw up a satisfactory budget for 1917, and expenditure was carried through on the basis of the 1916 estimates supplemented by extraordinary allocations.

When they assumed power in October 1917 the Bolsheviks were faced with acute economic crisis and severe inflation. They took over a budgetary system which had been modified considerably since 1914 by the introduction of new taxes, but which had failed to raise the revenue required for the conduct of the war, and was in consequence disorganised and ineffective.

4. THE POLICY OF THE BOLSHEVIKS

Marx and Engels had made few specific statements about socialist society which could provide guidance for the Bolsheviks in drawing up their economic policy. In their general comments on the nature of the socialist economy which would replace capitalism, made at various times between 1848 and 1890, Marx and Engels had confined themselves to saying that the 'means of production' would be centralised in the hands of the proletarian state, and that a system of planned economy would be needed to regulate the expansion of production by 'direct and conscious control', rather than by 'the movement of commodity prices', the regulating mechanism in capitalist society. Distribution of the social product in 'the higher phase of Communism' would take place 'according to needs', but society would have to pass through an intermediate socialist stage of distribution 'according to work done'.[1]

Marx and Engels assumed that in socialist and communist society commodity circulation, and money, the medium for this circulation, would no longer exist. There would perhaps be 'paper cheques'

---

[1] See Marx, *Capital*, Kerr edn. vol. II (1933), pp. 361–2; *Critique of the Gotha Programme* (London, 1933), pp. 27–8, 30–1; Marx and Engels, *Selected Correspondence* (1941), p. 232; *Communist Manifesto* (1948, London edn.), p. 19. On this whole question, see especially E. H. Carr, *The Bolshevik Revolution, 1917–1923*, vol. II (1952), pp. 3–27, 385–93.

indicating work done, and the 'keeping of accounts' in connexion with planning, but these cheques would not be money, for they would not circulate.[1]

However, Marx and Engels did envisage a transitional stage after the seizure of political power by the proletariat, in which the economic power of the bourgeoisie had not been destroyed. In this stage, the money system would be used to bring about 'despotic inroads on the rights of property' by measures different in different countries, but including, at least in the most advanced countries, 'a heavy progressive or graduated income tax'[2] and the 'centralisation of credit in the hands of the State by means of a national bank with State capital and an exclusive monopoly'.[3]

Like Marx and Engels, the Bolsheviks did not attempt to work out their economic policy in detail before their assumption of power. Instead, they treated 'every point in the economic platform' as 'a *fighting* slogan...to rally the masses'.[4]

Nevertheless, Lenin had already recognised by 1917 that Russia was in a different position from the industrialised countries which Marx had had in mind, and the economic programme adopted at the Sixth Congress of the Bolshevik party in July 1917, three months before the October revolution, envisaged that progress towards a socialist economy would be slow and cautious in Russia. In the initial stages, the war would be ended, certain large syndicates would be nationalised, 'workers' control' would be established in industry as a whole, and 'planned control of production and distribution' would be introduced; but most of industry would remain in private hands.

Thus Bolshevik statements about financial policy in 1917 should be seen in the light both of their function of political agitation against the provisional government and of the Bolshevik intention to make gradual progress towards a socialist economy after the seizure of power. Before the war Lenin had uncompromisingly criticised the

[1] Arnold, in *Banks, credit and money in Soviet Russia*, pp. 102–3, is ambiguous on the subject of Marx's views on money under socialism, but Marx himself was unambiguous. See *Capital*, Everyman edn. I, p. 70, Kerr edn. II, p. 412, III, p. 992, and the comments on Marx's views on money in K. Ostrovityanov, *Voprosy ekonomiki*, no. 1 (1948), pp. 31–2, and Z. Atlas, *Problemy ekonomiki*, no. 4 (1939), pp. 87, 88.

[2] Such a tax became the central financial demand of the European socialist movement. Thus it was included in the original programme of the Socialist Workers' Party of Germany (which Marx on other points strongly criticised) for achievement even 'within the limits of existing society...in place of all existing and particularly indirect taxes' (*Critique of the Gotha Programme*, p. 118).

[3] *Communist Manifesto*, p. 19.   [4] *Hist. Civil War*, vol. I, p. 401.

tsarist financial and budgetary system,[1] and the Bolsheviks adopted the same attitude to the attempts of the provisional government to get out of its financial difficulties, holding that without the ending of the war and the taking over of power by the proletariat, the financial problem could not be solved.[2] The Bolsheviks also made definite though not very detailed statements about the financial measures they would adopt after assuming power. At their Seventh Conference in April 1917 a resolution was carried stating that while 'the immediate achievement of socialist reform' was impossible, certain steps towards it could be taken, including

the establishment of state supervision of all banks, unifying them into a single central bank...with a gradual transition to a juster, progressive taxation of revenue and properties.[3]

In the economic resolution of the Sixth Congress in July, the situation of state finance was characterised as 'close to a final crash'. The resolution demanded not merely supervision and unification of the banks, but their 'nationalisation and centralisation'[4], and put forward proposals for tackling the immediate situation in these terms:

In order to struggle against financial disaster, the following measures are essential: immediate cessation of the further issue of paper money;

[1] In pre-war articles he used the annual budget statements to criticise tsarist financial policy as a whole (Lenin, *Sochineniya*, 4th edn. vol. v, pp. 304–9; vol. xviii, pp. 563–4) and attacked the structure of the budgetary system as a reflexion of the tsarist state (*ibid.* vol. xiii, pp. 311–13, 397–402). He also discussed the tactics to be pursued by Social-Democratic members of the Duma in budget debates, holding that only in very exceptional circumstances should they vote for an item of the budget (*ibid.* vol. xii, pp. 270–9; vol. xiii, pp. 397–403; vol. xv, pp. 298–9).

[2] Before Lenin's return, the Bolshevik press in Petrograd put forward drastic proposals for raising state revenue, including the use for the war of all the income received by the landowners and capitalists in 1916 (*Pravda*, no. 4, 9. iii. 1917) and drastic inroads into imperial property and the salaries of high officials (*Pravda*, no. 7, 12. iii. 1917). In the spring and early summer, contributors to *Pravda* condemned the use of paper money, the Liberty Loan, and indirect taxes, and declared that they should be replaced by a direct tax on the wealthy. They also demanded the stabilisation of prices except on luxury goods, and close supervision of the banks and the postal and telegraph services to prevent transfers of money (particularly abroad). See *Pravda*, 1917, nos. 22, 24, 27, 29, 31, 32, 41, 55, 75; *Izvestia*, no. 48, 1917.

[3] 24–29. iv (7–12. v) 1917, in *VKP(b) v rezolyutsiakh*, 6th. edn. vol. ii (1940), pp. 236–7 (Resolution 'On the present moment').

[4] 'Without big banks,' wrote Lenin in October 1917 (before the revolution), 'socialism could not be achieved. The big banks *are* the "state machinery" we *must have* to achieve socialism, and which *we shall take ready-made* from capitalism; our problem here is only to *lop away* the features which *distort* this excellent machinery in a capitalist direction, and to make it *still larger*, more democratic, and comprehensive. Quantity is transformed into quality. A single state bank, the largest of the large, with branches in every parish and factory, will be nine-tenths of our *socialist* apparatus' (*Soch.* vol. xxvi, p. 82).

refusal to pay both internal and foreign state debts (safeguarding, however, the interests of the small subscribers); the reform of the whole tax system by introducing a property tax, a tax on the increase in the value of property, and a high indirect tax on luxury goods; reform of the income tax, placing the assessment of income under real supervision in both the centre and the localities.[1]

Thus, by the eve of the October revolution the Bolsheviks were pledged to centralisation of the banks, the progressive income tax of the Communist Manifesto, a series of additional measures for taxing the rich, and the stabilisation of the currency.[2] But they went no farther than this. They had no explicit plans for the conduct of the Ministry of Finance after the seizure of power, and there was little discussion of the forms and methods by which the financial transition to a socialist economy should take place, or of the function of finance in a socialist economy. Marx's view that in a planned socialist economy money would no longer exist remained unchallenged, but it was expected that in the immediate future the currency would be stabilised and the credit and financial system centralised and used as a weapon against the property-owning classes.

[1] *Ibid.* pp. 256 ff. for the resolution, and pp. 265–8 for the manifesto issued by the Congress, 26. vii–3. viii (8. viii–16. viii), 1917.

[2] In September, Lenin laid stress on these points, declaring that 'the issue of paper money is the worst form of compulsory loan', and added the point that an adequate system of supervision was needed in order to put the proposed income tax measures into effect, including the enforcing of the use of cheques for deals between capitalists and the abolition of commercial secrecy, with the penalty of confiscation of property for concealing income (*Soch.* vol. xxv, pp. 327–31).

CHAPTER II

FIRST STEPS
OCTOBER 1917–OCTOBER 1918

FROM the point of view of the development of the Russian economy as a whole, the first twelve months after the October revolution fall into two distinct phases. October 1917 to March 1918 was a period of precipitate change, in which the new government eagerly sought to transfer the key positions in the economy into its own hands in accordance with its 1917 programme. The machinery of government was seized. Land was nationalised and the redistribution begun by the peasants before October was extended, with government support. The state attempted to regulate industry, and to this end instituted workers' control. The power of the local soviets, which took independent measures against the propertied classes, was rapidly extended throughout the country.

The breathing-space provided by the signing of the Brest-Litovsk treaty with Germany in March 1918 was used by Lenin to launch his programme of consolidation. The key tasks, as he saw them, were to establish 'all-embracing accounting and supervision of production and distribution', to raise labour productivity, and to organise the 'regular daily work of administration.'[1]

But while Lenin's April pamphlet outlined a new phase in Bolshevik economic policy, it was not really followed by a new phase of economic organisation. Its impact had scarcely been felt when the first shots of the civil war were fired. The summer of 1918 was not the 'period of slow construction' of a new economic system which Lenin had intended it to be, but the first stage of the emergency developments of war communism. By autumn 1918 a food dictatorship had been set up, all large-scale industry had been nationalised, and a decree had enacted the general compulsion of all to work.

Financial policy closely followed the main lines of economic policy in the first months after the seizure of power. But except in the case

[1] *Soch.* vol. XXVII, pp. 207–85.

of local finance, no major step towards the centralisation and emergency measures characteristic of the civil war period was taken until the end of October 1918, when the Extraordinary Revolutionary Tax was introduced, and our account in this chapter is taken to the end of October 1918 for this reason. This first year of revolution was by and large a period not of building new financial institutions, but of attempting to use the existing ones to hold back financial chaos.

In the first six months after October 1917 a series of measures was adopted to put the commanding financial positions into the hands of the new government:

(i) The Ministry of Finance was taken over and put in charge of a People's Commissar who was a member of the Council of People's Commissars (SNK).[1]

(ii) The State Bank was taken over by the government, and the main private banks were nationalised, after attempts to supervise the existing banking system had met with the opposition of the old management. All banks were gradually fused into the State Bank, later renamed the 'People's Bank'.[2]

(iii) The government renounced the national debt, reimbursing only holdings of less than 10,000 roubles.[3]

(iv) Shares were brought under close government control.[4]

[1] SU 1/1917 (28. x. 17). The first commissar was I. I. Skvortsov (Stepanov), but he was replaced by Menzhinskii after two days (*Hist. Civil War*, vol. II, 1946, p. 588). Some idea of the atmosphere of the time is conveyed by the story told about Menzhinskii's appointment by V. D. Bonch-Bruevich, then secretary of SNK. The new commissar was so fatigued with overwork that when he heard of his appointment, he scrawled 'Commissar of Finance' on a sheet of paper, and pinned it above a sofa on which he immediately went to sleep, snoring peacefully (*Molodoi kommunist*, no. 4 (1955), pp. 30–1).

[2] For material on bank nationalisation, see SU 56/1917 (25.xi. 17), 150/1917, 237/1919; *Sbornik dekretov i postanovlenii po narodnomu khozyaistvu, 25. x. 1917–25. x. 1918* (1918), 708; *Sbornik dekretov o finansakh 1917–20* (1920), no. 124–5; *Sbornik dekretov 1917–18* (pub. NKYu, 1920), no. 168; *Protokoly zasedanii VTsIKa...II sozyva*, pp. 148 ff.; *Pravda*, nos. 189, 195, 201 (1917); *Ekonomicheskaya zhizn'*, nos. 1, 6–11, 19, 21–2 (1918); Lenin, *Soch.* vol. XXVII, pp. 195–6; V. P. D'yachenko, *Sovetskie finansy v pervoi faze razvitiya sotsialisticheskogo gosudarstva*, part 1, 1917–1925 (1947), pp. 58 ff.; Z. V. Atlas and E. Ya. Bregel', *Denezhnoe obrashchenie i kredit SSSR* (1947), p. 120. Accounts of the course of nationalisation will be found in A. Baykov, *The Development of the Soviet Economic System* (1947), pp. 32–5; E. H. Carr, *The Bolshevik Revolution 1917–1923*, vol. II (1952), pp. 132–8; M. S. Atlas, *Natsionalizatsiya bankov v SSSR* (1948); and G. Sokol'nikov, *K voprosu o natsionalizatsii bankov* (1918).

[3] For details, see *Sbornik dekretov 1917–18*, 138 (26. x. 18); SU 353/1917–18, 386/1917–18 (7.iii. 18), 487/1919 (9.x. 19). For the size of the national debt in 1917, see L. N. Yurovskii, *Denezhnaya politika sovetskoi vlasti 1917–1927* (1928), p. 16; V. P. D'yachenko and G. A. Kozlov (eds.), *Finansy i kredit SSSR* (1938), p. 69. For the reimbursement of small-holdings, see D'yachenko, *op. cit.* pp. 65–8.

[4] *Sbornik...po nar. khoz.* 702 (29. xii. 17); SU 696/1917–18 (18. iv. 18).

(v) Withdrawals of deposits placed in current accounts before 1918 were restricted, and the government took powers to open private safes.[1]

(vi) Trade in gold and platinum was made a state monopoly.[2]

With the aid of this financial machinery, the Soviet government strove to bring state finance into order. It recognised from the outset the need to reduce currency issue and bring the state budget into balance. In January 1918 Lenin drew attention to the large potential deficit, and declared:

> Of course in this state of affairs you and I [he was speaking to a meeting of agitators] will fail, if we are not able to drag out this cart of state from the marsh in which the tsarist government has submerged it.[3]

But in these first six months little was done to solve the problem of inflation. There were few Bolsheviks who had any knowledge or experience of financial matters; counsels were more divided and leadership was weaker than in other spheres of policy.[4] The government consolidated the fiscal machinery in its hands only gradually—in the first weeks after the revolution it was able to obtain even limited sums only by threatening force against the officials of the State Bank and treasury.[5] The central treasury, which had refused to carry out the instructions of the government, was replaced by a new expenditure office,[6] which issued allocations by a rough system of priorities on the basis of existing estimates, supplementary grants for special purposes being made by decree.[7] In addition, loans and grants were made to nationalised enterprises via the State Bank and the war fund.[8] To control this emergency system of allocation, a

[1] D'yachenko and Kozlov, *op. cit.* p. 67; SU 151/1917 (14. xii. 17).

[2] SU 232/1917–18 (12. i. 18); 376/1917–18 (22. ii. 18).

[3] *Soch.* vol. XXVI, p. 469.

[4] Gukovskii, who replaced Menzhinskii as NKF in March 1918, stated 'I cannot envisage clearly how I can lead the department which has been handed to me', and declared that the Central Executive Committee of Soviets (VTsIK) should decide whether there was room for him in a socialist cabinet. At the first Congress of Councils of National Economy, Sokol'nikov gave an apparently official report on finance, but Gukovskii declared: 'I don't know in whose name cde. Sokol'nikov made his statements, personally or from some organisation, but my policy is somewhat different' (*Protokoly VTsIKa 4-go sozyva* (1918), pp. 112–17, 149–51; *Trudy vserossiiskogo s"ezda sovetov narodnogo khozyaistva 25. v–4. vi. 1918: stenograficheskii otchot* (1918), pp. 116 ff.).

[5] D'yachenko, *op. cit.* pp. 49–50.

[6] *Ibid.* p. 78. I have been unable to find out when this change became effective.

[7] *Ibid.* p. 51. For special allocations (for such purposes as teachers' bonuses, miners' wages, timber procurement, and organising the Red Army) see SU 60/1917 (24. xi. 17), 112/1917 (13. xii. 17), 141/1917 (15. xii. 17), 159/1917 (9–12. xii. 17), 161/1917 (20. xii. 17), 168/1917 (18. xii. 17), 194/1917–18 (2. i. 18), 247/1917–18 (16. i. 18), 345/1917–18 (19. ii. 18).

[8] SU 167/1917 (20. xii. 17), 332/1917–18 (16. ii. 18).

Special Committee for the Reduction of State Expenditure was established under the Supreme Council of National Economy (VSNKh), and was instructed to examine all estimates before allocations were made.[1] These institutions did not work very effectively. While allocations continued to be made to inoperative bodies surviving from the old regime, there was in general a chronic shortage of resources even for the most elementary needs.[2]

Allocations had to be made almost entirely by new currency issue. In the first six months after the revolution the central government confined itself on the revenue side of the budget to an attempt to collect existing taxes at the established rates. To do this it sought the assistance of the newly-formed local soviets, who were instructed to supervise the imposition of taxes by putting commissars in the local treasury chambers and using the Red Guard and the militia to enforce payment.[3] But in fact little revenue was raised through taxation, and the local soviets tended to retain the small amounts which were collected.[4]

Of much greater importance in the first six months were the taxes and contributions raised by the local soviets for their own use. The centre, unable to meet local requirements by grants, gave the local soviets *carte blanche* to introduce local taxes.[5] This policy relieved the

[1] SU 349/1917–18 (20. ii. 18).

[2] Thus it was complained that the Commissariat of Education received less from the budget than had been received under the tsar; that delegations 'stood whole weeks and months in the hallways' and 'went from one institution to another, and in the end could not receive the necessary resources'; and that regions received only a fraction of the allocations they required, while there had been no reduction in the number of persons engaged in unproductive work, and employees of defunct and superfluous institutions continued to receive their salaries (*Protokoly VTsIKa 4-go sozyva*, pp. 93, 112 ff.; and *Trudy*... (1918), speeches by Sokol'nikov, Syromolotov, and Ryazanov).

[3] SU 71/1917 (24. xi. 17), 205/1917–18; and see Lenin, *Soch.* vol. XXVI, p. 266. The local soviet could impose a fine up to the confiscation of the entire property of the taxpayer, and deliberate evasion could be punished with imprisonment for up to five years. The only tax increase in this period was in the tax on tobacco, as already envisaged by the provisional government; postal charges were also raised (SU 169/1917 (24. xi. 17), 199/1917–18 (9. i. 18), 320/1917–18 (26. i. 18), 390/1917–18 (6. iii. 18); *Rospis' obshchegosudarstvennykh dokhodov RSFSR na i.–vi. 1919 s ob"yasnitel'noi zapiskoi NKF* (1919), p. 78).

[4] D'yachenko, *op. cit.* p. 78.

[5] Local soviets, stated SNK, 'as the power in the localities, also have tax rights, as a result of which all appeals for subsidies to the central state power will not be met if they are not supported by adequate proof of the impossibility of receiving the required money resources from the introduction of local taxes'. The People's Commissariat of Internal Affairs (NKVD) exhorted local soviets to carry out 'merciless taxation of the propertied classes' (SU 47/1917 (23. xi. 17), 179/1917 (11. xii. 17); D'yachenko, *op. cit.* pp. 78, 93). Only two local taxes, one on land and the other (in Petrograd only) a surtax on state income tax, were specifically decreed by the government (SU 105/1917 (4. xii. 17), 162/1917 (19. xii. 17)).

central authorities of part of their burden, and was also of considerable political importance to the government, for it weakened the richer classes in the localities, and encouraged the local supporters of the government to learn to manage local affairs without relying on officials largely hostile to the new regime. It was here and not through central policy that the traditional socialist aim of direct taxation of the propertied classes was put into effect, through a variety of local taxes and levies.[1] The 'contributions' (*kontributsii*) exacted from the richer groups, often quaint and badly-organised,[2] provided revenue to maintain the bare needs of the new local authorities, which could not at this time have been met by the central government or through the old revenue channels.

This first period of *ad hoc* development came to an end when the government turned its attention to fundamental economic problems in the spring of 1918. What financial policy was appropriate for the Soviet government in these new circumstances? In May Lenin outlined his financial programme for the consolidation period in a speech which was the financial counterpart of his April pamphlet. The new ingredient as compared with the economic resolution of the Sixth Congress a year before was the emphasis on the centralisation of the financial system. Lenin's conception was that local taxes would be replaced by a central tax on income and property, which would partly cover the gap between revenue and expenditure and pave the way for a currency reform.[3] While the 'broadest autonomy of local organisations' must be preserved, a 'unified, strictly-determined financial policy' was essential if the economy was to be consolidated. The local financial apparatus must be properly organised if decrees from the centre were not to hang in the air.[4]

---

[1] These included levies on factory owners, traders, owners of hotels, persons with deposits of money, etc.; taxes on shops; and additions to state taxes. There is no reliable record of the revenue raised by local soviets; one source states that contributions in 57 provinces amounted to 826·5 million roubles between October 1917 and November 1918, including 738·9 million roubles in the towns (D'yachenko, *op. cit.* pp. 79–80; *Ek. zhizn'*, no. 54 (1919)).

[2] Thus in Kaluga, according to Gukovskii, anyone who did not subscribe to the Kaluga *Pravda* was 'considered to be a saboteur...and fined 3,000 roubles'. (For this and other examples see Gukovskii's speech in *Trudy*... (1918), evening session of 31 May.)

[3] Lenin first referred to the possibility of a currency reform in December 1917 (*Soch.* vol. XXVI, p. 354).

[4] *Soch.* vol. XXVII, pp. 200–1, 223–4, 347–51. Lenin's policy was strongly opposed by the Left opposition (see, for example, Smirnov's speech in *Trudy*... (1918)).

How was centralisation to be achieved? At this time local finance was not co-ordinated with or controlled by the centre. Local soviets received little practical help from the centre, and tended to take a hostile attitude to it, and to corner to themselves all sources of revenue.[1] The NKF tried to solve the problem by edict. It forbade the levying of *ad hoc* 'contributions', and tried to use the local financial bodies surviving from before the revolution as channels for centralisation. This policy was a failure. The circular forbidding contributions was revoked by the Central Executive Committee of Soviets (VTsIK), owing to local opposition supported by the NKVD,[2] and the levying of contributions continued.[3] Proper connexions were not established between the old financial institutions and the local soviet financial departments, and there were frequent clashes between them.[4]

In July 1918 the new constitution attempted to regulate the financial relationship between the centre and the localities. It laid down that local estimates were to be compiled by the local soviets, and approved by the higher soviet body. Central and local taxation was to be delimited by VTsIK and the all-Russian Congress of Soviets, and local taxation was to be used exclusively for local needs. Grants and loans could be made for indispensable expenditure if local resources were insufficient.[5] In September and October 1918 the new Commissar of Finance, Krestinskii, prepared legislation to put the constitution into effect by integrating the financial departments (*finotdely*) of the local soviets with the central NKF apparatus. The old local financial authorities were abolished, and the soviet

---

[1] For examples see *Trudy...* (1918), pp. 226–32; *Protokoly VTsIKa 4-go sozyva*, pp. 112–17; D'yachenko, *op. cit.* pp. 89, 95–6. The practice of imposing local taxes on centrally controlled state concerns was particularly objected to. SNK ruled against this in April (SU 408/1917–18 (11. iv. 18)).

[2] The NKVD was still at this time in general charge of local government and finance, as the Ministry of Internal Affairs had been before. For details of this controversy, see *Protokoly VTsIKa 4-go sozyva*, pp. 130–2, 149–51; *Trudy...* (1918) evening session of 31. v.; D'yachenko, *op. cit.* pp. 96–7. Mr E. H. Carr confuses the NKF circular with the SNK decree on taxes on *state* bodies, which was not abrogated (see previous note and Carr, *op. cit.* pp. 142–3).

[3] See, for example, I. A. Gladkov, *Ocherki stroitel'stva sovetskogo planovogo khozyaistva v 1917–1918gg.* (1950), p. 337.

[4] See Krestinskii's speech in *Trudy vserossiiskogo s"ezda zaveduyushchikh finotdelami* (1919), session of 21 May; and *Ek. zhizn'*, no. 1 (1919). Krestinskii, who succeeded Gukovskii as NKF in August 1918 and remained in the post throughout the civil war, stated that in the end 'Gukovskii understood that the course he had chosen [of continuing the old financial institutions] was a wrong one'.

[5] These provisions will be found in the 1918 constitution: SU 582/1917–18 (19. vii. 18), ch. 16, 'Budget Law'.

finotdely were put under the general charge of the NKF, while remaining subordinate to the local soviet Executive Committee (E.C.). Detailed legislation set out the organisation and functions of the *finotdely* at various levels (1 November), and the sources from which they could obtain revenue (8 December)—a list of permitted local taxes was approved, and local soviets were also given permission to impose a surtax on state income tax for local use.[1] To assist the unification of the system, persons sympathetic to the Soviet government were appointed to responsible financial posts in the localities.[2]

This legislation marked an important stage in the development of the Soviet financial system. Although it was abandoned for extreme centralisation during the civil war period, it was taken as a basis for local organisation under N.E.P.

Although Lenin's financial programme had influenced local finance, it had little effect on the financial situation as a whole. The central government enacted a series of further increases in both direct and indirect taxation between March and July 1918,[3] but these measures were less radical than those of the provisional government a year before. At the same time many taxes ceased to be imposed, and the yield from others declined.[4]

It proved impossible for the government to carry out its intention of solving the financial crisis by large-scale direct taxation. The income tax was a wartime innovation, and easily evaded, and attempts to prepare a new income tax law failed because of the difficulties of establishing a suitable apparatus for collecting the tax,

---

[1] This legislation was prepared primarily by a commission appointed by a congress of financial workers in May 1918, and was partly based on legislation passed by the provisional government in Sept. 1917. For details, see *Sistematicheskii sbornik uzakonenii i rasporyazhenii rabochego i krest'yanskogo pravitel'stva* (1919), 47; *Sbornik dekretov 1917–18* (1920), no. 175; *Trudy...* (1919), p. 13; *Ek. zhizn'*, no. 27 (1918), no. 175 (1921); *Fin. ents.* col. 720; D'yachenko, *op. cit.* pp. 97–8.

[2] See *Ek. zhizn'*, no. 27 (1918). At the financial congress in May 1919 there were 183 communists out of 272 representatives, and the majority were said to have been newly appointed, mainly in August and September 1918 (*Trudy...* (1919)).

[3] All the main excises were drastically increased; a 5% levy was imposed on trade turnover, the only new central tax introduced during the first year of Soviet government; and taxes on private profits were raised to a maximum of 95% against the previous 90%. For excises, see SU 430/1917–18 (13 and 21. iv. 18); *Rospis'...na i.–vi. 1919...*, pp. 80, 82; and article by L. Obolenskii (Ossinskii) in *Izvestiya NK finansov*, no. 10 (1919). For 5% levy, see *Rospis'...na vii.–xii. 1919...*, p. 15; *Ek. zhizn'*, no. 31 (1918); L. Obolenskii, *loc. cit.*; and D'yachenko, *op. cit.* pp. 99–100. For direct taxes, see SU 544 and 548, 1918 (17. vi. 18); *Rospis'...na i.–vi. 1919...*, pp. 47 ff.; *Rospis'...na vii.–xii. 1919...*, pp. 13–14.

[4] SU 547/1917–18 (17. vi. 18); *Sbornik dekretov o finansakh*, no. 65 (19/22. vi. 18), no. 67 (18. ix. 18); *Izvestiya NK finansov*, no. 10 (1919) (referring to abolition of tax on money capital, 13. ix. 18).

apart from other reasons.[1] The cash reserves of the richer groups of the population in the towns could not therefore be taxed away through 'constitutional' taxes imposed through the central fiscal apparatus. In any case, the economic measures of the government (abrogation of the state debt, confiscation of land, shares, etc.) deprived these groups of their main sources of income. On whom could a high level of direct taxation be imposed if not on the propertied classes? Obviously not on the industrial workmen, for political reasons; and yet any attempt to increase the direct taxation of the peasantry, who certainly had large cash hoardings at this time, met with great opposition, and could not be carried through without endangering existing peasant support for the regime.[2]

How then could the financial crisis be solved? The government could not hope, even in the 'breathing-space', to receive foreign loans, in view both of its own repudiation of previous loans and of the general hostility of foreign governments.[3] The Bolsheviks were committed to the high indirect taxation of luxuries, but it seemed unlikely that more than a small amount of revenue could be raised from this source. It seemed that the hated indirect taxation of necessities was the only possible source for further revenue on a large scale in an economy in which taxation of the rich yielded diminishing returns. Soviet financial officials showed increasing signs of recognising this as early as the spring of 1918,[4] and towards the end of the year the

[1] Gladkov, *op. cit.* p. 338. Lenin in May 1918 suggested that the income tax should be imposed monthly, and for state employees deducted from wages. In June this was put into effect for state employees (but this was not P.A.Y.E., for the tax was still imposed on earnings in the previous year). But technical difficulties prevented its introduction for private payers, and although income tax commissions were set up under the local soviets, and individual tax returns were subject to public scrutiny, in fact during 1918 only arrears for 1917 were collected. SU 547/1917–18 (17. vi. 18); *Sbornik dekretov 1917–18*, no. 124 (23. ix. 18); *Rospis'...na vii.–xii. 1919...*, p. 8; Lenin, *Soch.* vol. xxvii, pp. 348–9.

[2] A draft decree on a graded tax in kind on the peasantry was adopted by SNK in December 1917; it had to be withdrawn after the opposition of the peasant section of VTsIK (D'yachenko, *op. cit.* p. 158). At the Congress of Councils of National Economy in May, violent peasant resentment to local contributions was expressed (*Trudy...* (1918), speech by Serkov). As late as August 1918 Lenin expressed the view that if prices were to rise (e.g. through tax measures), the price of grain rather than of manufactured goods should be increased, 'to help us to neutralise in the Civil War the greatest possible number of peasants' (*Soch.* vol. xxviii, p. 28). Thus the Bolsheviks' hands were tied all round in respect of increased taxation on the peasantry.

[3] Sokol'nikov, who became NKF in 1921, spoke optimistically of the prospect of foreign loans at the end of May 1918, however (G. Sokol'nikov, *Finansy posle oktyabrya* (1923), pp. 60–1).

[4] Thus Gukovskii stated that the demand in the programme that expenditure on administration should be paid by the capitalist classes was by and large no longer

system of indirect taxation was radically reformed. Excises were abolished and replaced by a system of 'mark-ups' (*nachisleniya*) on fixed prices, which covered a wide range of industrial consumer goods as well as goods traditionally subject to excise.[1] This shadowy precursor of the turnover tax of the planning period was too late to be effective in the inflationary situation, and in any case the hopes of the leaders of the government and their supporters continued to be pinned on a new drastic tax on income and property.[2]

Meanwhile, the printing press continued to be the main source of revenue. As is shown in Table 4, no real success was achieved in limiting currency issue at any time during the first year after the October revolution, although there was a slight improvement from May 1918 onwards which may have resulted from the policy of consolidation.[3] In 1918 currency circulation more than doubled, as it had in 1917; by the end of 1918 it was some forty times the pre-war level. In these conditions, the currency reform envisaged by Lenin and actively prepared during April–June 1918 could not have succeeded in stabilising the currency, and the outbreak of civil war in any case made the postponement of the reform inevitable.[4]

In the circumstances of this period, it was impossible for a satisfactory budget to be compiled. An attempt was made to complete the unfinished estimates of the provisional government. After this proved impracticable, the Soviet government authorised com-

---

appropriate, as a result of expropriation. Bogolepov, a Bolshevik who had specialised in financial matters, and who represented the NKF on the commission which drew up the 1918 Constitution, declared in a far-sighted speech that it had been correct to oppose indirect taxes in the earlier period, but in the period of transition to socialism what were formerly called indirect taxes were needed. 'We must rearrange the financial system', he said, 'so that, for example, of the surplus value of a machine costing 1,000 roubles, a definite surplus should be taken for state expenditure... In a system of nationalisation, this is the necessary path.' Another speaker said that indirect rather than direct taxes were the most expedient way of raising money from the peasantry. (See for Gukovskii's statement *Trudy*... (1918); for the others, *Protokoly VTsIKa 4-go sozyva*, pp. 4, 135–9, 143.)

[1] Textiles and leather goods, paper, and sewing machines were, for example, made subject to these mark-ups during 1919. See decree of 21. xi. 18 and circular of 25. xii. 18 in *Sbornik dekretov o finansakh 1917–20*, no. 101; *Rospis'...na vii.–xii. 1919...*, pp. 27–9; *Narodnyi komissariat finansov 1917, 7. xi/25. x. 1922* (1922), p. 4.

[2] Lenin as late as August 1918 considered that the means to solve the crisis were a tax in kind on the peasantry and 'to impose an *income* and property tax, and make it progressive' (*Soch.* vol. xxviii, p. 29).

[3] The reduction of issue in January and February 1918 was apparently due to printing difficulties (see Krestinskii in *Izvestiya NK finansov*, no. 10 (1919)).

[4] For the schemes which were canvassed, and the steps which were actually taken (including the printing of new notes), see D'yachenko, *op. cit.* pp. 113, 118–19; Gladkov, *op. cit.* pp. 330–4).

missariats and other government departments to compile simplified estimates for the first six months of 1918,[1] which were to be examined by the Special Reduction Committee of VSNKh before being approved by the government.[2] In the event, the adoption of the budget was delayed far beyond original intentions.[3] The central authorities waged a protracted struggle to reduce departmental estimates,[4] which were drawn up schematically without data from the localities,[5] and were often exaggerated and inaccurate[6] (the confusion which existed is shown by the fact that estimates of the size of the six-months' budget varied from 12 to 80–100 milliard roubles).[7] Eventually an emergency commission was set up to

[1] The drawing-up of a half-yearly budget was embarked upon as a result of discussions held during the summer of 1917 (by the provisional government) on the draft of a new budget law. It was then decided that the most suitable date for beginning the budget year was 1 July, so that it should coincide with the agricultural year, and not 1 January as had always previously been the case; the 1918 budget should therefore be for six months. The intention was that this should be followed by an annual budget for 1918/9, but in practice six-monthly budgets continued till 1920 (*Obshchaya rospis' gosudarstvennykh dokhodov i raskhodov rossiiskoi respubliki na i.–vi. 1918g.* (1918); *Ek. zhizn'*, no. 2 (1919)).

[2] See *Obshchaya rospis'...na i.–vi. 1918...*; *Izvestiya NK finansov*, no. 10 (1919), p. 7; Gladkov, *op. cit.* p. 339. Complaints were made of the Reduction Committee that it was 'secret, both its composition and function are unknown' (see speech by Lozovskii in *Trudy...* (1918), evening session of 31 May).

[3] The delay was occasioned by (i) the general chaos and confusion; (ii) the rapidly changing situation, which made estimates out of date in the course of compiling them; (iii) the indifference of supporters of the government ('some comrades', said Gukovskii, 'look on estimates as a bourgeois prejudice'); (iv) the hostility of financial officials; (v) the transfer of the government to Moscow from Petrograd in March. See *Obshchaya rospis'...na i.–vi. 1918*; *Ek. zhizn'*, no. 2 (1919); *Narodnoe khozyaistvo*, no. 3 (1918), p. 20, cit. Gladkov, *op. cit.* p. 340.

[4] This is indicated by the following examples (in million roubles):

	Original demand	Granted by Reduction Committee	Final allocation in budget
NK of Agriculture	705	109	185
NK of Food	—	1,749	1,372
NK of Military Affairs and Navy:			
ordinary estimate	670	291	495
extraordinary estimate	—	6,500	459

Sources: *Trudy...* (1918); *Obshchaya rospis'...na i.–vi. 1918g.*

[5] See Krestinskii, interview in *Ek. zhizn'*, no. 1 (1919), and *Protokoly VTsIKa 4-go sozyva*, pp. 145–6.

[6] See, for example, Lozovskii's speech in *Trudy...* (1918), evening session of 31 May.

[7] *Protokoly VTsIKa 4-go sozyva*, pp. 112ff., 143ff.; *Trudy...* (1918) (speeches of Sokol'nikov, Gukovskii, and Lozovskii); *Obshchaya rospis'...na i.–vi. 1918g.* Gukovskii denied that he had ever intended the upper figure given to refer to a *six*-months' budget; but the extent of the confusion is indicated by the fact that the two rapporteurs at the Congress at the end of May gave 12,000 million roubles (Sokol'nikov) and 25,000–30,000 million roubles (Gukovskii) as their estimates of the size of the January–June budget. Lenin in January 1918 said 'the revenue of the Soviets equals 8 milliard, and the expenditure 28 milliard' (*Soch.* vol. xxvi, p. 469).

Table 4. *Currency circulation, 1917–18 (million roubles)*

	Amount of currency in circulation on 1st of month	Monthly issue as % of total circulation on 1st of month	Prices as % of preceding month [1]
Nov. 1917	19,577·4	29·2	151
Dec.	25,295·0	9·3	134
Jan. 1918	27,650·2	6·9	129
Feb.	29,563·5	4·9	122
Mar.	31,019·3	9·5	131
Apr.	33,975·6	12·6	132
May	38,266·2	6·5	122
June	40,743·4	7·3	125
July	43,711·9	6·1	114
Aug.	46,394·9	4·9	92
Sept.	48,674·0	5·9	100
Oct.	51,525·5	5·4	114
Nov.	54,295·7	5·7	125
Dec.	57,370·6	6·9	121

Source: D'yachenko, *op. cit.* p. 118.
Note: (1) Budget index of All-Russian Central Council of Trade Unions.

hasten the preparation of the budget,[1] but the final budget was not adopted until July 1918, after the period it covered had already expired.[2]

Although on the expenditure side the first Soviet budget reflected the political and economic changes which had taken place since 1917 (notably in the rise of expenditure on the economy), it was an unreal document, as is shown by the fulfilment figures.[3] Its chequered history is of interest to us chiefly as an indication of the importance attached by the new government at this stage to the principles of orthodox budgetary finance. These principles were enshrined in a series of decrees issued in May and July 1918. In May a decree 'On the unity of the exchequer' (*O edinstve kassy*) ordered that all monetary resources of state departments must be deposited in the People's Bank, and all their payments made through it.[4] In June detailed

---

[1] See *Izvestiya NK finansov*, no. 10 (1919), p. 7, reporting decree of 8. vi. 18.
[2] SU 579/1917–18 (11. vii. 18).
[3] The data in Table 9 are certainly an underestimate. Currency issues from January to June 1918 were some 16 milliard roubles, or slightly more than the planned budget deficit, whereas the budget fulfilment figures show a deficit of only 5 milliard roubles—it seems impossible that 11 milliard roubles could have been issued in bank credit not passing through the budget. And compare the fulfilment data in S. N. Prokopovich, *The Economic Condition of Soviet Russia* (1924), pp. 179 ff. (expenditure given as 8,700 million roubles against 5,788 in our table); and in M. S. Atlas, *op. cit.* pp. 143–4 (759 million roubles to industry alone, against 884 million for whole national economy in our table).
[4] SU 460/1917–18 (2. v. 18). For examples of the ineffectiveness of this decree, see *Ek. zhizn'*, no. 13 (1918).

and exacting rules were published on the compilation of the budget for July to December 1918.[1] In July the constitution included a chapter on budget law, which stated that revenue was to be fixed by the Congress of Soviets or VTsIK, that all expenditure must be made strictly for the purpose laid down in the estimates, and that expenditure outside the budget could be made only through a decree of the central authorities.[2] This legislation, like that on local finance, was prevented by the inflation and the intensification of the civil war from being effective, but in revised form took its place in the new budgetary systems of N.E.P. and the planned economy.

[1] SU 521/1917–18 (3. vi. 18).
[2] SU 582/1917–18 (19. vii. 18), ch. 16, 'Budget law' (*Byudzhetnoe pravo*).

CHAPTER III

TOWARDS A BUDGET IN KIND
1918–20

1. THE DECLINE OF THE MONEY ECONOMY

THE extension of the civil war from May 1918 onwards resulted in a further rapid decline in industrial and agricultural production. The extreme measures of war communism were in essence emergency methods by which the government acquired a maximum share of this reduced output and allocated it to what it regarded as the most essential uses.

There were two ways in which the government could mobilise labour and other resources. It could enter the market as a purchaser, or it could use its powers of requisition and compulsion. In the first six months after the October revolution, before the outbreak of large-scale civil war, attention was concentrated on the first alternative. Extremely large cash issues were made in order to obtain supplies from the peasantry, and to enable increased wages to be paid to workers and employees so that they could maintain their purchases on the market. But even in these first months administrative pressure was used to force the peasantry to sell their supplies, and factories were confiscated piecemeal so that their productive resources and output could be placed at the direct disposal of the government. By the summer of 1918 compulsion became more important than market pressure, with the establishment in June of Committees of Poor Peasants to confiscate grain from the less poor (these committees continued their activities till the autumn) and with the nationalisation of large-scale industry in July.

However, financial measures as drastic as this were attempted only in the autumn of 1918, when the government made a final effort to halt the inflation by reabsorbing its cash issues in the form of budgetary revenue. Further attempts to draft a new income and property tax and to impose the existing income tax more widely on the village population were without practical result,[1] but as an alternative the government introduced a ten-milliard rouble Extraordinary Revolutionary Tax, aiming at the final expropriation of the cash resources of the 'property-owning groups of the town and village population'.[2] The amount to be collected in each province was fixed in the original decree,[3] and provincial and lower soviets were instructed to apportion the tax among the population according to property status and income.[4] In practice, extreme measures including acts of violence were used to enforce the collection of the tax,[5] and in the villages it tended not only to be levied on the better-off households but also to be extended arbitrarily to the middle groups of the peasantry.[6] Even so, only 1,630 million roubles were collected by the end of 1920,[7] and this could not begin to meet the 'indispensable needs of revolutionary construction and struggle' as the original decree had intended.

In fact the policy of large-scale direct taxation was doomed to

[1] The party programme adopted in March 1919 declared that 'the R.C.P. supports the transition... to a progressive income and property tax', but added more realistically that 'to the extent that this tax dies out owing to large-scale expropriation of the possessing classes, the covering of state expenses must be based on the direct transfer of part of the income of various state monopolies to state revenue'. For details of income tax legislation during this period, see SU 17/1919 (23. i. 19), 118/1919 (27. iii. 19); *Sbornik dekretov o finansakh 1917–20*, nos. 97 and 98 (28. vii. 19 and 6. ii. 20); *Narodnyi komissariat finansov*, pp. 4, 80.

[2] Decree of 30. x. 1918 (*Sbornik dekretov 1917–18*, no. 142). For detailed circulars, etc., see *Sbornik dekretov 1917–20*, nos. 70–82.

[3] Factors taken into account in fixing the sum due from a province were said to be (*a*) the size of population; (*b*) the sown and cultivable area; (*c*) the returns of state and local land and Promtax (income tax schedules affected urban payers only, and were outdated by the changes of the preceding period); (*d*) exceptional circumstances such as the proximity to the front (*Ek. zhizn'*, no. 21 (1918)).

[4] Wage earners with incomes of less than 1,500 roubles per month, and poor peasants, were completely exempt from tax.

[5] In the original decree, sequestering of money and property, and hard labour were permitted penalties for failure to pay. In the course of the campaign, cases of whipping and even execution were reported. (See Prokopovich, *op. cit.* ch. IV; and *Ek. zhizn'*, no. 26 (1919), article by Yevreinov.)

[6] For examples, see *Ek. zhizn'*, no. 25 (1918), and nos. 26 and 38 (1919); *Rospis'... na vii.–xii. 1919*, pp. 18–20; Stalin, *Soch.* vol. IV, pp. 214–15. A resolution of the Eighth Party Congress in March 1919 emphasised the need to reduce the taxation of the middle peasantry, and this was followed by legislation (SU 121/1919 (10. iv. 19)).

[7] The original date for completing the collection was 15 December 1918, but little was collected by that date. 1,088 million roubles were said to have been raised by mid 1919, and 1,200 million roubles by the end of 1919. Including confiscated valuables and the sums in current accounts which were written off, the yield was said to be 'several milliard' roubles, in a much depreciated currency. The amounts raised varied from an insignificant percentage of the sums fixed for Moscow and Petrograd, to over half in certain provinces. (*Rospis'... na vii.–xii. 1919*, p. 19; Prokopovich, *op. cit.* ch. IV; D'yachenko, *op. cit.* p. 150; Krestinskii in *Izvestiya NK finansov*, no. 10 (1919), and in *Trudy vserossiiskogo s"ezda zaveduyushchikh finotdelami* (1919), session of 21 May.)

failure in view of the drastic reduction in the incomes of the propertied classes since the October revolution, and of the inaccessibility of the hoards of the peasantry in notes and gold. Half-hearted attempts to raise the level of indirect taxation were also unsuccessful. As is shown in Table 8, revenue expressed in money terms at current prices rose only slightly in 1919, so that in real terms it declined rapidly. Taxes fell to a tenth of total revenue in the budget for the second half of 1919, and one three-hundredth in 1920.

Thus inflationary currency issues, which could not be withdrawn from circulation by fiscal means, were the only means by which the government could make its necessary purchases on the market: the rapid decline in the proportion of state expenditure met by revenue and not by currency issue is illustrated in Table 6. The inflation in turn led to a further reduction of the market and extension of direct control by the state.

In the industrial sector of the economy, 'finance through inflation' soon took second place to physical allocation of resources. At an early stage in the civil war the government nationalised the main branches of industry, and brought them under central control. The allocation of raw materials and output within industry was carried out directly by the state at low fixed prices, by methods of extreme centralisation. Direction of labour and compulsory labour service were introduced. The market was excluded from industry.

But industry was not as yet excluded from the market. Agricultural raw materials for industrial use, and food for workers in industry and the town population generally, had to be obtained from small peasant holdings which could not be subjected to nationalisation and centralisation as industry had been. Larger issues were made in order to obtain supplies from the countryside. But the depreciation of the currency, and the scarcity of industrial consumer goods in the villages, made the peasantry unwilling to sell their produce to the state.

The government therefore resorted to compulsion in order to obtain agricultural supplies. The compulsion used through the Committees of Poor Peasants in the summer of 1918 became a regular feature of the Soviet war economy from the end of 1918 onwards, after the failure of the attempt to impose a progressive tax in kind (*natural'nyi nalog*).[1] The requisitioning system was entirely

[1] The amount levied was to depend on the size of the family, the sown area, and the number of cattle. Products were assessed in terms of rye and then valued at fixed prices for inclusion in budget revenue. Some of the methods proposed for this tax were revived for the tax in kind introduced in 1921. For details of the 1918 tax and its failure, see

non-fiscal in character, and involved the seizure of all the 'surplus' of each household in excess of its essential needs. These supplies were distributed at low prices or even without charge to factories for issue as wages in kind, and to individual urban consumers by a system of rationing, differentiated by the social class to which the consumer belonged.

The quantity of goods in circulation on the free market declined considerably. In 1919 industrial output fell to 23% and in 1920 to 20% of the pre-war level; and the gross yield of crops in 1920 was 54% of the average harvest for 1909–13.[1] Of this reduced output, a much smaller proportion went to the market, owing to the growth of direct allocation in industry, and the introduction of requisitioning. Currency issues had at first (through price rises) acted as a levy on fixed incomes and hoards and yielded large real revenues to the state,[2] but as the market narrowed larger issues commanded a smaller quantity of real resources. Central issues had continually to be increased to enable state employees, enterprises, and the Army to obtain unrationed supplies,[3] and local currencies were issued to supplement central note allocations.[4] All the causes of a classic price inflation were present—the rise in currency issues, the contraction of the market, and the increased velocity of circulation resulting from declining confidence in the currency.[5] As is shown in Table 5, between July 1918 and July 1920 (i.e. roughly the period of civil war), currency in circulation increased twelve-fold, but prices rose ninety-fold.[6]

Sbornik dekretov 1917–18, no. 147 (30. x. 18), no. 173 (12. xi. 18); SU 141/1919 (2. ii. and 8. iii. 19), 498/1919 (15. x. 19); *Rospis'...na vii.–xii. 1919*, pp. 10–11.

[1] A. Baykov, *op. cit.* pp. 8, 23. The crop percentage refers only to the area covered by the 1920 Census.

[2] In November–December, 1917, as much as 288 million gold roubles (Yurovskii, *op. cit.* p. 73).

[3] For details of the decrees authorising currency issue, of types of currency issued, and of the technique of issue, see Yurovskii, *op. cit.* pp. 71, 74–5; and *Finansovaya politika za period 5. xii. 1920g. po dekabr' 1921g. (otchot k IX Vserossiiskomu s"ezdu Sovetov)* (1921), pp. 138–41.

[4] On these, and on attempts to unify them with the central currency during the civil war period, see D'yachenko, *op. cit.* p. 169; Yurovskii, *op. cit.* pp. 74–5, 159–68.

[5] This declining confidence led to dishoarding of currency by the peasantry, but whether this dishoarding was greater than new cash receipts is doubtful in view of the small amount of industrial consumer goods supplied to the village. Thus early in 1919 it was stated that the new issues to the countryside were hardly being spent at all (*Ek. zhizn'*, no. 45 (1919)). It has also been argued that the mere presence of 'hoarded' money on a large scale itself tended to reduce the value of money (cf. Katzenellenbaum, *Russian currency and banking 1914–1924*, p. 23).

[6] Very varied price indices have been produced for these years. For alternative figures, see Yurovskii, *op. cit.* p. 72; and Sh. Ya. Turetskii, *Sebestoimost' i voprosy tsenoobrazovaniya* (1940), p. 164.

As the civil war progressed, the sphere of operation of money declined. The government mobilised the diminishing resources mainly by requisitioning and direct allocation. Exchange via the free market dwindled, and private trade was ultimately made illegal. In the final stages of this process, barter replaced money exchange even on the black market. The money economy was replaced by a centralised war economy in kind.

During the civil war the activities of the NKF were primarily concerned with the allocation of currency issues. Like the other institutions of war communism, the 'budgetary' system was adapted to the task of ensuring that resources were used solely for essential war needs, and was rigid and centralised. This centralisation was brought about both by extending the scope of the central budget to include the nationalised sector of the economy and local finance, and by tightening up control over budget grants.

2. THE GROWTH OF THE SCOPE OF THE BUDGET

In the first year after the October revolution, the state budget was responsible primarily for financing central administrative, social and cultural, and defence expenditures. Local budgets and the national economy received grants from the centre, but their accounts were not included in the state budget (the only exception were the railways; their gross incomes and expenditure had been included in the budget even before the revolution).

(a) *Industry and the budget*

During 1918 nationalised enterprises retained the receipts from the sale of their output as their main source of income, but were made additional grants to meet their current needs through both the State Bank[1] and the budget. Although attempts were made to regularise the compilation of estimates of grants needed from the budget[2] and

[1] Bank credits (in practice grants) to industry, issued through a special committee, were probably larger than budget issues in the first four or five months after October 1917. They were prohibited in August 1918, but in practice continued till the end of 1919. (D'yachenko, *op. cit.* p. 111; M. S. Atlas, *op. cit.* pp. 143, 149–52.)

[2] The method by which estimates of nationalised enterprises were adopted was approved in March (SU 396/1917–18, 18. iii. 18), and although all nationalised enterprises were instructed in April to draw up estimates, in the event only administrative expenditures of VSNKh were included in the budget for January–June 1918, and enterprises were financed through a special fund (M. S. Atlas, *op. cit.* pp. 146–8; D'yachenko, *op. cit.* p. 110; *Obshchaya rospis'...na i.–vi. 1918*).

Table 5. *Currency circulation, 1918–21 (million roubles)* [1]

Year and quarter	Currency circulation on 1st day of quarter	Quarterly issue as % of currency circulation on 1st day of quarter	Real value of currency circulation on 1st day of quarter (gold roubles) (col. 1 ÷ col. 5)	Real value of new issue (treasury index roubles)	Price index on 1st day of quarter (1913 = 1)
1918, 1st	27,650	22·9	1,317	} 62	21
2nd	33,975	28·7	790		43
3rd	43,711	17·9	491	} 27	89
4th	51,525	19·0	548		94
1919, 1st	61,326	22·6	374	} 19	164
2nd	75,185	34·4	224		336
3rd	101,030	46·7	154	} 18	656
4th	148,201	51·8	161		923
1920, 1st	225,015	51·4	93	} 10	2,420
2nd	340,662	50·2	71		4,770
3rd	511,816	45·6	63	} 10	8,140
4th	745,158	56·8	77		9,620
1921, 1st	1,168,597	44·3	70	} 6	16,800
2nd	1,686,684	39·2	47		35,700
3rd	2,347,164	—	29	—	80,700

Sources: D'yachenko, *op. cit.* pp. 167–70; Arnold, *op. cit.* pp. 91–3; Yurovskii, *op. cit.* pp. 71–4; Katzenellenbaum, *op. cit.* pp. 56–7, 70, 74–5, 95; *Vestnik finansov*, no. 1, 1922, pp. 3–5; no. 3, p. 2.

Note: (1) The figures given in different sources show some variation, particularly the figures for real value of currency in circulation, and the price index for 1921 (cf. Table 10).

Table 6. *Budgetary revenue as proportion of expenditure, 1918–20*

	Revenue as % of expenditure Plan (budget)	Fulfilment	Revenue as % of 'true expenditure' [1]
Jan.–June 1918	16·2	15·3	5·2
July–Dec. 1918	9·5 [2]	21·9	12·3
Jan.–June 1919	40·1	16·9	5·4
July–Dec. 1919	17·3	14·8	3·9
1920	13·1	—	—

Sources: as for Tables 8–9.

Notes:
(1) 'True expenditure' = revenue fulfilment as given in Table 8 + currency issue (from Table 5).
In view of the obvious considerable understatement of actual expenditure in the available fulfilment figures, this 'true expenditure' figure gives a closer picture of actual expenditure during the period. It must, however, be borne in mind that revenue receipts themselves may be an underestimate (not all revenue was in fact passed to the centre). It seems likely that the second column over-estimates the ratio of revenue to expenditure, and the third column under-estimates it.
(2) The planned receipts from Extraordinary Revolutionary Tax are excluded. If they were included, this figure would rise to 43·9.

to control their issue,[1] they were in practice made in a somewhat arbitrary manner. From the summer of 1918, however, most supplies were centrally distributed, and both the raw material input of an enterprise and its output were exchanged at low nominal prices. Hence the income of an enterprise from sales could not equal its expenditure on the money wages of its workers, which were continually rising in order to meet the increase in prices on the free market. The only possible source for the major part of the cash expenditure of industry was central allocations.

Now it was not, of course, an automatic corollary of this situation that the receipts of industry from sales should be included in the central budget; but in a situation where cost accounting was out of the question, and strict centralisation essential, a drive towards a full 'estimate-budget' financing of industry became a natural part of the policy of the central authorities.

The first steps towards this system were taken in August 1918 and January 1919, when book entry and accounts by cheque through the bank replaced cash payments for all institutions and nationalised enterprises. At this time the existence was recognised both of enterprises fully on the budget and of those with their own working capital whose losses alone were made up by the budget.[2]

This transitional stage lasted only a few months. A decree of 4 March 1919 put all state enterprises fully on the budget. All their receipts, in whatever form, were to pass into treasury revenue; all their expenditure was to be made by allocations from the budget based on approved estimates or by advances in lieu of estimates.[3]

These measures were enforced only gradually during 1919 and 1920.[4] Enterprises were extremely short of cash, and tended to retain the cash they received instead of passing it on to the centre.[5] Proper

[1] See Gladkov, *op. cit.* p. 344; and SU 477/1917–18 (17. v. 18).
[2] D'yachenko, *op. cit.* pp. 137–8; SU 22/1919 (23. i. 19).
[3] VSNKh was permitted to keep a limited floating fund. Later decrees extended this system to co-operatives and other bodies, and tightened up the procedure. See SU 107/1919 (4. iii. 19), 9/1920 (5. i. 20), 305/1920 (15. vii. 20), 530/1920 (13. xii. 20); *Ek. zhizn'*. nos. 43 and 53 (1919); D'yachenko, *op. cit.* p. 139.
[4] For criticisms made of the system, see *Trudy 2-go vserossiiskogo s"ezda sovetov narodnogo khozyaistva, 19–27. xii. 1918* (1918), pp. 266–86, 396–400. For evidence that it was introduced slowly and imperfectly, see article by Pyatakov in *Ek. zhizn'*, no. 9 (1918), and SU 208/1920 (17. v. 20) (repeating the terms of the original decree).
[5] In his report to the Congress of Heads of Financial Departments in May 1919, Krestinskii referred to the attempt of VSNKh and the food commissariat to retain their cash receipts, and not include them in the budget. Nationalised enterprises, he said, were using the sums on their current accounts, the money of the former owners, and their income from goods, before seeking credits from NKF or VSNKh. At the same congress

estimates of expenditure were not compiled, and in practice the centre issued grants *ad hoc* as currency became available.[1]

(b) *Local finance*

The position of local finance was similar to that of nationalised industry. Local soviets became increasingly dependent on central grants,[2] and the central authorities sought to take over the financial powers of the local soviets in order to concentrate expenditure on essential purposes. In November 1918, six months after the clash between the local soviets, supported by NKVD, and the NKF, about local 'contributions' from the rich (see p. 19 above), a new controversy flared up round the question of the revenue rights of local soviets, when SNK (at the request of the NKVD) decreed that local soviets had the right to impose local revolutionary taxes under central control.[3] This decree was opposed by the NKF, and was not put into effect.[4] Nevertheless, various illegal local levies continued to be imposed during 1919,[5] and local soviets and their financial departments (see pp. 19–20 above)[6] retained considerable financial powers within the framework of central control.

Early in 1919 the NKF raised the question of the appropriateness of continuing the semi-autonomy of local budgets, and asked whether it might not be better to include them in the central budget.[7] In May 1919 the Congress of Representatives of Financial Departments showed extreme confusion of thought and some differences of opinion on this question. Nevertheless, it passed resolutions calling for the fusion of local finance with general state finance, for all local

---

Milyutin referred to local resistance by enterprises to the system of cashless accounting (*Trudy*... (1919), sessions of 21 and 22 May). For a further example of failure to pass receipts to the centre, see *Ek. zhizn'*, no. 89 (1919).

[1] *Finansovaya politika*..., pp. 47–8; D'yachenko, *op. cit.* p. 139.

[2] D'yachenko, *op. cit.* p. 176, states that in 32 provinces local revenue amounted to 695 million roubles in the whole of 1919, while 1,075 million roubles was issued from the centre to the localities in loans and grants in the last three months of the year alone. Local revenue would of course tend to be understated in official returns.

[3] *Sbornik dekretov, 1917–18*, no. 144 (31. x. 18).

[4] See *Trudy*... (1919), session of 21 May, where Krestinskii declared that the decree 'was adopted on the initiative of Sverdlov and the NKVD, not on our initiative'; *Izvestiya NK finansov*, no. 10 (1919); and references in Prokopovitch, *op. cit.* ch. IV.

[5] See, for examples, *Ek. zhizn'*, nos. 51 and 86 (1919).

[6] The central budget-accounting administration of NKF sent special 'agent instructors' to the provinces for periods of three weeks to three months. The new financial organisation had been established in 45 provinces by early 1921 (*Ek. zhizn'*, no. 114 (1921)).

[7] *Rospis'*...*na i.–vi. 1919*..., pp. 25 ff. As early as 1918, it had been suggested that the division of finance into state and local was now senseless (N. Torgulov, *Finansovaya nauka*, p. 137, *cit.* D'yachenko, *op. cit.* p. 176).

financial expenditure to be made via the appropriate central commissariat, for the NKF to take over all local financial matters from the NKVD,[1] and for the constitution of 1918 to be changed accordingly.

These resolutions marked a major departure from the policy expressed in the legislation of December 1918 (see chapter II), and specifically called for its repudiation.[2] The real justification for this change in policy lay in the emergency conditions, which made drastic incursions into local spending powers inevitable. But in this matter, as in others, there was a tendency to treat decisions arising out of war needs as matters of high principle—thus the main speaker at the financial congress declared that the provisions of the constitution on local financial powers reflected 'the old point of view inherited from the bourgeois capitalist regime'.[3]

In practice the rights of local soviets were only partially restricted during 1919.[4] It was not until the middle of 1920 that the division of budgets into state and local was formally abolished.[5] From then onwards, the estimates of local bodies formed a part of the general estimate system, and were to be approved by the centre like those

[1] This it did during 1919. See *Rospis'...na vii.–xii. 1919...*, pp. 25 and 38, and *Ob. zapiska*, p. 51; *Sbornik dekretov o finansakh* (1917–20), no. 226 (26. viii. 19); SU 559/1919 (23. ix. 19).
[2] Krestinskii later declared that this legislation had been passed by SNK against the will of the majority of the NKF (*Izvestiya NK finansov*, no. 10 (1919)).
[3] The fusion of local with central finance was supported by Krestinskii as a necessary step towards making the budget into a 'real picture of the income and expenditure of the national economy' and by Potyaev, who opened the discussion on central and local finance, as an inevitable step in the transition from capitalism to socialism. Such was the feeling on this issue that the two resolutions, of the local and central finance and the budget estimate sections of the congress, were looked on by some persons as mandatory documents, and the Communist fraction at the Congress, faced with the situation that SNK itself had postponed discussion of the matter at the request of NKVD, had to move amendments to put the first resolution into a non-imperative form; and Krestinskii himself had to warn the delegates that a government decision must be awaited before the resolution could be put into practice.
Chutskayev, who opened the discussion on tax policy, took a different view. He defended the legislation of the previous autumn and asserted that local finance must be retained if local economy was retained, adding that 'ideally all power must be in the localities; the centre must play a definite part, but it may possess dictatorial power only in a definite transition period' (*Trudy...* (1919)).
[4] Only one-fifth of local requests for allocations from the centre was granted in 1919 (D'yachenko, *op. cit.* p. 175); and grants and loans were restricted to those matters fully under local control (SU 558/1919, 23. ix. 1919). At the same time attempts were made to get local revenue to pass to the centre (see, for example, *Ek. zhizn'*, no. 80 (1919)). On the other hand, as late as May 1919 a decree was published authorising the imposition of a supplementary Promtax as a source of revenue for local soviets (SU 261/1919 (30. v. 19)).
[5] Decree of VTsIK of 18. vi. 1920 (*Narodnyi komissariat finansov, 1917, 7. xi./25. x. 1922* 1922), p. 4).

of central bodies; the right of the local soviets to independent sources of income was rescinded. But by then the money budget had lost virtually all practical importance.

3. CONTROL OF BUDGET EXPENDITURE

Thus the budget was gradually extended to include the gross income and expenditure of the whole economy.[1] The financial authorities attempted to subject the compilation and fulfilment of this wider budget to a rigorous system of control. Departmental estimates were examined first by departmental commissions and then by a co-ordinating 'inter-departmental budget commission' under NKF, and finally combined into a budget which was approved in turn by SNK and VTsIK. Allocations had to be issued and spent strictly in accordance with the purposes stated in the estimates. The compilation and fulfilment of the budget was inspected and supervised by the NK of State Supervision, reorganised into the NK of Workers' and Peasants' Inspection (RKI) in 1920.[2]

This whole procedure was based on orthodox budgetary principles, and much of it was an adaptation of pre-revolutionary legislation. Close central control over state expenditure is not a feature peculiar to war communism, and the methods and organisation used in 1919 were revived with little change under N.E.P. But what was unusual was the wide range of activities and functions now included in the budget, and therefore, on paper at least, subject to budget control. Had the budget been compiled and executed in accordance with this legislation the concentration of resources on essential war needs would have been considerably facilitated. There was some improvement in financial discipline,[3] and the estimates commissions

[1] 'In the period when the socialisation of the means of production...is beginning,' stated the Party programme of March 1919, 'state power...begins to turn into an organisation directly fulfilling the function of directing the economy of the country, and in the same way the state budget becomes a budget of all the national economy as a whole.'

[2] For detailed material on all these procedures, see SU 521/1917–18 (3. vi. 18), 273/1919 (30. iv. 19), 318/1919 (24. v. 19); *Izvestiya NK finansov*, no. 10 (1919), p. 7 (decree of 28. i. 18); *Sistematicheskii sbornik*..., 49 (2. xi. 18); for the explanatory notes to the successive *Rospisi* published in these years and for the system of inspection and supervision, see E. E. Pontovich in *Vestnik finansov*, no. 10 (1926), pp. 35 ff.; and I. P. Kozlitin in *Istoricheskie zapiski*, XXVI (1948), pp. 65 ff.

[3] Krestinskii stated at the end of 1919 that for several months there had hardly been a single case, even in the newly freed areas, of expenditure without grants from the centre, and in retrospect permitted himself the rosy judgment that 'in 1920 we had achieved such a budgetary discipline...by our provincial comrades that [they] strictly restricted

played an important part in reducing the excessive claims of departments, at least in 1919,[1] but there could be no really effective budget control in the civil war years. The compilation and execution of the budget were made difficult by the lack of reliable trained financial personnel; by the rapid changes in territory and in the make-up of the state institutions themselves; and by the general confusion and chaos of the time. But the central factor which turned all attempts at centralised budgetary control into unreal paper work was the inflation of the currency. It was not only that the value of money depreciated; it depreciated irregularly from month to month and from commodity to commodity. This meant that the centre could not set meaningful financial limits to the activities of institutions in advance, for the real value of any estimate had declined (and declined unpredictably) by the time it was adopted. In this situation budget planning for a period of more than a few months became impossible. The six-monthly budget period had to be retained,[2] and even these shorter budgets were adopted only after considerable delay. Thus the July–December 1918 budget was adopted only on 3 December 1918; the adoption of the January–June 1919 budget was delayed until 21 May 1919 by attempts to reduce it; and the July–December 1919 and 1920 budgets were both adopted, purely formally, only on 11 August 1921.[3] The budget became little more than a *post factum* statement of the financial intentions of the government for a period which had elapsed.

The unreality of these civil war budgets can be seen from Table 8 (p. 42). As a result of the system of low fixed prices, the proportion of planned expenditure devoted to defence declined from 30% to

themselves to the allocations allowed them, and did not transfer allocations from one department to another' (*Izvestiya NK finansov*, no. 10 (1919); N. Krestinskii, *Nasha finansovaya politika* (1921), p. 35).

[1] This is illustrated in Table 7. Reduction was carried out with particular vigour in the case of the January–June 1919 budget, which was re-examined by a special committee of the Small Council (*Malyi sovet*) of SNK before being adopted. (See report of Krestinskii to VTsIK on 20 May 1919, in *Trudy...* (1919), Appendix 2; and *Ek. zhizn'*, nos. 14 and 36 (1919).)

[2] It was originally intended that an annual budget should begin in July 1918; but it proved impossible in practice to draw up a budget covering a period of more than six months (D'yachenko, *op. cit.* pp. 104–5). Again, it was at one time intended that a budget covering the first six months of 1920 should be succeeded by an annual budget for 1920/1 beginning in July; in the event an annual budget was compiled covering the whole of 1920 (this was not, of course, because the government felt it could now see ahead for a year rather than six months; the budgets by this stage had little practical importance). (See article by S. G[olovanov?] in *Izvestiya NK finansov*, no. 10 (1919); and SU 318/1919, Clause 62.)

[3] *Rospis'... na vii.–xii. 1918g....*; SU 245/1919; *Rospis'...na vii.–xii. 1919g....*

11%, although in fact defence absorbed a rapidly increasing share of total resources. The fulfilment data are even more unrealistic—budget expenditure actually recorded amounted to only 20–30% of total currency issue, largely as a result of the failure of economic bodies to include their expenditure in the budget accounts.

Table 7

(i) Reduction of original estimates in 1918–20, summary figures (million roubles)

	Original demands of departments	Budget: final estimates	% of original
1918	65,894	46,706	70·4
1919	321,815	215,402	66·9
1920	1,436,268	1,215,159	84·6

Source: *Na novykh putyakh. Itogi novoi ekonomicheskoi politiki*, vyp. 2, *Finansy* (1923), p. 17, cit. D′yachenko, *op. cit.* p. 178; and as for Table 9.

(ii) Reduction of original estimates in January–June, 1919, budget period (million roubles)

	Revenue	Expenditure
Original demands of departments	30,801	107,205
Proposals of departmental commissions	22,636	68,948
Proposed by budget inter-departmental commission	22,636	60,827
Finally adopted on proposal of special commission of *Malyi sovet* of SNK	20,350	50,703

Source: *Rospis′...na i.–vi. 1919...*, pp. 33 ff.

As the inflation progressed, discipline in the compilation of estimates gradually broke down. By 1920, as soon as estimates reached the inter-departmental commission, they were treated for practical purposes as if they had been adopted already by the government. Government departments ceased to be concerned about the formal adoption of their estimates by SNK, and the initial estimates for 1920 passed into the budget with little alteration.[1]

The delay in the adoption of estimates meant in fact that from the beginning of the civil war allocations had to be made by temporary monthly, and later six-monthly, credits. At first these were equal to those allowed in the estimates adopted for the preceding budget; later, in view of the depreciation of the real value of allocations,

[1] See Table 7 and *Ek. zhizn′*, no. 215 (28. ix. 1920). The compiling of the initial 1920 estimates was not completed until very late in the year, and that for VSNKh (in spite of a circular at the end of August which attempted to speed it up) not till September (*Ek. zhizn′*, nos. 191, 249 (1920)).

provision was made for credits above this level.[1] In practice even this kind of allocation became irregular. The physical shortage of new notes to meet permitted allocations made it necessary to set up an inter-departmental commission for the distribution of currency, which issued money to central government departments by a rough system of priorities.[2] These sums were then re-allocated to local bodies (or, in the case of VSNKh, to its *glavki*) as earmarked grants, in accordance with what the central bodies conceived to be the most important needs.[3] The attempt of the organs of state supervision to supervise in advance the issue of allocations came to nothing.[4]

Thus within the limits of the money system first the over-all budget, and then the estimates of the separate government bodies, ceased to have practical importance. By early 1921, government departments were ceasing to compile estimates; and in March 1921 the estimate commissions of the commissariats and the inter-departmental budget commission of NKF were abolished.[5] The compilation of money budgets in Soviet Russia had come to an end.

4. THE MONEYLESS ECONOMY AND THE MATERIAL BUDGET

The growth of transactions in kind meant that the money economy and the money budget included and reflected a steadily declining proportion of economic activity. From 1919, money accounts, even when accurate, ceased to reflect the real processes of the economy; behind the budgets there lay the material input and output of the state, taking place as a rule directly in physical terms—the requisitioning of foodstuffs, the passage of goods from state enterprise to

[1] For the second half of 1918 monthly temporary allocations had been at the average level for May–June 1918; for the second half of 1919, at one-sixth of the January–June 1919 budget estimate. For the first six months of 1920, two quarterly allocations were permitted, at a maximum of half the July–December 1919 budget estimate *plus* above-estimate allocations. For the first six months of 1921 much greater latitude was given to exceed the 1920 level; and the procedure laid down for approval of these temporary credits was a much-simplified version of that for adopting the budget. (See legislation already cited, and SU 80/1920 (1. iii. 20) and 448/1920 (28. x. 20)).

[2] The commission is said to have been abolished in mid-1920, when (it is said) currency distribution was centralised in NKF (see K. Shmelev in G. Y. Sokol'nikov, *et al.*, *Soviet policy in public finance 1917–1928* (1931), pp. 125–6).

[3] *Ek. zhizn'*, no. 115 (1921).

[4] This preliminary supervision was first abolished for allocations earmarked for wages, and completely abandoned by the end of 1919 (though not formally abolished until early in 1921) (D'yachenko, *op. cit.* pp. 139–41).

[5] *Ek. zhizn'*, no. 112 (1921); *Sbornik dekretov i rasporyazhenii po finansam*, vol. IV (1921), no. 183 (decree of 17. iii. 1921).

state enterprise in their various stages of manufacture, and their final transfer to the individual consumer (or to the army).

Much of this 'expenditure' took place purely as book transfers, which had no direct effect on the amount of currency in circulation. It bore little relation to expenditure in cash on the free market. A proposal was therefore mooted to keep separate national accounts for the fixed-price rouble and the free-market rouble by distinguishing so-called 'turnover' payments and receipts (book-keeping transfers from one soviet body to another for materials, products, services, etc. supplied or received) from 'direct' payments and receipts (in currency notes or to and from current accounts).[1] But the financial situation deteriorated to such an extent that this system was unworkable.[2]

Many enterprises and institutions ceased recording transfers of goods in money terms by the end of 1919;[3] and in 1920 and in the first months of 1921 all payments in fixed low prices, by enterprises and by most of the population, were formally abolished for many goods and services and replaced by a further extension of the rationing system.[4]

These developments were accompanied by a considerable change in the prevailing attitude to the function of finance and money. Before the revolution the Bolsheviks held that money and full socialism were incompatible, but that in Russia a transition period would be necessary in which finances would have to be strengthened, not weakened. And in the first eighteen months after the revolution,

---

[1] SU 318/1919 (24. v. 19).

[2] In July 1920 VTsIK resolved that 'turnover' allocations should gradually be excluded from the budget (D'yachenko, *op. cit.* p. 183).

[3] K. Shmelev, *op. cit.* p. 83.

[4] Postage on letters up to 15 gms. in weight had already been abolished in 1918 (*Sbornik dekretov, 1917–18*, no. 149 (21. xi. 1918)); children up to sixteen years of age had been supplied with free food from mid-1919 (SU 238/1919 (17. v. 19), 296/1919 (12. vi. 19)); payments for posts and telegraphs by soviet institutions, etc., were abolished from 1 April 1920 (SU 109/1920 (25. iii. 1920)). Then a sweeping decree of 11 October 1920 abolished payments for fuel supplied by the main fuel committee and for municipal services, both by state and co-operative bodies and by their workers and employees, forces' dependants, and all persons on pensions and covered by the commissariats of health and social security; and payment for the food supplied to certain bodies and ration categories was also abolished (SU 422/1920). Subsequent decrees extended free supply to virtually all food, postal services and fuel (SU 505/1920 (4. xii. 20), 539/1920 (23. xii. 20), 20/1921), to medicines on prescription (SU 60/1921 (5. ii. 1921)), to fodder for socially-necessary work (SU 81/1921 (14. ii. 21)), to newspapers (SU 211/1921 (23. iii. 21)), and to films for state institutions (SU 246/1921 (20. v. 21)). References to the 'norms' or rations to be made available are made in certain of the above decrees and in a decree of 27. i. 1921 (SU 47/1921).

attempts were made, as we have seen, to grapple with the problems of public finance in a transition period of 'mixed economy'. What were the appropriate methods for taxation, when large-scale property and income had been seized, or taxed to the limit? What should be the place of local finance in this system? How should the accounts of state enterprises with each other and with the private sector be kept? But no satisfactory financial theory (or even policy) for a socialist economy was developed, and these problems remained unresolved.

When it proved impossible to stabilise the currency, and a centralised 'war communist' economy began to be established, the earlier cautions about the dangers of a rapid transition to a moneyless system were heard less often. The view spread that the civil war system of complete state ownership and the abolition of the market was the full socialism of Marx and Engels, and that money was therefore an anachronism. And this view was strengthened by the inflation which seemed in any case to make the abolition of money inevitable.

By the middle of 1920, the view that the time was ripe for the complete establishment of a moneyless system was almost universally accepted, and attention turned to the problems of operating an economy in kind.[1]

[1] The victory of the supporters of the moneyless economy did not take place simply or automatically. In the first months, stabilisation of the currency was accepted as an aim by all except the 'Left Communists' (e.g. Bukharin, who in *The Programme of communists*, 1918, triumphantly declared 'Society is turning into a huge labour *artel*, which produces, and distributes what is produced, without gold, metal or paper money. The power of money is coming to an end'; or Smirnov's speech of May 1918—*Trudy*... (1918)).

By the end of 1918, there was already talk of labour units and a material budget (cf. *Ek. zhizn'*, no. 27 (1918) and no. 1 (1919)); and the prevailing attitude of the communists in the NKF, particularly after the Extraordinary Revolutionary Tax failed to yield the results which were hoped for, seems to have been that money must be retained temporarily, but would be abolished in the near future (see e.g. *Ek. zhizn'*, no. 40 (1918)). Warnings were given, however, that a moneyless system was 'a most responsible and complex task of communism', which 'it is impossible to approach...by simply annulling existing money' (Shefler, in *Ek. zhizn'*, no. 15 (1918)), and that it 'could be dangerous and even catastrophic if the decline and devaluation of our rouble took place before we finished our economic reconstruction' (*ibid.* no. 23 (1918)). The general view was reflected in the programme adopted by the Eighth Party Congress in March 1919, which stated that 'in the first period of transition from capitalism to communism, while communist production and distribution of products is still not yet fully organised, the abolition of money is impossible'; but nevertheless added that 'the R.C.P. [Russian Communist Party] is striving to introduce a number of measures extending the sphere of moneyless accounting and preparing the abolition of money'.

The policy of stabilisation was, however, given a new lease of life in the spring of 1919, when a further unsuccessful attempt was made to undertake a currency reform. This move was enthusiastically backed by Lenin, always a proponent of caution on the

In the sphere of the budget the central problem became the replacement of the money budget by a budget or balance of state income and expenditure in kind (the 'material budget'), a 'unified plan for utilising the material resources of the country'.[1] In October 1920 SNK set up a commission under NKF to prepare a draft decree annulling accounts in money terms between soviet bodies, and to work out a basis for material accounts. At the end of January 1921, at the request of the commission, SNK issued general instructions on the form which material accounts and the material budget should take. The budget was to show expenditure by administrative unit, by purpose, and by area, and it was to be a net budget, not including the mutual accounts of state bodies. The commission continued to meet until the middle of 1921, when a draft decree on the material budget was produced.[2]

The work of the commission was the centre of lively controversy during the first few months of 1921.[3] These discussions took place in extremely adverse circumstances. The unified economic plan of which the budget was to be the detailed expression hardly existed, and there were no past examples of material budgets to take as a starting point.

The key problem for the would-be builders of a material budget and of a moneyless economy was to find a substitute which would do the work of money. In the absence of prices freely formed on the market and of a common money denominator, how could production be evaluated and economic decisions taken? and how could consumer goods be distributed?

There were some (e.g. A. V. Chayanov) who answered that no common denominator was possible or necessary. On the production

question of the abolition of money (cf. *Soch.* xxix, pp. 16, 329; and various references in *Trudy*... (1919)).

But when this failed, the view that money must be abolished soon became almost universally accepted. By the middle of 1920 Strumilin could write that 'the unsuitability of money accounting for the planned control of the state economy of Soviet Russia in present conditions is so evident, that no one is in doubt of it. Money accounting of economic wealth must give way to moneyless accounting. That is beyond dispute' (*Ek. zhizn'*, no. 237 (1920), and see Carr, *op. cit.* pp. 262–3; M. H. Dobb, *Soviet Economic Development since 1917* (1948), pp. 121–2).

[1] *Narodnyi komissariat finansov*..., pp. 37 f.

[2] For details, see D'yachenko, *op. cit.* p. 193 (where the statement that the work of the commission continued till the end of 1921 is apparently an error); *Finansovaya politika*..., pp. 73–6.

[3] See, e.g., Azarkh's proposal for a central material bank in *Ek. zhizn'*, no. 12 (1921); and the discussion between M. Al'skii, Syromolotov, *et al.*, *ibid.* nos. 39, 54, 71, 91, and 101, 1921—the last of these articles did not appear till 12 May, nearly two months after the introduction of the tax in kind.

Table 8. *Revenue of state budget, 1917–21 (million roubles)*

	1917[15] Draft plan(a)	1 Jan.–30 June 1918[16] Plan(b)	1 Jan.–30 June 1918 Fulfilment(h)	1 July–31 Dec. 1918 Plan(c)	1 July–31 Dec. 1918 Fulfilment(h)	1 Jan.–30 June 1919[12] Plan(d)	1 Jan.–30 June 1919 Fulfilment(h)	1 July–31 Dec. 1919 Plan(e)	1 July–31 Dec. 1919 Fulfilment	1920 Plan(f)(b)	1920 Fulfilment	1921 Plan(f)	1921 Fulfilment(g)
I. DIRECT TAXES													
Income tax	130·0	150·0	—	255·0	—	400·0	88	250	52	207	—	—	77,418
Promtax	275·7	200·0	—	100·9	—	376·9		74					
Land and property tax and dues[1]	160·3	18·0	—	11·0	—	5·1		6		20[13]		—	8,863
Other direct taxes	n.a.	n.a.	—	n.a.(5)	—	950·0[11]	613[12]	511[12]	453				86,281
Total direct taxes	566·1	368·0	—	366·9	—[14]	1,732·0	701	851	505	227		275,492[8]	
II. INDIRECT TAXES[2]	1,099·1	410·2	—[14]	393·3	—[14]	2,572·2	191	1,730	345	356		2,680	1,830
III. DUES (*poshliny*)	442·2	175·7	—[14]	120·0	—[14]	97·9	54	132	128	49		9,410	n.a.
IV–V. REGALIA AND OTHER INCOME FROM GOVERNMENT PROPERTY													
Post and transport	1,253·2[6]	1,104·0	—	846·7	—	1,256·7	146[7]	1,920	562[7]	22,522		689,100	—
Nationalised industrial enterprises[10]	n.a.	n.a.	—	12·0	—	5,812·1	46[7]	8,855	253[7]	52,031		93,576	—
Receipts from supply of essential goods to population	n.a.	n.a.	—	n.a.	—	6,500·0	0	11,655	42	51,104			—
Other[3]	471·8	730·1	—	942·8	—	2,031·1	404	2,652	135	29,397		3,046,683	—
Total from government property	1,725·0	1,834·1	240	1,801·5	1,537	15,599·9	596	24,992	992	155,654		3,829,359	567,009
VI–VIII. VARIOUS AND EXTRAORDINARY REVENUE[4]	245·3	64·7	77	45·3	171	347·6	724	856	2,068	3,318		22,959	19,602
TOTAL REVENUE	4,077·8[28]	2,852·7	885	2,726·9	2,477	20,349·6	2,266	28,610	4,038	159,604		4,139,900	835,505[9]

n.a. = not applicable. Dash indicates not available.

Table 9. *Expenditure of state budget, 1917–21*[18] *(million roubles)*

	1917[17](a) Plan	1 Jan.–30 June 1918 Plan(h)	1 Jan.–30 June 1918 Fulfilment(h)	1 July–31 Dec. 1918 Plan(h)	1 July–31 Dec. 1918 Fulfilment(h)	1 Jan.–30 June 1919 Plan(h)	1 Jan.–30 June 1919 Fulfilment(h)	1 July–31 Dec. 1919 Plan(h)	1 July–31 Dec. 1919 Fulfilment(h)	1920 Plan(h)	1920 Fulfilment(h)	1921 Plan by departments(f)
I. ECONOMIC NKS AND DEPARTMENTS[19]	4,385	9,489	844	12,762	2,782	26,177	4,140	85,093	6,071	725,166		17,619,797
II. SOCIAL AND CULTURAL[20]	3,159	1,706	1,319	4,606	820	7,456	2,553	35,351	6,735	269,716		1,958,380
III. DEFENCE[21]	3,139	5,222	3,051	9,516	5,053	12,239	5,122	31,171	10,740	137,842		260,106
IV. ADMINISTRATION[22]	1,496	640	561	1,886	2,664	2,803	1,419	10,543	3,115	68,290		4,633,639
V. TO COVER EXPENDITURE OF LOCAL SOVIETS	n.a.	—	—	—	—	—	—	—	—	2,500		—
VI. INTEREST AND COMPENSATION ON LOANS, ETC.	916[25]	—	—	—	—	—	—	—	—	525		—
Other expenditure[23]	101[25]	546[27]	—	333	42	2,028	149	2,541	587	11,120		n.a.
Extraordinary expenditure[24]	14,675	—	13	—	—	n.a.	n.a.	n.a.	n.a.	n.a.		n.a.
TOTAL EXPENDITURE	27,871[29]	17,603	5,788[26]	29,103	11,301[26]	50,703	13,383	164,699	27,248	1,215,159		24,471,922
Excess of expenditure over revenue	23,793	14,750	4,903	26,376	8,834	30,353	11,117	130,089	23,210	1,055,555		20,332,022

n.a. = not applicable. Dash indicates not available.

Sources:

(a) *Proposed budget of the Empire for 1917*, part I, 1917; *Ek. zhizn'*, no. 4, 1918; *Proekt gosudarstvennoi rospisi dokhodov i raskhodov na 1917 god...* (1916).
(b) *Obshchaya rospis'...na i.–vi. 18*.
(c) *Rospis'...na vii.–xii. 18*.
(d) *Rospis'...na i.–vi. 19*.
(e) *Rospis'...na vii.–xii. 19*.
(f) *Narodnyi komissariat finansov...*, p. 45.
(g) *Ek. zhizn'*, no. 33, (1922).
(h) D'yachenko, *op. cit.* pp. 103, 106, 186–9.

Notes:

(1) Includes tax on immovable property, levy on income from money capital, and various dues.
(2) Includes revenue from alcohol, drinks, tobacco, cigarette papers, matches, sugar, tea, and oil; and customs revenue. The profit from the treasury alcohol and (from 1918 onwards) sugar monopolies appears under Sections IV–V.
(3) Includes revenue from alcohol and sugar monopoly, treasury works and properties, coinage, timber, state farms, and foreign trade.
(4) Includes refunding of expenditures by treasury, levy on enterprises for non-mobilised workers and employees, etc. Extraordinary Revenue refers only to 1917 (draft plan), where it amounted to 79.2 million roubles.
(5) The ten-milliard rouble Extraordinary Revolutionary Tax (E.R.T.) was originally due to be collected by 15 December 1918, but collection was hardly begun by that date. It is therefore not added in here to the budget total. Receipts from the tax are, however, included in the fulfilment figures (they amounted in this period to 183 million roubles).
(6) Includes 24.7 million roubles from participation of treasury in revenue of private railways.
(7) Includes various treasury enterprises, appearing under 'other' in planned figures.
(8) Presumably includes local taxes, incorporated in state budget from June 1920.
(9) Includes 160,783 million roubles local taxes.
(10) The gross revenue of nationalised enterprises was included in the January–July 1919 budget for a number of branches of industry (e.g. metal-working, coal, chemicals) and the NK of Food; and the gross revenue of all industry in the July–December 1919 and later budgets.
(11) Includes 850.0 million roubles tax in kind on peasant households and 100.0 million roubles E.R.T.

(12) E.R.T. only. For 1 Jan.–30 June 1919, such receipts as were obtained from the tax in kind are included with the 88 million roubles above.
(13) Tax in kind only.
(14) Total receipts from direct and indirect taxes and customs dues are stated to have amounted to 568 million roubles in January–June and to 586 million roubles (including E.R.T.) in July–December 1918.
(15) Where the data in the various sources cited vary, the latest figure is given here.
(16) Data for these years are as far as possible reclassified on the basis of the classification used in the budget for July–December 1919.
(17) Expenditures of old departments is classified as nearly as possible under equivalent heads for post-revolutionary departments.
(18) Except for 1921 (plan), all expenditure is shown by function (thus economic expenditure by a primarily administrative body appears under national economy and not under administration). This reclassification by function is based on D'yachenko and must be accepted with caution, as it could not be checked with the original sources. Fulfilment data is available in sources used by us only by function. Budget expenditure classified by government departments may be found in sources (b)–(f) listed above.
(19) Includes expenditure on VSNKh, nationalised enterprises, NK of Trade and Industry, State Equipment Committee, Transport and Posts, and NK of Food and Agriculture.
(20) Includes Education, Health, Labour, and Social Security.
(21) Includes NKs of Army and Navy, Evacuation Commission, and 'expenditure from war and its consequences'.
(22) Includes administrative expenditure of VTsIK, SNK, NKVD, NKs of Justice, Foreign Affairs, Nationalities, Finance, State Control, Central Statistical Commission, etc.
(23) Includes reserve funds, and expenditure in 'liberated areas'.
(24) Mainly 'war fund' expenditure (see chapter I).
(25) Includes Holy Synod and various state bodies abolished after revolution.
(26) Alternative fulfilment figures to these obvious under-estimates are given in Prokopovitch, *op. cit.*, namely: January–June 1918, 8,700 million roubles; July–December 1918, 22,000 million roubles.
(27) Includes payments to Germany under the Brest-Litovsk Treaty (325 million roubles).
(28) This total excludes short-term and long-term internal and external loans. In fact (see Table 2), total revenue amounted to 22,165 million roubles, of which 5,039 million roubles falls within the items covered by the above Table.
(29) Total expenditure in fact amounted to 30,606 million roubles (see Table 2).

side, the efficiency of one method or another of producing a particular good could be determined by reference to 'norms' (standard rates) of average productivity. Chayanov was, however, unable to suggest any criteria for determining the optimum ratio of capital to labour in a given outlay; and his system implied that the state should determine from above what goods should be produced (*how* it should do this was not clear), and distribute them by a system of rationing.[1]

The majority of writers, however, considered that some kind of common denominator was needed, as a basis for the allocation of resources and, many thought, for the payment of wages and some degree of consumers' choice. As is well-known, most of the schemes of 1920–1 were built up on the basis of some kind of 'labour-unit' (*trudovaya edinitsa*), known as *tred*.[2] Essentially, nearly all the versions (e.g. Strumilin, Kreve, Shmelev) proposed that the basic unit for economic measurement should be the normal output of a worker of a certain skill in a certain time. Higher or lower skills, and greater or less output for the given level of skill, should be reduced to the standard labour-unit by the use of appropriate factors (the only criteria suggested for these factors were the wage-scales of the pre-revolutionary period). According to the most sophisticated scheme, that of Strumilin, goods should be 'priced' in labour-units, and wages paid in them; and the allocation of resources to new production should be made in such a way as to enable a balance of supply and demand for all goods at these labour-unit prices.

It should be noted that the labour-unit scheme presumed that goods would exchange at a 'price' level determined by labour input, uninfluenced by the ratio of capital to labour in the particular industry.[3] No allowance was made for an interest rate on capital, although Strumilin conceded that this was theoretically conceivable.[4]

In practice no unified detailed proposal was compiled either by the special currency sub-commission of the NKF commission on the material budget, or by the economic bodies (VSNKh, the Central

[1] See articles in *Ek. zhizn'*, nos. 225, 231, 247 (1920).
[2] The freak 'labour and energy unit' and 'energy unit' (*ened*) schemes of M. Smit and S. Klepikov never went further than rough suggestions, and assumed that the same expenditure of energy always produced the same economic effect. Smit's scheme involved a parallel measurement of labour and energy, but did not explain how they could be compared; and Klepikov's involved the reduction of labour to energy but did not show how this could be done.
[3] I.e. in Marxist terminology they would exchange at the 'values' of vol. 1 of *Capital* and not at the 'prices of production' of vol. 3.
[4] See Dobbert, ed., *Soviet Economics*, pp. 146–8.

Statistical Administration, the Commissariat of Transport, etc.) which were considering the question.[1] SNK got no further than a resolution (21 January 1921) proposing the 'working-out of the most appropriate accounting-unit, as a general measure of evaluation, for the labour régime'; and the final resolution of the currency sub-commission of NKF was limited to a general suggestion that the Council of Labour and Defence (STO) should draw up rules on reducing complex labour to simple labour, and prepare a 'price-list' of normal labour expenditure for all goods and services.[2] When the policy of war communism was abandoned in 1921, not even the general principles for the compilation of a budget in kind had been worked out.

[1] For further discussion on *treds*, etc. see Yurovskii, *op. cit.* ch. II. See also *Ek. zhizn'*: articles by Strumilin in nos. 167, 237, 284, 290 (1920); and no. 14 (1921); by Varga in no. 259 (1920); by Tolstomyatov (on the application of the labour-unit to railway accounting), no. 276 (1920); and no. 126 (1921).

[2] Yurovskii, *op. cit.* pp. 88, 107.

PART II

THE MIXED ECONOMY
1921–9

CHAPTER IV

THE EMERGENCE OF A NEW BUDGETARY SYSTEM 1921-4

1. THE NEW ECONOMIC POLICY, 1921

AT the end of the civil war, the Bolsheviks were faced with a political and economic crisis. Industrial production had fallen to a fraction of the pre-war level, and agricultural production had declined considerably. The market economy had been replaced by an economy in kind, in which the town obtained supplies of foodstuffs from the countryside by barter and by requisitioning. Centralisation and compulsion had steadily reduced support for the government—in the spring of 1921 local peasant uprisings took place, and there was great discontent in the towns.

It was even more essential for the government to consolidate its position than it had been in April 1918, and this involved it in a retreat from the extreme measures which it had been forced to take by military necessity. At the end of 1920 it abandoned the policy of rigid control of labour and compulsory membership of trade unions, and in March 1921 the arbitrary system of requisitioning of foodstuffs was replaced by a tax in kind, the limits of which were fixed in advance at a level below that of 1920.

These limited concessions to industrial worker and peasant were not at first intended to be a major reversal of policy. Economic writings of the period continued to envisage a moneyless economy. It was held that 'commodity exchange' between town and country, and within state industry, would take place by a form of barter, and that trade in money, if it took place at all, would be confined to the local market.[1]

---

[1] D'yachenko, *op. cit.* pp. 200-1; SU 212/1921 (24. v. 21); K. Shmelev in *Vestnik finansov*, no. 8 (1926), pp. 14-15; *VKP(b) v rezolyutsiakh*, vol. I, pp. 396-9 (Resolution of Tenth Party Conference, 26-28 May 1921).

In practice, the barter system soon broke down. The goods offered to the peasant by the co-operatives were badly distributed, insufficient, and of poor quality, and the cumbrous system of 'exchange equivalents' operated against him.[1] He therefore preferred to sell his produce on the now legal local market, in spite of the fact that the currency was still depreciating. At the same time, the factory workers, who had previously relied almost entirely on requisitioned supplies for their personal consumption, now had to turn for part of their requirements to the market, where they bartered or sold products from their factories which were issued to them as bonuses in kind.[2] The factories themselves were gradually taken off centralised supply, and came increasingly to the market as both buyers and sellers. The economy in kind was driven out by the money economy, and the government was forced to recognise this in August 1921 by legalising trade on a national as well as a local scale.[3]

During 1921 the New Economic Policy took shape. The 'commanding heights' of industry were retained in state hands, but its management was substantially decentralised, and small-scale industry was transferred to private ownership. Rationing was abolished and private individuals were permitted to engage in wholesale and retail trade, becoming particularly important in retail trade. The new economy established in 1921 was a mixed system in which state-owned industry operated in an environment of small-scale private farming and of a capitalist market. The Soviet government regarded this economy as essentially merely transitional to socialism in the Marxist sense. The growth of the private sector was seen as an unfortunate necessity, forced upon the government by the need to rehabilitate the shattered economy. Once this had been achieved, the Soviet leaders argued, the planned economy of the workers' and peasants' state should seek to supplant private ownership and the market. Economic policy took this aim into account even in the first years of N.E.P.

[1] See Yurovskii, *op. cit.* pp. 131 ff. The equivalents on the basis of which exchange took place were usually measured in grain-units, and were at first based on the assumption that the current ratio of exchange had moved 3:1 in favour of industrial goods as compared with pre-war prices. When this proved unacceptable, market prices were taken as a standard—but this was already an admission that the money economy had triumphed over exchange in kind.

[2] SU 156/1921 (7. iv. 21).

[3] See D'yachenko, *op. cit.* pp. 202–4; and Lenin, *Soch.* vol. xxxiii, p. 72, where he states: 'Nothing has come of commodity-exchange; the private market has shown itself stronger than us, and instead of commodity-exchange we have ordinary purchase and sale, or trade' (speech of 29. x. 21).

2. THE INFLATION OF 1921–2

The introduction of N.E.P. placed a heavy burden on what remained of the fiscal system. When supplies in kind were reduced, enterprises had to obtain materials by money payments to the non-socialised sector of the economy, and by cash instead of purely book-keeping transactions with other units inside the socialised sector. At the same time the money wages paid to state workers and employees had to be increased in real terms owing to the reduction of centralised food supplies. The cash incomes of enterprises from sales on the market were still extremely small; industry was not efficient enough to pay for itself, and those factories which were not closed down or transferred into private hands had to be given money subsidies from the budget in place of the subsidies in food and materials which they had previously received. Monetary budget expenditure rose from 9 million pre-war roubles per month in the third quarter of 1921 to 30 million in the last quarter, and by the end of 1922 it had reached 70 million roubles per month—a quarter of the pre-war level.

In 1921 and 1922 it proved impossible to collect substantial budgetary revenues. The tax apparatus had dispersed during 1920 and early 1921, and it was only slowly revived, although priority was given to its reconstruction.[1] The market was unstable, the money incomes of the population were irregular, and the economy was generally disorganised. As a result, only a few simple taxes were introduced by the end of 1922. The imposition of excises did not present great administrative difficulties, and they were responsible for two-thirds of all taxation.[2] The remaining revenue was collected by means of the Promtax,[3] reintroduced in pre-war form, and of a

---

[1] See SU 488/1921 (19. ix. 21), 46/1922 (30. xii. 21), 550/1922 (17. vii. 22); D'yachenko, *op. cit.* pp. 240–2; *Ek. zhizn'*, no. 176 (1921). For material on the size and efficiency of the N.E.P. tax apparatus as compared with 1913, see *Vestnik finansov*, no. 3 (1924), pp. 100–5, and no. 3 (1926), pp. 84–93.

[2] For details of the excises on spirits, matches, tobacco, kerosene, tea, coffee and chicory, sugar and saccharine, and yeast, introduced in 1921 and 1922, see *Sbornik...po finansam*, vol. IV, no. 99 (decree of 9. viii. 21); SU 624/1921 (14. xi. 21), 631/1921 (21. xi. 21), 700/1921 (1. xii. 21), 156–7/1922 (3. ii. 22), 220/1922 (25. ii. 22), 258/1922 (9. iii. 22), 390/1922 (4. v. 22), 1007/1922 (30. xi. 22); and *Vestnik finansov*, no. 7 (1924), pp. 1–7. For material on the N.E.P. excise apparatus, see *Sbornik dekretov i rasporyazhenii po finansam*, vol. IV (1921), nos. 191, 187 (circulars of 22. viii. and 5. ix. 21); *Fin. politika...s xii. 1920 g. po xii. 1921 g.* pp. 130–4; and *Vestnik finansov*, no. 3 (1924), pp. 100–5.

[3] For details, see SU 354/1921 (26. vii. 21), 89/1923 (18. i. 23); *Sbornik...po finansam*, vol. IV, p. 58 (3. ix. 21); *Izvestiya VTsIKa*, no. 32, 1922 (8. ii. 22); D'yachenko, *op. cit.* pp. 245–9.

series of graded poll-taxes earmarked for famine relief.[1] In the first nine months of 1922 money taxes reached on the average only 3% of the pre-war level in real terms, but expenditure in real terms was some 14% of the pre-war level.

This level of expenditure was obtained by extremely large issues of currency, leading to a galloping inflation, as is illustrated in Table 10. Currency circulation increased particularly rapidly between October 1921 and April 1922, when the famine led to a decline in trade in real terms to a level below that of the worst months of war communism. The inflation made the development of a stable system of internal trade impossible. It made it difficult to reorganise industry along efficient lines, as both outlays (on wages and market purchases) and receipts (from market sales) were rising at unpredictable rates. It hindered the construction of a new financial system: as it was impossible to budget in depreciating currency, various methods were devised to measure budget expenditure in pre-war roubles (commodity roubles) and gold roubles, but they were not very successful.[2] Additional difficulties were caused by the fact that some transactions were still conducted in kind (the tax in kind, for example, and part of exchange inside state industry), and these had to be measured in money terms.[3]

Nevertheless, this rapid inflation proved to be a prelude to financial recovery. The steady triumph of the money economy had brought about a radical change in the attitude of Soviet economists to money; it was an obvious fact of life that trade between town and

[1] Per-head levies were first discussed in September 1921. In February 1922 the first 'general civil tax to help those suffering from famine...' was introduced as a levy on almost all adults in town and country, varying from 50 kopeks to 1r. 50k. (in pre-war units), according to the status of the person concerned. Three times the anticipated sum was raised. A second similar levy was imposed at the end of 1922. Various other taxes to relieve the famine were also imposed. During this period the labour and cartage tax (*trudguzhnalog*) was converted from a due of four days' labour per annum into a money tax. For details of all these taxes, see *Ek. zhizn'*, no. 200 (1921) *et seq.* (conference of Institute of Economic Research); *Izvestiya VTsIKa*, no. 35 (1922) (11. ii. 22); D'yachenko, *op. cit.* pp. 254–6, 263; SU 583/1922 (25. vii. 22), 892/1922 (2. xi. 22), 343/1921 (14. vii. 21), 696/1921 (29. xi. 21), 479/1922 (13. vi. 22), 1020/1922 (6. xii. 22), 191/1923 (15. ii. 23).

[2] For details, see Yurovskii, *op. cit.* pp. 195, 202 ff., and ch. v in general; *Sbornik dekretov ...po finansam*, vol. IV, no. 127 (5. xi. 21); *Rospis'...na i.–ix. 1922g....* (1922), supplement, pp. 10–11 (22. xi. 21 preliminary decree); SU 75/1922 (18. i. 22), 127–8/1922 (21. i. 22), 310/1922 (30. iii. 22), 961/1922 (10. viii. 22), 962/1922 (17. xi. 22); *Vestnik finansov*, no. 5 (1923), pp. 122–3 (circular of 16. i. 23).

[3] The attempt to retain the distinction between 'direct' and 'turnover' revenue and expenditure in the budget originally compiled for 1922 was unsuccessful. In the 1922/3 and the 1923/4 budgets, revenues in kind were included at their value in current market prices. See SU 961/1922, 961/1923.

Table 10. *Currency circulation, 1921–4*

(i) 1921–2

	Currency circulation on 1st day of quarter (milliard 1921 roubles)	Increase of circulation during quarter (%)	Estimated real value of currency on 1st day of quarter (million pre-war roubles)	Price index (1913 = 1) on 1st day of quarter [1]
Jan.–Mar. 1921	1,169	44·3	70	19,200
Apr.–June 1921	1,687	39·1	47 [2]	42,029 [2]
July–Sept. 1921	2,347	93·2	29	80,500
Oct.–Dec. 1921	4,529	287·2	55	88,700
Jan.–Mar. 1922	17,538	362·9	61	311,500
Apr.–June 1922	81,179	294·1	32	—
July–Sept. 1922	319,949	166·1	55	—
Oct.–Dec. 1922	851,486	134·3	116	7,829,500

(ii) 1923–4

	Circulation of *sovznaki* on 1st day of quarter (million roubles 1923 issue)	Circulation of *chervontsy* on 1st day of quarter (million roubles)	Estimated real value of *sovznak* circulation	Estimated real value of *chervonets* circulation	Total real value of currency
			(million pre-war roubles)		
Jan.–Mar. 1923	1,994	3·6	94	3	97
Apr.–June 1923	4,482	25·7	114	20	134
July–Sept. 1923	9,031	70·0	77	45	122
Oct.–Dec. 1923	29,754	207·4	45	126	171
Jan.–Mar. 1924	225,637	237·2	41	130	177 [3]

Sources: *Vestnik finansov*, no. 1 (1922), pp. 3–5; D'yachenko, *op. cit.* pp. 213, 352; Yurovskii, *op. cit.* pp. 147 ff.

Notes:
(1) Labour statistics index.
(2) This figure, taken from E. A. Preobrazhenskii, *Teoriya padayushchei valyuty* (1930), p. 119, is not strictly compatible with the other data in the column, as it is based on a different price index.
(3) Includes 5 million rubles 'transport certificates'.

country, essential to the N.E.P. system, could be conducted only in money.[1] The experience of 1920–1 had shown that no unit of account apart from a money unit could be put at the basis of state finance in the Russia of the 1920's, and that of 1921–2 demonstrated that the budget could be compiled and fulfilled satisfactorily only in a *stable* money unit which had replaced relations in kind throughout

[1] Discussions on labour-units and on the material budget continued intermittently for several months after March 1921 (cf. e.g. *Ek. zhizn'*, no. 126 (1921)), but by May 1921 the need for money exchange was generally accepted. The view that money would be abolished in a system of full communism was of course never abandoned by Soviet leaders (cf. Krestinskii, *Nasha finansovaya politika* (1921), pp. 19–20; Sokol'nikov, *Finansovaya politika revolyutsii*, vol. I, p. 114; and Stalin, *Soch.* vol. x, pp. 226–8 and *Ekonomicheskie problemy sotsializma v SSSR* (1952), p. 23).

the economy. This was soon recognised by Soviet economists.[1] But they held that a stable currency could not be achieved by an immediate currency reform. Currency issue was necessary because revenue and expenditure could not be balanced; and financial measures alone could not eliminate the budget deficit. Behind the financial crisis there lay the economic crisis, which could be solved only by raising agricultural and industrial productivity and on this basis expanding the market. Only this revival could enable state industry to pay for itself, they argued, and provide a level of income among the population sufficiently high for part of it to be taxed to finance normal state expenditure on administration, social services, and defence. Nevertheless, it was essential to restore the budgetary system and a banking network in which available monetary resources could be concentrated for productive use. The budget and the banks, it was stated, would be an important lever to encourage the restoration of the economy, and they would play their part in reducing currency issue as the prerequisite for a currency reform at a later date. This approach to financial policy was gradually developed and made coherent in a series of government and party resolutions in the autumn and winter of 1921–2.[2]

3. THE RESTORATION OF THE BUDGET, 1921–2

During the first two years of N.E.P., in spite of economic difficulties and the persistence of rapid inflation, important steps were taken towards the re-establishment of a budgetary system.

The need for a budgetary system arose automatically out of the abolition of the economy in kind. But how all-embracing was the restored budget to be? If it were to continue to be the 'national economic balance' which was tried out under war communism, it would have to carry the burden of financing all the activities of the state, economic and administrative, central and local. In March–June 1921, NKF in fact made an unsuccessful attempt to tighten its control over money allocations both to industry and to the local

---

[1] Preobrazhenskii had spoken in favour of a stable currency as early as March 1921 (see Carr, *op. cit.* vol. II, p. 345); and early in May E. Knorre called for a metal currency, and a balanced money budget, in terms which within a few months became government policy (*Ek. zhizn'*, no. 96 (9. v. 1921)).

[2] Circular of NKF, 22. viii. 1921 (*Sbornik dekretov...po finansam*, vol. IV, no. 20); VTsIK decree, 10. x. 1921 (SU 550/1921); decree of Ninth Congress of Soviets, 30. xii. 1921 (SU 46/1922); resolution of Eleventh Party Congress, 27. iii.–2. iv. 1922, *VKP(b) v rezolyutsiakh*, vol. I, pp. 425–8.

soviets,[1] but it was unable to issue sufficient currency to meet even the most elementary requirements. As has been described, industrial enterprises began of their own accord to sell their output on the market. Parallel with this, local soviets introduced illegal local taxes.[2]

The government and the financial authorities soon recognised both that a new, entirely monetary, budgetary system must be established, and that it should be responsible for financing only the most indispensable state expenditure on administration, defence and the economy. 'Without a decisive reduction of the state budget', stated a resolution of the Eleventh Party Conference in December 1921, 'the restoration of the economy is impossible.' Between July 1921 and the end of 1922 the budget was freed from 'in kind' transactions and from financing the expenditure of industry and the local soviets.

The system whereby enterprises had received all their supplies from the state and transferred all their output to it was gradually abolished. In July and August 1921 payment was reintroduced for transport, posts, and all goods sold to co-operatives and the private sector,[3] and enterprises were formally permitted to sell part of their products on the market for cash.[4] During the next few months sale and barter of industrial products on the market increased rapidly—enterprises preferred to take their output to market rather than to transfer it to another state body at a nominal price in the expectation of receiving central supplies. Between October 1921 and June 1922 at first the consumer goods industry and then the basic industries were taken off state supply and permitted to sell their output,

[1] For details of this attempt, and the subsequent discussion in which the *khozraschot* system was first canvassed, see *Ek. zhizn'*, no. 115 (1921) (M. Vindel'bot), and nos. 126, 144, and 214 (1921). I have been unable to trace no. 130 (1921) in which the tight system of budget accounting is defended.

[2] Characteristic early local taxes were per-head levies, often for specific purposes (especially education and health), marriage and birth registration fees, and taxes on trade and industry. Local trade taxes were permitted as early as June 1921 in the Ukraine (but were over-ridden by the introduction of the Promtax in July). See O. Popova in *Vestnik finansov*, no. 1 (1922), pp. 17–19; M. Al'skii in *ibid.* no. 2 (1922), pp. 3–5; Sokol'nikov, *op. cit.* vol. II, pp. 107–8; *Fin. politika...s xii. 1920 g. po xii. 1921 g....*, p. 119; D'yachenko, *op. cit.* p. 310; *Ek. zhizn'*, no. 220 (1921).

[3] See, for transport: SU 327/1921 (9. vii. 21), 330/1921 (22. vii. 21), 72/1922 (6. i. 22), 199/1922 (20. ii. 22), 334/1922 (13. iv. 22); Sokol'nikov, *op. cit.* vol. I, pp. 161–3; *Vestnik finansov*, no. 7 (1924), pp. 1–7. For postal and telephone charges: SZ 351/1921 (18. vii. 21), *Sbornik...po finansam*, vol. IV, no. 159 (13. xi. 21). For goods sold to co-operatives and private sector: SU 394/1921 (5. viii. 21) and *nakaz* of 9. viii. 21.

[4] At this time the detailed subdivisions of estimates were simplified, and the preliminary supervision of estimates by RKI was abolished. Decrees of 9. viii. 21, 12. viii. 21 (*Sbornik ...po finansam*, vol. IV, no. 131); SU 458/1921 (16. viii. 21—and see *Ek. zhizn'*, no. 188 (1921)), 551/1921 (28. ix. 21), 530/1921 (4. x. 21); and see *Fin. politika...xii. 1920 g....po ix. 1921 g....*, p. 18.

although the state compulsorily 'bought' a part of the production of the basic industries at prices below the market value.[1] Finally, from the autumn of 1922 onwards, all purchases and sales were made at market prices.

Meanwhile, the financial powers which local soviets had been granted in December 1918 were restored. In August 1921 the right to collect local revenues for local use was acknowledged,[2] although local finance formally formed part of the central state budget. In December local budgets were separated from the state budget, which was empowered but not obliged to make loans to them to cover their deficits.[3] During 1922 local soviets were made responsible for an increasingly large variety of expenditures, broadly covering local administration, elementary education and health, and local economy.[4]

The central budget was also relieved of most of its social security functions. Four funds (for sickness benefit, invalid pensions, unemployment pay, and 'health measures') were set up outside the budget and maintained by contributions from enterprises in propor-

[1] See *Sbornik...po finansam*, vol. IV, no. 134 (27. x. 21); SU 155/1922 (6. ii. 22), 291/1922 (21. iii. 22) (and see *Ek. zhizn'*, no. 46 (1922), for discussion of this decree); *Vestnik finansov*, no. 18 (1922), pp. 4–5, and no. 11 (1923), pp. 32–3; Sokol'nikov, *op. cit.* vol. II, pp. 39–41. Owing to the cuts in centralised state material supplies, enterprises suffered from an acute shortage of working capital in the spring of 1922, and they were able to obtain materials essential to production only by disgorging their stocks on the market at low prices (this process became known as *razbazarivanie*) (for details see M. H. Dobb, *op. cit.*, pp. 155 ff.; and see Pyatakov in *Vestnik finansov*, no. 6 (1922)).

[2] SU, decree of 22. viii. 1921; and see discussion in *Ek. zhizn'*, nos. 175 and 200 (1921). Payment for municipal services was formally introduced at the same period, but was held up by dissentients who argued that it would reduce real wages (see SU 445/1921 (25. viii. 21), 288/1922 (20. iii. 22), and SU 349/1922 (20. iv. 22), and article by Yu. Mitlyanskii in *Ek. zhizn'*, no. 44 (1922)). In July 1921 a decree had been adopted on the structure of provincial financial departments (SU 381/1921 (28. vii. 21)).

[3] See SU 550/1921 (10. x. 21), 553/1921 (10. x. 21), 693/1921 (9. xii. 21), 691/1921 (10. xii. 21). The December 1921 decrees were confirmed by the Ninth Soviet Congress (SU 46/1922 (30. xii. 21)). Local taxes included taxes on buildings used for business purposes, restaurants, etc., on cab-drivers (*izvozchiki*), on cartage, for the use of public weights, on bicycles, and on allotments. In the towns, levies were also permitted on mobile trade, on loads conveyed by rail or water, on domestic animals and cattle, on cattle sold in the market, and for witnessing contracts. In the countryside, a levy could be imposed for the right to hunt. Revenue also included a 25% deduction from and a local addition (maximum 100%) to the Promtax. Local expenditure rights were listed in these decrees for the first time in the post-revolutionary period.

[4] For details, see *inter alia* SU 711/1922 (31. viii. 22) (transferring provincial Economic Councils, the maintenance of army buildings, etc. to local charge), and 853/1922 (19. x. 22) (permitting certain higher education institutes, as a temporary measure, to be maintained by the local budget); 58/1923 (11. i. 23) (transferring local police, teachers in first-grade schools, personnel of children's homes, etc.), 437/1923 (transferring most telephone networks), and decree of 17. vi. 23, *cit.* D'yachenko, *op. cit.* p. 225 (transferring most local industry).

tion to their wage bill.[1] Only military personnel and their families, invalids from birth, and certain persons and groups receiving individual pensions continued to receive security benefits from budgetary funds.[2]

Finally, strenuous efforts were made to reduce the expenditure of bodies still financed by the budget. The ending of the war enabled a drastic reduction to be made in allocations to defence. The government also introduced measures to curtail greatly the number of administrative personnel.[3] Thus in June 1921 all institutions on the budget were ordered to reduce their staffs by 50%; and in July and August 1922 further heavy cuts in the number of state and local employees were ordered, and 'norms' (standard numbers) of administrative personnel were made binding on all state institutions.[4]

By the end of 1922 the process of disburdening the central budget called for by the Party had been completed. At the beginning of 1921 some 35 million persons were in receipt of rationed supplies issued without payment, nominally through the state budget. At the end of 1921 only 6 million, and at the end of 1922, only 2·8 million people received wages or maintenance from the state budget.[5] The new money budget covered a much more restricted sphere than the shadowy civil war budget in kind.

Meanwhile, although revenue was still low, it was rising steadily. Over 40% of expenditure was met by revenue at the end of 1922 (see data in note 1 on p. 64). Economic recovery and the restoration of the financial system had proceeded sufficiently far to make

[1] The contribution to the unemployment fund, for example, was $2\frac{1}{2}$% of the wage bill (SU 65/1922 (12. i. 22)).

[2] For further details of the social insurance system in these years, see D'yachenko, *op. cit.* pp. 287–91.

[3] 'A severe cut must be made in the administrative machine', the Eleventh Party Congress resolved, 'the number of directing institutions centrally and locally must be reduced...all expenditure not connected with the direct maintenance of the proletarian state must be removed from the state budget...a determined struggle is necessary against irrational distribution of resources by state institutions in the direction of too great expenditure on the central apparatus of government at the expense of enterprises and lower institutions.'

[4] SU 675/1922 (23. viii. 1922) and 792/1922 (28. ix. 1922); and D'yachenko, *op. cit.* pp. 229–34. The total personnel of central NK's was to be reduced from 68,000 to 26,000, that of each provincial E.C. from 4,000 to 1,600 (of which financial personnel were to number 285, including 136 tax agents), and of each district E.C. from 1,190 to 240. NKF central personnel, excluding the State Bank and the insurance administration, were to number 3,425; contrary to the general trend, this was a slight increase.

[5] *Vestnik finansov*, no. 3 (1922), p. 13, no. 2 (1923), pp. 2–18 (Sokol'nikov's speech to the Tenth Soviet Congress); Sokol'nikov, *op. cit.* vol. I, p. 164.

possible the first steps towards the abolition of the budget deficit and the establishment of a stable currency.[1] As a preliminary step, the paper currency (*sovznaki*) was devalued at the end of 1922, so that one 1923 rouble was worth one million 1921 roubles.[2] Simultaneously a new stable currency, the *chervonets*, a ten-rouble note covered 25% by foreign currency and gold, was issued by the State Bank, and circulated side by side with the inflated *sovznak*. During 1923 its issue was carefully extended so that by the autumn it occupied the dominant position in circulation (see Table 10).

4. THE ABOLITION OF THE BUDGET DEFICIT, 1923–24

To enable the currency reform to succeed, the budget had to be stabilised so that new currency issues were not made at a greater rate than the expansion of trade. 1923 and 1924 were years of an intensive effort to abolish the budget deficit by increasing revenue and limiting expenditure.

Budgetary revenue from taxation was increased in a number of ways. Excise rates were raised,[3] and the expansion of production and trade turnover resulted in a considerable growth in revenue from both excises and Promtax. The tax in kind on the peasantry was unified and then transformed into a tax in money—59% of the new tax was collected in money in 1923, and all of it in 1924.[4] Finally, an

---

[1] For details of the course of recovery in these years, see Yurovskii, *op. cit.* ch. III.

[2] From the end of 1921, '1922' roubles were issued, worth 10,000 roubles of previous denominations, and circulated simultaneously with the old roubles. This earlier reform had little practical effect, as was reflected in the fact that the population continued to refer to the 1922 100-rouble note as 'a million roubles'. The 1923 rouble was worth 100 1922 roubles, so that the overall devaluation was 1,000,000:1. For details of the currency reforms, see Dobb, *Russian economic development since the revolution* (1929), pp. 225–35; Arnold, *Banks, credit and money in Soviet Russia* (1937), pp. 200–243; Yurovskii, *op. cit.* chs. VI–VIII.

[3] Cf. the following excise rates, given as a percentage of total price:

	October 1922	January 1923	July 1923
First-grade tobacco	—	38	72
Raw alcohol	62	—	75
Kerosene	7	16	30
Salt	4	15	28
Refined sugar	3	15	18
Calico	nil	nil	2·1

All rates are for last week in month, except for raw alcohol, October 1922, which is for third week in month (*Statisticheskii sbornik...5. x. 1922g. po ix. 1923g*. Table 49, facing p. 102).

For the growth of revenue from excises in 1922–24, see Table 26.

[4] D'yachenko, *op. cit.* p. 270. For details about the agricultural tax in 1921–4, see SU 147–9/1921 (21 and 28. iii. 21), 233/1922 (2. x. 22), 240/1922 (6. iii. 22), 284/1922

income and property tax was introduced in the towns in November 1922, and unified with other direct taxes at the end of 1923.[1] As a result of all these measures the total amount collected in tax rose steeply, to 475 million roubles in 1922/3 and 786 million roubles in 1923/4.

In 1923 and 1924 substantial progress was made in developing a technique for compiling budget estimates which would enable the total size of budgetary expenditure to be limited to revenue possibilities.[2] The ambitious, hasty, crude, and erroneous budget of December 1921[3] bore little resemblance to the realistic and carefully prepared, if still not very refined, budget of 1924/5.[4] At the beginning of the period the bodies responsible for compiling the budget no longer existed;[5] by October 1924 the decree on budget

(17. iii. 22), 451/1923 (10. v. 23), 912/1923 (7. viii. 23); *Vestnik finansov*, no. 2 (1922), pp. 15–16; no. 2 (1924), pp. 45–51; no. 3 (1924), pp. 4–19, 178; Sokol'nikov, *op. cit.* vol. II, pp. 69–71, 110, 112–26.

[1] For details of the income tax in 1921–4, see SU 940/1922 (23. xi. 22), 981/1922 (23. xi. 22), 1054/1923 (12. xi. 23).

[2] This period covered five budgets: the first unsuccessful draft budget for January–September 1922; the second draft budget for the same period; and the budgets for 1922/3, 1923/4, and 1924/5. The material in this section is taken, unless otherwise stated, from the rules for compiling these budgets: SU 553/1921 (10. x. 21), 961/1922 (10. viii. 22), 961/1923 (21. viii. 23) and 189/1924 (29. x. 24) (the decree on the budget rights of the USSR and the constituent Union republics).

[3] Ambitious, because it endeavoured to embrace all the incomings and outgoings of the economy, and to be an integral part of an overall economic plan. Hasty, because only a few weeks elapsed between its initiation in October and its adoption in December. Crude, because it was drawn up on the basis of rough calculations by central organisations. Erroneous, because it was riddled with fundamental flaws, the most ludicrous of which was the subdivision of VSNKh into its constituent units to calculate its income (i.e. including intra-VSNKh receipts), although it was treated as a whole to estimate its expenditure (i.e. intra-VSNKh payments were excluded)—as a result VSNKh income appeared as 899 million roubles, while its expenditure appeared as only 154 million roubles, reducing the potential budget deficit by 745 million roubles, or over one-third of total expenditure. For details, see decree of 11. viii. 1921 in *Rospis'...na vii.–xii. 1919g.*...; SU 553/1921 (10. x. 1921) and 46/1922 (30. xii. 1921); *Sbornik...po finansam*, vol. IV, no. 126 (5. xi. 1921), no. 127 (5. xi. 1921) and no. 128 (14. xi. 1921); *Rospis'...na. i.–ix. 1922g.*..., supplement pp. 10–11, decree of 22. xi. 1921, and *ob"yasnitel'naya zapiska*; Sokol'nikov, *op. cit.* vol. I, pp. 122–3; *Ek. zhizn'*, nos. 19, 21, and 23 (1922), and the informative and amusing series of articles on this budget by L. Kritsman in *Ek. zhizn'*, nos. 17, 20, 24, 27, 30, 31, 38, 42, 45, and 46 (1922).

[4] Between 1923 and 1930 the budget and economic year dated from October 1 to September 30, so as to coincide with the agricultural year (but compare p. 23, n. 1, the decision to begin the budget year on July 1 taken in 1918 for the same reason). In practice it meant that the budget had to be compiled before the results of the harvest were known. The switch to the calendar year was made by the inclusion of a 'special quarter' covering 1 October to 31 December 1930. For the long controversy about the budget year, see, for example, *TsIK* 2/III, pp. 191, 216, 366, 814; 3/III, pp. 624, 698; 3/IV, p. 209; *Plenum byudzhetnoi komissii...*, pp. 60, 100, 114, 124, 163; P. Haensel, *The Economic Policy of Soviet Russia* (1930), p. 113.

[5] They were abolished by a decree of 17. iii. 1921, reported in *Ek. zhizn'*, no. 112 (1921); and in *Sbornik...po finansam*, vol. IV, no. 183.

rights included many of the arrangements which have continued in force throughout the Soviet period.

The general procedure by which the budget was compiled was taken over from the civil war system, itself inherited from pre-revolutionary practice, but was modified to permit the adoption of separate republican budgets. The estimates for the various commissariats and other government departments under the Union budget were drawn up by the departments themselves,[1] and then each estimate was considered individually by the Estimates and Budget Commission of NKF (on which sat representatives of NKF, NK RKI, Gosplan, the NK of Labour (for wage questions), and the department whose estimate was being examined). They were then transferred to the central apparatus of NKF,[2] which combined them into a unified budget (*edinyi byudzhet*), together with the estimates of Union revenue, and with the republican budgets (which had been drawn up in a similar way at republican level). The unified budget was examined by Gosplan, discussed and revised by SNK, and then adopted by VTsIK, which voted it paragraph by paragraph for commissariats on the Union budget, and then *en bloc* for each republican budget.

The most important difference of substance between this procedure and that of the civil war period was that the expenditure budget was now no longer based purely on what the commissariats themselves thought they needed. Unlike the civil war budgets, where the pressure on spending departments to keep their estimates down was almost entirely a moral one, the budgets of N.E.P. were mainly revenue-determined. The amount of expected revenue was first estimated from existing levels of taxation and previous actual yields, not usually, however, with great accuracy in this period (thus expected revenue was overestimated in 1922/3, and underestimated in 1923/4). The estimated total revenue was then used for fixing the overall size of the budget.[3] An agreed deficit to be met by currency

[1] The Estimates Commissions set up in each government department in 1918–20 were not continued in the N.E.P. period.
[2] Budgetary matters came under the Administration of Budgets and Estimates of NKF, and its subordinate Budget, Administrative Estimates, and Economic Estimates Departments (*Sbornik...po finansam*, vol. IV, no. 185 (26. vii. 1921)).
[3] The amount due from excises was either worked out directly in accordance with production plans, or reached by adding a roughly estimated percentage to the fulfilment for the previous year. The tax in kind (the agricultural tax) was estimated as a lump sum before the rates of imposition were fixed, the lump sum being reached in the light of what it was thought the peasantry would tolerate. Promtax and income tax were

issue was added to the expected revenue (the details are shown in Table 11 (i)), and total expenditure was then required to be limited to this total, usually broken down by months.¹ In drawing up their annual estimates, commissariats were expected to limit them strictly to the control figures drawn up by NKF in accordance with this total expenditure, and to the norms laid down centrally for separate types of expenditure.

This was the position in theory. In practice, what was attempted in compiling the budgets of the early years of N.E.P. was to reconcile the conflicting requirements of various bodies with the allowed total expenditure—to confine the budget within the limits which the NKF thought practicable on the revenue side and desirable on the expenditure side. The NKF did not at first manage to restrict the initial claims of spending departments to the desired limits. This was because its controlling levers were not effective enough to hold back the urgent demands of the different departments, each of which was being subjected to enforced cuts in staff and materials (and they included departments responsible for the revival of industry and education, of course, in addition to purely administrative ones). Control through expenditure norms was weak because, although they covered staffing, wages, heating, office expenditure, minor repairs, and transport costs, they were not consistent or well developed. NKF control figures or 'limiting sums' for the total expenditure of each NK were not introduced until 1923/4, and then they were unsatisfactory.² Additional difficulties were created by the fluctuations in the value of the currency, and by the parallel existence of a stable

---

calculated directly from estimates of industrial, trade, and individual incomes at various levels, and the prevailing rate of taxation. (See, in addition to the decree of 21. viii. 1923 already cited, A. A. Nikitskii in *Vestnik finansov*, no. 3 (1925), pp. 51–72.) For examples of inaccurate estimating of individual items of revenue in 1923/4, see I. Pergament in *Vestnik finansov*, no. 11–12 (1925), pp. 31–61.

[1] E.g., in July 1923 monthly issue was reduced to 30 million roubles; it was subsequently cut to 15 million roubles, SU 636/1923 (7. vii. 23); Sokol'nikov, *op. cit.* vol. II, pp. 63–6.

[2] In 1922 allocations were broken down very crudely (e.g. in the first draft budget, the Ukraine was simply allocated, as a percentage, 14·6% of total Soviet expenditure; in the second, non-unified commissariats were allowed 31% of the total). Even with the 1922/3 budget, control figures were not issued for each commissariat: the NKF compiled its version of the budget on the basis of quadrupling the actual expenditure of each NK in the first quarter, while the discussions in SNK and Gosplan were based simply on the demands of the commissariats. In 1923/4 control figures were issued, but they were badly worked out, and as a result some were too high and others too low. The budget law of 29. x. 1924 did not mention the control figures, but they were in fact issued as in the previous year. See *Ek. zhizn'*, no. 19 (1922); *Nar. kom. fin....*, pp. 62–8; Sokol'nikov, *op. cit.* vol. II, pp. 50–3; D'yachenko, *op. cit.* pp. 329–30; SU 192/1924 (29. x. 1924).

Table 11. *Variations in budget estimates 1922–4*

(i) Proposed and actual annual deficits, 1922–4 (million pre-war roubles)

	Permitted deficit issue	Actual issue [4]
First draft budget, i.–ix. 1922	300 [1]	} 220–270
Second draft budget, i.–ix. 1922	775 [2]	
Oct. 1922–Sept. 1923	310 [3]	250–400
Oct. 1923–Sept. 1924	180	127–147

Sources: *Rospis'...na i.–ix. 1922 g....* Sokol'nikov, *op. cit.* pp. 25–6, 37–8. *Vestnik finansov*, no. 7 (1924), pp. 1–7, 9; no. 12 (1923), pp. 34–5. *Svodnye materialy o deyatel'nosti soveta narodnykh komissarov i soveta truda i oborony za pervyi kvartal (x, xi, xii) 1924–1925 g.* (1925), p. 15. And as for Table 10.

Notes:
(1) This was reduced later to 240 million roubles.
(2) As approved by SNK; NKF had proposed a deficit of only 135 million roubles.
(3) This was later raised to 350 million roubles.
(4) No accurate figures on actual issue are available; those quoted are upper and lower figures cited in various sources used by us (see Table 10).

(ii) Proposed total budget figures at various stages of compiling the 1922/3 budget (million pre-war roubles [1])

Approximate date	Body proposing	Revenue proposed	Expenditure proposed	Deficit proposed
Jan. 1923 [2]	NK's and departments	1,050	2,202	1,152
Feb. 1923	NKF budget commission	993	1,334	341
Apr. 1923	Gosplan and SNK	1,015	1,620	605
June 1923	Tsyurupa commission [3]	1,050	1,569	519
June 1923 [4]	NKF	1,050	1,400	350
1922/3 (actual)		1,064	1,460	394

Sources: *Vestnik finansov*, no. 23 (1922), pp. 26–7; no. 12 (1923), p. 2; no. 7 (1924), pp. 8–9. Sokol'nikov, *op. cit.* vol. II, pp. 26–31, 37–8, 126–7. D'yachenko, *op. cit.* pp. 318, 452–3.

Notes:
(1) As far as possible in Gosplan general commodity index roubles, but the units used are not always stated clearly in the sources.
(2) NK's began compiling their estimates in August, and NKF began considering their proposals in November.
(3) In view of the disagreement between NKF and SNK on the amount of deficit permissible, a special Commission was set up by SNK under Tsyurupa (then deputy-chairman of SNK) to re-examine both the revenue and the expenditure estimates for the second half of the year.
(4) No agreement was finally reached on the size of the 1922/3 budget, but VTsIK resolved in July to limit the monthly issue to 30 million roubles, and to adopt budgets only with deficits within that limit.

(iii) Proposed total budget figures at various stages of compiling the 1923/4 budget (million *chervonets* roubles)

Aug.–Sept. 1923	NKF (control figures)	1,607	1,813	206
	NK's and departments (estimates)	1,472	2,139	667
Dec. 1923 [1]	NKF draft	1,529	1,709	180
	Gosplan	1,596	1,776	180
	SNK	1,623	1,803	180
1923/4 (actual)		2,192	2,318	126

Sources: D'yachenko, *op. cit.* pp. 329–40, 452–3. *Vestnik finansov*, no. 7 (1924), pp. 18–19. *Vtoroy s"ezd sovetov SSSR; sten. otchot (26. i. 1924–2. ii. 1924)*, 1924, pp. 137–54.

Note: (1) The delay between August and December was said to be due to the complications produced by the introduction of separate republican budgets.

and a depreciating currency. During 1923 the assessment, collection and allocation of revenue and expenditure in the new stable *chervonets* was introduced only gradually.[1] In the meantime the absence of a stable currency and the delays in the adoption of the budget[2] meant that the annual budget had to be replaced by monthly operative budgets, based on the monthly currency issue plan, and then by quarterly budgets.[3]

In spite of these complications, the procedure we have described for compiling the budget estimates succeeded in introducing an elementary budget discipline, and in limiting expenditure. This is illustrated in Table 11. In 1922/3, after several months of controversy, NKF persuaded Gosplan and the government to accept its figure for the budget deficit, and the expenditure demands of the departments were substantially cut. In 1923/4 the NKF proposals were much more easily accepted, and the deficit was again reduced substantially.

The reduction of the deficit resulted both from the government's determination to restore a stable currency, and from the overall economic successes of 1923 and early 1924. In 1923 industrial production rose to a third, and the marketable surplus in agriculture to three-fifths, of the pre-war level, and the real value of the currency in circulation doubled. In spite of the setback of the famous 'scissors crisis' of 1923,[4] the *chervonets* was stabilised, as is illustrated in Table 10, and in the early months of 1924 the paper *sovznak* was withdrawn from circulation and replaced by a stable currency of

[1] For details, see D'yachenko, *op. cit.* p. 330; SU 951/1923 (24. viii. 23), 961/1923 (21. viii. 23), 980/1923 (9. x. 23); Sokol'nikov, *op. cit.* vol. II (1926), p. 63; Yurovskii, *op. cit.* pp. 261 ff; Z. V. Atlas, *Ocherki po istorii denezhnogo obrashcheniya SSSR*, pp. 158 ff.

[2] The 1922/3 budget was still under discussion in June 1923, and the 1923/4 budget in June 1924, and they were never finally adopted by SNK (see *Vestnik finansov*, no. 11–12 (1925), p. 31; and Table 9).

[3] A quarterly budget, used as the basis on which the monthly budget was compiled, was first successfully introduced in the first quarter of 1923/4. From July 1924 onwards, the monthly budgets were dispensed with, and allocations were given on the basis of quarterly budgets direct. For details see *Vestnik finansov*, no. 44 (1922), p. 24, no. 8 (1926), pp. 15–17; *Nar. kom. fin.*...., pp. 68–70; Sokol'nikov, *op. cit.* vol. II, pp. 63–8; D'yachenko, *op. cit.* p. 317.

[4] During the summer and early autumn of 1923 not only the paper *sovznaks* but also the new *chervonets* had depreciated in value, and the 'scissors' (the graph showing the prices of manufactured and agricultural goods) had opened against the peasant. The main causes of this crisis were evidently the relatively low level of industrial as compared with agricultural production, combined with the monopoly position of state industry on the market and the lavish crediting of industry by the banks. Industrial prices had been forced up, so that the 'scissors' were opened and goods turnover temporarily declined. The 'scissors 'were closed by peasant resistance to the high industrial prices and by government intervention to force these prices down.

small denominations. In 1924 the part played by currency issue in financing budget expenditure was relatively small.[1]

5. PRE-WAR FEATURES IN THE N.E.P. SYSTEM

The new budgetary system, which had been firmly established by 1924, retained many features of the pre-war system, as is illustrated in Table 12, in which the fulfilment figures for the budgets of 1913 and 1924/5 are compared. Excises were collected by an apparatus similar to that of the pre-war period, use being made wherever possible of pre-revolutionary excise personnel,[2] and were imposed mainly on goods which had been taxed before the war, at rates for each type of good based on the pre-war rate (see Table 23, and n. 3 on p. 58). The different composition of excises in 1923/4 was mainly due not to different rates of tax but to changes in the composition of trade turnover (in particular vodka sales were only a fraction of the pre-war level). Objections that indirect taxes were regressive continued to be made,[3] but they were generally recognised to be essential; there were further signs of the emergence of the view that some form of fiscal mark-up on costs was necessary if accumulation was to take place in an economy in which the private sector was limited.[4] The Promtax too was re-introduced in a form hardly

[1] The following figures show the percentage of budgetary expenditure (measured in fixed prices) met by currency issue. Though they are necessarily rough, they indicate the steady decline in the part played by currency issue throughout 1922-4:
| 1922: | | Jan.–Mar. | 85; Apr.–June | 69; July–Sept. | 56. |
| 1922/3: Oct.–Dec. | 46; Jan.–Mar. | 29; Apr.–June | 26; July–Aug. | 20. |
1923/4: Oct.–Sept. (whole year) 5·5.
(Calculated from data in *Vestnik finansov*, no. 18 (1923), p. 53; *Statisticheskii sbornik po obshchegosudarstvennomu byudzhetu, denezhnomu obrashcheniyu i dvizheniyu tsen s oktyabrya 1922g. po sentyabr' 1923g.* (1923), pp. 14–35, 78–9, 99; and D'yachenko, *op. cit.* p. 331. These figures are only roughly comparable, as different index-roubles are used for different periods, and are intended only to illustrate the general trend during the period.

[2] For references to material on excise administration, see p. 51, n. 2 above.

[3] See, for example, *Fin. politika...s xii. 1920g. po xii. 1921g.* p. 126. At the end of 1923 the tax on salt was halved, and that on kerosene reduced by 25%. The Thirteenth Party Conference in January 1924, and the Soviet Congress later in the same year, called for further reductions in excises on necessities.

[4] Cf. I. Bogolepov's view that the deficit must be overcome by 'state fiscal monopolies' charging higher prices (*Ek. zhizn'*, no. 247 (1921)); O. Smit's that the main source of revenue must be nationalised industry 'whose goods must be sold at prices higher than their cost, achieving in this way a special form of indirect taxation' (*ibid.* no. 193 (1921)); and Sokol'nikov's prognostication in May 1923 that 'in the end a position is possible when there will be no direct tax on the peasantry, and when a sufficient share of profit will be included in state industry to allow the state on the one hand to cover its, as it were, "organisational" expenditure...and on the other hand to develop its economy further, invest new resources in it, etc. In any case it may be said that the price of the nationalised product will then include, in a sense, a certain rate of a form of tax' (*op. cit.* vol. II, p. 116).

Table 12. *Budgetary revenue and expenditure, 1913 and 1924/5*

	1913 Amount	1913 % of total revenue	1924/5 Amount	1924/5 % of total revenue
(i) Budgetary revenue, 1913 and 1924/5 (million current roubles [1])				
Indirect taxes				
(a) Excises including alcohol monopoly	1,254·0[2]	36·5	507·8	16·9
(b) Customs	352·9	10·3	101·9	3·4
Total indirect taxes	1,606·9	46·8	609·7	20·3
Direct taxes				
(a) Promtax	150·1	4·4	157·3	5·2
(b) Income tax	n.a.		94·3	3·1
(c) Agricultural tax	n.a.		326·2	10·8
(d) Other direct taxes	122·4	3·6	17·6	0·6
Total direct taxes	272·5	7·9	595·4	19·8
Other taxes, dues, etc.	231·7	6·8	122·6	4·1
TOTAL TAXES	2,111·1	61·5	1,327·7	44·2
State properties, revenue, profits, etc.				
(a) Timber revenue	92·4	2·7	104·8	3·5
(b) Deductions from profits of state bodies	n.a.		123·1	4·1
(c) Other revenue	146·4	4·3	21·6	0·7
Total from state property	238·8	7·0	249·5	8·3
State loans	—	—	130·5	4·3
Other revenue	147·9	4·3	206·5	6·9
Gross revenue of transport and posts	933·4[3]	27·2	1,088·0	36·2
TOTAL REVENUE	3,431·2	100·0	3,002·2	100·0
(ii) Budgetary expenditure, 1913 and 1924/5 (million current roubles [1])				
National economy	203·6	6·0	555·6	18·7
Social and cultural	143·0	4·2	198·7	6·7
Defence	825·9	24·4	443·8	14·9
Administration, including NKF	775·7	22·9	242·7	8·2
Transfers to local budgets	n.a.		265·3	8·9
Payments on loans	424·3	12·5	66·2	2·2
Other expenditure	288·7	8·5	123·3	4·2
Gross expenditure of transport and posts	720·8	21·3	1,073·9	36·2
TOTAL EXPENDITURE	3,382·0	100·0	2,969·5	100·0
Surplus	49·2		32·7	—

Sources: as for Tables 1, 14 and 15.

Notes:
(1) For a comparison of price levels in 1913 and 1924/5, see Table 16, p. 89.
(2) Includes *gross* revenue of alcohol monopoly, 234·9 million roubles of which was expended on administration.
(3) Excludes 26·5 million roubles from participation in private railways.

differing from that of the pre-war period, and it was unsatisfactory both technically,[1] and from the point of view of the economic and social policy of the government—it was imposed indiscriminately on private and state industry.[2] Budgetary expenditure was administered by pre-war methods, through central and provincial pay-offices (*kassy*),[3] and the highly formalistic apparatus for control and audit of the budget was partly based on the pre-war system.[4]

All this seemed to lend credence to the widely expressed view that the NKF, and financial policy in general, were a bulwark of conservatism and pre-revolutionary influence. These charges were sometimes unjustified,[5] and the cautious policy pursued by the financial authorities was in fact supported by the leaders of the government throughout this period. It is true, however, that many measures were introduced in this period (the Promtax, for example) in forms appropriate for pre-revolutionary economic and fiscal policy rather than for the policy of the Soviet government. It seems reasonable to suppose that this was the result of the influence of the former officials of the Ministry of Finance now working in the NKF, many of whom were out of sympathy with the new régime.[6]

[1] The standards used to determine the licensing fee (e.g. number of workers employed) corresponded only very roughly to profitability. The 'equalising levy' had been paid as a profits tax in the pre-war period, but it was now imposed as a percentage of gross turnover, which was not a satisfactory criterion for the level of profit, and led to the duplication of payments on goods as they passed from one enterprise to another.

[2] As the licensing fee rose progressively with the size of the firm, it tended to discriminate *against* state enterprises, which were usually larger than private enterprises (the fee charged early in 1923 worked out at 2–6 roubles per worker for firms employing three workers, and 8 roubles per worker for firms employing 1,000 workers). The equalising levy was a non-progressive percentage tax. Co-operatives, however, paid reduced fees (SU 559/1922 (18. vii. 22)).

[3] For details, see *Vestnik finansov*, no. 4 (1924), pp. 45–9; SU 783/1922 (26. ix. 22), 14/1923 (14. xii. 22); and order of 27. xii. 22 quoted in *Vestnik finansov*, no. 2 (1923), p. 122.

[4] The RKI transferred its main functions of detailed financial supervision to NKF during 1921. The new NKF Administration of Financial Supervision was formed in 1923. For details, see SU 349/1921 (19. vii. 21), 458/1921 (16. viii. 21), 551/1921 (28. ix. 21), 606/1921 (3. xi. 21), 984/1923 (6. ix. 23); *Ek. zhizn'*, no. 166 (1921); *Vestnik finansov*, no. 10 (1926), pp. 35–44; D'yachenko, *op. cit.* pp. 233–4; *Finansovaya entsiklopedia*, cols. 392–6. The pre-war classification of the budget, including (temporarily) the division of revenue and expenditure into 'ordinary' and 'extraordinary', was also retained (see *Vestnik finansov*, no. 1 (1926), pp. 200–1).

[5] Compare, for example, the Ukrainian attack on the first draft of the 1922 budget, which was alleged to have been drawn up by 'specialists of the old treasury school'. In fact, according to Sokol'nikov, it was compiled mainly by Larin, Preobrazhenskii, and Al'skii, the first two of whom were prominent communists (*Ek. zhizn'*, nos. 21 and 23 (1922)).

[6] In mid-1922, only 18 out of 5,000 tax-workers were members of the Communist Party. In 1922–5 great efforts were made to ensure that communists predominated

6. INNOVATIONS

(a) *Budgetary revenue*

In spite of these similarities, the budgetary system of 1924 already showed marked differences from the pre-revolutionary system. This was partly true even of so traditional a form of taxation as the excise. In 1923 it was extended to textiles and other goods,[1] and began to show signs of its later form of a tax not only on goods traditionally subject to excises, but also on the products of consumer goods industry as a whole. But the most important change on the revenue side of the budget was the increase in direct taxation. In the early 1920's conditions permitted small traders and private industrialists ('Nepmen'), and the upper groups among the peasantry, to develop their activities, and one of the aims of government taxation policy was to restrict these groups by limiting their incomes. In the towns this was to be done by the income and property tax;[2] in the countryside, by the agricultural tax.[3]

The income tax[4] introduced in 1922 was not heavily biassed against the Nepmen. It rose to a maximum rate of only 15% (the maximum rate of the income tax introduced in 1916 was 12·5%), and all persons receiving the same income paid the same rate of tax, irrespective of the source of the income. Moreover, the better-off groups evaded the payment of tax on a large scale in the first year of imposition.[5] At the end of 1923 the tax was therefore reconstructed. A basic levy was instituted with a separate scale for each of four classes of income:

---

among the new personnel employed by the NKF, particularly in the case of tax-workers who came into direct contact with the population, but many of these new recruits were poorly trained and inexperienced. See *Vestnik finansov*, no. 1 (1924), pp. 103–5; and D'yachenko, *op. cit.* pp. 241–2.

[1] See SU 211/1922 (23. ii. 22) (excise on salt, on which no tax had been paid since the 1880's); 214/1923 (28. ii. 23), 436/1923 (5. v. 23) (on textiles and rubber galoshes); for excise on candles see *Vestnik finansov*, no. 7 (1924), pp. 1–7.

[2] The resolution of the Tenth Soviet Congress in December 1922 declared that the income and property tax must be strengthened and that 'in particular it is necessary to strengthen the taxation of the new bourgeoisie and those bourgeois and petty bourgeois professions and crafts which have grown up under N.E.P.' (SU 329/1923 (27. xii. 22)).

[3] The tax in kind, stated the Tenth Party Congress in March 1921, should 'bear a progressive character; lower amounts of tax should be fixed on middle and poorer (*malomoshchnye*) households; the economies of the poorest peasants should be freed from some and in exceptional cases from all taxation in kind'.

[4] The original tax of December 1922 included a property tax, at 0·33% to 1·5% of value; it proved difficult to impose and was dropped in 1924.

[5] See, for example, speech by Vladimirov at the Second Congress of Soviets of the USSR, January–February 1924: *Vtoroi s″ezd sovetov SSSR; sten. otchot* (1924), pp. 140–1. Only 70% of the anticipated amount of tax was collected in the first six months of 1923 (*Vestnik finansov*, no. 7 (1924), p. 148).

(*a*) wages and salaries, (*b*) independent incomes from personal labour (independent artisans, etc.), (*c*) income from the ownership of industrial and trade enterprises, etc., and (*d*) incomes of companies and banking institutions.[1] In addition, a supplementary tax was paid on higher incomes up to a maximum rate of 25%.[2] Although this arrangement was technically unsatisfactory,[3] it was a step towards a policy of tax discrimination against incomes from the private sector of the economy.[4]

The agricultural tax[5] on peasant households replaced the tax in kind of 1921–3, the requisitioning of the civil war period, and the large indirect tax on spirits which the peasant had paid before 1914. The introduction of the direct taxation of largely self-sufficient farms involved special difficulties. The agricultural tax was imposed not according to the actual money income of each household but on the basis of so-called 'external indications' (*vneshnie priznaki*), primarily the amount of ploughland held per household and the number of persons in the household, taken in conjunction with the average yield for the district and the type of land.[6] The number of cattle owned was also taken into account, but receipts from sources other than grain and cattle (e.g. technical crops, non-agricultural work) were ignored, although they provided 19%–71% of income in various areas by 1923/4.[7]

In fixing the total amount of tax, important problems of principle were involved. On the one hand, the greater the amount that could be raised from the peasantry the sooner the budget could be balanced; on the other hand, it was argued that too high a level of

---

[1] Class A paid 3r. 6ok. to 15r. per month; B paid 3r. 6ok. to 18r.; and C 3r. 6ok. to 72r.

[2] Only persons paying the supplementary tax had to complete personal income declarations.

[3] A very large number of small taxpayers had to pay the basic tax, including persons (in categories B and C) with insufficient income to meet the amounts demanded. For details, see D'yachenko, *op. cit.* pp. 252–3.

[4] The fairly moderate grading of the tax was strongly criticised. See, for example, *Vtoroi s"ezd...*, pp. 154–60.

[5] For references to material on this tax, see n. 4, p. 58.

[6] The income of each household was assessed by the method of the so-called 'standard net income' (*uslovno-chistyi dokhod*), worked out on the basis of a district norm of profitability for each type of crop and a district survey of the type of crops grown. The main issue of controversy was whether the tax should be imposed on the basis of the *total* ploughland or of the *sown area*. Taxation by ploughland gave a stimulus to the extension of the sown area and less opportunity for tax evasion; on the other hand, it gave an advantage to the richer peasant groups, who were able to sow a greater proportion of their total land (since they could preserve more grain for seed, etc.). On the importance of the unit of taxation in later periods, see pp. 117, n. 1, 223, 281–2.

[7] D'yachenko, *op. cit.* p. 270.

tax would harm the 'worker-peasant alliance' which was sought after as the main condition for consolidating the régime, and would limit the ability of the peasant to provide a market for reviving industry. In practice, after the introduction of the tax in 1921 at a level below that of requisitioning, the yield from it was gradually and cautiously increased between 1922 and 1923/4, but the rate of increase was less than the rate of expansion of the market.[1]

Until 1926 little attempt was made to make the tax into a progressive tax. Government policy towards the upper groups of the peasantry was far more cautious than its policy towards the private sector in the towns, as it was feared that heavy taxation of the better-off groups would harm the recovery of agriculture. In 1923 the Commissar of Finance stated that the tax imposed often did not correspond to the real ability of each household to pay,[2] and an official analysis, referring to the 1924/5 period, stated that 'the agricultural tax in no way resembled an income tax', and that there was no question of the progressive taxation of peasant economies at this period.[3] The only important discriminatory steps at this period were the freeing of certain sections of the poorer peasantry from tax,[4] and the reduction of the rate of tax on the few existing collective farms.

Another important innovation was the system of state loans.[5] The NKF devised a variety of expedients to persuade the population to invest in loans. In the spring of 1922 and 1923 so-called 'grain loans' were successfully launched among the peasantry. These were short-term bonds sold to the peasantry for cash, but valued in stable 'grain units'—the government repaid cash purchases of bonds by cancelling the holders' obligation to pay the equivalent amount of tax in kind at the next harvest, or by repaying them in grain after the harvest.[6]

In the towns, long-term money loans were issued, bearing both

---

[1] E.g. TsSU (the Central Statistical Administration) and NKF both estimated that 600 million gold roubles could be raised from the peasant in all forms of taxation in 1923/4, but a target of only 400 million roubles was in fact set. (Sokol'nikov, *op. cit.* vol. II, pp. 109, 112–22, where the relation of this problem to retaining the political support of the peasantry is also discussed.)

[2] Speech at Twelfth Party Congress, reprinted in Sokol'nikov, *op. cit.* vol. II, p. 109.

[3] See I. Magidovich in *Statisticheskoe obozrenie*, no. 4 (1927), pp. 75–80, cit. [A. Baykov], *Byulleten' ekonomicheskogo kabineta prof. S. N. Prokopovicha*, no. 69 (1929), p. 11.

[4] SU 969/1923 (24. viii. 23).

[5] For material, see D'yachenko, *op. cit.* pp. 275ff.

[6] SU 430/1922 (20. v. 22), 278/1923 (22. iii. 23); Sokol'nikov, *op. cit.* vol. I, pp. 165–70, and (for 'sugar loan' of 1923) *Fin. ents.* col. 964. The first grain loan was over-subscribed—63% of it was 'paid out' in the form of cancelling payments of the tax in kind.

interest and lottery prizes. But they were unpopular, as the interest rate was far below the high market rate; subscription was therefore made compulsory, the higher-income groups paying according to their income-tax grading.[1]

All these changes taken together considerably increased the weight of direct taxation in budgetary revenue as compared with the pre-war period (see Table 12). Agricultural tax and income tax, which did not exist in 1913, accounted between them for 38% of tax revenue in 1923/4 and 31% in 1924/5. But as yet the use of these taxes for political and economic discrimination was in an incipient stage.

(b) Budgetary expenditure

The changes in the structure of budgetary expenditure as compared with the pre-war period are shown in Table 12(ii). Defence and administrative expenditure appreciably declined, the latter partly owing to the reduction of expenditure on the alcohol monopoly. Owing to the renunciation of the national debt in 1918, the young Soviet financial system was a net gainer from loans, whereas over 10% of expenditure in 1913 was devoted to interest and repayment on loans. On the other hand, expenditure on the transport and postal services had increased considerably—in 1913 railway transport had been an important source of net revenue, but in 1924/5 it barely made a profit, after having been considerably in deficit in 1922/3 and 1923/4 (the transport deficit in 1923/4 amounted to over half the currency issue).

But the most characteristic changes in 1924/5 compared with 1913 are the increase in expenditure on the economy, and the central grants issued to local budgets. These two changes reflect important innovations—the system of financing the economy, and the local and republican budgetary system.

7. THE BUDGET AND THE ECONOMY

State-owned industry under N.E.P. was financially independent of the budget, and organised by a system which was first known as 'commercial accounting' (*kommercheskii raschot*) and later as 'economic accounting' (*khozyaistvennyi raschot* or *khozraschot*), which may be

---

[1] See SU 887/1922 (31. x. 22), 960/1922 (4. ix. 22), 974/1922 (7. ix. 22), 981/1922 (3. ix. 22); *Fin. ents.* cols. 398–408. The value of compulsory loans on the market fell to 20% of their nominal value.

roughly translated as meaning that economic units had to finance their own production out of sales, on cost accounting principles.[1] The working capital of the *khozraschot* unit (at this time usually the 'trust' or group of enterprises) was at its own disposal, and it was legally required to use its resources with the aim of deriving profit.[2]

But cutting the economy loose from the budget did not mean that each *khozraschot* body now operated as a completely independent unit, with no obligations to or assistance from the state. In the first place, part of its outlays was regulated from outside—wage-scales, for example, were largely outside its control, being fixed centrally by VSNKh, STO, etc., in consultation with the trade unions. Secondly, it could not simply fix its prices at what the market would bear: VSNKh and STO had over-riding powers (rarely used at this stage) to fix prices. When industry used its monopoly position to force up prices in 1923, the state intervened to reduce them. Thirdly, profit was not at the free disposal of the trust. It was expected to set an annual sum aside for depreciation (this was not in fact done as a rule until 1924). It had to pay Promtax and income tax.[3] Of the remaining profit, a percentage fixed annually, but not less than 20%, went to reserve capital, used to cover losses and to expand the work of the trust; and further percentages had to be set aside for bonuses (*tantième*, usually 2%) and for the Fund for Improving Workers' Welfare (FUBR, usually 10%). The percentages for these purposes were fixed annually by VSNKh and NKF. Any residual profit was normally absorbed into state revenue.[4]

Economic units were also connected to the central state financial machinery through the banking network, the revival of which was inevitable in view of the growth of the market and of *khozraschot*. In the first three years of N.E.P., the State Bank and its branches were re-established and a number of specialised banks was opened.[5]

---

[1] Later the term came to imply that cost accounting was applied to definite tasks set by the plan, in physical as well as in monetary terms. See Baykov, *Development...*, p. 116.

[2] 'The whole activity of the trust is directed and evaluated from the point of view of profit' (Decree of VSNKh, 16. vii. 23, quoted in *Fin. ents.* col. 363). (In 1924 at the Thirteenth Party Congress, however, Rykov cited this kind of extreme formulation as an example of the erroneous policy prevailing in 1923. See Carr, *op. cit.* vol. IV, p. 9.)

[3] In May 1923 an income tax of 8% on the net income for the previous year was introduced for state and co-operative enterprises, corresponding to the Class D income tax on private firms (SU 573/1923 (20. v. 23); D'yachenko, *op. cit.* p. 253).

[4] Decree on Trusts, SU 336/1923 (10. iv. 23); D'yachenko, *op. cit.* pp. 222–5.

[5] The State Bank, founded in October 1921, itself subordinate to the NKF (SU 594/1921 (12. x. 21)); the Bank of Trade and Industry (*Prombank*, or Industrial Bank); *Elektrokredit* (later reorganised as *Elektrobank*); the Russian Commercial Bank (*Roskombank*, for foreign trade); the Consumers' Co-operative Bank (*Pokobank*, later reorganised as

It was intended that as far as possible all free money in the economy should be concentrated in the banks. The unused moneys of state enterprises had to be deposited with a bank, and payments had to be made for the most part by cheque through the State Bank, or by bills of exchange (usually transferable), which were discounted by the banks.[1]

The sources of grants and loans to the economy were rather complicated. First, direct budget grants and loans were issued for specific purposes, and were administered either by the banks or by the departments of NKF. Secondly, budget allocations were also made to expand the resources of the banks themselves. With the aid of these grants, and from the temporary deposits of economic bodies, the banks gave short- and long-term loans at their own discretion.[2] In analysing the state financing of the economy under N.E.P., both budget and bank financing and their inter-relation need to be borne in mind.[3]

It has been impossible to ascertain more than approximately the relative importance of the banks and the budget in financing the economy (including direct and indirect budget grants *via* the bank). Available data[4] indicate that in 1922 (January–September), when enterprises were being provided with new working capital, the bulk of state allocations to industry was made from budget grants (under this term I include direct budget grants and indirect grants through the bank, treating only bank loans not backed by the budget as 'bank loans'). But in 1923/4 the annual net increase in bank loans to industry was almost double the budgetary allocations.[5]

Budgetary relations with the economy gradually took shape in the

Vsekobank) (SU 163/1922 (6. ii. 22)); the municipal banks (SU 82/1923 (18. i. 23)); and the Agricultural Bank and mutual credit societies (SU 234/1923 (1. iii. 23)). For details on the banking system of N.E.P., see Arnold, *op. cit.*

[1] SU 311/1922 (30. iii. 22); 370/1923 (19. iv. 23); and (on bills of exchange) 285/1922 (20. iii. 22).

[2] Sokol'nikov, *op. cit.* vol. II, pp. 158–60.

[3] It is not possible to discuss in the brief account of the financing of the economy which is given here and in the succeeding chapter the attempts of the Soviet government between 1922 and 1928 to expand the economy by granting industrial and other concessions to foreign firms. Concessions played an auxiliary part in developing certain sectors of the Soviet economy, but the concessions policy as a whole was largely ineffective. For references to material on concessions, see [A. Baykov, 'Novoe postanovlenie o kontsessiakh...', in *Byulleten'...prof. Prokopovicha* (1928).

[4] D'yachenko, *op. cit.* p. 414. A fuller picture could doubtless be obtained from a closer study of available material, but this would be beyond the scope of my present research.

[5] For material on the role of the banks and agricultural loan societies in assisting the development of the economy, see Baykov, *Development...*, pp. 84–8, 98–100.

annual budgets and their fulfilment reports. The first draft budget for 1922, adopted in December 1921 before *khozraschot* had been fully introduced, still bore the marks of war communism: it attempted to show both the direct money payments and receipts of industry and its 'turnover' income and expenditure (i.e. the transfers in kind inside industry, shown in nominal money units). But, beginning with the second budget for 1922 adopted in May, only state allocations were shown, both direct to VSNKh in grants and loans and to the capital of the State Bank (to enable loans to be made to industry).[1] Only in the case of transport and posts and telegraphs were current receipts and expenditure kept on the budget, as they had been before the revolution. This was mainly in order to ensure fuller rights of control to the NKF, in view of the large transport deficit.[2] In practice, the periodic estimates of the NKPS (People's Commissariat of Transport) were approved like other budget estimates, and detailed estimates for each economic unit were approved monthly, but the estimates were administered on a semi-*khozraschot* basis: the NKPS did not hand over its receipts to the NKF, but simply received at intervals the planned deficit sum. If the actual revenue exceeded the plan, the excess was retained by the NKPS as a quasi-profit, part going to the central NKPS and part to its local bodies, mainly to cover unplanned operating losses and to improve labour and living conditions.[3]

Detailed data on actual budget expenditure on the economy are not available for 1922. Data for 1922/3–1924/5 are shown in Table 15. In 1922/3 substantial grants were made to cover the transport deficit, and to provide new working capital for industry; these between them accounted for at least half the large budget deficit. In 1923/4 the proportion of total budgetary expenditure received by the economy was reduced, owing mainly to the sharp fall in the transport deficit and to the relatively slow increase in expenditure on industry, which was now considered to have adequate working capital in the main; allocations to industry were cut back after the controversy in connexion with the 'scissors' crisis. More than half

---

[1] Allocations in grain (expressed in money terms) and in money, with which the state bought part of industrial output, were still shown in this budget.

[2] 'When our transport ceases to run at a loss and it becomes a question of a positive balance, it is possible we shall be faced with the problem of including only the balance of transport in the budget', said Sokol'nikov, adding that until then 'the state must interfere in all the affairs of [transport] enterprises' (*op. cit.* vol. II, pp. 161–2).

[3] SU 70/1922 (16. i. 22); 300/1923 (27. iii. 23). See also the discussion of NKPS finance in *Vestnik finansov*, no. 3 (1923), pp. 21 ff.; no. 9 (1923), pp. 2–17; no. 6 (1924), p. 167; no. 9–10 (1924), pp. 59–76.

of the much smaller currency issue was used to cover the transport deficit. In 1924/5 the main changes were that transport did not make a loss and that allocations to agriculture were substantially increased. As yet, there was little attempt to expand industry through grants from the budget.

How far were budget grants to state economy a mere re-allocation of resources collected from the economy itself in taxation, etc., and how far did they indicate a real transfer of resources from private profit or personal incomes to public accumulation? Only an approximate answer is possible. The amount of taxes on the state economy can be only roughly estimated,[1] and it is impossible to ascribe any particular proportion of the agricultural tax to a tax on agriculture *qua* agriculture, for it had the effect both of a personal income tax on the peasantry and of a tax on farming. The position is further complicated by the currency issue, which acted as a tax—the distribution of its 'incidence' between private persons and the various sectors of the economy cannot be ascertained. As far as state industry is concerned, it can be roughly estimated that some 40 million roubles in 1922/3, 110 million roubles in 1923/4, and 190 million in 1924/5 were paid in taxes and deductions from profits.[2] There was therefore a substantial but declining net grant to industry and electrification from the budget.

8. THE SYSTEM OF LOCAL BUDGETS

The main purpose of the separation of local budgets from the state budget was of course to facilitate the balancing of the central budget, but this separation also had more permanent advantages. Decentralisation of the budget reduced bureaucracy, inherent in detailed central control; it helped the development of local initiative and responsibility; it facilitated the collection of revenue, as revenue used for visible local services was less unpopular than revenue used purely for central government expenditure; and, as the local revenues were linked with central revenues, decentralisation aided

---

[1] Data for these years do not show fully what proportion of taxes on industry was received from the public sector.

[2] The assumption is made that no more than half of the Promtax, income-tax, and deductions from profits was paid by the socialised sector of the economy in 1922/3 (in 1924/5 somewhat more than half of these payments was made by the socialised sector, but in 1923/4 only one-eighth of income tax was paid by the socialised sector as against one-third in 1924/5—data from *Sotsialisticheskoe stroitel'stvo* (1935), p. 644). The surtaxes paid to the local budgets by state industry, and their expenditures on industry, are here ignored.

the fulfilment of the central budget. The limits of decentralisation were set by the degree of central control which the government considered it needed to fulfil its aims: the problem of Soviet local finance and government was to combine decentralised local functions with an economy the general direction of which was determined from the centre.

By October 1924 local budgets were responsible for all expenditure on local administration, elementary education and health, and local economy (including industry of local importance)—broadly speaking, this range of functions has remained within local competence throughout the Soviet period. At this stage local economy and social and cultural services each accounted for about one-third, and administration for about one-fifth, of local expenditure.[1]

With the increase in the responsibilities of local budgets, their sources of revenue were also expanded. As new direct state taxes were introduced, the central government permitted local deductions from them and additions to them to be made, and when functions were transferred to the local budgets, the rates of local deductions were increased. These 'linked' revenues yielded more than 40% of total local revenue in 1923/4. This system gave the local financial authorities a strong incentive to collect state taxes.

Purely local sources of revenue were also extended. In 1922 various local taxes were authorised in addition to those allowed in the legislation of December 1921,[2] and in 1923/4 the revenue from local non-tax sources, especially municipal services, rose considerably—in this connexion a statute was adopted on the property rights of local soviets.[3] These local revenues played little part in the social and political policies of the government. Local taxes were apparently used to discriminate against the private sector even less than state taxes, and were often imposed purely on a per-head basis.

As a result of these measures, the revenue of local budgets rose both absolutely and in relation to the state budget (see Table 13(i)). But the increase in local and 'linked' revenues was insufficient to

---

[1] In 1924/5, for instance, out of a total expenditure of 1,021 million roubles, economic expenditure amounted to 29·2%, social and cultural to 34·7%, and administration and justice accounted for 20·6% (for details see D'yachenko, *op. cit.* p. 438; *3 sessiya TsIKa SSSR 3-go sozyva...14–25. ii. 1927* (1927), pp. 578–9).

[2] E.g. to assist those affected by the famine (March–November) (SU 893/1922 (2. xi. 22)), on entertainments (SU 495/1922 (22. vi. 22)), per-household tax (SU 713/1922 (5. ix. 22)). These various local taxes were co-ordinated in November 1922 (957/1922 (16. xi. 22)), and a year later various minor taxes were abolished (SU 989/1923 (14. ix. 23)).

[3] For details, see D'yachenko, *op. cit.* pp. 326–9.

enable the budgets to be balanced; and state subsidies had to be increased in 1923/4. In this period subsidies were given in the form of block grants from the state budget to meet local deficits approved by the centre; but this method proved to be fundamentally unsound. Local soviets tended to inflate the estimates of their deficits in the

Table 13. *Local budgets, 1921–4*

(i) Local budgetary revenue (million roubles)

	1922/3 Amount	%	1923/4 Amount	%	1924/5 Amount	%
Local taxes and levies	—	—	71·3	11·5	80·1	8·1
Total local non-tax revenue (mainly municipal and housing)	—	—	244·7	39·6	382·4	38·7
Various local receipts	—	—	30·4	4·9	42·2	4·3
Additions to state taxes and levies	—	—	134·2	21·7	200·5	20·3
Deductions from state revenue	71·6	24·7	110·5	17·9	196·6	19·9
Grants from state sources:						
(a) Subventions	—	—	4·7	0·8	38·9	3·9
(b) Subsidies	—	—	21·8	3·5	19·3	2·0
(c) Earmarked grants (*tselevye posobiya*)	—	—	—	—	5·9	0·6
Total grants from state sources	6·7	2·3	26·5	4·3	64·1	6·5
TOTAL LOCAL REVENUE	289·5	100·0	617·7	100·0	986·5[2]	100·0
of which, direct from state sources	78·3	27·0	136·5	22·1	260·7	26·4
Total overall revenue [1]	1,278·7		2,052·4		2,621·4	
Local revenue as % of total	22·6		30·1		37·6	

Sources: D'yachenko, *op. cit.* pp. 324–9, 440. *3 sessiya tsentral'nogo ispolnitel'nogo komiteta SSSR 3-go sozyva...14–25. ii. 1927* (1927), pp. 578–9. And see sources to Tables 14, 15.

Notes:
(1) Excludes transfers from central to local, and self-balancing central budget items, including currency issue.
(2) Includes 21·6 million roubles revenue from loans. There is a discrepancy of 1 million roubles in this column, not explained in the source.

(ii) Maximum permitted rates of local deductions from central revenue, 1921–4

	As at December, 1921 %	As at December, 1922 %	As at May, 1923 %
Promtax	25	25	50 [1]
Income tax	—	25	25
Labour and cartage tax	—	25	50
Timber revenue	—	10	30
Rent revenue	—	—	25 [2]

Sources: SU 693/1921 (9. xii. 21), 957/1922 (16. xi. 22), 981/1922 (23. xi. 22), 482/1923 (10. v. 23), 855/1923 (27. vii. 23).

Notes:
(1) Of this 50% went to the provincial subsidy fund.
(2) Introduced in July 1923.

hope of securing a larger grant—the grant was sometimes a reward for bad work, but never an incentive to good work.[1] In October 1924 a new system was therefore introduced in most cases, under which state subventions were issued to cover a percentage of a particular expenditure.[2] By accepting the subvention, the local soviet obliged itself to spend an appropriate sum from its own resources for the same purpose. In this way central control over the expenditure of state grants was increased.

The initial legislation of the end of 1921 had provided for separate local budgets down to *volost'* (small rural district of about half-a-dozen villages) level, but it could not of course be put into effect at once. In 1922 budgets were in most areas established only at the level of the province (*gubernia*) and the provincial town, and expenditure was for the most part confined to the towns.[3] In 1923 budgets were also introduced in many districts (*uyezdy*) and small towns, but the extent to which district budgets were compiled at district level, independently of the province, varied considerably.[4] The compilation of *volost'* budgets, to which great importance was attached in view of their direct links with the peasantry,[5] began in 1924, at first in the Ukraine and later in the Russian Republic; but they did not develop to the planned extent, and became general only in 1924/5.[6] By 1924 the way in which total provincial revenue and expenditure was divided between the various lower budgets was as yet unsystematic.[7]

---

[1] 'Illusions and hopes for subsidies complicated the whole work' (*TsIK*, 2/III, pp. 882 ff., speech by Polyudov).

[2] This should not be confused with the earlier temporary system of 'double financing' (*dvoinoe finansirovanie*), under which a *particular* item of a group of expenditures was put on the central budget. Thus under 'double financing' the wages of teachers were paid by the state budget and other educational expenditure by the local budget; under the system of subventions all expenditure would be paid from the local budget, which would receive a grant from the state budget of a percentage of planned local expenditure on education.

[3] Sokol'nikov in *Vestnik finansov*, no. 2 (1923), pp. 2–18; K. Shmelev in *ibid.* no. 8 (1926), pp. 15–16. In August 1921 a decree ordered that the district financial department should be replaced by a smaller 'treasury office' (*kaznacheistvo*), but this curious anachronism was soon repudiated (SU 675/1922 (23. viii. 22), 791/1922 (28. ix. 22)).

[4] *Vestnik finansov*, no. 1 (1924), pp. 132–6, and (M. Sirinov) 136–40; and no. 8 (1926), pp. 16–17 (K. Shmelev).

[5] Thus a resolution of the Thirteenth Party Congress in May 1924 stated that 'with the establishment of the *volost'* budget, new possibilities are created of developing the economic and cultural work of *volost'* and village soviet organs, and of involving in their work the whole mass of the middle and small peasantry'.

[6] SU 1047/1923 (12. xi. 23); Sokol'nikov, *op. cit.* vol. II, pp. 61–2, 137–9; D'yachenko, *op. cit.* pp. 442, 444.

[7] In 1923 there were 75 *gubernia*, comprising 766 *uyezdy*, divided in turn into 13,700 *volosti* (roughly the same as before the revolution).

9. THE SYSTEM OF REPUBLICAN BUDGETS

The exclusion of local finance from the state budget was paralleled by the separation of individual budgets within the state budget for each of the main nationalities of the Soviet Union. Here the budgetary system was an instrument of the policy of the Soviet government towards national minorities and of the decisions on economic and political organisation which were taken in connexion with this policy.[1]

The declarations of rights in November 1917 and at the Third Soviet Congress in January 1918 had already led to some discussion of the need for federal financing of services such as education, and for autonomous regional budgets,[2] but the constitution of 1918 had made no mention of the budget rights of separate nationalities. During the course of the civil war independent allied republics were founded in the Ukraine, Belorussia, etc., and no central legislation was passed about their organisation, apart from a general declaration in June 1919 that their military organisations, economic councils, railways, labour commissariats and finance should be unified under single collegia.[3] The state budget for the second half of 1919 accordingly showed no separate republican budgets, and in practice most of the areas which later became Soviet republics were not under Soviet control during much of 1918 and 1919. However, allocations were listed (in a fairly random fashion) for separate republics under each main commissariat, and republics had the right to subdivide these allocations as they wished.[4] At the same time certain republics were compiling their own budgets.[5]

In 1920, with the achievement of victory on most fronts, the process of unifying the various Soviet republics began. Treaties of alliance were signed with the larger independent republics. The first of these, with Azerbaijan, had a supplementary agreement on financial questions, which provided that the Azerbaijan estimates of

---

[1] Soviet nationalities' policy in these years is analysed in detail in Carr, *op. cit.* vol. I, part III; see also the contemporary reports and speeches of Stalin, collected in his *Marxism and the National and Colonial Question* (1936).

[2] See Sukharkov's speech to VTsIK, April 1918, in *Protokoly VTsIKa 4-go sozyva* (1918), pp. 145–6; *Ek. zhizn'*, no. 38 (1919); and also the detailed material on the projected autonomous budget of the Northern Region in *Ek. zhizn'*, nos. 8, 34, and 40 (1919).

[3] SU 264/1919.

[4] Republics and districts to which allocations were given included the Ukraine, Belorussia, Lithuania, Latvia, Turkestan, Bashkiria, Kirghizia, the Don area, and the Siberian revolutionary committee. *Rospis'...na vii.–xii. 1919g....*, *passim*.

[5] *Narodnyi kommissariat finansov, 1917, 7. xi./25. x. 1922*, pp. 30 ff.

the major so-called 'unified' commissariats (military, VSNKh, labour, transport, posts, finance, foreign trade, etc.) should be approved centrally in Moscow, but that the estimates of the other 'non-unified' commissariats should be approved only by the Azerbaijan SNK. A plenipotentiary of the NKF of the R.S.F.S.R. was to sit in the republican SNK.[1] A similar treaty was signed with the Ukraine.[2] Treaties with Armenia and Georgia recognised the independence of the republican budget and that it should be approved by the republican governments.

In addition, Autonomous Republics (A.S.S.R.'s) were established (Bashkir, Tatar, Kirghiz, etc.). They had their own NKF's, but these were directly under the control of the NKF of the Russian Republic, and financial resources were supplied from the general resources of the R.S.F.S.R.[3] As a rule these republics had both unified and non-unified commissariats as with the larger republics. The estimates of all their commissariats had to be approved by the R.S.F.S.R., but those of non-unified commissariats passed first through the SNK of the A.S.S.R.

With these measures, and with the introduction of NKF plenipotentiaries into all the main republics by the middle of 1921,[4] the preliminary steps necessary for the unification of the budgetary systems of the Soviet republics had been taken some months before the adoption of the first budget of N.E.P., at a time when the restoration of local budgets and the introduction of *khozraschot* were still under discussion. In the draft budget for 1922, the estimates for each non-unified commissariat of each republic appeared as a lump sum in a special section of the budget; and roughly the same procedure was followed in the 1922/3 budget.[5] The estimates of unified commissariats were included entirely in the central estimates, without subdivision by republics. There was at this stage no clear distinction between autonomous and treaty republics, except that the latter were allowed to redistribute their allocations among their non-unified commissariats.[6] In 1922/3 provision was made for the combination of the estimates of non-unified commissariats into general

---

[1] SU 426/1920 (30. ix. 20); N. Gobza in *Vestnik finansov*, no. 7 (1926), pp. 61 ff.
[2] SU 13/1921 (23–29. xii. 20).
[3] SU 203/1920 (19. v. 20), 222/1920 (27. v. 20), 359/1920 (26. viii. 20); 41 and 49/1921 (20. i. 21), 556/1921 (18. x. 21); 370/1922 (27. iv. 22).
[4] *Ek. zhizn'*, no. 151 (1921).
[5] SU 553/1921 (10. x. 21), 961/1922 (10. viii. 22).
[6] Decree of 22. xi. 1921, *Rospis'...po i.–ix. 1922g....*, supplement, pp. 10–11.

republican budgets; but no sums of revenue were earmarked for particular republics, and therefore the 'budgets' were in fact estimates of expenditure only,[1] with the exception of the Ukraine and the Trans-Caucasian Federation, which continued to retain their own budgets and wide financial powers.[2]

There were two outstanding anomalies in this situation. First, all the republican budgets formed a part of the Russian budget, but the Russian Republic did not have a republican budget of its own; the 'Union' aspects of the Russian budget were not separated from its 'Russian Republic' aspects. Secondly, the division of all functions into *either* unified *or* non-unified was not satisfactory; there was a case for certain of the functions dealt with by unified commissariats being delegated to the republics, while remaining under central control, but there was no provision for this with the division of powers into only two types.

The experience of 1920-22 led to a widespread discussion on the organisation of republican finance in 1923,[3] and the full republican budgetary system was introduced after the adoption of the U.S.S.R. constitution in the middle of the year. By the provisions of the constitution and the subsequent rules for compiling the 1923/4 budget, the unified state budget was to be made up of the budget for the Union as a whole and the budgets of the constituent Union republics (at this time Russia, the Ukraine, Belorussia, and Transcaucasia). The budgets of the Union republics were themselves to contain the budgets of the Autonomous republics. What had previously been the 'unified' commissariats, under central jurisdiction but subject to some intervention at republican level, were now split into two groups—the Union and the Unified commissariats. The Union commissariats came entirely under the Union authorities, and were completely outside the control of the national republics. They included foreign affairs, defence, foreign trade, transport and posts. Plenipotentiaries represented their interests in the republics. The Unified commissariats,[4] which included VSNKh, and the commissariats of food, labour, finance and RKI, had both a central commissariat in

---

[1] *Vestnik finansov*, no. 7 (1926), pp. 71–8.

[2] The Transcaucasian budget, for example, included rail transport; it was not unified with the central budget until 1924–5. For the Ukraine, see SU 733/1922 (25. viii. 22).

[3] See, for example, articles by S. Golovanov, A. Orlov, and N. Sirinov in *Vestnik finansov*, no. 7 (1923), pp. 2–22; and TsIK discussion of November 1923.

[4] Also known as 'directive' commissariats, and later known as 'Union-Republican' Commissariats.

Moscow and commissariats in each of the republics. The part of their work considered to be of all-Union importance came under the central commissariat and the Union budget, and the remainder under the republican commissariats and budgets. Thus the Union budget included all the expenditure of Union commissariats and the central expenditure of Unified commissariats. The republican budgets included all the expenditure of non-Unified commissariats, and the republican expenditure of Unified commissariats. The republican budgets received the revenue of those commissariats subordinate to them, and in addition subsidies from the Union budget.[1]

The system as it stood suffered from major weaknesses. In the first place, the revenues granted to republican budgets were completely inadequate, consisting, apart from the receipts of the commissariat of agriculture, of only trivial sums. As a result, large subsidies had to be given from the Union budget to the republican budgets.[2] This gave no incentive to the republics to collect taxes for the state; instead, the republican NKF's devoted their main attention to demonstrating that the republic needed a large subsidy. This was corrected in the budget laws adopted in October 1924,[3] which made available to the republics substantial deductions from and additions to state direct taxes and non-tax revenue, the total timber revenue, and a number of additional minor sources of revenue. As a result, the subsidy from the general-Union budget was cut substantially.

The second main weakness of the rules of 1923, repeated in the 1924 decree, was that they left the organisation of the A.S.S.R. budgets to the republics to which they were subordinated. No settled or satisfactory A.S.S.R. budgetary organisation was developed until some years later.

By October 1924 the main outlines of both the republican and the local budgetary systems were established. The central government had kept firmly in its hands the main items of expenditure and sources of revenue, and had even taken over certain functions which had previously been under republican control. Expenditure of less importance had been left under republican management, though it was still included in the unified budget in general terms, and was

---

[1] SU 961/1923 (21. viii. 23).
[2] 46·8% of republican revenue in 1923/4 came from central grants, according to the supplement to Bryukhanov's speech in *2 sessiya TsIKa SSSR 3-go sozyva, 12–25. iv. 26* (1926).
[3] SZ 189/1924 (29. x. 24).

Table 14. *Revenue of state budget, 1922/3–1929/30 (million roubles)*

	1922/3		1923/4		1924/5		1925/6		1926/7		1927/8		1928/9		1929/30	
	Amount	%	Amount	%	Amount	%	Amount	%	Amount	%	Amount	%	Amount	%	Amount	%
TAX REVENUE																
Agricultural tax	176·5	12·1	231·0	10·0	326·2	10·7	251·7	6·2	357·9	6·6	354·2	5·3	449·4	5·3	405·6	3·1
Promtax on socialised economy	59·2	4·1	113·1	4·9	92·8	3·1	134·9	3·3	240·4	4·5	287·5	4·3	885·8	10·5	1,797·1	13·8
Promtax on private sector					64·5	2·1	94·3	2·3	108·5	2·0	85·9	1·3	170·1	2·0	144·3	1·1
Income tax on socialised economy	12·7	0·9	7·9	0·3	33·0	1·1	65·3	1·6	78·1	1·4	78·4	1·2	120·0	1·4	421·3	3·2
Income tax on population			56·8	2·5	61·3	2·0	86·1	2·1	114·1	2·1	153·0	2·3	165·5	2·0	193·3	1·5
Excises	103·5	7·1	240·7	10·4	507·8	16·9	841·6	20·7	1,209·8	22·4	1,491·2	22·4	1,802·6	21·4	2,643·0	20·4
Customs revenue	66·7	4·6	67·4	2·9	101·9	3·4	150·5	3·7	189·5	3·5	259·7	3·9	258·2	3·1	304·3	2·3
Dues and levies	23·1[(1)]	1·6	67·3	2·9	122·6	4·1	157·9	3·9	176·4	3·3	229·4	3·4	131·8	1·6	141·1	1·1
Other tax revenue	32·9	2·3	1·3	0·1	17·6	0·6	8·9	0·2	15·9	0·3	22·7	0·3	20·7	0·2	33·7	0·3
Total tax revenue	474·6	32·5	785·5	33·9	1,327·7	44·2	1,791·2	44·1	2,490·6	46·2	2,962·0	44·4	4,004·1	47·5	6,083·7	46·8
SELF-BALANCING REVENUE OF TRANSPORT AND POSTS[(2)]	392·6	26·9	746·4	32·3	1,073·9	35·8	1,563·5	38·5	1,868·4	34·7	2,121·7	31·8	2,538·1	30·1	3,399·8	26·2
SELF-BALANCING REVENUE FROM STATE LOANS[(2)]	4·2	0·3	71·8	3·1	66·2	2·2	117·6	2·9	101·0	1·9	299·6	4·5	317·5	3·8	405·7	3·1
NON-TAX REVENUE																
Deductions from profits	11·4	0·8	48·9	2·1	123·1	4·1	171·9	4·2	308·2	5·7	382·2	5·7	417·7	5·0	1,004·5	7·7
State property (timber and ores, etc.)	31·3	2·1	64·6	2·8	126·4	4·2	256·8	6·3	287·3	5·3	326·4	4·9	406·8	4·8	593·9	4·6
Other non-tax revenue[(3)]	28·4	1·9	179·3	7·7	152·5	5·1	103·5	2·5	94·9	1·8	92·0	1·4	98·6	1·2	403·8 [(6)]	3·1
Total non-tax revenue	71·1	4·9	292·8	12·6	402·0	13·4	532·2	13·1	690·4	12·8	800·6	12·0	923·1	11·0	2,002·2	15·4
STATE LOANS NET REVENUE[(4)]	77·7	5·3	111·7	4·8	64·3	2·1	28·4	0·7	218·2	4·1	426·8	6·4	407·3	4·8	872·7	6·7
OTHER REVENUE[(5)]	45·7	3·1	183·1	7·9	68·1	2·3	33·3	0·8	22·0	0·4	59·7	0·9	237·6	2·8	222·4	1·7
CURRENCY ISSUE[(7)]	394·1	27·0	126·3	5·4	n.a.		n.a.		n.a.		n.a.		n.a.		n.a.	
TOTAL REVENUE	1,460·0	100·0	2,317·6	100·0	3,002·2	100·0	4,066·2	100·0	5,390·6	100·0	6,670·4	100·0	8,427·7	100·0	12,986·5	100·0

n.a. = not applicable.

Table 15. *Expenditure of state budget 1922/3–1929/30 (million roubles)*

	1922/3		1923/4		1924/5		1925/6		1926/7		1927/8		1928/9		1929/30	
	Amount	%	Amount	%	Amount	%	Amount	%	Amount	%	Amount	%	Amount	%	Amount	%
NATIONAL ECONOMY																
Industry[8]	121·0	8·3	143·2	6·2	150·9	5·1	219·5	5·4	447·6	8·4	649·9	10·1	972·5	11·8	2,045·3	16·6
Electrification	23·3	1·6	50·8	2·2	51·7	1·8	68·3	1·7	102·5	1·9	136·1	2·1	179·2	2·2	229·4	1·9
Agriculture	50·6	3·5	58·3	2·5	171·4	5·8	209·8	5·2	204·0	3·8	279·2	4·3	547·1	6·6	1,099·0	8·8
Net expenditure on transport and posts[9]	142·9	9·8	68·5	3·0	0[10]		3·3	0·1	176·9	3·3	213·8	3·3	131·1	1·6	21·7	0·2
Trade and co-operation[11]	8·8[12]	0·6	35·2	1·5	16·0	0·5	54·8	1·3	90·0[13]	1·7	176·7[13]	2·7	257·6[13]	3·1	689·5[13]	5·6
Municipal economy and housing	0·2	0·0	2·2	0·1	48·0	1·6	74·8	1·9	42·8	0·8	110·0	1·7	67·5	0·8	76·1	0·6
Loan of economic restoration[14]	n.a.		n.a.		n.a.		5·0	0·1	58·1	1·1	62·4	1·0	28·5	0·3	65·1	0·5
Other expenditure on national economy	44·0	3·0	47·3	2·0	117·6	4·0	46·1	1·1	75·7	1·4	46·6	0·7	61·9	0·8	54·8	0·4
Total on national economy	390·8	26·8	405·5	17·5	555·6	18·7	681·1	16·8	1,198·5	22·5	1,674·7	25·9	2,246·2	27·3	4,280·9	34·7
SOCIAL AND CULTURAL MEASURES																
Education	—	—	113·6	4·9	153·9	5·2	227·7	5·6	293·8	5·5	340·1	5·3	398·2	4·8	704·6	5·7
Health	—	—	13·9	0·6	24·1	0·8	34·3	0·8	43·9	0·8	50·4	0·8	44·4	0·5	49·0	0·3
Other social and cultural measures	—	—	5·6	0·3	20·7	0·7	13·9	0·3	18·7	0·4	35·5	0·6	38·8	0·5	41·3	0·3
Total on social and cultural measures	83·0	5·7	133·1	5·7	198·7	6·7	275·9	6·8	356·4	6·7	426·0	6·7	481·7	5·8	794·9	6·4
DEFENCE[15]	230·9	15·8	402·3	17·3	443·8	14·9	638·0	15·7	633·8[(a)]	11·9	774·6[(b)]	12·0	1,206·9	14·6	{1,046·0[(c)]	8·5
															{350·9	2·8
ADMINISTRATION[16]	230·3	15·8	245·2	10·6	242·7	8·2	261·6	6·5	368·6	6·9	334·7	5·2	1,264·1	15·3	1,701·4	13·8
TRANSFERRED TO LOCAL BUDGETS	78·0	5·3	133·0	5·7	265·3	8·9	413·7	10·2	582·2	10·9	634·9	9·8	—	—	—	—
SELF-BALANCING EXPENDITURE ON TRANSPORT AND POSTS	392·6	26·9	746·4	32·2	1,073·9	36·2	1,563·5	38·6	1,868·4	35·0	2,121·7	32·8	2,538·1	30·8	3,399·8	27·6
SELF-BALANCING EXPENDITURE ON LOANS	4·2	0·3	71·8	3·1	66·2	2·2	117·6	2·9	101·0	1·9	299·6	4·6	317·5	3·9	405·7	3·3
OTHER EXPENDITURE[17]	50·2	3·4	180·3	7·8	123·3	4·2	99·5	2·5	225·7	4·2	198·8	3·1	186·4	2·3	355·4	2·9
TOTAL EXPENDITURE	1,460·0	100·0	2,317·6	100·0	2,969·5	100·0	4,050·9	100·0	5,334·6	100·0	6,465·0	100·0	8,240·9	100·0	12,335·0	100·0
EXCESS OF REVENUE OVER EXPENDITURE	n.a.		n.a.		32·7		15·3		56·0		205·4		186·8		651·5	

n.a. = not applicable.

Sources:
Except where otherwise stated, *Sotsialisticheskoe stroitel'stvo*, 1935, pp. 644 ff.; D'yachenko, *op. cit.* pp. 452–3.
(a) *TsIK, 4/IV, Bull.* 2, pp. 4–5;
(b) N. P. Bryukhanov, *Khozyaistvennyi pod"em Sovetskogo Soyuza i ego finansovaya baza* (1929), p. 6 (preliminary figure).
(c) *Otchet 1931*, p. 133.

Notes:
(1) Stamp tax (*gerbovyi sbor*) only.
(2) I.e. that part of revenue which is devoted to expenditure on this item.
(3) Includes 14·1 million roubles *net* revenue (i.e. gross revenue minus gross expenditure) from transport and posts in 1924/5. In all other years transport and posts received a net allocation from the budget.
(4) I.e. gross revenue from state loans minus expenditure.
(5) Includes revenue of mint, surpluses from budget of previous years, and (in 1929/30 only) 15·6 million roubles from local budgets.
(6) Includes 299·2 million roubles from special commodity fund.
(7) From 1924/5 onwards, as is explained in the text, the budget was always nominally in balance, and currency issue did not appear in the budget.
(8) Excludes food industry, which appears under trade and co-operation.
(9) I.e. gross expenditure minus gross revenue.
(10) In this year transport and posts provided a net surplus to the budget of 14·1 million roubles.
(11) Includes home and foreign trade, supplies (*snabzhenie*), and food industry.
(12) Co-operation only.
(13) Excludes co-operation.
(14) For an explanation of this loan, which is not shown separately on the revenue side of the budget, see text, pp. 103–4.
(15) For a discussion of the coverage of this item, see text.
(16) Includes, at this period, institutions controlling the national economy, and the administration of social and cultural measures.
(17) Includes grants to social insurance, State Bank (1924/5 only), and special state reserve (1926/7 to 1928/9).

subject to central approval.[1] The principal expenditures of local government were left in the charge of local soviets, and here there was no direct central control, though particular items of expenditure could be encouraged through subventions from the central exchequer.

While even the main outlines of republican and still more of local expenditure lay for the most part outside the direct control of the centre, the total expenditure of each budget lay within the control of the centre through the ingenious system of raising revenue. Each lower budget depended for the size of its revenue on the deductions and additions to central items of revenue, and on smaller taxes the limits and nature of which were fixed by the centre.

However, some years' further experience was needed before the system was fully adapted to the purposes of the Soviet state. The functions and organisation of the various types of budget were not properly delimited (e.g. the A.S.S.R. budgets, and those of the lower soviets), and the peasantry were not as yet directly involved in budgetary organisation (budgets had hardly reached *volost'* level, and were absent at village level)—public finance (including taxes) was for them something which came 'from above'. And while the means were there (e.g. by varying the deductions from central taxes available to different areas), the budgetary system was as yet hardly being used at all to assist the more rapid development of the backward areas and to enforce the social policy of the government. A new engine had been constructed; but it had not yet been put to work.

[1] The following points of terminology should be noted. The 'unified state budget of the U.S.S.R.' (*edinyi gosudarstvennyi byudzhet SSSR*) included both the Union budget and the budgets of the republics, but not the local budgets. The 'over-all budget' (*svodnyi byudzhet*) included both the unified budget and the local budgets. From 1938 onwards the terms 'unified' and 'over-all' budget were abolished with the inclusion of Union, republican, and local budgets in a single 'state budget of the U.S.S.R.'. Thus the concept 'state budget' *excludes* local budgets before 1938, and *includes* them from 1938.

I have used the same English term 'Unified' in this book for two Russian words: *edinyi* ('unified' budget) and *ob"edinennyi* ('Unified' commissariat).

CHAPTER V

THE BEGINNINGS OF CAPITAL INVESTMENT AND THE PLANNED ECONOMY 1925-9

1. THE DECISION TO INDUSTRIALISE

By 1925 the productive capacity taken over from the pre-revolutionary period had been brought back into use in most branches of industry, and agricultural production had recovered substantially. Industrial production, taken as a whole, rose from about 60% of the 1913 level in 1923/4 to about 90% in 1925/6, and agricultural production rose from some 70% to 90% in the same period.

Most industrial capacity available from the pre-war period had now been taken up, so that any large-scale increase in industrial production would involve substantial new investment. The Soviet government had therefore to make a decision of principle as important as that of 1921. Should the economic policy of previous years be continued, and the level of new investment be determined primarily by the market, or should the government attempt to enforce its own line of development, and if so, in what direction?

While the details of the bitter controversies inside the Party on questions of this kind need not concern us here,[1] the policy which emerged from them was of cardinal importance for the development of the Soviet economic system. In principle, this policy was endorsed by a resolution of the Fourteenth Party Congress in December, 1925,[2] which declared that internal policy must 'give first place to the task of securing by every means the victory of socialist economic forms over private capital' and must 'ensure the U.S.S.R. economic independence, so as to protect the U.S.S.R. from becoming an appendage

---

[1] For references to material on these controversies, see Dobb, *Soviet Economic Development...*, ch. VIII.

[2] *VKP(b) v rezolyutsiakh*, vol. II, pp. 47-53.

of capitalist world economy'. To these ends it must 'pursue a policy aimed at the industrialisation of the country, the development of the production of means of production and the formation of stocks for economic manœuvring'. A policy of rapid industrialisation was seen as an essential part of the attempt to establish 'Socialism in One Country', since that country was backward Russia. Thus industrialisation had its roots in the general programme of the Soviet leaders, rather than in economic considerations in the narrow sense, although economic pre-requisites such as Russia's potential self-sufficiency and the industrialisation begun before the revolution were a *sine qua non* of its realisation. The decision to industrialise determined the shape in the next fifteen years both of Soviet economic development and of the Soviet financial and economic system. If priority in capital investment had been given to light industry instead of heavy industry, or if it had been decided that accumulation as a whole should take place at a substantially lower level (or that the level of accumulation should be determined by the market), the organisation and methods of the economic and financial system would have taken different forms.

Two major problems therefore faced the Soviet leaders:

(*a*) How was the level of investment, extremely low in the preceding period,[1] to be raised to a substantial proportion of the national income? How were the 'savings' necessary to carry out this investment to be made, both in real terms and in money terms, and how were these savings to be directed to the desired ends?

(*b*) If industry and the non-food-producing population were to expand fairly rapidly, how were the necessary extra food supplies and agricultural raw materials to be secured, in view of the fact that the social and economic changes in the village since 1917 had shifted ownership from the landlords and the 'kulaks' to the poor and middle peasantry, and therefore considerably reduced the actual and potential off-farm sales? How were off-farm sales to be increased without an extremely large shift in purchasing power to the village, and without strengthening the better-off peasantry, politically unreliable and unamenable to planning?

These problems were, to a considerable extent, seen consciously by the Soviet leaders in this form, and discussed in these terms. But they were not tackled at the root until the second year of the first five-year plan (1929/30). The desired level of accumulation out of current

[1] Baykov, *op. cit.* p. 120.

income was reached only in the mid 1930's, and then only partially and temporarily, after the establishment of planning bodies with power to enforce their decisions, and after thorough fiscal and bank reforms. Adequate supplies of foodstuffs were made available to the government for the expanding industrial population only through the control which collectivisation made possible. But in 1925–9 the prerequisites for these fundamental changes did not exist. Hence this period was dominated by the attempt of the Soviet government to enforce the beginnings of industrialisation while the problems of accumulation and of the supply of agricultural products had not yet been solved. From 1925/6 onwards these problems became a major source of economic difficulty. But under the pressure of government measures, a substantial programme of capital investment began to be put into effect. Industrial production and investment rose by some 10–15% per annum from 1925 onwards. Agricultural production, however, expanded more slowly, and off-farm sales did not increase at all.

2. THE SUPPRESSED INFLATION OF 1925–9

The problem of securing an adequate rate of accumulation for investment while achieving the necessary surplus of agricultural supplies is the key to an understanding of the financial situation in this period. In the partly planned and partly state-owned economy of 1925–9, a high level of industrial activity was being enforced by the government over-riding the price mechanism and market conditions. The essential financial problem of the government was to try to provide conditions which would 'balance' the monetary situation at the level of industrial activity which had been obtained. In the attempt to bring about this 'balance', both the problem of accumulation and the problem of agricultural supplies had to be tackled. If a monetary balance were to be achieved, sufficient resources would have to be accumulated to cover new investment, by taxation, by loans, or by keeping productivity increases above real wage increases in state industry. If the government failed to accumulate sufficient resources by these means, and did not curtail the investment plan, a budget deficit and inflation would result. To obtain a balanced monetary situation, the government would also have to try to fix a ratio of agricultural prices to industrial prices at which the peasant would be willing to sell his surplus. Otherwise off-farm sales instead of rising, would decline, unless administrative pressure were used.[1] Finally, state and co-operative retail prices would need to be fixed at a level at which the available purchasing power in town and village would be mopped up, or else goods shortages would appear in the publicly owned trade sector, and prices would rise in the private trade sector.

In practice, the government was unable to fulfil any of these conditions completely. Consequently, the period from 1925 to 1929 was one of increasing inflation and goods shortages, culminating from early 1928 onwards in a situation of general scarcity, even of essential goods. Both the town-village relationship and the problem of accumulation were involved here. In 1924 and part of 1925 supply and demand were temporarily in balance, but the gross and *per capita* purchasing power of the agricultural population as compared with that of the wage and salary earners was relatively less than in 1913.[2] From 1925 onwards this situation was gradually but only partly righted: this is indicated by the fact that the percentage of total trade turnover taking place in the villages rose steadily from 1925 to 1929.[3] The resulting lack of balance between the supply of goods and the available purchasing power could have been avoided if industrial wages and salaries had been reduced to offset the increase in the purchasing power of the agricultural population. In fact, wages in 1925/6 rose more than production, worsening the goods shortage. And while industrial production rose more than the total wage-bill from 1927 to 1929,[4] this was not passed on to the market in the form of a relative reduction in the purchasing power of industrial workers. The decline in wage rates was offset by the increase in employment due to the employment of additional workers in capital construction and in administration and the social services; these new workers came partly from the unemployed and partly from the villages. The total wage fund of the non-agricultural sector of the economy therefore rose, without any corresponding increase in the output of consumer goods. The early stages of the investment programme were partly (but only partly, as will appear later) paid

---

[1] The government was able to influence the ratio of agricultural to industrial prices owing to the monopoly position which most sectors of state industry held on the market.
[2] This was a result of the changed exchange-ratios ('equivalents') for the main types of goods traded between town and country (see, for example, A. Kaktyn', *O politike tsen*, pp. 39–44).
[3] See data in *Narodnoe khozyaistvo* (1932), pp. 316–17.
[4] This is shown by the annual reduction in costs (see Table 18(i)).

for by a money inflation. The channels through which investment and inflationary issues were made will be considered later; here we are concerned only with the total inflationary situation, and it is necessary to note merely that the inflation resulted partly from the investment programme and partly from the shift in the terms of trade in favour of the countryside.

Table 16. *A Soviet index of prices, 1924–9*

(1913 = 100)

As at 1 April	Agric. whole-sale	Agric. retail: socialised trade	Agric. retail: private trade	Indust. whole-sale	Indust. retail: socialised trade	Indust. retail: private trade	Overall index: whole-sale	Overall index: retail
1924	162	—	—	213	—	—	178	201
1925	201	—	—	191	—	—	194	211
1926	191	—	—	201	—	—	196	216
1927	160	175	208	196	198	242	177	203
1928	156	177	233	188	189	242	171	203
1929	170	191	381	188	192	268	179	230

Source: Kaktyn', *O politike tsen*, pp. 68–9.

Increased purchasing power in town and country could have been absorbed by increased industrial prices, but in fact the government pursued a policy not of increasing but of reducing the retail prices of industrial goods. In consequence, industrial goods became scarce, and part of urban purchasing power was diverted to the purchase of agricultural goods on the free market. This raised the prices of these goods and the purchasing power of the village still further.[1] (The price-reduction policy is discussed later.) Table 16, taken direct from a Soviet source, indicates part of the process which took place during these years, though it probably underestimates the extent of the price-rise on the private and illegal markets, resulting from the goods shortages.

The inflation and shortages of the late 1920's were obviously harmful in their effects on the economy. The shortages of industrial goods were a major factor in the reluctance of the peasantry to supply grain in the required quantities from 1927 onwards. The goods famine acted as a deterrent to increased production by the industrial workers. It created conditions for speculation on the free market and

---

[1] According to Dobb, *Russian Economic Development...*, p. 220, village purchasing power rose between July and December 1927 by about 12%, while the supply of finished industrial goods rose by only just over 3%.

a drift of capital into the hands of private traders. It ultimately forced the government to adopt a complicated rationing system.

It should be noted, however, that the inflation did not carry with it some of the consequences which result inevitably from inflation in under-developed economies in which there is a smaller degree of state control than in the U.S.S.R. In addition to the objections already mentioned, inflation in such economies, to quote a U.N. survey,

(*a*) distorts the profitability of various types of enterprises and (*b*) encourages people to put too much capital into speculative enterprises and (*c*) into hoards of gold and foreign exchanges... (*d*) by reducing the real value of small savings, it also discourages the lower and middle income groups from continuing to save.[1]

In the N.E.P. type of economy:

(*a*) The transfer-prices of state industry were to a large extent rigidly kept down (i.e. the inflation was suppressed) with the result that inside industry costing was not subject to rapid fluctuation (though at a later stage during the first five-year plan the general inflationary conditions forced costs, especially wage costs, to rise).

(*b*) New capital formation was sufficiently controlled to make speculative investment, except by the state, impossible.

(*c*) State monopoly in gold and foreign exchange made hoarding them extremely difficult (although coins were withdrawn from circulation into hoards). On the other hand, the existence of obstacles to 'hard currency' hoarding increased the reluctance of the peasantry to exchange grain for a currency with which goods could not easily be purchased.

(*d*) As industrial investment was made almost entirely by the state through forced savings (taxes, and savings due to inflation), it did not much matter that there was little incentive for the population to save. The urban worker would in any case have been inclined to spend almost all his income, even had inflationary conditions been absent (the state loan campaigns, discussed below, attempted to compensate for this by providing a *political* incentive to save).

Was the suppressed inflation inevitable? It could, of course, have been mitigated by a reduction of investment in heavy industry. This would have enabled a greater immediate output of industrial consumer goods for the market and would have reduced the inclination of the peasantry to withhold supplies; but it is doubtful whether the

[1] *Measures for the economic development of under-developed countries*, United Nations Department of Economic Affairs (1951), p. 42.

practicable immediate increase would have been sufficient to persuade the peasantry to increase production and then market willingly sufficient supplies to permit a substantial increase in the urban population.[1] Measures of this character were advocated by the Kondratiev group in 1926–7 and by the Right Opposition in 1928–30, but they were politically unacceptable to the government. The proposals canvassed at the opposite extreme for more rapid capital investment in industry hardly offered a feasible alternative: the Left Oppositions of 1923, 1925, and 1927 argued that more rapid investment was in the long run the only way of securing an adequate production of industrial consumer goods. But any appreciably greater rate of investment would inevitably have antagonised the peasantry.

Could the shortages of consumer goods have been avoided *without* a change in the rate of industrialisation? Of course, if labour productivity had risen faster than it did, this would have improved the situation; and to the extent that the wage policy fostered by the trade unions hindered such an increase they were partly responsible for the goods shortages. But assuming the actual rate of increase in productivity, a balance of supply and demand could have been achieved only by reducing the purchasing power of either the agricultural or the non-agricultural population (or of both). Was this practicable?

The purchasing power of the peasantry could conceivably have been reduced in three ways:

(*a*) The prices paid for agricultural goods could have been reduced. Since the scissors were already open to the disadvantage of the peasantry, this course was politically and economically unacceptable. It would have made the procurements campaigns even less likely to succeed, and would have increased peasant hostility. Unless the retail prices of agricultural goods in the towns had been kept up by a sales tax, it would have increased the disproportion between town demand and food supplies.

(*b*) Extra taxes could have been imposed on the peasantry. This was attempted to some extent early in 1928, when a drive was made to increase 'self-taxation' for village use, to increase peasant subscriptions to state loans, to collect in arrears of agricultural tax, and to stamp out illegal distilling in order to compel the peasant to buy state-produced vodka on which there was a high rate of excise. But

---

[1] 'It was possible even that there might be *no* rate of exchange, however favourable, that would induce the village to part voluntarily with as large a proportion of its harvest as it had done before the war' (Dobb, *op. cit.* p. 216).

the use of these methods was limited by the fear of arousing peasant hostility. As it was, it was pressed to the point of antagonism.[1]

(c) The prices of industrial goods could have been raised. This proposal was frequently canvassed in these years. If the extra receipts from increased prices had been passed on to the workers as increased wages, this policy would, of course, have been useless. But if they had been skimmed off as tax, or used by industry itself for investment, it would have substantially improved the position on the retail market. But it was open to the same fundamental objections as the other two courses. To raise industrial prices without raising agricultural prices would open the scissors and antagonise the peasantry. But the government, already maintaining an artificial town-village price ratio (the gains from which Stalin admitted were 'super-profit' and 'tribute'[2]), could not risk peasant hostility in a situation in which it did not have an assured grain supply. Moreover, a rise in industrial prices would have led immediately to pressure from the industrial workers for higher wages.[3]

Could the purchasing power of the industrial workers have been reduced to lessen the goods shortage? Here the various possibilities were all open to the objection that they would have involved cutting real or nominal wages of the workers, which were seen as an 'untouchable' gain of the revolution. It would have been an economically sound course to reduce wages while keeping up prices by a sales tax for new investment. This would have relieved the goods shortage and at the same time the change in relative incomes would have led to a shift in the town-village price ratio in favour of the peasant. In the form that rises in productivity were not followed by equivalent rises in wages this policy was to a certain extent carried out. But actual wage-cuts were so politically unacceptable that they were not even discussed. Similarly increases in agricultural prices were in principle rejected as inevitably resulting in wage increases,[4] although they were in fact made to a limited extent in 1929 owing to the procurement difficulties. And although such increases would have cut down

---

[1] See, for example, Stalin, *Soch.* vol. xi, pp. 17–19.

[2] *Soch.* vol. xi, pp. 49 ff. The relevant section of this speech (April 1929) was first published in 1949.

[3] The assumption is made in the preceding argument that large-scale collectivisation was impracticable in the 1925–9 period. Of course collectivisation on the 1930 scale could have made possible a relative reduction in peasant purchasing power without reducing food supplies to the towns, but such a course was not openly advocated by any of the main political groupings.

[4] See, for example, Stalin, *Leninism*, 11th edn. (1944), p. 265.

the surplus purchasing power of the non-agricultural population they would have increased rural purchasing power (assuming they were not skimmed off as tax) and thus led to further shortages.

It seems, therefore, that given the existing level of industrial production and of available agricultural surplus, the suppressed inflation was, in the political situation that then existed, an inevitable result of the level of investment in the economy fixed by the government.

3. THE POLICY OF PRICE REDUCTION

In this context of inflation and goods shortages it may seem to have been perverse of the Soviet government to persist in a campaign not merely for the stabilisation but also for the reduction of prices throughout the period 1926–9.[1] The case for this policy rested on the following considerations:

(*a*) A wide wholesale-retail margin was skimmed off by state and co-operative trading organisations, due to excessive trading costs, overheads and profits. A campaign to reduce retail prices would minimise this.

(*b*) Owing to their semi-monopoly position, there was an inherent tendency on the part of the trusts to attempt to charge excessive prices, and to fail to economise to the full. A consistent campaign to reduce industrial wholesale prices would force economy on the trusts, it was argued, and ultimately lead to a continuous reduction of overhead costs and wages per unit of output (as productivity rose).[2] This reduction in prices would be passed on not only to the urban consumer (raising his standard of living more than his nominal wages) but also to the peasant consumer, helping to close the scissors.

In the event, the only effective price reduction campaign was that of 1927. The 1926 campaign had 'insignificant results', and those of 1928 and 1929, taken as a whole, succeeded only in preventing 'official' prices from rising (while prices on the free market rose considerably owing to the increasing goods shortage).[3] But the campaign of 1927 succeeded in reducing the retail prices of industrial

---

[1] Targets for the reduction in the prices of industrial goods were set at 10% in 1926, and 10% in January–June 1927 (later extended to the end of the year). The campaign was continued in 1928 and 1929, but without definite targets being set (see SZ 117/1927 (16. ii. 27), 125/1927 (25. ii. 27), 510/1927 (12. vii. 27), and 238/1928 (20. iv. 28)).

[2] Cf. Stalin, *Soch.* vol. x, p. 230.

[3] See Table 16, and also Yurovskii, *op. cit.* p. 37. It might be plausibly argued that all these campaigns were in fact 'effective' in view of the stabilising effect they had on prices, and that it was necessary for the government to advocate a *reduction* in prices in order that prices should be stabilised.

goods by about 10%. Of this about one-third seems to have been due to cost reductions in industry, and two-thirds to the reduction of trading costs and profits.[1] In the same period, supplies of industrial consumer goods to the retail market rose by about 10%,[2] so the total money value of goods marketed remained approximately constant while increasing in real terms. But meanwhile urban nominal purchasing power had risen. Part of this increase was absorbed by increased taxation (this will be discussed later) and was used to finance new industry. The remainder, however, was diverted to the purchase of goods in the countryside, increasing village purchasing power and worsening the goods shortage in the rural districts. Thus, in assessing the effect of this forced price reduction, the 'gain' from the reduction in wholesale and retail trading costs must be weighed against the aggravation of the goods shortage which resulted.

Why did the Soviet government not skim off the gains from reduced costs as tax rather than reduce retail prices? The only objection to this seems to have been that it would have made a nation-wide campaign for costs reduction less popular.

The ultimate *rationale* of the price-reduction policy as a long-term policy, that it was a means of passing the gains from increased productivity on to the consumer, could not be tested in practice in the stormy transition years of 1926–9. Such reductions in costs as took place were more than fully absorbed by increased accumulation for new construction. The policy remained a paper policy, to be resumed again only when the objective conditions for it appeared again after 1935.

4. THE POLICY OF INDUSTRIALISATION AND THE GROWTH OF DIRECT PLANNING

The most obvious effect of the decision to industrialise the Soviet Union, and certainly the most widely discussed in the U.S.S.R. at that time, was the growth of inflation. The changes that the early stages of the industrialisation programme brought about in the organisation of the economic system were, however, of more lasting importance.

Among western economists it is a matter of dispute whether effective planning is possible by the use of indirect planning methods in which the price system would continue to determine most economic

---

[1] A. Mikoyan, *Rezul'taty kampanii po snizheniyu tsen* (1927), pp. 33, 81.
[2] Calculated from data in internal trade section of *Narodnoe khozyaistvo* (1928).

decisions. Whatever may be true of other economic situations, it seems certain that in the Soviet economy, as in the British war economy,[1] expansion *in the desired direction* and *at the required speed* was possible only with resort to direct planning. Even if the special difficulties created by the agricultural supply problem had been absent, a system in which industrial prices had been allowed to find their own level would inevitably have resulted in the expansion of light industry before heavy industry, and in a level of accumulation lower than that desired. Nor does it seem a feasible or sufficient alternative to construct an 'artificial' price structure in which an incentive would be given to state-owned trusts to invest in the desired heavy industrial production by artificially raising the price for, or subsidising, this production. Apart from the complexities which this would involve, such a system would, it seems, lead to bidding for the materials required for expansion within the heavy industry sector, and to the consequent breakdown of the fixed price structure for these materials. Once a labour shortage appeared, bidding for labour would also result, breaking down the fixed wage structure, and therefore the total wage fund, on which the price structure depends. As a result, direct allocation would again have to be resorted to.[2] Only if prices were perfectly adjusted to supply conditions for both labour and capital, and to the preferences of the government, and if the cost structure in each industry could be kept rigid, would such a system be practicable.

But whether or not an attempt to direct an economy along a predetermined path through a price system alone is theoretically conceivable, this course was out of the question in the inflationary Soviet economy of the late 1920's. In this situation, and in view of the presence of a private sector in industry and trade, small but potentially dangerous to planning, and a large and unplanned (and almost

[1] 'Even if there had not been the danger of steep price increases, it was most unlikely that business men would have been willing to invest in capacity for the production of munitions on the large scale necessary, or that they would have taken the right risks in such investment.... For all these reasons the government was forced to attempt the allocation of resources in terms of the real alternatives involved' (E. Devons, *Planning in practice* (1950), p. 4). See also E. A. G. Robinson's article in D. N. Chester (ed.), *British war economy* (1951), pp. 40, 53–6.

[2] In the whole pre-war planning period, bidding did in fact take place, and tended to have the results indicated; but this bidding was marginal, and the general shape of the economy was determined through direct planning channels. With the hypothetical system of planning through price which we are discussing, however, it seems that the shape of the economy would be bound to depart from that desired by the government, at least in the circumstances of Soviet industrialisation.

uncontrolled) peasant agriculture, only direct planning, at least within the industrial sector, could conceivably have made a success of rapid industrialisation.

A direct planning system in the sense in which I use the term in this book[1] has the following characteristics:

(a) The growth of the economy is regulated by the conscious aims of a central authority.

(b) The planning structure is such that these aims are embodied in specific investment or production plans.

(c) These plans are based on a more or less realistic knowledge of the present situation and future possibilities. To this end there has to exist a properly developed system of accounts and statistical reports; and the planners have to be able to distinguish which are the key planning tasks, and to link general aims with the actual situation.

(d) The plans must be applied and enforced by appropriate machinery. This may and probably will involve central control over the allocation of materials, equipment, and labour.

(e) It will also involve the introduction of methods of providing incentives to replace those automatically provided by a competitive economy, so as to encourage the fulfilment of investment or production plans with respect to both output and costs. Planning methods must be devised which are sufficiently flexible to allow 'initiative from below' to find expression within the general aims of the plan, and to enable adjustments to be made for production of particular items in excess of or less than the plan. In general, the planning machinery must be so designed as to make possible a satisfactory compromise between centralisation and decentralisation.

[1] What I describe as 'direct planning' has elsewhere been variously described as 'fully-fledged planning', 'totalitarian planning', 'central planning', or simply as 'planning'. Cf. the following. 'National planning is an intention to promote the public interest by the more or less visible hand of the State. In its fully-fledged form it is an acknowledgment of intentions embodied in pre-arranged tasks, based on knowledge of existing conditions and controlled or carried out by an organized structure' (P. Sargant Florence, *The Logic of British and American Industry*, pp. 277–8). 'Planning, in the full meaning of the word, is a reality when the execution of the plan is effected by means of direct orders and instructions. If, however, the planned aims are achieved by applying indirect measures, this cannot be regarded as planning, but should be termed control' (Baykov, *op. cit.* p. 424). For the terms 'totalitarian planning' and 'central planning', see *Economic Survey for 1947*, cmd. 7046, and M. Polanyi, *The Logic of Liberty* (1951), ch. 8. The last two tend to assume, however, that the planning system they describe excludes our clause (e) above by its very nature. This is as unrealistic in its way as pre-war economic theorists were in discussions of the socialist economy, when they assumed that our clauses (b) and (d) were irrelevant to it. I return to this matter below, ch. VI, pp. 139–141, and ch. XI, pp. 327–9.

In 1926–9 only the rudiments of such a planning system were established, although they were already sufficient to enable the investment programme to be put into effect at a fairly rapid pace. The system for allocating equipment and raw materials was *ad hoc* and sketchy, leading to a scramble between industries and enterprises, but industry was fitting into the planning system,[1] and both the amount and the costs of industrial production were beginning to be planned. Agriculture, on the other hand, with the exception of a small state sector, lay outside the control of the planning system.

The greatest difficulties lay not in the details of planning, but in finding appropriate means for reconciling the aims of the policy-makers with the existing situation, and for expressing these aims in detailed plans and programmes. How should the long-term line of growth be decided upon in practical terms, taking into account both real possibilities and the key aims of the government? How should the annual operative plans be tied in with the general long-term plans? The first five-year plan, the first long-term plan to be adopted for the economy as a whole, was approved in April 1929 only after several years of discussion of alternatives, and it was not until the third year of experiment with annual control figures (i.e. 1927/8) that a set of figures was drawn up by the experts which took the policy of industrialisation as its starting point.

5. THE BEGINNINGS OF FINANCIAL PLANNING

In looking at the inflationary situation in 1925–9, I have so far been concerned with it purely as a relationship on the retail market between the purchasing powers of the peasantry and the different groups of wage-earners, with its effect on the wholesale 'market' within state industry, and with how these relationships resulted from the investment policy of the government. I have ignored the important problem of how, and through what administrative channels, financial accumulation was brought about, and of the channels through which the issues of currency were made which brought about the inflationary situation. To analyse this problem, it is necessary to examine the development of the financial system in these years in its administrative and economic contexts.

---

[1] This was reflected in the change in the legal definition of the aim of an industrial trust from 'deriving profit' in 1923 to acting 'on the basis of commercial principles in accordance with planned tasks' in 1927 (Baykov, *op. cit.* p. 113).

In a 'pure' socialist economy, or even (with reservations) in an economy like that of the post-1930 U.S.S.R., the raising of money to cover the expenditure side of the financial plan is largely a technical question (as will be seen in chapter VI), for all (in the U.S.S.R. of the 1930's, most) issues and receipts of money pass through government channels (the incomes and expenditures of the population are received from or paid to a government body). But in N.E.P. Russia agriculture was privately owned and unplanned, and a substantial part of industry and trade was in private hands. This meant that the government had only partial control over the money incomes and expenditures of the population. The flows of income between sections of the population partly depended on the market, and here the government's influence was only an indirect one. Only state finance (the budget and banking system) could be planned, and the distribution of income among the population had to be taken as given, at least in part.

Raising revenue for the expansion of the economy and other purposes could not therefore be a mere technical appendix to the plan. Financial plans were not simply a reflection in money terms of the real allocation of resources laid down in a material plan. The plans in physical terms were strongly influenced by the *financial* possibilities offered by the position of the whole economy, including the private sectors. This was particularly true in the first years of N.E.P. when (as we saw in chapter IV) the budget itself was the only economic plan. For several years it remained the determining plan:[1] the extent to which the state sector could expand depended primarily on the resources which the financial system could accumulate 'from outside' (i.e. from the population or from the private sector), and these 'outside' resources were limited in view of the low level of the economy as a whole. Unless the government were to resort to currency issue, which it was not prepared to do in view of the importance of a stable currency as an ingredient in popular confidence in the Soviet régime, it had to enforce a strictly limited budget.

From 1925 onwards the planning of production and of capital investment increased. In consequence the budget lost some of its earlier importance. The planned tasks of the state sector, conceived primarily in material terms, gradually took precedence, and financial

---

[1] As late as March 1925 the budget was described as the basis of the economic plan; the production approach to planning, it was said, was speculation (Sokol'nikov, *op. cit.* vol. II, pp. 161–2).

bodies were more and more relegated to the position of 'finding the money' through which the planned shifts in materials, manpower, etc., would be carried out. Overall financial planning, closely associated with physical plans, became more important than purely budgetary planning.

The subordination of finance to planning and of the budget to overall financial planning took place only after a protracted struggle. Although industrialisation was accepted by the Party in 1925 as a fundamental aim in its policy, both the tempo and the methods by which this aim was to be achieved continued to be disputed until 1930. In these discussions NKF took a conservative stand. Thus in 1924/5 it came into disrepute for under-estimating the tempo of economic recovery and hence the possible size of the budget.[1] At the end of 1925 the NKF (Sokol'nikov) played an active part in the opposition at the Fourteenth Party Congress.[2] In 1926 a three-year financial plan was drawn up in the NKF on the assumption that the budget must remain the same percentage of the national income as it had been in 1913.[3] In 1929 the older staff of NKF were officially chided for not being adaptable to the 'large-scale financial generalisations' necessitated by the five-year plan.[4]

Financial planning was only tenuously linked with economic planning in 1925–9, owing to the conservatism of the NKF, the disrepute which surrounded it, and the incompleteness of the planning system as a whole. In the material attached to the 1926/7 control figures, the budget is dealt with in complete isolation from the economic plans in physical terms,[5] and in the 1927/8 volume the problem of accumulation is almost ignored.[6] There was also no co-ordination between the different financial plans. As late as 1927/8 the credit plan (the plan of bank loans) was not taken into account when the government discussed the budget.[7] Detailed

[1] See Stalin, *Soch.* vol. VII, pp. 128–9.
[2] See *14 s"ezd...RKP(b)*... and Sokol'nikov, *op. cit.* vol. III, pp. 13, 35 ff. Sokol'nikov's thesis was that attention should be concentrated on the export of agricultural goods. He was replaced as NKF by Bryukhanov in January 1926.
[3] A. A. Nikitskii in *Planovoe khozyaistvo*, no. 11 (1925), and no. 1 (1926); and see critique by A. A. Neusypin in *Ek. oboz.* no. 5 (1928).
[4] *Edinyi finansovyi plan na 1929/30 g.* pp. 11–13 (Bryukhanov). On the other hand, Stalin spoke of the cut made by NKF in the 1928/9 allocation to VSNKh in these terms: 'That Narkomfin gave less is not astonishing, of course; Narkomfin's stinginess is known to everyone, and it cannot but be stingy' (*Soch.* vol. XI, p. 276).
[5] *Kontrol'nye tsifry narodnogo khozyaistva na 1926/7 g.* (1926), pp. 93–100.
[6] *Kontrol'nye tsifry...na 1927/8 g.* (1928), pp. 302–21.
[7] See Smit's report on behalf of budgetary commission in *TsIK* 3/IV, pp. 48–9.

information on the incomes and expenditures of the population was lacking, so that proper planning of them was impossible.[1] As a result of these weaknesses, the compilers of the 1928/9 control figures had to admit that they were unable to secure sufficient resources through the financial plan to cover the outlays involved by the physical plans.[2]

This does not mean that economic and financial activities were completely unco-ordinated. The budget was gradually adjusted to fit in with the economic plans. Thus the 1926/7 budget took as its basis the government directive on the expansion of industrial production and capital investment,[3] and from 1928 the budget was administered on the principle that priority was to be given to expenditure on the economy if revenue plans were under-fulfilled.[4]

But the budgetary and banking system was transitional in character, like the economy of which it was a part. It retained the appearance and methods of the earlier years of N.E.P., but the functions of those years were now only part of a much wider task. The financial system now had to collect and re-distribute resources not only for traditional government purposes, but also for the expansion of the economy, as a part of an all-embracing economic plan. However, it was not yet a co-ordinated system of financial planning. By 1928 the idea that a complete overhaul of the system was needed in order to adapt it to its new tasks began to be canvassed.

6. THE PROBLEM OF ACCUMULATION

As long as a private sector remained, the functions of the financial system could not be simply resolved into the re-distribution of income within the socialised sector. It was intended from the start that new investments should not be made on any major scale by the private sector (except in agriculture), but the inflation provided conditions for the accumulation of private capital. The financial system therefore had to accumulate resources from the private sector for the state investment programme, and in such a way as to discriminate against the 'undesirable' Nepman and kulak elements and to prepare for their eventual elimination.

---

[1] An attempt was made at drawing up a balance of incomes and expenditures of the population for 1927/8, but in 1928 NKF had to turn to Gosplan and TsSU for the available data (*Kontrol'nye tsifry...na 1927/8g.* pp. 542–8; Kuznetsov in *Vestnik finansov*, no. 6 (1928)).

[2] *Kontrol'nye tsifry...na 1928/9g.* (1929), pp. 53–5, 325–41.

[3] *Plenum byudzhetnoi komissii...*, p. 107.   [4] *Ot s"ezda k s"ezdu...* (1929), p. 59.

But the resources of the private sector were relatively small, and there was little possibility of acquiring foreign loans and credits. A large part of the resources for investment therefore had to be raised through channels fundamentally different from those through which accumulation is made in competitive economies.[1] It was therefore the task of the financial system to redirect resources within the planned publicly-owned sector from consumption purposes (e.g. light industry, administration, the wages of the state-employed population) into investment. The main administrative channels through which this could be done were:

(1) The free resources of economic bodies could be concentrated in bank deposits, and bank loans could be made to the expanding industries to the amount of the unspent deposited money. By exhortation and legislation the amount deposited could be increased (i.e. the outlays of the depositors could be reduced below the level they would otherwise reach), and the bank loans issued could rise by the same amount without altering the quantity of money in circulation.

(2) The savings of the population could be invested in savings banks or in loans and transferred to the expanding sector.

(3) The income of the state-employed population could be taxed.

(4) The income of state industry could be taxed (either by raising the price of output above costs, and skimming off the margin as tax, or by taxing the profits of light industry and transferring them to heavy industry).

(5) Production in industry could increase more rapidly than wages (i.e. costs could be lowered), and the resulting increased profits could either (*a*) be used for expansion within the industry itself or (*b*) be taxed off for use in other industries.

(6) The above channels imply leaving the amount of money in the economy unaltered, but in addition it was possible to provide the money needed by industry by increasing the quantity of money in circulation up to and beyond the point at which inflation began. In one sense, of course, all these methods of accumulation were dominated by the prevailing price relationships between industry and agriculture, which provided a kind of protective shell without which it would have been impossible for industry to develop on a paying basis (unless the wages of industrial workers had been radically

---

[1] See the well-known passage in Stalin, *Soch.* vol. VIII, pp. 124–8; and also the resolution of the Fifteenth Congress of the Party in *VKP(b) v rezolyutsiakh...*, vol. II, pp. 126 ff.

reduced). If the price structure is seen as providing a 'hidden subsidy' for industry, then in this sense the resulting difficulties in obtaining agricultural supplies may be said to have been the price that was paid for industrial development. Throughout 1925-9, especially in the winter of 1925/6 and from 1928 onwards, part of new investment was financed by bank loans (mainly short-term), which were larger than the surplus on the budget account, and this net currency issue via credit was directly responsible for further worsening the goods' shortages (the budget was always kept in nominal surplus although the amount of currency in circulation was rising, since for political reasons it was felt to be advantageous always to show a budget surplus).

In 1925-9 all the above methods were used to provide the funds needed for industrialisation. The banking system was responsible for accumulating the unused resources of industry (item (1) above) and for all issues which were not backed by equal receipts (item (6) above). The budget was responsible for accumulating the stable savings of the population, and of course for all taxation (items (2), (3), (4), and (5b) above). (But sums raised through taxation were sometimes issued to industry by transferring sums from the budget to banks to issue as loans.) Finally, accumulations from reducing costs inside industry (item (5a)) were, of course, the responsibility of industry itself, and appeared in VSNKh production and financial plans.

In Table 17 (i) an attempt is made to assess the relative importance of these budget, bank, and internal industrial sources to the expansion of the economy. Data for these years are, however, confused and patchy, and the figures given should be treated with caution.

It will be seen that these three main channels (bank, budget, and internal accumulation) were all of importance throughout the period, but that their relative importance changed as the economy developed.

(1) In 1922-4 (see chapter IV), after the initial issue of budget grants to enable industry to start working again, the budget did not play an important part in such restoration of basic capital as took place. Expansion was brought about through short-term credits (in practice not returned) and to some extent through the profits of industry.

(2) In the transition years 1925/6-1926/7, in which the first attempts were made not merely to restore pre-war capital in industry

Table 17. *Financing of socialised industry, 1924/5–1928/9*

(i) Sources (million roubles)

	1925/6 Amount	%	1926/7 Amount	%	1927/8 Amount	%	1928/9 Amount	%
Banking system	295	24·4	423	25·4	469	22·9	463	18·5
Budget	171	14·1	487	29·3	642	31·3	900	36·0
Profit in industry	574	47·4	662	39·8	812	39·6	1,040	41·6
Unallocated	170	14·0	91	5·5	126	6·2	100	4·0
Total [1]	1,210	100·0	1,663	100·0	2,049	100·0	2,503	100·0

Sources: *Planovoe khozyaistvo*, no. 5 (1936), pp. 88 ff.; *Ek. oboz.* no. 2 (1929), p. 50.

Note: (1) *Excludes* depreciation allowances (which did not exactly correspond to expenditures on capital repair).

(ii) Relations with budget (million roubles)

	1924/5	1925/6	1926/7	1927/8	1928/9
Taxes, etc. to budget	137	216	415	447	499
Receipts from budget [1]	106	171	487	642	900
Net gain (+) or loss (−) of industry from budget	−31	−45	+72	+195	+401

Sources: as for (i) above.

Note: (1) Calculated on slightly different basis from Table 15, resulting in discrepancies.

but to carry out new investments, the part played by the budget in financing new industry increased. However, as will be seen from Table 17 (ii), the *net* receipts of industry from the budget were still small. In this period the budget mainly acted as a re-distributor of income inside industry (taxes on the profits of both light and heavy industry were used to finance investment mainly in heavy industry).[1] In addition to budgetary allocations, and to short-term credits which were still of considerable importance,[2] an important part was temporarily played by the so-called 'loan of economic restoration'. This was an attempt to concentrate the free resources of economic organisations, through exchanging them for bonds issued by the bank, so as to provide a 'pool' in the hands of the banks from which they could issue long-term loans to new industrial projects approved in the plan. This 'pool' it was held would compensate for the absence of a market for long-term loans in Russia. This attempt was doomed to failure, for industry lacked substantial free resources; it was essen-

---

[1] These taxes were not, of course, ear-marked for this purpose, but their introduction made greater budget resources available for heavy industry.
[2] See discussion in Z. S. Katsenelenbaum, *Industrializatsiya khozyaistva i zadachi kredita v SSSR* (1928), pp. 57 ff.

tially trying to persuade industry to lift itself by its own bootlaces, for new sources of finance had to come primarily from increased productivity in industry (which was not presupposed by the loan) or from outside industry. In practice although the bonds of the loan were formally issued to industry, the overall deposits of industry with the banks (ordinary deposits plus bonds held) *fell* during 1926, and the state had to make up the gap by currency issue.[1]

(3) In 1927–9 accumulation inside industry and allocations from the budget both rose considerably, and bank loans took third place, although net credit issues continued to be the administrative channel through which the government made its net issues of currency which worsened the financial situation. The problem was now essentially whether the necessary accumulation could be made mainly 'inside' industry, or whether (and if so to what extent) a large part of it would have to come from the budget (or from further inflationary issues—but this was not explicitly discussed).

About this question more will be said in the following chapters. At this stage it is sufficient to mention the obvious point that the extent to which the budget had to be involved in the financing of industrialisation depended primarily on the degree to which cost reductions (or price increases) within industry were sufficient to pay for the expansion of industry. To the extent that they were not, the money would have to come either from the budget or from currency issue. (The budget might also be involved in transferring these internal accumulations between one industry and another, but that is a technical question and not one of principle.)

7. INTERNAL INDUSTRIAL ACCUMULATION

The struggle for internal industrial accumulation was of major importance from 1926 onwards. In April of that year a speech by Stalin emphasised the importance of the 'régime of economy' to the success of industrialisation. Industrial plans must be moderate and practicable; administrative bodies must be reduced in size, simplified, made less costly and more efficient; wastefulness must be avoided throughout the economy; labour discipline must be improved and productivity raised; the workman and the peasant must be won over to active support of the campaign.[2] In June 1926 a

[1] See SZ 398/1925 (14. viii. 25), and *Fin. ents.* cols. 417–20.
[2] *Soch.* vol. VIII, pp. 129 ff.

government decree referred to the régime of economy as involving the 'strengthening of the internal resources of socialist accumulation' in view of the 'task of the development and re-equipment of state industry'.[1] In February 1927 this decree was made more specific when for the first time an annual cost reduction target was adopted for industry.[2]

Table 18. *Reduction of industrial costs, 1923/4–1928/9*

(i) Plan and fulfilment

	Plan %	Fulfilment %
1923/4	—	−17
1924/5	—	−13·3
1925/6	—	+2·2
1926/7	−5	−1·5 [(1)]
1927/8	−6·3	−6·2
1928/9	−7	−5·3

Sources: Kaktyn', *O politike tsen*, p. 51. Turetskii, *op. cit.* SZ 724/1929 (1. xii. 29).

Note: (1) Turetskii gives −1·8%. In the first half of 1926/7, costs rose 1·2% (SZ 564/1927 (6. ix. 27)).

(ii) Composition (weighted)

	1927/8 %	1928/9 %
(a) From lower norms of raw materials, fuel, etc.	−1·8	−1·7
(b) From lower overheads	−0·8	−1·8
(c) From lower prices of raw materials, fuel, etc.	−1·6	−0·4
(d) From productivity rising more than wages	−2·0	−1·4
Total	−6·2	−5·3

Source: Turetskii, *op. cit.*

This innovation, which has obtained a permanent place in the Soviet planning system, was moderately successful in the first years of its application, as will be seen from Table 18(i). Costs were reduced each year in the following way:

(*a*) Raw materials and fuel were used more efficiently ('norms' per unit of output were adopted from the autumn of 1927 onwards).

(*b*) Overheads were reduced (a separate campaign was waged in an endeavour to cut down administrative expenditure in industry).[3]

(*c*) The prices of raw material input were forced down.

(*d*) Labour productivity rose faster than wages, encouraged by new (but still imperfect) systems of payment, and the extension of production meetings and other early forms of socialist emulation.

[1] SZ 291/1926 (11. vi. 26).
[2] *VKP(b) v rezolyutsiakh...*, vol. II, pp. 158 ff.
[3] See SZ 106/1927 (15. ii. 27), 248/1927 (22. iv. 27), 542/1927 (30. viii. 27), 133/1928 (29. ii. 28), 509/1928 (7. ix. 28), 542/1929 (11. ix. 29), 721/1929 (8. xii. 29).

Table 18(ii) gives an example of the relative importance of these four elements in the reduction of costs.

At the same time this period saw the introduction of financial incentives in addition to the Fund for Improving Workers' Welfare (*Fond uluchsheniya byta rabochikh* or FUBR) (see below p. 119) to encourage the fulfilment and over-fulfilment of the costs plan. From June 1927 to June 1928 all, and from June 1928 onwards part of, savings in costs in excess of those laid down in the costs plan remained with the director of the enterprise to be used at his discretion for rationalisation measures, and for welfare, educational, and health purposes.[1] In September 1929 a further fund was placed at the disposal of enterprises equal to 40% of the saving brought about by socialist emulation.[2]

8. THE BUDGET AND ACCUMULATION

These successes in cost reduction encouraged the optimism of the compilers of the first five-year plan about the future weight of internal accumulation in the financing of industrialisation (see chapter VII, pp. 194–7). But this source did not prove sufficient on its own to finance the expansion of the economy required by the government in 1925–9. Attention turned towards the budget, but only gradually. In May 1925 the Third Soviet Congress, in listing the channels through which accumulation for capital investment could be made, had confined itself to depreciation allowances (which do not in themselves represent accumulation for *new* investment) and to 'real accumulation' (this term apparently referred to costs reductions) inside the national economy.[3] As late as April 1926 Stalin, in listing the potential reserves for industrialisation, had merely made a cautious reference to 'state power which controls the state budget and collects a certain amount of money for the further development of the national economy in general and our industry in particular'.[4] But in November 1926 the Fifteenth Party Conference, while emphasising the prime importance of internal industrial accumulation, bluntly stated:

However, to whatever extent accumulation in industry may grow, it cannot be enough to secure the necessary speed of industrial development, at any rate in the near future.

[1] SZ 392/1927 (29. vi. 27), 384/1928 (14. vi. 28). [2] SZ 541/1929 (11. ix. 29).
[3] SZ 250/1925 (20. v. 25). [4] *Soch.* vol. VIII, pp. 124–5.

Therefore the further expansion of industry will to a considerable extent depend on the additional means which are directed into industrial construction.

One of the main tools for the redistribution of the national income is the state budget. In the all-Union budget the policy of industrialising the country must find full expression.[1]

This was re-emphasised by the Fourth Soviet Congress in April 1927.[2] During 1926–9 the use of the budget to accumulate resources for investment was extended, and the realisation grew that the budget could no longer fulfil merely the traditional function of financing defence, administrative, and social and cultural expenditure, but also had a large part to play in the financing of the national economy.[3]

Table 19. *National income and the budget, 1924/5–1928/9*
(milliard roubles—current prices)

	National income [1]	Overall budget [2]	Budget as % national income
1924/5	15·6	3·0	19
1925/6	21·2	4·2	20
1926/7	22·9	5·8	25
1927/8	25·3	7·2	28
1928/9	30·0	8·8	29

Sources: *Ekonomicheskoe obozrenie* (1928), no. 5, pp. 40–6. *Kontrol'nie tsifry...na 1929/30 g.* pp. 466, 470. Plotnikov, *Byudzhet sots. gosudarstva*, p. 54.

Notes:
(1) It is not possible to discuss here the validity of Soviet national income data. These figures are given solely in order to indicate a general trend.
(2) All-Union, republican and local budgets are included. Calculated according to classification in force in 1938, i.e. total social insurance expenditures, and only NKPS and NKSvyazi *net* expenditure, included.

The relative growth of the budget is indicated in Table 19. Between 1924/5 and 1928/9, according to Soviet sources, the national income, measured in current prices, doubled, but the budget

---

[1] *VKP(b) v rezolyutsiakh...*, vol. II, p. 126.
[2] SZ 235/1927 (26. iv. 27). See also Katsenelenbaum, *op. cit.* pp. 63–4.
[3] Thus Bryukhanov, Commissar of Finance, referred in 1926 to the task of 'throwing state resources into industry via the state budget', and stated that the budget was mainly 'economic...not administrative and military' (Katsenelenbaum, *op. cit.* pp. 62–3; *Plenum byudzhetnoi komissii*, p. 44). One economist went so far as to suggest that the budget was taking on the accumulative functions of an entrepreneur in a capitalist state (A. Neusypin in *Ekon. oboz.* no. 5 (1928), pp. 40 ff.). See also Zangvil''s speech in *Plenum byudzhetnoi komissii*, p. 100; N. A. Padeiskii in *Vestnik finansov*, no. 3 (1925), pp. 73–80; and *Ot s"ezda k s"ezdu...* (1929), p. 59.

almost trebled.[1] The increase in the proportion of the national income passing through the budget was due almost entirely to the growth of budget allocations to the economy (see section on expenditure below).

Throughout this period the budget was kept in surplus by increases in revenue. In an under-developed economy, in which the propensity of the population to consume is high, such an increase, representing a change in the level of accumulation in the economy as a whole, could be obtained only by a sustained effort on the part of the government. From 1926/7 onwards, the general conditions in which budget fulfilment took place were what was characterised in contemporary Soviet literature as 'strained' (*napryazhennyi*). Although the budget as a whole was over-fulfilled in each year, this was only as a result of the application of special measures (such as the introduction of unplanned higher tax levels in the course of the year) in a campaigning atmosphere. This strain was publicly admitted by the leaders of the government to be a result of the industrialisation drive.[2] Like the goods shortage and the subordination of the budget to production plans, which we discussed above, this was one of the pivotal points on which the disagreement of the Rights and the financial specialists with the government appeared most openly. In 1927/8 and 1928/9 both these groups sought to reduce the overall size of the budget by cutting the allocation to industry.[3]

Table 14 shows that there were no startling changes in the composition of budget revenue between 1924/5 and 1928/9, in terms of the traditional classification. The yield of all major taxes steadily increased in absolute terms, with the exception of the agricultural tax, which was reduced in 1925/6 but increased again in 1926/7 and 1928/9. The yield from Promtax and excises rose more rapidly than that from the budget as a whole, particularly in 1928/9. So did

---

[1] In real terms, the national income increased by only about 60%, as measured by Soviet sources (see Birmingham Bureau of Research into Russian Economic Conditions, *Memorandum* no. 3). The price rises which led to this discrepancy occurred principally at each end of the period—1924/5 and 1928/9. In the intervening years, the general index of prices remained stable or even fell.

[2] Cf. Stalin in November 1928 (*Soch.* vol. XI, pp. 246 ff.).

[3] In 1928/9 VSNKh demanded a budget allocation of 825 million roubles; Gosplan accepted a figure of 750 million roubles, but NKF would agree only to 650 million roubles (a figure which was defended by Frumkin, a leading member of the Right opposition). The Central Committee of the Party finally agreed to a figure of 800 million roubles, a figure which in the event was over-fulfilled (*Narodnoe khozyaistvo...* (1932), p. 572). Cf. Stalin, *Soch.* vol. XI, pp. 273 ff., 318–25; XII, pp. 1 ff.; and *Leninism*, p. 297; Haensel, *op. cit.* p. 114.

that from loans and deductions from profits, though the bulk of revenue continued to come from those taxes which had already become important in 1921–3. The stability of the major sources of revenue in terms of the traditional classification does not, however, reflect adequately the struggle for accumulation during these years, for it does not show clearly the real sources from which the rapid increase in revenue was derived.

9. BUDGETARY ACCUMULATION AND THE PRIVATE SECTOR

The dilemma of the Soviet government in taxation policy became apparent in the first months after it took power in 1917 (see chapters II and III). It wanted to raise its revenue as far as possible from the property-owning and wealthier groups, but its political, economic, and financial policies were driving these groups out of existence.

In the mid 'twenties this problem was not as acute as it had been in 1918, as capital had been accumulated since 1921 by the Nepmen (and to a lesser extent by the better-off peasantry). By 1925/6 the government had begun to drive out private trade and industry in the towns, and to replace them by state and co-operative industry and trade. In the countryside its policy was more cautious. It attempted to restrict the activities of the better-off peasants, to grant privileges to the poorer peasants, who were its main supporters in the countryside, and to win the support of the middle peasantry by concessions. This was a preliminary step towards eliminating petty capitalism from the villages and replacing it by co-operative farming, though this process was at first intended to be much slower than the corresponding one in the towns (it was accelerated in 1929/30 by the grain procurement difficulties). In both town and country, taxation played an important part in enforcing government policy towards the private sector, though a part secondary to the administrative and political measures of the government.

(a) *Taxation of the private sector in the towns*

In the early years of N.E.P. it was not possible to increase the progression of direct taxes sharply, as this would have hindered the recovery of the economy, in which the private sector was important. However, as early as February 1924 the Second Soviet Congress passed a resolution calling for the use of the income and property tax as a 'regulator of accumulation' and for increased taxation of non-productive consumption.[1] In 1924 little was done to implement this resolution. Although the income tax system was the subject of much complaint, no reform was instituted, apart from a slight increase in the rate of taxation on the richest groups.[2] Nor was any attempt made to use the Promtax to discriminate against private concerns. There was an obvious reluctance to launch a tax offensive against N.E.P. elements, due partly to the influence of conservative elements in the NKF itself.

In 1925, over a year after this first resolution, the Soviet Congress again called for increases in the rate of progression of direct taxes.[3] This time large changes were made. Income tax was radically reformed. The division of the tax into basic and supplementary (see chapter IV, pp. 67–8) was abolished, and replaced by a single progressive tax with rates varying according to the income and social group of the taxpayer. Incomes were divided into three groups:

(1) Wages and salaries (tax deducted at source monthly)—tax rose to a maximum of 30% of the increment to income.

(2) Income from personal labour, not hired—maximum tax, 35%.

(3) Income of persons engaged in trade and industry (employers of labour)—maximum tax, 45%.[4]

In addition to this, local soviets were permitted to charge, for their own revenue, a supplementary tax of 25% of the amount levied by the central authorities.[5] The rate of tax on the top ranges of income in the third group therefore amounted to a substantial proportion of income. In addition to this, in the same year, 1926, a tax on excess profits was introduced, additional to income tax. Latitude was given to local financial organs, trade departments, and provincial executive committees of soviets, to determine the level of 'normal' profit. They could levy excess profits tax to a maximum of 50% of income tax on

---

[1] *Vtoroi s"ezd sovetov SSSR: sten. otchot*, 1924.
[2] The maximum rate was raised to 30% (SZ 196/1924 (29. x. 24))—it had previously been 25% (see ch. IV, p. 68). The complaint was made against the basic tax (see p. 67) that it tended to be imposed more heavily on the poorer groups (see Larin in *Vtoroi s"ezd sovetov*... (1924), pp. 154–60; *Ot s"ezda k s"ezdu*... (1929), p. 66). However, a 'war tax' was introduced in November 1925, based on income tax, on men aged 21–40 not subject to military service for political and social reasons: this had the effect of increasing the income tax on the persons affected (SZ 577/1925 (6. xi. 25)).
[3] *Tretii s"ezd sovetov SSSR: sten. otchot*, 1925.
[4] Private juridical persons paid at the same rate. For details see SZ 484/1926 (24. ix. 26), 96/1927 (10. ii. 27); *Finansy SSSR*..., pp. 253–9; *Plenum byudzhetnoi komissii*..., p. 105.
[5] SZ 198/1926 (25. iv. 26).

persons or private concerns earning profits, providing that they were earning at least four times the exempted minimum.[1] Finally, in March 1927 the 'apartments tax' imposed on persons with 'non-working' incomes (i.e. unearned income and income from private industry and trade) was increased (the rate of this tax varied according to the level of income as assessed for income tax).[2]

The 1926–7 reforms were approved by TsIK early in 1927 as 'corresponding to the class principles adopted by the Soviet government'.[3] A series of changes was also made in the Promtax, considerably increasing the overall amount payable both as license fee and as equalising tax (tax on turnover), and applying discriminatory rates against luxury production and favourable rates to production considered to be of social importance.[4] Small co-operatives were exempted from tax and the tax rate on other co-operatives was reduced.[5] However, state industry continued to pay effectively higher rates than private industry (the rate of tax increased with the number of workers employed, and private industry consisted almost entirely of small firms). The resulting pattern of tax, in which the co-operatives paid the lowest rates, private industry higher rates, and state industry the highest rates had certainly not been in the minds of the leaders of the government, and was strongly criticised in the subsequent period.[6] From this point of view the reform of the Promtax was a failure.

The Promtax was not in fact made discriminatory against private industry and trade until August, 1928. The radical reform of the tax which was then carried out will be discussed in chapter VII. The new law imposed identical rates on state and co-operative enterprises (1·4–14·8% of turnover) and higher rates (2·15–17·15%) on private enterprises.[7] Meanwhile the rates of personal income tax on employers and private firms employing more than three hired workers

[1] SZ 307/1926 (18. vi. 26). The tax was regularised by a decree of 18. v. 27 (SZ 273/1927). See also *Finansy SSSR*..., pp. 269–70.
[2] SZ 172/1927 (23. iii. 27); *Finansy SSSR*..., p. 271. For the earlier history of this tax see *Fin. ents.* pp. 592–3; *Finansy SSSR*..., pp. 255–6.
[3] SZ 120/1927 (25. ii. 27). See also the resolution of the Joint Plenum of the C.C. and the C.C.C. of the Party of July–August 1927 (*VKP(b) v rezolyutsiakh*..., vol. II, pp. 179–85).
[4] Thus in July 1925 and March 1926 successively higher rates of tax had been applied to luxury goods (SZ 406/1925 (31. vii. 25) and 156/1926 (26. iii. 26)), while on the other hand electric stations were exempted from tax in February 1926 (SZ 63/1926 (5. ii. 26)).
[5] SZ 461/1926 (10. ix. 26).
[6] SZ 474/1926 (24. ix. 26); *Finansy SSSR*..., p. 267; *Ot s"ezda k s"ezdu*... (1927), pp. 16–17; *TsIK* 3/III, pp. 534–5; *Plenum byudzhetnoi komissii*..., pp. 237–8.
[7] SZ 442–3/1928 (10. viii. 28).

had been further raised from a maximum of 45% to a maximum of 54% (plus local addition).[1] Subsequently rates almost as high as these were applied to all employers of labour,[2] and the inheritance tax on this group was also raised.[3] The rent paid for dwellings was also made dependent on income and social class,[4] and the additional apartments tax on non-working incomes was raised still further.[5]

Table 20. *Direct tax on different income levels and groups, 1923–30*

Monthly earnings (roubles)	1923 Group A	1923 Group B	1923 Group C	1927 Group A	1927 Group B	1927 Group C	1930 Group A	1930 Group B	1930 Group C
200	1·6	5·5	5·5	1·4	7·1	13·3	1·4	7·1	14·1
1,000	14·2	14·2	14·2	11·0	24·8	57·0	11·1	31·6	61·2
3,000	24·3	26·0	26·0	27·2	41·5	94·6 (1)	27·2	57·3	>100·0

Group A = Workers, employees, and artisans in producers' co-operatives.
Group B = Artisans not in co-operatives, traders not employing hired labour.
Group C = Owners of enterprises and persons with other non-working income.

Source: Finansy SSSR..., p. 271.

Note: (1) This rate is for an income of 2,500 roubles per month.

The overall effect of all these measures is set out in Table 20. Whereas in 1923 the rates of tax paid on 'non-working income' were little higher than those on the incomes of state workers and employees, by 1927 (after the 1926 reform) the tax was sharply discriminatory against the Nepman groups, and by 1930 (after the 1928–9 reform), taxation on the highest income groups reached over 100% of income (i.e. constituted a continuing capital levy).

These rates were nominally very high, but in practice it proved extremely difficult to enforce them. Russia had no traditions of an efficient system of direct taxation, and mobility and complexity of earnings, which was characteristic of the private sector in the 1920's, increased as a result of the worsening goods shortage, which led to the growth of quick speculative profits. To meet this problem the Fifteenth Party Conference in November–December 1926 had resolved that it was 'necessary to carry out a number of measures which would secure, first, sufficient reporting of the activity of private capital, and, secondly, the concentration of [tax-collection] work in

---

[1] SZ 2/1928 (14. xii. 27).   [2] SZ 639/1929 (29. x. 29).
[3] SZ 78/1929 (6. ii. 29).   [4] SZ 35/1928 (21. i. 28).
[5] The maximum rate was fixed at 3 roubles 20 kopeks per square metre per annum (SZ 199/1929 (27. iii. 29)). The previous maximum was 2 roubles 50 kopeks.

those branches of the economy where the regulation of its activity, and accounting and taxation of its profit, would be made possible'.[1] In February 1927 TsIK stressed that 'the further increase of tax receipts is possible by a fuller inclusion of taxpayers, especially from the non-working elements, and a more precise declaration of their taxable income', and urged SNK's to take steps to 'improve the methods of assessing and collecting taxes'.[2] Some steps were taken. Promtax was imposed on current turnover instead of on the turnover of the previous year, to avoid the lapsing of payments through 'skipping' by small firms.[3] Local authorities were given an increased interest in tax collection. They were allotted a percentage of receipts from direct taxation, which encouraged them to impose the tax as fully as possible, and, as already mentioned, they were also given the right to assess 'excess' income for the tax on excess profits. In May 1928 the tax-collecting machinery was expanded to increase its efficiency in taxing private capital.[4] These are only illustrations of measures adopted to tighten up the taxation of the private sector—a detailed account is not essential to our main theme. Inevitably the taxation of this sector was crude and somewhat arbitrary.

Although the level of taxation was extremely high, the amount yielded by direct taxation of the private sector in the towns was relatively small, and it tended to decline as the private sector contracted, in spite of increased rates of taxation. The proportion of the Promtax paid by private industry and trade steadily decreased, from 41·0% in 1924/5 to 7·4% in 1929/30,[5] even though the rates of tax on the private sector were increased in 1928.[6]

(b) *Taxation of the private sector in the countryside*

In the towns the private sector was peripheral to the main state sector, but in the countryside small-scale private farming overwhelmingly predominated. The need to retain the support of the peasantry made a severe tax policy on private agriculture as a whole inappropriate, particularly in view of the 'supertax' already imposed in concealed form by the scissors. The intention of taxation

---

[1] *VKP(b) v rezolyutsiakh*..., vol. II, pp. 126 ff.   [2] SZ 120/1927 (25. ii. 27).
[3] This also enabled the large revenues from state industry to be received with a smaller time-lag, and therefore reduced the surplus money at the disposal of enterprises (SZ 442–3/1928 (10. viii. 28)).
[4] SZ 322/1928 (3. v. 28).   [5] See *Sots. str.* (1935), pp. 644–5.
[6] I have been unable to find similar data on income tax. In May 1928 instructions were issued by the government that statistical information on the division of taxation between the classes was to be improved (SZ 322/1928 (30. v. 28)).

policy was to assist the government in its aim of gradually squeezing out the better-off groups and winning the support of the poorer and middle groups.

A policy of progressive taxation had been formulated in 1921 (see ch. IV, p. 67, n. 3), and was reiterated by the Twelfth Party Congress in 1923, which resolved that taxation should 'protect the interest of the poor and middle peasant', and that the burden of tax should be 'justly distributed between the various strata of the village, with the greatest benefit to the poor peasantry'.[1] This was re-emphasised in subsequent government and Party resolutions. The tax must be progressive, resembling an income tax as closely as possible (Second Soviet Congress, February 1924).[2] Financial help to small peasant households must be increased (Fourteenth Party Conference and C.C. Plenum, April 1925).[3] The scale of taxation must be changed, 'fully freeing the more impoverished groups from taxation and strengthening the taxation of the well-to-do and kulak strata of the peasantry' (C.C. Plenum, April 1926).[4]

In practice, sharply progressive rates of taxation were introduced slowly in the countryside, as in the towns.[5] In 1923/4 exemption from agricultural tax was given to only about 2% of total households,[6] and the tax was not very steeply graded. It was not until 1925/6 that a change began. In the following years, the differentiation in rates was increased cautiously but steadily (the Opposition groups demanded that it should be increased further[7]). In 1928/9 an addition of between 5 and 25% was made to the tax imposed on some 10% of households, and the income of the richest households (some 2–3%) was assessed individually instead of by an area norm based on the cattle, land, and equipment held.[8] On the other hand, the number of poorer households totally exempt from tax was steadily increased, from 2% of total households in 1923/4 to

[1] *Vestnik finansov*, no. 19 (1923), pp. 3–6.
[2] *Finansy SSSR...*, p. 247; *TsIK* 2/III, pp. 640 ff.
[3] *VKP(b) v rezolyutsiakh...*, vol. I, pp. 642–9; vol. II, pp. 23–4. See also Stalin, *Soch.* vol. VII, pp. 157–9, 173–8.   [4] *VKP(b) v rezolyutsiakh...*, vol. II, pp. 95–6.
[5] See for example the complaint on this score in *Svodnye materialy...za tretii kvartal... 1924–5 g.* (1925), pp. 77–8.   [6] D'yachenko and Kozlov, *op. cit.* p. 120.
[7] For example, Sokol'nikov at the Fourteenth Congress. The reduction in the *total* yield from the tax in 1925/6 meant that in spite of the good harvest the absolute amount paid by the better-off peasant did not increase, and probably declined. See also *Ot s"ezda k s"ezdu...* (1929), pp. 84–6; and speech by the peasant Ovcharenko in *TsIK* 3/IV, pp. 84–6).
[8] For detailed information on the imposition of the agricultural tax during this period, see SZ 208–9/1925 (7. v. 25), 192/1926 (25. iv. 26), 189/1927 (2. iv. 27), 211/1928 (21. iv. 28), 103/1929 (10. ii. 29).

20–25% in 1925/6, and 28% in 1926/7. At the end of 1927 it was decreed that 35% of all households should be totally exempt in 1927/8, and in fact about 37% were.[1] Such collective farms as then existed were also given privileged rates of taxation, amounting in 1928/9 to 25–40% below the normal rates for artels, and 30–60% for communes.

The results of all these measures are summarised in Table 21. The tax burden on the poorer peasantry was considerably reduced while the upper 3–4% of households had to bear 38% of the total tax in 1928/9 as against 17% in 1924/5.

In the villages, as in the towns, the total amount of direct tax which could be collected from the better-off groups was fairly limited. In the earlier years too high a rate of tax would have restricted the expansion of agriculture and harmed the recovery of the economy.[2] In the later years, as the activities of the richer peasantry were restricted (by administrative means as well as by taxation), their total taxable income declined. The tax which could be raised from the middle peasantry was limited by the desire to win their support (even the relatively moderate amounts of tax which were collected led to numerous complaints that the tax on the middle peasant was too high).[3] The total possible yield of tax was further restricted by the special exemptions and privileges given to encourage cattle raising and the sowing of technical crops. As a result of these political and economic considerations, the revenue from the agricultural tax rose markedly less rapidly than total budget revenue (see Table 14), and in fact direct taxation was a smaller proportion of the total money income of the peasant in 1928/9 than in 1923/4 (though it was, of course, a far higher proportion of the incomes of the better-off groups). In 1925/6, at the beginning of the 'face to the village' campaign which sought to win over the middle peasantry, the total sum of tax was actually reduced.[4] The only attempt to increase the total agri-

---

[1] In 1923/4 and 1924/5 exemption had been available via the rebate (*skidka*) of 5% of total tax given to each province to assist the poorer peasantry. From 1925/6 onwards a specific non-taxable minimum peasant income was fixed for each province. See D'yachenko and Kozlov, *op. cit.* p. 120; *Finansy SSSR...*, pp. 261, 264; and *TsIK* 2/III, p. 12.

[2] Thus in April 1925 the Fourteenth Party Conference cautiously stated that the progression of the tax must be such as to 'enable the further development of the economy' (*VKP(b) v rezolyutsiakh...*, vol. II, pp. 23–4).

[3] *TsIK* 2/III, pp. 370, 641–58, and see Kalinin in *Pravda*, 23. ix. 28. In 1928/9 the provision for a special mark-up on the basic tax for the better-off groups in fact led to an over-assessment of the tax on the middle peasantry (*Ot s"ezda k s"ezdu...* (1929), pp. 66–8; N. P. Bryukhanov, *Khozyaistvennyi pod"em Sovetskogo Soyuza...* (1929), pp. 26–7).

[4] *Svodnye materialy...za tretii kvartal...1924–5 g.* pp. 77–8.

Table 21. *Agricultural tax by income groups, 1924/5–1929/30*

(i) Percentage of tax paid by main groups

	1924/5		1925/6	
	% of total households (2)	% of total tax	% of total households (2)	% of total tax
Poor peasantry	—	6·2	—	4·0
Middle peasantry	—	76·9	—	74·8
of which lower group	—	—	—	—
upper group	—	—	—	—
Richer peasantry ('kulaks')	—	16·9	—	21·2
of which upper group (1)	—	—	—	—
Total	—	100·0	—	100·0

	1927/8		1928/9	
	% of total households	% of total tax	% of total households	% of total tax
Poor peasantry	33·2	5·9	29·3	2·6
Middle peasantry	63·6	70·9	66·7	59·5
of which lower group	54·8	47·4	55·7	33·8
upper group	8·8	23·5	10·9	25·8
Richer peasantry ('kulaks')	3·2	23·2	4·0	37·9
of which upper group (1)	—	—	0·9	10·8
Total	100·0	100·0	100·0	100·0

(ii) Amount of tax paid per household (average) by main groups

	1925/6	1926/7	1929/30
Poor peasantry	1 r. 83 k.	90 k.	18 r. 9 k.
Middle peasantry	13 r. 25 k.	17 r. 77 k.	
Richer peasantry	63 r. 60 k.	100 r. 77 k.	172 r. 49 k.
Peasants on collective farms, per household	—	—	10 r. 74 k.

Sources: *Finansy SSSR za XXX let*, pp. 248, 262, 264. D'yachenko and Kozlov (eds.), *Finansy i kredit SSSR*, p. 141. For supplementary data, see *TsIK* 2/III, pp. 640–58; 3/III, p. 531; *Ot s"ezda k s"ezdu (iv. 1927–iv. 1929)...*, pp. 66–8; *Plenum byudzhetnoi komissii...*, pp. 195–6; *Ek. oboz.* no. 5 (1928), pp. 13–28, no. 3 (1929), pp. 14–26.

Notes:
(1) Those taxed by individual assessment of income.
(2) Not given in original source, but not likely to differ substantially from percentages in 1927/8 and 1928/9.

cultural tax sharply, in 1928/9, met with the hostility of the middle peasantry (supported by the Right Opposition inside the party), and the government was forced to reduce its projected total.[1]

The improvement in the system of taxing the peasantry did not result in any increase in the total amount of tax, although the

[1] *VKP(b) v rezolyutsiakh...*, vol. II, pp. 216–323. The planned total was cut from 400 to 375 million roubles. However, nearly 450 million roubles were in fact collected.

improvements in the methods of assessing peasant incomes made the tax less arbitrary and therefore more palatable.[1] It was also made more palatable by the transfer of an increasing proportion of the tax to the local authorities for district (*uyezd*) and *volost'* use.

10. ACCUMULATION FROM THE STATE SECTOR

As sufficient accumulation could not be secured by direct taxation, the government was forced to turn for a substantial part of its revenue to the state sector, which was under the direct influence of the planning organs. It has been remarked in previous chapters (above, pp. 20–2, and 64, text and n. 4) that in a planned economy in which prices and wages are fixed by the state (as they already were to a considerable extent in 1925–9), profits tax, excise, etc., begin to

---

[1] The main changes in the assessment of the agricultural tax were as follows:

(1) The basic method of assessing the income of the peasantry was changed. Until 1926/7 the unit of measurement was a *desyatin* or hectare of ploughland or of actually sown land (for a discussion of the relative merits of these two units, see p. 68, n. 6). Cattle were incorporated into this system by using a coefficient to convert heads of cattle to ploughland—or sown-area units, based on the relative earnings of cattle and crops in different areas. Different rates of tax were then charged in each province based on the likely earnings (calculated on the basis of yield, market prices, etc.) per unit area. The disadvantage of this system was that it excluded from tax auxiliary trades and specialised crops, which in certain areas and among the better-off groups earned a considerable proportion of the total income. In 1924 the Second Soviet Congress had called for a system of taxation which would include these auxiliary crafts (*Finansy SSSR...*, p. 247; *TsIK* 2/III, pp. 640–58), but the new system was not introduced until 1926/7.

The new system was based on the work that had been done in previous years in calculating the net income of the peasantry (these data were used under the old system to assess the appropriate local rate of tax). An assessment was now made for each republic or district of the total average income obtained by the peasantry from all sources, including auxiliary and non-agricultural work, per unit of land. The income of each household could then be assessed by multiplying this average income per unit by the amount of land held. This income was then taxed according to a scale uniform for the whole U.S.S.R.

(2) A related problem was whether income should be assessed on the basis of the actual harvest in the current tax year and the prevailing prices. This was the method used until 1925/6. In that year a change was made to an advance assessment on the basis of the average harvest over the previous three years. This had an incentive effect, as any income the peasant made above the average for the previous period did not carry any tax.

(3) Finally, how should allowance be made for households differing in number of members but occupying the same area of land? Two methods were used. In the first, used almost everywhere until 1925/6, the total income of the household was divided by the number of persons and tax was then imposed on each person's income separately (the 'per eater' method). In the second, applied as an experiment in the Ukraine in 1926/7 and then made optional throughout the U.S.S.R. in 1928/9, tax was imposed on the income of the whole household but with tax allowance for each member of the household (the 'per household' method). (In Central Asia, where the system of imposition was more crude, no allowance was made for differences in the size of households.) Although in form this was a purely technical distinction, in practice the application of the second system led to taxation falling more heavily on larger than on smaller households.

have identical functions. If retail prices are raised, while costs remain unaltered, the margin can be skimmed off as tax. If retail prices are lowered, *ceteris paribus* the tax as a margin between cost price and retail price must be reduced. Whether this tax takes the form of excise, deductions from profits, or Promtax, it remains a mark-up on cost price (although the different forms may vary considerably in their incentive effect on industry). To treat Promtax as a tax on industry, excises as a tax on the population, and deductions from profits as something different from both, is to make a purely formal distinction. Even a planned income tax on the planned income of a state employee does not have the social significance of income tax in a competitive economy. In a 'pure' socialist economy these taxes are all in essence different methods of concentrating that portion of the national income which is to cover expenditure both on normal budgetary functions and on investment functions performed by the state, which would be performed by a private entrepreneur in a competitive economy (although different taxes have, of course, different social effects). This does not mean, of course, that whether one tax or another is used is a matter of indifference. While in some theoretical models of an 'ideal' economy wages, prices and taxes can be adjusted instantaneously to correspond with the new required level of accumulation, in the real world these factors are not easily susceptible to large changes for political, institutional and social reasons. To alter the level of accumulation substantial effort and manœuvring are needed in purely financial terms, if real changes in terms of labour and materials are to be brought about. In N.E.P. Russia the financial authorities were not permitted to lower wages or raise industrial prices, although these measures, combined with a sales tax, could have brought about the required degree of accumulation. Also income tax and other direct taxes on the state-employed population could not be increased beyond a certain level without having a disincentive effect. Attention therefore turned to attempts to increase the revenue from taxes on the state sector (excises, Promtax, and deductions from profit) without raising industrial prices. Between them these taxes were responsible for 39% of budgetary revenue in 1928/9, and their essential similarity to each other was increasingly recognised by Soviet economists during 1925–9.[1] The

---

[1] Cf. Stalin, *Soch.* vol. VII, pp. 158–9; Rykov in *TsIK* 3/IV, pp. 339–49; *Edinyi finansovyi plan na 1929–30g.* (1930); P. N. Kutler in *Vestnik finansov*, no. 1 (1926), pp. 69–72; Bryukhanov in *TsIK* 3/IV, p. 354.

formal classification of revenue as 'tax' and 'non-tax' was retained, however, although it cut across the real division of taxes by function (deductions from profits, for example, were recorded in the 'non-tax' category, entirely separately from Promtax).

(a) Deductions from profits, and income tax

Total profits of state industry depended on the gap between cost-price (including overheads, depreciation, etc.) and transfer-price. As has been shown, cost-price, transfer-price, and the resultant total profits were made subject to increased regulation by the state in 1925–9. The proportion of a given level of total net profits[1] which could be transferred to the budget depended on the amount which needed to be left in each industry for its own expansion.

In 1923–7, as is shown in Table 22, the distribution of profits between budget and trust[2] was not fixed rigidly. 10% was transferred to the budget as income tax. 32% at least remained with the trust, as reserve capital, in the Fund for Improving Workers' Welfare (FUBR—later the Director's Fund),[3] and in funds for special bonuses.[4] The remaining 58% was divided between the trust (retained profits) and the budget (deductions from profits) in proportions fixed annually.

But from 1927 onwards this flexibility was abolished. In that year 41·75% of net profit were directly transferred to the state budget, and a further 22·5% were removed from the immediate disposal of the trust and put in a long-term bank for general state use (see n. 5 to Table 22). By 1929 direct transfers to the budget had been increased to 58% of net profit, and in addition to this 20% (as against the previous 22·5%) was placed in special long-term credit funds in the Industrial Bank, where it was centrally disposed of by the state. Only 19% of net profit remained at the disposal of the trust.

Thus most industrial profit was now centrally redistributed. As the profits-level was rising considerably during these years (costs fell more than the reduction of wholesale industrial prices), an expanding

[1] Net profit excludes Promtax and depreciation.
[2] Profits were imposed at trust level throughout this period.
[3] In 1925–8 75%, and from 1928 75–85% of this was intended for housing. The remainder was to be allocated to such purposes as canteens, education, children's homes, etc. for factory workers and their families, and was to be spent after consultation between management and trade union (SZ 176/1925 (27. iii. 25), 49/1926 (5. ii. 26), 333/1926 (2. vii. 26), 387/1928 (27. vi. 28)).
[4] These were also distributed after consultation with the appropriate trade union (SZ 324/1925 (10. vii. 25)).

Table 22. *Distribution of profits of state industry, 1923–9*
(in % of total profits)

	1923 (a)	1927 (b)	1929 (c)
Income tax	10	10 [3]	20
Deductions from profits	— [1]	31·75	38
Special state long-term credit funds in Prombank	n.a.	10	20
Levy for technical education	n.a.	3 [4]	2·8
To expand economic activities of enterprises in the trust	— [1]	25 [5]	10
Reserve capital	20	10 [6]	n.a. [7]
FUBR	10	10	9
Tantième and other bonus funds	2 [2]	0·25	0·20
	100·0	100·0	100·0

n.a. = not applicable.

Sources:
(a) D'yachenko, *op. cit.*, pp. 225–6.
(b) Aleksandrov, *op. cit.*, p. 116.
(c) SZ 729–30/1929 (6. xii. 29).

Notes:
(1) Fixed annually. Deductions from profits and sums retained to expand economic activities within the trust together amounted to 58%.
(2) Maximum figure (see SZ 324/1924 (10. vii. 24)).
(3) 8% plus 25% addition for local resources (SZ 198/1926 (10. iv. 26), SZ 524/1926 (15. x. 26)).
(4) First introduced in 1924/5 (see SZ 57/1926 (12. ii. 26)).
(5) Of this 50% had to be placed in the Bank for Trade and Industry as a long-term deposit.
(6) Until reserve fund is 50% of initial capital fund.
(7) State enterprises had been restarted in 1921–3 with issued capital, reserve capital, etc., along orthodox lines. Reserve capital acquired a more and more formal character as the planning system developed, being used in practice either by the bank or by the trust for investment and other purposes. Both issued capital and reserve capital funds were abolished in the early 1930's.

source of accumulation was thus transferred to the state budget. However, at this stage (after 1927) no differentiation was made between industries as far as deductions from profits were concerned.[1] If an industry had a large investment programme (e.g. the engineering industry), the percentage of its profits transferred to the budget still remained the same as in the case of a branch with a small investment programme (e.g. textiles). State allocations therefore financed most of the investment programme of heavy industry, so that this programme did not have to rely on the success or failure of heavy industry in fulfilling the profits plan. This weakness was not corrected until much later, and then only partially (see chapter IX, pp. 150–1).

[1] This had been attempted in an experimental way after 1923 (see D'yachenko, *op. cit.* pp. 225–6).

(b) *Promtax*

During 1925–9 the rates of the Promtax on state industry were increased, and the tax was made more discriminatory against luxury goods and in favour of goods of 'national-economic importance'.[1] But the methods by which tax was imposed remained complicated and out-of-date until 1928—the outmoded division of the tax into licence fee and 'equalising levy' (tax on turnover) continued.[2] The 1928 reform replaced this double tax by a simple tax on current net turnover (i.e. gross turnover minus the value of production of other enterprises re-worked by the firm).[3] The new Promtax thus resembled the sales taxes and turnover taxes of post-1918 Europe in form.[4] It differed from them, however, in attempting to discriminate much more sharply between different types of production; in this respect it resembled an excise. This was an important step towards the unification of taxes on state industry.

(c) *Excises*

The yield from excises steadily increased between 1925 and 1929. In the earlier years of this period (1924/5–1926/7) it rose both absolutely and as a proportion of budgetary revenue, principally as a result of a sharp increase in vodka sales. In the following two years (1927/8–1928/9) the revenue from excises expanded at the same rate as the total budget, and therefore at a considerably greater rate than the expansion of the national income or of retail trade turnover.

In an economy in which the available sources of direct taxation were fairly limited, the continued use of indirect taxation in one form or another was essential if the necessary resources for industrial expansion were to be raised through the budget. The traditional socialist policy of direct taxation, relevant in a transition period in which large sources of income remained in private hands, had now to take second place.

The augmentation of excise revenue was supported by the financial experts and had the cautious support of the government. However, strong opposition to the excise policy continued throughout the

[1] See SZ 406/1925 (31. vii. 25); 156/1926 (26. iii. 26); *Finansy SSSR...*, p. 267. But cf. *Plenum byudzhetnoi komissii...*, pp. 232–3, where it is suggested that taxes on luxury output are too low.
[2] For an analysis of the method of imposition see *Vestnik finansov*, no. 1 (1926), pp. 69–72 and *TsIK* 3/IV, p. 54.
[3] SZ 442–3/1928 (10. viii. 28).
[4] For similar taxes in other countries, see A. Comstock, *Taxation in the modern state* (1929), pp. 110–53.

period 1923–9. To a considerable extent this opposition simply stemmed from the traditional dislike of excises as a tax on the mass of the population. It is significant that no such opposition was aroused to increases in the Promtax, although they also had the effect of putting up the retail price of consumer goods. But the discussion on excises also turned on the extent to which excise rates should be imposed on luxuries rather than on necessities, and on goods consumed by the better-off rather than on those consumed by the poorer. In N.E.P. conditions a properly graded excise system could be weighted against the Nepmen, who were the main consumers of the dearer commodities, and could also penalise the consumption of less essential goods such as vodka and tobacco.

To some extent the rates of excise did have these effects. Higher grades of tobacco and yarn paid a higher rate of tax.[1] Kerosene paid a smaller rate of tax than petrol.[2] Most of the tax was levied on alcohol and tobacco. The excise on salt was abolished.[3] While the structure of excises was still fundamentally the same as it had been in 1913 (see Table 23), the opposition to excises on necessities expressed at successive sessions of TsIK undoubtedly played a part in restricting tax rates on these goods.[4] Thus an upper limit to the tax was fixed both by government policy, which precluded any considerable rise in the official price of any goods, and by public pressure. In a non-inflationary economy the rate of excise on goods for which demand is elastic is also limited by the consideration that if prices rise too much on these goods, the yield from the excise may fall because of the decline in consumption which results. But in the inflationary Soviet economy of 1925–9 this consideration was irrelevant, except for luxuries consumed only by upper income groups,[5] and these were not of great fiscal significance because these groups were less wealthy than the equivalent pre-war groups. The rates of tax on tobacco, vodka, kerosene, tea, and sugar could have been increased considerably more than they were with profit to the budget.

On the other hand, a lower limit was imposed on excise rates both for the primary reason that further revenue could not easily be obtained from any other source, and because any reduction of excise

[1] *Fin. ents.* cols. 1009–1010, and article on 'excises'.
[2] *Ibid.* and *Plenum byudzhetnoi komissii*, pp. 308–11.
[3] SZ 186/1927 (30. iii. 27).
[4] E.g. on kerosene in 1924/5, and on salt (see e.g. *TsIK* 2/III, pp. 121 ff., 153).
[5] This exception apparently occurred in the case of wine production, the excise on which was lowered to assist sales (SZ 389/1925 (13. viii. 25)).

Table 23. *Revenue from excises, 1913–1927/8 (million roubles)*

	1913	1922 i–ix.	1922/3	1923/4	1924/5	1925/6	1926/7	1927/8
TAXES ON LUXURIES								
Wines, alcohol, beer	710·5 [1]	2·4	15·8	59·4	178·6	364·2	585·0	697·0
Tobacco products [2]	83·7	2·1	18·0	38·5	83·4	125·2	155·1	167·5
Perfumery and toilet articles	n.a.	n.a.	n.a.	n.a.	n.a.	n.a.	n.a.	8·0
Total tax on luxuries	794·2	4·5	33·8	97·9	262·0	489·4	740·1	872·5
TAXES ON FOODSTUFFS								
Sugar	149·2	—	—	—	117·8	177·5	244·7	245·0
Tea and coffee	n.a.	—	—	—	22·0	22·7	31·5	29·5
Salt	n.a.	—	—	—	15·9	17·6	10·0	3·0
Total tax on foodstuffs	149·2	5·6	45·8	89·0	155·7	217·8	286·2	277·5
TAXES ON CLOTHING								
Textiles	n.a.	n.a.	—	—	46·1	72·2	100·2	109·0
Rubber footwear	n.a.	n.a.	—	—	3·1	5·6	16·1	23·0
Total tax on clothing	n.a.	n.a.	7·8	28·0	49·2	77·8	116·3	132·0
TAXES ON LIGHTING								
Matches	20·1	—	—	—	15·3	21·1	21·0	25·0
Kerosene, etc.	48·6	—	—	—	24·1	33·6	35·7	41·0
Candles	n.a.	—	—	—	1·5	1·8	2·6	2·6
Total tax on lighting	68·7	1·7	16·0	28·1	40·9	56·5	59·3	68·6
TOTAL EXCISES [3]	1,012·1	11·8	103·4	243·0	507·8	841·5	1,201·9	1,350·6

n.a. = not applicable.

Sources: I. Reingold in *Soviet policy in public finance...*, pp. 189, 288; Michelson (ed.), *op. cit.*; D'yachenko, *op. cit.* pp. 243–4.

Notes:
(1) Includes excises on vodka, liqueurs and wines, and beer; and net profit on alcohol monopoly.
(2) Includes small item for cigarette papers and tubes (4·9 in 1913; 0·8 in 1927/8).
(3) There are slight discrepancies between the totals here and those in the sources used for Table 14; for 1927/8 the figures here are preliminary.

rates on sugar, kerosene, etc., would increase the shortage of these goods.[1] Moreover, as the revenue from luxuries such as high-grade wines and tobaccos was limited, the bulk of excise revenue had inevitably to come from what might be termed 'staple luxuries' such as vodka and tobacco, and from 'staple necessities' such as matches, clothing and foodstuffs. Consequently the government resisted the demand for the abolition of the excise on tea and sugar.[2]

The controversy about excise rates took its sharpest form in the protracted and confused discussion about the vodka monopoly, which continued from its inception in 1923 till 1929. The background

[1] See *TsIK* 3/III, pp. 536–7; *Plenum byudzhetnoi komissii...*, pp. 159, 308–11.
[2] See *Fin. ents.* col. 12; and for an example of this demand, Ryazanov in *TsIK* 3/III, p. 703.

to the discussion was the prohibition of the sale of vodka by the tsarist government in 1914. It was argued that this prohibition should be continued and that a socialist state should not profit from drunkenness. At one stage this view even received the support of the Budget Commission of TsIK. Against this the government maintained that the alternative would be the growth of illicit stills, the profits from which would accrue to the richer peasantry; and that vodka was an essential source of revenue for industrialisation in the absence of foreign loans. But it did agree on various occasions to pursue a policy of reducing the sales of vodka and the revenue from this source. How this was to be done was not made clear. In fact the revenue from vodka rose steadily throughout the period and reached over half of total excises, as against 70% in 1913. It increased still further in 1928/9 when the rates of tax were increased.[1]

To sum up. Excises, Promtax and deductions from profits were steadily increased as the budgetary financing of the national economy grew. This partly resulted from the expansion of the sources on which these taxes were imposed, and was partly due to increased rates of taxation which (*a*) diverted industrial accumulation towards the financing of heavy industry, and (*b*) increased the proportion of tax to price (without as a rule raising prices at this period), and therefore restricted the purchasing-power of the consumer. Although each of these taxes took a different form, they all had the fiscal effect of a mark-up on cost price.

11. STATE LOANS

Taxation on private incomes and on state industry proved insufficient to meet the growing needs of the budget. The only feasible remaining non-inflationary source of revenue was the raising of loans from the economy and from the population. The importance of loans to the budget is indicated by the fact that from 1926/7 onwards they were responsible for between twice to four times the revenue raised by income tax, and in 1927/8 and 1928/9 for more than twice the revenue from the unified agricultural tax. They increased much more rapidly than any other item of budgetary revenue.

[1] For the legislation concerned, see SZ 599/1928, 94/1929 (6. ii. 29), 591–2/1929 (27. ix. 29), 630/1929 (21. x. 29). For examples of views expressed in this controversy, see *Fin. ents.* col. 264; Stalin, *Soch.* vol. vii, pp. 340–1, vol. ix, pp. 191–2, vol. x, pp. 231–4; *Sten. otchot* of Fifteenth Congress of VKP(b), p. 60; *Plenum byudzhetnoi komissii*..., pp. 191–2; *TsIK* 3/iv, pp. 54–5, 58–9, 225–7; Bryukhanov in *TsIK* 4/iv, Bull. no. 1; Bryukhanov, *Khozyaistvennyi pod"em*..., p. 32.

State loan policy during this period had two main purposes. First, the government tried to accumulate the temporarily free resources of economic bodies in loans. If these bodies could be persuaded, by favourable interest rates, etc., to deposit in state loans part of the resources which were legally at their disposal, this would mean in real terms that money resources which would otherwise have been used by these bodies in a semi-autonomous way could now be used by the state for centrally planned measures. This real transfer of resources towards the financing of the industrialisation programmes was, in the mixed metaphor of one commentator, 'a bridge joining economic spontaneity to the planned economy, a canal through which private capital flows into the system of state economy'.[1]

Secondly, and increasingly, loan policy aimed at diverting the purchasing power of the population into the budget. Income tax rates could not have been doubled without strong popular disapproval, but a yield corresponding to this higher rate was obtained through state loans.

In Soviet circumstances, from the point of view of the budget year in which the revenue from loans was received, there was no difference between a loan and a tax. The disadvantage of loans as compared with taxes was that they entailed an obligation on the part of the state to pay back the sum deposited in the loan, plus interest. Unless the revenue from loans rises sufficiently in successive years, the burden of repayment and fixed-interest payments will steadily rise in terms of current prices until eventually it exceeds the revenue from new loans.[2]

This was not thought to be an important objection to loan policy in 1925–9. It was argued that loans were to be used not to cover unproductive expenses but to finance capital investment. Successful industrialisation would make the future repayment of the national debt relatively easy.[3] In any case, owing to the renunciation of tsarist debts (see chapter II), the accumulated state debt was not heavy. By 1928 it amounted only to some 4% of the national income, whereas in 1913 it had been 30% of national income.[4] However, the annual additions to the debt increased in each successive year, and so did the net revenue from loans (see Table 24 (i)).

[1] G. Vul'ff in *Fin. ents.* col. 397.
[2] Of course in an economy in which prices are rising the inflation will reduce the real cost of repayment and interest to the state, as in fact happened in 1928–36, but this possibility was not envisaged in the published discussion of the subject at this time.
[3] See, for example, G. Vul'ff in *Fin. ents.* col. 396.   [4] *TsIK* 3/IV, pp. 32–3, 45.

The problem of interest rates was nevertheless serious. In the conditions of N.E.P., a private interest rate formed on the free market, and, for reasons adduced earlier, it was an extremely high one. If state loans could be issued at this rate, they would be taken up. If they were issued at substantially below this rate, they would be taken up only if social or administrative pressure were used.

Table 24. *State loans and national debt, 1924/5–1928/9*

(i) State loans

	1924/5	1925/6	1926/7	1927/8	1928/9
Revenue	130·5	146·0	319·2	726·4	724·8
Expenditure [2]	66·2	117·6 [1]	101·0	299·6	317·5
Net revenue	64·3	28·4	218·2	426·8	407·3
State debt— end of year	367·3	657·2 [3]	929·1 [3]	1,422·7 [3]	2,541·0

Sources: *Sots. stroitel'stvo SSSR*, 1935, pp. 644–7; *Ot s″ezda k s″ezdu (iv. 1927–v. 1929)*... (1929); W. H. Chamberlin, *The Soviet planned economic order* (1931), p. 94.

[N.B. Owing to differing methods of calculation, data in Soviet sources on the size of the state debt vary widely. For alternative figures (not, however, differing substantially) see: *Ot s″ezda k s″ezdu (v. 1925–iv. 1927)*..., p. 20; P. Haensel, *The economic policy of Soviet Russia* (1930), pp. 182–3; D'yachenko and Kozlov, *op. cit.* pp. 121, 142; *TsIK* 2/III, p. 37.)]

Notes:
(1) Interest and repayments rose considerably in 1925/6 owing to short-term loans of the earlier loan period falling due, and to the high interest rates borne by these earlier loans.
(2) Interest and repayments.
(3) Includes 'loan of economic restoration' (see pp. 103–4 above).

(ii) Structure of national debt (million roubles)

	1. x. 1925	1. x. 1928
Total from industry	142·2	400·8 [1]
Total from population	225·1	639·3
Loans from savings banks	—	257·7
Total	367·3	1,297·8

Sources: *TsIK* 3/IV, pp. 32–3, 45; 4/IV, pp. 2, 8.

Note: (1) Excludes loan of economic restoration, 124 million roubles.

As far as state bodies were concerned, this problem was tackled by increasing central powers over their free money, which had to be deposited with a bank and not held in cash. In addition, 60% of reserve capital had to be invested in state loans.[1] As a result of these administrative measures, from 1924 onwards internal government loans were taken up although they bore only 8% (well below the free market rate).[2]

[1] SZ 36/1925 (8. i. 25); *Fin. ents.* col. 402.
[2] *Vestnik*..., 43/1924 (15. ii. 24); SZ 286/1926 (2. vi. 26); 325/1927 (11. ii. 27); 566/1928 (12. x. 28).

With the population the position was more complicated. In 1923–4 (see chapter IV) the subscription to lottery loans floated with the population had been compulsory, in view of the high private interest rate, which had stood as high as 16% per month in the autumn of 1923. With the stabilisation of the currency, this rate gradually fell, and early in 1925 it proved possible to issue a successful small *short-term* 'test' loan to voluntary subscription at only 5%.[1] From 1925 onwards the policy was pursued of issuing loans on a voluntary basis at interest rates comparable with the market rate.[2] During 1925 and 1926 the interest rate on *long-term*[3] loans floated with the population was 10 or 12% per annum, and the period of repayment was gradually extended from 5 years to 10 years (thus further postponing budget outlays on repayment).[4] By 1927 the potential receipts from industry were very limited, as its resources and production programmes were under much closer control from the centre. Expansion in loan revenue could therefore take place only through extending the savings of the population. By October 1928 over 60% of the state debt was in loans held by the population (see Table 24(ii)). To achieve the required expansion of revenue from this source, the population had to be persuaded to invest more than any practicable interest rate would have encouraged them to do. The large loans of 1927–9 were therefore launched in an atmosphere akin to that of British war-time 'savings campaigns',[5] under the slogan of finding resources for industrialisation.[6] Interest was paid partly or wholly in the form of lottery prizes (which proved more attractive than a straight interest rate), but at a rate of only 6–8%. From 1928 onwards the general propaganda campaign was supplemented by trade union pressure on the workers and staff of state factories to subscribe 80–100% of a month's wages annually. From 1929 permanent elected 'commissions to assist state loans and savings' were

---

[1] SZ 100/1925 (23. ii. 25); *Fin. ents.* col. 410.
[2] For details of peasant loans, see SZ 505/1925 (2. x. 25); 182/1927 (11. iii. 27). For lottery loans, see SZ 449/1926 (3. ix. 26); 71/1927 (4. ii. 27).
[3] Long-term, that is, by Soviet standards.
[4] The average repayment period rose from 3 years 4 months in 1922–5 to 8 years 4 months in 1926–9 (D'yachenko and Kozlov, p. 142).
[5] See resolution of Fifteenth Party Conference (26 October–3 November 1926) in *Finansy SSSR...*, pp. 300–1.
[6] Industrialisation loan of 200 million roubles (25 million roubles of this were earmarked for Dnieprstroy) (SZ 508/1927 (24. viii. 27)); second industrialisation loan of 500 million roubles (SZ 406/1928 (18. vii. 28)) and subsidiary 50-million-rouble issue (SZ 5/1929 (19. xii. 28)); third industrialisation loan of 750 million roubles (SZ 442/1929 (24. vii. 29)).

set up at republican and factory level to assist the campaign,[1] and subscriptions were deducted from wages at source in instalments.[2] Loan campaigns among the peasantry were much less successful. The much smaller peasant loans[3] were only over-subscribed through the use of administrative and physical pressure,[4] condemned by the government,[5] and it proved difficult to persuade the peasantry not to sell back their loan obligations soon after they had purchased them.[6]

Deposits in savings banks also rose. They bore a tax-free interest of 6–9%, and special loans were held by the savings banks from the government to the amount of the stable balance of the deposits.[7] As a result of the reorganisation of the savings banks,[8] deposits rose considerably, but remained at only a fraction of the pre-war level in both town and country.[9] The work of savings banks took a secondary place to the main loan campaigns.[10]

12. BUDGET EXPENDITURE

Once the 'pool' of budgetary revenue had thus been accumulated, to what extent was it able to be used for its main purpose of financing the economy? Was part of the increased accumulation diverted to

[1] SZ 297/1929 (15. v. 29); 360/1929 (14. vi. 29).
[2] See SZ 633/1929 (16. x. 29); Haensel, *The Economic policy of Soviet Russia* (1930), pp. 182 ff.
[3] 100-million-rouble loan to strengthen peasant economy (SZ 24/1928 (30. xii. 27)), later extended by 50 million roubles (SZ 118/1928 (29. ii. 28)). Peasant loans amounted to only 47 million roubles out of a total state debt to the population of 225 millions on 1 October 1925; on 1 October 1928 they amounted to 139 out of 639 million roubles (*TsIK* 3/IV, pp. 32–3, 45, and 4/IV, pp. 2, 8).
[4] See *Ot s"ezda k s"ezdu*... (1929), p. 69; *TsIK* 3/IV, p. 35 (report by Bryukhanov). Less than a quarter of the section of the third industrialisation loan earmarked for the peasantry was taken up (SZ 540/1929 (13. ix. 29)).
[5] Stalin, *Soch.* vol. XI, p. 19.
[6] SZ 391/1929 (5. vii. 29).
[7] 12% 200-million-rouble loan (SZ 318/1927 (1. vi. 27)); 11% 300-million-rouble loan (SZ 540/1928 (9. ix. 28)).
[8] For details, see SZ 612/1925 (27. xi. 25); 220/1927 (11. iv. 27); 100/1929 (20. ii. 29); *Finansy SSSR*..., p. 300.
[9] The savings position as compared with pre-war was as follows (*TsIK* 3/III, p. 562; *Finansy SSSR*..., p. 301):

	Number of savings banks	Number of depositors (thousands)	Amount of deposits (million roubles)
1. i. 1916	app. 7,000	app. 9,500	app. 2,250
1. x. 1925	7,362	817	33
1. x. 1927	15,620	3,826	333

Of course the purchasing power of the rouble was considerably less in 1929 than it had been in 1916.

[10] An attempt to introduce 'savings certificates' was unsuccessful (SZ 472/1927 (6. viii. 27); *Finansy SSSR*..., pp. 302–3).

other state needs than industrialisation? Or did it, on the contrary, prove possible to limit and reduce expenditure on the 'normal' needs of the budget and thus provide an auxiliary source for the financing of industry?

Table 25. *Expenditure of overall budget, 1924/5–1928/9*
(*million roubles*)

	1924/5 Amount	%	1928/9 Amount	%
National economy [1]	916·4	29·9	3,686·8	42·0
Social and cultural [2]	948·2	30·9	2,773·0	31·6
Administration and defence	936·8	30·6	1,621·2	18·5
Expenditure on loans	69·6	2·3	317·5	3·6
Other expenditure	194·1	6·3	385·1 [3]	4·4
Total	3,065·1	100·0	8,783·6	100·0

Sources: *Finansy SSSR za XXX let* (1947), pp. 150, 160 (for calculations in text, use is also made of data in *Sots. str. 1935*, pp. 644 ff.).

Notes:
(1) Includes transport and posts by classification of 1933 onwards—i.e. only a part of net profit on operating costs is transferred to budget, and only part of expenditure on expansion is met from budget.
(2) Includes expenditure of social insurance budget.
(3) Given incorrectly in original as 355·1, which would make a total expenditure of 8,753·6.

A first examination of budgetary expenditure during this period (see Table 25) seems to show a budget still dominated by traditional expenditures. In the overall budget,[1] net of the gross revenue and expenditure of transport and the postal services (which still at this time passed through the budget), defence, administration, and the social services still accounted for some three-fifths of total expenditure in 1928/9.

A closer examination reveals the increasingly intimate connexion between the budget and the expansion of the economy. Between 1924/5 and 1928/9 the national income, measured in current prices, approximately doubled.[2] Had the budget grown at a comparable rate, it would have risen from some three milliard roubles in 1924/5 to some six milliard roubles in 1928/9. In fact it rose to over 8½ milliard roubles. The allocation of the 2½ milliard roubles 'excess

[1] On this term, see p. 84.
[2] It is not possible to enter here into a discussion of the validity of Soviet national income calculations. These figures are being used here merely as an indication of the order of magnitude of the growth of the economy in terms of current prices. For some discussion of Soviet national income data for this period, see Birmingham *Memorandum* no. 3 (1931); and Oleg Hoeffding, *Soviet National Income and Product in 1928* (1954).

growth' provides the key to the changes which were taking place in the budget. The use made of this 2½ milliard roubles can be found by doubling each budget item of the 1924/5 budget (to obtain the figure which it would have reached if it had increased at the same rate as the national income), and subtracting the result obtained from the actual expenditure on the corresponding item in 1928/9. The allocation of the 2½ milliard roubles is then seen to be made up approximately as follows:

	(million roubles)	
National economy		+1,850
of which		
Industry	+725	
Electrification	+ 75	
Agriculture (State budget only)	+200	
Trade	+250	
Municipal economy and housing	+125	
Transport, posts and other	+475	
Social Services		+ 875
Administration and defence		− 250
Outpayments on loans		+ 175
Other		− 25
Net total (approx.)		+2,625

It can therefore be concluded:

(1) Expenditure on the national economy accounted for 70% of the expansion of the budget in relation to the national income in 1925–9. Of this increase, some 45% was the result of increased allocations to industry and electrification, and the remainder consisted of extra allocations to transport, trade and agriculture.

(2) The remaining extra increase resulted from the expansion of expenditure on the social and cultural services at a rate greater than the rate of expansion of the national income. This mainly affected social insurance[1] and education—the latter principally through the local budgets.[2]

(3) Defence expenditure expanded at approximately the same rate as the national income.

[1] Until 1938 social insurance, which covered a large part of health expenditure and almost all pensions and benefits, appeared in an entirely separate budget, but it is included in these calculations (420 million roubles in 1924/5 and 1,221 million roubles in 1928/9).

[2] A decision to slow down appreciably the rate of expansion of the education and health services and of social security benefits (all of which principally affected the urban worker) would have released considerable resources for investment in industry, and have enabled the inflationary issues of currency to be reduced. But it is doubtful whether it would have been feasible to carry out the initial stages of industrialisation without incurring this additional burden in social costs. In any case, this would have been an academic question in the political climate of the time.

(4) Administrative expenditure expanded at a rate considerably below the rate of expansion of the national income.

The allocations to the economy and, to a lesser extent, to social and cultural services, were therefore able to rise not only as a result of the diversion of resources from the economy itself and from the population direct, but also as a result of the slower rise of allocations to defence and particularly to administration. If administrative and defence expenditure had risen at the same rate as the expansion of the national income, the amount allocated to the economy would inevitably have been less, and the pace of industrialisation would have been slower.

The level of defence expenditure was, of course, determined by the estimate made by the government of the international situation. It was held that in the long term the Soviet Union was likely to be attacked by a capitalist power or group of powers. But if the defence allocation could be kept reasonably small, industrialisation could proceed at a more rapid pace and provide a sounder basis for Soviet defence potential. The increase which took place, which roughly kept pace with the growth of the national income, was a compromise between long-term and short-term needs, and was reached only after controversy.[1] The defence allocation consisted of direct allocations to the People's Commissariat of the Army and Navy. In the words of the control figures for 1926/7, it included 'expenditure connected with the maintenance and functional activity of departments and administrations the personnel of which has been called up under the law on military service'.[2] Thus the pay, food, training expenses, equipment and ammunition of the armed forces are covered by this item. At one time[3] the Military Health Administration of the Armed Forces and the expenditure on convoy defence (transport protection within the country) were listed separately, but they were later incorporated in the main defence item.[4] The OGPU and its special armies were always listed as a separate item.[5] War industry presented

---

[1] Thus in 1924/5 military expenditure was increased during the course of the year, after the discussion at the third session of TsIK (*Svodnye materialy...za vtoroi kvartal... 1924/5 g.* (1925), p. 17; *Svodnye materialy...za tretii kvartal...1924/5 g.* (1925), pp. 97–8). In 1926/7 the defence allocation adopted was considered insufficient by Voroshilov, People's Commissar of the Army and Navy (see Bryukhanov in *TsIK* 3/III, p. 549).

[2] *Kontrol'nye tsifry...na 1926/7 g.*, p. 98.

[3] E.g. 1924/5, see *Vestnik finansov*, no. 6 (1925), pp. 170–3.

[4] See, for example, SZ 467/1927 (7. viii. 29).

[5] There was at one time some controversy over the scope of the defence item of the budget. One writer suggested that it should include both 'internal' and 'external'

a special problem. As late as 1925/6 an item 'war industry' appeared in the defence item of the budget.[1] Industrial production purchased by the armed forces remained part of the defence item after 1925/6, but new investment in the war industries, which were concentrated in trusts under VSNKh[2] has at least since 1926/7 appeared under the 'national economy' item of the budget.[3] At this stage, however, it amounted to only a small percentage of the total allocation to the economy.[4] Thus, although no breakdown of the defence expenditure in the Soviet budget is available,[5] it can be taken for this period as roughly coterminous with the normally accepted definitions of defence expenditure.

Administrative expenditure included all expenditure on central and local government, including state administrative bodies concerned with the economy, and (at this time) the administration of the social and cultural services. It did not, of course, include the overhead and managerial expenses of bodies with *khozraschot* rights, which formed part of their costs.

It was kept down as drastically as it was only as a result of an intensive annual campaign (a part of the larger campaign for a 'régime of economy') from 1926/7 onwards. The most drastic were the campaigns of 1926/7, to cut the total estimates of institutions on the state budget by 10%, and of 1927/8, to cut administrative allocations by 20%.[6] In 1928/9 the more modest aim was set that administrative expenditure should not exceed the 1927/8 level, all new needs to be met entirely from the saving resulting from further rationalisation.[7]

The main source of saving in administration was intended to be the reduction in personnel. The staff of general-Union commissariats (excluding NKPS and NKPT) was reduced from 33,000 in 1925/6 to 26,000 in 1926/7. However, this saving was partly cancelled out by the rise in wages of the remaining personnel, and the staffs of the

---

defence in the broadest sense, i.e. the courts and the NK of Foreign Affairs as well as the armed forces, but that on the other hand it should exclude the health and educational expenses of the armed forces (A. Nikitskii in *Vestnik finansov*, no. 7 (1926), pp. 68–72).

[1] *TsIK* 2/III, pp. 18 ff.   [2] SZ 76/1927 (15. xii. 26).
[3] See tables in *Otchot NKF SSSR ob ispolnenii edinogo gosudarstvennogo byudzheta SSSR za 1926/7 g.* (1928).
[4] In 1926/7, for example, to 36 million roubles (fulfilment) (the planned figure was 43·1) (*ibid.*).
[5] As early as 1926/7 it was examined in secret session by the Budget Commission of TsIK (*Plenum byudzhetnoi komissii...*, p. 566).
[6] SZ 396/1926 (28. vi. 26), 395/1926 (31. vii. 26), 542/1927 (30. viii. 27).
[7] SZ 257/1928 (15. v. 28).

republican commissariats were not reduced in this period.[1] At the same time, drastic cuts of 12–20% were made in the allocations for overheads such as posts and telegraphs, duty journeys, and general office expenses, to such an extent that some bodies claimed that it was almost impossible to function.[2] Finally, regulations were tightened up in order to confine administrative expenditure rigidly within the estimates. No transfer of expenditure from operational to administrative estimates was legally permitted, and no claims for supplementary allocations to administrative bodies were considered after the budget had been adopted. If any borrowings were made from operational estimates for administrative purposes, allocations were reduced by an equal sum.[3]

The targets set were not reached, and waste and bureaucracy continued to be characteristic features of Soviet administration. But the campaigns succeeded in keeping administrative expenditure down at a time when the administrative functions of the state, particularly in local affairs, were expanding rapidly. In 1927/8 an actual saving of 90 million roubles was effected.[4] This policy was thus an important contributory factor in the expansion of the national economy item of the budget.

The financial authorities had to be concerned not only with obtaining the resources needed to expand the national economy item of the budget, but also with finding means of ensuring that these resources were used to best effect to finance the expansion laid down in the plans.

In this respect 1925–9 was an experimental period. As physical and financial plans were not properly co-ordinated, tight control over budget expenditure on the economy was difficult to achieve. In 1928/9 the allocations to the economy were adopted only in the form of lump-sum grants to each branch when the budget was approved. These lump sums were broken down in detail only at a later stage, and control by the NKF was accordingly limited.[5] Financial control was made even more difficult by the complexity of the sources from which most new investment was financed.

[1] The reduction in staffs in the Russian Republic was offset by an increase in Central Asia, and the total remained unaltered at 375,000 (*Plenum byudzhetnoi komissii...*, pp. 49–50).
[2] Bryukhanov in *TsIK* 3/III, pp. 545–7, and 3/IV, pp. 23–4; *Plenum byudzhetnoi komissii...*, pp. 139–40.
[3] SZ 133/1928 (29. ii. 28), 511/1928 (11. ix. 28), 19/1929 (19. xii. 28).
[4] *Ot s"ezda k s"ezdu...* (1929), p. 63.   [5] SZ 218/1928 (30. iv. 28).

In industry, the first steps towards the solution of the problem were taken with the reforms of the banking system in 1927/8. These made the State Bank responsible for most short-term credit, while the Prombank and the Electrobank were reorganised into a single Bank of Long-term Credit for Industry and Trade. This bank worked in conformity with an annual credit plan based on the production and financial plan (*promfinplan*) of industry. All budget grants, special allocations from profits, and other resources were placed with the bank and administered by it in accordance with the plan. Part of these resources was issued as non-returnable grants, and part as long-term repayable loans, bearing a quasi-interest rate (it did not correspond to the market rate) and intended to be recouped from the future profits of the investment. Thus loans for new electric stations bore an interest rate of 6%, and repayment was to begin within one year of the opening of the station.[1] The question of whether allocations for new investments should be repayable or not was not yet resolved in principle (see chapter VI). The bank was expected to exercise a controlling function over the funds it administered, and to see that grants were spent efficiently and in accordance with the plan. The problem of the financial control of investment is discussed in greater detail in chapter VII.

The financing of agriculture was even more complex. As is shown in Table 26 (i), only a relatively small proportion of state expenditure on agriculture came from the budget itself. Part of these budgetary grants was issued in the form of non-returnable grants, for such purposes as large-scale irrigation schemes, the maintenance of the agricultural commissariats, the all-Union Resettlement Committee, and expanding the basic capital of the agricultural banks. The remainder of the budgetary allocation was put with credit and other resources in a number of special funds (e.g. for struggle with drought, for loans to the village poor, for long-term loans, for loans to state farms, for village electrification).[2] These funds were held by the Agricultural Bank, and loans were made from them which bore interest rates varying in accordance with the social importance of the purpose for which they were made, and with the type of borrower (see Table 26 (ii)). This afforded an additional means of discriminating against the richer peasantry and assisting the poorer peasantry.

[1] SZ 34/1927 (22. xii. 26).
[2] SZ 314/1925 (3. vii. 25), 171/1926 (17. iii. 26), 161–2/1927 (16. iii. 27); 240/1928 (25. iv. 28), 323/1929 (5. vi. 29); 455/1929 (25. vi. 29).

Table 26. *The financing of agriculture, 1927/8*

(i) Sources of financing of agriculture (million roubles)

	1927/8 (plan)
From 'Financing of national economy' item of state budget	131·2
From republican budget allocations to NK's of agriculture	78·3
From local budgets	84·0
Total from budgets	293·5
From agricultural credit system	274·0
Other sources (state enterprises, other credits, etc.)	149·9
Total from non-budgetary sources	423·9
TOTAL	717·4

Source: SZ 126/1928 (2. iii. 28).

(ii) Interest on agricultural loans (in %)

	Short-term loans	Long-term loans
General loans from Agricultural Bank	10 (a)	6 (a)
Loans from fund to credit village poor	—	6 (b)
Loans from budget to basic capital of agricultural co-ops	—	3 (c)
Loans for electrification	—	4 (d)
Loans for purchase of agricultural machinery:		
(i) to collective farms	7 (e)	4 (e)
(ii) to poor and middle peasantry	8 (e)	5 (e)
(iii) to richer peasantry	12 (e) (f)	7 (e) (f)

Notes and Sources:
(a) Reduced in November 1925 for 12 and 7% respectively (SZ 588/1925 (4. xi. 25)).
(b) Maximum. Loans given for 3–6-year periods (SZ 171/1926 (17. iii. 26)).
(c) 10-year period (SZ 594/1927 (30. viii. 27)).
(d) 25-year period (SZ 455/1929 (25. vi. 29)).
(e) SZ 206/1928 (20. iv. 28).
(f) Given only 'in exceptional circumstances'.

New investments in transport and posts were financed mainly from their own profits, but partly in addition from budget allocations.[1] It will be recalled that the gross revenue of this branch of the economy passed through the budget, although transport authorities had considerable powers to spend their receipts. In this period planning of the expansion of transport increased: new investments and research

---

[1] The net gain (+) or loss (−) of the budget on these services, taking into account both investments and operating costs, was as follows (million roubles):

	1924/5	1925/6	1926/7	1927/8	1928/9
Transport	+10·6	−8·2	−166·1	−208·5	−139·8
Posts and Telegraphs	+3·5	+4·9	−2·8	−5·3	+8·7

(Sources as for Tables 14 and 15.)

were placed under the economy item of the budget and administered by the same methods as those used for financing industry.[1]

By 1928/9 the budget had become a major source for financing the expansion of the economy. But a number of problems were still unresolved. How was the budget to be co-ordinated with other financial plans, and with the national economic plan? Was a state budget separate from the overall financial plan needed in a planned economy? If so, how far was the budget to be responsible for financing new investment, and how far was it to be financed from the increased profits of industry, or from inflation? How far should the resources for the budget be raised by taxation, and how far from the savings of the population? Should new investment be financed from the budget with non-returnable or with repayable grants? How should control over the new types of budgetary expenditure be established?

To these questions, which were the main subject for discussion in Soviet financial literature of 1928–30, we shall turn in the succeeding chapters.

[1] SZ 188/1929 (7. iii. 29).

PART III

THE PLANNED ECONOMY
1930–41

CHAPTER VI

FINANCIAL PLANNING AND THE BUDGET

1. ECONOMIC PLANNING IN THE U.S.S.R.

DURING the first five-year plan, the bulk of marketed agricultural production was incorporated into the socially owned sector as a result of mass collectivisation, and the remnants of private trade and industry in the towns were almost entirely absorbed by the state and co-operative sectors. This was a major turning-point in the development of the Soviet economic and financial system. While the economy was not a 'pure' socialist (in the sense of publicly-owned) economy, the proportion of state ownership and control was great. Industry, which was rapidly becoming the main part of the national product, was almost entirely state-owned, and could therefore be directly planned by the state, even if political considerations limited the extent to which the allocation of labour could be directly planned. Although agriculture, apart from the relatively small state farm sector, was not directly in state hands, the extent of state control over it was large: agricultural machinery, essential to farm work in the new conditions, was very largely state-owned, and a large part of agricultural production had to be delivered to the state in return for the use of this machinery or sold to the state at fixed low prices. The distribution of the national product could therefore also be in large part directly planned by the state. Distribution of equipment, raw materials, and labour was in state hands, but the powers of the state were in fact more limited in the case of labour and agricultural raw materials than in the case of industrial output. Retail distribution was also largely carried out either by state trading agencies or by retail co-operatives which were firmly harnessed within the shafts of the plan (for several years, until the introduction of the free market, known as 'collective farm market', all private trade was in fact illegal). The market economy, in the sense in which it had still existed in 1925–9, was abolished. Planned economy had replaced it.

In such an economy the processes by which resources are allocated must evidently be different in kind from those of competitive economies. If there are to be prices, they cannot be market-determined, and must be fixed by the government or the planning authority:[1] hence neither the level of investment nor its allocation between different uses can be determined through a self-adjusting price mechanism. If the central authority takes decisions on the amount of investment and its allocation, then *ipso facto* it also takes decisions on the volume and composition not only of heavy industrial production but also of the production of consumer goods. The wishes of consumers and the suggestions of producers may be and probably will be taken into account, but the central authorities must take the major decisions, whether they are the dictators overruling the popular will which they are conceived to be by many Western writers, or a body acting on behalf of society and 'subordinating socialist production to its fundamental purpose of securing the maximum satisfaction of the constantly growing material and cultural needs of society' as they were depicted by Stalin.[2]

In taking the main economic decisions, the government and the planners acting on its behalf will be confronted by a number of problems. Their decisions will involve, consciously or unconsciously, balancing the future needs of the consumer against his present needs, and against present and future defence needs. They will have to decide how far the individual wishes of consumers in regard to their future pattern of consumption (in so far as these can be ascertained) should be respected, and how far it is socially necessary that they should be overridden. They will have to find a way to calculate which methods of production are less 'costly' in the absence of a set of market prices. They will have to find criteria which will enable them to choose between one investment project and another. In

[1] I leave aside here the models constructed by western economists in the inter-war period in which (as in the case of Professor H. D. Dickinson's model) an artificial market and pricing system was set up by making state bodies into competing public corporations, or (as in the case of Lange's model) prices but not output were fixed by the state. As these models involve the indirect determination of all output and investment allocation decisions (except the decision on the total size of investment), they cannot be used to describe the Soviet planning system of the 1930's, which was largely a system of direct allocation and central determination of output decisions—though, as we shall see, a model which depicted the economy as one in which all *effective* economic decisions were made by central planners would also be inappropriate for the analysis of Soviet economy.

[2] *Ekonomicheskie problemy sotsializma v SSSR*, p. 78.

order to solve these problems, they may have to adopt common units to measure current costs (labour days, or an accounting unit), and some means of assessing the return to capital in different uses (which may resemble an interest rate on capital). Even so, economic decisions will be made by a different mechanism from those in a competitive economy. They will be made not by private businesses in the light of profit expectations, but in a centralised co-ordinated plan which may overrule immediate 'profitability' (however that is calculated) in the interests of what is conceived to be the long-term profit of society.[1]

I am not attempting here to argue that such a system is or could be as efficient as or more efficient than one in which market prices are the mechanism through which allocation decisions are made, or to investigate the methods by which such problems are overcome and planning decisions made in the Soviet Union: these matters need a special study. I am taking the plan as given, and seeking to show what kind of a financial and budgetary system, if any, is necessary in such a planned economy in order that the plan should be fulfilled.

2. MONEY AND DIRECT PLANNING

By the end of the first five-year plan, the plan was laying down in physical terms not only the amount of future production for each economic unit, but also the raw material, equipment and labour it was to receive in order to fulfil the plan. Retail distribution took place mainly through the sale of rationed goods at low, almost nominal, prices. Money seemed to be essential only in order to deal with the not yet fully planned agricultural sector. Was money in fact a vestige of N.E.P. which would die away when the N.E.P. economy was fully extinguished? Was a moneyless economy now an immediately practicable aim, so that the controversies of the war communism period (see chapter III) were again relevant? Views belittling the importance of money were canvassed by a group of Soviet economists in 1930–2 in the light of the triumph of direct planning in the first five-year plan,[2] but were sharply criticised by the Communist Party Central Committee and by Stalin at the Seventeenth Party Congress in 1934.[3]

[1] The development of heavy industry much more rapidly than light industry in the U.S.S.R. between 1929 and 1941 is the most striking example of this.
[2] For details, see Arnold, *op. cit.* pp. 444 ff.
[3] 'We shall use money for a long time to come,' said Stalin, 'right up to the time when the first stage of Communism, i.e., the Socialist stage of development, has been completed.... Money is the instrument of bourgeois economy which the Soviet government

Money forms an essential part of the Soviet economic system for several reasons. First, money is required in order to maintain differing levels of income within the population, and to give the consumer freedom of choice within the framework of the available supply. The citizen is paid a wage *qua* producer, depending on the amount and ability of his work as assessed by a planned wage scale. He can then spend this wage on the purchase of such retail goods as he wants at the state fixed prices. With a given supply of goods, the state has to fix prices at such a level that the part of purchasing power spendable on goods[1] is equal to the total supply of goods at fixed prices, and so that demand is equated to supply for any particular good. This can be achieved by varying the retail price by means of a tax. If the tax mark-up is greater than the average rate of tax when supply and demand for a good are in equilibrium, the excess of tax above average represents an 'artificial' increase in price in order to maintain equilibrium. The proviso must, however, be made at this point that in practice an equilibrium between supply and demand on the retail market has rarely been achieved by the Soviet government. Demand has usually run ahead of supply at fixed prices, and there has always been a large range of goods for which demand is heavily in excess of supply (e.g. houses, books, metal consumer goods).

The second reason for retaining money in the Soviet economy is that it facilitates economic relations between the state and the collective farm system. Part of agricultural production is supplied by the collective farm and the collective farmer to the state at fixed low prices (i.e. as a form of tax), and here the money relation between the state and the farmer is completely secondary to the administrative relationship. But part of production, both on collective farm land and on the collective farmer's personal plot, remains at the free disposal of the producers, either for their own use or for sale on the free market, or to state trading organisations. The prices obtained by free market sales, which are an important part of the money income of the rural population, are determined by several factors:

(*a*) The level of state retail prices as a whole influences the amount of purchasing power which the townsfolk have available for the free market.

has taken over and adapted to the interests of Socialism for the purpose of expanding Soviet trade to the utmost, and of thus creating the conditions necessary for the direct exchange of products' (*Leninism*, pp. 512–13).

[1] Money spent on the free market is here excluded from consideration, and will be taken into account later.

(*b*) If the level of state food prices is such that supply equals demand at the state price, the collective farmer will not be able to sell his products at above that price.

(*c*) At a given level of state retail prices, the prices on the free market are determined by the quantity of production which is brought to market (this in turn is influenced by the ratio of free food prices to other prices, as the farmer may prefer to consume the products himself rather than bring them to market if the price is too low).

Thus the overall town-country price structure is partly directly planned and partly indirectly planned, or 'regulated'. This complex system determines the total purchasing power of the collective farm population, which then enters into the retail market mechanism already described, as part of total purchasing power.[1] This relationship between town and country would, of course, be impossible without a money mechanism.

Thirdly, wages are not only a means of distributing the production of consumer goods. From the point of view of the state as a producer, they constitute the 'costs' to the state of employing a particular grade of worker on producing a particular good, these 'costs' being a money representation of the packet of consumer goods which the state has to supply to the worker to meet his wage. At the same time the raw materials, transport, fuel, etc., used in producing and delivering the good are broadly speaking purchased at a price corresponding to their wage-costs (or to a wage cost farther back along the production line).[2] Thus a wage-costs price, taking the existing allocation of capital between enterprises as given, can be fixed for any good.[3] The wage system therefore provides a framework for current costing within industry, and a measure of efficiency in

[1] Of course not all the money paid for sales to the state and on the market reaches the collective farm population, as part is used for investment by the collective farm (part of this itself takes place by means of purchases on the retail market), part goes to the state as payment for work done by MTS (in the case of certain types of output only; as a rule payment is in kind), and for insurance, etc.

[2] The price paid for agricultural raw materials is, as has been shown, partly market-determined.

[3] I assume throughout the discussion in this chapter that every factory in both the capital goods and the consumer goods industries is organised on a *khozraschot* or profit-and-loss basis, as was of course the case in the U.S.S.R. In the civil war period, as we have seen, all industry had been financed from the budget (inasmuch as finance had any real existence), and it is perhaps wrong to assume without discussion that such an arrangement was unsuitable for Soviet economy in the planning period. But the advantages of *khozraschot* from the point of view of decentralisation and efficiency were so apparent in the late 1920's that there was no attempt to put industry 'on the budget', even in the case of those factories whose production consisted entirely or mainly of armaments paid for from the budget.

terms of a common financial unit. By penalising and rewarding enterprises for non-fulfilment and over-fulfilment of their costs plan, it is possible to maintain what has become known as 'control by the rouble'.[1]

3. ACCUMULATION AND INVESTMENT

In an economy of the Soviet type, a money system is therefore required to operate the wages system and the concomitant system of retail distribution, for dealings with the non-state sector, and for current costing. Could not money have a greater significance than this in a planned economy, and in some sense act as a determinant of future economic activities?

For example, should the level of accumulation in the economy be made dependent, not on a tax the level of which is fixed by the state, but on the money savings which wage-earners and agricultural producers are prepared to make out of current earnings? Merely to put the question in this form shows its absurdity. The money incomes of the community are by and large directly fixed from the centre and can be made to correspond to the available supplies of consumer goods, which are also sold at centrally fixed prices. In an economy from which the individual entrepreneur is absent, the savings which the population are likely to be prepared to make will necessarily be relatively small. Thus in the U.S.S.R. an impossibly high interest rate would have been required in the late 1920's to raise savings even to the level of accumulation in the Russia of 1913. There is no reason to suppose that, in an economy in which state ownership predominates, the level of personal savings will correspond to the investment level desired by the state, even if this desire is shared by public opinion. Considering the matter from another angle, in a planned economy new investment is ultimately a question of transferring labour and material resources to the planned object: if these resources and labour are available, and if the planners (using their new criteria as assumed earlier) consider the object desirable, there could be no point in making the achievement of the plan dependent on personal savings.

---

[1] This costing system appears to suffer from certain fundamental limitations. Since capital as a factor of production plays as a rule only a negligible role in the sum of current costs (appearing as a small depreciation allowance), special allowance has to be made in planning the costs of a factory for its over- or under-equipment as compared with other factories. This weakness is increasingly recognised by Soviet economists (see, for example, Ya. Kronrod, *Osnovy khozyaistvennogo rascheta* (1952), pp. 88–92). On this point see also Dobb, *op. cit.* p. 353, nn. 1 and 3.

However, a number of Soviet economists, in the last years of the 1920's, thought differently.

The financial plan of Gosplan's five-year plan must be replaced by a directly opposite plan [wrote Professor Katsenelenbaum in 1928]. Instead of receiving resources by means of the budget and intra-industrial accumulation, we must switch over to credit (loans) and attract the national accumulation needed for industrialisation with the help of credit operations.... Savings in our conditions are the obverse side of industrialisation.

He added that in prevailing circumstances an interest rate on loans of 12 to 14% was too low.[1] Surplus purchasing power, it was thought, should be mopped up by loans, which should supply the necessary funds for industrialisation, and prices should be steadily reduced by cutting taxes. Essentially this extreme argument formed part of the right-wing trend which presented inflation as the main danger to the Russian economy. In the existing situation inflation was, however, inevitable if the funds for industrialisation required by the plan were to be obtained, and the rate of industrialisation would have to be reduced to avoid inflation. Behind this argument lay the belief that the government had fixed a suicidal rate of industrialisation. This viewpoint was an arguable one. Under a planned economy of the Soviet type the rate of accumulation is fixed by the government, and it is quite conceivable that it will fix an inappropriate or unachievable rate. But the attempt to gear the level of accumulation to the level of personal savings was not compatible with a system of direct planning.[2]

Interwoven with this discussion was a further problem of principle in relation to the money system. While it was agreed that the allocation of resources should be determined by the state, it was suggested that new capital as a factor of production should play a more prominent part in current costing than it would through a simple depreciation allowance. In fact, it was argued, branches of industry which were constructing new enterprises with the help of state grants should be required to repay the cost of this new investment over a series of years out of their future earnings. They should not be given non-returnable grants but long-term repayable loans on which

---

[1] Z. S. Katsenelenbaum, *Industrializatsia khozyaistva i zadachi kredita v SSSR* (1928), pp. 81–4, 87.
[2] See for further references D. P. Bogolepov's article in *Ekon. oboz.* no. 2 (1929), pp. 40–56; and *Plenum byudzhetnoi komissii*, p. 161.

interest was charged.[1] The discussion on this question was very confused. Generally the people who advocated the expansion of industry through credits were the same as those who advocated raising resources through loans. But of course the two policies are not necessarily connected. Revenue raised through loans can be issued as grants; revenue raised through taxes can be issued as loans. In the first case the state is taking on a future monetary burden (interest and repayment on the loans) in order to raise money in the present; in the second case it is securing for itself a future revenue from interest and repayment in return for present expenditure. But this is not a 'real' future revenue. In a future year, a certain level of investment is fixed involving a gap $y-x$ between cost price (say, x) and retail price (y). But cost price is put up by interest and repayments to the state on earlier investment by, say, z. Cost price will now be $x+z$. But the state will still need only $y-x$ to cover its new investment programme. From interest and repayments on previously issued capital it derives z, from gap between new cost price and retail price it will derive $y-(x+z)$ without altering the retail price. The total revenue will therefore be $y-(x+z)+z=y-x$ as before.

In a directly planned economy the method of financing investment is thus a technical question, as far as the raising of revenue is concerned (though it does, of course, have an important effect on the problem of costing mentioned above). An increase in current investment merely means a current shift in labour and materials from production of consumption goods to production of producer goods. Whether a grant should be returnable or not is therefore really a question of which is the more efficient form of financing. Would control over investment be better secured if in the future the price of goods produced by this investment were put sufficiently high to include repayments from industry on the original cost of the investment as well as an allowance for amortisation?

In terms of investment control this question was not discussed very widely by Soviet economists. It is clear that at a time when investment goods were to make up such a large proportion of production, a system in which capital grants were returnable to the state would have led to a very considerable interest burden gradually being

---

[1] This proposal should not be confused with the suggestion of some western economists that an interest rate should be artificially formed in a socialist society by public corporations bidding for new capital. There was no suggestion that the *allocation* of capital should be determined by present ability to pay.

placed on a small initial heavy industry base. Future prices of industrial goods would rise substantially, and if repayments were automatically included in cost price, they would in fact have little control value. Non-repayable grants would be the more convenient form in which to issue new investment, *if* some other means of controlling the efficiency and suitability of investment could be found. In practice, grants had gradually assumed greater importance in the Soviet investment programme as bank loans for investment declined in importance from 1926/7 onwards, and from 1930 all allocations to investment in state industry were made as non-repayable grants.[1] The problem of investment control will be discussed in later chapters.

To sum up the preceding discussion, the main principles on which Soviet financial planning is based are:

(1) Planning is in physical terms, and direct allocation of resources is primary. Prices are not 'determining' but 'determined'.

(2) A money economy is, however, needed for the payment of wages and for retail distribution, for relations with the non-state sector, and for costing of current production in the state sector (state industry has to pay its way by producing at planned costs).

(3) Accumulation is made out of current income. It must come from taxes, the internal profits of industry (and increases in them through reductions in costs), or from inflationary spending. It cannot come from personal savings to any appreciable extent.

(4) Investment is financed by the plan. It is made through non-repayable grants or from the internal resources of industry.

4. ACCUMULATION THROUGH PROFITS AND THE BUDGET

Given these conditions, there would seem to be two systems by which the raising and issue of money for investment (the key problems of financial planning) could be carried out.[2]

By the first method (call it method 1), the transfer prices of industrial goods would be fixed by the planning authorities so that profits could be earned in each branch of industry equal to the planned investment in that branch. Transfer prices would exceed cost prices by the extent to which investment was planned to take

[1] SZ 316/1930 (23. v. 30).
[2] Direct taxation is not treated as a principal method of financing investment in the following discussion; it is assumed that to use direct taxation would have strong disincentive effects owing to the money illusion (see p. 175 below).

place in the branch. The investment plan would then be financed entirely from these profits. In other words, the price system would be adjusted so that the 'non-repayable grants' discussed above would be made to the branch not directly in the form of a grant, but by permitting the branch to charge high transfer prices. (This method, in which investment is covered by *current* income, should not be confused with the proposals for capital loans discussed above. These would have been repaid by price adjustments in the future affecting future flows of income.)

With this method the budget would not play a prominent part in the financing of the economy, and taxation would finance only defence, administration, health, education, and other activities common to the budgets of both planned and competitive economies. Of course, in a period of economic expansion these traditional budget functions include heavy social costs (on education and health, for example) essential to the achievement of the programme of expansion, and these would have to be borne by the budget even if all industrial investment were paid for by industry itself out of its profits. The problem of accumulating resources to meet the expansion of budgetary expenditure would therefore still remain, although it would be less acute.

A special case of this system of accumulation is the use of 'intra-industrial accumulation' to finance investment. If costs are reduced, but transfer prices are left unaltered, the extra profits so earned can be used for investment. If the gap between the new level of costs and the old transfer price is too great, the transfer price can be reduced accordingly, ultimately leading to a reduction in retail prices, or the surplus profits can be transferred to other branches via a tax. If the gap is too small, the transfer price must be raised if sufficient resources are to be available for investment without resort to the budget.

With the second method (call it method 2), the transfer price of each good would equal its costs (or costs plus a very small margin for incentive purposes). No funds for investment would therefore be accumulated by industry itself. All purchases and sales inside industry would be made at cost price (in the wage-cost sense already defined). But when goods were transferred to the wholesale stage, a tax would be imposed on them, as part of the price at which they passed to the next consumer, and this price would supply the funds required for expansion of the economy, as well as for normal state needs. Planned investment would be financed from these funds through the budget. Thus in addition to 'normal' functions, the budget would include a major item 'capital investment', equal to the capital investment programme.

This method could also be used to absorb intra-industrial accumulation. Periodically, transfer prices would be reduced to absorb the new reduction in costs. All industrial investment would therefore still be made through the budget.

It should be noted that both these methods come within the framework of the type of planned economy already described. In both cases, all investment would be financed, either at the wholesale or at the retail stage, from the prices fixed for goods, and all investment would be carried out in accordance with a centrally fixed plan. Which method should be given more weight depends largely on the type and level of investment to be carried out, and on the historical conditions and existing financial institutions. Method 2 is applicable for *any* level or type of investment, and carries with it the possibility of much stricter central control over investment. It carries, however, the disadvantage that there would be no financial links between a branch of industry and its investment programme. Method 1 would seem to be applicable as the main method only under certain conditions:

(*a*) The capital investment programme would need to be fairly evenly distributed between light and heavy industry, otherwise the prices of the products of heavy industry would have to be fixed at a very high level, and an unreal structure of current costs would accordingly appear in light industry and in engineering (the costs of materials would be very high). Also, in the special case mentioned above, if costs were reduced evenly throughout industry, and more investment were to take place in heavy industry than in light industry, some method would have to be found (e.g. a differentiated profits tax) to transfer the 'gains' from light industry to heavy industry.

(*b*) If a new level of investment were introduced, the price system would have to be capable of easy adjustment to a new set of prices.

(*c*) It would have to be reasonably certain that the costs plan would be fulfilled in each industry. Otherwise there would be a danger that key projects in the investment programme would not receive the necessary funds.

(*d*) Supply and demand for particular goods on the retail market would have to balance at the retail prices resulting from this price system if consumers were not to be subject to a rationing system (without a retail tax, no 'artificial' price could be imposed for goods in relatively short supply). This would presuppose that more attention was being paid to consumer goods industries than was the case in the Soviet Union in 1929–41.

In practice the Soviet government has therefore evolved a 'mixed' system of financial planning incorporating features from both of these methods. The financial plan of the first five-year plan, adopted in 1929, corresponded most closely to method 1. It was intended that the bulk of accumulation for investment should come from reduction of costs within industry, and that the role of the budget and retail taxes (Promtax, excises) should be secondary. While the investment programme was largely fulfilled, the costs reduction programme was considerably under-fulfilled. The actual fulfilment of the plan was therefore carried out (apart from inflationary methods) mainly through the budget, and by the use of the turnover tax introduced by the reform of 1930. It therefore approximated to method 2.

Throughout the 1930's, while the bulk of investment was financed through the budget, each branch of industry was permitted to retain part of its profits, from which part of capital investment in the branch was financed. From 1931 onwards, profits were retained by each branch up to the extent needed to cover its investment programme, and budget grants were given only when profits were insufficient. In certain branches, all new investment was thus financed from profits. But the bulk of investment was financed from the budget, as was inevitable with a continued high rate of investment in heavy industry. Resources for the budget were raised principally through the turnover tax (a general sales tax on goods) and a profits tax ('deductions from profits'), imposed only when all planned investment had been covered from profits (except for a nominal 10% deduction made for control purposes). Profits and turnover tax play the same fiscal role in principle: they both constitute a mark-up on cost price which is used for the financing of other branches.

Although the pre-war Soviet budgetary system combined both methods, it had a strong bias towards method 2. Normally only a relatively small part of investment was financed by any industry from its own profits. Moreover, the connexion between profits and investment was relatively tenuous: the investment banks usually in fact paid extra grants to projects which had high priority, when the industry concerned did not make the profits planned; and the banks often withheld planned grants from industries which had reached the planned level of profits, and switched them to a more important industry.

Moreover, method 2 as I have described it is broader in its scope than it was in Soviet practice, for it could involve the imposition of a tax on both producer goods and consumer goods. If this were the case, the tax could then be used to make adjustments of supply and demand within industry as well as on the retail market. However, a large part of the output of heavy industry is consumed and paid for by the state (capital equipment is paid for from the national economy item of the budget and armaments from the defence item). Tax imposed on this output would be a mere book-keeping transfer, as it would be met not from the incomes of the population but from the budget itself. The wages of the workers in the investment and defence industries would still have to be met by imposing a tax to the same amount on consumer goods (or on those producer goods which are used to produce consumer goods). In the Soviet economy of the 1930's a very large part of the total output of the producer goods industries was consumed by budget-financed investment and defence, and a very large amount of 'double-taxation' would therefore have been involved if producer goods had been taxed. For this and other reasons the tax of method 2 was therefore made almost exclusively a tax on consumer goods. This meant that products were sold within industry at cost-price (plus a small profit margin); price could not therefore be adjusted to balance supply and demand for producer goods when disproportions arose in output; and this made a tight centralised physical allocation of materials an inevitable part of the system.

So far I have been concerned with establishing the main pivots on which the Soviet financial system turned. These main features arose partly in response to the general problems which must face any direct planning system, and partly from the special problems which faced the Soviet system due to intensive industrialisation. These special problems led to a high degree of centralisation throughout the economy. In a direct planning system in a more advanced economy, or in an economy in which industrialisation was proceeding at a quieter pace, an allowance for capital obsolescence might have been included in current industrial costs, method 1 might become of much more than formal importance, and the tax of method 2 might be imposed on both producer and consumer goods. These possibilities will be discussed further in chapter XI. In the present chapter we shall be concerned with explaining some of the more important pre-war Soviet financial arrangements by developing the crude model of the financial system which we have so far constructed.

5. THE UNIFIED FINANCIAL PLAN AND THE BUDGET

In the Soviet system of accumulation there are, therefore, two main sources for the capital investment programme: the budget and the retained profits of enterprises. The budget from the point of view of financial planning is thus part of a wider national accumulation plan. The budgetary system does not include the accumulation plans (retained profits plans) of industry, and (before 1938) the social insurance system and the local budgets were excluded from the state budget. All of these were, however, included in the wider accumulation plan, the unified financial plan (*edinyi finansovyi plan*), which is the key document in Soviet financial planning. The question therefore arises whether the budget should occupy the important place it does in Soviet financial practice. Should it not be administratively subordinated to the unified financial plan?

In 1929–31 this was the prevalent view among Soviet economists. As early as 1928 it was argued that the budget should no longer act as a substitute for an overall financial plan, but should take its place alongside the credit plan and the financial plans of industry as part of a 'general financial plan'.[1] In 1928/9 the first attempt was made to co-ordinate the separate sources of accumulation in the annual control figures. This succeeded only partially,[2] and the Budget Commission of TsIK placed on record its view that a unified financial plan was needed.[3] In the autumn of 1928 work was begun on a unified financial plan for 1929/30. In the document which was produced,[4] it was admitted that the plan lacked reality. Although the budget data were said to be accurate, the social insurance figures were 'conditional', and those on the national income and the wages fund were 'very conditional and extremely imprecise'. Nevertheless the 'overall financial plan of socialised economy' which formed a part of this document should, it was held, be improved in future years, and become a government enactment analogous to the budget.

[1] M. I. Bogolepov in *Ek. oboz.* no. 2 (1928), pp. 54–60.
[2] *Kontrol'nye tsifry...* (1928/9), pp. 53–5, 325–41; *Kontrol'nye tsifry...* (1929/30), pp. 270–313.   [3] *TsIK* 4/IV, Bull. no. 3, p. 2.
[4] *Edinyi finansovyi plan na 1929/30 g.* (1930), esp. pp. 11–13, 17.

These recommendations were accepted in May 1930. Decrees of TsIK and SNK declared that 'the successes achieved by planned economy make it possible and necessary to raise the planning of finance to a higher level and to include the finances of the socialised sector in a unified financial plan', and gave instructions for the compilation of a plan which would include the state and local budgets, the overall financial plans of the banks, the social insurance and state insurance budgets, and the financial plans of industry, transport, agriculture, trade and co-operation, and housing and municipal economy. The warning was, however, given that this plan should not replace the 'separate operative financial plans' such as the state budget.[1] In January 1931 the victory of the system of direct planning was marked by renaming the annual control figures the 'national economic plan', and by the joint adoption of the budget and the unified financial plan at a session of TsIK.[2] A decree hailed the unified financial plan as 'a very great step forward in the strengthening and further improvement of the whole system of planned socialist economy', 'redistributing for socialist construction two-thirds of the whole national income'.[3] This step was widely greeted as a turning-point in financial planning,[4] and an attempt was made to elevate the unified financial plan into a general financial planning document which would replace the operative plans including the budget.[5]

The weakness of this step was that it confused the methods of the planner with the methods of the administrator. In the evolution of the planning system, a stage had been reached at which it was considered possible to compile a project of the overall accumulation and

[1] SZ 315/1930 (23. v. 1930); and 370/1930 (24. v. 1930).
[2] SZ 60–1/1931 (10. i. 1931).
[3] This statement seems to have a somewhat doubtful basis. The plan amounted to 32 milliard roubles in current prices, and the national income to 49 milliard roubles in 1926/7 index prices (*TsIK* 3/v, Bull. no. 3, p. 4). But in current prices the national income would have considerably exceeded this figure.
[4] Thus the People's Commissar of Finance declared: 'This is not a technical change of financial organisation—it is a reflection of the gigantic strengthening of the position of socialist economy and the socialised sector...bringing us near to constructing in the future a state budget of the whole national economy' (*TsIK* 3/v, Bull. no. 3, pp. 1–3). Another speaker said 'I think that in a couple of years, in any case in three years, our unified financial plan will include the whole national income, and then we shall achieve a socialist plan' (*ibid.* Bull. no. 8, pp. 1–2).
[5] One report asserted that the plan provided 'a stable basis for real daily operative supervision and checking of the course of fulfilment of the whole national economic plan' (*Finansy SSSR mezhdu V i VI s"ezdami sovetov Soyuza* (1931), pp. 3–4), and a speaker at TsIK proposed that the budget commission of TsIK should be replaced by a 'commission of the economic and financial plan' (*TsIK* 3/v, Bull. no. 10, pp. 26–7).

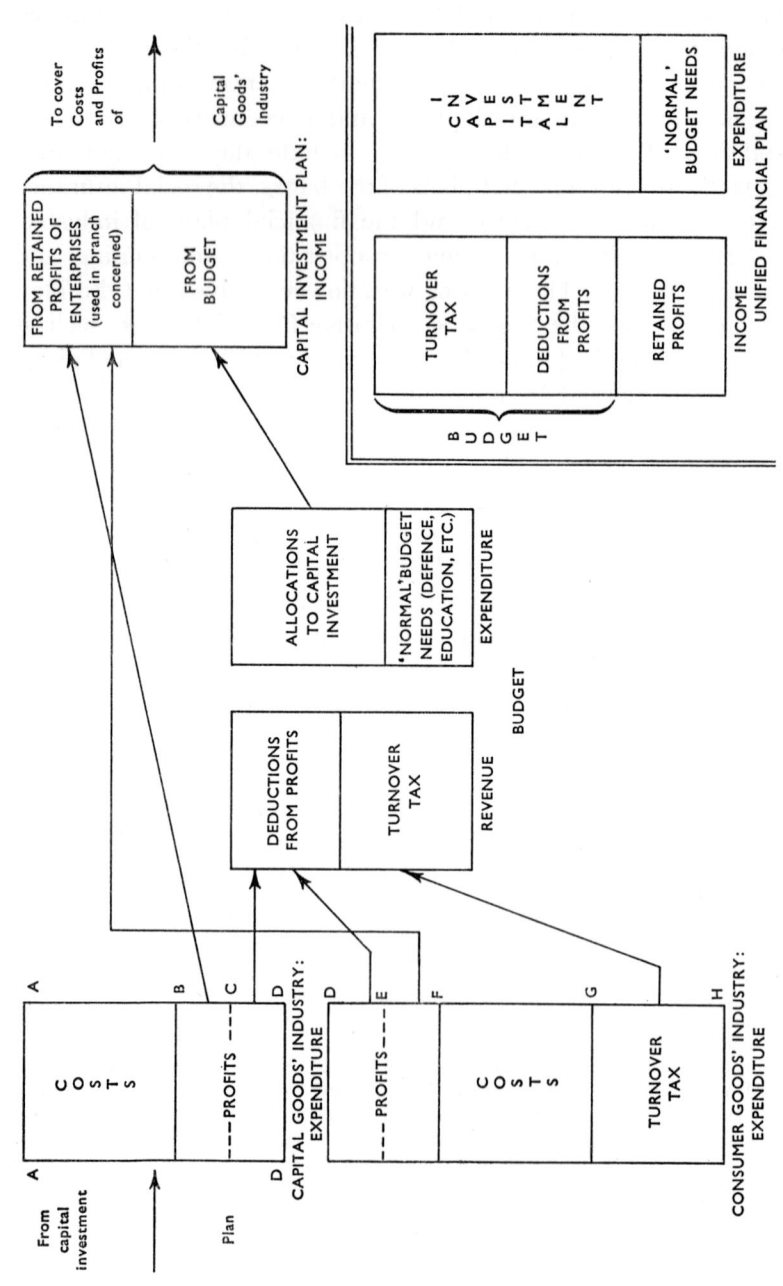

Fig. 1. The Soviet system of financial planning: a first approximation.

allocation of national finance. It was assumed that this project could be put into effect most easily if the separate financial plans were fused into a single operative (i.e. administrative) document. But in reality the separate parts of this single plan each needed its own method of control. Financial efficiency was possible only by maintaining budget control over taxation and expenditure, bank control over loans, and financial control over the profits of *khozraschot* enterprises (see chapters vii, viii and ix). The elevation of the unified financial plan to the status of an operative plan in 1931 was later held to have weakened auditing and control, already weakened by the errors made in the credit reform of 1930.[1] In addition, the unified financial plan of 1931 was not of high quality. The budget commission and TsIK itself did not receive a complete financial plan in 1931 as the basis for their discussions, and during the TsIK debate reference was made to the 'exceptionally difficult circumstances in which the financial plan was compiled...in these conditions the government must turn special attention to compiling quarterly operative plans'.[2] For these reasons the unified financial plan was from 1932 onwards again relegated to the position of a planning document, and the decree on the 1932 budget made no mention of it.[3] In subsequent years the state budget has been expanded to include the local budgets and the social insurance system, but bank-credit and currency-issue plans, and the financial plans of branches of the economy, are kept separate from it administratively.

Although the administrative subordination of the budget to the unified financial plan was brought to an end, it is clear that some means was needed of bringing together the separate sources for

[1] 'We need to delimit sharply the budget, and budget resources, from the working capital of economic organisations and from the credit resources of the State Bank', said Grin'ko (the People's Commissar of Finance) when making the 1932 budget speech, 'for in conditions of *khozraschot* each of these three forms of financial organisation has its own special field. The experience of 1931 has shown that the practice of carrying out the unified financial plan makes more difficult a sharp delimitation between budget resources, State Bank credits, and the own accounts of economic organs, and in particular prevents the introduction of the real responsibility of economic organs for the own and loan resources entrusted to them. That is why, while fully using the method of the unified financial plan for a general evaluation of the resources of the country, we are putting forward for your adoption only the state budget. By this we are ensuring greater flexibility in the use of the own resources of economic bodies, and greater responsibility for these resources, and on the other hand great flexibility in using the resources of the State Bank' (*TsIK* 3/vi, Bull. no. 10, p. 27). A few weeks later an economist wrote of the unified financial plan that it 'is only one of the methods of financial planning and does not possess any state sanctions' (I. Smilga in *Pl. khoz.* no. 3 (1932), p. 24).

[2] *TsIK* 3/v, pp. 1–2, and 820–1.

[3] SZ 301/1931 (28. xii. 1931).

financing capital investment and of allocating them to construction jobs in accordance with the plan. An instrument was to hand in the specialised long-term credit banks, which had been responsible for most long-term financing of the economy in the later 1920's. In 1932, after reorganisation, these banks were made fully responsible for collecting in the resources for capital investment from the budget, from profits and from other sources (e.g. part of the depreciation allowance), and for controlling the issue of these resources in accordance with the plan. Thus budgetary issues for capital investment were not subject to the forms of budgetary control used for expenditure on administration, defence, etc., but to a somewhat more flexible system of control used for all investment financing. This system is discussed in chapters VII–IX.

Figure 1 illustrates schematically the simplified version of the Soviet financial system so far discussed. It shows the main flows of money in the state sector of the economy:

(i) Income from profits of the consumer goods and capital goods industries is used to finance capital investments in those branches (BC, EF) (method 1).

(ii) Deductions from profits of the consumer goods and capital goods industries (DE, CD) and turnover tax on consumer goods (GH) pass to the budget where they are used partly for capital investment (method 2).

(iii) The capital investment plan is financed from both (i) and (ii) above, and supplies the money income of the capital goods industries by buying their products (AD).

(iv) These operations are summarised in the unified financial plan.

But this is only a first approximation to the Soviet system of financial planning. The system so far described is extensively modified in practice for reasons which we shall consider under four main heads:

(i) Financial methods of securing the satisfactory operation of state industry.

(ii) Complications arising from the existence of a non-state-owned sector of the economy.

(iii) Modifications to the revenue system.

(iv) Balancing the retail market.

6. REFINEMENTS OF THE SIMPLIFIED SYSTEM

Working capital   *(a) Industry*

Probably the most obvious deficiency of the system so far described is that it assumes that in a given planning period the costs and planned profits of industry will exactly equal its receipts from sales. In fact, in addition to its receipts from sales, in a given period industry also needs working capital for several reasons.

First, there must be a minimum stock of raw materials, fuel, finished goods, etc.[1] To enable stocks to be purchased, the enterprise must be provided with its own working capital (*sobstvennye oborotnye sredstva*). Unspent sums forming part of this capital are kept by the enterprise with the State Bank (or in the case of building firms with the appropriate specialised bank), and all accounts pass through the bank. As the work of an enterprise expands, and as new enterprises are founded, additional working capital has periodically to be made available. This comes principally out of profits. After the planned deductions from profits have been made to the budget, as much of the remaining profit as is required by the plan is allocated to the expansion of working capital in the subsequent period. Profit is not reckoned for this purpose simply on an enterprise basis; it is redistributed as required throughout the section of industry concerned (*glavk* or NK) in accordance with the needs of the plan. Any required increase in working capital which cannot be met by the profits of the NK or *glavk* is met by an allocation from the budget.

Secondly, in addition to these permanent requirements in working capital, in a number of cases expenditure by enterprises may not be met by receipts in the short run. In an industry producing a small number of costly products (heavy equipment, etc.), income will be received in large irregular amounts, and working capital in hand will therefore fluctuate considerably. In certain industries, large seasonal stocks will need to be accumulated (e.g. sugar manufacture). With all production, payment for sale will not coincide with the moment of sale. If the plan is over-fulfilled, extra working capital will be needed for stocks, wages, etc., which will not immediately be met by increased sales. If the central authorities change the plan during the course of the planning period, extra working capital will be needed to purchase stocks for the new type of production, to cover temporary

---

[1] Wages are paid fortnightly in arrears, and therefore do not increase but reduce the need of an enterprise for working capital.

losses in the switch-over, etc. All these requirements could be met by increasing the ordinary permanent working capital allocated to the enterprise ('own working capital'). But this would involve a very great increase in this capital, so that large uncontrolled sums were placed at the disposal of the enterprise. In order to fasten the enterprise firmly to the plan, these temporary needs are therefore met by short-term repayable credits from the State Bank (or in the case of building firms, from the specialised banks)—credits for 'seasonal stocks', 'accounts in transit', and 'unplanned credits', as they are called—and these are kept under close bank control. These credits are covered principally by the balances of 'own working capital' in the bank, from the current balances and reserves of the state budget, and from the reserves of the specialised banks (all of which are kept with the State Bank).

The complexities of the short-term credit system cannot be discussed here.[1] It was initiated in 1927–8 and consolidated in 1931 after an unsuccessful reform in 1930. By abolishing all credits from one enterprise to another (bills of exchange, etc.), and by limiting 'own working capital' to permanent needs, it assisted the harnessing of the current accounts of industry to the economic and financial plans. Bank policy had to steer a difficult course. Too much credit would lead to overstocking and waste; too little credit would lead to hold-ups in production from understocking. Too little bank control over the finances of enterprises would tempt them to depart from the plan; too great a control would deprive managements of initiative. By 1941 a workable system had been evolved, but it was still undergoing substantial modification. (These problems will be returned to in later chapters.)

An important form of bank control is that over wages. In theory, the system outlined so far already provides all the elements required for fitting wages into the overall financial plan. Cost price, transfer price, and profits are planned, and the 'cost price' level is based on calculations in which the wage element is the most important. If wages are greater than is planned for a given output, costs will exceed the plan and profits will be lower than planned. But fulfilment of the costs plan depends on the achievement of the planned rise in the productivity of labour. If productivity rises less than is planned, the output plan will be fulfilled only if wages costs rise

---

[1] Some of them are discussed in my article in *Soviet Studies*, vol. v, no. 1 (1953), pp. 18–31.

(*a*) to provide for more workers, (*b*) to pay overtime, (*c*) to give extra bonuses as incentives, (*d*) (if there is a shortage of skilled labour) to attract skilled labour from other enterprises. If productivity rises less than is planned, the manager must therefore choose between under-fulfilling the production plan, and 'over-fulfilling' the costs plan. Which he chooses to do will depend on the relative strength of the incentives in each case. In practice, wage-payments in the Soviet economy have had a chronic tendency to exceed the plan, not merely in times of acute goods shortages (such as 1930–4) when there was an inflationary pressure on wages, but even in relatively favourable times. But this is harmful, because if wage issues are too large the balance on the retail market is thrown out. Bank control of current accounts is therefore used in an attempt to enforce ceilings of total wages, which are set out industry by industry in the national economic plan.

Subsidies

The financial principle of *khozraschot* is that receipts of enterprises should exceed costs by a planned margin of profits. They may be less than costs, however, if (i) costs exceed the plan or (ii) the state fixes transfer-price below costs. In both cases losses will have to be met by subsidies. (In a planned economy of the Soviet type, enterprises cannot be allowed to go bankrupt. If they fail to pay, they can be closed down or reorganised, but this must be a deliberate decision of the planning authorities.) In the first case, they will be unplanned subsidies; in the second case, planned subsidies. Subsidies must be distinguished from allocations of new working capital which enable the expansion of stocks in hand but do not affect the transfer-price of the eventual output, which continues to be greater than costs.

Planned subsidies are found in Soviet practice in the following cases:

(i) During the first five-year plan, when prices on the retail market rose continuously, it was considered advisable to maintain the original (1928) transfer-prices of heavy industry products. As wage costs rose more rapidly than productivity (from 1931 onwards), this was possible only by giving large subsidies. These large-scale subsidies to industry continued until 1936.

(ii) New products often have an initially high cost, and they are subsidised while the new production methods are being mastered.

(iii) New factories may have high costs in the initial period of their operation.

(iv) The average level of costs may be exceeded in certain areas (e.g. with poor coal seams, high transport costs), or by factories with obsolescent equipment. If this high-cost production is to continue, it will have to be subsidised.

(v) The planning authorities may consider it advisable that a line of production should be sold below costs even when subsidies in general have been abolished (e.g. high-grade seeds to collective farms).

As far as possible these cases are met without resort to a direct budget subsidy. Within an enterprise, some goods may be produced at a loss and others at a profit, but an overall profit will still be made (the disadvantages of this will be discussed below). Profit and loss are cancelled out between enterprises within a *glavk* or NK, either by use of the 'dual price' system (the *glavk* buys at a loss from some of its enterprises and at a profit from others) or by a system of 'internal subsidy' (the *glavk* transfers the profit of some of its enterprises to others as a subsidy). The *glavk* itself has a high incentive to reduce losses at enterprise level so that its net profits will be as high as possible. But if the economic unit (*glavk*, trust, etc.) is planned to make an overall loss, it will receive a subsidy from the budget, which will be subject to budget control, the strictest form of control.

Capital replacement

In an economy of the Soviet type the costs of replacing the existing stock of capital can be met in two ways: from profits and budgetary grants through the capital investment plan, or from costs. The Soviet government has preferred to meet this expenditure from a depreciation allowance which forms part of the costs of production in every enterprise (though at one stage the capital repair plan formed part of the capital investment plan). For such a system to be efficient the rate of depreciation allowance must be just enough to allow for the replacement of used-up capital at current prices, the size of 'used-up' capital being calculated at a level of wear and tear 'reasonable' for the industry at its stage of development. Both the evaluation of existing capital stock at current prices and the assessment of what is 'fair' wear and tear have presented considerable difficulties. Under the system in force until 1938, actual expenditure on capital repair was sometimes below but often above the size of the depreciation fund. The system introduced in 1938 tied in the responsibility for repair more closely with the enterprise concerned, and made the allowances more flexible: they varied not only by industry but also by *glavk* and even by enterprise (e.g. in rail transport from 6–16·5% of assessed capital value). But the assessment of capital stock was still unsatisfactory, and depreciation allowances used for replacement purposes remained below the level required for replacement at current prices. An equally serious weakness was in the control of expenditure from the capital repair fund: expenditure on capital repair by the *glavk* or the director of the enterprise was controlled only by the indirect stimulus that if the fund were used inefficiently it would not cover the repair needed. Systematisation of experience and standardisation of methods were in a rudimentary state. More generally, it may well be that the size of the capital stock of an enterprise or a branch of industry plays too small a part in the determination of planned costs, where it appears only as a depreciation allowance—no allowance is made in current costs for obsolescence, which, of course, takes place far more rapidly than physical wearing-out, or for any kind of 'rate of interest' on capital.[1]

Soviet procedure in regard to depreciation is further complicated by the fact that since 1938 depreciation allowances have been used for capital investment as well as repair. From 40 to 60% of the total depreciation fund (varying by industry) is transferred to the specialised banks and used for investment in the industry. This procedure does of course raise the share of capital in costs somewhat, and ensures that every branch has to make at least a minimum contribution from its own funds towards its capital investment programme, irrespective of its level of profits.[2]

[1] See Rovinskii, *op. cit.* pp. 123–4; Kronrod, *op. cit.* pp. 87–107; *Fin. khoz. bull.* (1938), nos. 1–2, pp. 14–15 (8. i. 1938), no. 13, pp. 10, 13 (8. iii. 1938), no. 14, p. 29 (8. iv. 1938), no. 17, pp. 15–16 (15. iv. 1938); SZ 446/1940 (1. vi. 1940); Turetskii in *Pl. khoz.* no. 9 (1935), pp. 119–121; *TsIK* 4/vi, Bull. no. 19, p. 5; *Pl. khoz.* no. 5 (1936), pp. 8ff.; G. F. Grin'ko, *Finansovaya programma Soyuza SSSR na 1937g.* (1937), p. 38; *Second session of the Supreme Soviet of the U.S.S.R....*, Verbatim report (1938), p. 285.

[2] The argument is put forward by Soviet economists (e.g. Rovinskii, *op. cit.* p. 65, D'yachenko and Kozlov, *op. cit.* p. 211, Aleksandrov, *op. cit.* p. 205) that the allocation of part of the depreciation fund to capital investment is made possible by the reduction of the costs of capital construction and repair (in a situation in which capital is valued at its price at the time of construction). This argument is not valid (*a*) because although costs of construction have fallen in 'normal' times, 'abnormal' times (e.g. the period of the first five-year plan) have caused the costs of capital repair in current prices to exceed their valuation in prices of the time of construction, in most cases, and (*b*) because by a simple reduction of the percentage allocation to the depreciation fund at the time of the 1938 reform, depreciation deductions could have been made to equal the estimated costs of capital repair.

The problem of incentives

How far does the organisation of the finances of industry so far described provide a financial incentive to the management *qua* management to fulfil and over-fulfil the production and costs plan?[1]

First, if these plans were not fulfilled, the danger would exist that available working capital would fall short of what is required to continue the efficient working of the enterprise.

Secondly, profits would be less than planned. Under the system as explained so far this would have three consequences:

(i) Deductions to the budget (made as a percentage of actual profit) would be less than planned, and this would probably involve inquiry and intervention by the NKF into the affairs of the enterprise.

(ii) The profit available for the extension of working capital in the enterprise or branch would be less than planned, so that the deficit in working capital would increase.

(iii) The profit available for the capital investment plan of the industry would be less than planned. Unless the budget made up the deficit, the total funds available for investment in the industry would therefore be insufficient to enable the fulfilment of the investment plan.

It is difficult to estimate the extent to which the wish to prevent these consequences acts as an effective prod to the management. It seems unlikely, for instance, that the allocation of part of profits direct to capital investment in the branch (which it will be remembered was the core of method 1 described earlier) is of primary importance in securing the fulfilment of the costs plan. In the case of important projects, budget allocations are made to cover the gap if the actual profits available for investment fall below the planned level.[2] Little effort is made to discriminate between the different sources of investment once these sums have reached the specialised bank.[3] On the other hand, there must be a great desire, at least at

[1] Incentive to the workers and managers as individuals is of course provided by the wages and bonus system.

[2] Rovinskii, *op. cit.* p. 126. And cf. his statement in *op. cit.* pp. 316–17.

[3] In the plans for investment checked and approved by NKF, and in the general account for an investment project kept by the specialised bank, receipts from depreciation, profit, and the budget, are of course shown separately, and considerable pressure is exerted to see that profits are transferred to investment in accordance with fulfilment (these transfers are carried out immediately after the deductions from profit to the budget, which have priority, have been made). But in the account of financing received by the construction job itself the sources of the investment are not shown separately (*Finansovoe pravo*, pp. 228–9, 230–1; D'yachkov and Kiparisov, *op. cit.* p. 277; SZ 58/1938, 17/1939).

glavk level, to see that the profits plan is fulfilled so that new working capital and the required sums for capital investment are easily forthcoming: if all moneys were issued impersonally by the budget for these purposes, the industry concerned would be completely disinterested in the sources of its own investment. This arrangement does seem to give limited priority to the investment programme of the economic unit which is more efficient.[1]

But at best these arrangements are only a deterrent to inefficiency, not a stimulus to efficiency. Such a stimulus is provided by setting aside a proportion of total profits for the enterprise itself to use freely, in a fund known as the 'Director's Fund' (or earlier as the FUBR—Fund for the Improvement of Workers' Welfare). This fund, first founded in 1923, amounted in 1938–41 to 4% of net profit (or, in the case of subsidised enterprises, to 3% of the economy from the costs plan).[2] Therefore, the greater the extent to which an enterprise fulfilled its costs plan, the larger would be its director's fund. Moreover, if the costs plan were *over-fulfilled*, 50% of all profit in excess of the plan was allocated to this fund.

The fund was at the disposal of the director, in consultation with the elected works committee, with the single proviso (not usually carried out in practice) that 50% had to be allocated to housing. The remainder was at his discretion to be divided between cultural and welfare measures, individual bonuses, supplementary capital works outside the plan, and rationalisation measures and the spreading of technical information.[3] Of particular interest in this connexion are the arrangements by which investments outside the plan ('decentralised' or 'outside the limit' investment) were permitted from this fund from 1935 onwards. This means that in addition to any flexibility within the capital investment plan itself, a limited field was left within which autonomous decisions about investment (within the

[1] The truth would seem to lie between Rovinskii's statement that 'involving the "own resources" of economic organs in the financing of the growth of working capital and capital investment creates their interest in receiving profit' (*op. cit.* p. 135), and N. Kaplan's that 'the distinction between profits paid into the budget and profits left with the enterprise is [in this respect—R.W.D.] an accounting distinction only' (N. Kaplan, *Capital investments in the Soviet Union, 1924–1951*, p. 17).

[2] This was reduced to 2% on the eve of the war. In 1923–9 it had been 10% of profit, and in 1929–38 9%, but in the earlier years of the five-year plans profit had been a smaller proportion of the gross income of enterprises.

[3] See SZ 167/1931 (18. iii. 1931), 338/1931 (13. viii. 1931), 471/1931 (2. xii. 1931), 149/1934 (1. iv. 1934), 253/1934 (17. vi. 1934), 149/1934 (1. iv. 1934), 296/1935 (1. vii. 1935), 319/1935 (4. vii. 1935), 169/1936 (19. iv. 1936), 457/1936 (8. xii. 1936), 5/1937 (31. xii. 1936) and *Fin. khoz. bull.* (1937), no. 6, pp. 1–2 (7. ii. 1937), and no. 23, pp. 22–3 (14. vii. 1937).

framework of available supplies) could be made at local level. Similar limited powers were also given to local soviets down to district level in respect of sums collected in excess of their revenue plans.[1]

In practice, the incentives to fulfil the costs plan provided by the arrangements for the disposal of the profits of enterprises have been limited by various weaknesses:

(i) For a long period many enterprises in the U.S.S.R. were working not at a profit but at a loss (the subsidies system), and this remained true of the more backward enterprises receiving 'internal subsidies' even after most subsidies had been abolished. Devices such as giving bonuses from cost reductions to subsidised concerns were only partly effective.

(ii) Transfer prices were not properly adjusted between industries. As a result, some industries had much higher rates of profit than others, so that the Director's Fund tended to be much larger in relation to output (light industry as a whole had a higher rate of profit than heavy industry).

(iii) Within an industry, and within an enterprise, profits tend to be much greater on some lines of production than on others. By concentrating on profitable lines, the enterprise could fulfil the profits plan while under-fulfilling the production plan as a whole. This can be corrected by administrative measures (e.g. by instructing the enterprise to give priority to certain lines), or by adjusting prices to give uniform profits in relation to costs.[2]

(iv) Above all, the attention of managements throughout the period was concentrated on the output plan, and they were always willing to pay wages and issue bonuses in excess of the plan, and even to pay extra sums to acquire scarce materials, if this would facilitate the fulfilment of the output plan, even if it meant that the profits plan would then be unrealisable.

Miscellaneous adjustments

In addition to these important adjustments in our simplified system, mention must be made of a number of practical devices

---

[1] For details see SZ 417/1935 (19. ix. 1935), 405/1936 (13. ix. 1936), *Fin. khoz. bull.* (1937), no. 16, p. 19 (15. iv. 1937), and Rovinskii, *op. cit.* pp. 76–7 (for decree of 7. i. 1941).

[2] However, extra profits would have to be given to lines which enterprises might otherwise be less likely to produce (excessively labour-intensive lines) and to lines to which the state wished priority to be given. For some comments on this point, see Kronrod, *op. cit.* pp. 214–16.

which have been introduced to enable industry to operate more efficiently, and which modify the simplified system still further. These include principally:

(i) Social insurance. Pensions, sick benefits, pay during pregnancy, holiday facilities and allied expenses could be met in a centrally planned system either as a general charge on the budget or out of the costs of enterprises. In the system which has been evolved in the U.S.S.R., these social insurance expenditures are met out of planned costs, a percentage addition being made to the wage funds of enterprises to form the social insurance funds. These funds, and the payments from them, are centrally regulated, but they are administered by the trade unions. Before 1938 the social insurance budget was entirely separate from the state budget; since 1938 it has formed an earmarked fund within the budget.

(ii) It has been found more convenient that certain non-capital expenditures of an economic character should be made a charge on the budget rather than included in costs. In this way, they are kept under closer centralised control. These include, in the national economy item of the budget, what is known as 'operational expenditure' (*operatsionnye raskhody*), i.e. expenditures on 'training staff for economic bodies, on scientific-research work, on geological surveying, on prospecting, and on experimental measures'.[1] Other items of the budget also include semi-economic items (e.g. expenditure on training workers under the item 'education', and expenditure on the administration of economic *glavks* and NK's under 'administration').

Thus the practice of Soviet financial planning in industry involves the following main modifications in the simplified system of Fig. 1:

(i) The costs of an industry (or enterprise) include, in addition to wages, materials, and overheads, a depreciation allowance (as a percentage of the assessed capital value), and payments to social insurance (as a percentage of the wage fund) (see Fig. 2a).

(ii) The profits of an industry (or enterprise) are allocated not merely to the budget (deductions from profits) and to cover part of the capital investment in the branch, but also to provide new working capital in the enterprise or in the branch, and to the Director's Fund (Fig. 2a).

(iii) Some industries work at a loss, and receive subsidies from the budget. Some enterprises work at a loss although the *glavk* as a whole

[1] D'yachenko and Kozlov, *op. cit.* p. 311.

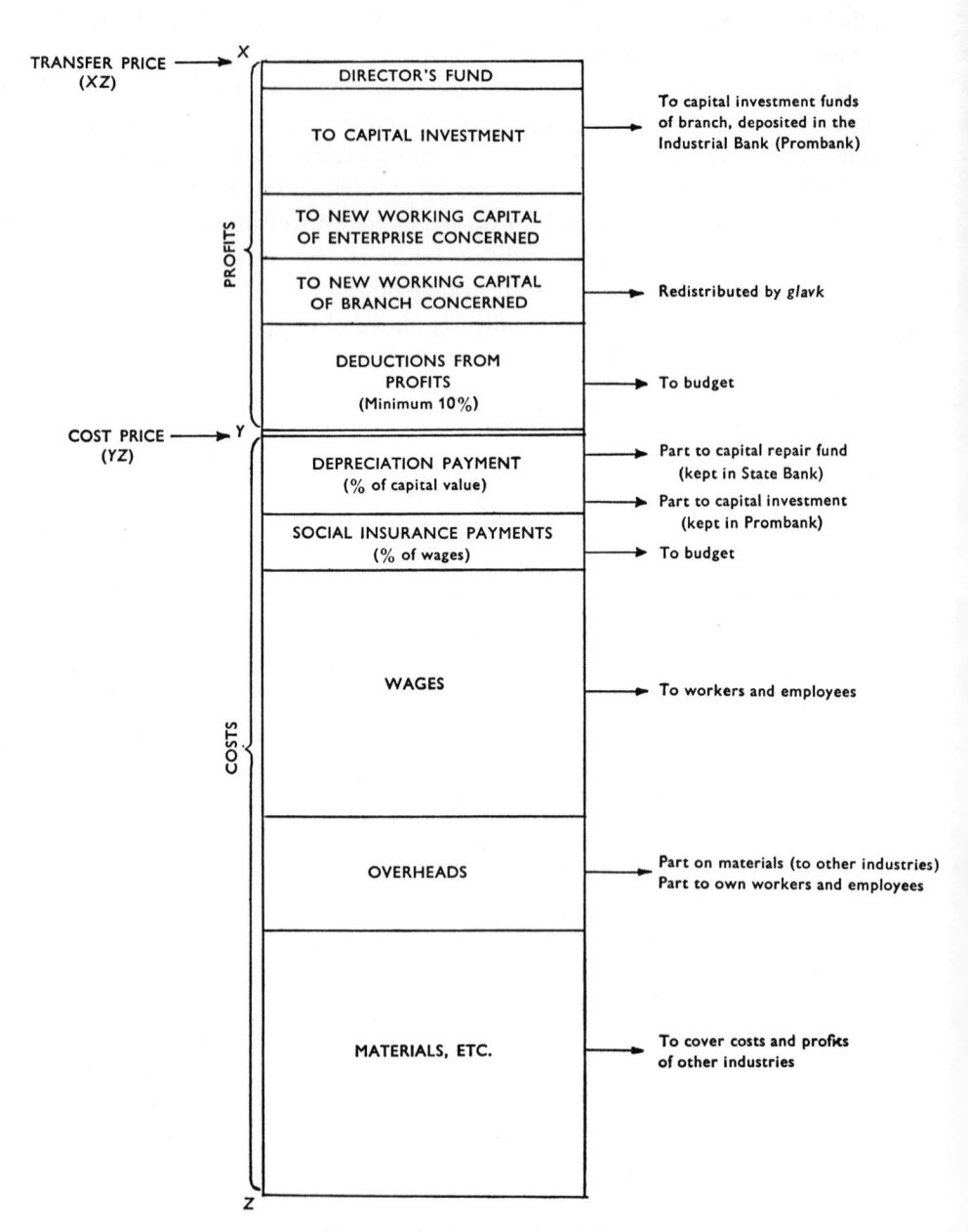

```
TRANSFER PRICE ──→ X
    (XZ)           ┌─────────────────────────────┐
                   │    DIRECTOR'S FUND          │
                   ├─────────────────────────────┤       To capital investment funds
                   │                             │  ──→  of branch, deposited in the
                   │    TO CAPITAL INVESTMENT    │       Industrial Bank (Prombank)
                   │                             │
              ┌    ├─────────────────────────────┤
              │    │   TO NEW WORKING CAPITAL    │
              │    │   OF ENTERPRISE CONCERNED   │
      PROFITS ┤    ├─────────────────────────────┤
              │    │   TO NEW WORKING CAPITAL    │  ──→  Redistributed by glavk
              │    │   OF BRANCH CONCERNED       │
              │    ├─────────────────────────────┤
              │    │     DEDUCTIONS FROM         │
              │    │         PROFITS             │  ──→  To budget
              └    │     (Minimum 10%)           │
  COST PRICE ──→ Y ├─────────────────────────────┤       Part to capital repair fund
    (YZ)           │   DEPRECIATION PAYMENT      │  ──→  (kept in State Bank)
                   │   (% of capital value)      │       Part to capital investment
                   ├─────────────────────────────┤  ──→  (kept in Prombank)
                   │  SOCIAL INSURANCE PAYMENTS  │
                   │       (% of wages)          │  ──→  To budget
              ┌    ├─────────────────────────────┤
              │    │                             │
              │    │                             │
              │    │          WAGES              │  ──→  To workers and employees
              │    │                             │
              │    │                             │
              │    ├─────────────────────────────┤
        COSTS ┤    │                             │       Part on materials (to other industries)
              │    │         OVERHEADS           │  ──→  Part to own workers and employees
              │    │                             │
              │    ├─────────────────────────────┤
              │    │                             │
              │    │                             │
              │    │       MATERIALS, ETC.       │  ──→  To cover costs and profits
              │    │                             │       of other industries
              │    │                             │
              └    └─────────────────────────────┘
                   Z
```

Fig. 2a. The finances of an industry.

is working at a profit, and receive a subsidy or favoured transfer price from the *glavk*.

(iv) All industries have their own working capital for permanent needs, and are lent working capital for temporary needs (this loaned capital appears in the credit plan).

(v) The capital investment plan is financed not simply from the budget and from the profits of industry, but also from part of the depreciation allowance made in each enterprise (Fig. 2*b*).

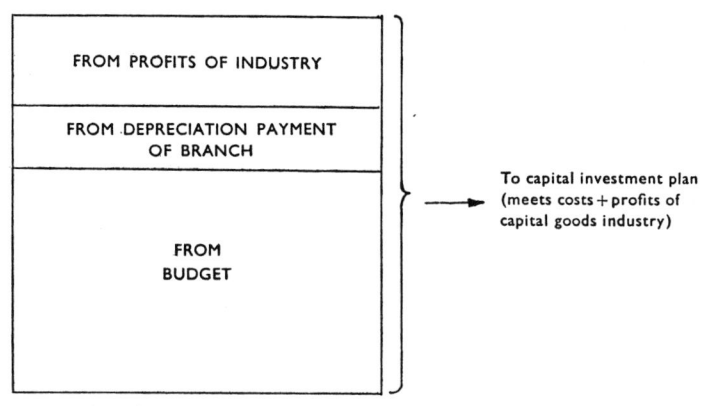

```
┌─────────────────────────────┐
│  FROM PROFITS OF INDUSTRY   │
├─────────────────────────────┤
│  FROM DEPRECIATION PAYMENT  │
│         OF BRANCH           │
├─────────────────────────────┤      To capital investment plan
│                             │ ───► (meets costs + profits of
│           FROM              │      capital goods industry)
│          BUDGET             │
│                             │
│                             │
└─────────────────────────────┘
```

Fig. 2*b*. Sources of the capital investment plan.

(vi) The revenue of the budget includes, in addition to turnover tax and deductions from profits, payments to the social insurance fund from the costs of enterprises.

(vii) The national economy item of the budget includes, in addition to allocations to capital investment, allocations to increase the working capital of enterprises, to subsidies, and to 'operational expenditure' (Fig. 2*c*). Various expenses of an economic character are borne by the budget, and social insurance revenue and expenditure form a part of the budget.

(*b*) *Relations with the non-state sector*

As was stated earlier, the Soviet economy is not fully centrally planned, because most agricultural production is at the disposal of the collective farms and not of the state direct. While the bulk of agricultural equipment is state-owned (via the MTS), the final product is owned either by the collective farm (if produced on lands worked in common) or by the individual collective farmer (if produced on the private plots belonging to each household). The planning of agriculture has therefore to be partly indirect.

As the position of the collective farm is intermediate between privately-owned and state-owned economy, its interconnexions with the state financial system are extremely complex. The state influences the disposal of the production of the collective farms in several ways (see Fig. 3*a*).

(i) It directly controls (in part) the disposal of the production of the collective farm and the individual collective farmer. Compulsory deliveries have to be made to the state from collective farm production and from the production of individual plots, and these

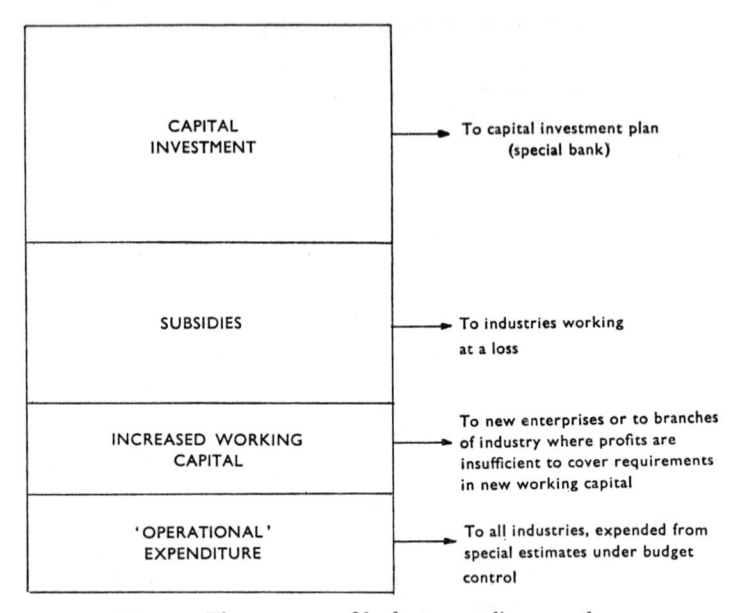

CAPITAL INVESTMENT	→ To capital investment plan (special bank)
SUBSIDIES	→ To industries working at a loss
INCREASED WORKING CAPITAL	→ To new enterprises or to branches of industry where profits are insufficient to cover requirements in new working capital
'OPERATIONAL' EXPENDITURE	→ To all industries, expended from special estimates under budget control

Fig. 2*c*. The structure of budget expenditure on the national economy (industry).

deliveries are paid for by the state at fixed low prices. Deliveries also have to be made to the state by the collective farms, in kind, or occasionally in money, in payment for work by the MTS on the farm. Proportions of gross output fixed as minima by the state have to be allocated to the seed and fodder funds of the farm.

(ii) It influences or regulates the disposal of the remainder of the production of the farms and the farmer. Part is bought by the state on a contract basis at prices nearer to the retail level. Agricultural prices on the free market ('the collective farm market'), on which the farm and the farmer are entitled to sell the remainder of their produce, are affected by the general retail market position and

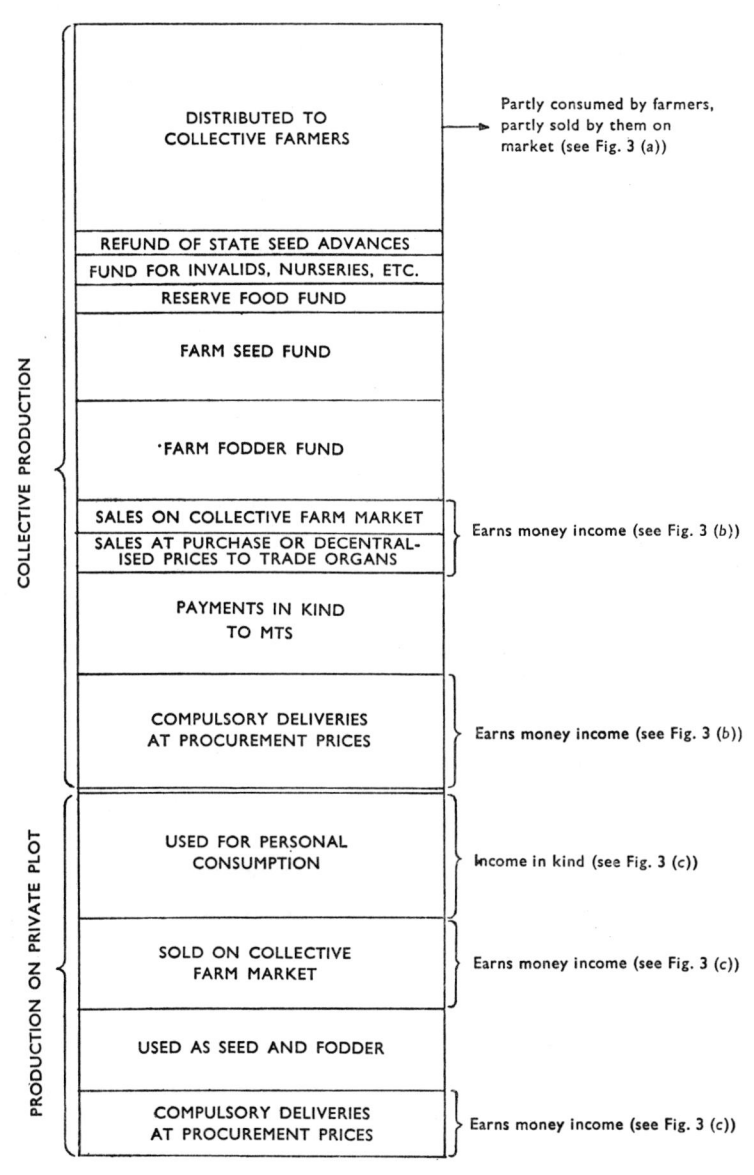

```
COLLECTIVE PRODUCTION {
    ┌─────────────────────────────────────┐
    │  DISTRIBUTED TO                     │ → Partly consumed by farmers,
    │  COLLECTIVE FARMERS                 │   partly sold by them on
    │                                     │   market (see Fig. 3 (a))
    ├─────────────────────────────────────┤
    │  REFUND OF STATE SEED ADVANCES      │
    ├─────────────────────────────────────┤
    │  FUND FOR INVALIDS, NURSERIES, ETC. │
    ├─────────────────────────────────────┤
    │  RESERVE FOOD FUND                  │
    ├─────────────────────────────────────┤
    │  FARM SEED FUND                     │
    ├─────────────────────────────────────┤
    │  ·FARM FODDER FUND                  │
    ├─────────────────────────────────────┤
    │  SALES ON COLLECTIVE FARM MARKET    │ } Earns money income (see Fig. 3 (b))
    ├─────────────────────────────────────┤
    │  SALES AT PURCHASE OR DECENTRAL-    │
    │  ISED PRICES TO TRADE ORGANS        │
    ├─────────────────────────────────────┤
    │  PAYMENTS IN KIND                   │
    │  TO MTS                             │
    ├─────────────────────────────────────┤
    │  COMPULSORY DELIVERIES              │ } Earns money income (see Fig. 3 (b))
    │  AT PROCUREMENT PRICES              │
    └─────────────────────────────────────┘
}

PRODUCTION ON PRIVATE PLOT {
    ┌─────────────────────────────────────┐
    │  USED FOR PERSONAL                  │ } Income in kind (see Fig. 3 (c))
    │  CONSUMPTION                        │
    ├─────────────────────────────────────┤
    │  SOLD ON COLLECTIVE                 │ } Earns money income (see Fig. 3 (c))
    │  FARM MARKET                        │
    ├─────────────────────────────────────┤
    │  USED AS SEED AND FODDER            │
    ├─────────────────────────────────────┤
    │  COMPULSORY DELIVERIES              │ } Earns money income (see Fig. 3 (c))
    │  AT PROCUREMENT PRICES              │
    └─────────────────────────────────────┘
}
```

Fig. 3a. Distribution in kind of gross agricultural production of collective farm sector.

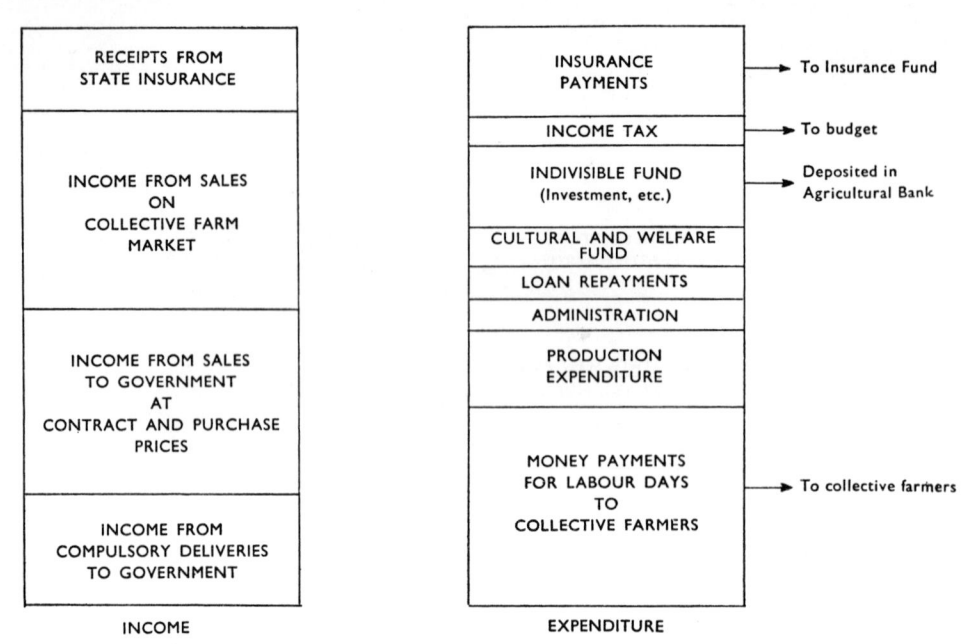

Fig. 3b. Money income and expenditure of collective farms.

INCOME
- RECEIPTS FROM STATE INSURANCE
- INCOME FROM SALES ON COLLECTIVE FARM MARKET
- INCOME FROM SALES TO GOVERNMENT AT CONTRACT AND PURCHASE PRICES
- INCOME FROM COMPULSORY DELIVERIES TO GOVERNMENT

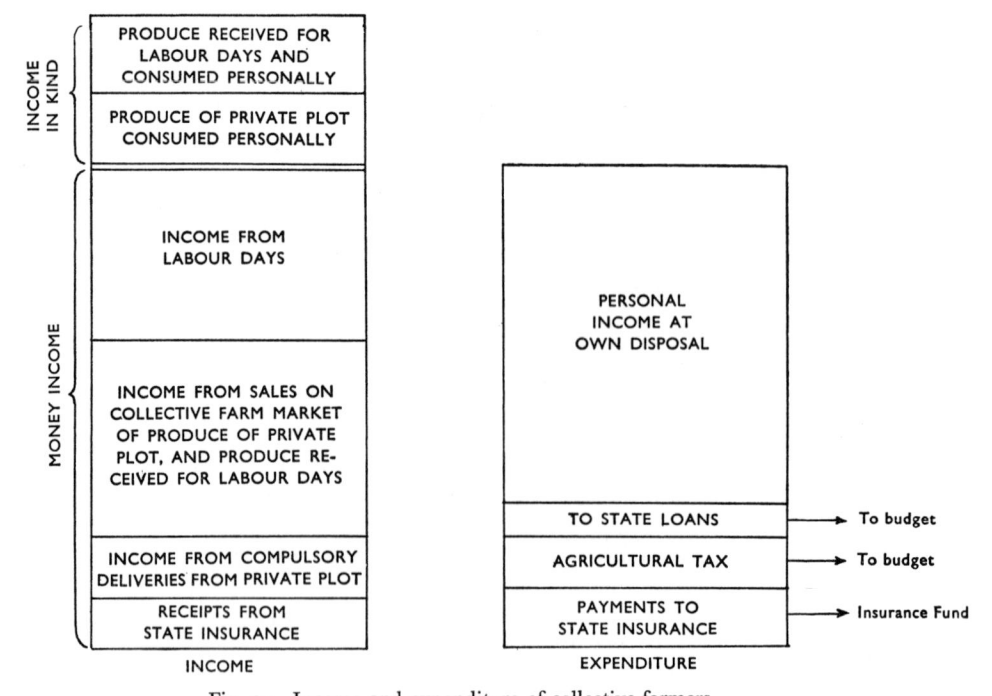

EXPENDITURE
- INSURANCE PAYMENTS → To Insurance Fund
- INCOME TAX → To budget
- INDIVISIBLE FUND (Investment, etc.) → Deposited in Agricultural Bank
- CULTURAL AND WELFARE FUND
- LOAN REPAYMENTS
- ADMINISTRATION
- PRODUCTION EXPENDITURE
- MONEY PAYMENTS FOR LABOUR DAYS TO COLLECTIVE FARMERS → To collective farmers

Fig. 3c. Income and expenditure of collective farmers.

INCOME

INCOME IN KIND:
- PRODUCE RECEIVED FOR LABOUR DAYS AND CONSUMED PERSONALLY
- PRODUCE OF PRIVATE PLOT CONSUMED PERSONALLY

MONEY INCOME:
- INCOME FROM LABOUR DAYS
- INCOME FROM SALES ON COLLECTIVE FARM MARKET OF PRODUCE OF PRIVATE PLOT, AND PRODUCE RECEIVED FOR LABOUR DAYS
- INCOME FROM COMPULSORY DELIVERIES FROM PRIVATE PLOT
- RECEIPTS FROM STATE INSURANCE

EXPENDITURE
- PERSONAL INCOME AT OWN DISPOSAL
- TO STATE LOANS → To budget
- AGRICULTURAL TAX → To budget
- PAYMENTS TO STATE INSURANCE → Insurance Fund

170

in particular by the price at which foodstuffs are sold in state shops. The level of prices on the collective farm market influences the proportion of the remaining produce which the producers are prepared to take to market, and thus determines the size of part of the overall money income of the collective farm and the collective farmer.

The money income of the farm as a whole, the produce in kind available for distribution to the collective farmers, and the money incomes of the farmers from sales from their own plots are thus influenced by the state directly and indirectly. It also influences the *disposal* of these incomes (see Figs. 3*b*, *c*):

(i) It regulates the system by which the available produce in kind and income in money are distributed among the collective farmers (the system of 'labour days', by which distribution is made according to amount and skill of work done).

(ii) It influences the proportions in which the money income of the farm is to be distributed between various uses, by fixing minimum proportions which are to be allocated to the 'indivisible fund' (used for investment), maximum proportions for administrative expenditure, etc.

(iii) It collects taxes (in money) from both the collective farm income and the personal income of the collective farmer, and operates a system of (partly compulsory, partly voluntary) state insurance of crops, cattle and equipment, which is a charge on the income of both the farmer and the farm.

In addition, the planning authorities attempt to influence the present and future production programmes of the collective farms, and therefore the present and future money incomes, both directly and indirectly. Particularly in the period 1938–41, the scope of the attempted direct planning of the production of collective farms was increased. In part the government sought to achieve the fulfilment of planned tasks by administrative means, and by using its political influence in the countryside (via party and soviet organs, etc.). But a large part in securing (or attempting to secure) their fulfilment was played by the indirect levers of state control in the countryside:

(i) By adjustments in the methods of assessing the amount of compulsory deliveries and the delivery prices of various crops and products, and in the rates and system of money taxation, the government attempted to direct the energies of collective farms towards the most urgent tasks of the plan, by making it more profitable for them to concentrate on those lines of production which the state considered most important.

(ii) The government influenced the collective farms via the MTS, both by supplying them with equipment suitable for coping with the tasks laid down in the plan, and by using the MTS personnel to instruct the collective farms both technically and generally.

(iii) The state budget financed the general agronomic network and special agricultural services such as veterinary points and laboratories, meat and dairy supervisory stations, anti-pest measures, and selection stations. These exercised considerable influence over collective farm production.

(iv) The Agricultural Bank issued loans at low interest rates for approved investment purposes, to supplement investments made through the indivisible funds of collective farms. These loans were met from the balances of indivisible funds (deposited with the Agricultural Bank), from the income of the bank from repayments and interest on past loans, and from funds provided by the budget. In this way both the size and the structure of collective farm investments were influenced.

It is impossible to attempt to assess here the extent to which these direct and indirect measures were successful in planning and regulating collective farm production in accordance with the general needs of the state. It is certain that these measures at least succeeded in providing the minimum requirements in foodstuffs and agricultural raw materials without which industrialisation could not have been carried through. It is also certain that the effects of planning in agriculture were far more limited than its effects in industry, and that the level of agricultural production was one of the main limiting factors on Soviet economic development.

It will be seen from the above account that much of the economic activity of the collective farms fell outside the centralised financial planning network. A considerable proportion of agricultural production did not enter the market. Of the remainder, part entered the collective farm market, which was not planned directly by the state. The indivisible funds of collective farms could not be precisely determined, or even accurately estimated, by the planning authorities. Their allocation was largely made by the autonomous decision of the collective farm management. All this non-state agricultural investment, like the decentralised investments in industry already mentioned, did not form part of the capital investment plan (though investments in the MTS were, of course, part of this plan).

However, the financial planning system influenced and was

influenced by the only partly-planned activities of the collective farms. The incomes of collective farmers entered the retail market together with the earnings of the state-employed population, and were partly obtained by diverting part of the wage fund via the collective farm market from immediate purchases from state trading organisations. These relationships had to be taken into account in planning the production of consumer goods by state industry and in fixing the prices of these goods. Further, the indivisible funds of collective farms were deposited with the Agricultural Bank, and there entered the financial plans of the banking system.

REVENUE	EXPENDITURE	
INCOME IN MONEY, RECEIVED FOR MTS WORK IN SPECIAL CASES		
INCOME FROM PAYMENTS IN KIND FOR MTS WORK, VALUED AT COMPULSORY DELIVERY PRICES		
TURNOVER TAX ON PAYMENTS IN KIND FOR MTS WORK	MTS CURRENT EXPENDITURE	To budget revenue as tax on fuel oil
TURNOVER TAX ON COMPULSORY DELIVERIES	MTS CAPITAL INVESTMENT	
INCOME TAX ON COLLECTIVE FARMS	GENERAL AGRICULTURAL MEASURES	
AGRICULTURAL TAX ON COLLECTIVE FARMERS	TO AGRICULTURAL BANK FOR LOANS TO COLLECTIVE FARMS	

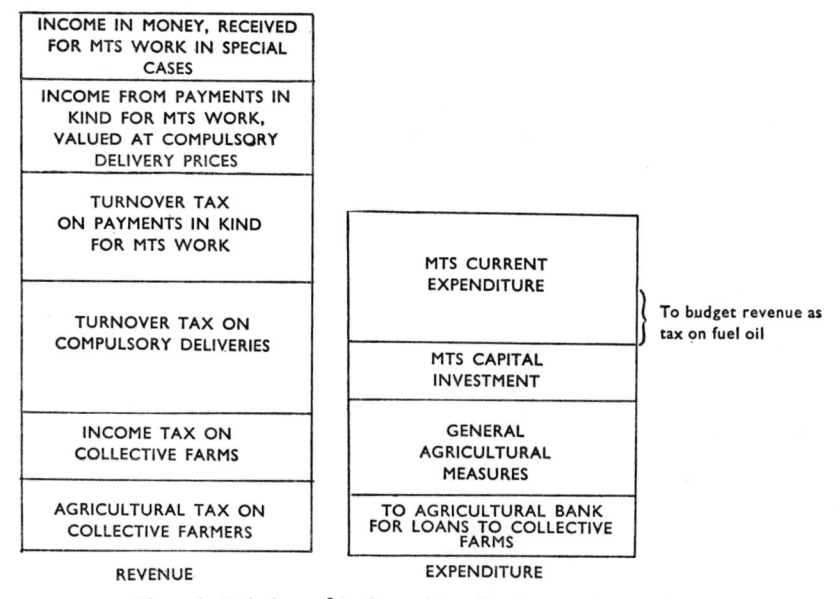

Fig. 3*d*. Relations of budget with collective farm agriculture.

The state budget was the main financial lever by which the collective farms were controlled by the planning system (see Fig. 3*d*). Considerable revenue accrued to the budget via compulsory deliveries at low prices. These deliveries were taxed at a high rate of turnover tax and sold at retail prices. Thus the revenue of the budget from turnover tax came not only from mark-ups on the prices of the product of light industry but also from mark-ups on the prices at which agricultural products were purchased. Turnover tax was therefore to a considerable extent a tax on the peasantry (this point is discussed in chapter IX). The agricultural tax on the incomes of collective farmers from their private plots, and the income tax on collective farmers (which until 1936 formed part of the agricultural tax) constituted a direct tax on agriculture.

Most collective farm investment was financed by the farms themselves. But budgetary grants covered the maintenance of the special services already mentioned, and small budget subventions were annually issued to the Agricultural Bank to enable it to expand its loans to collective farm investment (these subventions did not normally appear under 'agriculture', as they were ultimately returnable to the budget, but under 'miscellaneous').

Finally, the capital equipment and current expenses of the MTS were covered entirely by the budget (from 1938 onwards). In return for the work of MTS, the collective farms made deliveries in kind (paid in certain cases in money), from which the budget received substantial revenues.

These deliveries were valued at nominal prices and then entered in the budget under 'MTS income', but of course a much larger revenue accrued to the budget from the turnover tax on these products than appeared in the item 'MTS income'. The total revenue from collective farm payments to the MTS more than covered the total expenditure of the MTS on both current and capital needs (current MTS expenditure as shown in the budget was itself inflated, since it included fuel-oil sold to the MTS at current retail prices, i.e. including turnover tax). Thus in respect of the MTS the budget performed a controlling and auditing role, but, if turnover tax on payments in kind made for MTS work is considered as a tax on agriculture (on this see chapter IX), MTS activities would appear to be financed not from general budgetary funds, but from the payments in kind made by the collective farms.[1]

(c) *Modifications in the revenue system*

Turnover tax and profits tax were the main sources of Soviet revenue. But a number of other revenue items were retained or introduced during the planning period which between them yielded between one-third and one-half of total revenue.

The main reason for this was that industrialisation involved, as will be shown in later chapters, a chronic tendency to inflation: in both the first and the second five-year plans wage plans were over-

[1] Of course the manufacture of the elaborate equipment of the MTS would have been impossible without the general policy of industrialisation, but industrialisation itself was partly 'paid for' by the turnover tax on agricultural compulsory deliveries.

fulfilled, leading to the continuous appearance of a surplus of urban purchasing power in terms of existing retail prices. Getting rid of this surplus presented serious administrative and political problems. In the period 1930–5 it was withdrawn principally by raising retail prices. It also proved possible to retain large-scale loans from the population and to impose at moderate rates such direct taxes as the income tax and the cultural and housing levy without apparently harming wage incentives.

Direct taxes on wage-earners in the U.S.S.R. rose in 1940 to a maximum marginal rate of 13% (this was imposed on earnings above 1,000 roubles per month). No special study has been published of the effects of direct taxation on production in the U.S.S.R.; but experience in other countries seems to show that such a low level of direct tax does not act as a disincentive. Direct taxes were therefore retained even after the revision of prices and wages associated with the abolition of rationing in 1935.

In raising loans from the population the state attempted to make use of various psychological and social factors. It tried to canalise and encourage the desire to accumulate personal savings. It made use of gambling instincts by offering high lottery prizes. It stimulated subscription to the loans by appealing to patriotic principles and political enthusiasm. In this way the loans were made as palatable as possible, although strong group and social pressure was exercised to ensure that loan revenue was collected as planned.

Direct taxes no longer had the social and economic function that they had had in the 1920's; but they were still used to discriminate against certain types of income over which the state did not have direct control through the planning mechanism. In 1940 the normal marginal rate of income tax rose to a maximum of 7%. However, doctors and teachers paid a rate rising to 38% on the income from their private practice. Authors and artists paid normal rates on their earnings up to 1,000 roubles per month; but the tax rose to a maximum of 50% on very high earnings in order to limit the large incomes of the most popular writers from royalties and fees. The marginal rate of tax on artisans who did not belong to handicraft co-operatives rose to a maximum of 60%; thus they were discriminated against through the income tax as the individual peasant was through the agricultural tax. Ministers of religion paid this rate plus a surcharge of 40% of the standard amount of tax; and *izvozchiki* (cab-drivers) using their own animals, and persons manufacturing goods from their own materials, paid a surcharge of 35% (partly, in these cases, to counteract low declarations of income).

Tax exemptions were granted for various purposes. The most important of these was that the tax was reduced by 30% for workers and employees maintaining more than three persons (in addition the state paid family allowances for young children). No new important points of principle are disclosed by the details of Soviet income tax practice.

In short, these sources of revenue played an auxiliary part in the state budget. They provided a convenient source of additional revenue without any important disincentive effects; and they were utilised for various purposes of social and economic discrimination.

(d) Balancing the retail market

The peculiarities of money circulation and of the retail market in the U.S.S.R. gave rise to a final group of problems involving modifications in the simplified system of Fig. 1. Payments in the Soviet economy, as in any other modern economy, are of two kinds— transfer payments by book entry, and payments in cash. Soviet budget expenditure can ultimately be reduced to cash payments in wages or to collective farmers, or to book-keeping entries returning to budget revenue without being converted into cash.[1] The wages of school teachers and of workers in capital construction are immediate cash payments from the budget, but the purchase of school pencils and of industrial equipment from budget funds is at first a non-cash transfer, converted into cash only when it has been transformed (through one or more stages) into the wages of the workers in the industries producing these items. Payments to the budget of income tax, loans, and social insurance fees, do not take place in cash. They are deducted from wages or paid out of costs at source, before they have been converted into cash.

The budget is not the only source of cash issues and payments. If outpayments on the credit plan are larger than repayments plus the budget surplus (which is kept with the State Bank), a net money (ultimately cash) issue will have been made while the budget account will still show a surplus. The day-to-day cash payments (wage payments) of enterprises are not made through the budget but from their non-cash receipts for sales, in accordance with their financial plans. Part of the cash collected from the population from sales in the retail market is transferred to the budget as turnover tax,

[1] The turnover tax on fuel used by the MTS is an example of this.

but the remainder goes to the consumer goods industries to meet the transfer prices of their production.

Cash issues and circulation in the Soviet economy are not therefore coterminous with the budget, the credit plan, or the financial plans of industry. For this reason, the State Bank compiles a separate cash plan, both for the country as a whole (showing the net increase or decrease in currency circulation) and for each main area, showing the issues and receipts of cash through the bank. The key figure in this plan (the net cash issue) influences the general state of surplus or deficit of purchasing power in the population as a whole.

However, the cash plan alone is insufficient to determine the state of equilibrium on the retail market. This is because:

(*a*) Within the limits of the supply, consumer choice is free. Supply of each good in each area must be sufficient to equal demand at the fixed retail price.

(*b*) The effect on the state retail market of private sales at free prices on the collective farm market must be taken into account. These sales transfer cash between one section of the population and another.

As a result of this, an elaborate balance of Money Incomes and Expenditures of the Population is compiled, in the course of compiling the national economic plan. It is based on and influences the trade turnover plan. This retail market balance, together with the unified financial plan (or plan of accumulations, as it has been called here), are the key general plans in securing the financial balance of the economy.

THE FINANCIAL PLANNING SYSTEM AS A WHOLE

Fig. 5 attempts to summarise the interrelations of the Soviet financial system. It includes in abbreviated form all the main Soviet financial plans:

(1) The unified financial plan;

(2) The balance of money incomes and expenditures of the population;

(3) The budget (including local budgets and the social insurance budget);

(4) The cash and credit plans;

(5) The capital investment plan;

(6) The financial plans (balances of income and expenditure) of industry;

(7) The incomes and expenditures of the collective farm sector.

In its entirety this diagram therefore corresponds to the kind of financial balance sheet for the whole economy, or overall financial plan (*Svodnyi Finansovyi Plan*), which Gosplan must have been compiling on the eve of the second world war, in the course of drawing up the national economic plan. Thus it is one of the principal input-output balances (the others being primarily in physical terms), on the basis of which decisions were made on the actual figures to be included in the national economic plan.

Several important reservations must be made in treating Fig. 5 as a representation of overall financial planning in the U.S.S.R. on the eve of the second world war. The first is that it became possible to draw up a fairly accurate balance such as that in Fig. 5 only after a decade of experience of direct planning. During the first and second five-year plans, knowledge of the financial interrelations of the economy, apart from those included in the unified financial plan, was somewhat limited. Financial plans of branches of industry did not until 1939 show their gross incomes and receipts, but only their accumulations (depreciation, profit, grants from the budget, etc.) and the disposal of these accumulations (capital investment, capital repair, Director's Fund, payments to budget, etc.). While wages funds, and indices for reduction in costs, were also planned centrally, as of course were industrial prices, the central planning authorities did not have before them detailed plans of the outlays and incomes of industry. Profits plans were not related to the turnover of the branch, and the financial plans of industry were not linked with the indices of the production plans.[1] The financial planning of agriculture was, as has been shown, even more rudimentary: at best it was possible only to *estimate* the future size of, for example, the indivisible funds of the collective farms, and even this was not possible until the mid-1930's.[2] These limitations to the financial planning of agriculture and industry, combined with the prevalent goods shortages, vitiated the attempts to draw up satisfactory balances of the income and expenditure of the population which had been made since 1928. For all these reasons the planners devoted their main attention to securing the fulfilment of the unified financial plan (see Fig. 1), and of the crucial indices of the capital investment plan. It was not until the years immediately before the war that overall financial planning began to become a possibility.[3] The in-

---

[1] See Shenger, *op. cit.* pp. 35–7. [2] *Pl. khoz.* no. 4 (1935), pp. 96–7.
[3] Margolin, *op. cit.* pp. 12–24, gives an indication of the kind of problem that was by then being tackled.

completeness of financial planning was not of course fortuitous, but was connected with the relatively slow development of 'synthetic' planning of supplies and requirements.[1] It was only when the main disproportions in economic growth were being tackled, and material balances of supplies and requirements could be drawn up with some degree of precision, i.e. from about 1936 onwards, that the auxiliary overall *financial* balancing of the economy could be attempted.

The second reservation which needs to be made about the overall financial balance of Fig. 5 is that it is a combination of plans with widely differing functions. It was shown in the earlier discussion of the unified financial plan and the budget that only the budget section of the unified financial plan is given operative sanction by the government as an administrative document. The remaining items of this plan are sanctioned, on the revenue side, only as a part of the operative plans of industry, the banks, etc.; and on the expenditure side as a part of the capital investment plan. The same must be said of the balance of money incomes and expenditures of the population. On the income side, the wages plan, and on the expenditure side, the trade turnover plan, have administrative sanction; the remainder is a planning balance. This distinction between 'operative plans' and 'planners' plans' is of crucial importance to the understanding of the methods by which the financial plans are compiled and administered.

There is a third important respect in which the financial planning system so far described is a drastic and dangerous over-simplification of reality. The financial and economic plans of the Soviet government are centrally determined, in the sense that all the major balances and economic programmes are approved and enforced by a central planning body. But it would be extremely difficult even on paper to operate a system in which all decisions, including minor decisions, were proposed and approved by a central planning authority—the planning authority in such a system would indeed be faced with 'thousands of equations'. And in practice the rigidity of such a system would stifle economic initiative.

A key problem facing direct planning systems in general is to attempt to secure operative decentralisation and flexibility in a system in which all major decisions of economic policy are taken by the central government. However, in the Soviet Union in 1929–41 the exceptional strain under which industrialisation was carried out,

[1] A discussion of the evolution of the system of synthetic balance planning will be found in Dobb, *op. cit.* pp. 329–36, and Baykov, *op. cit.* pp. 444–8.

political and economic, internal and external, resulted in a much greater degree of centralisation and inflexibility than need necessarily be present in a planned economy of the Soviet type. It may be added that as the technical level of the Soviet economy approaches that of other advanced countries, a flexibility which encourages innovations becomes more essential.

Decentralisation in Soviet pre-war planning practice took five main forms. First, lower authorities were given possibilities for initiative in making proposals for future plans in the spheres in which they operate,[1] so that a variety of alternatives for investment were presented to the planning authorities. The system for compiling the plan was designed so that at each successive stage in moving up towards the central authority, the alternative projects were co-ordinated (or made into sub-variants of major variants), so that at top level the government could take its decision between a few major possibilities. Naturally this kind of activity cannot be included in the static representation of the Soviet financial system so far outlined, for this takes the economic plan as given. In money terms, these proposals appear to the central authorities as different sums to be allocated, or as different uses for these sums. How this system works is discussed in more detail below.

Secondly, once the plan has been adopted, operative flexibility was given to the lower bodies. The central authority says to the ministry, the ministry to the *glavk*, and the *glavk* to the enterprise: here is your programme in quantities and costs, here is your allocation of materials, trained labour, capital, and money—within this framework, reach the target how you like. This is the essence of the *khozraschot* as distinct from the budgetary system of control. It involves granting some operative flexibility to each body in using the resources allocated to it and in redistributing them among the lower bodies. In financial terms, the enterprise has full control over the financing of the workshops subordinate to it, and the *glavk* and the ministry are given powers to re-distribute the working capital and profits of the enterprises subordinate to them.

Thirdly, and this is presupposed in granting some operative flexibility to economic units, less important planning decisions were

---

[1] The question of whether the plan as a whole is democratically determined (i.e. whether the central planning decisions accord with the wishes of the people) is not relevant here. Whether or not the plan as a whole is democratically determined, it is still possible for proposals for more effective future action in its own sphere to be made from each unit of the economy.

devolved on to lower bodies, such as the disposal of the Director's Fund in each enterprise, the distribution of less essential materials, and the detailed breakdown of industrial targets.

So far we have been concerned with the legal opportunities for decentralisation provided in the central plan. In fact the actual operation of a direct planning system of the Soviet type inevitably involves the emergence of illegal or semi-legal operations by which the producing units put into practice the plans of the central authorities and adjust them to reality—the scramble for materials, bidding for labour, illegal investments. Such operations must not be looked upon purely as hindering central planning, although they sometimes do—they are rather part of the means by which the plans must be put into effect, and efficient planners will recognise this and adjust their plans to the situation. Methods of central control which made this flexibility impossible owing to strict proscriptions and high penalties would tend to paralyse economic advance, just as plans would fail if they did not recognise the practical limitations of the existing situation, and attempted to advance the economy faster than was objectively possible. This was quickly recognised in Soviet planning practice,[1] if not in its theory. It may be said to constitute a fourth form of decentralisation, one which in pre-war Soviet conditions was the most important one.

Finally, collective-farm agriculture was in a special position in decentralisation arrangements. Although the state influenced the economic decisions of collective farms, they were to a large extent made autonomously as a result of market influences over which the state had only very limited control. Whereas industrial development was firmly controlled from the centre, in agriculture the government was normally unable to forecast with any accuracy the main lines of growth (except for certain industrial crops), still less to plan them.[2] Hence it attempted to extend its centralised planned influence on agriculture—but by 1941 satisfactory methods of planning and control had not yet been devised.

---

[1] For a practical analysis of the relationship between plans and economic reality in the pre-war period, see David Granick, *The Management of the industrial firm in the U.S.S.R.* (1954).

[2] This can easily be demonstrated by comparing the percentage deviation of the actual net rate of growth from the planned net rate of growth in the five-year and annual plans, for the principal items of production of heavy industry and agriculture. Industrial planning will be seen to be much more accurate than agricultural 'planning', and increasingly so, throughout the pre-war period (and, for that matter, the post-war period as well).

A special case of the devolution of decisions is the organisation of local finance. The main features of Soviet local finance were established already by 1925, and the system as it then existed was incorporated without major change into direct planning. Part of each of the major items of budgetary revenue does not reach the central authorities, but is retained by the local soviet, and used at its (limited) discretion for local industries, education, health, and administration. Certain central taxes were retained (e.g. the personal income tax) and even introduced (e.g. the cultural and housing levy) in the 1930's as mainly local taxes, and various minor taxes and levies of purely local significance were retained in the local budgets. This local and republican financial system has been of importance not only because of its decentralised character, but also because skilful use of it by the central planning authorities has financed the local authorities of backward areas in order to bring them up towards the cultural and administrative level of central Russia. This system is discussed in chapter x.

Having surveyed the structure of Soviet financial plans and the budget, we can now turn to a consideration of the methods by which these plans are drawn up. By what procedures are they compiled? What is the relation of the budget to the indices of the national economic plan? How is the budget balanced?

8. HOW FINANCIAL PLANS AND THE BUDGET ARE COMPILED[1]

In the first stage of planning, balances in physical terms and overall financial plans are compiled by Gosplan. These show the state of the economy as it is expected to be in the current year, and set out variants for the year being planned, based on different assumptions about the level and type of investment, etc. On the basis of these projects the government adopts a general directive, indicating the main targets envisaged for the planned year. This directive in general fits in with the longer-term perspective five-year plan of which the plan for the year is a part. The directive consists of a series of interrelated production and investment targets based on the overall balances of Gosplan.

In theory at least, the detailed plans compiled by economic units on the basis of this directive should already be at least roughly in

[1] Fig. 4 illustrates schematically the process described in this section.

balance, and cohere with the plans for other parts of the economy. After the issuing of the government directive, each ministry issues more detailed directives to the bodies under it, and these bodies in consultation with lower units down to factory and workshop level compile plans embodying their production programmes, their requirements for material and labour, and the money income and expenditure corresponding to the material plans. These are re-

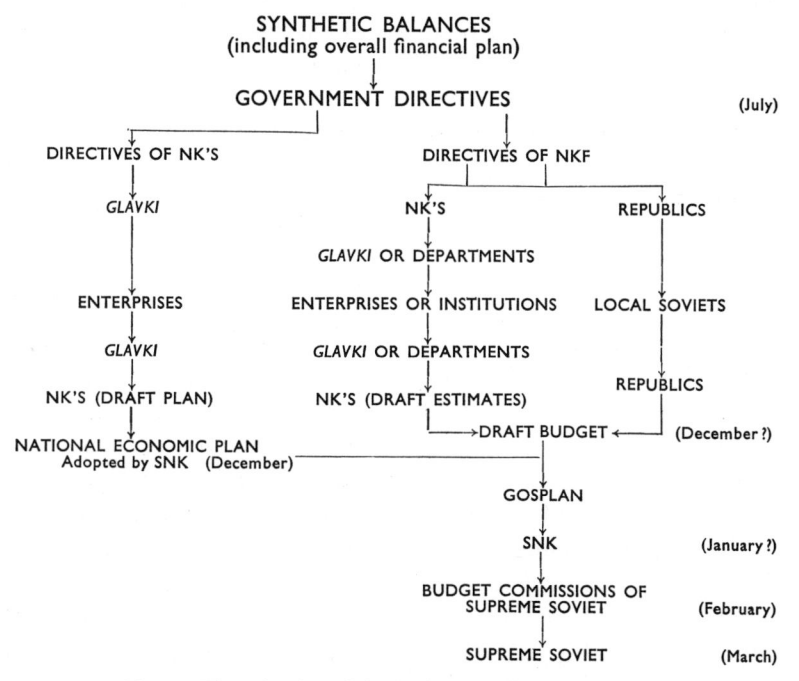

```
                    SYNTHETIC BALANCES
                (including overall financial plan)
                            │
                    GOVERNMENT DIRECTIVES                    (July)
            ┌───────────────┤
            ▼               ▼
  DIRECTIVES OF NK'S    DIRECTIVES OF NKF
            │           ┌───┴───────────────┐
            ▼           ▼                   ▼
          GLAVKI       NK'S              REPUBLICS
            │           │                   │
            │      GLAVKI OR DEPARTMENTS    │
            ▼           ▼                   ▼
        ENTERPRISES  ENTERPRISES OR     LOCAL SOVIETS
            │        INSTITUTIONS           │
            ▼           ▼                   ▼
          GLAVKI    GLAVKI OR DEPARTMENTS
            │           │                REPUBLICS
            ▼           ▼                   │
      NK'S (DRAFT    NK'S (DRAFT            │
         PLAN)        ESTIMATES)            │
            │           └──►DRAFT BUDGET◄───┘  (December ?)
            ▼                   │
   NATIONAL ECONOMIC PLAN ──────┤
   Adopted by SNK (December)    ▼
                             GOSPLAN
                                │
                                ▼
                               SNK                  (January ?)
                                │
                                ▼
                       BUDGET COMMISSIONS OF
                          SUPREME SOVIET           (February)
                                │
                                ▼
                        SUPREME SOVIET              (March)
```

Fig. 4. The adoption of the budget and the national economic plan (main stages).

submitted to the ministry, which then puts alternative proposals to the government, based partly on the modifications suggested by the lower bodies. The government adopts the final national economic plan at the conclusion of this process, and the lower bodies then adjust their original plans to fit in with the final plan.[1]

Parallel with this, the operative financial plans are compiled. The financial plans of an industry are, of course, compiled within the

[1] At each stage in the planning process, the body concerned compiles in detail an account of the expected fulfilment of the plan for the current year. The plan for the forthcoming year is compiled on the basis both of the draft targets set by the higher body, and of an analysis of the course of plan fulfilment in the current year.

industry (with NKF participation), parallel with the production, supply, labour, and other plans. The other operative financial plans (the budget, and the cash and credit plans) are compiled in conjunction with this.

The NKF issues directives (*ukazaniya*) to the Union and Union-republican ministries and the Union republics on the basis of the general directive of the government. This is usually in August.[1] The financial directives show the proposed general growth of the budget, and the main purposes for which the extra sums available are to be used, and indicate specific measures which are to be taken in connexion with separate items of revenue and expenditure in order that the plan shall be fulfilled. The lower bodies issue more detailed financial directives to the enterprises and executive committees under them. In compiling its estimate (for bodies 'on the budget') or financial plan including proposed budget grants (for *khozraschot* bodies), each unit should have before it the details of its expected results for the current year, and the basic draft production indices, wage funds, numbers of employees, and capital investment allocations with which it will be expected to conform in the forthcoming year. The estimate or financial plan thus compiled is now examined by the higher body, and incorporated by it in an overall estimate or plan. This stage is, in theory, completed by the end of October.[2] In practice delays are frequent at each step, so that a factory may have to draw up its financial plan without adequate knowledge of the draft production plan (or the financial plan may be drawn up for it by the *glavk* without its participation), and the whole stage may be either considerably delayed or take place in a very formal manner.

The appropriate financial organ now examines these overall estimates and financial plans. At the centre, for instance, the estimates commission of the NKF examines the estimates and financial plans of all-Union ministries, and the budgets of republican SNK's. This is the point in budgetary planning at which the most serious clashes arise. The ministry or republic asks for larger budgetary grants than were originally proposed for it in order to fulfil its plan; NKF tries to pare down the new allocation demanded.[3] The

---

[1] For the 1932 plan, for instance, on 8. viii. 1931.   [2] E.g. 25. viii.–20. x. 1931.

[3] 'Here...there are customarily very sharp struggles between NKF and the departments, for every NK is more interested in receiving more from budget financing, since that is more guaranteed, than in depending on its own internal accumulations' (*TsIK* 3/vi, Bull. no. 17, pp. 6–7). 'In the analysis of branch financial plans a number of disagreements generally arise between Narkomfin of the U.S.S.R. and the departments

gap which had to be bridged in the case of the republican budgets as a whole, for example, remained moderately large throughout the period,[1] in spite of the safeguards introduced to prevent this, and as late as 1938 individual republics were demanding allocations up to twice as large as those they were granted.[2] This illustrates the extent to which departure from the original government directive was possible in the course of compiling the plan.[3]

After the draft estimates have been examined in this way, the figures accepted by NKF as suitable budget allocations and possible receipts are combined by it into a draft budget unifying the estimates of all departments. This budget incorporates, of course, only those items in the financial plans of *khozraschot* bodies which are redistributed through the budget (e.g. turnover tax and deductions from profits on the revenue side and allocations to capital investments and subsidies on the expenditure side), though the financial plans themselves are attached to the budget in appendices. By this time (usually December) the final national economic plan has generally been adopted by the government, and the draft budget is adjusted to allow for the variations of the plan from the original directives.

The concluding stages in the adoption of the budget have now been reached. It is submitted to Gosplan, and then passes on with the conclusions of Gosplan to SNK. This is usually in December.[4] In this version the revenue and expenditure of the all-Union and

[receiving budget grants]' (Shenger, *op. cit.* p. 105). In 1938 the NK of the timber industry presented six different claims for grants, varying from 1672 to 1732 million roubles, but SNK eventually granted only 1067 million roubles; the NK of light industry demanded 808 million roubles in additional working capital, but were eventually granted only 369 million (*Second Session of the Supreme Soviet...* (1938), p. 115).

[1] This is illustrated by these examples (in milliard roubles):

	Demanded by republics	Allocated by government
1929/30	3·6	3·1
1938	45·1	37·7

(*TsIK* 2/v, Bull. no. 3, pp. 21–2; *Supreme Soviet...* (1938), pp. 114–15).

[2] Thus the Kirghiz S.S.R., which expended 235 million roubles in 1937, claimed 617 million roubles in 1938, but was actually allocated only 313 million roubles (*Supreme Soviet...* (1938), pp. 114–15).

[3] This departure may have been because (*a*) the original directives were put in very general terms leaving considerable flexibility in drawing up the plans at lower levels, (*b*) the republics considered that more money than was allocated in the directives was needed in order to fulfil the plan (or felt it was necessary to claim this in order to ensure a reasonable grant), or (*c*) new proposals were added to the original plan by the local bodies.

[4] E.g. 1. xii. 1931. From the later 1930's, the budget and the plan have been sent *direct* to SNK, with a *copy* to Gosplan.

republican budgets are shown in detail, but the local budgets are included only in general terms. SNK has to resolve any differences still remaining between the all-Union ministries, the republican SNK's, Gosplan, and the NKF.

Finally, the budget as approved by SNK is ratified by the U.S.S.R. Supreme Soviet, after being examined by the budget commissions of the Soviet of the Union and the Soviet of Nationalities.[1] This generally takes place in March. By this time the national economic plan has been finally approved by the government, and the economic year has already begun, and so only minor amendments can be introduced on the expenditure side. Proposals for new expenditure are in fact generally referred back to SNK. Of course, increases in revenue thought practicable by the budget commissions are easily incorporated into the final budget. The budget debates are generally used by deputies to air grievances about under-allocations to expenditures on local matters and to individual projects, and to expose weaknesses in the financial and general work of ministries, including all-Union ministries, and in particular in the work of NKF and its local organs. The budget debates and the work of the budget commissions act as an auxiliary control, but they are not essential to the operation of the budget. Other economic and financial plans, including the national-economic plan itself, do not have to be approved by the Supreme Soviet, but only by SNK.

After the approval of the budget, the Ministries and *glavki* then have to make readjustments in the provisional amounts which they have allocated to economic or administrative units, who generally are notified of their final allocation only after a considerable delay. From the point of view of the lower unit, what is taking place is a series of adjustments in its output and financial plans as a result of changed orders from above. After the final plan has been approved, financial and costs plans are generally left unchanged, but changes in output plans continue to be made throughout the year, so that the financial and output plans of a factory are often incompatible.

9. THE BUDGET AND THE NATIONAL ECONOMIC PLAN

Although the budget is an operative plan, it does not form a part of the national economic plan, or of the original government direc-

---

[1] Before 1938 it was approved by a general session of TsIK, after being examined by a single budget commission.

tives. However, the crucial budget figures, as we have seen, do not have an independent existence but are built up at each stage on the draft or final figures of the national economic plan. In view of the complexity of this process, the main principles by which the budget figures are reached from the economic plan targets can be indicated only schematically here.[1]

The national economic plan itself consists of a series of crucial tables of production indices, some in physical terms and some in money terms.[2] It is supplemented by an equally crucial supply plan, which shows how production is to be distributed between ministries and departments if the national economic plan is to be fulfilled.[3]

The principal item of budget expenditure, 'expenditure on the national economy', is a composite item including the budgetary grants required by all the branches of the economy in order to fulfil their plans. The allocation to each branch is derived from the data in the national economic plan roughly as follows:

(1) The national economic plan shows the planned production of the branch both in physical terms and in money terms, in current prices.[4] It also shows the main items of production costs, the unit costs of the principal types of production, the planned lowering of costs (as a percentage of costs in the previous year), and the wage fund for the industry. Finally it shows in current or index prices the amount of capital investment which the industry may carry out. Table 27 illustrates this by an example from the 1941 plan.

(2) From these figures, the planned marketed production can be calculated in real terms. The transfer prices of the type of production concerned are known from a separate list (not part of the plan). Hence the planned receipts from the sale of output can be calculated.

(3) The data in the plan also enable the planned overall commercial cost of production (factory cost plus overheads plus trading costs) to be ascertained.

(4) Receipts (from stage 2 above) minus commercial cost (stage 3) gives total planned profit.

---

[1] For details, see Rovinskii, *op. cit.* chs. v–x, xiv–xviii, Shenger, *op. cit.* and G. F. Doundoukov, *La planification financière*....

[2] This is best illustrated by the *1941 Plan*, published by the American Council of Learned Societies.

[3] For details of the supply plan, see E. Yu. Lokshin, *Planirovanie material'no-tekhnicheskogo snabzheniya narodnogo khozyaistva SSSR* (1952).

[4] Until the late 1930's, it showed the value of production only in 1926/7 index prices. Values in current prices had to be derived from this by means of a conversion factor.

(5) The distribution of this total profit must now be calculated. It can be distributed in four ways:

(i) To the Director's Fund. This is a simple percentage of planned profit.

Table 27. *National economic plan data used in compiling the state budget: example of NK of coal industry, 1941*

1. Coal output (million tons)	171·2 (a) (1)	
Gross production in 1926/7 prices (million roubles)	2,687·0 (b)	
Commodity production in current wholesale prices	16,200 (c)	
2. Reduction in costs (% of average level of 1940)	−6·3	
Economy (million roubles)	408	
Comparable commodity production in 1941 at costs of 1941 (in million roubles)	6,069	
Full cost of all commodity production	6,206	
Sum of expenditure:		
Raw and other materials	1,435	
Fuel and electric energy	219	(d)
Wages plus additions	3,622	
Depreciation	209	
Other	439	
	5,924	
Trading-*sbyt* and other extra factory costs	285	
Coal: cost per ton	29 r. 85 k.	
Timber: cost per m.³	33 r. 50 k.	

3 (e).

	Number of persons (thousands)	Average wage (roubles)	Wage fund (million roubles)
Workers in industry	487·6	5,475	2,669·6
Engineering and technical workers	19·5	13,876	270·58
Charge hands	21·9	10,247	224·4
Clerical workers (*sluzhashchie*)	14·53	5,231	76·0
[Other	36·47	2,904	105·93]
Total for the industry	580·0	—	3,346·51
Other branches of economy	125·3	4,203	526·6
[Other	25·3		204·23]
Total	730·6	—	4,077·34

Productivity per worker in industry: 5,511 roubles
Ibid. as % of expected fulfilment in 1940: 110·6 %

4. Capital investment (excluding decentralised expenditure) 1,680·00 } (f)
   Put into operation   1,625·00 }

Sources: All from *1941 Plan:* (a) p. 13; (b) p. 9; (c) p. 11; (d) p. 568; (e) p. 514; (f) p. 483.

Note: (1) For NK Coal Industry only. Electric power, slate, etc., produced by this NK are shown on pp. 12 ff. of the plan.

(ii) To increased working capital. The needs of the enterprise in new working capital depend on the stocks, etc., it requires to meet its expanded production programme, less any extra resources it acquires from increases in unpaid wages (due to increases in the wage fund), etc.

(iii) To capital investment. The total requirements of the branch in capital investment are known from the plan.[1] From this sum is deducted the investment resources made available through the depreciation allowance, from economies in the stocks held by the construction body ('mobilisation of the internal resources of construction'), and other minor items. The remainder is then met from profits.

(iv) To the budget. Any remaining profit, and in any case a minimum of 10%, is deducted into the budget.

(6) In the course of the above calculations, deficits may have appeared (*a*) in deducting commercial costs from receipts (stage 4), (*b*) in meeting requirements in increased working capital from profits (stage 5 ii), (*c*) in making allocations to capital investment (stage 5 iii).

In all these cases an allocation must be made from the budget to cover the gap. The total for each of these purposes (subsidies, increased working capital, and capital investment), plus various miscellaneous allocations, comprises the total budget allocation for the branch.

A further complication may arise in the course of compiling the financial plans on which the budget allocation rests. The government may decide to lower the transfer prices of industrial goods in some branches, so that the reduction in costs does not appear entirely in the form of profits to the branch, but is partly passed on to other industries in the form of lower input prices (in the case of consumer goods, it is passed on either to the public in reduced prices or to the budget in extra turnover tax). On the other hand, the transfer prices of certain goods may be raised, in order to increase the profit of the branch concerned, or to reduce its losses and hence the subsidy if needs. In either case, both the receipts of the branch concerned and the costs of the branches to which it is selling will have to be adjusted. This will affect the size of the profits of all the enterprises concerned, and hence budget allocations and receipts will have to be adjusted accordingly.

The calculation of the other items of budgetary expenditure is based on more simple principles. For a number of services financed by the budget the economic plan shows the targets in physical terms—the number of schools and pupils, the number of places in hospitals, the number of doctors, etc. These are then transformed into money

---

[1] These requirements take into account the reduction in construction costs as laid down in the plan.

terms by the use of an elaborate system of 'norms'.[1] These norms, which do not form part of the plan, show in physical terms the permitted average amount of food per patient per day, the quantity of equipment of various types per pupil, the number of teachers per class, etc. These physical norms are supposed to vary widely by season and by region.[2] They are translated into 'financial' or 'budget' norms[3] by calculating their cost at the fixed prices and rates of wages. For overall planning, a number of individual norms is combined into a single consolidated measure of cost', which shows for example the average current expenditure per pupil or per hospital bed per year. These 'consolidated measures' resemble the 'unit costs' of school dinners approved by the British Ministry of Education.[4] The budget allocation for each item is found by multiplying the planned number of physical units (pupils, etc.) by the budget norm.[5]

The calculation of budgetary revenue does not present any special difficulties. The method of estimating deductions from profits has already been outlined. For turnover tax the retail sales of goods are calculated from the plan of commodity production, and the expected amount of tax is then assessed by using data on average retail prices and average rates of tax for each main type of production. The income tax on the population is calculated from the planned wage fund and the estimated ratio of the average rate of tax to the rate of tax on the average wage (the 'coefficient of operation of progression'). The agricultural tax is calculated by estimating the probable future income of collective farmers and its structure from the point of view of taxation, from a variety of data obtained from the taxation and statistical organs, and from the agricultural departments of the local soviets. Similar methods are used to estimate the expected revenue from other taxes.

[1] The 'norms' of Soviet industrial costing and budget estimates correspond very closely to the cost standards, unit costs, output rates, and job rates of British and United States practice; the one term 'norms' is used to cover all of these concepts.
[2] Certain norms are *obligatory* either as maxima (e.g. number of administrative staff) or as minima (e.g. amount of food and frequency of changes of bed-linen per person). Others are *orienting*—i.e. used for planning purposes and without the force of law—and are supposed to be differentiated for each area according to local conditions, although in practice local differentiations were often absent or rather crude.
[3] The term 'financial norms' refers to all norms in money terms for all bodies. The term 'budget norm' refers to the financial norm for institutions all of whose expenditure is covered by the budget (e.g. elementary schools), or to that part of the financial norm of institutions partly financed from other sources (e.g. kindergartens) which is covered by the budget. [4] See V. J. Oxley, *Local government financial statistics* (1951), p. 44.
[5] Capital investment in schools, etc., is financed directly from the budget in accordance with the data of the national economic plan.

10. BALANCING THE BUDGET

The process by which the budget is balanced after these initial estimates of revenue and expenditure have been made can be discussed only in very general terms, as detailed information on the methods and practices by which this is done has not been published.

In the course of compiling the overall synthetic balances on which the original government directives and the final national economic plan are based, the planners are supposed to have ensured that the price structure shall be such as to bring about a rough financial balance. For example, the plan may provide for an increased level of expenditure on investment, defence or the social and cultural services. This increase in 'unproductive' expenditure will cause the total wage fund to rise more rapidly than the wage fund and the output of the consumer goods industry at current prices. Therefore retail prices would have to be raised to draw back in the form of a tax the extra money wages issued to the population (or looked at in another way, the shift to investment will lead to extra budget expenditure which would have to be covered by extra revenue in the form of a higher tax). Speaking more generally, any change in output and its allocation, and in costs, must involve a corresponding change in prices on the retail market and in direct taxation if both the money incomes and expenditures of the population and the expenditure and revenue of the budget are to be balanced.

Obviously, therefore, if the budget is badly out of balance after it has been compiled, this must be due to misplanning at the stage of synthetic planning. Retail prices should have been raised (to yield more tax) or lowered (to enable the population to buy all the available goods with their existing wages).[1] In practice, of course, this 'misplanning' may be deliberate—the government often decided that a lack of financial balance and consequent goods shortages were preferable to an increase in retail prices to the extent needed.

A small deficit could be met by various auxiliary means which did not involve altering prices or the production targets of the national economic plan. For instance, costs could be reduced more than

---

[1] If there is a large planned surplus in the budget, it would not in fact be received unless the population had sufficient purchasing power to buy the available supply of goods at prevailing prices; if it did not, there would instead be a goods surplus. A large deficit would generally mean both an actual deficit and a goods shortage. It must also be borne in mind that the budget surplus or deficit alone does not show the real money position in the economy, but must be considered in conjunction with the extra credits issued by the bank via the credit plan.

originally planned by raising productivity (so that wages per unit of output would fall) or by reducing the amount of materials, fuel, etc., used per unit of output. This would yield greater profits in the branch, and hence in 'deficit' branches would reduce the need for a budget allocation, and in 'surplus' branches would increase revenue from deductions from profits. The deficit could also be reduced by cutting the expenditure of institutions on the budget, within the framework of the national economic plan, by reducing their norms of expenditure per unit. This could be done by reducing the staff per pupil (e.g. by increasing the size of classes), per government department, etc., or by reducing expenditure on materials. This could only be done on a limited scale if the quality of the service were not to be impaired.[1] On the other hand, if there were a surplus in the budget, the quality of a service could be raised by increasing the expenditure per unit.

Disclosing these auxiliary 'reserves' is a major task of the financial organs in the course of compiling the budget. To the extent that the financial organ is able to reduce the budget allocation needed without lowering standards, it can be responsible for an improvement in efficiency which enables resources to be used for other purposes. But if this is not possible, the budget can be balanced only by increasing taxation, primarily by manipulating the retail price structure.

In this analysis of Soviet financial planning and the budget, we have come rather a long way from our original discussion of the role of the budget and finance in the planning system. We then saw that the key problem of financial planning was to accumulate and redistribute the resources of the economy in financial terms, to raise and control the money needed to enable the production plans to be carried out. The original model which showed how this is done through profits and turnover tax should not be lost from view among the refinements of the financial system which have been outlined. These refinements were often essential to the efficient working of the system in practice. They were often innovations as compared with financial practice in other countries (e.g. the strictly delimited short-term credit system), and sometimes merely continued in a somewhat

---

[1] According to Rovinskii, *op. cit.* p. 188, 'when the amount of expenditure is changed to balance the budget the norms serve as a criterion of the limit of these changes and guarantee the maintenance of a minimum of budget allocations'.

changed form the financial methods of N.E.P. (e.g. the income tax on the population). But they must be seen as secondary to the main problem. What primarily distinguishes the Soviet planning system from other economic systems is that capital investment is planned centrally by the state. The main criterion in assessing the efficiency of the financial system must be the success or otherwise with which it is adapted to this main function of the planning system.

It must also be borne in mind that although a study of the Soviet financial and economic system often discloses principles of general importance and applicable to any system of direct planning, it was a specific system, emerging from Russian historical conditions and adapted to the specific task of turning an underdeveloped peasant country into an advanced industrial nation. The Soviet budgetary system can be fully understood only if it is firmly placed in its historical context. The predominance of accumulation through the budget and through turnover tax rather than through the profits of industry, the financial relations of agriculture with the state, and various other features of Soviet budgetary planning discussed in this chapter, resulted from the specific tasks of Soviet planning.

In the next chapters, Soviet financial and budgetary planning is put into its context. The emergence and operation of the 'working model' of the financial system which we have constructed is illustrated by discussing the actual development of the budget during the three pre-war five-year plans against the background of the growth of the economy as a whole.

CHAPTER VII

THE BREAKDOWN OF THE OLD BUDGETARY SYSTEM 1928-30

I. FAILURE OF THE ACCUMULATION PLANS

THE central financial problem of the first five-year plan (1928/9–1932), finally adopted in April 1929,[1] was the problem of accumulation. The plan was an ambitious programme for the industrialisation of the U.S.S.R.: gross investment in fixed capital was to rise from 28% of the national income in 1927/8 to 39% in 1932/3; of this a quarter was to be investment in industry direct, primarily heavy industry.[2] The realisation of the plan was primarily conceived in terms of the large shifts in material resources which it would involve —in terms, for example, of the rapid increase in the urban population and the consequent need to double the marketable surplus of food supplies during the five years. But it was hoped that appropriate measures for financial accumulation would enable industrialisation to be carried through without inflation. This was considered to be most important, for the necessary food supplies, for example, would be voluntarily yielded by the peasantry only if the inflationary situation of 1928 and 1929 was eliminated and the retail price of non-agricultural goods did not rise. But the extra purchasing power earned by the new labour force in industry provided for by the plan, was likely to worsen the inflationary situation. How could the necessary financial resources for investment be raised without resort to currency issue on a large scale?

The solution to the accumulation problem envisaged by the drafters of the first five-year plan was based on two material proposals made in the plan: first, that there should be a considerable

---

[1] SZ 268/1929 (23. iv. 29), 311/1929 (28. v. 29).
[2] See *Pyatiletnii plan narodno-khozyaistvennogo stroitelstva SSSR*, vol. 1 (1930), pp. 164-5. These figures include depreciation.

increase (103%) in the output of consumer goods,[1] and secondly, that labour productivity should rise rapidly (by 110%), and more rapidly than the rise in wages. The mechanism envisaged for accumulation was essentially simple. As a result of the planned rise in labour productivity, costs would be reduced 30–35% by the end of the plan, falling more rapidly in the consumer goods industry (group B) than in the producer goods industry (group A). But transfer prices in both branches, and retail prices of industrial consumer goods, would be reduced by an average of 19% to 'take up' part of this planned reduction in costs. The 'gap' (*razryv*) between cost price and transfer price would therefore increase by 11% (14% in group B and 5·5% in group A).[2] Part of this accumulation was to be transferred from group B to group A through the budget, and the long-term bank and the budget were to retain the right to make further redistribution where necessary. But a large part of the accumulation from the reduction in costs was to be retained by industry for its own expansion. As a result,

> By the end of the five year period the relative weight of the budget system in the general financial system will be somewhat reduced...the budget will slowly yield its position on this front [the socialised sector], giving way to the more rapid growth of the system of finance of production organisations....The importance of the budgetary system will be slowly weakened in view of the growth of the own resources of economic organs, rising during the five years from 17·8% to 23·3% [of the whole financial plan].[3]

In short, the method of accumulation during the five-year plan was to be a combination of investment through profits (method 1 of chapter VI) with investments through the budget (method 2 of chapter VI), but the importance of method 1 was to increase steadily throughout the period. The financial plan did 'not propose any radical reconstruction of the financial system'.[4] The existing structure of budgetary revenue, the principal taxes (such as the Promtax and excises), and even the traditional divisions into 'tax' and 'non-tax' revenue, were retained in the financial plan of the five-year plan. No radical reform of the banking system was contemplated. But

---

[1] This was, of course, considerably less than the planned increase of 204% in the producer goods industries (these figures refer to *all* industry, in the maximum version of the plan).

[2] These figures for cost and price reduction refer to the minimum version of the plan, which involved a costs reduction of 30%; I have not managed to find a similar breakdown for the maximum variant's cost reduction target of 35%.

[3] M. I. Bogolepov, *Finansovyi plan pyatiletiya* (1929), pp. 12 ff., 28; *Pyatiletnii plan...*, vol. I, chs. v, VII and IX, and appendix tables.   [4] Bogolepov, *op. cit.* p. 11.

although no change was intended in the administrative structure of the financial system, the relative size of the parts would have changed markedly if the plan had been achieved; financing of industry through the budget and the general financial strain which this involved in 1927–9 would have taken second place to financing through the increased internal savings of industry.

A number of economists and financial experts were very sceptical about the possibilities of the success of the financial plan of the first five-year plan. They considered that the proposed reduction in costs was not feasible, and therefore that the five-year plan could be financed only through continued inflation. This they regarded as dangerous to the point of folly, and they therefore (at least privately) opposed the high targets of the plan.[1] In this they were joined during 1929 by the Right opposition inside the Communist Party.[2]

The compilers of the financial section of the five-year plan did not admit that further inflation was an inevitable consequence of the high targets of the plan. The financial plan was as it were 'adjusted' to make the carrying-out of the plan without inflation seem feasible. The original target for cost reduction in industry of 26% was raised to 30, 32, and eventually to 35%, and the target for price reduction was cut from 23 to 19%.[3] But the achievement of the financial plan depended on the fulfilment of a programme for increasing labour productivity which, to say the least, was optimistic. In fact the planners admitted that their work was experimental and needed considerable improvement;[4] it is characteristic that six months after the date on which the plan formally began, the government instructed the planners to make the financial plan more precise.[5]

The position of the leaders of the government seems to have been that they were conscious that there was a considerable risk that the goods shortage would continue, and that the programme for costs reduction in industry would not be achieved. But they considered that these risks were necessary for the long-term security of the Soviet

[1] For examples of this view, see articles by A. A. Sokolov, L. N. Yurovskii and S. T. Kistenev in *Finansy i narodnoe khozyaistvo*, nos. 38 and 43 (1928). For further references, see article by D. P. Bogolepov in *Ekon. obozrenie*, no. 2 (1929).

[2] See Bukharin's *Zametki ekonomista* in *Pravda*, November 1928, and references to this article and to letters of Frumkin in Stalin, *Soch.* vol. XI, pp. 245 ff., 318 ff., and vol. XII, pp. 1 ff.

[3] D. P. Bogolepov, *Ekon. oboz.* no. 2 (1929); M. I. Bogolepov, *op. cit.* and article in *Ekon. oboz.* no. 4 (1929), pp. 36–51, and SZ 268/1929 (23. iv. 1929).

[4] 'The problems of the reconstruction of the financial system must be the object of special care throughout the five-year period' (Bogolepov, *op. cit.* p. 11).

[5] SZ 268/1929 (23. iv. 1929).

system. Industrialisation must be carried out whether or not it resulted in inflation.[1]

The experience of the first two years of the plan (1928/9 and 1929/30) justified the view that the financial provisions of the plan were optimistic. Labour productivity rose, but not to the extent demanded by the plan,[2] and as a result the industrial labour force increased more than had been planned. Even so, the production programmes of industry were under-fulfilled, and as during the course of the plan the government had raised the targets for investment in heavy industry, the output of consumer goods lagged considerably behind the plan. At the same time foodstuffs were not surrendered by the peasantry in the required quantities, even under extreme pressure, and consequently the government was compelled in 1930 to embark on a policy of mass collectivisation in order to make sure that essential food supplies would be forthcoming.

The financial plan of the five-year plan had been based on the premiss that both labour productivity and the supply of consumer goods would increase rapidly, and the failure to fulfil the plan in both these respects led to a swift deterioration in the financial situation. Neither industrial consumer goods nor foodstuffs were available in quantities sufficient to meet the planned increases in the purchasing power of the urban population. In theory, this situation could have been dealt with by restrictions on wages. In practice the pressure on managements to fulfil their output programme was much greater than the pressure on them to keep within their costs plans. As a result the average wage rose above the planned level in 1928/9 and 1929/30, and costs fell less than was planned, particularly in new enterprises producing investment goods. Hence urban purchasing power was considerably in excess of the planned level. The government again suppressed the inflation by price-control: the goods shortages of 1926–8 were repeated on a larger scale, and the decline in food supplies to the towns forced the government to introduce rationing from 1929 onwards.

[1] Thus at the end of 1928 Stalin admitted that the goods shortage would continue for three or four years (*Soch.* vol. XI, pp. 266–8). See also *Pravda*, 11. xi. 1929: 'The phenomena of currency circulation are not the cause but the consequence of economic difficulties, having their roots in the depth of production and class relationships in our country.'

[2] Measured in 1926/7 index prices, it is stated to have risen by 12·2% in 1928, 12·9% in 1929, 9·7% in 1930, 7·6% in 1931, and 2·6% in 1932 (*Sots. str* (1935), p. xx). W. Galenson, *Labour productivity in Soviet and American industry* (1955), calculates labour productivity in industry as follows (1928=100, 1928 employment weights)—1929: 111·9, 1930: 116·4, 1931: 118·3, 1932: 110·4, 1933: 119·8.

From the point of view of the budgetary and credit system, this situation was a reflection of the fact that extra money was being pumped into the system. The budgets of the first five-year plan were essentially expenditure-determined. The money needed to finance the required shifts of labour from agriculture to industry, and within industry, was issued through the financial system, often to an extent greatly exceeding the plan. Part of this money was subsequently withdrawn from circulation in taxes, etc. But the issue of new money led to inflation. Although the state budget itself was always balanced *post factum* over a year or a quarter, or even showed a surplus, budget and net credit expansion taken together exceeded budget receipts and loan repayments to the banks in each period. Currency circulation therefore rose.[1] This was a clear indication of 'deficit financing'. Moreover, even when new money issues were subsequently withdrawn, this was done only by imposing retail taxes which had the effect of raising the price level inside the state sector of the retail market. The effect of increased budgetary expenditure (ultimately increasing the wages paid out to workers in investment industries, etc.) was to spread the supply of consumer goods over both the old and the new workers in industry, and to concentrate it on those with higher wages within the new wage pattern.[2] In the sense that budget expenditure and taxation were accompanied by a rising price-level, the methods used to finance the five-year plan can be described as 'inflationary' or 'deficit' financing.

In this system, the budget played the major part. It was shown earlier that the five-year plan had originally envisaged that the budget would decline in importance during the period in favour of 'intra-industrial accumulation'. But as costs did not fall to the planned extent in 1928/9 and 1929/30, the anticipated 'gap' between cost price and transfer price did not appear, and hence industrial profits were less than planned. Moreover, to prevent a decline in budgetary revenue from profits, the percentage of profits deducted into the budget was increased. The internal accumulation available to industry to meet its investment programme was therefore absolutely less than had been planned. But, as we have seen, both

---

[1] For details of currency circulation in this period, see Arnold, *op. cit.* pp. 404–27.

[2] The position was complicated by the fact that prices in state trade did not rise sufficiently for shortages to disappear. Hence there was rationing and queueing in the state sector, and a 'black market' outside it. Part of urban wages was diverted to the peasantry through this free market, and the peasantry were by this means partly compensated for the tax in kind imposed on them through compulsory deliveries.

the costs of investment and the amount of investment in real terms were greater than those provided for in the original plan. This expenditure could be financed only by unplanned increases in budgetary allocations to industry in 1928/9 and 1929/30.[1] By the last quarter of 1930 (the 'special quarter', October to December), the budget was already established as the most important means of financing the expansion of industry.

The breakdown of the financial programme of the five-year plan was of cardinal importance for the future of the Soviet budgetary system. The main burden of regulating the financial system now had to be borne by the budget. The task of the budgetary system was both to limit expenditure to the minimum compatible with the fulfilment of the material production programmes, and to provide the mechanism by which the cash issues involved in this expenditure could be withdrawn from circulation. For the more modest tasks placed on the budget by the original five-year plan, the methods of collecting revenue and disbursing expenditure used in the 1920's may have been adequate, as was thought in 1929. But could the old budgetary system cope with the new tasks imposed upon it as a result of the failure to reduce costs to the planned extent? Could it deal satisfactorily with the inflationary situation of 1930?

2. THE SYSTEM OF BUDGETARY REVENUE

The N.E.P. system of taxation had evolved in an *ad hoc* fashion. After the civil war, certain taxes were revived from the period before the October revolution (for example, Promtax and excises), and certain new taxes were introduced, largely based on foreign experience (for example, the income tax). The distinctive contribution made by the Soviet experience to budgetary practice in the 1920's was the development of methods of taxation which discriminated against social and economic groups considered undesirable by the government. But clearly, as the importance of the private sector diminished, attention had to be increasingly directed towards the efficient taxation of the state sector. During 1925–8, as was shown in chapter v, the rates of excise, Promtax, stamp tax, and other established taxes on the state sector were frequently increased, but without any

---

[1] Planned expenditure on industry in 1929/30, for example, was 1,886 million roubles; fulfilment was 2,166 million roubles (unified budget). I have not been able to trace comparable data for 1928/9. (SZ 720/1929, 8. xii. 1929; *Otchot*... (1931), p. 133.)

fundamental changes in the method of taxation. The compilers of the first five-year plan recognised that revenue could not be increased appreciably by greater direct taxation of the private sector or of the population, and accepted the general principle that accumulation had to be made through the adjustment of wholesale and retail prices by the government. But partly as a result of their illusions about the prospects of costs reduction in industry, they believed that the N.E.P. system of taxation could be retained in the planning period without any changes in principle.

The first two years of the five-year plan provided the final proof in practice that a thorough-going reform of the taxation system was required. The unplanned increases in budgetary expenditure could be met only by drastic increases in the level of indirect taxation. The rate of deduction from profits was sharply increased,[1] but owing to the under-fulfilment of profits plans, the revenue from this source barely reached the planned level.[2] A budget deficit was avoided by increasing the level of excises and Promtax on goods with mass sales such as vodka and tobacco.[3] The strain which these increases placed on the old system of indirect taxation finally revealed that it was inadequate to cope with the new tasks imposed on it. It became essential to introduce new taxes designed to collect as revenue, through the price mechanism, the large additions to purchasing power issued to the population in the course of fulfilling the plan.

Even before the accumulation plans of the five-year plan broke down, the system of taxing state enterprises had been strongly criticised, notably in two reports issued by the RKI[4] in 1928 and 1930. These reports recognised that the efficient operation and extension of indirect taxation was seriously hindered by complications and

[1] For details, see ch. v, Table 22, p. 120.
[2] The planned amount of profit deductions to the budget was 275 million roubles in 1928/9 and 821 in 1929/30; the actual budgetary revenue from this source was 287 million roubles in 1928/9 and 847 in 1929/30 (N.P. Bryukhanov, *Khozyaistvennyi pod"em...* (1929), pp. 20–3; *Sots. str.* (1935), pp. 644–5; SZ 720/1929 (8. xii. 29); *TsIK* 2/v).
[3] Excises and Promtax taken together were planned at 2,841 million roubles in 1928/9 and 4,041 in 1929/30; the actual yield was 2,859 and 4,584 (SZ 638/1928 (15. xii. 28); *Sots. str.* (1935), pp. 644–5; SZ 720/1929 (8. xii. 29); *TsIK* 2/v). For increased tax on vodka, SZ 599/1928, 94/1929 (6. ii. 1929), 591–2/1929 (27. ix. 29) and 630/1929 (21. x. 29). As a result of all these measures the tax rose from 2r. 81k. per litre to 3r. 81k. (but the Promtax was abolished). For cigarettes and tobacco, see SZ 431/1929 (29. vii. 29) and 123/1930 (18. ii. 30). A tax of 10–50% of the wholesale price was introduced on cosmetics (SZ 54/1930 (16. i. 30)). For other sources of additional revenue in 1930 see *TsIK* 2/v, Bull. no. 3, pp. 3–5, 15.
[4] The RKI was at this time responsible *inter alia* for supervising the operation of the financial system.

inconsistencies. The system introduced in 1922, they stated, was entirely based on pre-revolutionary legislation. This had been inevitable at that time, both because there had been no previous experience of an economy of the N.E.P. type, and because in the early 1920's taxation had to be levied principally on the private sector. It was true that the original financial system of 1922 had been modified as the economy developed, and major changes had been made in the methods of taxing the socialised sector. However (and this was the main point of the 1930 report), the financial machinery, 'consisting for the most part of old employees of the former Ministry of Finance, not only showed no initiative in adapting the tax system to the structure of the economy and to the changes taking place in it, but also opposed any large-scale changes in any way'.[1]

In the opinion of the RKI, the existing system of taxation was principally designed for the taxation of the private sector, and this made it unsuitable for the new conditions. The existence of sixty-two different taxes[2] could be justified by the need to make sure of catching the complex and tax-evading private sector in the taxation net, but socialised enterprises were 'only agents through which taxes and levies are imposed on the price of the commodity'. In the state sector, the system of taxation could be simple and straightforward. But in fact many separate taxes, such as the local tax on loads, which fell almost entirely on state enterprises, and the special levies on cotton and other products, were mere supplements to the Promtax, and others could be abolished without harm. The complexities of the existing system meant that every enterprise needed specialists in tax legislation, that every department of the NKF down to provincial level had to employ consultants on different types of taxes, and that NKF tax-collectors were forced to become narrow specialists in a particular tax. The planning of taxation was difficult, and anomalies inevitably appeared (the RKI mentioned as an instance that in 1928/9 the coal industry made a loss and the metallurgical industry made a profit, but the taxes on coal were larger than the taxes on metals). The complexities were particularly great in the case of excises and Promtax, the two main forms of tax. Both excises and

[1] As an example the report quoted *Vest. fin.* no. 5 (1928), p. 35, where it was suggested that no special form of taxation was necessary for state enterprises.

[2] This frequently quoted figure is somewhat exaggerated, for these 62 taxes included, for example, 12 excises. While each was formally a separate tax, the variation between them was not much greater than the variation between the turnover tax on different types of commodity.

Promtax had to be paid on commodities subject to excise, and Promtax usually had to be paid on a commodity every time it was transferred from one productive unit to another. As a result, the tax on, for example, leather footwear produced by different concerns, varied from 4·3–18·5% of value. These anomalies made price-fixing and imposing a proper level of taxation extremely intricate.

To solve these difficulties, RKI put forward a series of proposals for the reform of the taxation of the state sector. As early as 1928 it suggested 'the complete abolition of excises and the fusion of them with the Promtax into a single system of deductions from price', and made interim proposals designed to prevent the taxation of the same good more than once. Neither its immediate proposals nor its long-term policy seems to have met with the approval of the conservative Commissariat of Finance. Changes in the taxation system were forced through in 1928 and 1929, it was said, 'in spite of categorical and frequent protests from the NKF of the U.S.S.R.'. These changes were all in the direction of the unification and simplification of the taxation of state enterprises. First, various minor taxes were abolished: in August 1928, for example, the tax on valuables and the local additions to Promtax were fused with the basic Promtax.[1] Secondly, an attempt was made to reduce the complexity of both Promtaxes and excises by transferring the payment of these taxes from enterprise level to the centre—this was possible because trade in the main goods was now handled by centralised syndicates. Thus the payment of excises was gradually centralised: more than 2,000 taxpayers were replaced by a few dozen, and the number of NKF excise workers was cut from 3,500 to less than 200.[2] The most important step here was the final abolition of 'double taxation' on a number of important goods—in 1923, 1926 and 1928, this weakness had been partly corrected; and in 1929 the Promtax on textiles, tobacco, butter and sugar was changed so that it should be paid once and once only on each good.[3] Thirdly, excises and Promtax were gradually modified and brought nearer to each other in their structure. In 1928 the old-fashioned 'licence fee' by which part of Promtax had been paid was abolished and replaced by a single 'tax on turnover' (not to be confused with the turnover tax itself), which was imposed on net turnover and varied according to the type of enter-

[1] SZ 442–3/1928 (10. viii. 28).
[2] See *Uproshchenie finansovoi sistemy* (1930), p. 15 and SZ 11/1928 (21. xi. 27), 469/1928 (22. viii. 28).   [3] SZ 574/1929 (25. ix. 29).

prise. Promtax, like excises, was made payable on the turnover of the current instead of the previous year.[1] In 1929 the excise on textiles was fused with the Promtax and replaced by a single 'state Promtax on turnover on the sale of textile goods', paid monthly by the all-Union Textile Syndicate.[2] In the same month the Promtax on vodka was fused into the vodka excise, which thus became the only payment on vodka sales to the budget.[3]

Thus, by the end of 1929, in some branches of state industry an excise was paid as a fixed sum per item or unit weight of product sold; in others a Promtax was paid as a percentage of the net turnover on all the goods sold by the branch concerned; and in others both Promtax and excise were still paid. In addition all branches had to pay to the budget a number of minor and supplementary taxes and levies and a proportion of their profits. This system was generally recognised to require radical reform. But there was no agreement on the form which this reform should take; and the old system continued in operation until September 1930.

3. CONTROL OF EXPENDITURE

The rapid expansion of the budget during the first five-year plan made it essential to devise an efficient system for the control of expenditure. This involves three distinct types of control. The first, which may be called 'technical' control, is aimed at ensuring that budgetary allocations are in fact spent on the purposes for which they were made available. The second, which I call 'efficiency' control, aims at seeing that an allocation for an approved purpose is used as efficiently as possible. The third and broadest control will seek to ensure that the total available resources are put to the best possible use—in other words, to find criteria for choosing between one purpose of allocation and another: I call this 'economic' control. In attempting to establish each of these forms of control, the authorities have to steer a careful course between over-centralisation and too great a devolution of powers.

In the 1920's pre-revolutionary practices had been continued. Financial authorities had by and large confined their attention to 'technical' control. Approved grants were issued, as they were before the revolution, through the central and local pay-offices

---

[1] See ch. v, p. 121. [2] SZ 573/1929 (25. ix. 29).
[3] SZ 591–2/1929 (27. ix. 29).

(*kassy*) of NKF, and their expenditure was scrutinised by special central and local financial control authorities subordinate to NKF. 'Efficiency' control was more or less empirical and was not enforced through any definite machinery. There was some attempt to control the use of allocations by the unit-costing of such expenditures as general office and postal and telephone outlays, making them dependent on the size of the institutions,[1] but even this was unsystematic. 'Economic' control had been allowed to find its own solution through the elaborate mechanism for adopting the budget (see chapter IV, pp. 60–3). NKF had tried to confine the total budget within what it thought were practicable limits; the various government departments put in claims, which were then reduced during discussions with the estimates commission. The final decision on financial programmes rested with the Central Executive Committee of Soviets, helped by its budget commission; but in practice its powers were difficult to exercise, and the real power of choice between major alternatives lay with SNK and (unofficially) with the central organs of the Communist Party. In the method of arriving at the final budget figures there was at this time little difference in principle from the budgetary practice of most twentieth-century states.

From 1927 onwards budgetary expenditure on 'traditional' items increased rapidly, and the budget played an increasing part in financing economic expansion. All budget items, including 'normal' expenditures, became increasingly dependent on the economic plan; the size of money allocations was determined primarily by the physical and financial indices of the plans. All these developments led to changes in the control functions of the financial authorities. Broad policy decisions of choice between competing claimants for allocations came less and less within the province of the financial authorities: preparing the budget became less an independent act of policy, and more an administrative task arising out of planning decisions previously reached. Thus 'economic' control passed out of the province of the budgetary system as such. On the other hand, the growth of the budget increased the need for both 'technical' and 'efficiency' control. Important steps were taken during the initial stages of the five-year plan towards improving the efficiency of budgetary administration as a whole. The most outstanding of these was the abolition of the anachronistic and

[1] For criticisms of the methods used, see *TsIK* 2/III, p. 216; *Plenum byudzhetnoi komissii*..., pp. 95–7, 369–73, 381.

cumbersome pay-offices in 1928 and the consequent transfer of the administration of budgetary revenue and expenditure to the central and local organs of the State Bank,[1] a step which was made possible by the extensive establishment and expansion of branches of the bank in the preceding period.[2] The State Bank therefore now acted as a book-keeper for transfers of money between the exchequer and individual institutions and enterprises, as well as for the transfers between one enterprise and another through their current accounts with the bank.

But the central task of financial control during the first five-year plan was to ensure that budgetary expenditure on the economy was efficiently administered. In the early stages of accumulating resources for industrialisation, it had proved possible to use methods of raising revenue borrowed from a competitive economy; in spending these resources it was necessary to devise *ab initio* new methods of administration appropriate to the special problems of the state as the principal investor in the economy.

The only precedent in the Soviet Union was the financing of state-owned railway transport. It will be recalled that both before and after the revolution the railway system was financed by including its gross receipts and expenditures in the budget. The application of this system to state industry would simply have increased central jurisdiction over current production without solving the problem of investment control. In the period 1926–9 there was some attempt to provide a quasi-automatic means of securing efficient investment. Allocations to industry, from the budget as well as from other sources, were often made as loans. The industry receiving the allocation had to meet it from future profits or depreciation allowances, and therefore had some incentive to use the allocation efficiently, so that future profits, from which the loan would have to be repaid, would be at a maximum. As industrial prices were fixed by the government, this simply transferred the problem to the price-fixers, who would themselves be determining how much investment an industry could 'afford' when they fixed the level of its profits via price. This 'automatic' system was never fully worked out, and in any case the concentration of investment in heavy industry from 1929 onwards made the issue of repayable allocations impracticable.[3] The choice between one investment project and another was made by the

[1] SZ 481/1928 (22. vii. 28); 134/1929 (6. iii. 29); 282–3/1929 (24. iv. 29).
[2] Aleksandrov, *op. cit.* pp. 431–2.   [3] For reasons, see pp. 145-7.

planners, in accordance with government decisions, and in this the financial authorities played little part. Their task was to supply the necessary financial resources for a given plan.

But what were the 'necessary financial resources'? How was a given investment to be made at minimum cost? The mechanism developed for investment control from 1926 onwards accepted the current prices of labour and materials employed in construction and in making capital equipment as an adequate criterion for cost.[1] The problem was therefore to find the cheapest way in which a given construction job could be carried out as measured in current roubles.[2] In a planning system of the Soviet type there is an inherent opposition of interests between the central planning authorities and the individual industry or enterprise. The industry tries to secure the maximum possible financial allocation for a given job, especially since no charge is made for budget grants. Even when a grant is fixed, the industry will tend to overspend it and ask for a further allocation. The central planners, on the other hand, will try to persuade the industry to manage with a very tight allocation, especially as it is aware that the claim made by the industry is probably exaggerated. Thus the struggle between competing claims at the stage when investment *decisions* are made is followed by a good deal of pushing and pulling when agreed jobs are costed. Only a long period of practical experience can gradually evolve a reasonably satisfactory compromise.

In the course of forming the planning system, an important task was to bring investment under central control and to reconcile the projects of each industry with the national plan. In the period from 1923 to 1927, each industry, and subordinate regional and functional groups of enterprises, had been instructed to proceed in such a way as to make the maximum profit. The reconstruction of industry had been guided by state intervention, but had been considerably influenced by the market. The programme of industrialisation on the other hand had to be carried through by controlling the expansion of industry rigidly from the centre, while permitting the current pro-

[1] Only a small depreciation charge had to be paid on machinery and other capital used for construction and for making equipment. This capital was allocated by the planners; and the financial authorities assessing construction costs and the price of equipment took this allocation as given.

[2] I ignore here the problem of how the choice was made between variants for the same investment project, as this was the concern of technical staff and planners and not the financial authorities.

duction of industry to be carried on on a profit-making basis. This meant, as was explained in chapter v, that not only the investment programmes but also the programmes of current industrial production and its allocation had to be gradually brought under central control. Therefore the part played by the profit motive in determining current production as well as investment was fairly small. Money became an auxiliary to centralised planning in physical terms, and this created a need for fundamental changes both in the organisation of the current finances of industry and in the methods of making grants to industry from central funds.

To bring about centralised control of investment a thorough reorganisation was necessary. In the first place the method of planning new construction projects was systematised.[1] Gradually each stage of drafting was systematised throughout industry, and model projects were drawn up for those construction jobs which were repeated in a similar form elsewhere. To each stage of project-making there corresponded an estimate or plan showing the resources required in financial terms, on the basis of which the allocation required from the budget could be worked out.

Secondly, the general principle was established that all projects valued above a certain ceiling (*limit*) in money terms (known as 'above-limit' projects) were subject to central approval. This 'limit' varied according to the branch or sub-branch of the economy concerned. The most important projects were included by name in a list (*titul'nyi spisok*) approved by the U.S.S.R. government as a part of the capital investment plan. A lower set of limits was also fixed, and projects whose value was in excess of these had to be approved in more detail by the Council of Labour and Defence or by VSNKh.[2] These arrangements cut across the division of industry into Union, republican, and local: whether a project had to be approved by the all-Union authorities was determined not by whether it was under Union, republican, or local control, but by its value. This gave VSNKh, the planning organs, and the government a considerable degree of control over all major investment projects throughout the U.S.S.R.

---

[1] The precise stages by which a fully worked-out system of drafting these projects was evolved are of little interest; and the developed system will be discussed in later chapters. The main decrees in which this development may be studied are SZ 97/1926 (17. ii. 26); 201/1927 (22. iii. 27); 672/1927 (23. xi. 1927); 199/1928 (23. iv. 28).

[2] Details of these developments may be found in the following decrees: SZ 341/1926 (24. v. 26); 610/1926 (30. xi. 26); 255/1927 (3. v. 27); 373/1927 (8. vi. 27); 696/1927 (25. xi. 27); 180/1928 (20. iii. 28); 297/1928 (1. vi. 28); 244/1929 (11. iv. 29); 412/1929 (6. vii. 29); 413/1929 (8. vii. 29).

The third problem was to find a satisfactory method of supervising the use of approved allocations. The most urgent task here was to bring under central control the various sources from which investment projects were financed. To this end budget grants, bank loans, the profits of industry, and other sources for financing investment had to be brought under central control. In 1927 the Department of Long-term Credits of the Industrial Bank, attached to VSNKh, was made responsible for issuing all moneys for financing the expansion of industry, both loans and grants.[1]

The main gap in the set of procedures established by these three groups of measures was that no satisfactory provision was made for the supervision of the issue of budget grants to the economy from *outside* the banking and budget authorities responsible for this issue. In 1927 the financial control bodies responsible for formal documentary checking of expenditure were raised in status to the State Financial Control of the NKF, and the NKF was simultaneously instructed to 'deepen its work on inspecting expenditure on financing the national economy'. The control organs were made responsible not merely for formal control but also for checking the economic suitability of expenditure. This attempt to pour new wine into old bottles was unsuccessful. It was made half-heartedly—only a fraction of the grant to industry was properly inspected—and where it was made it led to a duplication of the work of the RKI. But for the most part the control organs continued formal inspection in the old way. In 1929 *khozraschot* bodies were withdrawn from the province of state financial control, so that there was no effective outside financial control of the national economy.[2]

The new machinery for financing investment did not yet work very effectively. Successive annual plans for reducing construction costs were only partly successful.[3] There were frequent complaints in government reports of money being spent on unplanned investment, of construction jobs costing more than had been planned, and of excessive overheads.[4] These faults were inevitable in a relatively backward country in which large-scale construction was still in an experimental stage, especially in view of the inflationary situation.

[1] See ch. v, p. 134, and V. V. Ikonnikov (ed.), *op. cit.* pp. 202–3. The Department was reformed into the Bank of Long-term Credits in February 1928.
[2] SZ 260/1927 (13. iv. 27); Aleksandrov, *op. cit.* p. 135; and *Uproschenie finansovoi sistemy*, pp. 44–8.
[3] See, for example, SZ 183/1928 (23. iii. 28); 345/1929 (21. xii. 28).
[4] See, for example, SZ 98/1927 (15. ii. 27); 640/1928 (15. xii. 28); 721/1929 (8. xii. 29); *TsIK* 3/IV, pp. 56–7.

But they were in part due to imperfections in planning and controlling investment grants. Financial plans often did not correspond to plans in physical terms, which were adopted late, and the financial estimates for a job could often therefore be compiled only months after the beginning of the economic year. The preparation of estimates and technical projects was still very imperfect. The investment bank, responsible for issuing grants under the new system, was attached to VSNKh, and it was therefore less interested in keeping within the approved money grants than it would have been if it had been subordinated to NKF—its work did not as a rule go beyond the routine issue of grants and loans as planned. The financing of investment was not yet adequately controlled by an independent control body, by industry itself, or by the investment bank.

An obvious prerequisite of adequate control was that the finances of industry itself and of each enterprise should be properly organised to receive these allocations. In the period after the civil war working capital had been made available to industry by initial grants, and these were later supplemented in a somewhat *ad hoc* fashion from industry's own profits, from credits granted by the State Bank or by the Industrial Bank, and from commercial credit from other enterprises, etc., via bills of exchange. New investment, when it took place, was financed principally from profits, depreciation allowances and bank loans. But there was no sharp demarcation between working capital and investment in fixed capital; and the distribution of profits between current and investment needs was not closely controlled.

During the period 1927–30 the importance of the profit motive declined. The fulfilment of production plans became more important to enterprises than making profit; and the profit level itself gradually came to be determined by the transfer prices fixed by the government in the course of planning. Nevertheless, the financial plans of industry remained important to the government and the planning authorities. They provided a means of controlling production efficiency and of estimating the amount of financial support needed from outside the enterprise in order that the plan should be fulfilled. In real terms, this financial support (budget grants and bank credits) meant that labour and materials could be transferred to an enterprise when it could not pay for them out of profits on the sale of its current production.

During the first two years of the five-year plan a number of practices continuing from the pre-planning period hindered the accurate compilation of financial plans. First, no efficient method had yet been introduced for calculating the amount of working capital needed by an enterprise to fulfil the plan. Secondly, there were two major 'leaks' in the system through which unplanned working capital was made available. The continued extensive use of commercial credit meant that enterprises had access to financial resources other than from sales of their production or bank and budget credits; and the existence of several different banks issuing credits made it possible for an enterprise to receive credits from more than one source.[1] Finally, working capital and capital for new investment in fixed capital still tended to be treated as being a 'common pool' on which an enterprise could draw indiscriminately for both capital and current needs. As a result of all these practices, it was extremely difficult to assess the resources which an industry needed to supplement its own funds. A thorough-going reform of the credit system and of the current finances of industry was clearly necessary.

For details see, for example, Ikonnikov, *op. cit.* pp. 219f.

CHAPTER VIII

THE EMERGENCE OF A NEW BUDGETARY SYSTEM 1930-4

1. REFORM OF THE REVENUE SYSTEM

By 1930 the difficulties in fulfilling the first five-year plan made it urgently necessary to unify and centralise the taxation of the state sector. In December 1929 the central committee of the Communist Party had instructed NKF and VSNKh to work out a new system for collecting budgetary revenue from industry,[1] and the need for reform was generally accepted by those active in the conduct of the economy, except for certain cautious experts in the NKF. But opinion was divided on the reform.

There were three main directions which it could have taken. First, existing excises, Promtax, and other taxes could have been abolished, and all revenue from industry raised as a single tax on profits. Secondly, all taxes, including deductions from profits, could have been unified into a single 'addition to costs', or turnover tax.[2] Thirdly, existing taxes could be unified into a turnover tax, while deductions from profits were retained as a separate source of revenue.

The first possibility, that existing taxes should be replaced by a single tax on profits, was clearly impracticable in the circumstances of the early 1930's. In the first place, the level of profits depends on the fulfilment of costs plans as well as output plans. In an economy in which there was no guarantee that costs plans would be fulfilled, a profits tax could be only a supplementary source of revenue. And if the largest mark-ups (for reasons explained in chapter VI) were to

---

[1] *Pravda*, 6. xii. 1929.
[2] The Soviet *nalog s oborota* does not correspond exactly to turnover taxes in other countries, for the tax came to be applied not as a flat rate on all the turnover of an enterprise, but as a rate which varied by *product*.

be imposed in the consumer goods industries, the use of a profits tax as the main source of budgetary revenue would involve a much higher ratio of profits to costs in these industries than in heavy industry; the collection of the tax would depend not even on the fulfilment of costs plans of industry as a whole, but primarily on those of the consumer goods industries to which relatively little attention was being paid at this period. Further, it would be extremely difficult to devise a system of taxing profits in which payments were made as frequently as with, say, excises, since the tax due on profits is usually calculated from *post-factum* accounts. If profits tax were the main source of budget revenue, large temporarily unpaid amounts of tax would be left at the disposal of enterprises for considerable periods.

Some kind of turnover tax, dependent not upon profits but on the amount of goods sold, clearly had to be the main source of budgetary revenue in the early 1930's. The main contest of opinion in 1930 was therefore between those who wanted to incorporate deductions from profits into the 'mark-up on costs' or turnover tax, and those who wanted to retain a profits tax as a separate source of revenue.

The protagonists of the incorporation of profits tax into the turnover tax received considerable support.[1] Why after all was it necessary to retain a tax on profits? Could not transfer prices be adjusted so that each enterprise would receive the same margin of profit if its costs plan were fulfilled? The required budget revenue could then be obtained entirely by manipulating the rates of turnover tax. Soviet sources state that the main reason for retaining deductions from profits as a separate source of revenue after September 1930 lay in the varying level of costs between enterprises. It would be administratively inconvenient to charge different rates of tax on similar goods produced by different enterprises. Hence the argument runs that if all enterprises were paid the same price for a given product, and profits were not taxed, some enterprises would have a much higher level of profits than others.[2] The trouble with this explanation is that it does not as it stands take account of the practice of equalising profits between enterprises by redistribution at *glavk* or combine

[1] For a presentation of their view, see S. Shakhnovskaya in *Pl. khoz.* no. 5 (1930), pp. 159–82. The decree of the Party Central Committee already mentioned had instructed NKF and VSNKh to 'draw up a system of taxation on state enterprises on the principle of a single tax on profits', reducing all revenue from the state sector to a 'turnover tax which is a mark-up on the cost of production', and 'a tax on the profits of the enterprise' (*Pravda*, 6. xii. 29).

[2] See, for example, Plotnikov, *op. cit.* pp. 23–4.

level (via the 'two-price system' or 'internal subsidies'). If the *glavk* were paid a price equal to the average level of planned costs in its enterprises, plus an agreed percentage of profit, no tax on profits would be necessary. The turnover tax on any particular product could be applied at the same rate throughout the *glavk*, and profits could be equalised by the *glavk*. (This would not apply, however, to a product manufactured by more than one *glavk* at different levels of average costs. Adjustments here would have to be made at Commissariat level.)

The main explanation for the retention of the profits tax in the form adopted in 1930 seems to be that its abolition would have involved an alteration in the transfer prices of all goods in order to bring down the level of profits; this would have involved administrative difficulties. The profits tax was therefore continued, and this meant that all other taxes on industry could be joined into a single turnover tax (a mark-up on costs plus profits), imposed mainly on consumer goods, without altering transfer prices and profits levels. It was later decided that profits should be extensively used by branches of the economy to finance their own planned expansion. Now, in these circumstances, if the plan for expansion were reduced in any period as compared with the previous level, 'free' profits would rise in those branches whose expansion was financed entirely or mainly out of profits. These 'free' profits would have to be absorbed either by lowering the transfer prices of the products, or by a tax. Here again a profits tax was administratively more convenient and flexible.

The decrees introducing the tax reform, effective from 1 October 1930, accordingly abolished the numerous existing taxes on the state sector, including the Promtax and all excises, and replaced them by two main taxes or variations on them: the turnover tax and deductions from profits. These two forms of tax will here be considered separately.

2. TURNOVER TAX

In attempting to bring together the various taxes on the state sector into a single flexible instrument for collecting revenue through the price mechanism, the government made use of its previous experience with excises and Promtax. It endeavoured to cut across the confusions of the old system of taxation by applying universally the modifications made in the Promtax in the previous two years. It was thought that the new tax could be collected without complicated administrative machinery; the extension of planning, it was held, meant that a task which had previously been devolved on to thousands of persons at all levels of the financial hierarchy could now be concentrated and centralised. What had been attempted in the textile industry in 1929 (see p. 203) was in 1930 applied to the whole of industry.

The tax was therefore collected not from the enterprise or from the trust covering a group of enterprises, but from the combine (*ob"edinenie*). Each combine established by the 1929 reform of industrial administration covered a whole branch of industry.[1] The tax was imposed and collected at combine level; all enterprises of Union subordination, and these paid between them the vast bulk of the tax, had to pay the tax not to the local financial organ but to the Union budget through the combine. It seemed a natural corollary of this that a single rate of tax should be charged for each combine, giving the combine the right to vary the rates charged on the different types of goods produced by its enterprises, provided that the total sum was collected as planned. It could, therefore, arrange that a particular product should be sold more cheaply to an industrial consumer, for example, than to the population. Centralised collection of the tax was thus combined with decentralisation of the power to fix the rate of tax on particular products. This method of collecting the tax was an extension of the practice increasingly followed since 1928 in collecting both excises and Promtax. The practice of fixing a single rate of tax on net turnover[2] at combine level was based on the Promtax, as reconstituted since 1929, rather than the excise; the 1929 Promtax on textiles had in fact been known as the 'Promtax on turnover'.[3] The origins of the turnover tax as it was constructed in 1930 can be traced back through the later forms of the Promtax to the pre-1928 'equalising levy', which had existed in simpler form before the revolution.

This first essay in the unification of taxation[4] was not very successful. A few months' experience disclosed that the method adopted for imposing and collecting the tax was unsatisfactory. In the words of

[1] Enterprises which were not in combines were taxed separately. For details of the 1929 reform of industrial administration, see Baykov, *op. cit.* pp. 169–76.

[2] The qualification 'net' is important. It was hoped to avoid the taxation of the same good more than once, a procedure which had been a recurring weakness of the Promtax, by imposing the tax as a rule only on the turnover of goods prepared or acquired by the combine concerned.

[3] SZ 573/1929 (25. ix. 29).   [4] SZ 476–7/1930 (21. ix. 30).

the NKF itself, the attempt to 'achieve the greatest possible simplicity in the method of assessing and imposing the tax' resulted in a 'depersonalised approach'. The centralisation of tax collection resulted in the almost complete abolition of the local machinery for taxing state enterprises, and deprived local soviets and financial departments of any interest in the results of the collection of the tax. The combines alone were responsible for ensuring that turnover at regional level was fully included. The absence of local financial control over the tax was stated to have resulted in the loss to the budget of fairly considerable sums. On the other hand, the power of the combine to fix tax rates was too great. The financial authorities had only a reserve power (which does not seem to have been used) to change the rates charged inside a combine on different products. But these rates were of great importance, as the collection of the planned amount of tax depended not only on the overall volume of turnover but also on achieving the planned composition of turnover within the branch of industry. If the output of goods on which a relatively high rate of tax was charged did not reach the planned level, receipts from the tax would be less than planned, even though the planned volume of turnover was reached by the branch as a whole. Moreover, as tax rates on individual goods were fixed by the combines, this meant that the retail prices of goods were to a large extent out of the hands of the planning authorities. Such a degree of decentralisation was incompatible with a planning system of the Soviet type (see p. 142). In short, the weakness of the turnover tax as introduced in September 1930 appears to have been that it was over-centralised at the point where the system could afford to be flexible, in its method of collection, while the fixing of the level of tax on particular goods, which needed to be kept in the hands of the planners and the financial authorities, was decentralised.[1]

The tax was accordingly modified in the course of 1931 and 1932. Collection was decentralised: the enterprise or trust replaced the combine as the unit of collection, and the tax was imposed and collected by local financial organs, whether the enterprise or trust was of general-Union, republican or local subordination. Local and republican soviets were allowed to retain a percentage of the tax collected from all-Union enterprises, and hence had a material incentive to secure the full imposition of the tax: this strengthened

[1] *Otchot...* (1931), pp. 148–57. See also K. N. Plotnikov, *Byudzhet sotsialisticheskogo gosudarstva* (1948), pp. 24–5.

the connexion which local authorities in any case had with Union enterprises in their area by supplying them with water, gas, etc. The tax ceased to be imposed at an overall rate on each combine, and instead, like an excise, it now varied by goods and groups of goods (although it retained the form and name of a percentage tax on turnover)—45 branch rates were replaced by 146 rates on groups of goods. Thus full control over the economic and social effects of the tax was placed in the hands of the financial and planning authorities, and taken away from industry. Finally, the State Bank was no longer allowed to deduct the tax automatically from every account it handled. In future, deductions were made only on the authority of the taxpayer, and not for every account, but monthly (later, three times a month[1]) on the basis of the turnover in the previous month; the monthly account was audited, and necessary adjustments made, every quarter.[2]

These modifications put the administration of the tax on a sounder footing. Already in 1931 almost twice as much was collected in turnover tax as had been raised by equivalent taxes in 1929/30.[3] During the period up to 1934, as Table 42 shows, the revenue from the tax rose constantly, both absolutely and as a percentage of budgetary revenue; throughout this period, turnover tax alone was responsible for more than half of all budget revenue.

How were these large revenues raised through the turnover tax? Ultimately the tax was a means of withdrawing from circulation part of the wages and other payments made to the population for production and services which were not bought by other producers, or by the consumer, but paid for by the state through the budget. To any given wage-bill and plan for production, investment, and services for the country as a whole, there corresponds an appropriate

[1] It was found that the uneven receipts resulting from monthly payments led to cash difficulties for the budget.

[2] SZ 199/1931 (3. v. 31), 497/1931 (19. xii. 31), 173/1932 (17. iv. 32).

[3] The revenue from turnover tax, excluding the commercial fund was 10,601·7 million roubles in 1931. In 1929/30 the equivalent revenue was 5,354·1 million roubles, made up as follows:

Excises	2,629·2
Promtax and additions for bills of exchange	1,841·3
Timber revenue	290·0
Revenue from ores	83·0
Dues and other state revenue	87·9
Local taxes and levies	126·0
Extra budgetary sums	296·7
Total	5,354·1

Otchot... (1931).

level of retail prices and average rate of turnover tax at which total supply and demand on the retail market will balance and the required budget revenue will be received. But a policy of charging the same rate of tax on all consumer goods would be open to objections on social grounds, and would lead to shortages of some products and gluts of others, unless the output of each product were finely adjusted to consumer demand for it at the price equal to costs plus average-rate-of-tax.[1] Different rates were therefore charged on different products. For any particular type of good, the revenue raised was a function of its price, the quantity sold, and the rate of tax. With a given output of consumer goods, the pattern of tax rates had to be so co-ordinated that the tax on all goods taken together reached the required level.

In later years, the solution to this problem was very complicated: the balancing of supply and demand for particular goods, the overall fiscal problem, and social considerations had to be weighted against one another. But in the period 1930 to 1934 the problem did not require a sophisticated solution. The continuing inflation and goods shortages, together with the rationing of essential goods, meant that supply and demand hardly had to be taken into account; within limits, almost all goods would sell, whatever the price. The fixing of tax rates therefore took place on what might be called an *ad hoc* basis. The initial rates were fixed at approximately the same level as the combined rates of the taxes it replaced. At the moment of its introduction, the tax was formally, in the words of the NKF, 'not a new source of state budgetary revenue, but only a new form of taking resources from the socialised sector'.[2] Nevertheless, its introduction was of considerable fiscal importance. It made the collection of additional budgetary revenue required by the plan (i.e. the absorbing of the required amount of surplus cash held by the population) a comparatively simple matter, as it could be accomplished by appropriate increases in the retail prices of various goods, brought about by increasing the rates of tax on them. The large increases in tax rates which were made after 1930 are illustrated in Table 28, and provide some indication of the extent of the continuing inflation.

The rates shown in the table are the basic rates on goods distributed at low fixed prices—rationed goods and goods distributed by quasi-ration methods via 'closed' shops (shops open only to workers in a particular factory or institution).

---

[1] This point is elaborated in ch. IX.   [2] *Otchot*... (1931), *loc. cit.*

Table 28. *Rates of turnover tax on selected goods, 1930–2 (as percentage of turnover or of wholesale price)* [1]

	1 Oct. 1930[a]	1 Mar. 1931[b]	1 May 1931[d] [16]	1 Jan. 1932[g]	1 Feb. 1932[h]	Feb. 1932 to 1 Jan. 1933[o]
Cigarettes and tobacco	71·5[2]	74·7[2]	82·3[2]	79·0[17] 64·5[18] 49·5[19]	Unchanged	Unchanged
Alcohol	87·2[3]	—[12]	—[12]	88·4[20] 53·2[21] 65·0[22]	Unchanged	88·8[20] [j] 54·1[21] [j] 88·3[27] [p]
Oil	32·0[4]	36·0[4]	39·5[4]	53·8[23] 16·0[24]	84·1[27] 77·0[28]	85·3[28] [p]
					Unchanged	Unchanged
Sugar	51·0[5]	Unchanged	Unchanged	48·0	70·3[29] 66·0[30] 66·3[31] 58·9[32]	86·5[37] 77·5[38]
Salt	14·5[6]	Unchanged	Unchanged	19·6	77·1[33]	73·5[k]–82·9[39]
Matches	55·1[7]	Unchanged	Unchanged	45·0	59·9	69·8
Flour	8·0[8]	Unchanged	Unchanged	8·0	37·9[34] 24·9[35]	43·0–60·0[40] 30·0[41]
Sewing machines	—[9]	—	—	12·0	Unchanged	56·0[42]
Woollen cloth	15·8[10]	22·9[10]	24·8[10]	28·8[25] 17·4[26]	Unchanged	64·4[25] [m] [36] 58·7[26] [m]
Cinemas	None	30·0[13] (c)	20·0[14] (e)	Unchanged	Unchanged	42·0[n]–30·0[q]
Non-commodity operations[11]	—	—	5·0–10·0[15] (f)	Unchanged	Unchanged	Unchanged

N.B. All from source indicated at head of column unless otherwise stated.

Sources:
(a) SZ 483/1930, 3. ix. 30.
(b) SZ 136/1931, 27. ii. 31.
(c) SZ 188/1931, 13. iv. 31.
(d) SZ 231/1931, 3. v. 31.
(e) SZ 352/1931, 20. viii. 31.
(f) SZ 326/1931, 3. viii. 31.
(g) SZ 497/1931, 19. xii. 31.
(h) SZ 37/1932, 28. i. 32.
(j) SZ 112/1932, 9. iii. 32, effective 1. iii. 32.
(k) SZ 111/1932, 6. iii. 32, effective 15. iii. 32.
(m) SZ 235/1932, 21. v. 32, effective 15. v. 32.
(n) SZ 146/1932, 29. iii. 32, effective 1. iv. 32.
(o) SZ 48/1933, 5. ii. 33, effective 1. i. 33.
(p) SZ 90/1933, 26. ii. 33, effective 1. ii. 33.
(q) SZ 243/1932, 27. v. 32, date of effect not stated.

Notes:
(1) Until January 1932 the tax was imposed as a percentage of the turnover of all goods prepared or produced by a branch of industry (*ob"edinenie*) or the enterprises under it, defined as the total sales of these goods to enterprises outside the branch (with some exceptions) (see SZ 477/1930, 2. ix. 30). From January 1932 it was imposed on commodities and groups of commodities as a percentage of their transfer price (SZ 497/1931, 19. xii. 31). Thus the rates before January 1932 are not strictly comparable with those which follow.
(N.B. In both cases the tax is reckoned as a percentage of selling price, the tax being *included* in this price. Thus a tax rate of 50 % represents a mark-up of 100 % on cost price plus profits, a tax rate of 90 % a mark-up of 900 %, etc.)
(2) Turnover of *Soyuztabak*.
(3) Turnover of *Tsentrospirt*.
(4) Turnover of *Soyuzneft'*. This included gas production from oil.
(5) Turnover of *Soyuzsakhar*.
(6) Turnover of *Soyuzsol'*.
(7) Turnover of *Vsespichprom*.
(8) Turnover of *Soyuzkhleb*.
(9) Included in engineering production, subject to a low tax rate (5–8 %).
(10) Turnover of *Gosshveiprom*, R.S.F.S.R.
(11) Not included for accounting purposes in turnover tax, but analogous to it.
(12) Decree effective 1. i. 31 transferred the right to fix the turnover tax rate for *Soyuzspirt* from the government to NKF (on consultation with NK Snab) (SZ 176/1931, 21. iii. 31).
(13) On basis of full receipts from admission tickets. Effective 15. iv. 31.
(14) Reduction effective from 21. viii. to 21. x. 31 only.
(15) On gross receipts hairdressing, photography, tailoring of customers' materials, laundering, etc. Effective 1. vii. 31.
(16) On 1 August 1931 all changes in taxation since 3. ix. 30 were cancelled and the earlier rates were restored (this decree was effective until the end of 1931, but presumably did not lead to a reduction in price on these goods. Presumably the increases were replaced by special mark-ups (*natsenki*)).
(17) Grade I cigarettes.
(18) Grade VI cigarettes.
(19) *Makhorka* (cheap tobacco) and snuff.
(20) *Vodka*.
(21) Brandy.
(22) Benzine (except for use by tractors).
(23) Kerosene (except for use by tractors).
(24) All oil used by tractors.
(25) Fine cloth.
(26) Coarse cloth.
(27) Kerosene sold in the villages.
(28) Kerosene sold in the towns.
(29) Lump sugar sold in the villages.
(30) Lump sugar sold in the towns.
(31) Granulated sugar sold in the villages.
(32) Granulated sugar sold in the towns.
(33) Salt used by industry continued to pay the old rate of 19·6 %.
(34) Wheat flour.
(35) Rye flour.
(36) Goods supplied to market fund only. Goods to non-market fund (e.g. overalls supplied via factory, uniforms) retain former rates.
(37) Lump and granulated sugar to villages.⎫ Sugar for use by confectioners, etc., retains lower rate of 28 or 51 %.
(38) Lump and granulated sugar to towns. ⎭
(39) *Vyvarochnaya* salt only. *Fasovannaya* only 35·0 %.
(40) Wheat flour, varies by degree of extraction.⎫ Lower rates in force in Far East and Central Asia, and for industrial
(41) Rye flour.   ⎭ use. See original decree.
(42) Sales on mass market only.

In addition to the basic rates of tax, additional 'budget mark-ups' (*byudzhetnye natsenki*) were imposed on a large number of goods sold unrationed or via closed shops, thereby raising their wholesale price.[1] The official rates of tax, particularly on manufactured goods, therefore do not disclose the full incidence of the tax. Thus in 1931, of the total turnover tax paid by VSNKh industry of 2,660 million roubles, budget mark-ups accounted for 677 million roubles; and of the 6,229 million roubles paid by NK Snab (mainly responsible for food products), 424 million roubles was in budget mark-ups.[2]

In addition to the rationed goods sold at low (but rising) prices, a proportion of the supply of these goods was included in a special 'commercial fund' and sold at very high prices approaching those on the black market. The amounts received in this way were transferred to the budget. After the success of this policy in the initial year, a steadily increasing sum was raised from this source.[3]

Thus a commodity costing a certain sum to produce or a foodstuff purchased at a low fixed delivery price, might be sold by the state trade network at one of several retail prices, the most important of which were rationed price and commercial price.[4] The gap between cost price (or delivery price) plus trading costs, and retail price, was skimmed off by a different rate of turnover tax in each case.

Variations of the turnover tax were introduced in circumstances where this tax itself was not appropriate. The most important of these were the tax on non-commodity operations and the tax on cinemas.

---

[1] Thus all clocks and watches paid a tax of 7%. But alarm clocks and wall-clocks bore an additional mark-up (L. Gatovskii, G. Neiman, V. Nodel' (eds.), *Ekonomika sovetskoi torgovli*, 1934). Similarly confectionery paid a mark-up on the wholesale price of 10% in the towns and 23% in the villages, in addition to the basic rate of 48·5% (i.e. a total tax in the towns of $(48·5+10·0) \times (100/110) = 53·2\%$ of wholesale price plus mark-up) (SZ 48/1933 (5. ii. 33), effective 1 January 1933).

[2] *Otchot*... (1931), *loc. cit.*

[3]

	1929/30	1930 (last quarter)	1931 (plan)	1931 (actual)	1932 (plan)	1932 (actual)
Total turnover tax (million roubles)	5,653	2,420	9,990	11,672	16,111	19,595
Of which, from 'commercial fund'	299	248	600	1,070	985	1,902

(*Sots. str.* (1935), p. 650; SZ 61/1931 (10. i. 31); *Otchot*... (1931), pp. 4–7; SZ 501/1931 (28. xii. 31); SZ 14/1934 (4. i. 34)).

[4] For further details of the retail price system in the rationing period, see Baykov, *op. cit.* pp. 243 ff.

The former was imposed on services such as repairing, cleaning, laundry, hairdressing, photography, and road transport plying for hire, and on enterprises making-up customers' own materials, at rates varying from 5 to 10% of the full gross receipts.[1] The tax on cinemas was imposed as a percentage of the total receipts from admission tickets, at first as a flat rate for all cinemas, and later at rates varying by the type of cinema—higher rates were charged for town cinemas than for village cinemas, and children's cinemas charging low prices, and Red Army cinemas, were exempt. The rate did not vary according to the price of admission.[2]

3. PROFITS TAX (DEDUCTIONS FROM PROFITS)

No fundamental changes in the profits tax were made at the time of the tax reform in September 1930. The income tax previously imposed on state enterprises was abolished, and the level of profits tax was raised. 81% of planned profits in all branches of industry were transferred to the budget, 19% remaining with the trust for the expansion of its basic capital (10%) and for the FUBR (9%). But the tax remained a simple flat-rate, which was now large enough to transfer the bulk of the gap between cost price and transfer price in every industry to the budget.[3] This inevitably had the result that a still larger part of the funds required by industries to finance their expansion had to be met by the budget.

This arrangement meant that the resources made available for the expansion of a trust did not depend on the fulfilment of its current production and costs plans. It also meant that the bulk of the profits of all branches of industry was used not in the branch concerned, but impersonally through the budget for the economy as a whole. This deprived profits of much of their potential value as an incentive to efficiency. In May 1931 the tax was therefore again revised. The profits of a branch, instead of being transferred mainly to the budget, were now used primarily to finance the investment programme of the trust concerned, and to supply its planned requirements in new working capital. The profits of the trust, and the extra resources it

---

[1] SZ 326/1931 (3. viii. 31).
[2] SZ 188/1931 (13. iv. 31), 352/1931 (20. viii. 31), 146/1932 (29. iii. 32), 243/1932 (27. v. 32), 343/1933 (13. ix. 33), 424/1933 (20. xi. 33), 54/1935 (28. i. 35), *Fin. khoz. bull.* nos. 1–2 (1939), p. 14 (8. xii. 38), no. 3 (1939), pp. 16–17 (26. xii. 38). Part of the tax was transferred to local Red Cross Societies between 1935 and 1939.
[3] SZ 478/1930 (2. ix. 30).

required for expansion, were assessed annually on the basis of the production, investment, and financial plans. Broadly speaking, only profit surplus to the extra resources needed was transferred to the budget. Thus at least part of the plan for expansion of each trust was met from profits; 'a break in accumulations inside enterprises', in the words of an NKF report, 'means for them a break in their working capital or the underfulfilment of their capital investment plan'.[1] The future expansion of an economic unit depended to some extent on the successful fulfilment of its costs plan.[2] A further incentive was provided by permitting trusts to retain 50% of all profit in excess of the plan for the FUBR and other uses.

These general principles were applied in practice as follows. All enterprises paid a minimum rate of 20% (later 10%) of profits to the budget; this provided a link between financial organs and all enterprises irrespective of the level of their profits. Enterprises receiving allocations from the budget paid only this rate, and the remainder of their profit was used to cover part of their expansion programme and their FUBR. Other enterprises paid between 10% and the maximum rate of 81%—they received no allocation from the budget, and paid a rate of tax varying by the proportion of their profits needed to finance their plans for expansion.[3]

In the first two or three years of operating the tax there was considerable experimentation in the method of collecting it. Most of the changes made are of a purely technical interest. The only important change of principle was in the method of assessing the tax due. At first the tax was paid monthly on the basis of *planned* profit, and readjustment to the actual level of profits was made only annually. In a period in which profits often fell below the planned level, this could produce considerable financial difficulties for the taxpayer. From 1931 onwards the tax was therefore collected on the basis of the actual profit made in the preceding quarter.[4]

In this period overall profits were so small, owing to rises in costs, that the profits retained by enterprises were in most cases only a negligible proportion of the total funds expended on the expansion of industry. The system of retained profits tended therefore to be of

[1] *Finansy SSSR...1931/4...*, p. 10.
[2] For a further discussion of this point, see above, ch. VI. pp. 148-51.
[3] A variation on the profits tax was applied to industrial co-operatives. These paid an income tax amounting to 20% of net profit (SZ 479/1930 (2. ix. 30), 350/1931 (23. viii. 31)). Later the level of tax was made dependent on the ratio of profit to commercial cost, rising to a maximum of 60% when this ratio exceeded 35% (SZ 253/1933 (7. vii. 33)).
[4] See, for details, SZ 205/1931 (3. v. 31), 367/1931 (3. ix. 31).

potential rather than actual significance; and the low level of profits meant that the tax was in this period of little fiscal importance. Only 8·6% of budgetary revenue in 1931 and 5·3% in 1934 was covered by the profits tax.

4. TAXES ON AGRICULTURE

Turnover tax and profits tax proved a powerful fiscal instrument; between them they raised some 55% of total budgetary revenue throughout this period, and thus were the main method by which accumulation was raised to finance the five-year plans.

While the taxation of agriculture is of considerably less fiscal importance than the taxation of state industry, the fiscal arrangements in agriculture played a significant if auxiliary part in the collectivisation drive of 1930–3, by encouraging the growth of the planned or semi-planned sector through taxation designed to eliminate the 'kulak' elements from the economy, and to encourage the peasantry to join the collective farms. Thus, taxation in agriculture performed an entirely different function from taxation in state industry, which was already under the direct control of the planning authorities.

Crippling rates of taxation were imposed on the 2–3% of peasant households which were designated as 'kulak' households by the appropriate regional executive committee of soviets. At the highest tax level, these rates constituted a heavy capital levy. In 1932, for example, a household designated as 'kulak' could pay an agricultural tax of 50% on all income above 1,000 roubles per annum and 70% on all income above 6,000 roubles per annum, an equal sum in the form of a 'cultural levy' and double this amount as a special tax. Non-collectivised individual peasant households had to pay rates substantially higher than those paid by collective-farm households, and these rates were increased as collectivisation was intensified. Thus in 1932 and again in 1934 a special 'single tax on individual households', the maximum rate of which was 175% of the agricultural tax, was imposed as a further inducement to individual peasant households to join the collective farm. A characteristic feature of these taxes on the peasantry was that they were adjusted to the local tempo of the collectivisation drive: local authorities were given powers to vary the amount of tax imposed on different households, within the limits of the sum of tax planned for the area. Thus the district soviet could at its discretion double the tax on households 'deliberately under-fulfilling' their sowing or compulsory delivery plans, and exempt those households fulfilling these obligations on time.[1]

Table 29. *Sources of agricultural tax, 1931–5*
(million roubles)

	1931	1933	1935
Collective farms	80	239·4	398·9
Collective farmers	37	? (2)	? (2)
Individual farmers	300	279·8	673·1
'Kulaks'	69	46·9	10·0
Total	486	560·0 (1)	1,082·0

Source: Finansy SSSR..., pp. 276–7.

Notes:
(1) This column actually adds up to 566·1, but total is given as 560·0. Plotnikov gives fulfilment for 1933 as 547·0.
(2) Presumably payments by collective farmers are included with collective farms, but this is not made clear in the source. According to other data, agricultural tax raised from collective farms was 230·0 million roubles in 1933 and 258·5 in 1935 (SZ 70/1935 (8. ii. 35); and *Otchot...* (1935)).

The incomplete data available (see Table 29) indicate that throughout this period the bulk of direct taxes on agriculture was collected from non-collectivised households, although the number of these households declined rapidly. Taxation on the income of collective farmers from their private plots and on the joint income of collective farms was kept at a low level,[2] and the methods used for imposing the tax were fairly simple. In 1930–2 the incomes of collective farmers were taxed as in the previous period on the basis of norms of assessed income, and a proportional tax of 2 or 5% of the joint collective farm income was paid irrespective of the size of farm (varying by the type of collective farm). In 1933, when the contract form of compulsory deliveries to the state was replaced by a more regularised system, the level of tax on the income of collective farmers was substantially lowered: the tax was collected as a simple lump sum of 15 to 30 roubles per household, the exact amount being fixed at republican or regional level. At the same time the method of taxing the joint income of the farm was changed so that the tax, like the amount of compulsory deliveries to be made, was assessed on the basis of the planned size of the sown area.

[1] For criticisms of faults made in applying this policy of discrimination against the non-collectivised sector (over-taxation of middle-peasant households, and insufficient taxation of 'kulak' households), see Bryukhanov in *TsIK* 2/v, Bull. 3, pp. 5–7, and *Finansy SSSR...* (1931), pp. 14–16.
[2] In 1933 more than 50% of collective farm income was exempted from tax (Grin'ko in *TsIK* 4/vi, Bull. 13, pp. 16–17).

These methods of taxing the money incomes of the peasantry suffered from considerable imperfections, as later experience disclosed. But already in this period efforts were made to use the system of taxation not only to encourage the form of organisation of production desired by the government, but also to assist the overcoming of bottlenecks in the output of various crops and products—thus privileged rates of taxation were granted to livestock, technical crops, and to extensions of the sown area.

The amount which could be collected by direct money taxes on agriculture was, however, extremely limited. The peasantry had to make contract and compulsory deliveries to the state at low prices for sale as rations to the growing urban population, and had to pay a higher price than the urban population for consumer goods. This high concealed 'tax in kind' restricted the possibilities of raising the level of direct money taxes on the rural population as a whole.[1]

5. OTHER SOURCES OF REVENUE

From 1930 onwards, the private sector in the towns was so diminished by administrative means that its importance as a source of revenue declined to vanishing point.[2] Although the rates of tax on the private sector in industry and trade were raised even above the 1929 level,[3] the amount collected tended to fall behind the planned level in each year.[4]

Because of this, and because the government was not prepared to increase the rates of tax on the incomes of state employees or able to increase the taxation of the money incomes of the rural population,

---

[1] Detailed information on the methods of imposing the agricultural tax will be found in SZ 143–4/1930 (23. ii. 30), 230/1930 (2. iv. 30), 261/1930 (23. iv. 30), 6/1931 (23. xii. 30), 171/1931 (29. iii. 31), 286/1931 (30. vi. 31), 189a–b/1932 (4. v. 32), 233/1932 (20. v. 32), 188a–b/1933 (25. v. 33), 231a–b/1934 (31. v. 34).

For details on the method of imposing compulsory deliveries introduced, see 25/1933 (19. i. 33), 228/1933 (20. vi. 33), 323/1933 (28. viii. 33), 406/1933 (23. xi. 33).

[2] Thus between January and October 1931 the number of private craftsmen in 58 large towns declined from 2·7 million to 1·84 million (*Otchot...* (1931), pp. 144–5).

[3] See details in *Otchot...* (1931), pp. 145–8.

[4] Thus the following were the results for 1931 (million roubles):

	Plan	Fulfilment
Tax on excess profits	18·0	10·1
Promtax on private crafts	180·0	128·4

(SZ 61/1931 (10. i. 1931); *Otchot...* (1931), pp. 4–7).

In 1930 84·9% and in 1931 only 46·5% of all direct taxes on income in the towns was paid by persons not working in state or co-operative enterprises (*Otchot...* (1931), pp. 140–1; *Finansy SSSR mezhdu V i VI s"ezdami sovetov Soyuza* (1931), pp. 5–6).

the yield from all the most important direct taxes on the population and the private sector rose only slowly during this period. While the budget as a whole absorbed an increasing proportion of the national income, the revenue from both income tax and agricultural tax rose much less rapidly than did the money incomes of the population. The rates of income tax on workers and employees were in fact reduced in 1931,[1] presumably because it was considered that income tax tended to have a disincentive effect. The maximum rate of tax in 1931 was 3·5%[2] and tax rates were further reduced in 1934 and 1935.[3]

The total revenue from taxes and loans direct from the population nevertheless rose absolutely, and roughly maintained its position as a proportion of budgetary revenue (it amounted to 18% of total revenue in 1928/9 and 17% in 1932). This increase was made possible by the introduction of new taxes, and by the extension of state loans. In 1931 housing and cultural levies were introduced in both town and countryside, on the rural population as lump sums based on the agricultural tax, and on the urban population on the basis of the income tax. These levies were 'earmarked' for popular purposes in order to make them more palatable. The cultural levy in the villages was, for instance, stated to have been introduced in connexion with the proposal to make elementary four-year education universal in 1931, and it was transferred entirely to district and village budgets. Village soviets also retained and extended various forms of 'self-taxation', imposed by general meetings of villagers and used for local purposes.[4]

During the period the state loan system described in chapter v was consolidated and extended. The more rigorous planned control over the working capital of enterprises led to a rapid decline in the revenue raised from industry in loans. But as a result of the wage inflation the population, unlike industry, had considerable surplus money resources at its disposal which could be tapped within limits for budgetary revenue. In 1930 the numerous and varied loans of the N.E.P. period were converted into a single new loan,[5] and in

---

[1] See *Otchot...* (1931), pp. 139–40.

[2] This was on earnings above 500 roubles per month. The average wage in 1931 was 119, and in 1932, 132 roubles per month (*Sots. str.* (1935), p. xxx).

[3] SZ 211*b*/1934 (17. v. 34), 30/1935 (14. i. 35).

[4] For details of all these taxes see, for the towns, SZ 35/1931 (13. i. 31), 137/1931 (26. ii. 31), 238/1931 (23. v. 31), 9/1932 (17. i. 32), and for the countryside see SZ 451/1930 (16. viii. 30), 34/1931 (9. i. 31), 320/1931 (3. viii. 31) and 10/1932 (7. i. 32).

[5] SZ 137/1930 (21. ii. 30), 353/1930 (13. v. 30), 379/1930 (3. vii. 30).

subsequent years loan-raising was concentrated on the mass annual lottery loans from the population which had been introduced in 1927. Throughout the pre-war period these mass loans were a permanent feature of the budget.[1] Of necessity, they had to be raised mainly from workers and employees, who could be most easily organised and persuaded to make systematic contributions from their wages. While workers and employees contributed an average of 2–3 weeks' wages[2] per annum, the peasantry were responsible for only a fraction of loan revenue throughout the 1930's. Various devices were introduced to make the loans more acceptable to the population,[3] but there was no important change in the methods of collection introduced in the previous period.

In summary, the revenue system was by 1934 a mixture of taxes and practices taken over from the N.E.P. period and of innovations introduced since 1930. Turnover and profits tax were the kernel of the system of budgetary accumulation, but the tense situation of 1928–34 led the government to search for and retain other forms of revenue. The urban population contributed income tax, cultural levy, and loan subscriptions to the budget, and the rural population, as well as making compulsory deliveries at low prices to the state, also paid to the budget agricultural tax, cultural levy, and loan subscriptions. In retaining these direct taxes and loans, the government sought to adapt them to its social and economic policy.

6. BUDGETARY EXPENDITURE

The growth of the budget in 1930–4 needs to be seen against the background of the prevailing economic and monetary situation.

By 1930 substantial transfers of materials and labour had been made into the heavy industry sector, and capital investment was taking place on a large scale. But these transfers did not take place in the smooth way envisaged by the original five-year plan. As productivity did not increase to the planned extent, a larger labour force was needed in heavy industry than had been anticipated, and as a result the industrial population expanded more rapidly than had been planned. But the output of consumer goods and the available

---

[1] For example, the 3,200 million-rouble loan of 1932, and the 3,500 million-rouble loan of 1934 (SZ 268/1932 (8. vi. 32) and 153/1934 (14. iv. 34)).

[2] In 1932, for example, 2·86 weeks.

[3] For example, the lottery was drawn monthly in public at various regional centres; and the local loan commissions carried out an annual check of loan accounts to disclose unclaimed winnings and interest (*TsIK* 2/vi, Bull. 10, p. 22; *Soviet Union, 1936*, pp. 498–9).

supply of foodstuffs did not reach the planned level, as priority in materials, machinery, and labour was given to the capital goods sector. In consequence there was a deficit on the retail market of almost all goods by 1930, and a tight system of rationing had to be introduced. Soviet economy had by 1930 all those characteristics which have been regarded in Britain as consequences of war-time inflation—shortages of labour and materials, bottlenecks, rationing, and direct allocation.

In the next four years inflation was brought under control only gradually. The inflationary situation had a momentum of its own. Increases in prices of rationed and unrationed goods in state retail trade and on the black market led to an inflationary pressure on wages from the side of the workers. This pressure was reinforced by several factors. First, the scarcity of skilled labour, combined with the fact that it was subject to direct allocation only to a limited extent, led managements to bid for labour by offering inducements of higher wages. Secondly, the decision to encourage higher productivity by introducing piece rates, bonuses, and higher rates of pay for the more skilled and efficient (while not reducing the wages of the less skilled) pushed the wage fund further above its planned level. Managements were subject to a much greater pressure to fulfil their output plan than to fulfil their costs plan; if they could achieve their output plan by exceeding their planned wage fund, they did so. Costs in consequence actually rose in 1931 and 1932. The average wage and the labour force in 1932 were both double the 1927/8 level, and as a result the wage fund was four times as large as in 1927/8, or more than two-and-a-half times as great as had been planned.

The reform of the revenue system in 1930–1 was designed to cope with this situation, but it provided only the negative half of the solution of the financial problems raised by the first five-year plan. The revenue system could make only *post-factum* adjustments to the monetary situation: as cash flowed on to the market owing to extra budget or credit issues, the prices of both rationed and unrationed goods were increased and the margin skimmed off as tax. Table 30 provides some indication of the extent of the price-rise during this period; but should be read with the caution indicated there. But in a sense the more important task facing the financial system was to stem the flow of cash on to the market. Ways of reducing production costs had to be found, so that profits would rise, and industry could therefore finance a greater proportion of its own investment, reducing the part played by the budget in financing the national economy. Construction costs had also to be reduced, so that expenditure on investment would be limited. Budgetary expenditure on administration, defence, and social services had to be kept down as much as possible.

Table 30. *Some changes in price levels, 1928–41*

	1928	1936–7	1941
Wholesale prices of industrial goods:			
Coal (per ton)[1]	10 r. 52–12 r. 00	21 r. 78	36 r. 25
Motor oil (per ton)	35 r. 40	233–271 r.[2]	233–271 r.[2]
Portland cement (per ton)	30 r. approx.	43–70 r.	92–120 r.
Roofing iron (per ton)	179 r. 20	385–601 r.	—
Red bricks (thousand)	38 r. 00	49 r. 30–59 r.	89 r. 06–128 r.[3]
Lorry (1½ tons)	12,316	—	6,000+5,538[4]
Retail prices of consumer goods			
Rye bread (kg.)	0 r. 08	0 r. 85	1 r. 00
Sugar (kg.)	0 r. 62	4 r. 20–5 r. 90	5 r. 00
Milk (per litre)	0 r. 22	1 r. 30	2 r. 30
Eggs (10)	0 r. 50	4 r. 00	7 r. 50
Bicycles (women's)	205 r.[6]	250 r.	—
Men's leather shoes	9 r. 95–13 r. 50[5]	80–105 r.[5]	280 r.[7]

Sources: Universal'nyi spravochnik tsen (1928), pp. 42, 447, 553, 554, 604, 720, 721; *Spravochnik roznichnykh tsen i torgovykh nakidck na promtovary po g. Moskve* (1936), pt. 1; *Promyshlennost' SSSR v 1926/7 g.* (1927), p. 32; *Trest Mosgortop: spravochnik-tsennik* (1936); *Spravochnik tsen na stroitel'nye materialy i oborudovanie i transport, Leningrad*, no. 34 (1941); and see N. Jasny, *The Soviet price system* (1951) and *Soviet prices of producers' goods* (1952); Baykov, *op. cit.* p. 261; *Conjuncture et études économiques*, annexe à no. 4 (April 1955); *Economic Survey of Europe in 1951* (1952); *Byulleten'... Prokopovicha* (1937), no. 138, p. 110.

Notes: Prices exclude transport costs except where otherwise stated. They are given only as a rough indication of the kind of price-change which took place.

(1) Donbass, grade PZh.
(2) Price of sale in Leningrad, including transport costs, which were something of the order of 100 r.
(3) Retail price.
(4) Price of GAZ-AA 1½ ton lorry is given as 6,000 roubles, and the cost of chassis and cabin at 5,538 roubles.
(5) '*Polubotinki rantovye.*'
(6) Made by *Gosshveiprom*.
(7) Type and quality not stated.

Some success was achieved in fulfilling these aims. Official returns state that industrial costs fell in 1933 by 1·0% and in 1934 by 3·7%. In 1932 the budget financed 88% of all investment in industry; this fell to 71% in 1934. This cannot of course be attributed entirely to improvements in the financial system. Financial indices reflect the processes taking place in the economy as a whole; and the reduction of costs reflects the results of the series of measures launched by the government in 1931 to increase industrial efficiency. But without efficient financial organisation these successes would have been impossible: the absence of effective financial control had been instrumental in permitting costs to rise in 1930–1, and its presence in 1933 and 1934 assisted their fall.

In 1927–30 the bare framework of financial control had been constructed—the central supervision of investments had been introduced, and allocations to the economy had been concentrated in the long-term bank. But before this system could work effectively the outstanding problems of the organisation of finances of industry discussed in chapter VII had to be solved.

In the first place, commercial credit had to be abolished. In January 1930 the government stated its position on this question as follows:

> The rapid development of socialist elements in the national economy of the U.S.S.R. and the level of planning which has been achieved makes a basic reform of credit necessary.
> The system of issuing goods on credit which has hitherto been extant in the socialist sector, and has resulted in the complication of the channels of credit movement and in difficulties in planning it, must be abolished and replaced exclusively by bank credit. Bank credit must be organised so that enterprises and organisations needing credit should receive it without going through intermediate stages.[1]

The issue of short-term credit was accordingly placed in the hands of the State Bank. Enterprises temporarily requiring funds in excess of the money they received from the sale of their output and their own working capital could obtain them only in the form of loans from the bank, issued in accordance with the central credit plan. The legal gap through which resources were issued without the sanction and control of the planning authorities was closed. The main funds of enterprises were henceforth to be received from the sale of their planned output at fixed prices and on the basis of contracts drawn up in conformity with the state supply plans; and all transactions between enterprises passed through the bank. The only other legal sources from which enterprises could receive funds were long-term credits and grants, already administered by one or another of the central banks, and short-term credit, now concentrated in the State Bank.

But the credit reform of January 1930, like the taxation reform later in the same year, suffered from a number of serious flaws. The reform provided no checking mechanism which would ensure that

[1] SZ 98/1930 (30. i. 30).

credits and other financial resources were used efficiently at enterprise level. First, under the system which now replaced the previous semi-commercial arrangements for purchases and sales there was no provision for the satisfactory control of transactions either by the bank or by the enterprises concerned: sums were automatically transferred to the seller from the purchaser's account as soon as the invoice for a despatched order was presented to the bank. The purchaser had no preliminary control over the payment of his accounts, and the branch of the bank in which the purchaser's account was lodged could not prevent him running into debt, and had to provide him with credits to cover any deficit which might be run up by payments of bills in excess of the amount of his account. Secondly, bank control over the fulfilment of the credit plan was purely formal. Credits were issued by the bank to enterprises in lump sums in accordance with the plan; there was no attempt by the bank either to ensure that credits were used for the purposes laid down or to make issues of credits dependent on the fulfilment of the plans of enterprises. Finally, credits to enterprises were included with their own working capital in a single current account at the bank. As credits were issued automatically, this weakened their interest in preserving their own working capital and fulfilling their costs plans.[1]

The first year's experience of the credit reform provided an excellent illustration of the principle that, in a planned economy from which the automatic checks of a market economy are absent, a mechanism in which there are no built-in checks on fulfilment and penalties for non-fulfilment will run out of control. In 1930, while production of large-scale industry, according to official data, increased by 30·6%, State Bank credits rose by at least 50%.[2]

Excessive bank credits were an important contributory factor to the inflationary situation, both directly, and also because, in the words of a Soviet government decree,

> the application of the new system of crediting not only did not achieve the strengthening of rouble control...of fulfilment...and accumulations... but, on the contrary, violations of the principles of *khozraschot* and the weakening of attention to financial work and of financial discipline in economic bodies have taken place.

---

[1] 'In a number of enterprises and economic organisations the concepts "régime of economy", "reduction of non-productive expenditure", and "rationalisation of production" have long gone out of fashion. Evidently they calculate that the State Bank "will issue us the necessary sums anyway"' (Stalin, *Soch.* vol. XIII, pp. 74–5, speech of 23. vii. 1931).   [2] Ikonnikov, *op. cit.* p. 227.

The main faults of the reform were corrected during 1931 and 1932. New regulations provided that all transactions were to take place on the basis of contracts and orders which were themselves based on the production and supply plans. Payments for orders were to be made only if they were specifically accepted by the purchaser or if he gave his authority for automatic payment for specific transactions. Credits were to be issued only as contracts between enterprises were fulfilled, and not as lump sums but for specific periods and for specific purposes, principally for seasonal stocks and (to the seller) to cover the period between dispatch and payment for goods. The bank was to endeavour to use short-term credits to secure daily 'control by the rouble' of production, circulation, and financial plans. All credits were to be deposited in a special account separate from the current account of the enterprise.[1]

The precise delimitation of the functions of bank loans, and their separation into a special account, were pre-requisites for the efficient organisation of the 'own working capital' of enterprises, from which normal expenses were met. Working capital had to be sufficient to enable the enterprise to hold the minimum supply of materials, fuel, and unfinished and finished goods necessary for it to be able to fulfil its production and trading programmes. To determine the amount of capital needed for a programme was a difficult task: resources had to be large enough to give the enterprise some measure of operative independence, but not so large as to permit significant unplanned expenditure, and wastage and inefficiency. A system of norms was worked out for calculating stocks and working capital needed on the basis of the production and financial plans, and enterprises were permitted to bring up their working capital to the level required by the plan by allocations from their profits, and, where necessary, by budget grants.[2] By the eve of the second world war, however, this system was in practice still in need of substantial improvement.[3]

Nevertheless these reforms, taken as a whole, were an important step towards financial efficiency. As short-term credit and working capital were strictly restricted, enterprises could obtain extra resources only by over-fulfilling their costs plan and making more

[1] SZ 98/1930 (30. i. 30), 52/1931 (14. i. 31), 166/1931 (20. iii. 31), 282/1931 (16. vi. 31), 316/1931 (31. vii. 31), 250/1932 (25. v. 32).
[2] SZ 316/1931 (23. vii. 31), 419/1931 (21. x. 31), 433/1931 (29. x. 31), 447/1932 (13. x. 32).
[3] See, for example, V. Batyrev in *Problemy ekonomiki*, no. 5 (1939).

profits; and if they failed to fulfil their costs plan, they would run into financial difficulties from which they could not now be relieved by excessive bank credits. As a large proportion of production was used in capital investment, the tendency to cheapen production which resulted from these reforms had a direct effect on construction costs and therefore on the resources which the budget needed to contribute in order that the investment programme should be fulfilled. In addition, the larger profits which resulted from reduced costs were used to expand working capital and to finance the investment programme, and hence also reduced the burden on the budget.

The reform of credit and working capital was also essential for the effective control of budgetary allocations to the economy. It brought to an end the old tendency for working capital and capital investment to overlap; and since the transactions of enterprises were now more firmly based on *khozraschot* principles, it was possible to calculate with greater precision the financial needs of an enterprise or branch of industry for capital investment, additional working capital, and other purposes, and the profits available to meet these needs—hence the budget allocation needed to make up the deficit could be determined.

To bring about effective 'efficiency' control over these economic expenditures was difficult. Different methods were adopted according to the type of expenditure. Allocations to working capital, subsidies, and so-called 'operational expenditures' were all disbursed by the State Bank, in common with allocations to non-economic functions. 'Operational' expenditures were of essentially the same character as administrative expenditures, and were treated in the same way. Allocations to working capital were issued monthly on the basis of the production results for the previous month. They were issued to the branch, which itself redistributed them to the enterprises under it on the basis of the plan, retaining up to 10% of the total for use at its own discretion. Allocations could be stopped if the analysis of the accounts of an enterprise by the financial organs disclosed that its working capital exceeded the norm, that it had used working capital for unspecified purposes, or that it was considerably in debt. Subsidies were issued in a similar way, except that the *glavk* was given greater rights over their redistribution (on subsidies policy, see below, pp. 237–8).

To a certain extent, if the amount allocated was appropriate, grants to additional working capital and to subsidies could be relied upon to 'control themselves'—the enterprise had a direct interest in making the most effective use of them, as any wastage was reflected in lower profits, shortages of stocks, and so on. But the control of allocations to capital investment had to be much more thorough. This was emphasised by the decision in 1930 to make all budget allocations to state industry non-returnable.[1] This meant that in future (as had in any case previously been the case to a considerable extent) there would be no 'automatic' check on expenditure resulting from the obligation to repay on the part of the economic organ receiving the grant.

In 1928 allocations to investment from all sources had been placed in a common fund in the Long-Term Credit Bank, which was made responsible for disbursing them. Until 1931 the bank issued these grants automatically on the basis of the plan, irrespective of the progress of the construction; and whatever control it exercised was confined to checking quantitative progress without reference to the quality of the work. The use of allocations was so poorly controlled that allocations for investment were often used for other purposes, and during the first year of the credit reform short-term credits and working capital were often used for investment. In June 1931 a decree stated that all grants should be issued only in accordance with the actual fulfilment of the plan; that no grants for investment should be spent on non-investment purposes; that all projects should be backed by drafts and estimates; and that inspection of the work of the bank by the NKF should be increased.[2] This decree, which was put into practice only half-heartedly, was the prelude to a thoroughgoing reorganisation of the administration of investment. In May 1932 the government declared that the essentials for efficient financing were

unity in the credit system; *supervision* of the use for the purpose laid down of state resources issued for capital construction; and the *introduction of khozraschot* on construction sites, and the cheapening of construction.

To assist these purposes, four 'special banks for long-term investment' were established—the *Prombank*, replacing the Long-Term Credit Bank, and covering industry and electrification,[3] the *Sel'khoz-*

---

[1] SZ 316/1930 (23. v. 30). This decree also applied to state trade, transport, and agriculture, and was extended to local budgets and municipal economy and housing in 1934 (SZ 105/1934 (9. iii. 34)).

[2] SZ 275/1931 (9. vi. 31).

[3] It later took over the financing of transport and communications, except for roads of republican and local significance (SZ 163/1933 (21. iv. 33) and 413/1933 (21. xi. 33)).

bank, for agriculture, the *Vsekobank*, for co-operatives, and the *Tsekombank*, for housing, municipal, and cultural-welfare construction. Each bank was to have branches in the main centres where expenditure took place, and to work through the branches of the State Bank in less important areas. All investment resources were to be concentrated in the banks. Budget allocations were transferred to the special bank periodically by the appropriate financial organ, where they were put with the depreciation allowances concerned. These transfers were carried out on the basis of the annual and quarterly plan for financing capital investment, compiled by the commissariat disposing of the credits (the 'chief disposer'); and this plan in turn corresponded to the national economic plan and the budget. Thus the financial organ was responsible for the formal task of control—it had to see that allocations were not issued by the bank in excess of the provisions of the budget.[1]

The banks, in issuing the allocations to the construction organisations themselves, were expected to exercise the much more important function of 'efficiency control'. They were instructed to issue funds only in accordance with the actual progress of the work on the basis of the plans. Allocations were to be made only to projects whose financial estimate had been approved on the basis of the technical draft, and which were included in the 'title list'; and were not to be issued to enable separate parts of a job to be carried out unless the draft for the whole construction had been approved. Accounts for building materials and loads were to be paid only at fixed prices, and for equipment only at the prices laid down in the contract or in pricelists. Wages must be issued only within the limits of the approved wage funds. Finally, if expenditure on a job exceeded the estimated cost, or the quarterly allocation as fixed by the commissariat or trust concerned, no further allocations were to be given during the period.[2]

In the attempt to put these provisions into practice, an important part was played by the organisation of the construction job. In the early 1930's, two methods of organisation were given roughly equal prominence: the 'economic' or direct labour method, in which a construction was directly subordinated to the economic institution for which it was being erected; and the contract method, in which the job was contracted out to a special construction organisation.

[1] Rovinskii, *op. cit.* pp. 313–17.
[2] SZ 191/1932 (5. v. 32); *Finansy i kredit*..., pp. 176–7.

The allocations were administered differently by the bank according to the method of construction employed (see chapter IX).

For 'efficiency control' it was not sufficient that the bank should ensure that grants were issued in the planned amounts, and that no significant expenditure took place outside its main provisions. It was of primary importance that the money figure given in the plan should be an optimum figure for the particular job at the given stage of development of the economy. Now the choice of one investment project rather than another, and of one way of doing a particular job rather than another, was the task of the planners, not of the financial system. But once these choices had been made, the efficient compilation of the estimates and plans on the basis of which the work was done was a vital concern of the financial system and the special banks.

Consequently a further group of decrees set out the methods by which drafts and estimates should be approved. A decree now stipulated that the 'title lists' of 'above-limit' constructions approved by the government should show for each job the place of construction, the draft power involved, the dates at which the job would begin and end, its total estimated cost, and the sum required in the year concerned. Limits varied from 0·5 million to 3 million roubles. In general they tended to be higher for heavy industry than for light industry[1] (i.e. more could be spent in heavy industry without inclusion in the title list approved by the centre), but all new enterprises (and new shops in existing enterprises) producing new lines of output had to be included in the list. While all 'above-limit' constructions had to be approved by the government, the commissariat responsible was not rigidly bound to the precise sum laid down in the title list for each job. It could keep an undistributed reserve of 3% of the total budgetary allocation for use at its discretion; and it could redistribute allocations between the separate 'above-limit' jobs, provided that no job had its allocation reduced by more than 10%.[2] In addition, each commissariat was allocated a fund which it could expend at its own discretion on 'below-limit' investments. Thus, while central control was considerable, it was not completely rigid.

To obviate the wastage which was a characteristic feature of the early period of industrialisation, construction jobs were also sub-

[1] Thus the limit for the coal industry was 3 million roubles; for oil-working 4 million; for the sugar industry 3 million; for the paper industry 2 million; for the glass industry 1·5 million.

[2] SZ 196/1932 (27. vi. 32), 386/1934 (27. ix. 34), 414/1934 (23. x. 34).

jected to more systematic control from the centre over their detailed drafts and estimates. Technical drafting offices were reorganised, and each made responsible for a precise sphere of work. At the first stage of the process, in the case of above-limit jobs, the combine or commissariat had to send a 'planning directive' (*planovoe zadanie*) to the drafting organisation, showing the purpose, place and planned productivity of the job. The technical drafting office then drew up a 'drafting directive' (*proektnoe zadanie*) which had to be approved by the combine or by VSNKh (later by the *glavk* or by the commissariat) according to cost. Approval having been given, the drafting office now drew up the detailed technical draft and estimate. These had to make systematic use of so-called 'consolidated measures' (*ukrupnennye izmeriteli*)—unit cost indices—based on previous construction experience, as guides to estimating the expenditure allowable for particular parts of the job.[1] This draft and estimate also had to be approved by the combine or VSNKh, and was used by the body carrying out the construction as the basis for its working plans—these did not have to be approved by a central body.[2] Later, centralisation was taken still further, so that the general plans and estimates of the most important jobs had to be approved by STO itself, i.e. by what was in some respects the economic committee of the central government.[3]

All these measures helped to make the administration of budgetary expenditure on the economy more efficient. But construction was on the whole still not carried out 'smoothly'. Certain organisational defects in administering these expenditures were important here, and will be discussed in chapter IX. But wastage and inefficiency in construction were mainly the result of more fundamental difficulties. The inflationary situation meant that shortages were inevitable throughout the economy. The system of synthetic planning had not yet been properly worked out, and as a result industry developed unevenly. Bottlenecks and scrambles for materials were a characteristic feature of the whole period before the abolition of rationing. As a result emergency measures had to be adopted to ensure the fulfilment of the most important sections of the investment pro-

[1] An important part was played in drawing up the unified system of calculation for investment by the Central Administration of National Economic Accounting (or Reporting) (TsUNKhU), which had accounting and supervising commissions jointly with the special banks at 200 important construction sites (SZ 318/1932 (3. vii. 32)).

[2] SZ 465/1931 (26. xi. 31).

[3] SZ 354/1934 (3. ix. 34). For a list of these objects for 1935, see SZ 152/1935 (22. iii. 35).

grammes; for example, as late as 1933 the government had to condemn unplanned construction as an anti-state act, and to apply severe legal penalties against it,[1] and in 1933–4 urgent construction jobs could only be fulfilled by making them into 'shock' jobs, to which special priorities in transport and supplies were given.[2]

The inflationary situation was also reflected in the budget in the large-scale issue of subsidies. This was the result of the policy pursued by the state of partly isolating the costs structure of industry from the inflationary pressure on the retail market. Transfer prices of basic industrial materials were kept constant, and these materials were therefore a fixed element in the costs of industries purchasing them. But within each branch of industry labour costs and overheads rose, particularly after 1930. These artificial transfer prices were maintained by subsidies from the state budget. From 1931 onwards subsidies replaced bank credits as the source through which losses were made up.[3] The subsidies policy was justified by two major considerations.[4] First, stable prices for the main industrial materials made possible some stability in the costing of current production and in estimates for construction jobs: frequent increases in prices would have produced great administrative difficulties (though they would have brought the cost of materials purchased by an industry more into line with its own wage costs). Secondly, low prices for metal and coal meant that the prices of machines could be kept down; and hence their use would be encouraged. In theory it might appear that this was of no importance, for capital goods were allocated to enterprises in accordance with the plan, and paid for almost entirely from the budget. But in practice the plan was not completely rigid. The director could choose between machines and labour to some extent in disposing of his resources, and low prices encouraged him to purchase machines. The subsidies system may also perhaps have been made necessary by the position of agriculture. If prices had been permitted to rise inside industry, the peasant would have had added reason for thinking that the low prices he was being paid for

[1] *TsIK* 3/vi, Bull. 11, p. 29.

[2] SZ 181/1933 (28. iv. 33), 269/1934 (26. v. 34).

[3] During 1930 the uncontrolled short-term credits already mentioned played a major role in covering up the rises in industrial costs. The obvious disadvantage of this credit policy was that it was uncontrolled, whereas the point at which close central control is needed is obviously the point at which costs plans are not fulfilled.

[4] For the arguments advanced in favour of the subsidy system, see, for example, Sh. Turetskii in *Pl. khoz.* no. 9 (1935), pp. 115–16; M. Bogolepov in *ibid.* no. 5 (1936), pp. 75 ff.; and citations in Baykov, *op. cit.* pp. 293–5.

his compulsory contract deliveries of agricultural raw materials and foodstuffs were too low (he was given considerable reason by the rise of prices on the retail market).[1]

On the other hand, the subsidies system carried many disadvantages. It meant from a budgetary point of view that each capital good was paid for through two channels: (i) the budgetary allocation to capital investment through which capital goods were bought at artificially low prices, and (ii) the budget subsidy, through which the producers of capital goods were compensated for low prices. Budget subsidies were under close control by the NKF, and therefore industries with high costs were under especially strict financial supervision. But subsidies weakened *khozraschot*. If an enterprise over-fulfilled its plan, it did not make a greater profit, it made a greater loss, and therefore required a larger subsidy. NKF therefore had no incentive to encourage enterprises to over-fulfil their plan of output. Enterprises, on the other hand, had no particular incentive to fulfil their costs plan, for they made no profit. The structure of industrial costs was distorted by varying levels of subsidies. A considerable proportion of subsidies was swallowed up in inflated overheads.[2] The subsidy system was sensible and suitable as a means of enabling sub-marginal enterprises within a branch to operate, and as a means of enabling new lines to be brought in while their costs were still high. But the system of giving subsidies to whole branches of industry could be justified only by the temporary conditions of the first stage of forced industrialisation.

In evaluating Soviet data given in current rouble prices, the effects of subsidies must be borne in mind. Subsidies artificially deflate costs in the capital goods sector, so that a rouble used to buy a subsidised capital good is worth more than a rouble used to buy a non-subsidised consumer good. In addition, the value of the rouble spent on the retail market is further relatively reduced as turnover tax is added to transfer price; and roubles have different values in different years owing to changes in the level of costs. Thus expenditure in money terms may not be directly related to expenditure in real terms, and data in current prices of different years may not be comparable.

[1] For data on this point see Turetskii, *op. cit.* pp. 115–16.
[2] Turetskii, *Pl. khoz.* no. 9 (1935), pp. 107–11.

7. EXPENDITURE ON AGRICULTURE AND TRANSPORT

Budgetary allocations to industry, with which we have so far been primarily concerned, amounted in 1930–4 to some 50–55% of total allocations to the national economy. Some 10–15% of allocations were expended on agriculture, and some 5–10% on road and rail transport and communications.

Expenditure on agriculture will not be considered in detail here. Collectivisation had made unnecessary the complex system of 'funds' and credits through which grants had been issued to private agriculture. From 1930 onwards budget allocations were mainly made as subsidies or investment grants to the state farms and Machine-Tractor Stations, and the methods by which they were disbursed did not differ essentially from those for industry.[1]

The system of administering transport finance before 1931 was a revival of the pre-revolutionary system used on the state railways—all income and expenditure passed gross through the budget. In the period from 1927/8 onwards, as Tables 14–15 show, the gross income of the railways considerably exceeded current expenditure on running costs and maintenance, and was sufficient to cover investment on the railways and the various social and cultural services they maintained, in addition to their operating costs. But in 1931 costs began to rise, in common with those of industry, and tariffs had to be increased.[2] At the same time it was decided that efficient *khozraschot* on the railways was not compatible with financing their running costs through the budget, and in April 1931 railway finance was brought into line with that of industry.[3] Only net income (gross income less running costs) was transferred to the budget in future, and the budget was responsible only for expenditure on investment, increased working capital, central and local administration, and cadres and scientific research.

However, during 1931 the financial position of the railways worsened instead of improving.[4] A decree of May 1932 stated that there was no personal responsibility for either income or expenditure; financial and material incentives were absent; the financial interrelations of separate parts of the system were confused; material

---

[1] Thus in 1934 (Plan) total state allocations to NK of Agriculture and NK of State Farms from the budget, State Bank and other services amounted to 2·6 milliard roubles, of which 1·26 were to the state sector, 0·98 to *Traktortsentr*, 0·08 to servicing trusts and 0·07 to science and training (*Pl. khoz.* no. 7 (1934), pp. 47–8).
[2] *TsIK* 3/v, Bull. 4, pp. 8–11; *Pl. khoz.* nos. 1–2 (1933), pp. 8–9.
[3] SZ 214/1931 (30. iv. 31).   [4] SZ 408/1931 (1. x. 31).

and financial plans had broken down; the payment of wages was delayed; bottlenecks had prevented the smooth financing of investment. In the following years frequent changes of an experimental character were made in the organisation of railway finance. The line was made the basic economic unit, and income was distributed between lines in accordance with the actual loads carried. The payment made to the line per ton-km. or passenger-km. was determined by 'accounting rates' (*raschotnye stavki*) based on planned costs plus a fixed percentage of profit, and varying according to the type of transport and the load carried. The permitted percentage of profit was raised for the most important loads in order that they should be given priority. Special methods of financing depots, stations, and operational districts were introduced.[1] From 1933 onwards investment allocations to transport were administered by Prombank and supervised in the same way as grants to industry.[2]

These changes improved the efficiency of the financial organisation of railway transport, but during 1932–5 wages continued to rise more rapidly than charges. In 1932, for example, costs rose much more rapidly than was planned, and the planned net income to the budget was not fulfilled. The gap between operating expenses and operating receipts steadily narrowed, and investment had to be increasingly covered by allocations from the budget. In 1934 the investment programmes of the most important lines were fulfilled only by making up from the budget the deficits resulting from the failure to earn the profits planned.[3]

8. OTHER BUDGETARY EXPENDITURES

Even in this period of intensive development of the economy, a large proportion of budgetary expenditure was devoted to traditional expenditures on defence, administration, and the social and cultural services, the latter mainly through the local budgets. A considerable expansion of social and cultural services was a concomitant of the industrialisation programme. Universal literacy, and the provision of substantial facilities for trade training and higher technical

[1] SZ 251/1932 (29. v. 32), 237/1933 (3. vii. 33), 241/1933 (8. vii. 33), 419/1934 (25. x. 34), 350/1935 (31. vii. 35). See also A. A. Grigoriev, *Sbornik rukovodyashchikh materialov po khozyaistvennomu raschotu na zheleznodorozhnom transporte* (1951), introduction.

[2] *TsIK* 4/vi, Bull. 13, p. 36.

[3] *Finansy SSSR...* (1931–4), p. 30. For the reform in the administration of the finance of posts and telegraphs, which took place along similar lines to that of rail transport, see SZ 456/1930 (6. viii. 30), 252/1932 (27. v. 32).

education, were, for example, essential to the building of a modern industrial state.

Table 43 shows that during this period 21–23% of allocations were made to the social and cultural services, and between 3·4% and 9·1% to defence. Allocations to administration remained fairly steady at 4%.

Unlike allocations to the national economy, allocations to these purposes are not a special feature of the Soviet budget, and the methods by which they are administered and controlled are accordingly of less interest, and will be summarised only briefly here.

The method by which budget estimates were compiled and adopted has already been outlined in chapter VI. The system of norms or 'unit costs' provided the basis for the estimation of the money required by the departments and these estimates were checked by the financial organs in the course of compiling the budget.

This 'preliminary control', as it was called, aimed at ensuring that allocations were of an optimum amount. If this was the case, budgetary efficiency depended on the success of 'operative control' of the disbursement of these expenditures. This control, which had been primarily in the hands of the State Bank since 1928, is discussed in chapter IX.

Expenditure was checked post-factum during the examination of quarterly and annual accounts and balances by the appropriate department of NKF.

Until 1932 the supervision of this process had been entirely in the hands of the bodies operating it, i.e. principally the bank and the disposer of the grant. But in 1932 the rights of central and local financial organs in supervising budgetary expenditure were considerably extended. They were made responsible for seeing that expenditure of budgetary institutions took place in accordance with the norms, and that accounts were correctly compiled; they also had to supervise the expenditure of economic allocations for non-investment purposes (investment allocations were of course subject to the control system of the special banks).[1]

Experience showed, however, that control by the banks and by the spending departments of the NKF was insufficient to prevent overexpenditure and the use of allocations for unauthorised purposes. What was clearly needed was some kind of external control department which would carry out selective investigations and audits of the

[1] SZ 501/1931 (28. xii. 31), 505/1932 (9. xii. 32).

use of budget grants. For this the bureaucratic 'State Financial Control' organisation of NKF was inadequate; the functions of this body were limited to the formal preparation of inspection reports, and had little effect on the efficiency of expenditure, and duplicated the work of the budget department of NKF and of the RKI. Accordingly 'State Financial Control' was abolished in 1930, and for three years external control was left to the occasional investigations of the broad government Commission of Fulfilment,[1] and to the financial department of the RKI and the volunteer brigades attached to it.[2] In 1933 the hiatus was filled by the establishment of financial and budget inspection departments at local and central level, which controlled expenditure by surveys and sample inspections of documents and other methods. A variety of methods of inspection was evolved, based partly on the previous experience of the RKI. These included the establishment of 'supervision posts' of voluntary workers in factories and institutions, reports at general meetings of workers, 'public inspections' of phases of budget work, and the publication of reports of investigations in the press. The new organisation achieved some improvements in financial discipline, but on the whole its work was unsatisfactory.[3]

In this chapter we have traced the main developments in the Soviet budgetary system during the period of rationing and intensive industrialisation. It has been shown how the turnover and profits taxes were established by the tax reform of 1930-1 to facilitate the raising of revenue to finance the plans. It has also been shown how methods were gradually evolved for controlling both traditional and investment expenditures.

The inflation of the first five-year plan period, which continued during the early years of the second five-year plan, was responsible for the presence of a number of transitional and temporary features of the budgetary system. Shortages on the retail market had led to

---

[1] This commission, which had local commissions at republican and regional levels, was responsible for generally checking the fulfilment of government directives, and its special investigations covered financial among other matters (for example, it investigated local budget accounting in 1933). It was later made into the Commission of State Supervision (after the abolition of RKI), and finally into the Commissariat of State Control (SZ 18/1931 (24. xii. 30), 100/1931 (13. ii. 31), 405/1931 (5. x. 31), 462/1932 (19. x. 32), 233/1933 (17. vi. 33), 58/1934 (11. ii. 34), 75/1934 (27. ii. 34), 471/1935 (29. x. 35), 673/1940 (15. x. 40); and *Fin. khoz. bull.* nos. 27-8 (1939), pp. 1-2 (10. vii. 39)).

[2] See report by Chutskayev in *TsIK* 3/v, Bull. 5, pp. 2-5.

[3] *Finansy SSSR*... (1931-4), pp. 11-12; *TsIK* 2/vi Bull. 15, pp. 9-10, 3/vi, Bull. 13, pp. 1-3; D'yachenko and Kozlov, *op. cit.* p. 182.

rationing and the multiple price system, which considerably complicated the imposition of the turnover tax and made it impossible to use it as a regulator of the state of supply and demand on the retail market. Rises in costs had almost wiped out profits and prevented their use as incentives to the efficient operation of industry. At the same time these costs rises had involved large budget subsidies to industry and agriculture, and made the maintenance of effective control over investment expenditure difficult.

A thoroughgoing reform of the budgetary system had been carried out, so that it would be correct to speak of the emergence in this period of a new budgetary system, appropriate to a planned economy in which industrialisation is taking place. But before this new system could be stabilised and made efficient, it was essential that rationing should be abolished and the relationship between industrial costs and transfer price normalised.

CHAPTER IX

IMPROVEMENTS AND MODIFICATIONS IN THE BUDGETARY SYSTEM AFTER THE ABOLITION OF RATIONING 1935-41

From 1932 onwards there was a steady improvement in the economic situation. Industrial efficiency increased and costs began to fall. As a result of collectivisation, larger and more stable supplies of agricultural products were available to the state at low fixed prices. The intensive pressure of the first years of industrialisation was somewhat relieved—the output of consumer goods was considerably increased, while the rise in the urban population slowed down. These factors made the abolition of the inflationary situation of 1930-4 an objective possibility.

However, the tremendous expansion of the wages fund since 1928 meant that supplies of consumer goods were still completely inadequate to meet the purchasing power of the population at the price levels of the pre-planning period or even at the increased 1932 level of rationed prices. As nominal wages could not be reduced, the abolition of rationing could only be brought about either by reducing costs of production and increasing the output of consumer goods very considerably, or by raising retail prices, or both.

The second five-year plan (1933-7), adopted in 1934, concentrated attention on the first of these alternatives. It was intended to raise labour productivity per person employed by 63%, and expand the labour force by 28%, while increasing the total wages' fund by only 55%. As a result, costs would be reduced by 26%, and, as was planned in the first five-year plan, a 'gap' would appear between cost price and transfer price in industry. This 'gap' was to be used in various ways. Primarily, it would enable a greater proportion of investment to be financed from profits and not from budget allocations. The proportion of money accumulation passing through the budget would decline, and budget receipts from turnover tax would be reduced in relative terms. At the same time supplies of consumer goods would rise more rapidly than the purchasing power of the population, so that the average level of retail prices could be reduced by 35%.[1]

However, even if this programme had been fulfilled, the reduction in commercial prices would not have brought them down to the level of rationed prices, even by 1937. In 1933 and 1934 the wages' fund in fact expanded more rapidly than had been planned, and the output of consumer goods increased less than had been planned, primarily owing to the shift of production to the defence industries after the assumption of power by the National Socialists in Germany in 1933.[2] It was therefore impossible to achieve the 35% reduction in retail prices envisaged in the plan, and unless rationed prices were increased the abolition of rationing would have to be postponed for a number of years.

Meanwhile the government became convinced that the retention of rationing was harmful now that the economic situation was more stable. Rationing involved over-centralisation and the weakening of consumer choice, bureaucracy, and a complicated multiple pricing system. It considerably weakened the incentive effects of wage differentials. The supply of rationed goods at low prices was of greater value to the special categories of workers receiving them than very large wage increases spent on goods sold at commercial prices or in the free market; and the privileged supplies of scarce goods to important factories were available to all the shock-workers in a factory: the right to purchase them could not be graduated satisfactorily according to skill and work done.[3]

At the end of 1934 the government therefore decided to increase the general level of retail prices considerably. Commercial prices were reduced, but ration prices were raised substantially. This resulted in an enormous increase in the revenue from turnover tax: between 1933 and 1936 it rose from 27 milliard to 66 milliard roubles, and amounted by 1936 to 70% of budgetary revenue. This was almost entirely due to the increased level of retail prices. The prices of the most important rationed goods were raised in an *ad hoc* fashion so that the given supply of marketable output roughly equalled

[1] For details, see *Second Five-Year Plan...*, pp. xli, 464, 508, 637–9, 656, 658; and *Proekt vtorogo pyatiletnego plana* (1934), p. 403.
[2] The wage fund in 1934 was 44·0 milliard roubles against 38·1 milliard planned (*Pl. khoz.* 5–6 (1934), pp. 196–232; no. 2, 1936, p. 281).
[3] For further details, see Baykov, *op. cit.* pp. 249–50.

demand (for many goods, however, lower prices were fixed than the market required, leading to a shortage). The sharpest increases were in the prices of essential foodstuffs such as grain and meat. During the rationing period, agricultural products had been compulsorily purchased from the peasantry at stable low prices, and sold at somewhat higher prices to the urban population as rations. This 'tax' on the peasantry was for the most part a tax in kind, and was reflected in the budget only in the moderate turnover tax collected on these products. When rationing was abolished, food prices were raised considerably, but the compulsory delivery prices paid to the peasantry were increased only slightly. Hence from 1935 onwards the bulk of turnover tax was collected not from industrial consumer goods but from agricultural products, as is shown in Table 41. The demand for agricultural goods was so great that it apparently proved possible to reduce the rate of tax on certain non-agricultural goods in 1935, even though receipts from the tax considerably increased in that year. Revenue from goods traditionally subject to excise, such as tobacco and kerosene, rose relatively slowly,[1] and the revenue from vodka actually declined, apparently owing to a reduction in consumption.[2] These commodities had yielded about half the total turnover tax in 1931; in 1936 they were probably responsible for less than 20% of the tax.

Thus the abolition of rationing transformed the appearance of the revenue side of the budget. It resulted in an increase in turnover tax relative to other items of revenue; and turnover tax itself became much more a tax on agricultural products, and much less a tax on industrial consumer goods and goods traditionally subject to excise.

The reform of retail prices by abolishing rationing in 1935 was logically followed by the reform of industrial wholesale prices. This was begun in 1936 with the abolition of subsidies to heavy industry, the disadvantages of which were discussed in chapter VIII. The second five-year plan had not specifically set the abolition of subsidies as an aim, although it had provided for a substantial rise in profits which would presumably have lessened the need for subsidies.[3] In the long

[1] The rise in the yield from oil products as a whole in 1931–6 is mainly accounted for by the abolition of privileged prices for oil products sold to state enterprises (for use by tractors, etc.) (SZ 337/1933 (28. viii. 33) and 210/1936 (15. iv. 36)).

[2] The *rate* of tax on vodka was not reduced until 1937.

[3] 'Savings' in industry from reductions in costs were to be 13·0 milliard roubles in 1937 as compared with 1932. The profits of industry were to amount to only 11·6 milliard roubles: this figure presumably refers to *net* profits (gross profits less subsidies), which had certainly been negative in 1932 (*Second Five-Year Plan*..., pp. 464, 637–9, 656, 658).

run, the abolition of subsidies, like the abolition of rationing, could have been achieved by cost reductions. But in the short run it could be brought about only by raising the transfer prices of subsidised goods. In 1936 these prices were actually raised more than the minimum needed in order to abolish subsidies, so that there would be a reasonable profit margin in the industries previously subsidised.[1]

This reform was reflected in the budget in two ways. There was a direct saving on subsidies; and the cost of equipment purchased through budget allocations to investment rose by approximately the same amount. The reform did not therefore alter the size of the allocation to the economy, but produced a shift in it from subsidies to capital investments. A secondary effect of the reform was that the costs of fuel and raw materials sold to the consumer goods industries rose, so that the transfer prices at which consumer goods were sold to trading organisations had to be increased; this was compensated by appropriate reductions in the rate of turnover tax.

These two reforms made possible a return to the approach to financial planning which seemed to underlie much of the unsuccessful policy of price reduction pursued by the Soviet government in the late 1920's. The government, said Stalin in November 1927, 'considers that industry must serve the population and not *vice-versa*. It considers that the undeviating reduction of the prices of industrial goods is the basic means without which the normal growth of industry is impossible.'[2] But such a policy can be carried out in a planned economy only if (i) supply and demand are not badly out of balance on the retail market; (ii) no rapid transfer of resources is taking place to production not intended for immediate consumption, whether of capital goods or of defence goods; and (iii) *either* a rapid shift is taking place from the production of investment goods to the production of consumption goods, *or* output is rising more rapidly than wages, or both, so that costs will fall.

The absence of these prerequisites in 1927–9 led to the failure of the policy of price reduction. In 1935–7, however, the abolition of rationing restored the balance of supply and demand, and a certain

---

[1] A similar reform was carried out in transport in 1938 and 1939. Passenger fares and goods tariffs were raised by an average of 20% and 14% respectively. As a result, the transport system, which had previously received large net grants for investment, etc., from the budget, became self-supporting, and in 1940 it even made a substantial net allocation to the budget (*Fin. khoz. bull.* (1938), no. 13, p. 11 (20. iii. 38); (1939), nos. 23–4, pp. 21–7 (5. iii. 39); SZ 230/1940 (2. iv. 40)).

[2] *Soch.* vol. x, p. 230.

shift was taking place from the production of investment goods to the production of consumer goods. However, the wages position was less satisfactory. In every year of the planning period, as Table 31 shows, the planned wage fund was over-fulfilled, even in those years when production rose less than planned. It appears to be an inherent tendency in an economy of the Soviet type, where labour is scarce and not as a rule subject to direct allocation, for managers to over-fulfil their wages' plan in order to attract and spur on labour.[1] In theory it was intended that output norms should be raised each year so that in successive years workers would receive the same money wage only for a higher output. But in practice it proved possible to introduce this policy only gradually. The simplest course for managers was to over-fulfil wages plans by paying out bonuses, etc. They would not do so only if the incentives to fulfil the costs plan were as great as the incentives to fulfil the output plan, or if wage issues were under a tight control by a body independent of factory management (e.g. the bank). Throughout the period neither of these conditions was operative. However, the abolition of subsidies, the introduction of the Director's Fund, and other measures discussed elsewhere, increased the incentives to fulfil the costs plan in 1935 and 1936, and costs in industry fell fairly substantially.[2] On 1 June 1937, therefore, the retail prices of textiles and other consumer goods were reduced by 5–10%, principally by reducing the rate of turnover tax.[3] The financial policy underlying the price reduction proposals of both the first and the second five-year plans began to be put into operation, and it seemed as if the financial system was entering what might be described as a 'normal' period of operation, in which accumulation was no longer being carried out under emergency conditions, and inflation and scarcities were decreasing rather than increasing.

[1] On wage over-fulfilment, see Shenger in *Pl. khoz.* no. 3 (1938), pp. 73–82.
[2] Costs fell by 4·1% in 1935 against the 5·2% planned; and by 4·4% in 1936 against the 6·2% planned (*Pl. khoz.* no. 9 (1935), p. 107; no. 2 (1936), p. 141; no. 1 (1937), p. 91).
[3] This is illustrated by the following examples:

	Reduction in retail price (%)	Turnover tax Old rate (%)	Turnover tax New rate (%)
Linen towelling	10	42	31
Linen sheets	9	51	45
Linen narrow cloth	10	48	43
Matches	33·3	41–53	22·8–24·4

(SZ 292/1936 (13. v. 36), 294/1936 (19. vi. 36); *Fin. khoz. bull.* (1937), no. 24, p. 7 (23. vii. 37)).

Table 31. *Wage fund, 1933–40 (milliard roubles)*

	Five-year plan	Annual plan	Fulfilment
1933	—	?	35·0 [b]
1934	—	38·1 [c]	44·0 [d]
1935	—	49·8 [d]	56·2 [d]
1936	—	63·4 [d]	71·4 [e]
1937	50·7 [a]	78·3 [e]	82·0 [f]
1938	—	94·0 [f]	96·4 [g]
1940	—	—	123·7/161 [h]

Sources:
(a) *Second Five-Year Plan*..., p. 625.
(b) Stalin, *Leninism*, p. 642.
(c) *Pl. khoz.* nos. 5–6 (1934), pp. 196–232. This was given earlier (*TsIK*, 4/vi, Bull. 13, p. 26) as 37·7.
(d) *Pl. khoz.* no. 2 (1936), p. 281.
(e) *Pl. khoz.* no. 3 (1937), pp. 222 ff.
(f) *Supreme Soviet, 1938*, p. 525.
(g) *Leninism*, pp. 640, 642.
(h) It is not certain which of these figures is compatible with the 1938 figure, most probably the former. See Bergson, *Rev. Econ. Stat.* vol. xxix (1947), pp. 234–42.

But from 1937 onwards, the international situation made necessary tremendous increases in direct defence expenditure. Unfortunately details of Soviet allocations to defence have not been published since the mid-1920's, and so it is impossible to analyse budgetary expenditure on defence. Table 32 brings together the three main budgetary items from which defence and associated expenditures were financed:

(i) The allocation to the commissariats of the army and navy covered the bulk of defence expenditure. It apparently included the pay, peace-time pensions, feeding and quartering of the commanding staff and the rank and file of the army and navy; part at least of the army health and educational services; the cost of building army barracks, clubs, and houses; transport and fuel costs; the cost of stocks held by the armed forces; and the costs of armaments and technical equipment which were purchased out of this allocation from the enterprises producing them. It is not known, however, what proportion of army purchases were made at privileged prices, although most privileged prices of food, fuel including oil, and other army supplies, and reduced transport charges were abolished in 1936 and 1937.[1] It cannot therefore be said whether the defence item includes as great a percentage of turnover tax as other items of the budget, or whether it contains any 'hidden subsidies'.

[1] For such details as are available on the coverage of this item of the budget, see *TsIK* 3/vi, Bull. no. 11, p. 26. Grin'ko, *Finansovaya programma...na 1937...*, pp. 40–1; *Soviet Union, 1936*, pp. 511–12; Rovinskii, *op. cit.* (1951 edn.), pp. 36–7.

Table 32. *Expenditure on defence and the NKVD, 1937–41 (million roubles)*

	1937 (plan)	1937 (fulfilment)	1938 (plan)	1938 (fulfilment)	1939 (plan)	1940 (plan)	1940 (fulfilment)	1941 (plan)
(i) Direct defence expenditure:								
Army	20,102·2	17,481	27,044·0	23,151	33,448·7	46,957·1	56,102	58,275·8
Navy					7,436·2	10,109·1		12,589·8
(ii) NKVD[1]	2,669·4	2,995	4,320·0	4,315	5,455·4	7,045·4	—	7,318·8[2]
(iii) Defence industry:								
Aviation	—	—	—	—	2,387·8	2,127·5	—	5,581·2
Shipbuilding	—	—	—	—	2,167·1	2,902·5	—	1,309·6
Military supplies	—	—	—	—	2,537·6	1,880·5	—	1,684·5
Armaments	—	—	—	—	1,420·9	1,049·8	—	1,190·4
Glavvoenstroi	—	—	—	—	—	291·3	—	222·8
Total	2,328·8	—	7,415·0	—	8,513·4	8,251·6	—	9,988·5
TOTAL	25,100·4	—	38,779·0	—	54,853·7	72,363·2	—	88,172·9
TOTAL BUDGET EXPENDITURE	97,119·5	93,921	131,138·0	123,996	155,477·8	179,913·4	173,259	216,052·2

Sources: *Fin. khoz. bull.* (1937), no. 2, p. 7 (13. i. 37). *Zas. verkh. sov.* (1938, 1939), pp. 328–53, 357–90; (1940), pp. 64ff., 233–63; (1941), pp. 260–94.

Notes:

(1) The functions covered by the NKVD include 'securing revolutionary order and state security'; defence of public property; registrations of births, deaths, marriages and divorces; frontier defence; convoy armies; the Administration of main and unpaved roads and motor transport; the Administration of state surveys and cartography; resettlement; the Administration of forest defence and fire protection; weights and measures; and the militia (for details see S. S. Studenikin et al., *Sovetskoe administrativnoe pravo* (1950), pp. 271ff.). Not all of the expenditures of the NKVD were met from this item of the budget. For example, allocations were made under the 'national economy' item of the budget to 'separate constructions of the NKVD', amounting to 1,884·3 milliard roubles in 1938, 2,884·0 in 1939, 3,440·0 in 1940, and 6,998·0 in 1941 (planned figures). There is no evidence that these constructions were of a military character.

(2) In February 1941 the NK of State Security was separated from the NKVD. They were rejoined in July 1941 after the outbreak of war.

(ii) The home armies of the NKVD were financed from the allocation to that commissariat. The extent to which these should be regarded as part of the defence forces is a matter of controversy, and the proportion of the NKVD item allocated to these armies is unknown. But it would certainly be incorrect to treat the total allocation to the NKVD as a defence allocation.

(iii) The commissariats of the defence *industries*, as distinct from the armed forces themselves, formed part of the system of industrial commissariats. Allocations to investment, subsidies, increased working capital, and 'operational expenditures' in these commissariats were made through the national economy item of the budget.

These three items taken together increased three and a half times between 1937 and 1941 (plan), and rose to 40% of total budgetary expenditure. The shift to defence had repercussions throughout the economy. As far as the financial system was concerned, it meant that the available supply of consumer goods increased at a much slower rate, while the wage fund rose considerably more than had been planned. An inflationary situation again developed. On the retail market, the wage fund grew much more rapidly than state and co-operative trade turnover, so that prices and the quantity of trade on the collective farm market considerably increased:[1] in 1940 and 1941 retail prices of foodstuffs and industrial consumer goods were somewhat increased in order to reduce the excess purchasing power of the population.[2] In industry, administrative measures were taken through the State Bank to prevent unplanned expenditure on wages,[3] but no reductions in costs were reported (in the building industry, costs rose in 1939 and 1940).[4]

Thus in the new circumstances of intensive defence preparations, the financial phenomena of the first five-year plan period were repeated on a smaller scale. The measures taken in connexion with the budgetary system in this period therefore had two contradictory aspects: a number of measures was adopted of a more or less

---

[1] The wage fund rose from 82 milliard roubles in 1937 to 124/161 (alternative figures) in 1940; retail trade (state and co-operative) rose from 126 to 175; trade on the collective farm market from 18 to 41; and collective farm money income from 14 to 21 milliard roubles (*Leninism*, pp. 640, 642; M. M. Lifits, *Sovetskaya torgovlya*, pp. 33, 54, 82–3, 102; N. Voznesensky, *Economic results of the U.S.S.R. in 1940* (1941), pp. 7–11).

[2] For details, see Baykov, *op. cit.* pp. 260–1; *Economic Survey of Europe in 1951*, United Nations Department of Economic Affairs (1952), p. 215.

[3] See below, p. 270.

[4] No data on industrial costs were published for these years, but the wage fund appears to have been over-fulfilled in each year.

emergency character to stem the rising inflation, and at the same time intensive attempts were made to improve the efficiency of the budgetary system by making changes of a more permanent kind.

Emergency measures.[1] Expenditure was limited in several ways. Drastic alterations were made in the terms on which sickness and other benefits were given, so that from 1939 onwards the amount paid out in sickness benefits fell. Expenditure by social insurance organs on rest homes, education, etc., was prevented from rising. As a result, by 1941 social insurance fees at the level of 1937 were able to be used to maintain services which they had not been originally intended to cover,[2] and also yielded a substantial surplus for general budget revenue (see Table 33). At the same period various relatively minor changes were made which had the effect of somewhat reducing the burden on budgetary expenditure.[3] Charges were introduced for various services previously maintained entirely free by the state budget, such as crèches, kindergartens, and tuition in the senior classes of secondary schools and in universities.[4] The Director's Fund in industry was reduced from 4% to 2% of standard profit; and the special fees paid to trade union funds for cultural purposes from the costs of economic bodies were reduced.[5]

On the revenue side of the budget, various increases in taxation were made. The most important of these was in the turnover tax, resulting from the rise in retail prices in 1940–1. Taxes directly on the income of the population were also increased. In the towns, income tax and the cultural and housing levy were both raised, from a maximum combined marginal rate of 6·1 % on incomes of workers and employees above 1,000 roubles per month, to 13%.[6] Direct taxes in the countryside were also raised.[7] The charges made for compulsory

[1] All the measures mentioned here had some justification apart from the fiscal one, but I confine myself to explaining their fiscal effects.

[2] Pensions to retired workers, which were met in 1937–8 from general budgetary revenue.

[3] The limitation of expenditure of bodies 'on the budget' directly reduced budget expenditure; the limitations on wage and other costs of *khozraschot* bodies in effect reduced the budget grant they required.

[4] Tuition fees were not included in the income of the educational bodies concerned, but were paid directly into the state budget. Payments to kindergartens and crèches were included in their income, and the budget allocation was reduced accordingly. In addition, the expenditure on student grants was reduced by giving them only for 'excellent progress' (*otlichnye uspekhi*).

[5] For details of these measures, see *Fin. khoz. bull.* (1938), nos. 11–12, pp. 3, 45–7 (8. iii. 38, 7. ii. 38); (1939), nos. 19–20, pp. 22–3 (11. iv. 39), nos. 13–14, pp. 3–5 (21. iv. 39); SZ 590/1940 (14. x. 40), 637/1940 (2. x. 40).

[6] *Zas. verkh. sov.* (1940), pp. 505–14 (4. iv. 40); and pp. 515–19 (4. iv. 40).

[7] See *Zas. verkh. sov.* (1939), and (1941), p. 36.

and voluntary insurance (of cattle, etc.) were raised, without increasing payments for claims, so that the net revenue of the budget from this source increased.[1]

Although some of these measures were continued after the war as more permanent features of the budgetary system, they were all occasioned at least in part by the financial situation resulting from increased defence expenditure.

Improvements in the system. The improvements made in the system were substantial, although they were necessarily restricted, at least from 1937 onwards, by the financial atmosphere described. They were made possible by the price reforms in industry and retail trade already described, which were themselves based on the successful stabilisation of the economic system in the mid-1930's. They will here be considered under three main heads:

(1) *Budgetary Expenditure.* The abolition of subsidies meant that the budget was now concerned primarily with direct allocations to investment as far as the economy was concerned. Attention could be concentrated on the efficient administration of investment expenditures. At the same time the successful solution of the most urgent financial problems of industrialisation meant that the financial authorities could now devote more of their attention to the control of budgetary expenditures on other items of the budget.

(2) *Financial control of industry.* The abolition of subsidies also meant that industry was now entirely dependent (apart from short-term bank loans) on the success of its costs plans to receive the funds it needed for current operation. A normal rate of profit, and the financial incentives associated with it, could be restored in all branches of industry. The problem of financial incentives and of supervision of industry by the financial organs was at the centre of the attention of the NKF in the immediate pre-war period.

(3) *Budgetary revenue.* The abolition of rationing meant that the complexities and *ad hoc* adjustments in the imposition of turnover tax could be brought to an end. Attention could be turned to improving the efficiency and refining the methods of imposing the turnover tax, and other sources of revenue.

[1] Budgetary revenue from state insurance (not to be confused with *social* insurance), rose from 2·4 milliard roubles in 1939 to 3·4 in 1940; but expenditure remained constant at 1·3 milliard roubles (*Zas. verkh. sov.* (1940), pp. 72–3 and (for 4. iv. 40, law) pp. 520–33; *ibid.* (1941), pp. 38–9).

Table 33. *Social insurance budget, 1930–41 (milliard roubles)*

	1930[a] (fulfilment)	1934[b] (plan)	1936[c] (plan)	1937[d] (plan)	1938[e] (plan)	1939[f] (plan)	1940[g] (plan)	1941[h] (plan)
REVENUE	1,796	5,050	8,380	5,292	6,323	7,206[10]	9,136	9,998
EXPENDITURE:								
I. *Grants and pensions*								
Sickness benefits } Pregnancy benefits }	391	824	1,939[3]	{ 1,973[4] 822	2,137 992	—	2,143 693	—
Invalid and old age pensions	319	676	1,250	248[5]	315[5]	—	684	—
Unemployment payments	49	—	—	—	—	—	—	—
Other	55	14	80	24	22	—	22	—
Total	814	1,514	3,269	3,067	3,466	—	3,542	3,639
II. *Health, etc.*								
Medical help and supervision	356	1,040	1,938	17[6]	20	—	19	—
Rest homes, tourism, physical training, etc.	53	403[1]	1,022[1]	1,044[7]	1,259[7]	—	1,235	1,033[11]
Children (including kindergartens, crèches)	—	327	709	531[8]	654	—	700	677
Special food for invalids	—	58	90	90	100	—	100	97
Other	5	—	n.a.	n.a.	n.a.	—	n.a.	n.a.
Total	414	1,828	3,759	1,682	2,033	—	2,054	1,807
III. *Education*	58	750	612[2]	73	84	—	48	20
IV. *Administration*	} 510	{ 50	47	70	80	—	82	80
V. *Housing*		698	800	—[9]	—	—	—	—
VI. *Other*		40	93	153	469	—	96	59
Total, excluding reserve	1,796	4,880	8,580[3]	5,045	6,132	5,294	5,822	5,605
Reserve	—	170	—	247	32	—	—	—
To State Budget	—	—	—	—	159	1,912	3,314	4,393
of which to retired pensioners	—	—	—	—	—	?	2,022	2,263
Net surplus to state budget	n.a.	n.a.	n.a.	n.a.	159	?	1,292	2,130
Wage fund (to nearest 100 million roubles)[j]	15,000	38,100	63,400	78,300	94,000	—	—	175,000[12]

n.a. = not applicable.

Sources:
(a) *Sots. spr.* (1932), pp. 604–5.
(b) SZ 152/1934 (10. iv. 34) (for 1935 (plan), see SZ 312/1935 (6. vii. 35)).
(c) SZ 404/1936 (4. ix. 36).
(d) *Fin. khoz. bull.* no. 23 (1937), pp. 25–9 (15. vii. 37).
(e) *Fin. khoz. bull.* no. 17 (1938), pp. 24–30 (12. v. 38).
(f) *Zas. verkh. sov.* (1939), pp. 152–76, 328–53.
(g) *Zas. verkh. sov.* (1940), pp. 233–63, 425–56, and *Spravochnik po sotsial'nomu strakhovaniyu dlya FZMK* (1940), cit. *American Review of the Soviet Union*, vol. VIII, nos. 3–4 (1947), p. 50.
(h) Rovinskii, *op. cit.* p. 234; *Zas. verkh. sov.* (1941), pp. 260–94, 498–532.
(j) For sources see appropriate parts of main text.

Notes:
(1) Includes:

	1934	1936
Current expenditure on rest homes, sanatoria and resorts	215	554
Construction of hospitals, etc.	134	343
Construction of rest homes, etc.	44	75
Construction of invalid homes	4	4
Construction of parks of culture and rest	3 }	41
Construction of physical training institutes	4 }	
Construction of tourist bases	—	5

(2) Includes unexplained item of 554 million roubles 'cultural needs'. Reduction otherwise mainly due to cutting of grants to workers who were studying, from 705 in 1934 (plan) to 105 million roubles in 1935 (plan) (transferred to state budget).
(3) Includes 200 million roubles from balance of current account in social insurance, to cover over-expenditure in first half of 1936 in connexion with influenza epidemic.
(4) Increase results mainly from putting employees on same terms as workers.
(5) Pensions to retired workers met through state budget.
(6) All health expenditure met through state budget.
(7) Includes:

	1937 (plan)	1938 (plan)
Rest homes, sanatoria and resorts	700	836
Equipment and construction	185	198
Tourism	39	50
Physical culture	100	148
Parks of culture and rest	20	27
	1,044	1,259

(8) Expenditure on kindergartens and crèches taken off social insurance budget.
(9) Taken off state budget.
(10) Fulfilment 7,606 million roubles (*Zas. verkh. sov.* (1940), pp. 64ff.).
(11) Rest homes, sanatoria, summer resorts, parks of culture and rest, and physical training only.
(12) Coverage of this figure is probably wider than that of figures for previous years. Cf. note (h) to Table 31, p. 249.

1. THE ADMINISTRATION OF BUDGETARY EXPENDITURE AFTER THE ABOLITION OF RATIONING

(a) Capital investment

Between 1935 and 1941 continuous attempts were made to improve the administration of capital grants, notably in two series of decrees in 1936 and 1938. In the account which follows the main changes in the system are summarised.

No changes of principle were made in the compiling and approving of drafts and estimates for investment projects, but the technique of project-making was refined and improved. All estimates were prepared according to a standard form adopted in 1938. The unit cost indices described in chapter VIII were made much more elaborate and gradually unified. Originally the norms of materials, labour, and machine shifts needed to complete each part of a job had been laid down by each commissariat separately, so that widely differing norms were used for similar work in different industries. From 1938 onwards the norms used in heavy industry were made obligatory in all branches of industry. State price lists, wage scales, and handbooks were used to convert the cost in real terms into money.[1] In this way costs per unit of construction (so-called 'unit evaluations', *edinichnye rastsenki*) could be worked out for each part of the job, and the cost of the whole job built up from them. In 1938 a Committee on Construction Affairs (*Komitet po delam stroitel'stva*) was set up under SNK with the task of unifying construction norms and supervising their application. It was responsible for preparing norms and prices for SNK approval, for adopting model building drafts, for examining regional schemes of large-scale construction, and for working out and presenting to SNK measures for improving and cheapening construction. A special inspectorate under the Committee supervised the fulfilment of decrees on construction.[2]

The procedure for compiling investment estimates did not differ essentially from that by which the planned cost of any item of industrial production was calculated, although it was more complicated. The essential difference was in the method of financing. The costs of industrial production had to be met out of the payment made for it at fixed transfer prices, and this provided an incentive to efficiency. Investment, on the other hand, was financed from non-

---

[1] Estimates were compiled in 1936 prices, and compensatory adjustments to allow for changes in costs were made in later years.
[2] *Fin. khoz. bull.* (1938), nos. 5–6, pp. 10–11 (26. ii. 38), no. 16, p. 12 (20. iv. 38).

returnable grants. The problem was to provide incentives to secure efficient and economical use of these grants.

Some incentive was provided by making industries responsible for supplying a large part of the funds needed for their own investment: between 1932 and 1940 the proportion of industrial investment met from profits, depreciation allowances, and other internal resources of industry rose from 11% to 30% (see Table 35). The interest of industries in the disposal of investment funds issued to them was also encouraged by increasing their powers over the use of these funds.[1] This was done in three ways. First, the procedure for financing 'below-limit' investment was considerably simplified, and the powers of the special banks to control 'below-limit' allocations were confined to keeping the spending body within the total and the wage allocation. Secondly, from 1938 onwards, capital repair was excluded from the capital investment plan and financed by special funds formed at enterprise or *glavk* level from depreciation funds, and deposited with the State Bank to be spent at the discretion of the body concerned. Thirdly, a special category was established of decentralised investment (investment 'outside the limit'), which did not form part of the capital investment plan. This simplified the financing of very minor construction work and the acquiring of small items of equipment. Decentralised investment included, for example, equipment valued at 200 roubles per item or less, new building costing up to 5,000 roubles per enterprise, and similar items, all of which were financed from current resources as provided in the financial plan of the enterprise. In addition, the Director's Fund and profits from the sale of consumer goods made from waste products could be spent on construction or equipment outside the plan and without any limit on its costs. Sums for these purposes were deposited in the State Bank in the ordinary account of the enterprise if they were 100,000 roubles or less; sums above 100,000 roubles were kept in an account in the appropriate special bank. Only the authority of the director of the enterprise was required to spend sums up to 100,000 roubles; expenditure above 100,000 roubles had to be sanctioned by the head of the *glavk*, and above 500,000 roubles by the commissar of the industry.[2]

These measures were, however, peripheral to the main problem. The greater part of investment funds was allocated to above-limit

---

[1] Commissariats had already been given limited powers to redistribute investment allocations during the first five-year plan.

[2] SZ 417/1935 (1. ix. 35), 405/1936 (13. ix. 36).

jobs, and it is by the efficiency with which these funds were spent that the system of financing investment must be judged.

The experience of the first two five-year plans showed conclusively that expenditure could be most satisfactorily controlled if it was administered on what might be called a quasi-*khozraschot* basis. Therefore from 1936 onwards, most jobs were financed by the contract method rather than by what we have called, for want of a better term, the direct labour method.[1] Even where the direct labour method was retained, attempts were made to avoid controlling investment grants by the rigid methods used with budget allocations to administration. From a general economic, as well as from a strictly financial point of view, construction by specialised building organisations had more to commend it than construction by direct labour, as it made it possible to concentrate at least part of machinery and skills in the hands of a permanent building labour force and management.[2] In 1936 special departments responsible for building work, and for controlling general and special construction units, were set up in each industrial commissariat and on a territorial basis: these departments were gradually raised to the status of independent commissariats or chief administrations under SNK. General units were responsible for erecting the buildings, carpentry, etc., and special units installed heating, ventilating, and sewage plant, etc.

Under this system, grants for investments were allocated in the first place to the commissariat concerned, which transferred them to the appropriate *glavk* or enterprise. Each *glavk* or enterprise set up a department of capital construction[3] in general charge of construction affairs (referred to below as the 'investor'). This department purchased the equipment to be installed in the new workshop or enterprise, and prepared plans, estimates, and working drawings for the construction work. It then concluded a contract with a general contractor, who was made responsible for the completion of the whole job within a definite time and at the cost estimated, and had to pay

---

[1] *Khozyaistvennyi sposob*, when work is done directly by the labour and resources of the enterprise or organisation concerned.

[2] 'It is necessary to set up from the dispersed and unstable construction organisations, on the basis of the division of labour, a stable system of construction organisations specialised at their job, and then the basis of a large-scale construction industry will have been laid' (Molotov, 1936, quoted in D'yachkov and Kiparisov, *Uchot kapital'nogo stroitel'stva* (1948), p. 7).

[3] When new enterprises were being built, a so-called 'Directorate' (*direktsia*) was set up to undertake the functions performed by this department for established enterprises. It was itself maintained from the investment grant.

fines and penalties to the investor if the contract was violated or not fulfilled to schedule. The general contractor sub-contracted specialised work to the appropriate construction unit. Equipment purchased by the investor was usually installed by the manufacturer or by the investor himself.

The contractors operated on a *khozraschot* basis. They were provided with working capital from several sources. First, their 'own working capital' was allocated to them from the budget, in the first instance as a lump sum, and afterwards in accordance with their requirements under the plan. This varied from 10·3 to 14% of their annual building programme, according to the type of construction involved. Secondly, they received advance payments from their customers to cover stocks of materials and unfinished work. The size of the advance was negotiated between the parties and stipulated in the annual contract, the maximum payable being 15% of the annual programme. Thirdly, the investor could pay special advances to cover the purchase of up to three months' stocks of prefabricated parts and similar special supplies. Finally, the contractors were given short-term credits to cover seasonal stocks and the repair of construction machinery.

Working capital enabled the contractor to build up stocks and to start fulfilling the contract. He was thereafter paid by the investor on a monthly basis. These monthly payments, together with the advance payments, were of prime importance, for they were the equivalent in the construction industry of the purchase of finished goods in the rest of industry. In the first half of the 1930's, these payments were made as a percentage of the total allocation for the year, provided that the plan was being fulfilled to schedule. From 1936 onwards they were more rigidly controlled. They could be made only after the conclusion of special 'acceptance deeds' (*akty priemki*) between investor and contractor, and covered only those parts of the job which had been completed. Payments were, of course, made at the prices stipulated in the contract. Efficiency in the construction organisations was stimulated by permitting them to retain 50% of any saving on estimated costs.

The contract method would provide an effective means of controlling investment expenditure only if the contractor had sufficient incentive to fulfil the plan within the limits of the estimate and/or if the investor restricted the payments he made to the contractor to the planned level. During the pre-war period neither of these conditions was fully effective.[1] The contractor had no greater incentive to keep within the estimates than the industrial producer had to keep within his costs plan; and we have seen that this incentive was not great. The investor had *less* incentive to prevent the contractor from overspending than the purchaser of an industrial product had to insist that the producer charged only the fixed price, for the purchaser of an industrial product was spending his own funds, and wastage immediately affected his working capital and profit, whereas the investor was spending an allocation of general state funds in which he had less interest. The investor had it is true a general interest in keeping the cost of investment in his industry as low as possible in order to make best use of the state allocation, but he had little immediate material incentive to put close pressure on the contractor. But investor and contractor had a common interest in persuading the budgetary authorities to grant as large a sum as possible to their industry, and therefore tended to work together by legal and illegal means to convince the authorities that extra grants were necessary.[2] In these circumstances the part played by the Committee of Construction Affairs and its endeavour to insist on the universal application of state norms were evidently of considerable importance. The executive arm through which state norms were enforced throughout the investment industry was the special bank. It had to act as a prop to the investor, checking to see that he was properly controlling the expenditure of allocations. In the first few years the supervisory functions of the bank were exercised formally and insufficiently,[3] but in 1935–41 these functions were gradually extended.

[1] In the post-war period the estimate itself became more and more a formal document. See my reports in *Soviet Studies*, vol. VI (1955), pp. 448–51, and vol. VII (1956), pp. 422–3.

[2] 'Such facts [registering in deeds and accounts work that has not actually been done] still occur in the activity of contracting organisations. Frequently the customers close their eyes to such facts, and in these cases consciously and criminally raise the cost of construction and crudely violate the directives of the party and the government on lowering the cost of construction.... In registering unfulfilled work it is not only a question of violating the directives of the party and government on putting into effect the strictest régime of economy and on mobilising the broad masses to struggle for thriftiness and against lack of economy and wastefulness. It is a question of criminal deception, which involves the criminal responsibility of the particular officials guilty of this registration.

'Instead of demanding the fulfilment of all the clauses of the contract by the contractors, the customer often turns a blind eye to a whole series of violations of the clauses of the contract by the contractor, and even in a number of cases directly or indirectly helps him to receive from the bank the largest sum possible to pay for the work envisaged in the contract. Often in indulging a negligent contractor the customer counts on a mutual amnesty of violations of the clauses of the contract and the rules of financing' (I. L. Braude, *Dogovory po kapital'nomu stroitel'stvu v SSSR* (1952), pp. 76, 78–9).

[3] See, for example, Grinko in *Soviet Union, 1936*..., pp. 510–11.

The procedure by which bank control was enforced may be summarised as follows. First the bank checked the approved allocation against the state plan of capital work and the summary list of expenditures planned for separate parts of the job during the year. In doing this, it sought to ensure that resources were concentrated on jobs which would be completed and put into operation during the year (*puskovye raboty*). Next it received a declaration from the investor to the effect that technical drafts and estimates had been approved by the appropriate authorities; and an official of the bank, sometimes trained as an engineer, checked the estimates, often at the site itself. The bank had to ensure that the costs of transport and materials and the price of equipment were calculated correctly, and that the norms of labour, materials and machine-shifts, and the standard wage scales, were correctly applied. It had to see that the estimates for separate parts of the job were correctly combined in the general estimate, and that no unnecessary expenses were included. Its conclusions after examining the estimate were discussed with the investor and the contractor, and if any of its proposals were rejected, it had the right to refer them to the central management of the bank and if necessary to the NKF. Finally, the bank checked the annual contract. It had to see that the contract corresponded with the construction plan, that it complied with the law, and that the investor made transport services and other facilities available to the contractor. It was instructed to pay particular attention to the size of the advance payment agreed between the two sides to ensure that it was not in excess of the real requirements of the contractor.

After this preliminary supervision was completed, the bank authorised the issue of the grant. In controlling this, the bank was primarily concerned with the investor's account, though the bank carried out for contractors the function performed by the State Bank for industrial enterprises, including the issue of short-term credits. In issuing resources from the investor's account, the bank had to ensure that the sums laid down for each part of the job in the estimates and contract were not exceeded, and that wage issues and administrative expenditures did not exceed the planned level (the procedure here resembled that enforced in industry by the State Bank). The investor's accounts were examined by bureaux of price checks (*byuro proverki tsen*) set up in each main branch of the bank to ascertain that all payments to the suppliers of equipment and the building contractors were made at the stipulated prices—these checks were made on all transactions in the most important materials, and selectively for the less important. Advances to contractors were deposited in a special account, which the bank controlled to prevent its use for unauthorised purposes. The most important act of supervision carried out by the bank was the examination of the monthly 'acceptance deeds' drawn up by the two sides to authorise payment for completed work. Here it did not confine itself to a documentary check, but also carried out control inspections (*kontrol'nye obmery*) on the spot: these covered about a third of the whole work. The bank had the right to charge the contractor a fine of 5% of all excess payments disclosed by these inspections. This fine was partly met from the wages of the construction officials responsible, and was paid into the funds of the bank.[1] On the other hand, the bank could authorise the issue of supplementary grants (within the limits of the annual estimate) and supply short-term credits to the contractor at reduced interest rates if the job was being completed ahead of schedule.[2]

The introduction of the contract method for most above-limit constructions and the extension of the control functions of the special banks eliminated much of the wastage and excessive expenditure which had been characteristic of investment practice in the rationing period. But on the eve of the second world war many faults still remained. Construction costs actually rose between 1938 and 1940,[3] although this was partly a reflexion of the general rise in industrial costs which appears to have taken place.[4] The rise in construction costs was to some extent due to the fact that control by the banks tended to be confined to formal and routine checking of documents, as a result of the lack of persons experienced in construction work on the control staff of the bank. Contracts, for example, tended to be

---

[1] As the bank itself was organised on a *khozraschot* basis, these funds increased the bank's own profits.

[2] For material on the organisation of investment finance and the functions of the special banks, see N. Rovinskii (ed.), *Organizatsiya finansirovaniya i kreditovaniya kapital'nykh vlozhenii* (1952); D'yachkov and Kiparisov, *op. cit.*; Braude, *op. cit.*; M. F. D'yachkov, *Statistika kapital'nogo stroitel'stva* (1952); SZ 70/1936 (13. ii. 36), 162/1936 (5. iv. 36), 258/1936 (23. v. 36), 259/1936 (28. v. 36); *Fin. khoz. bull.* (1937), no. 22, p. 7 (8. vii. 37), no. 36, p. 4 (3. xii. 37); (1938), nos. 5–6, pp. 10–34 (26. ii. 38), no. 15, p. 28 (26. viii. 38); SZ 487/1940 (26. vii. 40), 108/1941 (12. ii. 41), 297/1941 (19. vi. 41).

[3] In 1938 costs of construction financed by Prombank fell by 1·3% against 6·9% planned; in 1939 costs rose; and in 1940 they rose again, by 2–3% (*Zas. verkh. sov.* (1939), pp. 376–7; (1940), pp. 77–8; (1941), pp. 42–4).

[4] This is indicated by the fact that the total wages paid to construction workers in 1940 fell, although the total amount of construction rose, in construction financed by Prombank (*Zas. verkh. sov.* (1941), pp. 42–4).

formal documents of little importance, and advances tended to be given as lump sums at the maximum permitted level without satisfactory control.[1] The special banks had not yet been transformed into the organs of 'efficiency control' which the issuers of investment grants must to some extent be in an economy of the Soviet type.[2]

(b) Non-investment allocations to the economy

The only important change made in non-investment allocations to the economy in this period was the adoption of a new system for financing machine-tractor stations. They could obviously not be financed in the same way as an industrial enterprise. An enterprise produces goods for which a transfer price is fixed on the basis of costs, but it is difficult for a 'price' to be fixed for the services supplied and work done by the MTS on collective farms, and it was impossible in the pre-war period, when no satisfactory method of costing collective-farm production had been devised. A large part of MTS activity consists of servicing the farms with machinery. In state industry, machinery is 'charged for' only as a small depreciation allowance, but the non-state-owned collective farms were required to pay for the use of state machinery.[3] But no attempt was made to fix a price (including a capital charge) for MTS work based on a detailed calculation; instead, payments in kind and sometimes in money were fixed somewhat arbitrarily by the state, as a rule as a percentage of the harvest.[4]

Given this system of payment, largely in kind, how should the MTS be financed? From the outset capital equipment was made available to the MTS through non-returnable budgetary grants for investment—the MTS did not differ from state industrial enterprises in this respect. There remained the question of financing current expenditure on wages, fuel, etc. Between 1930 and 1937 a quasi-*khozraschot* system was used, in which the income of the MTS was related to the payments in kind made by the collective farms. The State Bank issued a credit to the MTS to provide it with working funds, and this was then paid back partly from collective farm payments (payments in kind were sold by the MTS to the state procure-

[1] Braude, p. 78; Rovinskii, *Gos. byudzhet*, pp. 117–18.
[2] For a discussion of the faults in investment financing in the context of the building industry as a whole, see my report in *Soviet Studies*, vol. VII, no. 4 (1955), esp. pp. 448–51.
[3] In a sense the collective farms were already 'paying for' the state facilities provided via the MTS, by the compulsory deliveries they had to make at low prices.
[4] SZ 234/1933 (25. vi. 33), 68/1934 (17. ii. 34).

ment organs) and partly by budget subsidies. The MTS also received allocations for special purposes from the Agricultural Bank. The budget was therefore connected with the MTS by both the grants it made for investment and the grants it made for subsidies, which by 1935 provided a high proportion of the current income of MTS.[1]

This attempt to combine *khozraschot* and budgetary financing is said to have been largely unsuccessful. The complexity of accounts made efficient financial control difficult to achieve. Large debts accumulated both to MTS workers and to other organisations, and resources tended to be wasted or used for unauthorised purposes.

In 1938 it was therefore decided to transfer the MTS to the budget.[2] Collective-farm payments in kind and money were paid into the budget (through the state procurement organs, which credited the budget with the value of payments in kind at compulsory delivery prices), and the MTS received their income mainly in the form of direct budget grants. The MTS compiled annual estimates on the basis of the production plan, and presented these to the regional financial department; they were then approved in the same way as other budget estimates. Six accounts were opened for each MTS in the State Bank, each covering a different heading of the estimates,[3] and the budget allocations were then paid quarterly into each account in accordance with the estimates, on condition that the production plan had previously been fulfilled. Their use by the MTS was checked monthly by the appropriate organ of the NKZ, and periodically on a selective basis by the financial organs.

The system diverged from normal budgetary practice in two important respects. First, with the permission of the regional land department, the MTS were permitted to meet over-expenditure on one account by economy on another. Secondly, extra allocations

---

[1] The following allocations to MTS appear in the 1935 budget report (million roubles):

Capital expenses (productive construction)	757·7
Financing own working capital [includes subsidies]	2,914·3
Operational expenditure	39·9
Total	3,711·9

(*Otchot*... (1935), pp. 64–5).
For further details on the system of financing MTS before 1938 see SZ 75/1935 (29. i. 35) and Rovinskii, *op. cit.* p. 246.

[2] The description of MTS financing given here takes into account the modifications made in the system in 1939. For details see *Fin. khoz. bull.* (1938), nos. 3–4, pp. 3–6 (5. ii. 38 and 11. ii. 38), nos. 8–9, pp. 6–14 (26. ii. 38), no. 10, pp. 13–17 (28. ii. 38); (1939), no. 3, pp. 18–20 (13. i. 39); Rovinskii, *op. cit.* pp. 246–60.

[3] These were (i) fuel; (ii) repair; (iii) wages of production workers; (iv) wages of MTS administration; (v) increases in stocks; and (vi) other expenditure.

were issued if the MTS over-fulfilled the production plan. In addition, elements of *khozraschot* were introduced into the system. Unlike other bodies on the budget, the MTS were allowed to hold working capital in the form of stocks of fuel, spare parts, etc. They were also permitted to pay bonuses and rewards to their workers for fulfilling and over-fulfilling the plan, for economising in fuel, and for keeping tractors in good order. These were paid from three sources: (i) a bonus fund formed in the MTS from payments made from the NKZ reserve fund in proportion to the over-fulfilment of the plan, and from a percentage of the collective farm payments deducted from budgetary revenue; (ii) special budget allocations; and (iii) 75% of any saving made as against the estimates, which the MTS was allowed to retain if the plan had been fulfilled.

The new system brought elementary order into MTS finance. But in the period immediately before the war violation of norms and over-expenditure on fuel and other items continued, and supervision by NKZ was insufficient.[1] There was room for a considerable increase in financial incentives to the MTS.

(c) *The financing of institutions maintained by the budget*

The most obvious change in the state budget in the period after the abolition of rationing was the great increase in the number and type of institutions maintained by the budget.

This increase resulted mainly from the systematising of the financing of social and cultural services undertaken during the second five-year plan. During the early 1930's, these services had received financial support from numerous sources, and had been administered by several distinct authorities, often overlapping. General education and health services were financed by the local budgets, which were not part of the state budget, although they were linked closely to it. A considerable part of the housing and health services, and of students' grants, was maintained by the social insurance budget, administered by the Commissariat of Labour and financed by fees paid by enterprises and institutions as a proportion of their wage fund. The social insurance budget, which did not form part of the state budget, was also responsible for nearly all pensions, sickness pay, and other benefits.

Between 1934 and 1938, all social and cultural services were gradually brought into the state budget. In 1934, when the Com-

---

[1] *Zas. verkh. sov.* (1939); (1940), pp. 176–8; (1941), p. 47.

missariat of Labour was abolished, management of the social insurance budget as a whole was transferred to the trade unions, and administered in a decentralised manner by officials and voluntary workers appointed by trade union branches at factory level, on the basis of estimates compiled by the trade union in each industry and approved by the A.U.C.C.T.U. The object of the system is said to be to link social insurance with the

> struggle to increase the productivity of labour and improve labour discipline, and also to adapt the material and welfare services of the working people to the varied production and living conditions of the persons insured, and to create the most favourable situation for the direct participation of the working people themselves in the administration of insurance funds.[1]

However, the social insurance budget was not autonomously controlled by the trade unions. The government laid down both the amounts of pensions and benefits to be paid in different industries and circumstances, and also the scale of social insurance fees, which varied by trade union according to working conditions in the industry. Even so, a number of services financed by the social insurance budget when it was controlled by the Commissariat of Labour, were considered inappropriate for administration by the trade unions. Between 1934 and 1937, health services, students' grants, crèches, and housing were gradually transferred to the general state budget, which was also made responsible for paying pensions to retired workers (but not those remaining at work). As a transitional measure, part of the social insurance fees was transferred to the state budget to cover the extra expenditure involved,[2] but in 1937 insurance fees were scaled down, and the transferred services were thenceforth financed from general state revenue.[3] The social insurance

---

[1] Rovinskii, *op. cit.* p. 232.

[2] According to *Otchot...* (1935), pp. 46–7, Union and republican budget receipts in 1935 from social insurance fees transferred by the A.U.C.C.T.U. and the C.C.'s of trade unions were as follows (million roubles):

For health measures	1,742·5
For payment of stipends	37·0
To improve housing and cultural and living conditions of workers and employees	131·9
To maintain crèches of health organs	16·4
To maintain kindergartens of education organs	49·9
Total transferred to budget	1,977·7

This was out of a total social insurance budget of 6,097·3 million roubles (plan) (SZ 312/1935 (6. vii. 35)).

[3] From 1939 pensions to retired workers were again covered by the social insurance budget. See above, pp. 252, 254.

budget therefore covered primarily sickness and pregnancy benefits, and invalid and old age pensions to people still at work. In addition, a network of rest homes and holiday camps for factory workers and their children continued to be maintained by the trade unions, and were financed through the social insurance budget.[1]

Although they were supervised in a decentralised manner, both the social insurance budget and the local budgets had gradually been brought under the control of the planning and financial authorities of the central government during the decade before 1938, as central norms and rules were more universally applied. The actual unification which had taken place in the budgetary system was formally recognised by the inclusion of the social insurance budget and the local budgets in the state budget approved by the U.S.S.R. government; they appeared in the budget, however, only as lump sums.

This meant that the bulk of all social and cultural services was now included in the budget (for example, more than two-thirds of all expenditure on education).[2] The only services which were excluded from the budget were those which were paid for directly by the persons using them, or by non-state organisations, and those which it was considered more expedient to finance from industrial costs.[3]

The extension in the range of services covered by the budget was not directly important from the point of view of financial planning, as all these services were included in some form in one of the synthetic financial plans or balances. But it was of great importance from the point of view of administration, for it meant that a greater range of expenditure was made subject to the strict provisions of

---

[1] For further details on these changes in the social insurance budget, see SZ 333/1933 (10. ix. 33), 220/1934 (13. v. 34); *Fin. khoz. bull.* (1937), nos. 8–9, pp. 37–9, no. 27, pp. 27–9. See also Table 33, p. 254.

[2] *Bol'shaya sovetskaya entsiklopediya*, vol. 'SSSR' (1948), col. 1250.

[3] These included:

(*a*) Payments by the population to cover services in whole or part (e.g. kindergarten fees, the cost of theatre tickets).

(*b*) Local village levies to cover the cost of local services ('self-taxation', excluded from the budget since 1935 (SZ 233/1935 (31. v. 35)).

(*c*) Expenditure by trade unions from their membership fees and by collective farms from special funds.

(*d*) Payments by industry from costs for labour safety and hygiene, for training workers, and for research on a contract basis (until 1940, enterprises had also paid special fees as a percentage of costs to the trade unions for social and cultural services (*Fin. khoz. bull.* (1938), nos. 11–12, pp. 3, 45–7 (8. iii. 38, 7. ii. 38); SZ 590/1940 (14. x. 40)).

(*e*) Expenditure from Director's Funds for social and cultural purposes. (See Plotnikov, *op. cit.* p. 218.)

budget control, and indirectly therefore brought more closely under the central planning authorities. At the same time the expansion of the budget itself brought about modifications in the methods by which these traditional budgetary expenditures were administered. The account which follows summarises the position on the eve of the second world war and the main changes made as compared with the pre-planning period.

The budget was voted by the Supreme Soviet in lump sums for each main disposer of credits, but the budget estimates approved by the NKF and the budget commissions and placed before the deputies of the Supreme Soviet particularised expenditure in greater detail. Pre-revolutionary budgets had shown the main purposes or institutions (central or local institutions, equipment and repair of buildings, etc.) on which the allocation to each government department was to be spent, and within these limits the department itself decided how the allocation was to be used. For the Soviet economy of the 1930's this was insufficient, for the budget is not merely a document distributing state expenditure between various departments, it is also an instrument by which the national economic plan, including the wages and investment plan, is applied to bodies financed from the budget. By 1931 the budget was therefore already showing expenditure divided not merely by its main purposes, but also by so-called articles (*statyi*) showing the main 'economic categories' of expenditure (wages, investment, etc.) (the so-called 'functional' division). But these articles were confused, overlapping, and inconsistent, and some expenditures were not subdivided in this way (for example, education). By 1935 a unified system had been developed: the comparison in Table 34 illustrates the greater detail in which expenditure was set out in 1935 as compared with 1917. In 1938 legislation was adopted setting out the system of classification by articles to be used universally throughout the budget.[1]

Once the budget had been adopted, only minor variations were allowed from the allocations in the estimates. Moneys could be transferred from one article to another only with NKF approval, and

[1] *Fin. khoz. bull.* (1938), no. 15, pp. 6–9 (2. iv. 38). The main articles for traditional budget expenditures were: (1) Wages. (1i) Additions to wages. (2) Office and economic expenditures. (3) Duty journeys. (4) Scientific research work, etc. (5) Training and production practice of pupils. (6) Acquiring books for libraries. (7) Grants to students. (8) Feeding. (9) Medicines and bandages. (10) Acquiring and repair of equipment (*inventar'*). (11) Capital investments. (12) Decentralised expenditures. (13) Other. An analogous list was adopted for *khozraschot* bodies, including such items as financing own working capital, subsidies, and 'operational' expenditures.

Table 34. *Allocations to foreign affairs as set out in 1917 and 1935 budgets (roubles)*

(i) *1917 Draft Budget*

Ministry of Foreign Affairs

1. Maintenance of central institutions	820,174
2. Maintenance of local institutions	27,531
3. Various expenses of '*administratsiya*'	953,000
4. Various expenses of '*upravlenie*'	598,511
5. Maintenance of diplomatic and consular institutions abroad	4,727,358
6. Equipment and repair of buildings	18,463
7. Grants for various purposes	197,466
Total	7,342,503

(ii) *1935 Budget (fulfilment)*

	Total	Wages	Administrative-economic expenses	Capital investment	Acquiring and repair of inventory and operational equipment	Operational expenditure	Welfare services
1. Central institutions	4,292,171	1,496,702	1,280,757	176,968	31,008	1,131,736	175,000
2. Local organs of central institutions	778,268	445,864	199,772	108,632	24,000	—	—
11. Representatives, consuls, agents and other diplomatic institutions of U.S.S.R. abroad	4,211,971	1,278,358	1,314,424	31,000	54,683	1,533,506	—
12. Commissions formed on basis of peace treaties	27,655	—	—	—	—	27,655	—
Totals	9,310,065	3,220,924	2,794,953	316,600	109,691	2,692,897	175,000

Sources: Proekt... na 1917 god, tables p. 6. *Otchot...* (1935), pp. 98–101.

in the years before the war any transfer from or to wages, grants to students, and investments, was forbidden, in order to limit unplanned expenditure.[1] Extra grants could be issued from the reserve fund, and transfers could be made from one government department to another, only with the approval of SNK in each case. This arrangement was to prevent the receiving bodies from over-spending their total allocation, and to force them to confine their expenditure within the limits of the national economic plan for the key financial items of the plan—wages and investment.[2] This was particularly important because of the tendency in an economy of the Soviet type for wages and investment plans to be overspent, unless some 'external' control is operated.

How were these expenditures administered? The methods used for institutions on the budget on the eve of the war had not been radically changed since the functions of the old treasury pay-offices had been transferred to the State Bank in 1928; and in many respects pre-revolutionary practice was still followed. After the budget had been approved, the chief disposers put in two claims to the NKF—one for the grant due to themselves, one for those due to institutions subordinate to them (these were called *raskhodnye raspisaniya*). When the claim had been approved by the NKF, it authorised the State Bank to issue the grants. This it did quarterly: 75% of the grant was made available at the beginning of the quarter, and the remainder after the accounts for the previous quarter had been approved. The disposer then drew on his own grant by cheque until it was exhausted, and made sums available from the second account to its subordinate institutions by issuing authorisations (*porucheniya*) to the appropriate branches of the bank.

The bank had to see that the grant as a whole was not overspent, but detailed accounts of expenditure were kept, not by the bank, but by the disposers themselves, who were responsible for seeing that no *article* was overspent, and for examining the accounts of the institutions subordinate to them. From 1932 onwards, as was explained in chapter VIII, the use of expenditures was controlled *post factum* by the

[1] Rovinskii, *op. cit.* p. 328.
[2] Of course part of the allocations to investment was spent on wages to construction workers, and all allocations to materials were ultimately transformed into wages. But the control here was exercised at the appropriate point in the system, i.e. at the point where the money was actually paid out as wages. A more pertinent criticism of the classification described is that some direct expenses of a wage character appeared outside the article 'wages' (e.g. under decentralised expenditures and duty journeys), where they were subject to less rigid control.

appropriate department of NKF.[1] The NKF had the right to reduce further allocations by the amount of any over-spending, and to cut grants if wages were paid in excess of the approved rates. In flagrant cases it could cease to issue grants.[2] Disciplinary proceedings and criminal prosecutions could be undertaken against accountants and officials responsible for violating budget discipline.

During the period after the abolition of rationing, control was tightened up over two major categories of expenditure. First, from 1935 onwards all institutions and enterprises were required to register particulars of the size and wages of their administrative staff, and details of their approved administrative expenditure, with the local financial department. The bank was instructed to issue allocations for administrative expenditure only if this registration had been carried out and confirmed. Central and local establishment commissions were set up to enforce the conformity of staffing to the approved norms.[3] Savings in administrative costs were encouraged by allowing bodies to retain 50% of any economy made on the estimates as a bonus fund for their employees. Secondly, in 1939 much tighter control was instituted over the payment of wages, in order to limit over-expenditure of the planned wage fund. The wages of all established and non-established staff were unified in a single article of the estimates. The bank, which normally controlled only the *total* grant issued to each body, was instructed to issue wages separately from other items of expenditure, and made responsible for seeing that wages were not issued in excess of the approved funds and that staffs had been registered with the financial organs.[4]

Control by the bank and by the spending departments of the NKF was found to be insufficient by itself to ensure proper budget discipline. Bank control was very limited. The spending departments of NKF were not linked to the majority of institutions financed by the budget directly, but only through the chief disposers to which the institutions were administratively subordinated; hence NKF control was indirect. Efficient financial control of expenditure therefore depended primarily on the efficiency of the book-keeping apparatus of the institutions themselves. As early as 1932 legislation had been adopted setting out the rights of the chief book-keepers of institutions

---

[1] For further details, see *Fin. khoz. bull.* (1938), no. 3, p. 17 (22. xii. 38).
[2] SZ 33/1936 (16. i. 36).
[3] D'yachenko and Kozlov, *op. cit.* p. 200; *Fin. khoz. bull.* (1938), nos. 1–2, pp. 2–3 (27. xii. 37); (1939), nos. 13–14, pp. 1–3 (23. iv. 39).
[4] *Fin. khoz. bull.* (1939), nos. 29–30, pp. 18–19 (15. viii. 39).

and enterprises. They were administratively subordinated to the institution in which they were employed, but subordinated in respect of methods of book-keeping to the higher body to which the institution was subordinate. They had to countersign all financial documents, and point out violations of the law to the head of the institution. If illegal orders were reaffirmed after their illegality had been pointed out, they had to fulfil them,[1] while informing the higher body and the appropriate financial organ that the violation had taken place.[2]

Efficient control of the expenditure of lower bodies also depended on satisfactory internal auditing and supervision by the chief disposers. During the rationing period, this control was badly and unsystematically organised.[3] In 1936 regulations were adopted ordering that a documentary audit of each of their subordinate bodies should be carried out annually by commissariats and regional E.C.'s of soviets (this was known as 'intra-departmental financial supervision', *vnutri-vedomstvennyi finanansovyi kontrol'*). These audits were to be conducted by the book-keeping or financial department of the higher body, with the aid of permanent inspectors, and as well as checking accounts and stocks and examining the general state of financial and budget discipline, this department had to seek out cases of waste. Deeds summarising the results of the audit were to be sent to the NKF.[4]

Finally, financial work was supervised by independent auditing departments of the NKF. The financial and budget inspection department which had been established for this purpose in 1933 notoriously suffered from many defects, and in 1938 it was replaced by a new department of the NKF called the Supervision and Inspection Department. Unlike its predecessor, the new department was highly centralised, presumably in order to ensure its independence from the bodies it inspected. The head of the department was appointed by SNK, and the heads of republican departments were appointed by NKF of the U.S.S.R., and so on down to regional level. The central department was responsible for inspecting all-Union commissariats and republican budgets; the republican departments were responsible for inspecting republican commissariats and regional budgets, and so on. The apparatus was responsible for

---

[1] Unless they involved an offence punishable under criminal law.
[2] SZ 440/1932 (29. ix. 32).   [3] D'yachenko and Kozlov, *op. cit.* p. 182.
[4] SZ 262/1936 (15. iv. 36).

lightning inspections and selective documentary audits of all institutions and enterprises, and for supervising the work of the financial organs and of the internal auditing apparatus we have described. Legislation set out in detail the methods of inspection to be adopted for different types of institutions, and the use that was to be made of voluntary 'control posts' and 'public inspectors' (see chapter VIII). It was empowered to impose fines of up to three months' wages on officials responsible for violations of financial discipline, and in particularly serious cases it could initiate criminal proceedings.[1]

The State Bank, the spending departments of NKF, the internal control organs of the commissariats, and the Supervision and Inspection Department of the NKF between them provided an elaborate apparatus for auditing and financial control. As a result of their activities gross violations of budget discipline by ministries and lower bodies became rarer, and expenditure was generally made in conformity with the plans approved by the appropriate higher body. But, on the whole, control work was the weakest side of Soviet budgetary administration.[2] The two main weaknesses seem to have been in accounting procedure in institutions, which was said to be complex and bureaucratic, hindering rather than assisting any broader control than the purely formal,[3] and in the Supervision and Inspection Department, which was considered to be over-centralised in its structure and superficial in its inspection work.[4]

2. THE FINANCIAL CONTROL OF INDUSTRY AFTER THE ABOLITION OF RATIONING

The budgetary system played an important part in the experiments between 1935 and 1941 to find successful methods for central financial supervision of *khozraschot* enterprises. State control of the financial plans of enterprises was essential because incentives at

---

[1] For further details, see Rovinskii, *op. cit.* pp. 361–4, and vol. II, ch. XXI *et seq.*; *Fin. khoz. bull.* (1937), nos. 29–30, pp. 3–4 (23. x. 37); (1938), no. 7, pp. 3–10 (23. ii. 38), no. 15, pp. 1–2 (9. v. 38), no. 16, pp. 2–3 (31. v. 38), nos. 26–7, p. 1 (4. ix. 38), nos. 31–2, pp. 6–8 (27. x. 38); (1939), nos. 13–14, p. 3 (17. iv. 39).

[2] 'When we discussed questions of estimates and plans...the officials of the financial organs showed that they knew their business. But when it came to questions of control, of checking up on how the financial organs are directing the carrying-out of budget provisions, we established the fact that this work was unsatisfactory' (Report of the Budget Commission, *Supreme Soviet* (1938), p. 68). See also *Zas. verkh. sov.* (1940), pp. 193–4.

[3] Soviet accounting procedures lie beyond the scope of this work. For examples of criticisms, see *Zas. verkh. sov.* (1941), pp. 52–4.

[4] See *Zas. verkh. sov.* (1939), pp. 59, 148; *Supreme Soviet* (1938), p. 115.

enterprise level were not sufficient to compel enterprises to eliminate wastage, and to keep within their costs plans, and because of the inevitable tendency in a system of the Soviet type for economic units at every level to bid for material and financial allocations from the state by presenting exaggerated claims. Only plans at least to some extent imposed by administrative means on economic units can bring in order and balance to overcome the inflationary scramble; and a satisfactory compromise between the interests of the centre and those of the economic units can be achieved only after a long period of practical experience. How this was done for investment expenditure has already been considered. Financial control of *khozraschot* bodies obviously had to take more flexible forms. Nevertheless, it had to be enforced through the existing channels of economic communication between centre and enterprise: the local financial departments responsible for compiling the budget, collecting revenue, and administering expenditure; and the State Bank, responsible for issuing short-term credits and holding the current accounts of enterprises.

The periodic and *post factum* supervision of the finances of enterprises was already well catered for by the late 1930's. In calculating the allocations required by economic bodies, financial departments thoroughly examined the accounts and financial position of enterprises, as was shown in chapter VI (this was in addition, of course, to the interdepartmental control of enterprises carried out by the commissariats and *glavks* by similar methods to those used in controlling institutions on the budget). The Supervision and Inspection Department of NKF carried out selective inspections.

But what might be called *day-to-day* supervision of the finances of enterprises, in order to find unused reserves and eliminate faults, was in a far less satisfactory condition. New methods of supervision had to be found, and the bodies carrying out the supervision had to be given a material interest in the work.

Some such supervision was exercised through the budget grants for subsidies and increased working capital, for they were issued subject to the fulfilment of the production programme, but the issuing authorities did not attempt to examine the production costs of the recipients, normally issuing them to the *glavk*, or on its authorisation. They were not closely connected with the enterprises, and could not have been, without a complete reorganisation of the system for issuing budget grants. They did not have a strong incentive to force economic bodies to accept a lower allocation than that which they had been allowed by the plan. And, of course, by no means all enterprises or even branches of industry were in receipt of these grants.

The turnover tax was more prominent among the channels through which financial supervision was attempted. The intention was that the financial department collecting the tax from an enterprise would check the fulfilment of the production plan, examine the accounts and analyse the work of the enterprise. Thus in 1936 Molotov received a delegation of tax collectors and

> emphasised in particular that the importance of the turnover tax lies not only in securing the revenue of the state budget but also in the supervision of the production and circulation of goods, and demanded from the NKF of the U.S.S.R. and the inspectors and auditors of state revenue that they should really penetrate into questions of the economy of the branches of industry, transport, trade and agriculture they served and raise the state financial supervision of the work of branches and enterprises of the national economy to the necessary level.[1]

Until 1936 the tax had been imposed mainly on the light and food industries. But in that year the exemptions previously given to heavy industry were abolished, and a minimum 'control percentage' of at least 0·5–3% had to be paid on all goods—this was of little fiscal significance, and was primarily introduced so that all industry would be subject to supervision from the tax-collecting agencies.[2]

The use of the tax for supervision purposes may have been of some value in the period before the abolition of subsidies. Profits were low and badly planned, and were not an adequate criterion of the fulfilment of the plan. Achieving the planned level of turnover tax depended on the fulfilment of the production programme, and the financial departments and the local soviets (which depended on the tax for a high proportion of their revenue) had a strong incentive to see that industries due to pay large amounts should pay up, and therefore, indirectly, to see that the production programme was fulfilled. But it is doubtful whether the financial departments, even at this stage, paid close attention to the finances of those industries (the more important economically) which contributed only a small proportion of the tax. And the successful fulfilment of the tax plan could provide only a rough indication of the efficiency of enterprises,

---

[1] Reported in Grin'ko, *Finansovaya programma...na 1937...*, pp. 23–6. See also Grin'ko in *TsIK* 3/vi, Bull. 11, pp. 16, 17–18; M. Bogolepov in *Pl. khoz.* no. 5 (1936), pp. 75 ff.; and *Soviet Union* (1936), pp. 492–4, for the expression of similar views.

[2] Grin'ko, *op. cit.* pp. 22–3.

for the tax depended on the output plan and not on the costs plan. Moreover, the tax was often paid on the turnover in the previous month, and therefore did not provide a good method of current supervision. It was impossible to supervise *all* industrial production in this way, as sales from one enterprise to another within *glavks* were not taxed, and there was not always a direct relationship between the financial department and the producing enterprise, for in many cases the tax was paid by the regional or *glavk* sales organ (*sbyt*).

The tax appears to have been an unsuitable means through which to supervise industry, particularly in heavy industry. It is not, therefore, surprising that administrative attempts to encourage financial supervision via the tax were unsuccessful. The attention of financial organs in branches where 'control percentages' were imposed was concentrated almost exclusively on the technical difficulties of collecting the tax, and only in rare cases was any investigation made of the financial efficiency of the enterprise concerned. By 1939 a number of these 'control percentages' had been abolished, and the question of their general abolition was being raised.[1]

Profits tax would appear to afford a more suitable means of financial supervision, as the fulfilment of the profits plan is possible only if both the production programme and the costs plan are fulfilled. But profits tax, unlike turnover tax, was highly centralised. It was normally collected at *glavk* level, for reasons explained in chapter VI, so that at enterprise level there was little contact with the organs collecting the tax. While regional financial organs participated in collecting the tax on behalf of the NKF, none of the tax received from enterprises of Union significance was paid into the revenue of local budgets, and they therefore had no financial incentive to ensure that the profits plans of these enterprises were fulfilled. To serve as a means of supervision of the current work of enterprises, the tax would have needed radical reform. This was contemplated,[2] but no steps towards it had been taken by 1941.

On the eve of the war attention in fact turned away from the budget and towards the banking system as a means of securing financial supervision. The State Bank had two main connexions with the current finances of enterprises. The first was in its capacity as

[1] See A. Gordin in *Pl. khoz.* no. 6 (1939), p. 137. For an appreciation of the inappropriateness of using the tax for financial supervision written as early as 1935, see Turetskii in *Pl. khoz.* no. 9 (1935), p. 116.   [2] See Gordin, *op. cit.*

banker for current accounts, over which the bank was given increased powers from 1939 onwards. It was instructed to meet wages payments only up to the limit of the monthly wages' plan for the body concerned. Even if an enterprise had a balance in its account, it was permitted to draw on it for wages in excess of the plan only if the plan was over-fulfilled, or if the *glavk* concerned agreed to reduce the wages' plan of some other body subordinate to it by the same amount.[1]

Secondly, attempts were made to increase the supervision of enterprises by the State Bank as issuer of short-term credit. The main difficulty here was that credits were of little importance in heavy industry; by and large, day-to-day supervision was carried out by the bank only in those industries where seasonal stocks, and therefore short-term credit, were important.[2]

In 1939 it was decided that in a group of engineering enterprises the bank should credit part of normal current outlays in addition to temporary and seasonal expenses. 20% of the normal amount of unfinished production and 50% of the normal stock of finished goods were financed not by the 'own working capital' of these enterprises, but by credits from the bank. The participation of the funds of the bank in financing current production gave it a direct interest in the successful fulfilment of the financial plans of these enterprises, for the failure to repay credits on time would cause difficulties to the bank and endanger its own profit.

In 1941 this attempt to bring about financial supervision through short-term credit was still at an experimental stage.[3] The Soviet government had not succeeded in finding a satisfactory method of supervising the day-to-day work of enterprises through either the State Bank or the financial departments—and it is perhaps possible that there is no way of arranging satisfactorily this kind of financial supervision from outside the industry.

More fruitful were the improvements made in what might be called 'self-supervision' by increasing the significance of profits as an incentive. Profits, indeed, were the *point d'appui* at which the tendency

---

[1] *Glavks* were required to establish a quarterly wage-fund, subdivided by months, for each of the enterprises subordinate to them, and to inform the appropriate branch of the State Bank of the amount fixed. On the first occasion of over-expenditure, the bank was permitted to issue an additional 10% of wages above the plan, provided that the enterprise agreed to take measures in the following month to remedy the position (*Fin. khoz. bull.* (1939), nos. 29–30, pp. 19–20 (15. viii. 39); SZ 108/1941 (12. ii. 41)).

[2] See article by Sitnin and Simkin in *Pl. khoz.* (1940), no. 2, pp. 21–32.

[3] For further details, see my article in *Soviet Studies*, vol. v, no. 1 (1953–4), pp. 25–6.

to scramble for resources could be partly eliminated. Enterprises and *glavks* would still try to secure as large an allocation as possible in the plans; but once the plans were adopted, managements would strive to fulfil the costs plans, if the incentive to make profits were strong enough. After 1935 this incentive was increased by the establishment of the Director's Fund in place of the old FUBR, by the increased level of profits, and by the increased importance of retained profits in financing investment.

But it was not, of course, sufficient that managements should merely have the desire to make profits, it was also necessary that profits should be made only if the production plan was fulfilled in the quantities, at the cost, and in the assortment (product-mix) laid down—'better' work in this sense must be reflected in greater profits. It is generally assumed that this will obtain if the ratio of profit to commercial cost is the same for all goods. This would be true if within industry the ratio of labour costs to total costs were the same for each item produced. But where there is a considerable variation in this respect (for example, in the textile industry), the tendency will be to concentrate production on those lines in which labour costs are relatively the smallest. It was therefore suggested in Soviet economic literature on the eve of the war that transfer prices should be adjusted so that the profit:wage-fund ratio was the same for each good.[1]

The situation after 1935 was in practice extremely confused, and it was a question of bringing elementary order into the organisation of profits. Price levels were such that within many industries certain lines carried a large percentage of profit, while others actually made a loss—financial incentives ran counter to the production programmes.[2] The level of profits was extremely low, and whole branches of heavy industry were actually making a loss.

From 1935 onwards the planning and financial authorities made an energetic effort to remedy these defects, by altering prices and tax rates. Now the final price of any good consists (in simplified form) of costs plus profits (part of which is transferred to the budget as tax) plus turnover tax. For any given plan, the final retail price and the costs price of a good must be taken as given, being determined by the whole matrix of prices and plans of other parts of the economy. But the gap between cost price and retail price can be

---

[1] See, for example, A. Gordin, *op. cit.*
[2] Thus, in the first quarter of 1937, the profitability of various textiles ranged from -8.5% to $+56.5\%$ (Plotnikov, *op. cit.* pp. 184–5).

distributed in any proportion between retained profits, profits tax, and turnover tax. The level of profits may be fixed high, so that the expansion programme of the industry is fully financed from profits, or it may be fixed low, so that only the control percentage of profits tax is deducted to the budget, and the budget has to make in addition an allocation to the industry. The overall level of accumulation will not be affected by these adjustments,[1] although they may affect the proportion of accumulation which is channelled through the budget.

It was by adjustments of this kind that the organisation of profits was improved between 1935 and 1941. First, transfer prices (i.e. costs plus profits) were adjusted between goods within industries to eliminate the worst cases of variation in profit levels. Secondly, the level of profits in whole industries was raised in an attempt to provide each branch with an equal incentive from profits. In 1935 transfer prices were raised and turnover tax correspondingly lowered in light industry to enable a higher level of profit;[2] and a further series of adjustments was made in 1938 and 1939. In heavy industry, where turnover tax was low, the profits level could be raised in the short run[3] only by increasing transfer prices without altering the level of turnover tax. This was done in 1936 when subsidies were abolished. Prices were raised again in some branches of heavy industry (e.g. the coal industry) in 1938 and 1939. This in turn raised the level of input costs in the light and food industries, so that the rates of turnover tax had to be reduced in these branches in order that their profits level and retail prices should be unchanged. It also raised the cost of the capital investment programme, but reduced the amount needed for this programme from the budget, as more was now covered by the retained profits of heavy industry. In short, the net result was that profits in heavy industry were increased at the expense of the turnover tax on consumer goods.

The possibility of increasing profits in this way gave rise to a re-examination of the emphasis which should be given to method 1 and method 2 (see chapter VI) in accumulation. Should profits be increased much further, so that a considerably higher proportion of investment was met from profits and not from the budget? On the eve of the second world war, the view was canvassed that light industry should

[1] Except in so far as they increase the size of the Director's Fund, the disposal of which is unplanned.
[2] See *Pl. khoz.* no. 9 (1935), pp. 107–11.
[3] In the long run annual reductions in costs would increase the level of profits if transfer prices remained unaltered.

be made as independent of budget allocations as possible. If the level of investment planned for a given year was likely to be maintained in future years, profits should be raised and turnover tax lowered so that the investment did not need to be supported from the budget. As far as possible, it was argued, a branch of industry should finance its own investment.[1]

Table 35. *Sources of capital investment, 1932–40*
(milliard roubles)

(i) National economy as whole

	1933 [a]	1934 [a]	1935 [a]	1936 [a]	1937 [a]	1938–9 [b] (average)	1940
Budget allocations	14·2	16·2	16·3	21·5	20·7	24·0	25·7
Own resources and other [1]	3·0	5·6	7·7	8·8	7·1	11·0	12·3
Total	17·2	21·8	24·0	30·3	27·8	35·0	38·0

(ii) Industry

	1932 [c]	1933 [c]	1934 [c]	1937 [d]	1938 [e] (plan)	1939 [f] (plan)	1940 [g] (plan)
Budget allocations	8·0	7·8	7·1	8·9	12·2	13·0	13·4
Own resources and other [1]	1·0	1·3	2·9	6·1	5·2	4·5	5·8
Total	9·0	9·1	10·0	15·0	17·5	17·6	19·2

Sources:
(a) See N. Kaplan, *Capital investments in the Soviet Union, 1924–51* (1951), (RM 735), Tables VI and 6.
(b) *Finansy SSSR...*, p. 64, gives capital investment via budget for 1938–40 as 73·7 milliard roubles. Fulfilment in 1940 was 25·7 milliard roubles. Therefore 1938–9 average budget expenditure on investment was $(73·7 - 25·7) \div 2 = 24·0$.
(c) *Finansy SSSR...* (*1931–4*), p. 23.
(d) See Bergson, *Soviet National Income and Product in 1937*, p. 128.
(e) *Zas. verkh. sov.* 2/1, 1938 (Zverev's report, 10. viii. 38).
(f) *Zas. verkh. sov.* (1939), p. 379.
(g) *Zas. verkh. sov.* (1940), pp. 76, 78.
Note: (1) Includes principally retained profits and that part of depreciation allowances which is allocated to investment.

Thus between 1935 and 1940 the level of profits tended to be raised in all industries: in heavy industry, by increasing transfer prices; in the consumer goods industries, by reducing turnover tax; in all industries, by reducing costs while not reducing prices. This is illustrated in Tables 35 and 36, which show that profits rose as compared with turnover tax, and that a greater percentage of investment was financed from profits, particularly in 1934–7. However, the inflationary tendencies and shift in resource allocation in 1937–41 hindered further change. Nevertheless, this was a period in which the importance of profits as a financial incentive greatly increased.

[1] See, for example, Shenger, *op. cit.* pp. 82–3.

Table 36. *Total turnover tax and profits, 1934–41*
(*milliard roubles*)

	1934	1935	1936	1937	1938	1939 (plan)	1940 (plan)	1941
Turnover tax	37·6 (c)	52·2 (c)	65·8 (c)	75·9 (c)	80·4 (d)	92·8 (d)	108·6 (e)	124·8 (f)
Profits	6·4 (a)	7·8 (a)	14·5 (b)	14·5 (c)	15·7 (d)	26·3 (d)	33·3 (e)	44·8 (f)
Total turnover tax and profits (h)	44·0	60·0	80·3	90·4	96·1	119·1	141·9	169·6
Profits to budget (g)	3·1	3·3	5·3	9·3	10·6	17·7	22·4	31·3
Profits retained by enterprises (h)	3·3	4·5	9·2	5·2	5·1	8·6	10·9	13·5

Sources:
(a) *Soviet Union* (1936), pp. 485–6.
(b) *Pl. khoz.* no. 3 (1937), p. 107.
(c) Plotnikov, *op. cit.* pp. 102, 112, 118, 186.
(d) *Zas. verkh. sov.* (1939), pp. 328–66.
(e) *Zas. verkh. sov.* (1940), pp. 66, 233–63.
(f) *Zas. verkh. sov.* (1941), pp. 31, 260–94.
(g) As for turnover tax.
(h) Derived.

3. CHANGES IN THE REVENUE SYSTEM AFTER THE ABOLITION OF RATIONING

(a) *Revenue directly from the population*

No important changes were made in most of the minor taxes during this period, apart from the increases on the eve of the war already discussed. But improvements were made in the methods of collecting taxes from the population. The collection of direct taxes was concentrated under the district financial departments, and considerable attention was devoted to raising the qualifications and improving the work of the tax inspectors and auditors (*revizory*) attached to these departments. The treatment of defaulting tax-payers was regularised by replacing the right of tax-collectors to distrain on their household goods by distraint only through the courts, and by exempting a wider list of property than before from seizure.[1]

The stabilisation of prices after the abolition of rationing raised in a

[1] For details see SZ 471/1935 (29. x. 35); *Fin. khoz. bull.* (1937), no. 13, pp. 3–5 (29. iv. 37), no. 16, p. 6 (11. iv. 37); (1938), nos. 1–2, pp. 32–4 (28. x. 37), nos. 33–4, pp. 36–8 (11. xi. 38). Part of the unlawful levying of taxes was attributed to 'wrecking activities' in the trial of Grin′ko and others in March 1938. Grin′ko, a former leading Ukrainian Communist, was NKF from 1930 to 1937; he was accused of being a nationalist and a spy, and was executed in 1938. At the trial Rykov, former chairman of SNK, denied that he had passed on a directive from Bukharin to Grin′ko to 'strike at the Soviet government with the Soviet rouble' (see Stalin, *Soch.* vol. VIII, pp. 150, 153–4; *Report of Court Proceedings...in re: N. I. Bukharin...G. F. Grinko...* (1938), pp. 7, 18, 67–87, 672–3, 718–21, 795). Grin′ko's successor Chubar′ disappeared during the 1938 purge, and the former NKF Krestinskii was executed and Sokol′nikov imprisoned (and then disappeared) in 1937–8.

particularly sharp form the problem of loan repayments. In the period of rationing, the constantly declining real value of money-repayments and the rapid growth of the money incomes of the population had made possible a large annual increase in the revenue from loans sufficient to yield a net revenue to the budget. But by 1936 interest and repayments had risen, and the net revenue from loans was declining. The government therefore decided to carry out a large-scale loan conversion. Bonds of all previous loans were called in and replaced by the issue of a new loan bearing only 4% against the 10% paid on previous loans.[1] At the new rate the budget made a substantial gain from the loans. However, sustained campaigns and pressure were still needed in order to raise the revenue required; public reluctance to retain bonds led to the failure of an attempt to lighten the conditions under which subscribers could mortgage their bonds with the government.[2] In spite of the campaign, loans from the village population tended to decline as a proportion of total loans revenue, and loans from workers and employees tended to decline as a proportion of the wage fund (see Table 37).

Major changes were made in the taxation of the peasantry and the collective farms. The agricultural tax on collective farms was replaced in 1936 by an income tax. Improvements in collective farm accounting made it possible to calculate fairly accurately the income in money and kind of each farm in the preceding year, and so a tax on the gross income from sales at a flat rate of 3% replaced the previous system by which the tax was proportional to the planned sown area. As a result of this reform, cattle and technical crops, which had been partly freed from tax, were now included.[3] In 1941 the tax was modified to discriminate in favour of production for the state and for reinvestment in the farm. Compulsory deliveries, payments in money and kind for MTS work, and feeding-stuffs for socially-owned cattle, were exempt from tax. Incomes from sales to the state, and produce used for seed and other internal economic uses was taxed at 4% (and the value of this produce was estimated at the low procurement prices). Produce distributed to the collective farmers was valued at the intermediate 'state purchase prices' and

[1] SZ 329 and 332/1936 (1. vii. 36); Grin′ko, *Finansovaya programma...na 1937...*, pp. 29–30.

[2] SZ 330/1936 (20. vii. 36); Grin′ko, *op. cit.* pp. 30–1. This attempt was also cited as an example of wrecking activities (see footnote on p. 280).

[3] Under the old law, 67% of the total tax was paid on grain and only 4% on cattle and technical crops. Under the new law, only 39% was paid on grain and 32% on cattle and technical crops (Grin′ko, *op. cit.* pp. 26–9).

Table 37. *Loans to state, 1931–41*

(i) Loans from population (million roubles)

	1931 [a]	1932 [b]	1935 [c]	1939 [d]	1940 [e]
From workers and employees	—	1,824	3,032	—	—
From other non-peasant population	—	133	183	—	—
Total from non-peasant population	1,223	1,957	3,215	4,994 [1]	7,830 [2]
From collective farmers	—	336	592	—	—
From other peasant population	—	199	71	—	—
Total from peasantry	498	535	662	806	1,603 [2]
TOTAL REVENUE	1,721	2,492	3,877	5,800 [1]	9,433 [2]
WAGE FUND	21,000	32,700	56,200	—	123,700 [3]

Sources:
(a) *TsIK*, 2/v, Bull. 3, pp. 7–9. (b) Plotnikov, *op. cit.* p. 48.
(c) *Otchot*...(1935), p. 175. (d) *Zas. verkh. sov.* (1941).
(e) Plotnikov, *op. cit.* pp. 290–1.

Notes:
(1) Approximate figure only.
(2) Amount *subscribed*. Only 1,392 million roubles was actually collected from peasantry by 1. i. 40.
(3) Cf. note (h) to Table 31, p. 249.

(ii) Net revenue from loans

	1937	1938	1939	1940	1941 (plan)
Total revenue from loans to state	5,867	7,596	8,365	11,450	13,330
Interest, repayments, etc.	3,458	1,955	1,855 (Pl.)	2,785	3,350
Net revenue	2,409	5,641	6,510 (approx.)	8,665	9,980

Sources: Plotinkov, *op. cit.* p. 181; *Supreme Soviet* (1938); *Zas. verkh. sov.* (1939), pp. 364–90; *Zas. verkh. sov.* (1941).

taxed at 8%; produce sold on the market was valued at full market prices and also taxed at 8%.[1]

In an attempt to limit the attention devoted by collective farmers to their personal plots, the agricultural tax was revised in 1939. Since 1932, as a concession to the peasants' interest in the private plot, the tax had been imposed as a lump sum per household irrespective of the income from the plot. This was now replaced by a system similar to that used for non-collectivised individual farm households. The income of the household from the plot was assessed by annual norms of income estimated on the basis of the area sown with different crops and the number of livestock held. These norms varied

[1] *SZ* 339/1936 (20. vii. 36), 364/1936 (4. viii. 36); *Zas. verkh. sov.* (1941), p. 36.

by area according to the conditions prevailing. The income thus assessed then paid a progressive tax rising to a maximum of 15%.[1] Non-collectivised households paid a maximum rate of tax of 45%; they also had to pay tax on their income from market sales, and a special tax on their horses.[2]

(b) *Method of payment of turnover tax*

The abolition of rationing enabled the removal of many of the so-called 'external complexities' of the turnover tax (budget mark-ups, etc.). However, in 1935 and 1936 the NKF continued to fix a very large number of different rates of tax on similar goods, and to change rates very frequently.[3]

From 1938 onwards, drastic efforts were made to simplify the methods of assessing and paying the tax. The number of rates was reduced considerably, and, to reduce the number of tax-payers, all turnover between enterprises in the same *glavk* was exempted from tax.[4] In branches where tax rates remained complicated, the imposition of the tax as a part of the wholesale price was replaced experimentally by imposing it as the difference between the wholesale price, which no longer included the tax, and the retail price minus trading costs.[5] It was stated that this method enabled greater flexibility in imposing the tax. At the same time the payment of the tax was speeded up. Monthly payment and payment every ten days was retained only for goods of less fiscal importance. The most important supply organs, covering grain and alcohol, paid the tax simultaneously with the receipt of each separate payment for the goods they sold.[6] Others, such as textiles and footwear, paid the tax daily on the basis of the turnover two days previously.[7] To make this possible in industries producing a large variety of goods bearing different tax rates, the tax was paid provisionally at a weighted

[1] *Zas. verkh. sov.* Extraordinary 4th session, 28. viii.–1. ix. 1939, pp. 7–37, 56–65, 89–115, 132–45, 167–76, 213–21. The norms fixed in 1939 were raised in 1941 in connexion with the rise of income from the collective farm market (*Zas. verkh. sov.* (1941), pp. 36–7).

[2] *Finansy SSSR za XXX let*, pp. 285–6; *Fin. khoz. bull.* (1938), no. 24, pp. 9–10 (21. viii. 38); *Zas. verkh. sov.* 4th session (1938), no. 24, pp. 237–66, 488–520, 599–604, 679–80.

[3] See, for example, Grin'ko, *op. cit.* pp. 62–3; *Supreme Soviet* (1938), pp. 20, 114; *Zas. verkh. sov.* (1939), p. 35.

[4] Previously only turnover within the same *trust* had been exempt (Suchkov, *op. cit.* p. 19; *Fin. khoz. bull.* (1939), no. 12, pp. 5–16 (28. iii. 39)).

[5] See, for example, the arrangement for textiles, *Fin. khoz. bull.* (1939), nos. 6–7, pp. 18–21 (31. i. 39).

[6] SZ 12/1935 (27. xii. 34); *Fin. khoz. bull.* (1938), nos. 1–2, pp. 17–19 (13. xii. 38); (1939), nos. 6–7, pp. 22–5 (11. ii. 39), nos. 31–2, pp. 8–13 (5. ix. 39).

[7] See, for example, *Fin. khoz. bull.* (1938), no. 30, pp. 9–11 (14. x. 38), nos. 31–2, p. 9.

average percentage, and corrections were made at intervals. As a result of these measures, the NKF was able to claim a considerable improvement in the method of imposing the tax, at least as far as the major contributors were concerned.[1]

(c) *Rates of turnover tax*

The abolition of rationing also raised urgently the problem of revising the pattern of tax rates which had emerged during the rationing period, and confronted the financial planners with the task of adopting a new pattern of rates adjusted to the conditions of free consumer choice on the state retail market.

The general principle involved is obvious. High rates of tax will tend to discourage consumption of a good if the demand for it is elastic, and low rates will encourage consumption. But rates can be varied for several reasons. First, tax rates can be used to adjust the pattern of consumer demand to a given pattern of supply of consumer goods. Secondly, tax rates can be used to encourage consumption of goods which are considered socially 'desirable' and to discourage 'undesirable' consumption; and new goods with high costs or not yet accepted by the population can be 'pushed' through a low rate of tax. This pattern of rates will affect the distribution of goods among the population. High rates (except on goods for which the demand is inelastic) will tend to concentrate consumption among the higher-paid groups. On the other hand, a low rate of tax leading to a shortage will tend to lead to a greater consumption of a good by the lower-paid groups than a higher rate bringing demand and supply into equilibrium.

How did the financial authorities reconcile these various considerations in fixing the rate of tax? Were they influenced mainly by the desire to balance supply and demand, or did social policy play an important part?[2]

The study of Soviet practice in fixing rates of turnover tax is hindered by the lack of discussion of the subject in the Soviet press, where comment is confined to such general statements as 'In fixing

[1] *Zas. verkh. sov.* (1940), pp. 64–6; (1941), p. 31.
[2] We assume in the argument which follows that the average rate of tax will be so fixed that the revenue required by the plan will be ensured, and consider here only variations from the average rate. But the pattern of rates is of course itself influenced by fiscal considerations—the financial authorities will inevitably have to impose a considerable amount of tax on mass consumption goods in order to get the high revenues required as well as from considerations of balancing supply and demand (taxing essential goods is of course attractive just because the demand for them is relatively inelastic).

the rate of tax a role is played by the level of the cost of production and the policy of wholesale prices on it, by the tasks of introducing production into commodity circulation, or, on the other hand, by striving to create conditions limiting its consumption, and also many other causes'.[1] While such statements indicate that supply and demand are consciously influenced by Soviet planners when they fix tax rates, the reason for imposing a particular rate on a particular good is rarely discussed, and little is said about the basis on which it is decided to push ahead with producing one line of consumer goods rather than another.[2] Soviet policy in fixing tax rates must therefore be *deduced* from the published rates, and only very tentative conclusions can be drawn.[3]

(i) *Supply and demand*

In the Soviet economy of 1935–41, priority in production was given to the capital goods and defence industries, so that consumer goods production was to some extent a residue of that production. But goods were distributed not by rationing but by sale. This made the adjustment of supply and demand with the help of the turnover tax particularly important.

Examination of Soviet practice discloses that turnover tax was often used to bring about major adjustments of supply and demand when these were out of equilibrium. The most striking example of this was the abolition of rationing in 1935. The level of tax on grain,

[1] Shenger, *op. cit.* pp. 95–6. See also *TsIK*, 2/VI, Bull. no. 10, pp. 30–1: the tax rate 'varies from 2 to 50% [in 1931] depending on the character of taxed production, on its profitability, and on its importance in the national economy'.

[2] The pattern of tax rates can itself affect the supply of different types of consumer goods. Suppose there is a low rate of tax on bicycles and a higher rate of tax on iron beds, and an acute shortage of bicycles develops while the supply and demand for iron beds at the given price are in equilibrium (skilled workers with high wages may demand bicycles, while the market for iron beds is saturated at that price). There are no economic grounds for increasing the supply of bicycles more than that of beds, until the rate of tax on bicycles is no lower than that on beds. The only immediate way of bringing this about, unless beds are to be made scarce by lowering their price, is to raise the price of bicycles. But owing to the price reduction policy of the government, prices are not as a rule allowed to rise. The planners may therefore try to increase the supply of bicycles more than that of beds. Present tax rates can influence future production programmes.

[3] The main principle to be followed here is that for any given set of material plans, a certain average rate of tax on consumer goods will yield the required level of tax. (Ascertaining this average rate is in practice very difficult owing to the paucity of information on the absolute size of taxed consumer goods production in current rouble terms.) If some goods are taxed at a rate different from this, this deviation from the average will distort the consumption pattern from what it would be if all goods were taxed at the average rate. This will therefore constitute discrimination in favour of or against the good concerned.

meat, and other rationed goods had to be raised from an almost nominal rate (8% on grain, for example, in 1930), to over 85% of the final wholesale price (i.e. to over 500% of the procurement price) between 1930 and 1935, in order to bring supply and demand into equilibrium. The demand for grain had risen much more rapidly than the marketed surplus, and demand exceeded supply much more than in the case of other consumer goods. Demand and supply could, therefore, be balanced only by increasing the price relative to that of other goods, as supply could not be raised to the required level in the short term.

Turnover tax was also used to adjust supply and demand in the case of individual goods and varieties of particular goods. Only in this way can, for instance, the multiplicity of rates in the mid-1930's and the frequent changes in individual rates in 1935 and 1936 be explained.[1] By 1937 there were nearly 1,400 rates in the NK of the food industry alone (including, for example, 66 for margarine), and 650 rates in the fish industry.[2] Presumably the complex and varied budget mark-ups which were added to the price of individual types of good during the rationing period were also adjusted so that goods of which there was a greater scarcity paid a higher rate of tax. Some variations in rates may result from the need to adjust the demand to the supply of certain goods with a high cost of manufacture. Their sale was encouraged by imposing a relatively low rate of tax. Thus higher-priced cosmetics sometimes paid a lower rate of tax than cheaper ones.[3] But, in general, the turnover tax seems to have been used to bring about broad adjustments of demand to supply with major categories of goods rather than to achieve rapid marginal adjustments. Shortages or over-stocking of particular items in particular areas or in the country as a whole would seem to have led to alterations in their retail price via the turnover tax only in exceptional cases.

(ii) *Social discrimination*

Discrimination between goods for socio-economic reasons seems also to play an important part in the determination of tax rates on individual commodities. Extremely high rates of tax are charged on

---

[1] As late as 1939 the turnover tax on potatoes purchased via the centralised fund was raised or lowered in accordance with the seasonal variations in the retail price of potatoes (*Fin. khoz. bull.* (1939), nos. 17–18, pp. 21–2 (13. v. 39)).
[2] *Supreme Soviet* (1938), p. 20.   [3] *Fin. khoz. bull.* (1937), no. 24, p. 9.

the traditionally excisable non-essential goods such as vodka (80–90% of wholesale price, i.e. 400–800% of transfer price). High rates (50–70%) were also charged on essentials which had previously been subject to excise, such as kerosene and matches. Standard consumer goods (household utensils, clothing, bicycles and radio sets, etc.) paid tax rates varying from 20–60%. Musical instruments, certain types of gramophone records, and other 'cultural goods' paid low rates of tax, and books and newspapers were exempt from tax, and were in fact often sold below costs.

There was also some degree of discrimination against the more expensive products within a branch. A higher rate of tax was paid on expensive cigarettes and tobacco, for example, than on *makhorka*.[1] To this general rule, however, there were some exceptions (Table 39 shows examples of these). Children's goods as a rule paid a lower rate of tax than the equivalent goods for adult use (see example in Table 39).

The wide variations in rates illustrated in Table 38 seem to be influenced both by considerations of social policy and by the adjustment to demand of available supplies. At the extreme ends of the scale, social policy appears to predominate. More vodka could easily have been produced so that the retail price and therefore the rate of tax could be reduced, but a high rate of tax was deliberately imposed, not only for fiscal purposes, but also to discourage consumption. Demand was fairly elastic, and hence the supply was reduced in the mid-1930's. At the other end of the scale, books paid no tax and entertainments paid a relatively small rate of tax,[2] although throughout the 1930's there was an extreme shortage of books and theatre places. The government preferred that these goods should be scarce rather than that the purchase of them should be restricted to the groups with higher earnings. In the middle of the scale, however, considerations of fitting demand to the available supply appear to have predominated. There is no 'social' reason which would account for charging a higher rate of tax on gramophones than on radios, for example, or to account for the fall in the rate of tax on beer while

---

[1] Between 1932 and 1938 the rate of tax on top-grade cigarettes varied between 79·0 and 94·0%; on *makhorka* it varied between 49·5 and 88·0% (SZ 497/1931 (1. i. 32), 80/1935 (1. ii. 35); *Fin. khoz. bull.* (1937), no. 10, pp. 13–14, nos. 20–1, p. 26; (1938), nos. 22–3, pp. 8–19).

[2] Theatres, lectures, etc., paid no tax in the pre-war period, and cinemas paid a flat rate on gross takings, varying by the type of cinema, in 1938, from 15·0 to 18·0% (children's cinemas with admission fees up to 50k., and army cinemas, were exempt) (*Fin. khoz. bull.* (1939), nos. 1–2, p. 14 (8. xii. 38, effective 1. i. 39)).

Table 38. *Turnover tax rates on selected goods, 1932–41*

	Effective in 1932	Effective in 1934 [4]	1938–41
Group I (80–90 %)			
Top-grade cigarettes	79·0 [a]	94·0 [b]	88·0 [b] [9]
Vodka	88·4 [a]	88·8 [c]	{83·0 [b] / 84·0 [j] [11]}
Group II (20–79 %)			
High-grade scent	55·0 [a]	55·0 [a]	70·0 [b]
Silver and gold watches	45·0 [a] [1]	55·0 [a] [1]	70·0 [n] [14]
Cameras	15·0 [a]	15·0 [a]	7·0–50·0 [t] [17]
Radio sets	?	?	25·0 [o] [15]
Bicycles	12·0 [a]	12·0 [a]	58·0 [p] [15] [16]
Gramophones	?	?	{32·5 [r] / 60·0 [s] [15] [18]}
Sewing machines	12·0 [a]	56·0 [d]	39·0 [r]
Aluminium utensils	22·0 [a] [2]	22·0 [a] [2]	50·0–60·0 [u] [15] [19]
Iron bedsteads	22·0 [a] [2]	22·0 [a] [2]	10·0 [v]
Makhorka	49·5 [a]	79·0 [b]	70·0 [b] [10]
Wine	39·6 [a]	42·0 [c]	42·0 [b] [13]
Beer	75·0 [a]	75·0 [a]	{59·0 [k] / 42·0–55·0 [m] [12]}
Salt	19·6 [a]	82·9 [d] [5]	{15·0–83·0 [b] [20] / 35·0–80·0 [w] [20]}
Matches	45·0 [a]	69·8 [d]	{22·0 [x] / 45·0 [21]}
Kerosene	53·8 [a]	90·5 [e] [6]	{88·3 [y] / 71·7 [z]}
Cotton goods	22·6 [a]	27·3 [f] [7]	{56·0 [aa] [22] / 47·0–60·0 [bb]}
Silk goods	36·7 [a]	51·0 [f]	{24·0 [aa] / 23·0–77·0 [bb]}
Footwear	17·0 [a] [3]	36·0 [g] [8]	26·0–40·0 [cc]
Group III (0–20 %)			
Soft toys and dolls	14·4 [q]	14·4 [q]	4·0 [q] [17]
Gramophone records	15·0 [a] [24]	7·5 [dd] [24]	0·0–60·0 [ff] [26] [15]
Pianos	15·0 [a] [23]	7·5 [dd]	1·0 [ee] [25]

Sources:
(a) SZ 497/1931 (1. i. 32).
(b) SZ 358/1933 (8. ix. 33, effective from 1. vii. 33).
(c) SZ 112/1932 (9. iii. 32).
(d) SZ 48/1933 (5. ii. 33).
(e) SZ 337/1933 (28. viii. 33, effective from 7. vii. 33).
(f) SZ 356/1934 (4. ix. 34, effective 1. vii. 34).
(g) SZ 121/1934 (18. iii. 34, effective 1. i. 34).
(h) *Fin. khoz. bull.* (1938), nos. 22–3, pp. 8–19 (15. vii. 38).
(j) SZ 212/1940, effective 1. i. 40.
(k) *Fin. khoz. bull.* (1937), no. 23, p. 2 (14. vi. 37, effective 1. i. 37).
(m) *Fin. khoz. bull.* (1939), nos. 10–11, pp. 5–6 (17. iii. 39, effective 16. iii. 39).
(n) SZ 70/1941 (23. i. 41).
(o) SZ 294/1940 (29. iv. 40, effective 1. i. 40).
(p) *Fin. khoz. bull.* (1939), nos. 17–18, p. 21 (10. v. 39, effective 16. v. 39).
(q) *Fin. khoz. bull.* (1939), nos. 10–11, p. 8 (27. iii. 39, effective 16. iii. 39).
(r) *Fin. khoz. bull.* (1937), nos. 22, p. 2 (23. vi. 37, effective 1. vii. 37).
(s) *Fin. khoz. bull.* (1939), nos. 29–30, pp. 13–14 (16. ix. 39, effective 13. vii. 39).
(t) SZ 711/1940 (22. x. 40, effective 16. ix. 40)
(u) SZ 30/1941 (4. i. 41, effective 16. x. 40).
(v) SZ 232/1936 (5. v. 36, effective 1. iv. 36).
(w) SZ 394/1940 (2. vi. 40, effective 1. v. 40).
(x) *Fin. khoz. bull.* (1939), nos. 1–2, p. 14 (28. xi. 38, effective 1. i. 39).
(y) *Fin. khoz. bull.* (1937), nos. 20–1, p. 24 (effective 1. iii. 37).
(z) SZ 296/1940 (29. iv. 40, effective 1. v. 40).
(aa) *Fin. khoz. bull.* (1937), no. 31, pp. 6–7 (1. xi. 37, effective 1. xii. 37).
(bb) *Fin. khoz. bull.* (1939), nos. 19–20, pp. 3–4 (17. v. 39).
(cc) SZ 29/1941 (4. i. 41, effective 11. vii. 40).
(dd) SZ 103/1935 (4. iii. 35, effective 1. i. 35).
(ee) SZ 368/1936 (26. vii. 36).
(ff) SZ 475/1940 (23. iv. 40, effective 1. vi. 40).

Notes:
(1) This is the rate for jewellery. Ordinary watches paid 7·0 %.
(2) Metal consumer goods.
(3) Leather footwear.
(4) These rates exclude 'budget mark-ups'.
(5) *Vyvarochnaya: fasovannaya* only—35·0.
(6) For sale in towns. Sale in villages 93·0 %.
(7) Pure cotton knitted goods. Cotton weaves pay 64·6 % (SZ 262/1934 (27. v. 34, effective 15. iv. 34)).
(8) All footwear except certain specialised kinds.
(9) Top grade 1st quality in packets of 25 and above. For packets less than 25, the rate was 83 %.
(10) Normal smoking *makhorka*.
(11) Percentage of retail price excluding cost of packing, etc., but including basic and transport discounts of trading organisations and special bonus for vodka sales.
(12) Percentage of retail price including trade discount (but excluding extra charge in bars, etc.). Rates vary by area, and are higher for barrel beer than for bottled beer.

(13) Except Trans-Caucasian wine from Isabella grape.
(14) 'Zif' watches. On retail price minus 15% trade discount.
(15) On retail price minus trade discount.
(16) Standard bicycles—sporting and children's bicycles, and bicycles with motor, pay lower rate.
(17) On retail price.
(18) Excluding gramophones produced by Ukrainian local industry, which paid 10·0%.
(19) State industry only.
(20) Packet salt paid lowest rate; uncrushed next; crushed paid highest rate.
(21) By SZ 40/1940 (effective 6. i. 40), 22% rate was retained only for 'Malyutka' factory. All other factories (including the 'Malyutka' factory when it began producing matches of the new format) paid the higher rate. Book matches were exempt from tax.
(22) Cotton weaves. This is *average* rate.
(23) All musical instruments.
(24) All gramophone records.
(25) Local production of R.S.F.S.R. and Ukrainian SSR.
(26) Records are divided into four categories, which pay 0, 40, 50 and 60% tax. Linguaphone records pay 5% tax.

Table 39. *Uses of turnover tax for discrimination*

(i) To discriminate in favour of cheaper grades of potatoes

	Tax in %	
Retail price per kg.	Compulsory deliveries	State purchases
80 k.–1 r. 10 k.	62·0	40·0
65 k.– 80 k.	58·0	35·0
50 k.– 65 k.	48·0	25·0
35 k.– 50 k.	42·0	15·0
Less than 35 k.	0·0	0·0

Source: SZ 298/1940 (21. iv. 40, effective 24. i. 40).

(ii) To discriminate in favour of more expensive grades of playing cards

	Retail price	Tax as % [1]
2nd grade (36 cards)	5 r. 00	82·0
1st grade (36 cards)	6 r. 00	82·0
1st grade (52 cards)	8 r. 00	82·0
'Atlas' cards (37 and 53 cards)	10–12 r.	75·0
Other named varieties	10–15 r.	55·0

Source: Fin. khoz. bull. (1939), nos. 29–30, pp. 12–13 (28. vii. 39, effective 5. viii. 39).

Note: (1) Tax as % of retail price minus 10% trade discount.

(iii) Privileged rates for children's goods (example of footwear, leather uppers)

	1934 [a]	1936 [b]	1937 [c]	1940 [d]
Adult (maximum and minimum rates)	10·0–36·0	1·0–33·0	1·0–35·0	0·0–56·0
Children (maximum and minimum rates)	10·0–23·0	1·0– 5·0	1·0	0·0–15·0

Sources:
(a) SZ 121/1934 (18. iii. 34, effective 1. i. 34).
(b) SZ 271/1936 (29. v. 36, effective 15. iv. 36).
(c) Fin. khoz. bull. (1937), no. 24, pp. 5–7 (23. vii. 37, effective 1. vi. 37).
(d) SZ 29/1941 (4. i. 41, effective 11. vii. 40).

that on wine remained steady, although presumably high-grade scent and gold watches paid the higher rates of tax in this middle range because they were luxuries. A high rate of tax was paid on kerosene, not, of course, because kerosene was considered to be as little of a necessity as scent, but either for fiscal reasons (because demand for it was inelastic) or in order to avoid a shortage of available kerosene supplies in the villages.

The general pattern of tax rates after 1935 seems then to have been a mixture of historical, social and economic factors. Goods subject to excise before 1917 and in the 1920's paid an even higher rate during the planning period. Taxes were introduced on goods which previously had not been taxed, the government being influenced both by social considerations (discrimination against luxuries) and by the need to bring about a rough adjustment of supply to demand and to encourage the sale of certain high-cost goods. In summary, the rates of tax as they stood in 1941 were influenced by the changes in total consumer incomes during the 1930's, by the excise rates of N.E.P., by social policy, and by the need to compensate for the deviation of the composition of the supply of consumer goods from that demanded by the consumer.

(iii) *Discriminatory rates on the same product*

Turnover-tax rates are used not only to discriminate between products, but also to vary and adjust the price of sale of an individual product.

(i) Products used within industry were taxed as a rule at lower rates than the same products sold to consumers. As a rule the principle was followed that intra-industrial transactions take place at transfer prices, i.e. at costs plus a small rate of profits. Thus potatoes for industrial use were freed of the tax paid when potatoes were sold to the consumer.[1] A particular case of this is that higher prices are applied to certain agricultural 'raw materials' when sold retail, in order to discourage their direct purchase and encourage the purchase of state-manufactured products. A notable example of this is the additional levy ('budget margin') charged on flour in order to encourage the purchase of state-baked bread.[2]

---

[1] SZ 298/1940 (21. iv. 40, effective 24. i. 40). Similarly salt for use by the chemical and fish industries was freed from **tax** (see SZ 394/1940 (2. vi. 40, effective 1. v. 40)), and paper for industrial use paid a low rate of tax (SZ 112/1941 (14. ii. 41, effective 10. ix. 40)). And see especially SZ 183/1936 (11. ii. 36, effective 1. iv. 36) and SZ 437/1936 (17. ix. 36). [2] See Suchkov, *op. cit.* pp. 44–5.

(ii) Similarly, goods purchased by institutions 'on the budget' are often subject to lower rates of tax. At one time supplies of foodstuffs and other goods to the army and navy, for example, were not subject to tax, but these privileged prices were as a rule abolished in 1935–7.[1] Oil products were an exception to this general rule—a high rate of tax was from 1936 onwards imposed both on sales to the population and on sales to MTS, industry, etc.[2] (see Table 40).

Table 40. *Oil products: percentage rates of turnover tax*

	1932 [a]	1933 [b]	1936 [c]	1937 [d]	1940 [e]
Kerosene for mass consumption	53·8	93·0 [1]	88·3	88·3	71·7
Benzine for mass consumption	65·0	80·0	78·0	80·0	80·0
Kerosene for tractors	16·0	41·5	88·3	88·3	71·7
Benzine for tractors	16·0	16·0	78·0	80·0	80·0

Sources:
(a) SZ 497/1931 (effective 1. i. 32).
(b) SZ 337/1933 (28. viii. 33, effective 7. vii. 33).
(c) SZ 210/1936 (15. iv. 36, effective 1. iv. 36).
(d) *Fin. khoz. bull.* (1937), nos. 20–21, p. 24 (effective 1. iii. 37).
(e) SZ 296/1940 (29. iv. 40, effective 1. i. 40).
Note: (1) 90·5 % in towns.

(iii) Lower rates of tax were imposed on the production of industrial artels, whose costs are higher than those of state industry, in order to enable them to continue to make a profit.[3] The tax was also used, as an exception, to equalise costs within state industry,[4] but this was usually done via the profits tax.

(iv) The tax is used in order to enable consumer goods to be sold at standard or even at reduced prices in remote areas to which transport costs are high.[5] This was not applied as a consistent policy, however. Some goods, especially in the early 1930's, were sold at higher prices and with higher tax rates in the villages, than in the towns.[6] Other goods were taxed at rates proportionate to their final

---

[1] See *Soviet Union* (1936), pp. 511–12; Grin'ko, *Finansovaya programma...na 1937...*, pp. 40–41.

[2] This was said to be in order to encourage economy in fuel; but the possibility of peculation provided by not taxing petrol for certain uses may also have been taken into account. Similar considerations may have been involved in charging unified prices to all consumers of sugar (see SZ 503/1935 (16. xi. 35, effective 1. x. 35)).

[3] Suchkov, *op. cit.* pp. 27–8.

[4] E.g. rates of 0, 3, 10, and 21% of the retail price on sheet-glass, according to the factory producing it (SZ 214/1940 (23. iii. 40, effective 1. i. 40)). For another example see Suchkov, *op. cit.* p. 30.

[5] Suchkov, *op. cit.* pp. 31–2.

[6] E.g. kerosene (see Table 40), rubber footwear and sugar (SZ 48/1933 (5. ii. 33, effective 1. i. 33)).

Table 41. *Turnover tax by branches of the economy, 1929/30–41*
(million roubles)

	1929/30 [9]	1931	1934	1935	1936	1938 (plan)	1941 (plan)
HEAVY INDUSTRY							
Oil industry	174·0	261·9 [1]	2,856	3,965	4,700 [25]	—	8,305 [18]
Rubber industry	44·0	161·8 [2]	619	646 [15]	—	—	875 [19]
Engineering industry	59·4	103·7	—	—	—	1,121 [23]	—
Other heavy industry	115·9	153·5	606	662	1,800	8,391 [10]	2,284
Total heavy industry	393·3	680·9 [3]	4,081 [10]	5,273 [10]	6,500	9,512	11,464
LIGHT INDUSTRY							
Textile industry	614·1	903·3 [4]	2,345	1,717 [16]	4,200 [25]	—	13,581 [20]
Leather industry	134·2	312·5 [5]	265	23 [17]	—	—	—
Other light industry	93·9	212·5 [6]	1,355	185	4,800	—	—
Total light industry	842·2	1,428·3 [3]	3,965 [11]	1,925 [11]	9,000	10,597 [11]	18,774
TIMBER INDUSTRY							
Matches	—	—	128	126	—	—	—
Other timber industry	—	—	249	92	—	—	—
Total timber industry	289·0	383·6 [3]	377 [12]	218	—	—	543 [21]
FOOD INDUSTRY							
Vodka	—	—	6,861	5,998	—	—	—
Sugar	—	—	1,194	2,093	5,900 [25]	—	—
Tobacco and cigarettes	—	—	1,687	2,169	—	—	—
Other food industry	—	—	3,804	4,517	10,900	—	—
Total food industry	2,979·9	6,397·0 [7]	13,545	14,777 [13]	16,800 [26]	23,247 [24]	50,550 [22]
AGRICULTURAL PROCUREMENTS	—	113·1	4,575	20,729	22,600	26,572	31,138
COMMERCIAL TRADE	299·1	1,070·2	8,322	5,307	n.a.	n.a.	n.a.
OTHER [14]	849·8	1,599·0	2,730	3,938	10,900	14,038	12,281
TOTAL TURNOVER TAX	5,653·3 [9]	11,672·1 [8]	37,596	52,167	65,800	83,966	124,750
Total state and co-operative retail trade	18,872·5 [27]	27,465·2	61,815	81,712	93,200	140,500	197,000

n.a. = not applicable.

Sources:
1929/30 and 1931: *Otchot...* (1931), and *Sots. str.* (1935), p. 551.
1934 and 1935: *Otchot...* (1935), pp. 56–7, 162–3.
1936: *Pl. khoz.* no. 2 (1936), pp. 282–3; no. 3 (1937), pp. 110, 222ff.; SZ 33/1936 (16. i. 36); *Fin. khoz. bull.* (1937), no. 2, p. 7 (13. i. 37); Grin'ko, *Finansovaya programma...*, pp. 22–6.
1938: *Supreme Soviet* (1938).
1941: *Zas. verkh. sov.* (1941); N. Voznesensky, *op. cit.*

Notes:
(1) *Soyuzneft'*.
(2) *Rezinob"edinenie*.
(3) VSNKh only.
(4) Textiles and tailoring.
(5) *Soyuzkozh*.
(6) Excluding fats and perfumes, transferred from food industry to make 1931 comparable with later years.
(7) NK *Snabzheniya* plus VSNKh fats and perfumes.
(8) Includes budget additions to turnover tax, and commodity fund.
(9) Divided as for 1931 (equivalent taxes).
(10) NK *Tyazhprom* only.
(11) NK *Legprom* only.
(12) NK *Lesprom* only.
(13) NKPP only.
(14) Includes co-operation, local industry, etc.
(15) Rubber and asbestos industry.
(16) Cotton, silk, knitwear, and wool industries.
(17) Leather footwear only.
(18) NK *Neftprom*.
(19) The three engineering commissariats.
(20) NK *Tekstil'noi promyshlennosti*.
(21) NK *Lesprom* and NK *Bumprom*.
(22) The three food industry commissariats.
(23) NK *Mash* and NKOP.
(24) NKPP excluding *Glavspirt* (6190 million roubles, 1937 (plan)).
(25) Plan figure.
(26) It is not clear whether this figure includes or excludes the income from alcoholic drinks.
(27) 1930.

retail price, with the result that retail prices were higher in the area remoter from the main regions of production of the commodity in question.[1]

(iv) *Rates of tax on agricultural goods*

Supply and demand, social discrimination, transport costs, and other factors were also involved in determining tax rates for agricultural goods. But the position was complicated by the use of the tax

[1] E.g. grain (see SZ 477/1935 (28. ix. 35), and later decrees).

as a kind of levy on agricultural producers. Industrial consumer goods, with the exception of those produced by the producers' artels, were usually all sold at the same transfer price. Variations in costs were allowed for by varying the profit level. A standard rate of turnover tax could therefore be applied to any good, irrespective of its producer, in order to reach the fixed wholesale or retail price. But agricultural goods were purchased at varying prices—the compulsory delivery price, the contract price, and the state purchase price discussed in chapter VI. But they were sold to the consumer at a standard price irrespective of their source. The rates of tax therefore varied according to the source of the product, and the state 'gain' depended on the price at which the good was purchased.

This raises the problem of the extent to which turnover tax must be seen as a tax on the rural population rather than the urban population. With industrial consumer goods, the position is simple— the 'share' of village and town in payment of tax is proportionate to their share in the purchase of goods.[1] But with agricultural goods, the matter cannot be resolved by a simple formula. It is clear that the turnover tax imposed on grain and meat, etc., is to a large extent a levy on the countryside. In 1930–4 the compulsory delivery of grain to the state by the peasant was virtually a tax in kind. From 1935 onwards, when the retail price of grain was raised without a corresponding increase in procurement prices, the large amount of tax raised was obviously mainly a tax on the peasantry. But this tax can hardly be considered as *entirely* a tax on the peasantry. The price paid for grain by the urban population was to some extent relatively higher than that paid for other products, as compared with the 1920's (as the elasticity of demand for foodstuffs was small, the government was able to increase their price relatively more than that of most other products without producing a glut). What proportion of the tax on foodstuffs should be considered as a tax on the agricultural population is really a question of how much higher the price which the peasants *should* have received for their products was than the price they were actually paid. For this, what the price would have been on a free market can hardly be regarded as a criterion. The question may really be put as whether, given the existing retail price structure, purchasing power was fairly divided between the

---

[1] We are discussing here the turnover tax *only*; whether purchasing-power *received* by the village and town population was in fair proportion to their relative contribution to economic wealth is another question.

agricultural and non-agricultural population. In answering this question, the receipts on the collective farm market would obviously have to be taken into account as well as those from agricultural deliveries or sales to the state. Sales on the collective farm market are made at prices at or above the state retail price, and therefore include the equivalent of the turnover tax 'paid' by both the urban and the rural population on state sales of foodstuffs. The production costs of state farms might help to establish a criterion here, if the receipts from market and compulsory sales of collective farm products could be averaged out.[1]

This problem would require a special study. It is, however, clear that the system of compulsory deliveries at low prices succeeded in greatly limiting the overall money incomes of the rural population, which were relatively very small throughout the pre-war period. It can be said with certainty that the extra production of consumer goods resulting from industrialisation passed mainly into the hands of the wage earners, even though a greater proportion of total agricultural production had to be supplied by the collective farms to the towns than had previously been supplied by the individual farmer. The fiscal instrument through which this result was achieved was the turnover tax.

[1] An interesting attempt to do this is made in F. D. Holzman's valuable work, *Soviet Taxation* (1955), which was published too late to be used here.

Table 42. *Revenue of state budget in standardised classification, 1928/9–41 (million current roubles)*

	1928/9 Amount	%	1929/30 Amount	%	Special quarter 1930 Amount	%	1931 Amount	%	1932 Amount	%	1933 Amount	%	1934 Amount	%
Turnover tax	3,146·1	35·6	5,653·2	40·7	2,420·4	45·9	11,672·0	46·2	19,595·1	51·5	26,982·7	58·2	37,595·6	64·3
Tax on non-commodity operations	n.a.		n.a.		n.a.		n.a.		n.a.		n.a.		n.a.	
Deductions from profits	557·4	6·3	1,562·4	11·3	562·3	10·7	2,175·5	8·6	2,023·4	5·3	3,349·7	7·2	225·0[2]	0·4
Income tax on socialised enterprises	—[3]		—[3]		2·1	0·0	16·3	0·1	130·8	0·3	135·5	0·3	3,090·4	5·3
MTS income	n.a.		n.a.		n.a.		n.a.		n.a.		n.a.		137·1[2]	0·2
Customs revenue	258·2	2·9	304·3	2·2	89·6	1·7	281·3	1·1	281·8	0·7	162·6	0·4	375·0	0·6
Agricultural tax and single tax }	449·4	5·1	405·6	2·9	170·2	3·2	457·9	1·8	625·1	1·6	{ 717·3	1·5	895·0	1·5
Income tax on collective farms }											{ 230·0	0·5	300·0[2]	0·5
Income tax	165·5	1·9	193·3	1·4	68·5	1·3	328·9	1·3	941·6	2·5	631·1	1·4	773·2	1·3
Cultural and housing levies	n.a.		n.a.		n.a.		518·1	2·1	—		1,369·5	3·0	—	
State loans from population	270·2	3·1	656·0	4·7	212·4	4·0	1,616·4	6·4	2,370·5	6·2	3,534·8	7·6	1,464·9	2·5
State loans from economy	277·8	3·1	336·1	2·4	108·5	2·1	1,428·5	5·7	1,128·4	3·0	872·7	1·9	—	
Social insurance	1,221·0	13·8	1,418·0	10·2	408·0	7·7	2,242·0	8·9	3,577·0	9·4	4,293·8	9·4	4,310·1	7·4
Other revenue[1]	2,484·8	28·1	3,350·5	24·1	1,227·0	23·3	4,480·3	17·7	7,233·7	19·0	3,923·9	8·5	5,689·9	9·7
													3,577·3	6·1
TOTAL REVENUE	8,830·4	100·0	13,879·4	100·0	5,269·0	100·0	25,246·4	100·0	38,041·5	100·0	46,363·6	100·0	58,433·5	100·0

	1935 Amount	%	1936 Amount	%	1937 Amount	%	1938 Amount	%	1939 Amount	%	1940 Amount	%	1941 (plan) Amount	%
Turnover tax	52,166·7	69·5	65,672·5[2]	69·6	75,910·0[2]	69·4	80,411	63·1	96,869	62·1	105,881	58·7	124,750	57·5
Tax on non-commodity operations	242·5	0·3	200·4[2]	0·3	—		424	0·3	555	0·4	724	0·4	817	0·4
Deductions from profits	3,258·1	4·3	5,268·6	5·6	9,294·1	8·5	10,466	8·2	15,838	10·2	21,719	12·1	31,259	14·4
Income tax on socialised enterprises	74·0	0·1	—		—		—		—		—		—	
MTS income	n.a.		n.a.		n.a.		—		39	0·0	37	0·0	46	0·0
Customs revenue	869·4	1·2	820·0[2]	0·9	860·0[2]	0·8	1,391	1·1	1,782[2]	1·1	2,007	1·1	2,603	1·2
Agricultural tax and single tax }	737·1	1·0	627·6	0·7	509·1	0·5	2,350[2]	1·8	3,210[2]	2·1	2,500[2]	1·4	3,000	1·4
Income tax on collective farms }	258·5	0·5	450·0[2]	0·5	530·0	0·5	665	0·5	1,515[2]	1·0	2,095	1·2	3,599	1·7
Income tax	874·7	1·2	1,205·3	1·3	1,496·5	1·4	760[2]	0·6	754[2]	0·5	837[2]	0·5	1,660	0·7
Cultural and housing levies	1,450·2	1·9	1,785·1	1·9	1,875·8	1·7	1,952	1·5	2,537	1·6	3,677	2·1	4,489	2·1
State loans from population	4,872·6	6·5	4,892·0	5·2	5,866·0	5·4	2,327	1·8	2,829	1·8	3,546	2·0	4,289	2·0
Social insurance	6,962·7	9·3	8,889·8	9·4	6,609·9	6·0	7,596	6·0	8,365	5·4	11,450	6·4	13,330	6·1
Other revenue[1]	3,244·1	4·3	4,527·7	4·8	5,987·0	5·5	7,167	5·6	7,606	4·9	8,518	4·7	9,998	4·6
							11,972	9·4	14,115	9·1	17,250	9·6	17,060	7·9
TOTAL REVENUE	75,010·6	100·0	94,399·0	100·0	109,329·4	100·0	127,481	100·0	156,014	100·0	180,241	100·0	216,840	100·0

n.a. = not applicable.

Sources of Tables 42 and 43:
Plotnikov, *op. cit.*
Sots. str. (1935), pp. 644ff.
Finansy SSSR. . . .
Zas. verkh. sov. (1939), (1940) and (1941).
Supreme Soviet (1938).
Otchoty. . . . (1931) and (1935).
Pl. khoz. nos. 5–6 (1934), pp. 229–30.
SZ 14/1934 (4. i. 34); 70/1935 (8. ii. 35); 33–4/1936 (16. i. 36).
Fin. khoz. bull. (1937), no. 2, p. 7 (13. i. 37).

Notes to Tables 42 and 43:
General note. These tables are not intended as an exhaustive summary of Soviet revenue and expenditure in the planning period, but merely to show the general trend in budgetary development. As far as possible data are expressed in comparable terms (e.g. various taxes in 1928/9–29/30 are combined and shown as turnover tax); but the sources used are not full enough to enable this to be done consistently.

(1) As various sources have been used, including planned figures for certain items for which fulfilment figures are not shown in sources used by us, this residual item is only approximately accurate. It includes on the revenue side local taxes and levies, *poshliny*, coinage revenue, tax on state farms, receipts from state insurance, state tax on horses of non-collectivised peasants, etc. On the expenditure side it includes expenditure on the NKVD, reserve funds, and items not listed in general accounts for certain years.
(2) Planned figure.
(3) Not available in comparable terms in sources used by us.
(4) Individual items add up to 24,989·5 (see *Finansy SSSR*. . ., p. 218)

Table 43. Expenditure of state budget in standardised classification, 1928/9–41 (million current roubles)

	1928/9		1929/30		Special quarter, 1930		1931		1932		1933		1934	
	Amount	%	Amount	%	Amount	%	Amount	%	Amount	%	Amount	%	Amount	%
NATIONAL ECONOMY	1,247·9	14·2	2,623·6	19·7	1,030·2	20·4	8,117·1	32·4	13,300·4	35·0	13,701·4	32·6	13,686·6	24·7
Industry	714·2	8·1	1,353·0	10·1	614·7	12·2	2,914·3	11·6	3,944·0	10·3	4,143·6	9·8	6,408·6	11·6
Agriculture	922·7	10·5	1,433·5	10·8	604·4	12·0	2,214·2	8·8	3,814·6	10·0	1,855·0	4·4	4,724·9	8·5
Transport	51·0	0·6	87·7	0·7	33·2	0·7	205·3	0·8	255·7	0·7	231·3	0·5	295·4	0·5
Communications	260·8	3·0	545·7	4·1	320·4	6·3	1,790·9	7·2	2,273·2	6·0	2,600·0	6·2	3,562·7	6·4
Trade, supply, procurements	439·2	5·0	560·1	4·2	90·0	1·8	694·6	2·8	1,063·6	2·8	1,023·9	2·4	1,578·0	2·8
Municipal economy and housing	51·0	0·6	50·8	0·4	64·4	1·3	34·1	0·1	112·8	0·3	1,502·2	3·6	985·0	1·8
Other expenditure														
Total expenditure on national economy	3,686·8	42·0	6,654·4	50·0	2,757·3	54·7	15,976·5	63·7	24,784·3	65·2	25,047·4	59·5	31,241·2	56·3
SOCIAL AND CULTURAL SERVICES														
Education	1,116·6	12·7	1,737·8	13·0	604·7	12·0	2,830·3	11·3	3,817·2	10·1	4,934·9	11·7	6,325·1	11·4
Health and physical culture	328·6	3·7	417·3	3·1	110·8	2·2	568·9	2·2	784·2	2·3	980·6	2·3	1,335·0	3·4
Defence of labour and social security	106·8	1·2	127·4	1·0	26·1	0·5	115·1	0·5	153·7	0·4	179·8	0·4	212·8	0·4
Social insurance	1,221·0	13·9	1,418·0	10·6	408·0	8·1	2,242·0	8·9	3,577·0	9·4	3,206·3	7·6	3,354·7	6·0
Grants to mothers	n.a.	—	n.a.	—	n.a.	—	n.a.	—	n.a.	—	n.a.	—	n.a.	—
Total social and cultural services	2,773·1	31·6	3,700·5	27·7	1,149·6	22·8	5,756·3	22·9	8,332·1	21·9	9,301·6	22·1	11,727·6	21·2
DEFENCE	879·8	10·0	1,046·0	7·9	433·7	8·6	1,288·4	5·1	1,296·2	3·4	1,420·7	3·4	5,019·1	9·1
ADMINISTRATION	741·4	8·5	903·7	6·8	190·5	3·8	1,124·1	4·5	1,576·1	4·2	(3)	—	(3)	—
STATE LOANS	317·5	3·6	405·7	3·0	74·9	1·5	408·3	1·6	961·8	2·5	1,273·	3·0	1,877·	3·4
OTHER EXPENDITURE (1)	385·1	4·4	612·0	4·6	432·2	8·6	543·4	2·2	1,044·6	2·8	5,037·9	12·0	5,579·8	10·1
TOTAL EXPENDITURE	8,783·6	100·0	13,322·3	100·0	5,038·2	100·0	25,097·	100·0	37,995·1	100·0	42,080·6	100·0	55,444·7	100·0

	1935		1936		1937		1938		1939		1940		1941 (plan)	
	Amount	%	Amount	%	Amount	%	Amount	%	Amount	%	Amount	%	Amount	%
NATIONAL ECONOMY	16,332·5	22·2	14,929·1	16·1	16,742·9	15·8	23,616·5	19·0	31,111·6	20·3	28,575·9	16·4	39,181·	18·1
Industry	7,682·4	10·4	9,157·8	9·9	9,506·0	8·9	11,408·8	9·2	13,334·1	8·7	12,203·5	7·0	13,455·	6·3
Agriculture	7,070·0	9·6	8,508·3	9·2	7,652·8	7·2	7,412·7	6·0	6,587·2	4·3	6,818·3	3·9	8,155·	3·8
Transport	259·2	0·4	434·5	0·5	447·9	0·4								
Communications	5,135·8	7·0	3,810·7	4·1	3,158·9	3·0	2,891·1	2·3	2,512·7	1·6	2,525·0	1·5	12,084·	5·6
Trade, supply, procurements	1,636·1	2·2	2,306·8	2·5	2,759·5	2·6	6,394·4	5·2	6,870·7	4·5	8,144·9	4·7		
Municipal economy and housing	1,241·7	1·7	2,784·0	3·0	3,143·9	3·0								
Other expenditure														
Total expenditure on national economy	39,357·7	53·5	41,931·2	45·3	43,411·9	40·9	51,723·5	41·7	60,416·3	39·4	58,261·6	33·5	72,875	33·7
SOCIAL AND CULTURAL SERVICES														
Education	8,804·6	12·0	13,905·4	15·0	16,454·7	15·5	18,738·7	15·1	20,313·9	13·2	22,488·9	12·9	26,670·	12·3
Health and physical culture	4,076·8	5·5	5,690·2	6·2	7,026·5	6·6	7,580·7	6·1	8,249·2	5·4	8,955·3	5·1	10,947·	5·1
Defence of labour and social security	175·0	0·2	236·1	0·3	1,252·2	1·2	8,005·8	6·4	7,759·5	5·1	8,230·2	4·7	3,470·	1·6
Social insurance	3,690·8	5·0	4,999·1	5·4	5,207·8	4·9	922·2	0·7	1,106·1	0·7	1,228·5	0·7	5,605·	2·6
Grants to mothers	n.a.	—	149·7	0·2	955·8	0·9							1,225·	0·6
Total social and cultural services	16,747·2	22·8	24,989·7 (4)	27·0	30,896·7	29·1	35,256·4	28·4	37,428·7	24·4	40,902·9	23·5	47,917·	22·2
DEFENCE	8,185·8	11·1	14,882·7	16·1	17,481·0	16·5	23,200·	18·7	39,200·	25·6	56,800·	32·6	70,866·	32·8
ADMINISTRATION	(3)	—	(3)	—	(3)	—	5,307·	4·3	6,122· (2)	4·0	6,752·	3·9	7,142·	3·3
STATE LOANS	1,798·	2·4	(3)	—	3,458·	3·3	1,955·	1·6	1,855· (2)	1·2	2,785·	1·6	3,350·	1·6
OTHER EXPENDITURE (1)	7,483·0	10·2	10,676·6	11·5	10,990·7	10·3	6,597·	5·3	8,277·	5·4	8,846·6	5·1	13,902·2	6·4
TOTAL EXPENDITURE	73,571·7	100·0	92,480·2	100·0	106,238·3	100·0	124,038·9	100·0	153,299·0	100·0	174,350·1	100·0	216,052·2	100·0

n.a. = not applicable. For Notes, see p. 295.

CHAPTER X

THE SYSTEM OF LOCAL AND REPUBLICAN BUDGETS

BY 1925, as was shown in chapter IV, the main outlines of the system of republican and local budgets had been established. Three types of commissariat were established in the 1923 constitution—all-Union (or general-Union), which came completely under the Union budget; Union-Republican (or Unified), for which there were commissariats at both Union and republican levels, financed by the Union and republican budgets respectively; and republican (or non-Unified), which were financed by the republican budget.

Central administration, defence, transport and the most important branches of industry and other sectors of the economy were financed from the Union budget, and the remaining budget expenditures were financed from republican and local budgets. The expenditure rights of local soviets had been made precise by the legislation of October 1924, and covered elementary education, health, local and municipal economy and local administration. However, there was still considerable vagueness about which functions of 'Union-Republic' commissariats should be met from the republican budget and which left to the Union budget. The period from 1925 to 1929 was one of experiment in which trusts and other bodies were frequently moved into and out of the republican budget.[1]

The amounts expended by the local and republican budgets on the functions delegated to them were controlled from the centre in two ways. First, each budget had to be approved by the next higher state authority—thus republican budgets had to be approved, at least in outline, by SNK and TsIK of the U.S.S.R. Secondly, the revenues of republican and local soviets were broadly speaking managed by the central government. The Union government decided what proportion of central direct taxes (Promtax, agricultural tax,

[1] See for details of the changes made in this period *Ek. oboz.* no. 2 (1929), pp. 56–67.

etc.) was to be allocated to the republics, and through them to the local soviets, and issued both general subsidies (*dotatsii*) and earmarked subventions (*subventsii*) and grants (*posobiya*) to the republics and the local soviets. Within the framework of this unified system, considerable latitude was left to the lower soviets to determine *how* their total budget was to be spent, and they retained a certain amount of power to decide the amount and structure of purely local revenues.

In the 1920's and early 1930's, with the consolidation and increased efficiency of Soviet administration, the number of local authorities and of republican and local budgets increased considerably. This expansion took place in two directions. First, as the economies of national areas became more stable, they were raised in status to the position of Union republics. In 1923 there were only four Union republics—the R.S.F.S.R., the Ukraine and Belorussian S.S.R.'s, and the Trans-Caucasian S.F.S.R. In 1924 the Uzbek and Turkmen S.S.R.'s were formed,[1] and in 1927 the Tadjik S.S.R. was separated from Uzbekistan.[2] Finally in 1936 the Trans-Caucasian Federation was divided into three Union republics (Georgia, Armenia, and Azerbaijan), and the Kirghiz and Kazakh S.S.R.'s were formed in Central Asia. The four Union republics of 1924 had been subdivided into eleven.[3] At the same time a number of national regions were elevated to the level of Autonomous republics, mainly within the R.S.F.S.R. From 1928 onwards, after a period of experiment in which the commissariats of the A.S.S.R.'s had been financed from the R.S.F.S.R. budget, the A.S.S.R.'s were permitted to have separate budgets similar to those of the Union republics, but covering a more limited range of functions.[4]

The second main cause of the increase in the number of local budgets was the decentralisation of local administration in the countryside, aimed at involving sections of the rural population actively in the work of government, and at strengthening support for the Soviet régime. From 1925 onwards, *volost'* (small rural district) budgets, covering a group of villages, were formed throughout the

[1] SZ 187/1924 (27. x. 24).   [2] SZ 717/1927 (5. xii. 27).
[3] In 1940–1 five further Union republics were formed from areas annexed by the U.S.S.R. on its western borders.
[4] For statistical and other purposes, the budgets of the A.S.S.R.s were included with 'local' and not with 'republican' budgets. For details of A.S.S.R. budgets, see SZ 250/1925 (20. v. 25); and *Vest. Fin.* no. 2 (1924), pp. 76–80; no. 6 (1924), pp. 28–33; no. 7 (1926), pp. 61–8; no. 11 (1926), p. 106; *Osnovnye itogi raboty pravitel'stva SSSR k perevyboram sovetov 1928–29* (1928), pp. 43–4; *Ek. oboz.* no. 4 (1928), pp. 13–24; D'yachenko, *op. cit.* pp. 430–1.

U.S.S.R., and the proportion of local revenue spent through these budgets was steadily extended.[1] From 1927 onwards, budgets were formed at village level; and the 1930's was a period of experiment in village administration, in which the financial powers of village soviets were frequently changed. By the eve of the war village budgets covering a very limited range of functions were in existence throughout the U.S.S.R.[2]

This increase in the number of local budgets was accompanied by important changes in the structure and functions of the republican and local budgetary system. As has been shown in previous chapters, between 1926 and (say) 1933 all aspects of Soviet economic life were gradually subordinated to the national economic plan. Soviet planning was not confined to key sectors. In order that resources should be concentrated on investment in heavy industry, direct allocation and central control were extended throughout the economy. The investment plan set out the amounts which were to be spent on capital construction in the housing, education, and health services as well as on heavy industry. Not only were the number of workers in each branch of industry fixed in the plan, but also the number of students in each main speciality, and of pupils in elementary schools.

The extension of economic planning profoundly affected the position of local and republican budgets. The most obvious change was the decline in the proportion of total budgetary expenditure passing through these budgets. This was for two reasons. In the first place, there was a great increase in the proportion of resources devoted to heavy industry and allied matters and financed through the budget—this resulted in a rapid expansion of the Union budget—while the consumer goods industries, and the social and cultural services, which were financed primarily through the republican budgets, expanded more slowly. In the second place, various functions which had previously been financed through the local and republican budgets were transferred to the Union budget during the period of the first five-year plan in order to bring them under the closer control of the Union government. When industry was

---

[1] *Volosti* were abolished by the 1930 reform of local government. From 1930 onwards, the main units of local government were the *oblast'* (region), the *raion* (district), the town, and the village. In 1941 there were 107 regions and territories, 4,007 rural districts, and 70,034 village soviets.

[2] For details, see SZ 85/1930 (25. i. 30), 172/1930 (3. ii. 30), 275/1933 (17. vii. 33), 358/1935 (3. vii. 35), 23/1936 (4. i. 36), 168/1936 (10. iv. 36), 312/1936 (28. vi. 36); *Fin. khoz. bull.* (1937), no. 22, p. 1 (20. vii. 37); *TsIK* 4/VI, Bull. 14, pp. 11–13; *Soviet Union* (1936), pp. 523–5; *Supreme Soviet* (1938), p. 105.

reorganised in 1929, a number of enterprises previously financed through the republican budgets were attached to the new combines and financed through the Union budget. At the same period all-Union agricultural trusts were established and many republican functions were transferred to them, and the timber industry was reorganised and centralised under Union control. In 1931 the main enterprises of the building materials industry (cement, slate, etc.), which had proved a bottleneck in the plan, were also put under Union control. The rapidly expanding network of universities and technical colleges (VUZy—*Vvsshie uchebnye zavedeniya* and VTUZy—*Vysshie tekhnicheskie uchebnye zavedeniya*) was also in the main transferred to the Union budget.[1]

Table 44. *Expenditure of Union, republican and local budgets, 1925/6–41 (million roubles)*

	1925/6	1928/9	1931	1933	1935	1941 (plan)
Union budget	1,674·0	4,112·9	16,000	29,200	55,025	170,500 [2]
Republican budget	653·7	1,121·9	1,900	2,300	3,703	13,297
Local budget	1,212·0	2,327·8	4,200	6,800	14,872	33,063
Total budget [1]	3,539·7	7,562·6	22,100	38,300	73,600	216,860

Sources: Plotnikov, *op. cit.* pp. 86ff. *Otchot...* (1935). *Zas. verkh. sov.* (1941).

Notes:
(1) Excludes Social Insurance expenditure except in 1941 (plan).
(2) Includes 5,605 million roubles' expenditure on Social Insurance.

The results of these changes are summarised in Tables 44–6. Republican budgets had financed 15% of overall budgetary expenditure in 1928/9 (including Union, republican, and local budgets, but not the social insurance budget). In 1933 they included only 6% of overall expenditure. This was accompanied by a decline in expenditure on the economy from 50% to 30% of total republican expenditure. In the same period local budget expenditure declined from 31% to 18% of overall expenditure, and here also expenditure on the economy declined relatively. This transfer of functions reached its peak at the end of the first five-year plan. From 1932 onwards, the process took place on a much more restricted scale. When the commissariats of the Heavy, Light and Timber Industries were formed from the old VSNKh in 1932, it was ordered that enterprises previously under republican or regional control should not as a rule be transferred to the Union budget, although they should be subordinated to

[1] *Otchot...* (1931), p. 227.

the Union commissariats for general planning purposes and for the control of investment.[1] During the mid-1930's, the health and education functions of the social insurance system and the payment of pensions to retired workers were transferred to the republican and local budgets. The increase in total expenditure on social and cultural services between 1933 and 1937 took place mainly through these budgets. But defence expenditure, which rose from 1934 onwards, was financed entirely through the Union budget. The net result was that the share of each type of budget in overall budget expenditure remained fairly constant after 1933.

Table 45. *Expenditure of republican budgets, 1925/6–41*
(*million roubles*)

	1925/6	1928/9	1931	1933	1935	1941 (plan)
National economy	213·2	560·4	850·1	715·7	1,012·7	4,600
Social and cultural services	210·8	328·0	689·8	1,090·0	2,394·1	6,900
Administration	174·1	153·7	133·5	316·8	168·7	1,700
Other expenditure	32·7	80·0	271·5	223·2	127·7	100
Total expenditure [1]	630·8	1,122·1	1,944·9	2,345·7	3,703·2	13,300

Sources: Sots. str. (1935), pp. 661–5. Otchot... (1935), pp. 108 ff. Rovinskii, *op. cit.* p. 34.

Note: (1) Excludes allocations to local budgets. Slight discrepancies between this Table and Table 44 result from using different sources taking somewhat different basis for calculation.

Table 46. *Local budget expenditure, 1924/5–39*
(*million roubles*)

	1924/5	1928/9	1931	1933	1939
National economy	148·4	649·4	1,187·8	1,625·0	5,060
Social and cultural services	341·2	992·5	2,196·7	3,718·0	19,570
Administration	248·2	367·9	589·4	1,007·1	2,850
Other expenditure	107·1	294·8	604·7	494·2	1,360
Total expenditure	844·9	2,304·6	4,578·6	6,844·3	28,840

Sources: Sots. str. (1935), pp. 674–7. Finansy SSSR... (1931–4), p. 62. Rovinskii, *op. cit.* p. 39.

The position on the eve of the second world war was therefore that the Union budget was responsible for all expenditure on defence[2] and for five-sixths of expenditure on the national economy. The Union budget financed under the national economy item: (*a*) all heavy and defence industries, and the largest enterprises of light industry;

[1] For details, see SZ 134/1932 (27. iii. 32).
[2] The local budgets were, however, responsible for expenditure in connexion with the annual call-up for the services, and for financing other minor defence matters.

(*b*) all Machine-Tractor Stations and the most important state farms; (*c*) all rail, sea, and air transport, the construction and maintenance of main roads, and the postal and telegraph services; (*d*) foreign trade and most functions in connexion with internal trade and procurements; (*e*) stocks. However, only about a third of social and cultural expenditures were met from the Union budget. This included expenditure on the most important higher and middle education institutes (*vuzy*, *vtuzy*, and technicums), all social and cultural bodies attached to Union commissariats, and grants to mothers. The expenditure of the social insurance budget was also formally included in the Union budget, although, as was shown in chapter IX, it was administered in a decentralised way.

Republican and local budgets were therefore responsible for only a limited range of expenditures on the national economy. These included republican and local enterprises of the consumer goods industry, less important state farms, a wide variety of agricultural services to the collective farms, most housing and municipal economy, and local transport and roads. On the other hand, most social and cultural services were financed through the republican and local budgets. These included all elementary and secondary education,[1] part of the higher education network, all health services,[2] and pensions to retired persons and dependants, and to invalids of the first world war and the civil war.[3]

The more limited functions financed through the republican and local budgets in the planning period were themselves subjected to closer central control. In chapters VII–IX we have described the system by which investment was controlled—'above-limit' projects had to be approved by name by SNK of the U.S.S.R., even if they were financed from republican and local funds. As the planning mechanism was extended, social and cultural and administrative expenditures similarly became more dependent on the national economic plan. The 1941 plan, for example, sets out for each republic *inter alia* the following programmes:

(1) The number of new trolley-buses, tramcars, laundries, public baths, etc., and the length of new sewage drains, tramlines, watercourses, etc.

---

[1] Excluding schools for the children of employees on the railways—these schools were financed from the Union budget.

[2] Only health services in transport and a few central bodies concerned with health matters were financed from the Union budget.

[3] For details of the functions of the various budgets, see Rovinskii, *op. cit.* ch. II.

(2) The number of passengers to be carried by tramcars and trolley-buses.

(3) The number of hospital and maternity beds in towns and villages, the number of places in town crèches, etc.

(4) The number of elementary schools, incomplete secondary, secondary, and further educational schools and their pupils; the number of kindergartens and children in them.[1]

These programmes were translated into financial terms by norms which were supposed to differ in each republic according to local conditions, but were part of a unified system both because wage scales, prices and so on were centrally controlled, and because the norms were adjusted (at least in theory) to give a similar standard of social service throughout the U.S.S.R. Expenditure on administration (which was very closely controlled throughout the period) was similarly regulated. The greater degree of unity in the budgetary system was formally acknowledged by the inclusion of local budgets in the state budget, as was described in chapter IX.

It would be a mistake to conclude, however, that the integration of local finance with the planning system meant that 'local' and 'republican' budgets differed from the Union budget only in name. The existence of republican and local budgets meant that the organisation and administration of the main social and cultural services could be decentralised and made subject to a much greater measure of public control than expenditure on the Union budget—through, for example, voluntary groups attached to the departments of the local soviet. Within their limited competence, the local authorities had some autonomous financial powers: while they had to carry out the centrally approved plan of the amount and type of their expenditure on various items, they were given some latitude within these general limits—thus they normally decided where and how municipal services were to be extended by the planned amount. In addition, local soviets retained independent control of part of their expenditure—for instance, any revenue they raised and any economy in expenditure they effected in excess of the plan could be spent at their discretion—these sums resembled the Director's Fund of a *khozraschot* body.[2] But of most importance was the influence they were able to exert on the amount and composition of local expenditure in the course of compiling the budget. As each local

[1] *1941 plan*, pp. 600 ff.
[2] *TsIK*, 4/VI, Bull. 13, pp. 39–41; SZ 505/1931 (21. xii. 31).

soviet prepared its budget for the forthcoming year, it introduced new proposals for the extension of facilities in its area, and attempted to secure from the higher soviet concerned the maximum amount of resources to finance the agreed programme. Throughout the 1930's there was a continuous clash between the centre and the localities over the size of their budgets. In this clash, which was illustrated in chapter VI (p. 185, n. 1), the final authority rested with the centre. The influence which local bodies managed to exert is difficult to assess, but it clearly depended largely on the degree of tension in the economy as a whole. Thus in the period of the first five-year plan, local rights were frequently over-ridden—Union commissariats treated the claims of republican commissariats as unimportant, and to be satisfied only from any surpluses left after Union needs had been satisfied, and the central government exacted local resources for use by the Union budget.[1] Even at periods of less tension, when local demands were more easily satisfied, local authorities continued to complain that the centre failed to take local conditions into account in fixing norms, and that insufficient discretion was given to local soviets to depart from the control figures of the centre and republics.[2] On the other hand, the centre complained that local soviets failed to keep strictly within the budget and to budget norms, and that they were resorting to legal and illegal[3] devices to gain greater resources than they were entitled to.[4] Similar clashes occurred between republican and local authorities, and culminated in a decision in 1936 that heads of lower financial organs should be appointed centrally, and that regional and district financial departments should be financed through the republican and not the local budgets, in order to increase their dependence on the centre.[5] It is evident that, as in the case of *khozraschot* bodies considered in previous chapters, the opposition between centre and localities could only be resolved by a long period of practical experience.

Local and, in particular, republican budgets played an important part in assisting the policy of the Soviet government towards the backward areas. Throughout this period the government attempted to raise the educational and health facilities of these areas to the level

---

[1] For examples, see *TsIK* 3/v, Bull. 5, pp. 9–10; *TsIK* 3/vi, Bull. 17, pp. 4–7.
[2] For examples, see *Supreme Soviet* (1938), pp. 80–2, 358–9.
[3] Such as compiling two budgets, one for their own use, and one for approval by the higher soviet (Rostov, 1935), and retaining turnover tax for local use.
[4] See *Soviet Union* (1936), pp. 525–9; Grin'ko, *Finansovaya programma*..., pp. 58–60.
[5] *Ibid.* pp. 63–5.

Table 47. *Expenditure of all-Union bodies by republics, 1926/7 and 1936 (million roubles)*

	Population (millions)	1926/7 Expenditure on national economy [1] Total	Per head (roubles)	All expenditure [2] Total	Per head	1936 1939 [3] population (millions)	Capital investment Total	Per head (roubles)
R.S.F.S.R.	100·9	367·0	3·6	625·3	6·2	109·3	21,431	196·1
Ukrainian S.S.R.	29·0	72·0	2·5	143·7	5·0	31·0	4,891	157·8
Belorussian S.S.R.	5·0	0·4	0·8	26·2	5·2	n.a.	—	—
Trans-Caucasian S.F.S.R.	5·9	6·6	1·1	34·9	5·9	n.a.	n.a.	n.a.
Azerbaijan S.S.R.	n.a.	n.a.	n.a.	n.a.	n.a.	3·2	816	255·0
Turkmen S.S.R.	1·0	2·2	2·2	10·2	10·2	—	—	—
Uzbek S.S.R.	5·2	14·3	2·8	28·4	5·5	6·3	839	133·1
Kazakh S.S.R.	n.a.	n.a.	n.a.	n.a.	n.a.	6·1	854	140·0
Total for listed republics	147·0	462·5	3·1	868·7	5·9	155·9	28,831	184·9

n.a. = not applicable.

Sources: Population: see Table 48. 1926/7 expenditures: *Otchot...* (1926/7). 1936 expenditure: *Supreme Soviet* (1938), p. 275.

Notes:
(1) Excluding expenditure on NKPS, and 185·1 million roubles spent by Central *Kazchast'* (Treasury) of NKF.
(2) Excluding 1,105·2 by Central *Kazchast'*, and 59·3 by military-field *kassy*, and expenditure of NKPS.
(3) Accurate data for 1936 are not available. The figures for capital investment per head must therefore be taken as a rough approximation.

of the more advanced areas of the Russian republic, and to develop their economies. The industrial development of the Central Asian republics and the national regions of the Russian republic was financed mainly through the Union budget. Basic industrial enterprises in the backward regions were built from and controlled by general state funds. This is illustrated in Table 47. Such data as are available appear to show that investments per head in the backward republics expanded somewhat more rapidly than investments in the R.S.F.S.R., even though they did not reach the absolute level per head of investment in the R.S.F.S.R. As a result of these investments, industrial production expanded most rapidly in these more backward areas, from an initially low level.[1]

The social and cultural services of the non-Russian areas were

---
[1] For official data, see, for example, *Supreme Soviet* (1938), p. 353.

primarily financed through the local and republican budgets. As early as 1924/5 it was reported that republican budget expenditure per head of population was greater in the Turkmen and Uzbek republic than in the Russian republic,[1] and annual reports in the second half of the 1920's frequently drew attention to the fact that health and other expenditures were relatively higher in the republics of the national minorities than in the Russian republic[2]—indeed, representatives of the Russian republic complained that this shift had gone too far and that their interests were being overridden.[3] This process continued in the early 1930's. Table 48, in which republican and local budget expenditure and total population are compared, indicates that, as would be expected, the concentration of expenditure in the non-Russian republics was at its maximum in the early 1930's, when the drive for improved health conditions and education facilities in these areas was at its most intense.

Satisfactory arrangements for providing the necessary resources to meet the expenditures of the less advanced republics and areas were developed only after a fairly long period of experiment. As we have seen, the revenues of republics and local soviets were derived from two main sources—from purely local revenues retained by the soviet concerned for its own use, and from additions to and deductions from direct state taxes, such as agricultural tax and income tax, which were collected by the local authorities. As a rule it was impossible for a local soviet to increase its revenue substantially by using its discretionary powers to raise the level of local revenues or to impose higher surtaxes on state revenues. While the republics were allowed a certain latitude in imposing, for example, the agricultural tax,[4] those areas which were most in need of extra revenue were generally the poorer areas in which extra taxes would be most difficult to impose. Also in the backward republics and areas the revenue per head raised from general state taxes was lower than in the more advanced areas. The problem was to raise the revenue to meet republican and local budgetary expenditure in the backward areas up to and beyond the level of this revenue in the more advanced areas. In the latter half of the 1920's, additional resources were provided to republican and local budgets mainly by direct subsidy

---

[1] *Vestnik Finansov*, no. 3 (1925), pp. 12–20.
[2] See, for example, *Plenum byudzhetnoi komissii*, pp. 95–7.
[3] See, for example, *Vest. Fin.* no. 4 (1926), pp. 52–6; *TsIK* 2/III, pp. 387–8.
[4] See, for example, SZ 382/1925 (7. viii. 25).

Table 48. *Expenditure per head of local and republican budgets, by republics, 1926/7–39*

	1926/7			1933			1939		
	Local and republican budget expenditure (million roubles)	Population (millions)	Expenditure per head (roubles)	Local and republican budget expenditure (million roubles)	Population (millions)	Expenditure per head (roubles)	Local and republican budget expenditure (million roubles)	Population (millions)	Expenditure per head (roubles)
R.S.F.S.R.	1,714·0	100·9	17·0	5,687·3	113·7	50·0	23,978	109·3	219·3
Ukrainian S.S.R.	473·9	29·0	16·3	1,722·3	31·9	54·0	6,542	31·0	211·0
Belorussian S.S.R.	70·6	5·0	14·1	355·6	5·4	65·9	1,301	5·6	232·3
Trans-Caucasian S.S.R.	137·3	5·9	23·2	691·2	7·1	97·3	n.a.	n.a.	n.a.
Azerbaijan S.S.R.	n.a.	n.a.	n.a.	n.a.	n.a.	n.a.	993	3·2	310·3
Georgian S.S.R.	n.a.	n.a.	n.a.	n.a.	n.a.	n.a.	1,148	3·5	328·0
Armenian S.S.R.	n.a.	n.a.	n.a.	n.a.	n.a.	n.a.	440	1·3	338·5
Uzbek S.S.R.	84·2	5·2	16·2	402·7	5·0	80·5	1,442	6·3	228·8
Tadjik S.S.R.	n.a.	n.a.	n.a.	152·0	1·3	116·9	483	1·5	322·0
Turkmen S.S.R.	26·1	1·0	26·1	147·3	1·3	113·3	496	1·3	381·5
Kazakh S.S.R.	n.a.	n.a.	n.a.	n.a.	n.a.	n.a.	1,514	6·1	248·1
Kirghiz S.S.R.	n.a.	n.a.	n.a.	n.a.	n.a.	n.a.	382	1·5	254·7

n.a. = not applicable.

Sources:

1926/7 population data: *Narodnoe khozyaistvo* (1932), pp. 402–3 (population on 1.i. 27 by 1926 census).

1933 population data: *Sots. str.* (1935), pp. xlviii–1 (as at 1.i. 33). These figures are probably somewhat exaggerated (see F. Lorimer, *The Population of the Soviet Union* (1946), pp. 133–7, which gives smaller estimates for total population than that given in our source).

1939 population data: Birmingham Bureau of Research into Russian Economic Conditions, Memorandum no. 12 (1939), p. 20 (results of 1939 census).

1926/7 and 1933 expenditure: calculated from data in *Sots. str.* (1935), pp. 644 ff.

1939 expenditure: *Zas. verkh. sov.* (1939) (planned expenditure only).

from general-Union funds. While these subsidies did not constitute a considerable percentage of total budgetary revenue for the U.S.S.R. as a whole, they were of great weight in certain republican budgets, particularly those of the Turkmen and Tadjik S.S.R.'s.[1] Part of these subsidies were then transferred by the republics to the local budgets under their control.

The disadvantages of the subsidies system have been discussed in some detail in previous chapters. During the period from 1924 onwards, the authorities sought means of decreasing the subsidies by increasing the revenues collected by the republics and local soviets themselves, so that their expenditure would be dependent on their success in collecting revenue in their area. As it was impossible to raise local revenues substantially, the only way to balance the budgets of backward republics without subsidies was obviously to permit them to retain a greater proportion of the general state revenue collected in their area. Experiments were made to find the best way of doing this. Republics were allocated, for example, a greater proportion of the stamp tax (*gerbovyi sbor*) collected for the whole of the U.S.S.R. than they were entitled to on a population basis.[2] But the simplest and most effective method of providing extra funds for the backward republics was to permit them to retain a greater percentage of the state taxes collected by their local financial departments than was retained by the R.S.F.S.R., so that their revenue was linked with their success in collecting taxes for the Union budget. This was attempted with the agricultural and income tax as early as 1924/5—whereas the Russian republic retained only 50% and 25% respectively of the amount of these taxes it collected, other Union republics retained 100%.[3]

However, this experiment was short-lived. As the role of direct taxes in the budget as a whole declined, it was necessary to permit all republics, even the more advanced ones, to retain an increasing pro-

[1] In 1924/5 subsidies were 115 out of a total republican budget revenue of 651 million roubles; by 1935 they had fallen to 200 out of 12,907 million roubles. In the Turkmen S.S.R., they were 4·3 out of a total revenue of 7·8 million roubles in 1924/5, and by 1935 still amounted to 32 out of 213 million roubles. In the Tadjik S.S.R. in 1935 they still amounted to 68 out of a total revenue of 210 million roubles.

[2] Thus in 1927/8 the R.S.F.S.R. was allocated only 20% of the total stamp tax receipts for the whole U.S.S.R., whereas the Uzbek S.S.R. received 12% and the Trans-Caucasian Federation received 13% (these two republics would have been entitled to only about 7% between them on a population basis)—see *Ek. oboz.* no. 4 (1928), pp. 13 ff. And compare the method of allocating Promtax receipts from Union enterprises, SZ 731/1929 (23. xii. 29).

[3] With the exception of the Ukraine, which received 65% of the agricultural tax.

portion of direct taxes to cover their expenditure.[1] From 1926 onwards, 99% of the income tax, Promtax, and agricultural tax collected on the territory of each republic was transferred to its own revenue.[2] The budgets of the backward republics could only be balanced if indirect taxes as well as direct taxes were made available to them. While a proposal to this effect was made as early as 1926,[3] it was not taken up by the NKF.[4] Excises continued to be treated as a tax of purely Union significance, and to be collected by the central excise administration and its subordinate bodies, and not by the financial departments of local soviets.

The tax reform of 1930 raised the question of balancing the republican and local budgets in a particularly sharp form. The reform provided that the turnover tax should as a rule be collected centrally by the NKF, and no arrangements were made for the allocation of turnover tax revenue to the republics. In practice, during 1931 lump sums from the tax were allocated to the republics as a kind of subsidy. In the Trans-Caucasus over 80% of revenue was received in the form of subsidies of one kind or another in 1931, and in Central Asia nearly 100%.[5] This system was clearly unsatisfactory from the point of view of linking republican expenditure with the success of republican and local organs in raising revenue.

During 1931, therefore, the revenue sources of Union republics were increased by making the income tax into a purely local and republican revenue, and by increasing the percentage of state loan revenue retained by the republican authorities. These measures, which were not of great fiscal significance, were followed in December 1931 by a major reform in the method of collecting the turnover tax. From 1932 onwards this tax was collected from enterprises in a decentralised way by local financial organs, instead of being collected centrally from combines covering the whole U.S.S.R. As a result, the bulk of the very large revenues from this tax now passed through the local financial departments, as had previously been the case with income tax and other direct taxes. The government could therefore compensate for the lower total revenue collected per head in the more backward republics by permitting them to retain a greater proportion of turnover tax. The rate of deduction from the

---

[1] See *Vest. Fin.* nos. 5–6 (1926), pp. 221–3.
[2] SZ 198/1926 (25. iv. 26), 286/1927 (25. v. 27).
[3] *Fin. ents.* cols. 1051–2; *Vest. Fin.* no. 4 (1926), pp. 52–6.
[4] Except in the form of differentiated deductions from the enlarged Promtax of 1929.
[5] *TsIK* 2/vi, Bull. 10, pp. 23–5; *Otchot...* (1931), p. 227.

tax collected on the territory of each republic was fixed annually by the government (see Table 49).

In the first half of the 1930's the budgets of the most backward republics—Turkmenistan and Tadjikstan—still did not balance even though they received 100% of the turnover tax collected on their territories. They therefore continued to receive subsidies from the all-Union budget. Thus their development was being assisted from the centre in three ways: (a) all-Union commissariats financed developments on their territory through the Union budget; (b) they were permitted to retain a larger percentage of state revenues collected on their territory than was retained by other republics; (c) they received direct subsidies from the Union budget. Direct subsidies to these two republics could be abolished only after the growth of their economies raised the level per head of retail trade and hence of turnover tax. By 1938 it proved possible to abolish all subsidies, and by 1940 no Union republic retained more than 55·5% of the turnover tax collected on its territory.

Table 49. *Percentage of turnover tax deducted to republics from amount collected on their territory, 1932–40*

	1932 [1] (a)	1935 (b)	1940 (c)
R.S.F.S.R.	5·0	13·5	5·9
Ukrainian S.S.R.	5·0	20·7	8·5
Belorussian S.S.R.	25·0	42·0	21·0
Trans-Caucasian S.F.S.R.	25·0	37·6	n.a.
Azerbaijan S.S.R.	n.a.	n.a.	20·7
Georgian S.S.R.	n.a.	n.a.	33·4
Armenian S.S.R.	n.a.	n.a.	45·9
Turkmen S.S.R.	100·0	75·0	37·3
Uzbek S.S.R.	40·0	36·4	6·3
Tadjik S.S.R.	100·0	75·0	55·5
Kazakh S.S.R.	n.a.	n.a.	42·7
Kirghiz S.S.R.	n.a.	n.a.	49·7

n.a. = not applicable.

Sources: (a) SZ 98/1932 (7. iii. 32). (b) SZ 196/1935 (23. iv. 35). (c) SZ 272/1940 (15. iv. 40).

Note: (1) Enterprises of all-Union significance only.

The system of deductions from state revenues was used to finance the expenditure of local budgets as well as that of Union republics. The rates of deduction from turnover and other taxes are fixed by the Union government so that the total revenue of the republican budget and the local budgets of each Union republic equals their total expenditure. Each republican government therefore has at its disposal a fund of general state revenue in excess of its requirements for the republican budget—this is expressed in the annual budget statements by showing the total revenue of each republic as considerably in excess of its expenditure. The excess revenue is used by the republics to balance the local budgets in their area. Here the relationship between republican and local budget is similar to that between Union and republican budget. The Union government controls certain of the deductions made from state revenue to local budgets via the republics. For example, the legislation of December 1931 stipulated that village soviets should receive as a rule 50% of the agricultural tax collected on their territory,[1] and that district soviets should receive the remainder. In this way the Union government ensured that the revenue of every soviet should not fall below a minimum level. But the main responsibility for redistributing state revenues among the local soviets was borne by the republican governments. They decided the amount of turnover tax revenue, for example, which should be retained by various local soviets. Thus the republics could assist the more backward areas within their territory, just as the Union government assisted the development of Union republics which were generally backward. The part played by the Russian republic in developing more backward areas was of particular importance, as it contained a great variety of autonomous republics and national areas which were economically and culturally at a low level.

In addition to these taxes redistributed through the budgets of the Union republics, local soviets also received revenue from two other main sources. First, they received certain state revenues direct and not through the republican budget—for example, state dues (*poshliny* —stamp taxes, notary's fees, payments for licences, etc.).[2] Secondly, they had the right to impose certain purely local revenues, such as the tax on buildings, land rent,[3] taxes on vehicles and cinemas, a profits tax on municipal enterprises, a levy on collective farm markets, and a tax on the sale of timber. Two types of revenue appear to have been included in the category 'local revenue'. First, this category included revenues associated with services rendered by the local

[1] Similarly the division of receipts from state loans between republic, town, village, and district soviet was laid down by the government (see, for example, SZ 174/1933 (14. v. 33), 195/1935 (4. v. 35)).
[2] Income tax was also allocated direct to local budgets between 1931 and 1940. The income tax on handicraft co-operatives was also directly included in the local budget.
[3] Agricultural land and land of state and collective farms were exempt from land rent.

soviets (revenues such as the tax on buildings and land rent, and the levy on collective farm markets, which are the nearest Soviet equivalent to rates). Secondly, it included taxes the details of which were decided by the local soviet and not by the Union government, which merely fixed upper limits and ordered certain exemptions.[1]

Table 50. *Local revenue, 1924/5–39 (million roubles)*

	1924/5	1931	1933	1939
Local revenue from local sources	375·9	2,209·8	2,621·5	7,310
Self-taxation [1]	—	362·3	505·9	—
State taxes, etc., direct to local budget	205·0	741·7	896·3	4,100
Deductions from state taxes, etc., transferred *via* republican budget	260·7	1,212·2	2,608·9	16,740
Other revenue	42·1	153·3	158·6	1,540
Total revenue	883·7	4,679·3	6,791·2	29,690

Sources: Sots. str. (1935), pp. 674–7. *Finansy SSSR...* (1931–4), p. 61. D'yachenko and Kozlov, *op. cit.* p. 343. Rovinskii, *op. cit.* p. 52.

Note: (1) Self-taxation by the village population (imposed by a general village meeting for local use) was not included in the budget for the years for which a blank is shown for this item.

The proportions of 'state revenues' and 'local revenues' in total local revenue changed considerably during the planning period (see Table 50). In the period of the first five-year plan, general state resources were concentrated primarily on heavy industry and other branches of the economy financed through the Union budget, and a much smaller percentage of state taxes as a whole was made available to local budgets. In these years local soviets had to rely to a considerable extent on purely local sources of revenue, and had to work to an extremely tight budget. From 1932 onwards, social and cultural services financed through the local budgets expanded more rapidly. This expansion was financed by increasing the deductions made to local soviets through the republican budget. By 1939, 70% of all local revenue was covered by state taxes, either directly or through the republican budget. These state taxes were of most importance in village or district budgets, where purely local revenues provided only 10–15% of total revenue, and of least importance in the towns, where local revenues amounted to 30–35% of total revenue.

By the use of this system of deductions from state taxes, both the Union and the republican authorities were able to influence local expenditure by controlling the revenues of local budgets as well as by

[1] For details of these local revenues, see V. A. Shavrin, *Mestnye byudzhety SSSR* (1946), ch. XIV.

establishing norms of expenditure. Control by the Union government, as we have seen, was fairly limited. It determined the total revenue available to a republic by fixing percentage deductions from regulating revenues such as turnover and agricultural tax.[1] But the division of this revenue between the various types of local soviet was primarily in the hands of the republic, although it had to ensure that each local soviet had available to it resources corresponding to the tasks set out in the national economic plan, and to enable it to perform its functions as set out in legislation about local government organisation enacted by the all-Union government.[2] The system of republican and local budgets enabled local government, health, and education to be administered more flexibly, but the limited autonomy which was permitted was kept under close central control.

[1] In 1933 turnover tax provided 1,605 million roubles and deductions from mass loans provided 805 million roubles out of total deductions from state revenue of 2,609 million roubles. Other taxes which were partly transferred from republican to local budget were the tax on non-commodity operations, the cultural and housing levy, and (from 1940) MTS income.

[2] For details about the functions of the various types of local soviet, see Rovinskii, *op. cit.* ch. II.

CHAPTER XI

THE BUDGETARY SYSTEM IN PERSPECTIVE

THE development of the budgetary system after the German invasion in June 1941 does not fall within the scope of this study. But a brief consideration of the main features of developments after June 1941 will help us to look at the pre-war system in some kind of historical perspective.[1] In examining the Soviet economic system, Western observers are particularly concerned to establish how far this experience is relevant to other economies in which different forms of what I have called 'direct planning' are being or may be established. An examination of the pre-war Soviet budgetary system from the vantage point of 1955 will help us to distinguish how far the main features of this system are inherent in any system of direct planning, and how far they result from the particular Russian environment, and from the pace of development dictated by the policies of the Soviet leaders.

1. THE WAR YEARS, 1941–5

At first glance, one is struck by the apparent consistency and stability of the budgetary system in 1941–55; very little new development seems to have taken place. The impact of the war on the system had effects very similar to those produced by the first five-year plan. The defence effort of 1941–4, like the large investments of 1928–32, led to a decline in consumer goods output (though a much greater one), while the money incomes of the population continued to rise. As a result, the retail price level was bound to rise. The government again introduced a system of strict rationing at low prices for the private consumer, while on the free market, and in the special 'commercial' stores which were again established, the prices of con-

---

[1] These developments are treated in more detail in the article by G. R. Barker and A. Baykov in *Bulletins on Soviet Economic Development*, no. 3 (1950); and in my articles in *ibid.* no. 7 (1952) and nos. 9–10 (1956).

sumer goods rose rapidly; thus, on the collective farm market, the prices of foodstuffs are stated to have risen by 1943 to 12·6–13·2 times the already high 1940 level.[1] Within industry, prices were pegged (and in the heavy and armaments industries, actually reduced),[2] so that extensive subsidies had again to be paid as in the early 1930's. As in the critical years of industrialisation, inflation and conflicting claims on available resources led to a breakdown in budgetary, bank and investment controls: the planners again had to devote most of their attention to concentrating supplies on key factories and jobs, and to switching men and materials from bottleneck to bottleneck—and the war economy, unlike that of the first five-year plan, was one in which output of basic materials was rapidly declining.

There were important differences between the two periods 1941–4 and 1928–32 in their financial development. Data on wartime inflation is too meagre to enable a comparison to be made between the extent of the inflation in 1941–4 and 1928–32: between 1928 and 1932 currency circulation trebled; all we know of the war period is that, in three years, currency in circulation increased by 140%, while available consumer goods in relation to the employed population declined much more rapidly. Wage inflation was apparently less in 1941–4: between 1940 and 1944 the average monthly earnings in industry are said to have risen by 42%;[3] between 1928 and 1932 they doubled. This evidently indicates a considerable improvement in wage controls and in the cohesion of the labour force. On the other hand, very much more cash seems to have passed into the hands of the peasantry through the free market, and to have been partly hoarded by them. During the first five-year plan, the compulsory delivery system was not yet properly established, and the government took firm administrative measures to prevent the existence of a free market (which was not legalised, it will be remembered, until 1932); but during the war years, the delivery system on unoccupied territory worked fairly satisfactorily, and the collective farm market was permitted to operate freely. The 1947 currency reform (which had no parallel in the 1930's) was aimed principally at eliminating the peasant hoards of currency which resulted.

Budgetary expenditure quadrupled between 1928/9 and 1932;

---

[1] N. Voznesensky, *War economy of the U.S.S.R. during the period of the patriotic war* (1948), p. 101.
[2] Voznesensky, *op. cit.* pp. 101–2.   [3] *Ibid.* p. 94.

between 1940 and 1945 it rose by only about 60%. This was because (a) the inflation in wage levels in matters financed by the budget was less intense; (b) expenditure on social and cultural services declined absolutely, even in terms of current prices, whereas it rose considerably during the first five-year plan; and (c) the economy as a whole had contracted in real terms. But the financial authorities had great difficulty in meeting this limited increase in money expenditure (budgetary expenditure measured in real terms probably declined absolutely over these years). The revenue from turnover tax declined absolutely owing to the fall in output of consumer goods and to the state policy of fixed prices for rationed goods (the prices of rationed goods were not raised until 1946, and state 'commercial' trade was not introduced until 1944). Much more reliance had therefore to be placed on direct taxation and loans, mainly from the urban population, than in 1928–32; and direct taxes were probably more acceptable to the population for patriotic reasons. Surcharges were made on the income and agricultural taxes; a special war tax was introduced; and a tax was imposed on bachelors and adults with small families, which was retained in the post-war period.

However, these revenues did not prove sufficient to meet state expenditure. In the later war years, as in the first five-year plan period, large short-term credits were issued by the State Bank, not through the budget, and swelled currency in circulation although the budget was formally in surplus. But in 1941, 1942 and 1943 the budget was actually in deficit, whereas in the 1928–32 period it had always shown a book-keeping surplus.

These war-time peculiarities of the budgetary system were not, however, of major significance; the Soviet budgetary system came through the war with all its main features intact, and was rapidly restored to its pre-war shape.

2. POST-WAR CHANGES

Post-war developments also seem to indicate a considerable degree of stability and permanence about the main features of the budgetary system. The currency and retail price reform of 1947 restored the balance between the cash available to the population and the supply of goods (at a much higher price-level than that of 1940), and enabled the turnover tax to resume its former paramount position as a source of revenue. The wholesale price increases of 1949 enabled budget subsidies to industry to be abolished. Pre-war stringency in the control of investment issues was gradually restored. Ten years after the end of the second world war, the budgetary system was largely administered by pre-war legislation and methods: still in force were the 1926 and 1927 laws about the adoption of the budget, and about republican and local budgets, the taxation legislation of 1931, the short-term credit system and system of budget norms and norms of stocks introduced in the early 1930's, and the 1936–8 decrees on investment control (which were themselves a modification of the system which had been instituted at the end of the 1920's).

Some changes have, it is true, been made in budgetary administration in the post-war period. First, in 1949, the attempt to impose a nominal rate of turnover tax on heavy industry for control purposes was finally abandoned; as has been shown earlier, this was already the subject of much criticism before the war. Secondly, greater consistency has been achieved between the profits rates of different industries: a standard rate of 4–5% is now usual. Moreover, the Director's Fund (the part of profits with which a factory is most concerned) has been adjusted in the post-war period to make a rough allowance for the variation in profits level between industries.[1] As a result of these measures the financial incentive to costs reduction and plan fulfilment is now applied much more evenly throughout industry. At the same time attempts have been made to improve bank control over the current financial operations of heavy industry.[2] Thirdly, central control over investment has been considerably increased: since 1950 the estimates and plans for the more important construction jobs have to be approved by the U.S.S.R. Council of Ministers after being registered with, and examined by, the re-established State Committee on Construction Affairs.

But all these changes are minor in character. They are improvements to aspects of the existing system and cannot be considered as a new departure. The only important respect in which the budgetary system has departed from pre-war practice in the post-war years has been in the successful containment of inflation, which has made possible a consistent policy of annual price reductions for goods in

---

[1] When the Director's Fund was re-introduced in 1946 it was fixed at rates varying from 2–10% of planned profits and 25–75% of profits above the plan. (This was later changed to 1–5 and 15–45% respectively.) The higher rate was paid in heavy industries such as iron and steel, where the rate of profit was lower, and the lower rates in the light and food industries, where profit was higher. See, for example, A. M. Aleksandrov, *Finansy SSSR* (1952), pp. 203–4.

[2] For details, see my article in *Soviet Studies*, vol. v, no. 1 (1953–4), pp. 24–9.

Table 51. *Profits, turnover tax and price reductions, 1949–55*
(*milliard roubles*)

	Total profits	Profits to budget	Turn- over tax to budget	Turn- over tax and profits tax	Net growth in budget- ary ex- penditure	Price reduction
1949	69·6	42·2	245·5	287·7	41·4	48 (plan) [2]
1950	65·5	40·4	236·1	276·5	0·4	80 (plan) [2]
1951	74·7	48·0	247·8	295·8	29·8	28 (plan)
1952	83·5	58·5	246·9	305·4	17·2	24
1953	89·8	70·3	243·6	313·9	5	50
1954 (plan)	123·4	89·8	234·3	324·1	53	15·7
1955 (plan)	143·3	117·5	233·7	351·2	23·8	Nil
Overall net growth in 1949–55	73·7	75·3	−11·8	63·5	128·7 [1]	—

Sources: *Zasedaniya verkhovnogo soveta SSSR*, for appropriate years. *Izvestia*, 6–9. viii. 53, 22. iv. 54, 4. ii. 55, 27. xii. 55. *Pl. khoz.* no. 3 (1954) (Zverev). *Voprosy Ekonomiki*, no. 6 (1954) (Plotnikov). K. N. Plotnikov, *Ocherki istorii byudzheta sovetskogo gosudarstva*, pp. 407 f., 479, 488, 528 f. *Pravda*, 1. iv. 52; and see Kaser in *Soviet Studies*, vol. VII, no. 1 (1955), pp. 46–7.

Notes:
(1) Not strictly comparable with columns above, as some figures in that column are planned figures only.
This 128·7 is made up of: profits and turnover tax 63·5; direct taxes on population 14·7; loans 2·9; social insurance (about) 7; other (about) 40.
The artificial additions to budgetary expenditure made in the official budget figures have been excluded from the 'net growth' in 1953–5.
(2) State trade only; excludes co-operative trade.

state (and co-operative) shops on the retail market. As has been shown, retail prices rose rapidly in the early 1930's, and in the best pre-war years were at most stabilised; the one attempt at a price-cut (in 1937) was a failure in the sense that all it resulted in was increased shortages. Between 1947 and 1952, retail prices were reduced by over 40%,[1] without apparently any increase in retail shortages. It is worth considering in some detail how this remarkable result, without parallel in the history of modern economies, was achieved.

What happened is illustrated in Tables 51 and 52. The main reason why such price reductions were possible was that costs per unit of output were systematically reduced in industry throughout

[1] See P. J. D. Wiles, *Bulletin of the Oxford University Institute of Statistics*, vol. 16, nos. 11–12 (1954), p. 376, for a useful estimate of retail price levels in state and co-operative trade in the post-war period. According to Mikoyan, retail prices in 1954 were 43% of the 1947 post-currency reform level, but the heavy price-cuts of 1953 evidently did result in a considerable increase in the scarcity of supplies on the retail market: there were no price reductions in 1955 (on this point, see my article in *Soviet Studies*, vol. VII, no. 1 (1955), pp. 61–4).

Table 52. *Reduction in industrial costs, 1949–55 (in %)*

	Plan	Fulfilment
1949	6·0	7·3
1950	5·7	5·4
1951	?	5·4
1952	?	4·4
1953	6·1	3·7
1954	4·4	3·2
1955	4·5	4·7

Sources: as for Table 51; *Pravda*, 27. ii. 55 and *Narodnoe khozyaistvo SSSR: statisticheskii sbornik* (1956), p. 93. Fulfilment figures are as percentage of cost in previous year, annual average, in comparable prices.

this period (see Table 52). The 'saving' to industry from this is said to have amounted to 35½ milliard roubles in 1951, and 46 milliard in 1952 (i.e. the output actually produced would have cost this amount more at the costs of the previous year).[1] No details have been published about the way in which these reductions in industrial costs have been achieved.[2] They partly resulted, no doubt, from savings in the consumption of raw materials and fuel per unit output, and perhaps also from savings in overheads. But it is evident from the available data on the slow rise of the average wage in this period[3] as compared with total output[4] that a large part of the reduction of costs must have been due to the fact that earnings rose less than productivity. In pre-war years attempts to cut the rate for the job (the annual 'revision of norms') were partly unsuccessful,[5] and the planned wage fund was usually overspent in each year (see above, pp. 197, 249). Little information has been published on post-war revision of norms: according to one economist, 'workers' rates of pay are not changed after every over-fulfilment of the output norm—they remain unchanged at least for the year concerned',[6] but cases have been reported of workers who are indignant because their payment per piece has been cut shortly after they introduced an improvement which led to a rapid increase in output.[7] Whatever the methods used, it is evident that such cuts in the rate indicate a considerable increase in the state's control over wages and productivity, which would not

[1] Zverev, *Pravda*, 9. viii. 53.
[2] Thus there are no data available for the post-war period like those reproduced in Table 18 (ii), p. 105.
[3] The rise in the average money wage between 1948 and 1953 apparently lies within the limits of 12 and 25% (see M. C. Kaser, *Soviet Studies*, vol. VII, no. 1 (1955), pp. 40, 42).
[4] Industrial output approximately doubled during this period.
[5] For details, see David Granick, *The management of the industrial firm in the U.S.S.R.*, pp. 83–5.
[6] M. Liberman, *Voprosy Ekonomiki*, no. 6 (1955), pp. 34–44.
[7] See, for an example, *Stroitel'naya gazeta*, 10. iv. 55 (I. Kharlamov and E. Abdullua).

be possible without an increase in the cohesion and discipline of the industrial labour force.[1]

The second factor, which together with costs reduction in industry formed the *sine qua non* of price reductions, is the relative stability of the prices paid to the collective farms for produce delivered to the state in 1948–52. By keeping compulsory delivery prices down (often to the pre-war level), the state limited the growth of the money incomes of the peasantry: had compulsory delivery prices been raised in these years, the money incomes of the peasantry would have been higher, and price cuts would of necessity have been smaller.[2]

The process by which price-cuts were passed on through the budget to the population deserves some attention, as the new features of post-war budgetary structure result from it, but its study is made difficult by lack of data: turnover tax rates have not been published in the post-war period. Apparently the process has taken place roughly in the following way. In the years after 1947 a substantial annual rise in output of consumer goods took place, but (except for 1953 and 1954) at a slower rate than the increase in producer goods: if costs had not fallen in industry, retail price reductions would therefore not have been possible, as the rise in output of consumer goods would have been more than 'balanced' by the outlay on wages. The retail price reductions therefore resulted from the reduction in costs, and not from a change in the structure of industry in favour of consumer goods. This reduction was passed on as follows:

(*a*) After their initial rise in January 1949 industrial wholesale prices were reduced in 1950 (in both January and July—the latter reduction affecting building materials only), 1951 and 1952, in step with the reduction in production costs.[3] As a result there was a considerable reduction in the money cost of investments (financed mainly from the budget) and the cost of equipment, office fittings, etc. purchased from budget grants; and this meant that budgetary

[1] This general point is not, I think, vitiated by the fact that productivity per worker has tended to rise less rapidly than has been planned (see data given by Khrushchev in his speech to the Builders' Conference, *Pravda*, 29. xii. 54), and (in 1953–4) less rapidly than *real* wages: productivity per worker has evidently risen more rapidly than *money* wages in these years, but price cuts were greater than the increased output of consumer goods plus the reduction in costs warranted (see article quoted on p. 318, n. 1, above).

[2] The rise in compulsory delivery prices in 1953–4 led to a substantial rise in the money incomes of the peasantry, considerably increased the state's difficulties in making price cuts, and was a contributing factor in increasing the scarcity of retail supplies.

[3] Each of the reductions was used to bring about particular adjustments in the level of profits for different industries and products, but this complication does not affect the general argument.

expenditure in money terms did not rise as much as it would have done if costs had been constant. Retail prices could therefore be reduced both because the transfer prices of consumer goods had been cut (owing to reduced costs in the consumer goods industries), and because the need for budgetary revenue was limited by reduced costs in the expenditure side of the budget.

(b) Between 1 January 1952 and 1 July 1955 wholesale industrial prices were kept constant in the producer goods industries; they were not reduced in step with cost reductions (this may also have happened in the consumer goods industries, but I have not been able to establish this from the available data). Therefore, profits in industry rose substantially in these years.[1] Budgetary expenditure rose steadily because investment costs fell only to the extent that building costs fell, and because the costs of materials purchased on budget appropriations fell only in those cases where turnover tax was paid, and only to the extent that the appropriate rate of tax was cut. But the rise in budgetary expenditure was able to be met by an increase in the rate of tax on profits, and by the 'natural' growth of income tax, social insurance fees, etc., with the expansion of the national income,[2] and retail prices could therefore again be cut by reducing the rate of turnover tax (i.e. the proportion of turnover tax in final retail price). Of course, these price reductions were made on foodstuffs as well as on industrial consumer goods: the state was able to manipulate its 'mark-up' on compulsory delivery prices.[3]

The net result of all these processes was as follows (see Table 51). Budgetary expenditure remained stationary in 1950. It rose from 1951 onwards, but this rise was met by an increase in profits tax (from 40 milliard roubles in 1950 to 117·5 milliard roubles (plan) in 1955), and in smaller items of budgetary revenue. Although retail trade in real terms more than doubled between 1949 and 1955, the yield from turnover tax actually declined, owing to the cut in turnover-tax rates, which resulted in the reduction of retail prices.

---

[1] The profits of industry were as follows (only available years): 1950 (actual) 35·3, 1951 (plan) 41·2, 1954 (plan) 73·3, and 1955 (plan) 88·7 milliard roubles (*Izvestia*, 8. iii. 51; *Pl. khoz.* no. 3 (1954), p. 21, and no. 2 (1955), p. 42).

[2] I ignore here complications such as the increased rate of agricultural tax in 1950–2, and the apparent growth of customs revenue and the decline in reparations.

[3] As we have seen, the reduction in prices could be made only because the money incomes of both industrial workers and peasants were kept down, the former through cuts in piece-rates, the latter through pegging the payments made for compulsory deliveries. A cut in food prices cannot *ipso facto* be attributed to the limitation on prices paid to the peasantry.

The successful policy of price reductions is the principal novelty of the post-war budgetary system; but it does not mean a radical departure from the pre-war system. It is rather its crowning glory. It will be recalled that the Soviet government had consistently aimed at passing on the increased supply of consumer goods through reduced prices ever since the mid-1920's: it failed because it could not control wage inflation. The price reductions of 1948–52 must be seen as the achievement of what budgetary policy had unsuccessfully aimed at before the war, and not as a change in the system.

3. LIMITATIONS OF THE SYSTEM

It would seem then from a first examination of post-war developments that the Soviet budgetary system has shown great stability, and it might be tempting to go further and conclude that the system is in all its main characteristics properly applicable to *any* direct planning system, and can therefore be used as a model by other countries adopting such a system.

I think this would be a mistaken view. Its erroneousness can best be illustrated by a consideration of what seem to be the limitations of the Soviet budgetary and financial system, as a result both of pre-war experience in the use of the system, which we have already discussed in detail, and of subsequent experience.

(1) First, the price and taxation system is so arranged that the use of *economic* methods to adjust supply to demand within industry is difficult. In the turnover tax on consumer goods, the planners have a fairly flexible instrument with which they can roughly adjust the pattern of consumer demand to the pattern of state output. But within industry, all materials and equipment are sold at a price equal to average costs (measured without an allowance for capital in use) plus a small rate of profit. If a particular material is in short supply (such as timber, for example), it is still sold at the same price as if there were a glut of it. As production plans are inevitably imperfect, shortages are bound to appear, so the central production plan has to be supplemented by a fairly tight allocation or rationing system within industry.

(2) Secondly, the system of financial incentives at factory level requires reconsideration in the light of post-war developments. As we have seen, the Director's Fund and the wage and salary system provide financial incentives which combine with administrative

pressure from above to persuade factories to fulfil their output plan and to reduce costs. In the pre-war period, the incentive to fulfil the output plan was generally much greater than the incentive to reach the costs reduction target. Factory managements were prepared to break through legal rules on the sale and transfer of equipment and materials, to exceed the wage ceilings fixed in the plan, and to make unauthorised changes in production methods, so that the output plan would be fulfilled.[1] The financial expression of the paramountcy of the 'output-plan' motive over the 'costs-reduction' motive was the continuing inflation. In the post-war period, the 'costs-reduction' motive has evidently increased considerably in importance, as the successful achievement of cost-reduction targets indicates. In the coal industry this has happened to such an extent that mine managers are artificially restricting the output of their workers in order to avoid the increases in costs which would result from paying higher piece rates;[2] but this appears to be an extreme case.

The increase in importance of financial incentives raises particularly sharply the question of the satisfactoriness of the present costs system within industry: do the present incentives provide a sufficient incentive to economic progress?—if they do not, their increased importance may be inhibiting the drive to increased output (as in the case of the coal industry) without resulting in a corresponding increase in efficiency and in incentives to innovation.

Many of the faults in the present costing system could be corrected and are being corrected within the framework of the system. The Director's Fund is not made available to the factory until some months after the year in which it is earned, and this limits its effectiveness. A factory is deprived of its Director's Fund if it is a bad debtor, even if its debts are not its own fault, but result from other factories failing to pay up their accounts with it. The Director's Fund, in spite of the 1946 reform, still tends to be smaller in heavy industry than in the consumer goods industries, and hence to provide a smaller incentive there. The rate of profits may not be as high on some products as others, so that the factory will be encouraged to violate its assortment plan in order to make easy profits (this tendency has been counteracted in the post-war period by the regulation that all the items in the factory's plan must be produced if the Director's Fund is to be awarded). Even when the rate of profit is the same for

---

[1] On this point, see Granick, *op. cit.* chs. IX and X.
[2] A. Zvorykin and A. Kirzhner, *Pravda*, 13. viii. 55.

all items in the plan, the factory will not be provided with an equal incentive to produce all goods: it will tend to concentrate on those in which the work done by the factory is least, and the proportion to total costs of the cost of components and materials produced elsewhere is highest (least 'labour-intensive' items, as they are called). Finally, although this is a fault in the production plan rather than in the financial arrangements as such, the tendency to plan the production of many items by weight (e.g. so many tons of domestic utensils) leads factories to produce unnecessarily heavy individual items so as to meet the output plan more easily: 'the heavier the bed, the better it is for the factory'.[1]

Of course, it is impossible ever fully to achieve a proper reflexion of the output plan in the profits incentive, so that the factory will have a financial incentive to produce each item of the plan which is exactly proportionate to the importance attached to that item by the planning authorities. But in the period since 1949, as in 1938–41 (see pp. 277–9 above), the profits incentive has been substantially improved: profits in heavy industry have been raised so as to bring them more to the level of profits in light industry, and a standard rate of profit of 4–5% is now said to be made on most goods.

But a more important set of 'weaknesses' in financial incentives seems not to be susceptible to minor improvements of this kind, but to be inherent in the present industrial costs structure. In the first place, the whole question of the size and structure of the capital stock of a factory is largely outside its purview. The equipment of a factory is almost entirely supplied on the decision of higher authorities, without the financial results of the factory's work influencing the matter directly. The factory does not have the right to invest its profits in its own further expansion: investment financed through profits (method 1 of chapter VI) is handled by the *glavk*, and the factory as such has little influence on it. Moreover, there is no precise relationship between the capital stock held by a factory and its planned costs. If a factory has less than the average capital stock, its costs will tend to be higher, and the *glavk* will pay it more for its output (some factories are paid less than the average price fixed for the particular product for the *glavk* as a whole, and some more, through either the 'dual price' or the 'internal subsidy' system). But the costs of an *inefficient* factory with the same amount of equipment as an efficient factory will also tend to be higher, and it will also

[1] *Novyi Mir*, no. 7 (1955), p. 37.

receive a higher price for its output. Capital stock, as we saw above (p. 144, n. 1), plays an insignificant part in costing. The efficient and highly capitalised factory is penalised to cover the losses of the inefficient and less capitalised factory.

It is not only that the costing and pricing system does not force a factory to acquire and use equipment in as efficient a way as possible. Under present arrangements, a factory is also disinclined to make itself rapidly more efficient. If it reduces costs by 12% in year A, while other factories reduce costs by only 3%, the ministry or *glavk* will still fix for it the blanket cost reduction of 3% in year $(A+1)$, and the price it is paid will be put down accordingly—the *glavk* does not measure the factory's achievement against its real possibilities as measured by the capital stock it possesses.[1]

The present pricing and costing arrangements affect technical innovation particularly strongly. If a factory proposes technical improvements, the costs reduction from these improvements does not swell the factory's profits: it is included in the factory target, and the factory is *penalised* if it does not achieve the target.[2] Moreover, production by new and ultimately cheaper methods often costs more in the initial stages, and may hold up the production programme for a time. To avoid these disadvantages, for which no compensating reward is paid, factory managements sometimes tend to prefer to use extra labour rather than introduce new machines and methods.[3]

---

[1] Compare the following quotations: 'Plans for factories in approximately similar conditions often vary—one is smaller, the other larger; one is "easy", the other "a heavy load"....*Glavki* base their plans mainly on the level of output already achieved. A factory which has already achieved a high level of productivity is set a growth rate of 10%, just the same as a more backward factory. Here it is generally forgotten that the advanced factory has already taken up most of its slack and that each percentage rise will need a greater effort to achieve' (*Stroitel'naya gazeta*, 27. vii. 55). 'Material incentives [to cut costs] operate only after the plan is approved, not *before* it is approved, when they sometimes even act in the opposite direction. As is well known, plan targets are distributed between factories mainly on the basis of the results already achieved. Factories which are working badly sometimes get very low plan targets, and the burden of plan fulfilment is shifted on to those which are working efficiently. Because of this they often try to conceal their capabilities in order to avoid getting targets which are too high....So *glavki* and ministries have the difficult task, which is often beyond their capacity, of deciding from the centre what the real capabilities of a factory are and what its plan must be like. This also leads [the higher authorities] to increase the number of reports and planning estimates. Factory plans are often reached by a kind of "contest" between the *glavk* and the factory. Experience shows that this system of planning does not always obviate the random distribution of plan targets' (E. Liberman in *Voprosy Ekonomiki* (1955), no. 8, pp. 34–44).

[2] 'The method of reward for plan fulfilment often turns into a method of *rewarding technical stagnation*' (Liberman, *loc. cit.*).

[3] See, for an example, *Trud*, 11. ix. 55.

(3) A further limitation of the present financial system, which is, of course, intimately connected with the limitations already discussed, is its extreme centralisation. The restrictions on the financial powers of lower units of government and industry have already been discussed for the pre-war period: in the post-war period they were taken farther. In 1948 the category of 'decentralised investment' was abolished; and the minor capital expenditures which were included under that heading (see above, p. 256) were placed under the strict control of the special banks as part of the investment plan: this made it far more difficult to use the Director's Fund and the surplus revenue of local budgets for the purchase of minor items of equipment—one commentator writes that it 'limited the possibility of satisfying the welfare needs of the working people, and improving the upkeep of towns and factory settlements'.[1] Moreover, as we have seen (p. 317 above), the State Committee on Construction Affairs, established in 1950, controls 'above-limit' investment much more strictly than its pre-war predecessor did; and until 1954 the 'limits' were not raised, while prices had risen considerably since the war, so that a much larger proportion of total investment (something like 80%) came within the 'title lists' approved by the all-Union Council of Ministers. It seems that, in general, central control over local and republican budgets has been considerably increased since before the war. The national-economic plan apparently contains (or contained until the 1956 plan) more details of republican and local expenditure than before the war; and the system of norms (of unit costs for schools, hospitals, etc.) has remained highly centralised—apparently it is only in the Ukraine that a separate system of norms exists in which allowance is made for local conditions.[2]

A cost and pricing system which makes necessary strict allocation of materials; severe limits on economic initiative and technical innovation by the lower units of the economy; and a highly centralised budgetary system—these features of the Soviet financial and budgetary system in the pre-war period, and after the war until 1952, did not exist in isolation, but were intimately bound up with the structure and function of the economic and planning system as a whole in these years. The Soviet economy was highly centralised in order to enable industrialisation to advance at a rapid pace, and

[1] V. Sosnovskii, *Finansy SSSR*, no. 8 (1955), p. 13. According to the 1951 budget report, the abolition of decentralised investment did not take place until that year (Zverev, *Pravda*, 8. iii. 51).   [2] Sosnovskii, *loc. cit.*

economic development was concentrated on producer goods, which were consumed by state markets (within industry itself, and by the defence ministries)—the production of consumer goods was primarily a by-product of this intensive industrialisation drive, and consumer demand did not greatly influence production plans. In this economy, in which the principal problem was to catch up the technical level already achieved by several Western countries, industrial advance could take place at a rapid pace primarily by introducing from above technique which had already been developed abroad (although initiative at lower levels played, of course, an important secondary part in economic progress); and industry was able to import unskilled manpower from the countryside on a large scale in order to meet labour shortages and failures to raise productivity as planned.

Important changes clearly need to be made in a planning system of the Soviet type, if it is to be flexible enough to allow for large-scale innovations and economic experiment at factory level; and if consumer demand is to find adequate expression in production planning. This does not, I believe, mean that a direct planning system is inappropriate for an advanced economy; but it does mean that the equation of 'direct planning' with 'extreme centralisation' is a vulgarisation of the concept. Direct planning, as I have used the term (see above, p. 96), may be defined as 'a system of planning in which the growth of the economy is regulated by conscious aims embodied by a central authority in specific investment or production plans compiled on the basis of a realistic knowledge of the present situation and future possibilities, and applied and enforced by appropriate machinery'. There has been a tendency among economic theorists to assume that such a system must be a highly centralised one, and that in such a system it is simply a question of how much power is given to the super-planners: the greater their powers, the more they will be able to plan the economy; the possibility of planners issuing orders and simply getting them carried out is, it is implied, limited merely by the limitations on their powers. It is, of course, true that certain quite extensive powers must be at the disposal of planners if they are to 'regulate the growth of the economy': Soviet planners were able to be much more precise in 1946 about what their economy would be like in 1950 than British post-war economic surveys were able to be about our economy; and the 1955 targets set for each of the main Soviet industrial raw materials in 1952 were fulfilled within a few per cent—no Western government has ever been able to plan industrial growth in this way. But if planning from the centre is taken too far on paper, the possibility of shaping the economy can be destroyed. This is not simply because over-centralisation can stifle innovation, and thus limit economic growth. If central powers are extensive, the inevitable weaknesses in the paper plan can up to a point be corrected by the emergence of unofficial markets, contact-men and pushers (*tolkachi*), and *blat'* (the Russian term for under-the-counter and illegal methods), and realistic planners will allow these devices to be incorporated into the system.[1] But if the authority of the central planners is taken too far, so that these devices are put to an end, it may stifle itself. The clearest example of this is the post-war planning of Soviet agriculture—the 1949–51 livestock plan and the fifth five-year plan for agriculture were not carried out, because the actual powers of the planners to intervene in agricultural matters were greater than their knowledge warranted, were so great as to stifle initiative at the point of production.

For direct planning to be effective, then, the planners must be able to adjust their plans to the actual conditions of economic life; they must know how far they can move the economy forward from the starting-point. Further, in a country in which innovations must largely be made from within the economy, there must be sufficient encouragement for innovations to be suggested, there must be scope for them to be tried out (risk is essential to economic progress), and there must be the means to incorporate innovation from below with the main lines of economic growth as they are being shaped by the central plan.[2] The financial and budgetary system must be designed to meet these conditions.

In the light of this argument, the model of the Soviet budgetary system which we constructed in chapter VI for purposes of exposition, is clearly inapplicable as a general model for all direct planning systems. This model took the concept of a one-way relationship between the central planning authority and the society as a whole for

---

[1] For an interesting discussion of Weber's model of bureaucracy in the light of Soviet industrial experience, see Granick, *op. cit.* ch. XI.

[2] As one Soviet economist put it, 'To simplify planning does not make it less effective; in point of fact, it makes it work better. If the details of the plan are more decentralised, it is possible to concentrate attention on the key questions in the plan. If the principles of incentives and profit-and-loss are used to improve planning by encouraging initiative at the bottom, the result is better than if attempts are made to work out every detail of the factory's work at the centre. Properly understood, planning in less detail is a superior form of planning' (Liberman, *loc. cit.* p. 44).

granted, and assumed that the central planners could control production, allocation, wages and prices. Freedom to change one's job was introduced as a mere 'friction' modifying the model, because in the 1930's the centralisation of industrial training and the possibility of large intakes of unskilled trainees from the countryside, meant that in the long run all the labour required by industry was available to it. Innovation and initiative from below were also seen as 'frictions' modifying the basic model rather than as inherent parts of the initial structure; and this was appropriate to a description of the economy of 1928–41 in which innovation from below occupied a secondary place to the centralised drive to bring Soviet industry up to Western levels.

4. POSSIBLE CHANGES IN THE SYSTEM

But obviously in an economy in which innovation occupies a central place, and in which a wide range of economic decisions is devolved on to lower levels, the budgetary system must clearly take a different form. The Soviet economy is now facing precisely the problems of innovation and decentralisation which we have been discussing; and an examination of the changes which are needed in the present Soviet budgetary and financial system, in order that it should be adapted to decentralisation and innovation, will help us to see how far its structure as it developed in the 1930's resulted from the particular circumstances of industrialisation. Possible changes have been widely discussed in recent Soviet economic literature; and reference will be made to these discussions at appropriate points.

(a) Decentralisation

There is clearly considerable scope for transferring functions at present controlled in detail by the Union budget to the republican and local budgets: this would mean that the disposition of a substantial proportion of materials and equipment would not be controlled from the centre (although its total size would be decided by the central plan).

Since 1953, steps have been taken in this direction. Ministries of the coal industry, the iron and steel industry, and higher education have been formed in the Ukraine; a ministry of non-ferrous metallurgy in the Kazakh SSR; a ministry of the oil industry in the Azerbaijan SSR; and ministries of posts and telegraphs have been set up in each of the sixteen republics. At the same time, several thousand industrial, trading and other enterprises and organisations, and a large number of state farms, have been transferred from the jurisdiction of Union ministries to the appropriate ministries of the Russian republic. These changes are still proceeding: according to Bulganin, 'all this is only a beginning.... A great number of factories is still directly under Union ministries, although they could be better managed by republican bodies.' Other writers have made a variety of suggestions for increasing the powers of local and republican budgets, which taken together would make a substantial inroad into the powers of the Union government.[1]

Moreover, during 1953 and 1954 the functions of the central planning authorities have been substantially reduced. The number of items in the industrial section of the annual national-economic plan has been cut from 4,500 to 1,500; and costs plans and labour plans have been considerably simplified. Most important, from the point of view of the budget, is that the ceilings or limits above which capital investment projects must be approved individually by the U.S.S.R. Council of Ministers have been raised from the 1·5–10 million roubles range to the 5–25 million roubles range. As a result, somewhat over half the total expenditure on capital investments is now covered by the 'title lists' approved by the Union government as against about 80% before 1953.[2]

These measures have been accompanied by parallel changes in methods of administering the budget. All-Union authorities now plan and approve the budgets of Union republics without deciding how much of each republican budget is going to be allocated to the local soviets; the size of local budgets is now determined by each republic. The detailed disposition of allocations within sections of the budget will henceforth be decided by the republic without higher approval (except for expenditure on wages), and Union authorities have been instructed to devote more attention to the proposals of republican agencies and ministries of finance—a proper explanation must be given for the rejection of any proposal. 'In response to the requests of local soviets', decentralised investments falling outside the state investment plan are to be restored in their 1935–48 form, but

---

[1] For details of decentralisation measures and proposals, see Khrushchev, *Izvestia*, 21. iii. 54; and Bulganin, *Pravda*, 17. vii. 55, and budget speeches by Pegov, Zverev, Lomako, Safronov, Senin, and Gedvilas, *Izvestia*, 5. 8. and 10. ii. 55.

[2] For details of these planning measures, see B. Glukser and P. Krylov, *Planovoe khozyaistvo*, no. 5 (1954), pp. 76–86; and my report in *Soviet Social Sciences Bulletin*, S.C.R. vol. II, no. 2 (1955).

apparently covering a wider range of matters. The tax collected on profits made in excess of the plan by industries controlled by republican and local authorities is to pass to the local or republican budget instead of the Union budget, and may be used for further investment in the industries concerned. Any revenue which republican and local budgets can raise in addition to the estimates made by the Union government is now placed entirely at their disposal (previously their rights in this respect were strictly limited). Finally, differentiated norms of expenditure are to be systematically worked out for each type of expenditure in each area.[1]

The decentralisation measures of 1953–5 do not yet amount to a radical change in the present budgetary system, although they do modify it considerably. More far-reaching proposals, however, have been made in order to simplify the system of allocating materials. Minor simplifications have already been made: ministries now each receive a 'block grant' of each material, which they themselves subdivide among the factories under their control; minor items of production have been excluded from the central supply plan; and details of supply (such as the types and grades of coal) will be decided by direct negotiation between the producing and consuming ministries. But these changes do not affect the central principle that both scarce and plentiful items are sold at cost-price plus a standard rate of profit within industry. It would evidently be difficult within a system of direct planning to give factories powers to charge 'what the market would bear' for their output: this would mean that the resources available to each industry (and to each factory within each industry), and hence, their new investments, would be considerably affected by the market which would form for purchase-and-sale within industry. But it would be fully possible for the state to charge a tax on scarcer industrial materials (this would then pass into general budgetary revenue), in order to discourage their use. For this purpose, it has been suggested that part of turnover tax revenue should be levied on the prices of producer goods as well as those of consumer goods.[2]

---

[1] Details of these changes in budgetary procedure are given in articles by V. Sosnovskii, N. Kisman, and M. Pomanskii, in *Finansy SSSR*, no. 8 (1955).

[2] The only published reference I have seen to this proposal appears in a review of Maizenberg's book on prices by D. Kondrashev (*Kommunist*, no. 16 (1954), pp. 125–6), but this indicates that there have been discussions on this proposal among economists:

'The question of the principles of the formation of wholesale prices on producer goods is recognised as controversial in our literature. There are unsolved problems here. Some economists, for example, consider that the structure of prices in both the producer goods and the consumer goods groups must be the same: accumulation, and in particular the

Such a tax could also be used to discourage the use of particular products for particular purposes: thus a general tax could be charged on timber which is particularly scarce to discourage its use, and a special tax could be charged on steel to discourage its use for building purposes.[1] Of course, the tax on goods which eventually were used for capital investments or defence production financed by the budget, would in effect appear on both sides of the budget (as indeed at present happens with oil sold to MTS and the armed forces); but this is not a serious argument against the proposal. Wholesale prices within industry, as well as the prices of consumer goods, would then include a substantial part of state accumulation (or what Soviet economists call 'net revenue'), and our model in chapter VI would have to be substantially modified.

(b) *Innovation and investment at the level of the enterprise*

We consider separately here changes to the present budgetary system which encourage innovation and attention to capital stock at factory level, but they would *ipso facto* reinforce the trend to decentralisation.

First, capital investment and capital stock. In order to solve the problem of measuring and rewarding the efficiency of different factories within the same industry, and in order that the planning authorities may be able to make proper cost estimates when deciding on future investments, there seems to be a strong case for including capital stock in costs in a much more extensive way than it is at present. The depreciation allowance which forms part of costs is at present arranged so that the cost of capital employed will be completely recouped only when it is physically worn out; i.e. it is

---

turnover tax, must be included in both sets of prices on an equal footing. [Maizenberg] does not develop this side of the problem sufficiently, and presents the existing price system as the only possible one....

'As is well known, we still have certain scarce goods, although their production grows from year to year. [Maizenberg] is silent about the following question: how justifiable is it to fix prices which result in a commodity being scarce with amounts of production normal in the particular conditions, and what must be the limits within which the prices of these goods deviate from their cost [*stoimost'*]?'

[1] At present reinforced concrete parts are sold *below cost* to encourage their use and discourage the use of steel and timber, and legal proscriptions are imposed to prevent steel being used for certain building purposes; but this means reinforced concrete factories make a loss. In transport, specially high railway freight charges are made where waterways could alternatively be used, so as to discourage the use of railways in these areas. The proposal we are discussing would have a similar effect with scarce products or products which the planners wish to discourage the use of for other reasons.

generally calculated on the assumption that the capital stock will be replaced only in 15 or 20 years.[1] This arrangement does not correspond to reality; equipment and other capital stock in fact become obsolescent in a much shorter period. If current costs of output were to correspond to the real costs of capital and labour, an 'obsolescence allowance' would have to replace the present depreciation allowance; factory managements would then be more concerned to use capital as effectively as possible—at present an improvement in the use of capital funds (excluding equipment) by 20–30% is reflected in a reduction of say 0·25–0·35% in the cost of production.[2] If this obsolescence allowance were to correspond to the period of recoupment (or, in Western terms, the rate of interest) required by Soviet planners when approving capital projects, it would need to be some 14–20% of the value of the capital stock annually (a period of recoupment of 5–7 years is normally required by Soviet planners).

So radical a proposal has not so far been specifically made in Soviet literature: it carries the disadvantage that it might discourage factory managements from making extensive use of new capital, but this could be countered by the other proposed measures outlined below. But proposals have been made which would enable the capital stock of each factory to be taken systematically into account in costing and pricing its output. It has been suggested that norms of output and costs should be worked out for similar pieces of equipment in similar factories, and payment for output should depend on these norms:[3] factories with inferior equipment would be paid higher prices for their output, or would pay a smaller rate of tax on their profits.[4] This would not, however, mean making a greater allowance

---

[1] This arrangement finds theoretical backing in the view widely advocated among Soviet economists that what Marx called 'moral depreciation' (i.e. obsolescence before the equipment is physically worn out) does not occur in socialist economy (see, for example, *Bol'shaya Sovetskaya Entsiklopedia* (2nd edn.), vol. II, p. 291). This view has been strongly criticised in the Soviet press recently: thus N. Nekrasov (*Voprosy Ekonomiki*, no. 6 (1955), p. 14) condemns economists who 'consider it almost an achievement that old equipment works for decades at our enterprises, and try to prove, contrary to reality, that this is a special feature of our system and gives a great economic effect.'

[2] Kronrod, *op. cit.* p. 88.

[3] This proposal was made by the editorial board of *Stroitel'naya gazeta* (the Builders' Newspaper), in response to complaints made by a conference of workers in the slate and asbestos industry that output and production plans varied for factories with similar equipment and capacity, and that this led to different rates of pay being given for the same work (*Stroitel'naya gazeta*, 27. vii. 55). See also Liberman, *loc. cit.*

[4] There has been some discussion recently of present methods of assessing productive capacity, which must be made more systematic if these proposals are to be carried into effect (see, for example, *Voprosy Ekonomiki*, no. 6 (1955), pp. 19 ff., no. 8 (1955), pp. 38 ff.).

for capital in costs, for the *average* price paid for a product (and its average costs) would still include only the small depreciation allowance.

The attention paid by a factory to its capital stock can also be increased, and to some extent has already been increased, by increasing its powers of investment on its own account. The category of decentralised investment has apparently already been restored in industry. Directors have been given the power to spend on recapitalisation and modernisation that part of depreciation allowances which is allocated to capital repair (until 1955 capital repair was normally in practice controlled by higher bodies), and to undertake on their own initiative measures to improve technology costing less than a ceiling varying from 1–2 million roubles for each measure according to the size of the factory (until 1955 the maximum that a director was allowed by law to spend on a piece of equipment for experiment was 300 roubles). The State Bank has been given the right to make loans for capital investments outside the plan in existing factories for a maximum period of 2 or 3 years, providing that the loans are fully recouped within the period.[1]

It has been suggested that the size of the Director's Fund, or, as it has now (1955) been renamed, the Factory Fund (*fond predpryatiya*), should be increased to, say, 50–70% of profits above the plan, instead of the present 15–45%, and that the present maximum limit on the fund (5% of the wage fund) should be abolished.[2] Half the Factory Fund may be spent on modernising equipment and introducing new technology and on housing.

The most radical suggestion which has been made in this respect is that the Factory Fund should be awarded on the basis not of an annual costs-reduction plan but of, say, a five-year costs-reduction plan. A standard level of profits would be fixed for each factory or group of factories, and costs targets would not be altered during the five-year period. A factory's profits would rise as it cut costs, and a substantial proportion of the increase would be included in the Factory Fund, and could be used for investment and other purposes. The management would then want its output plans to be as high as possible, it is argued, so that overheads would be reduced and profits rise. It would be encouraged to introduce new methods which would reduce costs over a relatively long period, because it would know

[1] See A. Zverev, *Finansy SSSR*, no. 9 (1955), pp. 7–8.
[2] See, for example, *Sovetskoe gosudarstvo i pravo*, no. 4 (1955), pp. 127 ff.

that its planned costs and future profits would not be affected as a result (at present costs-reduction targets are being increased annually in accordance with successes in the previous year).[1]

Finally, method 1 of chapter VI (financing part of investments through profits) could be increased in importance, not so much by increasing the proportion of total investment which is financed from retained profits and depreciation allowances, as by using the method to penalise factories which fail to reach the planned level of profits by reducing the new investment they received. At present, profits are mainly allocated for these purposes at *glavk* level, and the factory is little affected by its failure to make sufficient profits to pay its due share of the contribution paid by the *glavk* to the long-term bank towards new investment. A step towards increasing the attention paid at factory level to profits (in addition to the incentive already provided by the Factory Fund) has been the recent decision that profits tax in certain industries shall be paid at factory level and not by the *glavk* or ministry.[2]

(c) Consumer demand

Obviously, as the size of the consumer goods industries increases, some more systematic way must be found of adjusting the production programmes of these industries to the requirements of the consumer. The transfer of the selling agencies (*sbyty*) of these industries to the Ministry of Trade (they were until 1953 under the management of the industries concerned) has considerably increased the powers of retail trading agencies over the consumer goods industries: production is now more likely to correspond with the detailed orders placed by the retail trade. But there is much that could be done to improve

---

[1] Liberman, *loc. cit.* While these proposals are being made to increase incentives in manufacturing and mining, steps are already being taken to improve the position in the more backward building industry. At the Builders' Conference in December 1954, the complaint was voiced that building contractors have little incentive to reduce costs: they are paid in accordance with the estimate, and therefore try to make the estimate as high as possible. It has therefore been decided that estimates must in future be compiled on the basis of standard prices per square metre of different types of building. If the contractor reduces costs below the prices, payment will still be made in accordance with the estimate. Thus building contractors will be advanced to the target-cost system at present used in mining and manufacture. This system will produce important changes in the arrangements for administering capital investments described on pp. 255–62 above. (See *Soviet Studies*, vol. VI, no. 4 (1955), pp. 448–51, and V. Uspenskii in *Stroitel'naya gazeta*, 28. ix. 55, reporting the Council of Ministers' decree of 24 August 'On improving planning, *khozraschot*, financial discipline, and the use of estimates in construction'.)

[2] This applies to enterprises of the ministries of the chemical industry and of vehicle, tractor and agricultural engineering, with effect from 1 July 1955 (V. Paevskii, *Finansy SSSR*, no. 8 (1955), pp. 59–62).

the pricing system. Soviet economists have made many suggestions that wholesale prices in the consumer goods industries should be improved, so that considerably higher prices are paid for goods which are high-grade, labour-intensive, or of better quality.[1] But if the orders placed by retail trade are to have some kind of consistent relationship with consumer demand, it seems that the system of turnover-tax rates needs to be thoroughly overhauled. Present rates are influenced by past history, by social motives, and by the need to adjust supply to demand. It would seem that Soviet planners ought to undertake a gradual simplification of the turnover-tax system, with the ultimate aim of reducing it to a few rates, which vary from the average rate only to encourage or discourage the sale of particular types of goods for social reasons. Only when supply and demand for a product are in at least rough balance on the retail market *at the average rate of turnover tax* can production be said to correspond to demand.

Clearly the 'price' paid for these measures and proposals is bound to be the establishment of a section of the economy in which developments are not directly planned from the centre, in which what might perhaps be termed 'quasi-market pulls' are introduced into the system. Some budgetary decisions are being devolved on to republican and local soviets; factories are being given powers to take certain investment decisions, the size of which partly depends on their efficiency; direct negotiation between consumer and producer within industry is being increased; and the voice of the consumer *qua* consumer in production decisions is growing. But such changes certainly do not mean that direct planning is being done away with. Even taken to their extreme, they would not affect the fact that the size of investment, the main lines of economic growth (the division of total investment between consumer and producer goods industries, and the main investment provisions in each industry), and the location of industry were decided by a central economic plan.

But they would lead to profound changes in the structure and organisation of the budget. Expenditure would be considerably decentralised—the powers of local and republican authorities would be increased, and the administration of expenditures on the national economy such as capital investments would be thoroughly reformed.

---

[1] For details of administrative and economic measures to increase the influence of trade on industrial production, see Ya. Orlov, *Voprosy Ekonomiki*, no. 8 (1955), pp. 90–100.

The turnover tax would continue to decline in importance (as it has throughout the post-war period); it would be imposed on both producer and consumer goods, and its structure as far as the retail market is concerned would be considerably simplified. The structure of the profits of industry would be transformed, with the change in arrangements for the Factory Fund and for investment from profits, and with the introduction of a charge for capital in costing. The whole system would look very different from the model we drew up in chapter VI.

5. THE PRE-WAR BUDGETARY SYSTEM IN PERSPECTIVE

It is clear then that a large part of Soviet budgetary and financial arrangements results from the special Soviet conditions of 1928–41, and would be applicable only in similar conditions. The intensity of Soviet industrialisation and defence preparations made inevitable a continuous struggle for materials, labour and financial resources between economic units, and between each economic unit and the central authorities; and forced the emergence of a plethora of rather rigid controls on the one hand, and exaggerated claims for resources on the other. The heavy investment programme and the inexperience of Soviet financial controllers led to an almost continuous inflation. During the rationing period, little success could be achieved in controlling costs: the incentives to the fulfilment of the production programme were far more effective than the incentives to reduce costs, and as a result wages plans were consistently over-fulfilled. The temporary improvement in the position between 1935 and 1937 could not be maintained during the rapid conversion to defence production in 1938–41. Throughout the pre-war planning period there tended to be more money on the retail market than had been planned: wages plans were over-fulfilled and production plans for the consumer goods industries were under-fulfilled. The situation could have been met by raising prices, but the government took this course reluctantly (in, for example, 1932, 1935, 1940 and 1941), and price-rises were insufficient to get rid of shortages.

The situation affected the budgetary system itself. Control over budgetary expenditure on health, defence, education and administration was extremely centralised, and the methods which were evolved for controlling capital expenditure (which were an innovation of the Soviet system) were also very tight: most investment was financed through the budget (by our method 2), and investment finance supplied from the resources of economic organisations was administered in a highly centralised fashion (so that our method 1 was more a book-keeping device than a fully fledged system of providing enterprises with an economic interest in investment plans). On the revenue side of the budget, the prominent place of turnover tax and its structure were 'features of the epoch': turnover tax was a successful means of raising the revenue required, but it could be at best only a blunt instrument in its function of adjusting supply and demand on the retail market—shortages of particular goods and in particular areas, and general shortages, were characteristic of the whole period. Moreover, the imposition of the tax almost exclusively on consumer goods was, it seems, a reflexion of the industrialisation drive. Finally, financial and budgetary controls over the work of enterprises (through bank, costing and profits) were peculiarly adapted to an economy in which investment decisions were almost exclusively controlled from the top, so that the economic unit took its capital stock as given from outside. This arrangement was suitable for an economy which can make large-scale technical borrowings from other economies, owing to its relative backwardness, or which has available a large potential labour force to compensate for technical deficiencies (and the Soviet economy of the 1930's had both these characteristics).

These features of the pre-war budgetary system owed their existence, then, to the particular tasks and problems facing the Soviet economy in 1928 to 1941, rather than to the direct planning system as such. Other, generally secondary, features of the system have been inherited from the N.E.P. period or from pre-revolutionary practices, and are also not essential to a planning system as such. The methods of compiling and adopting budget estimates, income tax, and various minor revenues are Russian pre-planning practices which have been adapted to the new system; other arrangements could function equally well. The *khozraschot* system itself was, it will be remembered, largely taken over from the mixed economy of N.E.P., and while the general principle that enterprises must work on a profit-and-loss basis seems essential to economic efficiency, many of the arrangements (e.g. for financing capital repair and for supplementing working capital) are not inherent in a planning system as such. The same is true of the details of republican and local budget relationships with the centre: the present system was originally devised to reduce the burden on the budget in the crisis years of 1921 and 1922, and proved able, with modification, to provide varying degrees of administrative decentralisation throughout the N.E.P. and planning periods; but different arrangements for linking local and central revenue, for example, are conceivable and would be workable.

How far is price reduction on the retail market, which emerged as a policy in the mid-1920's, was attempted unsuccessfully in the mid-1930's, and blossomed in the post-war period, essential to a direct planning system as such? Its advantages are clear. By price-cuts, the benefits of the increased production of consumer goods can be passed on to the whole population, including all salary earners, pensioners and other persons who do not work directly in production. If prices were not reduced systematically, all money payments and salaries would need to be adjusted in order to raise the standard of living of those who did not work directly in production. A second important advantage of the policy of making annual price-cuts is that it gives an annual public demonstration to the country as a whole that the standard of living is rising.[1] But even under present Soviet circumstances the policy carries with it serious disadvantages. The norms of productive workers have to be raised periodically so that they produce more for the same money; this offends the money illusion, and even after a quarter of a century meets with the discontent of Soviet workers. Moreover, the policy of reducing prices in annual jumps deprives the government of the possibility of making gradual adjustments to prices so as to keep a continuous balance between supply and demand, and it therefore makes partial shortages inevitable; and the policy obviously involves and depends on the retention of quite tight central controls over retail prices (which may not be essential to a direct planning system). And in practice the government has often been tempted to reduce retail prices more than the availability of goods warranted, as in 1937 and 1953, which resulted in a general shortage of essential goods throughout the country.[2]

[1] 'Only in a socialist country is the working class conscious of the fact, and actually experiences it, that the greater the increase in productivity of labour, the more goods the worker gets, the lower prices are, and the better-off he is', said Mikoyan in reporting price reductions (*Pravda*, 27. iv. 54).

[2] Mikoyan stated: 'We reduce the prices even of goods which are still in short supply, if these goods are important for mass consumption. This creates additional demand, and stimulates us to increase more quickly the production of goods in short supply needed by the people' (*Izvestia*, 27. x. 53). But the shortage of goods encourages only *administrative* steps to be taken for their production; financial inducement to produce these goods would involve *higher* prices being paid to the producer (actually on a particular good retail prices could be lowered *and* higher prices be paid to the producer by reducing the turnover tax rate—as actually happened with potatoes and vegetables).

Further, even if the policy of price reduction is on the whole the best one in Soviet conditions, it is certain that such a policy would be much more difficult to enforce in an economy in which there was an historical tradition of money wages rising in proportion to the increase in output. The maintenance of this tradition would involve a mild continuing inflation, if and when the producer goods sector was growing more rapidly than the consumer goods sector, or if progressive piece rates were paid. But this inflation would probably be preferable to the bad effect on productivity and industrial morale which cuts in the rate might have, and to the shortages and rigid price-controls which seem to be inherent in the policy of annual price-cuts.[1]

Nevertheless, there is much in Soviet budgetary experience between 1928 and 1941 that is of more general relevance. The Soviet budgetary system emerged, as we have shown, in an *ad hoc* way, and the mistakes made in constructing it can be avoided through the study of Soviet experience by countries facing similar problems. In particular, under-developed countries in which the attempt is being made to industrialise via direct planning can learn from Soviet financial experience during the first five-year plan.

Soviet experience seems to lead to the conclusion that it is very difficult to avoid inflation when a large-scale investment programme is launched by the state in a predominantly peasant country. Even with the extensive controls that the Soviet government could manipulate, it proved impossible to keep down urban wages and to keep up peasant supplies to the town. However, it would be unwise to conclude that inflation must take place on the Soviet scale, in view of the pace of industrialisation there, which other countries will probably not attempt to imitate.

It also seems to follow from Soviet experience that an inflation in a direct planning system is not so harmful as might at first appear. It is often said that inflation beyond a fairly limited point in under-developed countries is harmful, because its effect on the distribution of income, on savings, and on the amount and pattern of investment is unpredictable. This is, of course, true for an economy in which the level of *private* savings has an important influence on the total amount of investment, and in which the investment pattern is determined via the profit-expectations of entrepreneurs. 'Easy profits' and the gains of middlemen may well upset hopes of industrialisation. But in the

[1] Attempts at price-reductions seem, however, to be a feature of the economic policies of all the East European countries. See *Economic Survey of Europe in 1953* (1954), pp. 63–6.

Soviet economy, the government's decision as to the amount and structure of investment, conceived in physical terms, was the ultimate cause of the inflation; and the inflation itself was fundamentally nothing more than a painful adjustment of the financial environment to the new level of accumulation and direction of investment. The inflation was inconvenient, and led to inefficiency and waste; and it drove the government much farther and faster along the road to direct planning than had originally been intended. But it did not prevent the required level of accumulation being reached, through central government taxation, or the concentration of investment on heavy industry. In a directly planned economy, the government controls investment, and the financial system is of subordinate importance, instead of investment being controlled by the market and the financial system. The general lesson seems to be that the experience of inflation in a competitive economy cannot be transferred to a direct planning system.

However, all major features of the Soviet system may not be applicable to peasant countries in which direct planning for industrialisation is introduced. The budgets of these countries may be faced with a more complicated fiscal problem in agriculture than that dealt with by the Soviet budget. The drastic collectivisation drive in 1930 actually resulted in a simplification of the budgetary revenue system: it was by administrative and not fiscal devices that the peasantry were induced to part with their grain; compulsory deliveries at nominal prices, which were virtually a tax in kind, were taxed at high rates of turnover tax and sold at high prices on the retail market. In other under-developed countries, however, a high degree of state planning in industry may be accompanied by widespread individual peasant farming, by the existence of a free market for foodstuffs as the main source of supply to the towns, and by relatively weak administrative powers over peasant produce (this situation exists to some extent in Eastern Europe at present). Here special financial incentives and fiscal arrangements will need to be devised; and in so far as lessons can be learned from the Soviet Union, they will be learned from the agricultural taxation policies of 1924–9, and not from the planning period.[1]

[1] If an advanced country with a highly developed agricultural industry were to adopt a system of direct planning, it might be expected on the other hand either that agreed fixed prices would be relatively easily accepted by the farmers through the existing marketing boards (cf. Britain during the second world war), or that a fairly rapid transition to state agriculture would take place.

More generally, it may be concluded from Soviet financial experience that the functions of the financial system are restricted and secondary in a directly planned economy, although money is, of course, still essential (to enable differential wages to be paid and consumer's choice to be exercised, to provide a means for the measurement and control of industrial efficiency, and to permit dealings with collectivised or private agriculture and the limited market associated with them, where they exist). The main economic decisions are made by the government, and the task of the financial system is to assist their enforcement. Wage rates and prices are not market-determined, but fixed by the government (though the government, like the market, is subject to social and political pressures in reaching its decisions). The quantity of goods and services received by each wage earner is determined by his wage in relation to the price and supply of retail goods and services; and price, supply, and wage are all controlled by the plan. Money relations are no longer the means by which the interplay of wills and choices shapes the economy, but only one of the means through which centralised decisions about the shape of the economy are put into effect (except in the collective farm sector). The financial system has the task of ensuring that the right amount of money is available in the right place to enable economic units to make investments, to pay wages, and to purchase materials in accordance with the plan; and it has to see that supply and demand on the retail market are balanced as far as possible: these are the minimum functions of money in any direct planning system in which consumers' choice and wage differentiation are maintained.

Moreover, in this economy the budgetary system will have to finance at least these functions for which it is responsible in a competitive economy. Part of what is described in recent Soviet economic literature as 'the net income of society' will have to be diverted to the budget to meet the costs of administration, defence, and the social services. The form of taxation used cannot be taxation of the propertied classes, for these no longer exist: it must be either direct taxation of incomes, or some form of a mark-up on costs (a profits or turnover tax), and in practice direct taxation will need to be limited, because of the money illusion. Moreover, in any directly planned economy, some part of investment will need to be financed through the budget (by our method 2), and it is likely to be a considerable part, particularly in an economy in which unanticipated wage inflation is occurring, for in such circumstances the budget will have to pump money into the economy to affect the required redistribution of the national income. Retail prices will have to be raised or incomes directly taxed in order to withdraw this money from the population, and this will involve a corresponding increase in the ratio of taxation to retained profits.

In carrying out these budgetary functions, all direct planning systems will find useful material in Soviet pre-war budgetary arrangements. The methods devised for the control of consumption and collection of revenue through the turnover tax, for the central administration of investment through the special banks, and for providing financial incentives to factory managements, are innovations of the Soviet financial system which will in part prove universally applicable in direct planning systems.

BIBLIOGRAPHY

(1) BOOKS BY INDIVIDUAL AUTHORS OR GROUPS OF AUTHORS

Aleksandrov, A. M. *Finansy SSSR* (Finance in the U.S.S.R.), 1952.
Arnold, W. Z. *Banks, credit and money in Soviet Russia*, 1937.
Atlas, M. S. *Natsionalizatsiya bankov v SSSR* (Nationalisation of banks in the U.S.S.R.), 1948.
Atlas, Z. V. *Ocherki po istorii denezhnogo obrashcheniya SSSR* (Essays in the history of currency circulation in the U.S.S.R.).
Atlas, Z. V., Bregel', E. Ya. *et al. Denezhnoe obrashchenie i kredit SSSR* (Currency circulation and credit in the U.S.S.R.), 1947.
Batyrev, V. M. and Sitnin, V. K. *Finansovaya i kreditnaya sistema SSSR* (Financial and credit system of the U.S.S.R.), 1945.
Baykov, A. *The Development of the Soviet economic system*, 1947.
Belevsky, A. and Voronoff, B. *Les organisations publiques russes et leur rôle pendant la guerre*, 1917.
Bergson, A. *Soviet national income and product in 1937*, 1953.
Birman, A. M. *Sostavlenie i ispol'nenie finansovogo plana predpriyatiya* (Compilation and fulfilment of the financial plan of an enterprise), 1951.
Bogolepov, D. P. *Den'gi sovetskoi Rossii* (Money in Soviet Russia), 1924.
Bogolepov, D. [P.] *Voina i finansy* (The war and finance), 1917.
Bogolepov, M. I. *Finansovyi plan pyatiletiya* (Financial plan of the five-year plan), 1929.
Bogolepov, M. I. *Finansy, pravitel'stvo, i obshchestvennie interesy* (Finance, the government and the public interest).
Bol'shaya sovetskaya entsiklopediya (Large Soviet encyclopedia), vol. 'S.S.S.R.', 1948.
Braude, I. L. *Dogovory po kapital'nomu stroitel'stvu v SSSR* (Capital construction contracts in the U.S.S.R.), 1952.
Bryukhanov, N. P. *Khozyaistvennyi pod''em Sovetskogo Soyuza, ego finansovaya baza (gosudarstvennyi byudzhet 1928/9 goda)* (The economic advance of the Soviet Union and its financial basis (state budget of 1928/9)), 1929.
Burns, E. *Russia's productive system*, 1930.
Carr, E. H. *A History of Soviet Russia. The Bolshevik Revolution 1917–23*, vol. II, 1952.
Chamberlin, W. H. *The Soviet planned economic order*, 1931.
Chernomordik, D. I. (ed.). *Narodnyi dokhod SSSR: ego obrazovanie i uchot* (National income of the U.S.S.R.: formation and accounting), 1939.
Chester, D. N. (ed.). *British war economy*, 1951.
Comstock, A. *Taxation in the modern state*, 1929.
Devons, E. *Planning in practice*, 1950.
Dobb, M. H. *Soviet economic development since 1917*, 1948.
Dobb, M. and Stevens, H. C. *Russian economic development since the revolution*, 1929.
Dobbert, G. (ed.). *Soviet economics*, 1933.
Dolgorukov, P. D. and Petrunkevich, I. I. (eds.). *Voprosy gosudarstvennogo khozyaistva i byudzhetnogo prava* (Questions of state economy and budget law), 1907.

Doundoukov, G. F. *La planification financière (établissement de la balance des recettes et dépenses des ministères et des directions générales)*, translated from the Russian in *Stat. et études financières*, suppl. finances comparées, nos. 17–18, 1953.

D'yachenko, V. P. *Sovetskie finansy v pervoi faze razvitiya sotsialisticheskogo gosudarstva* (Soviet finance in the first phase of the development of the socialist state), vol. I, 1947.

D'yachenko, V. P. and Kozlov, G. A. (eds.). *Finansy i kredit SSSR* (Finance and credit in the U.S.S.R.), 1938.

D'yachkov, M. F. *Statistika kapital'nogo stroitel'stva* (Statistics of capital construction), 1952.

D'yachkov, M. F. and Kiparisov, M. *Uchot kapital'nogo stroitel'stva* (Capital construction accounts), 1948.

Eliacheff, B. *Les finances de guerre de la Russie*, 1919.

Epstein, E. *Les banques de commerce Russes*, 1925.

Galenson, W. *Labour productivity in Soviet and American industry*, 1955.

Garbutt, P. E. *The Russian railways*, 1949.

Gindin, I. F. *Russkie kommercheskie banki* (Russian commercial banks), 1948.

Gladkov, I. A. *Ocherky stroitel'stva sovetskogo planovogo khozyaistva v 1917–18 gg.* (Essays on the construction of Soviet planned economy in 1917–18), 1950.

Gladkov, I. A. *Voprosy planirovaniya sovetskogo khozyaistva v 1918–20 gg.* (Questions of planning Soviet economy in 1918–20), 1951.

Golovachev, A. A. *Desyat' let reform, 1861–71* (Ten years of reforms, 1861–71), 1872.

Golovachev, A. *Voprosy gosudarstvennogo khozyaistva* (Questions of state economy), 1873.

Golutvin, V. A. *Kazna tsarskaya i kazna sovetskaya* (Tsarist exchequer and Soviet exchequer), 1925.

Gorky, M., Molotov, V. et al. *The history of the civil war in the U.S.S.R.*, vol. I [1936], and vol. II, 1946.

Granick, D. *The management of the industrial firm in the U.S.S.R.*, 1954.

Grin'ko, G. F. *Finansovaya programma Soyuza SSR na 1937 g. Doklad i zaklyuchitel'noe slovo o gosudarstvennom byudzhete SSSR na 1937 god na III sessiya TsIKa SSSR VII Sozyva, 11. i. 1937 goda* (Financial programme of the U.S.S.R. for 1937. Report and reply to the debate on the state budget of the U.S.S.R. for 1937 at the third session of TsIK U.S.S.R., Seventh Convocation, 11. i. 37), 1937.

Grinko, G. F. *Financial program of the U.S.S.R. for 1936*, in *Soviet Union* (1936), [1936].

Gur'iev, A. *Reforma denezhnogo obrashcheniya* (Reform of currency circulation), 2 vols., 1896.

Gusakov, A. D. and Dymshits, I. A. *Denezhnoe obrashchenie i kredit SSSR* (Currency circulation and credit in the U.S.S.R.), 1951.

Haensel, P. *The economic policy of Soviet Russia*, 1930.

Hoeffding, O. *Soviet national income and product in 1928*, 1954.

Holzman, F. D. *Soviet taxation*, 1955.

Hubbard, L. E. *Soviet money and finance*, 1936.

Ikonnikov, V. V. (ed.). *Denezhnoe obrashchenie i kredit SSSR* (Currency circulation and credit in the U.S.S.R.), 1952.

Jasny, N. Soviet prices of producers' goods, 1952.

Jasny, N. The Soviet price system, 1951.

Kaktyn', A. *O politike tsen* (On price policy), 1929.

Kaplan, N. M. *Capital investments in the Soviet Union, 1924–51* (Rand Publication RM-735), 1951.

Katsenelenbaum, Z. S. *Industrializatsiya khozyaistva i zadachi kredita v SSSR* (Industrialisation of the economy and tasks of credit in the U.S.S.R.), 1928.

Katzenellenbaum, S. S. *Russian currency and banking, 1914-24*, 1925.
Khromov, P. A. *Ekonomicheskoe razvitie Rossii v XIX-XX vekakh, 1800-1917* (Economic development of Russia in 19th-20th centuries, 1800-1917), 1950.
Kokovtsev, V. N. *Iz moego proshlego. Vospominaniya 1903-19 gg.* (From my past. Recollections of 1903-19), vols. I-II, 1933.
Kokovtzoff, W. *Five years of Bolshevik dictatorship. An economic survey.*
Krestinskii, N. *Nasha finansovaya politika* (Our financial policy), 1921.
Kronrod, Ya. *Osnovy khozyaistvennogo raschota* (Foundations of profit-and-loss accounting), 1952.
Lenin, V. I. *Sochineniya* (Works), 4th edn., vols. I-xxxv. [*Soch.*]
Lifits, M. M. *Sovetskaya torgovlya* (Soviet trade), 1948.
Litoshenko, L. N. *Natsional'nyi dokhod SSSR* (National income of the U.S.S.R.), 1925.
Lokshin, E. Yu. *Planirovanie material'no-technicheskogo snabzheniya narodnogo khozyaistva SSSR* (Planning of material and technical supply of the Soviet economy), 1952.
Lorimer, F. *The Population of the Soviet Union*, 1946.
Lyashchenko, P. I., *Istoriya narodnogo khozyaistva SSSR* (History of the economy of the U.S.S.R.), vol. II, 1952.
Margolin, N. S. *Balans denezhnykh dokhodov i raskhodov naseleniya* (Balance of money incomes and expenditures of the population), 1940.
Marx, K. *Capital*, Kerr edn., vol. II, 1933.
Marx, K. *Critique of the Gotha programme*, London, 1933.
Marx, K. and Engels, F. *Selected correspondence*, London, 1941.
Marx, K. and Engels, F. *Communist manifesto*, 1948 London edn.
Measures for the economic development of under-developed countries, United Nations Department of Economic Affairs, 1951.
Michelson, A. M. *et al. Russian finance during the war*, 1928.
Mikoyan, A. *Rezul'taty kampanii po snizheniyu tsen (doklad sovetu truda i oborony)* (Results of the campaign to reduce prices (report to STO)), 1927.
Nusinov, I. M. *Metodika finansovogo planirovaniya* (Method of financial planning), 1937.
Oxley, V. J. *Local government financial statistics*, 1951.
Ozerov, I. Kh. *Ekonomicheskaya Rossiya i ee finansovaya politika na iskhode XIX i v nachale XX veka* (Economic Russia and her financial policy at the end of the 19th and beginning of the 20th century).
Ozerov, I. Kh. *Kak raskhoduyutsya v Rossii narodnie den'gi?* (How does the state spend our money in Russia?), 1907.
Ozerov, I. Kh. *Osnovy finansovoi nauki* (Foundations of financial science), vols. I-II, 1909, 1910.
Ozerov, I. Kh. *Russkii byudzhet: dokhodnyi i raskhodnyi* (Russian budget: income and expenditure), 1907.
Plotnikov, K. N. *Byudzhet sotsialisticheskogo gosudarstva* (Budget of the socialist state), 1948.
Plotnikov, K. N. *Ocherki istorii byudzheta sovetskogo gosudarstva* (Essays in the history of the budget of the Soviet state), 1955.
Polanyi, M. *The Logic of Liberty*, 1951.
Popov, N. *Outline history of the communist party of the Soviet Union*, 2 vols., 1934.
Preobrazhenskii, E. A. *Finansy v epokhu diktatury proletariata* (Finance in the period of proletarian dictatorship), 1921.
Preobrazhenskii, E. A. *Teoriya padayushchei valyuty* (The theory of a devaluing currency), 1930.

Prokopovich, S. N. (ed.). *Opyt ischisleniya narodnogo dokhoda 50 gubernii Evropeiskoi Rossii v 1900–13 gg.* (Experiment in calculating the national income of 50 provinces of European Russia in 1900–13), 1918.
Prokopovich, S. N. *Voina i narodnoe khozyaistvo* (War and the economy), 1918.
Reddaway, W. B. *The Russian financial system*, 1935.
Rovinskii, N. N. (ed.). *Finansovoe pravo* (Financial law), 1946.
Rovinskii, N. N. (ed.). *Finansy SSSR za XXX let 1917–47* (30 years of Soviet finance 1917–47), 1947. [*Finansy SSSR...*]
Rovinskii, N. N. *Gosudarstvennyi byudzhet SSSR* (State budget of the U.S.S.R.), 1944 edn.
Rovinskii, N. N. (ed.). *Organizatsiya finansirovaniya i kreditovaniya kapital'nykh vlozhenii* (Organisation of the financing and crediting of capital investments), 1951.
Ryabov, N. *Sotsialisticheskoe nakoplenie i ego istochniki v pervoi i vtoroi pyatiletkakh* (Socialist accumulation and its sources in the first and second five-year plans), 1951.
Shavrin, V. A. *Mestnye byudzhety SSSR* (Local budgets of the U.S.S.R.), 2nd edn., 1946.
Shenger, Yu. E. *Planirovanie finansov* (The planning of finance), 1940.
Sokol'nikov, G. Ya. *Denezhnaya reforma* (Currency reform), 1925.
Sokol'nikov, G. Ya. *Finansovaya politika revolyutsii* (Financial policy of the revolution), vols. I–II, 1925 and 1926.
Sokol'nikov, G. *Finansy posle oktyabrya* (Finance after October), 1923.
Sokol'nikov, G. *K voprosu o natsionalizatsii bankov* (On the question of the nationalisation of banks), 1918.
Sokol'nikov, G. Ya. *Zadachi finansovoi politiki* (Tasks of financial policy), 2nd edn. [1922].
Sokolnikov, G. Y. et al. *Soviet policy in public finance 1917–28*, 1931.
Sokol'nikov, G. Ya., Bogolepov, D. P., Bukovetskii, A. I., Derevenko, N. N., Tarasov, D. G. (eds.). *Finansovaya entsiklopediya* (Financial encyclopedia), 2nd edn., 1927. [*Fin. ents.*]
Stalin, I. V. *Sochineniya* (Works), vols. I–XIII.
Stalin, J. *Leninism*, London, 1944.
Stalin, J. *Marxism and the national and colonial question*, London, 1936.
Suchkov, A. K. (ed.). *Dokhody gosudarstvennogo byudzheta SSSR* (Revenue of the state budget of the U.S.S.R.), 1945 edn.
Teplov, G. V. *Tekhpromfinplan promyshlennogo predpriyatiya* (Technical, industrial and financial plan of an industrial enterprise), 1948.
Turetskii, Sh. Ya. *Sebestoimost' i voprosy tsenoobrazovaniya* (Cost and questions of price-formation), 1940.
Voznesensky, N. *War economy of the U.S.S.R. in the period of the patriotic war*, 1948, Moscow edn.
Voznesensky, N. *Economic results of the U.S.S.R. in 1940 and the plan of economic development for 1941. Report delivered at the 18th All-Union Conference of the C.P.S.U.(b), February 18, 1941*, 1941.
Yasnopol'skii, L. *Vosstanovitel'nyi protsess v nashem denezhnom obrashchenii i zadachi valyutnoi politiki* (The restoration process in our currency circulation and the tasks of foreign exchange policy), 1927.
Yurovskii, L. N. *Denezhnaya politika sovetskoi vlasti, 1917–27* (Currency policy of Soviet power, 1917–27), 1928.
Yurovsky, L. N. *Currency problems and policy of the Soviet Union*, 1925.
Zimand, S. *State capitalism in Russia, 1917–26.* Foreign Policy Association Information Service. Supplement no. 2.

(2) GOVERNMENT AND OTHER OFFICIAL PUBLICATIONS

(a) GOVERNMENT AND SOVIET MEETINGS
(in chronological order)

Protokoly zasedanii VTsIKa R., S., kr., i kaz. deputatov 2-go sozyva (Protocol of the sittings of VTsIK of Workers', Soldiers', Peasants' and Cossacks' Deputies, 2nd Convocation) [27. x.–29. xii. 1917] [1918].

Stenograficheskii otchot 4-go chrezvychainogo s"ezda sovetov raboch., krest'yansk., i kazach'ikh deputatov (Verbatim report of 4th extraordinary congress of workers', peasants', soldiers' and Cossacks' deputies) [15. iii.–16. iii. 1918] [1920].

Protokoly VTsIKa 4-go sozyva (Protocols of VTsIK 4th convocation) [20. iii. 1918 et seq.].

Pyatyi sozyv VTsIKa: stenograficheskii otchot (Fifth convocation of VTsIK: verbatim report) [15. vii.–4. xi. 1919], 1919.

1 s"ezd Sovetov SSSR, stenograficheskii otchot. 30. xii. 22 (1st Congress of Soviets of U.S.S.R. verbatim report. 30. xii. 22), 1922.

2 s"ezd... [26. i.–2. ii. 1924], 1924.

3 s"ezd... [13. v.–20. v. 1925], 1925.

1 sessiya tsentral'nogo ispolnitel'nogo komiteta 3-ogo sozyva...21. v. 1925 (1st session of TsIK, 3rd convocation...21. v. 1925), 1925. [*TsIK* 1/III.]

2 sessiya...3-ogo sozyva, 12–25. iv. 1926, 1926. [*TsIK* 2/III and similarly for other *TsIK* reports.]

3 sessiya...3-ogo sozyva...14–25. ii. 1927, 1927.

Plenum byudzhetnoi komissii TsIKa SSSR. Stenograf. otchot (Plenum of the Budget Commission of TsIK SSSR. Verbatim report) [ii. 1927], 1927.

SSSR: 4 s"ezd sovetov. Sten. otchot [18–26. iv. 1927], 1927.

Pervaya sessiya...4-ogo sozyva (1st session...of the 4th convocation) [27. iv. 1927], 1927.

2 sessiya...4-ogo sozyva. Sten. otchot (2nd session...of the 4th convocation, verbatim report) [15. x.–20. x. 1927] [1927].

4 sessiya...4-ogo sozyva [3–15. xii. 1928], Bulletins 1–34, 1928.

SSSR: 5 s"ezd sovetov. Sten. otchot (U.S.S.R.: 5th Congress of Soviets. Verbatim report) [20–28. v. 1929]. 1929.

1 sessiya...5-ogo sozyva. Sten. otchot (1st session...of 5th convocation. Verbatim report) [29. v. 1929], 1929.

2 sessiya...5 sozyva [29. xi.–8. xii. 29], 1929.

3 sessiya...5 sozyva. Sten. otchot i postanovleniya (3rd session of 5th convocation. Verbatim report and resolutions) [4–12. i. 1931], 1931.

6 s"ezd sovetov SSSR. Sten. otchot (6th Congress of Soviets of U.S.S.R. Verbatim report) [8–17. iii. 31], 1931.

2 sessiya TsIKa SSSR 6 sozyva. Sten. otchot i post. [22–28. xii. 1931], 1931.

3 sessiya...6 sozyva... [23–30. i. 1933], 1933.

4 sessiya...6 sozyva... [28. xii. 1933–4. i. 1934], 1934.

Second Session of the Supreme Soviet of the U.S.S.R. August 10–21, 1938. Verbatim report, 1938. [*Supreme Soviet* (1938).]

Zasedaniya verkhovnogo soveta SSSR. Sten. otchot (Sittings of the Supreme Soviet of the U.S.S.R. Verbatim report), 1939, 1940, and 1941. [*Zas. verkh. sov.* (1939), etc.]

(b) LEGISLATION

Edinyi sel'sko-khozyaistvennyi nalog 1923–24 g. *Sbornik nalogogo zakonodatel'stva* (Unified agricultural tax 1923–24. Collection of tax legislation), 1923.
Khronologicheskii perechen' zakonov SSSR deistvuyushchikh na 1. vii. 1936g. (Chronological list of U.S.S.R. laws effective on 1. vii. 1936), 1936.
Sbornik dekretov i rasporyazhenii po finansam (Collection of decrees and enactments on finance, vol. IV, 1921), 1921.
Sbornik dekretov 1917–18 (Collection of decrees 1917–18), 1920.
Sbornik dekretov o finansakh 1917–20 (Collection of decrees on finance 1917–20), 1920.
Sbornik dekretov i postanovlenii o narodnom khozyaistve 25. x. 1917–25. x. 1918 (Collection of decrees and resolutions on the economy 25. x. 1917–25. x. 1918), 1918.
Sistematicheskii sbornik uzakonenii i rasporyazhenii rabochego i krest'yanskogo pravitel'stva (Systematic collection of laws and enactments of the workers' and peasants' government), 1919.
Sobranie uzakonenii i rasporyazhenii rabochego i krestyanskogo pravitel'stva (Collected legislation and enactments of the workers' and peasants' government), 1917–24 (this was the title of the main series of decrees published before the formation of the U.S.S.R. government in 1924). [SU.]
Sobranie zakonov i rasporyazhenii SSSR (Collected laws and enactments of the U.S.S.R.), 1924–41 (this was published in two parallel series, the second being concerned with changes in posts, etc.; all references here are to the first series in each year). [SZ.]

(c) SOVIET AND OTHER GOVERNMENT REPORTS, PLANS, ETC.

Economic Survey for 1947, H.M.S.O., 1947.
Economic Survey of Europe in 1947, (ibid.) *in 1951* and (ibid.) *in 1953*, United Nations Economic Commission for Europe, 1948, 1952 and 1954.
Edinyi finansovyi plan na 1929–30 g. (Unified financial plan for 1929–30), 1930.
Les finances de l'Union des Républiques soviétiques socialistes en 1924–5, 1925.
Finansovaya politika za period s xii. 1920 g. po xii. 1921 g. (otchot k IX Vserossiiskomu s"ezdu Sovetov) (Financial policy from xii. 1920 to xii. 1921 (report to 9th all-Russian Congress of Soviets)), 1921. [*Fin. politika.*]
Finansy SSSR mezhdu V i VI s"ezdami sovetov Soyuza (U.S.S.R. finance between the Fifth and Sixth Congresses of Soviets of the Union), 1931.
Finansy SSSR mezhdu VI i VII S"ezdami sovetov (1931–4) (U.S.S.R. finance between the Sixth and Seventh Congresses of Soviets (1931–4)), 1935. [*Finansy SSSR... (1931–4)*.]
Gosudarstvennye i mestnye nalogi i dokhody za 1922–3 byudzhetnyi god. Statisticheskii sbornik (State and local taxes and revenues for the budget year 1922–3. Statistical abstract), 1924.
Gosudarstvennyi plan razvitiya narodnogo khozyaistva SSSR na 1941 god (State plan of development of the economy of the U.S.S.R. for 1941), American Council of Learned Societies reprints, Russian series no. 30. [*1941 Plan.*]
Kontrol'nye tsifry narodnogo khozyaistva na 1926–7 g. (Control figures of the economy for 1926–7), 1926.
(*Ibid.*) *na 1927/8 g.* (1928).
(*Ibid.*) *na 1928/9 g.* (1929).
(*Ibid.*) *na 1929/30 g.* (1930).
Narodnoe khozyaistvo (National economy), statistical handbook, 1928.

349

Narodnoe khozyaistvo SSSR: statisticheskii sbornik (The U.S.S.R. economy: a statistical abstract), 1956.
Narodnyi komissariat finansov 1917 7. xi./25. x. 1922, 1922.
Obshchaya rospis' gosudarstvennykh dokhodov i raskhodov rossiiskoi respubliki na i.–vi. 1918g. (General list of state revenue and expenditure of the Russian republic for i.–vi. 1918) [including explanatory notes], 1918.
Osnovnye itogi raboty pravitel'stva SSSR k perevyboram sovetov 1928–9 (Basic results of the work of the government of the U.S.S.R.; for the re-election of the soviets 1928–9), 1928.
Otchot Narodnogo Komissariata Finansov SSSR ob ispolnenii edinogo gosudarstvennogo byudzheta SSSR za 1926–7g. (Report of NKF U.S.S.R. on the fulfilment of the unified state budget of the U.S.S.R. for 1926–7), 1928. [*Otchot...* (1926/7).]
(*Ibid.*) *za 1931g.* 1932. [*Otchot...* (1931).]
(*Ibid.*) *za 1935g.* 1937. [*Otchot...* (1935).]
Ot s"ezda k s"ezdu (v. 1925–iv. 1927) Materialy k otchotu pravitel'stva na IV s'ezda Sovetov SSSR (From Congress to Congress. Materials for the report of the government to the Fourth Congress of Soviets of the U.S.S.R.), 1927.
Ot s"ezda k s"ezdu (iv. 1927–v. 1929)..., 1929 (for Fifth Congress of Soviets).
Proekt gosudarstvennoi rospisi dokhodov i raskhodov na 1917 god s ob"yasnitel'noyu zapiskoyu Ministra Finansov (Draft of state list of revenue and expenditure for 1917 with explanatory notes of the Minister of Finance), 1916, and similar drafts for 1908, 1913, 1916.
Proekt vtorogo pyatiletnego plana (Draft of the second five-year plan), 1934.
Promyshlennost' SSSR v 1926/7g (U.S.S.R. industry in 1926/7), 1927.
Proposed budget of the Empire for 1917, Part I, 1917.
Règlement définitif du budget de l'Empire pour l'exercice 1903, 1904.
Report of Court Proceedings... March 2–13, 1938, in re: N. I. Bukharin,... G. F. Grinko.... Verbatim Report, 1938.
Rospis' obshchegosudarstvennykh dokhodov i raskhodov rossiiskoi sotsialisticheskoi federativnoi sovetskoi respubliki na vii.–xii. 1918 s ob"yasnitel'noi zapiskoi NKF (List of general state revenue and expenditure of the R.S.F.S.R. for vii.–xii. 1918 with explanatory notes of NKF), 1919. [In footnotes Budget appears as *Rospis'...*, and explanatory notes, which are separately numbered, as *Ob. zapiska*, followed by year concerned.]
(*Ibid.*) *na i.–vi. 1919g.* (1921).
(*Ibid.*) *na vii.–xii. 1919g.* (1921.)
(*Ibid.*) *na. i.–ix. 1922g.* (1921).
The second five-year plan for the development of the national economy of the U.S.S.R. (1933–7), [1936].
SSSR: Tri byudzheta 1923–6gg. (U.S.S.R.: three budgets 1923–6), 1926.
Sotsialisticheskoe stroitel'stvo (Socialist construction), statistical handbook, 1935.
Spravochnik roznichnykh tsen i torgovykh nakidok na promtovary po g. Moskve (Reference-book of retail prices and trade mark-ups for industrial goods in Moscow), pt. 1, 1936.
Spravochnik tsen na stroitel'nye materialy i oborudovanie i transport, Leningrad (Price reference-book for building materials, equipment and transport, Leningrad), no. 34, 1941.
Statisticheskii sbornik po obshchegosudarstvennomu byudzhetu, denezhnomu obrashcheniyu i dvizheniyu tsen s oktyabrya 1922g. po sentyabr' 1923g. (Statistical abstract on the general state budget, currency circulation and price movements from October 1922 to September 1923), 1923.
Svodnye materialy o deyatel'nosti soveta narodnykh komissarov i soveta truda i oborony za

pervyi kvartal (oktyabr', noyabr', dekabr') 1924-5 goda (Collected materials on the work of SNK and STO for the first quarter (October, November, December) of 1924-5), 1925.
(*Ibid.*) *za vtoroi kvartal...1924-5g.* (for second quarter of 1924-5), 1925.
(*Ibid.*) *za 3 kvartal...*, 1925.
(*Ibid.*) *za 4 kvartal...*, 1925.
Trest Mosgortop: spravochnik-tsennik (Moscow town fuel trust: reference-book of prices), 1936.
Universal'nyi spravochnik tsen (Universal reference-book of prices), 1928.
Uproshchenie finansovoi sistemy (Simplification of the financial system), 1930.
Vtoroi pyatiletnii plan narodnogo khozyaistva SSSR (1933-7 gg.) (Second five-year plan of the economy of the U.S.S.R. (1933-7)), 2 vols., 1934.

(*d*) CONGRESSES, CONFERENCES, ETC.

Communist Party

Desyatyi s"ezd Rossiiskoi Kommunisticheskoi Partii. Sten. otchot (8-16 marta 1921) (Tenth Congress of R.C.P. Verbatim report (8-16 March 1921)), 1921.
11 s"ezd... (27. iii.-2. iv. 1922), 1922.
13 s"ezd... (23-31. v. 1924), 1924.
14 s"ezd... (18-31. xii. 1925), 1926.
16 s"ezd... [26. vi.-11. vii. 1930], 1931.
The Land of socialism today and tomorrow. Reports and speeches at the 18th Congress of the C.P.S.U.(b), March 10-21, 1939, 1939.
VKP(b) v rezolyutsiakh i resheniyakh s"ezdov, konferentsii i plenumov TsK (C.P.S.U.(*b*) in resolutions and decisions of Congresses, conferences, and plenary meetings of the CC), 2 vols., 1941.

Other bodies

Trudy vserossiiskogo s"ezda sovetov narodnogo khozyaistva 25.v.-4. vi. 1918: stenograficheskii otchot (Proceedings of the all-Russian Congress of Councils of National Economy 25. v.-4. vi. 1918: verbatim report), 1918. [*Trudy*... (1918).]
Trudy 2-go vserossiiskogo s"ezda sovetov narodnogo khozyaistva. 19-27. xii. 1918 (Proceedings of the Second all-Russian Congress of Councils of National Economy, 19-27. xii. 1918), 1919.
Trudy vserossiiskogo s"ezda zaveduyushchikh finotdelami (Proceedings of the all-Russian Congress of Heads of Financial Departments) [21-25. v. 1919], 1919. [*Trudy*... (1919).]

(3) PERIODICALS AND NEWSPAPERS

American Review of the Soviet Union.
Bulletin of Oxford Institute of Statistics.
Bulletins on Soviet economic development.
Byulleteny VSNKh (VSNKh Bulletin), 1918.
Byulleteny ekonomicheskogo kabineta prof. Prokopovicha (Bulletins of Prof. Prokopovich's economic office).
Conjuncture et études économiques.
Ekonomicheskoe obozrenie (Economic outlook). [*Ek. oboz.*]

Ekonomicheskaya zhizn' (Economic life), newspaper published from 6. xi. 1918 by various economic bodies in the U.S.S.R. [*Ek. zhizn'*.]
Finansovaya gazeta (Financial newspaper).
Istoricheskie zapiski (Historical notes).
Izvestiya (News), newspaper of first the Petrograd Soviet and later the Soviet government, from 1917.
Izvestiya NK Finansov (Bulletin of the P.C. of Finance), 1919–1920.
Kommunist (formerly *Bolshevik*), periodical published by C.P.S.U.
Memoranda of the Birmingham Bureau of Research into Russian Economic Conditions.
Molodoi kommunist (Young Communist).
Planovoe khozyaistva (Planned economy), published by Gosplan from 1926. [*Pl. khoz.*]
Problemy ekonomiki (Problems of economics). [*Prob. ek.*]
Pravda (Truth), newspaper of R.C.P. and C.P.S.U., from 18. iii. 1917.
Review of economics and statistics.
Slavonic and East European review.
Sovetskoe gosudarstvo i pravo (Soviet state and law).
Soviet social sciences bulletin.
Soviet studies.
Stroitel'naya gazeta (Building newspaper).
Vestnik finansov (Financial herald, weekly and later monthly publication of NKF), 1922–30.
Voprosy ekonomiki (Questions of economics).
Voprosy istorii (Questions of history).

INDEX

Abdullua, E., 319 n.
accounting, 14, 32, 70, 96, 113, 143, 236, 240, 270–2
   moneyless, 40 n., 41 n., 44–5, 141
   see also *khozraschot*
accumulation, 3, 74, 87, 88, 99, 100 ff., 144 ff., 192, 194 ff., 200, 205, 248, 331–2 n.
   co-ordination of sources, 152
   inadequate, 94, 106, 109, 117, 230
   income tax as regulator, 109–10
   intra-industrial, 101 ff., 124, 147 f., 150–2, 193, 195, 198, 221, 244, 256, 278–9
   level of, 86–7, 95, 108, 144, 145, 278, 341
   limits of planning, 118
   methods, 97, 101, 102, 104, 106–7 n., 195, 278–9
   nepmen, 109
   'outside', 98, 100, 102, 104, 128, 145, 148, 193, 195, 226, 244–5, 278–9
   personal income, 175
   plan, 152–4, 177–8, 200
   see also taxation and taxes, etc.
administration, 14, 30, 42, 55, 88, 97, 101, 104, 133, 142, 164, 165, 179, 214, 214 n., 239, 265, 266–7, 296, 298
   budget allocation, 130–2, 204–5, 241, 253, 257, 297, 317, 330, 337
   control, 57, 132–3, 155, 270, 303
   expenditure on, 3, 21 n., 54, 70, 75 n., 83, 104–5, 107, 107 n., 129, 131, 132, 148, 165, 228, 232, 240, 254, 301, 303, 337
   local, 56, 75, 182, 297–8, 301
   norms, 190 n.
   of plans, 153–4
   reduction of staff, 57, 57 n., 61, 104, 132, 133 n., 270
agriculture, 3, 4, 59 n., 72 n., 89, 93, 99, 139, 274, 335 n.
   allocations to, 74, 83, 130, 134–5, 172, 186, 193, 233 n., 239, 296
   bank, 72 n., 134–5, 172–4, 233–4, 263
   decentralisation, 181
   expansion, 63, 85, 87, 95, 115
   funds, 134, 239
   labour, 198
   machinery, 135, 139, 143 n., 167, 172
   materials, 86, 139, 143 n., 172
   planning, 95–8, 100, 139, 141, 153, 167, 178, 181, 328, 341, 341 n.

prices and pricing, 87, 88 n., 89, 91–2, 101, 139, 142–3, 168, 171, 246
production, 26, 29, 49, 54, 85–7, 139, 142, 167, 172, 181, 244, 246
rent, 311 n.
scissors crisis and, 63 n., 113
services to, 172, 174, 302
subsidy policy, 237–8, 243
tax, 58 n., 60 n., 67–8 n., 69, 70, 74, 82, 91, 108, 113–17, 124, 170, 173, 174, 190, 222–5, 281, 282, 295, 297–8, 306, 308–9, 313, 316, 321 n.
taxation policy, 68–9, 113–17, 172, 292–4, 341
Agriculture, NK of, 23 n., 42, 81, 134–5, 239 n., 263, 264
alcohol, tax on, 6, 41, 42, 51 n., 58 n., 65, 68, 70, 91, 122, 123, 218, 283, 292
   see also vodka
Aleksandrov, A. M., 120, 161 n., 205 n., 208 n., 317 n.
allocations, 6, 10, 16–17, 19, 32, 39, 39 n., 44, 61 n., 63, 97, 133, 155, 168, 191, 233, 235, 256
   basis of, 139–41, 267
   budget, 72–3, 103, 104, 108, 108 n., 129–30, 135, 184, 189, 207
   control, 35, 37–8, 38 n., 54, 203, 207, 229–33, 241, 260, 267, 269, 329
   direct, 140 n., 147, 227, 248, 299
   'operational expenditures', 232, 251
   planning, 96, 140, 141, 153–4
   to republics, 78–9, 185, 298
   see also under separate purposes of allocations
allotments, tax on, 56 n.
Al'skii, M., 41 n., 55 n., 66 n.
amortisation, see depreciation
armaments, see defence expenditure
Armenian S.S.R., 79, 298, 307, 310
Army, Red, 16 n., 29, 39, 56 n., 220, 249, 250, 287 n., 291, 332
   NK of, 131, 131 n.
   Red Guards, 17
   see also defence expenditure
Arnold, W. Z., 11 n., 31, 58 n., 72 n., 141 n., 198 n.
artels, industrial, 291, 293
Atlas, M. S., 15 n., 24 n., 30 n.
Atlas, Z. V., 11 n., 15 n., 63 n.

auditing, 154, 271–2
  see also control
Autonomous Republics (A.S S R.'s), 79, 80, 81, 84, 298, 298 n., 311
aviation, allocations to, 250
Azarkh, 41 n.
Azerbaijan S.S.R., 78–9, 298, 305, 307, 310, 329

backward areas, financing of, 84, 304–8
banks and banking, 3, 11, 12, 12 n., 15, 15 n., 71–2, 87, 103–4, 155, 158, 191 n., 205, 229, 275–6
  control, 154, 158, 159, 208, 230, 260, 269, 270–1, 275–9, 315, 317, 326, 338
  credit plan, 134, 229–31
  deposits, 101, 104, 120, 126, 128
  efficiency control, 234, 241, 248, 262
  financing the economy, 72, 72 n., 102, 103
  investment, 150, 209, 233
  loan plan, 99, 101, 104
  loans and credits to industry, 30 n., 63 n., 71, 72 n., 102, 154, 198, 208, 209, 210, 229–32, 237
  long-term, 155, 195, 229, 335
  methods reconstruction, 234–6, 236 n., 256–9, 260–1
  plan, 153, 179
  reform, 134, 196
  Russian Commercial Bank, 71 n.
  share of trust profit, 119, 195
  special, 155, 157, 158, 161–2 n., 233, 236 n., 241, 255, 259, 261, 261 n., 262, 326, 343
  system, 3, 54, 68, 98, 100, 102, 134, 173, 196
  Trade and Industry, 71 n., 119, 120, 134, 166, 208, 209
  see also under specific banks
Barker, G. R., 314 n.
barter, 30, 49, 50, 55
  see also transactions in kind
Batyrev, V., 231 n.
Baykov, A., 15 n., 29 n., 69 n., 71 n., 72 n., 86 n., 96 n., 97 n., 179 n., 214 n., 219 n., 228, 237 n., 245 n., 251 n., 314 n.
beer, tax on, 123, 287, 288
Belevsky, A., 7 n.
Belorussia, 78, 80, 298, 305, 307, 310
Bergson, A., 249, 279 n.
bicycles, price of, 228
  tax on, 56 n., 285 n., 287, 288
bills of exchange, 72 n., 158, 209, 216 n.
black market, *see* market
Bogolepov, D. P., 7 n., 22 n., 64 n., 145 n., 196 n.

Bogolepov, M. I., 152 n., 195 n., 196 n., 237 n., 274 n.
Bolshevik Party, *see* Communist Party
Bonch-Bruevich, V. D., 15 n.
bonuses
  Director's Fund, 163
  in kind, 50
  incentive, 159, 162 n., 164
  from profits, 71, 119, 119 n., 120
  tantième, 120
  wage, 227, 248, 264, 270
books, excess demand for, 142, 287
Braude, I. L., 259 n., 261 n., 262 n.
bread, price of, 228
Bregel, E. Ya., 15 n.
Brest-Litovsk treaty, 14, 43
bricks, price of, 228
Bryukhanov, L. P., xxi, 81 n., 83, 99 n., 107 n., 115 n., 118 n., 124 n., 128 n., 131 n., 133 n., 200 n., 223 n.
budget, 3, 16, 23–5, 32, 35 n., 66 n., 107, 124, 234, 242, 337
  accumulation via, 103–4, 106–13, 120, 145, 148–9, 152, 245, 278, 341
  balancing, 191–2
  centralisation, 30–5, 74, 84, 326, 337–8
  commission(s), 35, 36, 38, 38 n., 153–4, 267
  control, 35–7, 60–1, 66, 74–5, 77, 133, 154, 155, 160, 165, 173, 180, 186, 203–4, 241–2, 253, 267–72, 315, 337, 338
  dates, 23 n., 36, 36 n., 59 n.
  deficit, 58, 64 n., 198
  estimates, 7, 10, 16, 17, 22–5, 32–6, 38, 58–64, 73, 78–9, 133, 241, 338
  grants and loans, 72, 102–4, 124–5, 134–5, 160, 174, 178, 184, 187, 203, 205, 206, 210, 234
  growth, 30–5, 107–8, 129–30
  in kind, 38–45, 53 n., 55, 57
  inflation, 52, 87
  Law, 19 n., 23, 25, 25 n., 80, 81
  money basis restored, 53, 55
  norms, 190, 190 n., 241
  orthodoxy, 24, 35
  'over-all budget' defined, 84 n.
  planning, 98–9, 108, 136, 152–4, 179, 186–90, 197–9, 234
  pre-revolutionary, 3–6, 6 n., 7, 10
  subsidies, 51, 160, 167, 185, 189, 238, 243, 247, 253
  surplus, 3, 7, 102, 108, 176, 191 n.
  technique, 59–60, 60–4, 182–4, 184 n., 185–6, 241, 267
  'turnover' budget, 39, 39 n.
  'unified state budget' defined, 84 n.
  working capital from, 72, 157–8, 232, 258

354

budget expenditure, 16, 41, 51–2, 52 n., 73, 118, 130, 176, 296
  accumulation, 148
  administration of, 16, 66, 204–5, 268–72
  attempts to reduce, 57, 58, 129, 228, 232
  changes, 3, 6, 7–8, 10, 70, 315, 316, 320–1
  control, 133, 136, 154, 155, 203–5, 208, 236–7, 241, 253, 256–7, 264–72, 337
  currency issues, 28, 54, 64
  decentralisation, 336, 338
  local, 56, 56 n., 241, 307
  'operational', 232, 267 n., 268
  republics, 78–84, 307
  subsidies, q.v.
budget revenue, 7–10, 12, 12 n., 20, 22, 26, 27 n., 119, 155, 176, 213, 219, 246, 321
  backward areas, 306–9
  collection, 74, 280
  control, 60–3, 84, 205
  increase in, 57–9, 108
  in kind, 52, 52 n.
  inflation, 36, 317–18
  local, 17–18, 19, 20, 34, 51, 56, 75, 75 n., 182, 298, 306, 308, 309, 311, 312
  reform of, 155, 200, 213, 227, 242
  sources of, 3, 6, 6 n., 17, 18, 21, 28, 31, 51–2, 108, 128, 174–5, 199, 200 n., 225, 226, 295, 316
  see also under separate sources of revenue
budget system, 6, 10, 11–12, 12 n., 30, 35, 64–81, 100, 141, 150, 152, 180, 193, 198–9, 204, 242–3, 251–2, 314–22, 329–32
building, 56 n., 256, 267, 311, 312, 321, 332
  concrete, price of, 332 n.
  conference (1954), 335 n.
  costing, 333 n.
  drafts, 255
  force, 257
  industry, 157, 158, 251, 262 n.
  materials, 300, 320
  programme, 258
  see also capital; construction
Bukharin, N. I., 40 n., 196 n., 280 n.
Bulganin, N., 330, 330 n.
bureaux of price checks, 260

capital, 20 n., 44, 90, 95, 120, 141, 163, 322
  allocation, 143, 180
  construction, 88, 176
  costing, 144 n., 145, 324–5, 333
  investment, 85–6, 87, 91, 98, 100, 106, 148, 149, 165, 166, 167, 177, 178, 221, 232, 256, 332
  private, 90, 100, 109, 112, 113, 125

repair, 160–1, 161 n., 166, 178, 256, 334, 338
replacement, 160–1, 333
reserves, 71, 119, 120, 126
stock, 160–1, 324–5, 332–5, 338
working, 71–3, 119, 154 n., 157, 157 n., 159, 162, 163, 163 n., 165–7, 180, 185 n., 188–9, 209, 210, 220–1, 229, 230–3, 239, 251, 258, 262, 263 n., 264, 267, 273, 278, 338
capital goods, 143 n., 146, 151, 155, 167, 195, 195 n., 197, 206, 227, 237, 238, 247, 285, 320, 321, 327, 331, 331 n., 337, 340
  see also industry, heavy
capitalism and capitalists, Bolshevik view of, 10, 12 n., 13 n., 21 n., 40 n., 86, 107 n., 131
Carr, E. H., 10 n., 15 n., 19 n., 41 n., 71 n.
cartage tax, 52 n., 56 n., 76, 201
cattle, 56 n., 68, 114, 115, 117 n., 171, 224, 252, 281, 281 n.
  livestock plan, 328
cement, price of, 228
Central Asia, 7, 117 n., 133 n., 218, 298, 305, 309
  see also under separate republics
centralisation, 11–13, 15, 18–20, 49, 119, 165, 182, 235–6, 245
  allocation, 151, 207
  budget, 30–5, 74, 84, 326, 337–8
  credit, 11, 229
  dangers, 179–81, 326–7
  direct planning and, 96, 140, 140 n., 151, 167, 179, 193, 326–7
  excise, 202, 309
  industry, 28, 50, 206, 207
  investment control, 317, 337–8
  supervision, 229, 271–2
  taxation, 211, 214, 215, 275, 309
Chamberlin, W. H., 126
Chayanov, A. V., 41, 44
chemical industry, 335 n.
Chester, D. N., 95 n.
Chubar', A., xxi, 280 n.
Chutskayev, 34 n., 242 n.
cinemas, tax on, 218, 219–20, 287 n., 311
clothing, tax on, 123, 287
coal industry, costing and planning, 160, 188, 201, 235, 237, 278, 323, 329, 331
coal, price of, 228
coffee, tax on, 51 n., 123
collective farm(s), 69, 109, 115, 116, 135, 142, 167–74, 176, 266 n., 282, 311 n., 342
  assessment of income, 223, 282–3
  decentralisation, 181
  income and expenditure, 170–4, 177

collective farm(s) (*cont.*)
  indivisible funds, 171–3, 178
  machine tractor stations, q.v.
  market, *see* market
  prices, 142–3, 168–74, 320
  private plots, 167, 170, 173, 223, 282
  purchasing power, 142–3, 143 n.
  seeds, 160, 168, 169, 281
  services to, 172, 174, 302
  tax, 190, 222, 223, 223 n., 281–2, 295
  see also agriculture
collectivisation, 87, 92 n., 222, 239, 244, 341
  and first five-year plan, 139, 197
combines (*ob"edineniya*), 212, 214
  and the budget, 300
  and construction estimates, 236
  and taxation system, 214–16, 218, 309
Commissars, People's, 15, 15 n., 17, 42, 57 n., 132, 157, 160, 165, 183, 184 n.
Commissars, People's Council of (SNK), 15, 15 n., 21 n., 33, 34 n., 42, 62, 280 n.
  budget control, 35, 36 n., 37, 60, 61 n., 63 n., 185–6, 204, 269, 271, 297, 302
  Committee on Construction Affairs, *see* construction
  construction control, 257
  financial planning, 153, 183, 184
  material budget, 41, 45
  relations with republics, 79, 297
  small council (*malyi* SNK), 36 n., 37
Communism, 10, 40 n., 53 n., 141, 196
  War, 14, 26, 30, 35, 40, 45, 52, 54, 73, 141
Communist Manifesto, 13
Communist Party (VKP (b) or RKP (b)), 9, 10, 11–14, 16, 21, 27 n., 35 n., 39, 40 n., 49, 57, 114 n., 115 n., 116 n., 124 n.
  Central Committee, 108 n., 111 n., 114, 141, 211, 212 n.
  Conference, Seventh 1917, 12; Eleventh 1921, 55; Thirteenth 1924, 71 n.; Fifteenth 1926, 106, 112, 127 n.
  Congress, Sixth 1917, 11, 12, 18; Eighth 1919, 27 n., 40 n.; Tenth 1921, 49 n., 67 n.; Twelfth 1923, 69 n., 114; Fourteenth 1925, 85, 99, 114, 114 n., 115 n.; Fifteenth 1927, 101 n.; Seventeenth 1934, 141
  see also Left oppositions, Right opposition
Communists versus old officials, 20 n., 66 n.
compulsion by state, 88, 109, 115, 126, 128, 171, 323
  discontent from, 49
  labour, 14, 28
  loans, 9, 70, 70 n., 127
  membership of trade union, 49
  purchase under, 26, 28, 56

compulsory deliveries, 168–73, 174 n., 198 n., 223, 224 n., 237–8, 246, 262, 263, 281, 289, 293–4, 315, 320, 320 n., 321, 321 n., 341
  see also procurement; requisitioning
Comstock, A., 121 n.
concessions policy, 72 n.
concrete, price of, 332 n.
Constitution, Soviet, 19, 19 n., 21, 22 n., 25, 34, 78, 80
construction, 233
  above limit, 207, 235, 236, 261
  below limit, 256
  compilation of estimates, 235–7, 255, 259 n., 260, 317
  control, 234, 260–1
  costing of, 206, 332–3
  costs reduction, 208, 228, 232, 259, 261, 261 n.
  illegalities, 259 n.
  investor, 257–61
  organisation, 209, 234, 255–9
  plan, 299
  road, 302
  unit evaluations, 255
  see also building; capital; capital goods; contract; investment
Construction Affairs, State Committee on (*Gosstroi*), 255, 259, 271, 326
consumer and consumption, 39, 110, 122, 139, 140, 142, 177, 214, 314
consumer goods,
  defence expenditure and, 251, 314
  distribution, 41, 50, 140, 143, 294
  industry, 67, 91, 143 n., 150, 155, 177, 247, 279, 299, 302, 323, 335, 340
  made from waste, 256
  metal, 142, 288
  output, 88, 90, 91, 94, 140, 143, 144, 146, 173, 191, 195, 197, 198, 227, 245, 285, 320, 320 n., 322, 327, 335, 337, 339
  price, 122, 199, 224, 238, 244, 246, 248, 251, 314, 331, 332, 336
  reduced costs, 321
  scarcity, 28, 29 n., 142, 244
  selling methods, 55–6, 335–6
  taxation of, 22, 67, 151, 212, 213, 217, 246, 278, 284–5, 285 n., 287–91, 293, 316, 322, 337, 338
  see also industry, light
consumers' choice, 245, 284, 327, 335, 342
contract method of construction, 258–9, 335 n.
  acceptance deeds, 258, 261
  compared with direct labour method, 234–5, 257
  control, 260–1
  illegalities, 259 n.

356

control, 10, 11, 28, 90, 96 n., 97, 150, 161, 175, 207, 241, 299, 315, 324, 337
  allocations, 54–5, 55 n., 192, 205, 232–3
  bank, 134, 154, 158, 159, 208, 230, 241, 260–1, 270, 315, 317, 326
  budget, 35–7, 60–1, 66, 74–5, 77, 133, 154–5, 164–5, 173, 180, 186, 203–4, 241–2, 253, 267–72, 315, 337, 338
  by the rouble, 144, 230, 231
  collectivisation as means of, 87, 168, 173, 181
  construction estimates, 235, 258–62
  contractor, 258–62
  costs, 337
  credit, 229–32, 237 n.
  efficiency, 232, 234–5, 262, 342
  enterprise and trust, 90, 161, 180, 272–80
  expenditure, 203, 337
  figures, 61 n., 97, 99, 100, 131, 152, 153
  financial, 154, 204, 208, 228–33, 242, 263, 272, 338
  investment, 134, 146–7, 149, 155, 205, 206, 207, 208, 229, 233, 243, 255, 261, 301–2, 315, 317, 326, 338, 341
  local budgets, 74–7, 81–2, 297, 299, 302, 312–13, 326
  operative, 241
  price, 197, 328, 339, 340
  private sector, 98, 139
  production, 11, 14, 127, 207, 272–4, 329
  productivity, 319
  republican budgets, 80–1, 82, 297, 299, 302, 312–13, 326
  state, 90, 139, 171, 181; NK of, 242 n.
  tax inspectors, 274
  turnover tax, 274–5, 317
  wage issues, 248, 315, 319, 322, 328
  working capital, 225, 229–33
co-operative(s), 32 n., 39 n., 55, 55 n., 83, 135, 139, 224 n.
  bank, 71 n., 234
  financial plan of, 153
  industry, 66 n., 109, 111, 175, 221 n., 311 n.
  prices, 88, 93
  trade, 50, 88, 93, 109, 139, 251, 251 n., 292, 318, 318 n.
  see also collective farms
cosmetics, tax on, 123, 200 n., 286, 288, 290
cost price, 118, 119, 146, 147
  gap between c.p. and transfer price used for accumulation, 158, 166, 195, 198, 220, 244, 277–9
  costs and costing, 88 n., 90, 95, 130 n., 132, 143–4, 145, 147, 149, 157, 159, 160, 165, 176, 187, 189, 262, 277, 322–6, 337

capital stock replacement via, 151, 159–61, 324–5, 332–5, 337
  depreciation, 144, 145 n., 160, 161, 332–3
  industrial, 94, 97, 101, 102, 104, 166, 196, 237, 251 n., 319, 323, 324
  of investment, 106, 199, 206, 321; *see also* construction costs
  new products, 160
  plan, 96–7, 105, 147, 149, 150, 162–3, 180, 186–8, 197, 221, 227, 230, 248, 275, 277, 330
  profits tax and, 212, 291
  reductions in, 93–4, 102, 104–6, 119, 144, 144 n., 147–50, 158–9, 162–4, 178, 187–9, 191, 195, 195 n., 196, 198–200, 208, 211–12, 227–9, 230, 232, 244, 246 n., 247–8 n., 251, 253, 258, 278 n., 279, 317–23, 325, 333–5
  rise in, 227, 229, 243, 251, 261
  subsidies, q.v.
  trading, 93–4, 187–8
  transfer prices and, 147–9, 209, 217, 237, 243, 262, 278, 293
  transport, 143, 160, 239–40, 260, 291–2
  wage, 143–4, 158–9
  without prices, 140–1, 324, 338
crafts, tax on, 6, 67 n., 117 n., 224 n., 311 n.
credit, 3, 198, 227
  agricultural, 134–5, 239
  bank, 24 n., 209, 229–31
  budget, 32 n., 37–8, 102
  centralisation, 11, 13, 229
  commercial, 209, 210, 229
  foreign, 101
  industry, 154, 229–33
  long-term, 119, 120, 134, 229, 233
  plan, 99, 134, 145, 152, 167, 176, 177, 184, 191 n., 229, 230
  reform, 154, 229–30
  short-term, 134, 158, 158 n., 192, 229, 231, 237 n., 258, 260–1, 273, 276, 316–17
  State Bank, 154 n., 209, 229, 230
culture, 163, 170, 234, 252, 254, 301, 302
  levy, 175, 182, 222, 225, 226, 252, 295, 313 n.
  tax on cultural goods, 287
  see also social services
currency, 3, 8–10, 12–13, 17, 22, 22 n., 26, 28–30, 36, 38, 40, 44, 61, 74, 90, 127
  chervonets, 58, 63, 63 n.
  circulation, 9, 22, 24, 24 n., 29, 29 n., 31, 39, 52–3, 63, 101–2, 177, 197 n., 198–9, 315–16
  commission on, 38, 44
  depreciation, 28, 36, 50, 52, 63, 63 n.
  devaluation of paper, 58, 58 n.

357

currency (*cont.*)
  issues, 8, 12–13, 16–17, 22, 26, 28–9, 30, 52, 54–5, 58, 58 n., 60–1, 63–4 n., 70, 74, 82, 89, 97–8, 102, 104, 130 n., 154, 194, 198
  reform, 18, 18 n., 40 n., 41 n., 54, 58, 315–16
  sovznak, 58, 63, 63 n.

Davies, R. W., 158 n., 276 n., 314 n., 317 n., 330 n.
defence expenditure, 3, 5, 7, 8–10, 30, 36–7, 42, 49, 54–5, 57, 65, 70, 78, 80, 83, 107, 110, 129, 130–2, 140, 143 n., 148, 151, 155, 191, 228, 240–1, 249–51, 253, 296, 297, 301, 301 n., 314–15, 327, 332, 337, 342
  industries, 245, 247, 250–1, 285, 301
  and NKVD, 249–51, 295
depreciation allowance, 71, 103, 106, 119, 119 n., 144–6, 155, 160–1, 161 n., 162 n., 165–7, 178, 188–9, 205, 206 n., 209, 234, 256, 262, 279, 332–5
Devons, E., 95 n.
Dickinson, H. D., 140 n.
Director's Fund, 163, 163 n., 164–6, 178, 181, 188, 248, 252, 256, 266 n., 277, 278 n., 303, 317, 317 n., 322–3, 326, 334–5
  factory fund, 334–5, 337
  see also Fund for Improving Workers' Welfare
discrimination
  by interest rates, 134
  against luxury goods, 121, 190
  among peasantry by state, 109, 113–14, 134, 175, 222
  against private sector, 100, 110–12, 223 n.
  socio-economic, 284, 286–90, 292
  by tax, 68–9, 70, 110–12, 175, 199, 222, 223 n., 285 n., 289 ff.
distilling, illegal, 91, 124
districts (*raiony*), 299
districts (*uyezdy*), 77
Dneprstroi, 127 n.
Dobb, M. H., 41 n., 56 n., 58 n., 85 n., 89 n., 91, 144 n., 179 n.
Dobbert, G., 44 n.
doctors
  tax on, 175
  planning of, 189
D'yachenko, V. P., 15 n., 16 n., 17 n., 19 n., 20 n., 22 n., 24, 27 n., 29 n., 30 n., 31 n., 32 n., 33 n., 36 n., 37 n., 39 n., 41 n., 43, 49 n., 50 n., 51 n., 52 n., 53, 55 n., 56 n., 57 n., 58 n., 61 n., 62, 63 n., 64 n., 66 n., 67 n., 68 n., 69 n., 71 n., 72 n., 75 n., 76, 77 n., 83 n., 114 n., 115 n., 116 n., 120, 120 n., 123, 126, 127 n., 161 n., 165 n., 242 n., 270 n., 271 n., 298 n., 312 n.
D'yachkov, M. F., 162, 257 n., 261 n.

economists, 107 n.
  Bolshevik policy, 10–13
  on budget's importance, 152
  on capital stock costing, 333, 333 n.
  on changes needed in system, 329
  on costs, 144 n.
  on depreciation, 161 n.
  on financial plan, 154 n., 196
  on investment control, 146, 146 n.
  on money, 40–5, 49, 52, 54, 141
  on net income of society, 342
  on net revenue, 332
  on planning, 94, 96 n., 140 n., 314, 327–8, 328 n.
  on pricing, 331 n., 336
  on profit ratio to wage fund, 277
  on savings, 145
  on taxes, 64 n., 118
economy, the, 3, 7, 10, 12–13, 14, 18, 30, 38, 49–51, 55, 85, 88–9, 109, 115, 115 n., 118, 129–30, 139, 194–5, 226–7, 229, 244, 247–51, 274, 314–16, 336
  financing the, 70, 72–4, 83, 100, 103, 104, 106–8, 121, 124, 128–31, 136, 148–9, 152–5, 160, 162–3, 166–7, 187, 192, 195–6, 198–9, 204–5, 213, 220–2, 228, 273, 296, 297, 301, 305, 320, 337, 342
  in kind, 30, 40, 49, 50, 54
  loans to the, 72–4, 124
  local, 56, 75
  regime of, 104–5, 132, 230 n., 259
  war, 7–10, 30, 40, 315
education, 5, 17 n., 42, 55 n., 61, 78, 106, 165, 190, 265 n., 266, 303
  army, 249
  backward areas, 304, 306
  expansion of, 130 n., 240
  expenditure, 83, 119 n., 130, 148, 252, 252 n., 254, 264, 267, 296, 299, 302–3, 337
  higher, 56 n., 300, 302, 329
  local budget, 7, 56 n., 77 n., 182, 264, 301, 302, 313
  local elementary, 56, 75, 190 n., 225, 297, 302–3
  republican budget, 297, 302
  schools, 189, 252, 303
  technical, 120, 240, 302
efficiency
  administrative, 298
  budget, 204, 241, 252
  construction, 258
  control, 232, 234, 235, 342

358

efficiency (*cont.*)
  credit, 229–30
  financial, 154, 203–4, 231
  incentive to, 323–5, 332
  industrial, 141, 143, 143 n., 147, 162, 163, 165, 192, 193, 209, 220, 228, 244, 255, 332, 338, 342
  investment, 205, 232, 257
  railway, 240
eggs, price of, 228
electrification, 74, 83, 111 n., 130, 134–5, 188, 233
Elektrobank, 71 n., 134
energy unit, 44 n.
Engels, F., 10, 10 n., 11, 40
engineering, 120, 149, 218, 276, 292, 335 n.
enterprises, 39, 40, 51, 55, 57 n., 66 n., 71, 97, 120, 121, 125, 135, 143, 152, 176, 180, 206, 209, 212–13, 220, 249, 280, 338
  compilation of plan, 183–4
  control, 154, 225, 230–1, 272–6, 338
  costs, 106, 144, 163, 164, 165–6
  credit to, 229–30, 230 n., 231
  decentralisation, 55, 180, 256, 330
  new, 145, 197, 235, 257 n.
  social insurance, 57, 165, 264, 266 n.
  State Bank and, 205, 230–1, 260, 275–6
  subsidies, 159–60, 163–7, 237–8
  supervision by tax inspectors, 274
  taxation, 68, 113, 200–1, 201 n., 202–3, 211–13, 214, 214 n., 215, 218, 220, 309
  working capital, 56 n., 70–1, 119, 157, 157 n., 159, 166–7, 180, 229–30, 231
  see also factory
equipment, 96–7, 105, 114, 131, 139, 141, 144 n., 151, 157, 167, 171–2, 174, 176, 190, 206, 206 n., 234, 247, 249, 256, 260, 267, 268, 320, 322–4, 329, 333, 333 n.
excises, 6, 7, 20 n., 22, 51, 51 n., 58, 58 n., 60 n., 64, 64 n., 67, 82, 91, 108, 117, 121–3, 122 n., 124, 150, 195, 199, 200–3, 211–14, 216, 216 n., 246, 287, 290, 309
  see also turnover tax
Extraordinary Revolutionary Tax, 15, 27, 31 n., 40 n., 42

factory, 4, 12 n.
  confiscation, 26
  costs, 144 n., 187, 188
  efficiency, 324–5, 325 n., 332
  Fund, 334
  incentives, 322
  levies, 18 n.
  loan commissions, 128
  new, 160
  obsolescence, 160

  plan compilation, 183–6
  powers, 336
  social insurance, 265
  subsidies, 51
  supervision posts, 242
  supply of goods, 245
  trusts, 143 n.
  wages in kind, 29
  workers, 50
  see also enterprises
farming
  co-operative, 109
  off-farm sales, 86–7, 168
  prices, 142–3
  private, 50, 113, 168
  seed and fodder funds, 168
  state farms, 134, 139, 168, 239, 302; NK of, 239 n.
  subsistence, 6
  taxing, 68, 74, 113, 222–3
  see also agriculture; collective farms; peasants
Finance, Ministry of, 6, 7, 13, 15, 66, 201
Finance, People's Commissar(-iat) of (NKF), xxi, 8, 9, 20, 21 n., 22 n., 30, 32 n., 33, 33 n., 34, 34 n., 42, 62, 65, 71 n., 80, 81, 99 n., 100 n., 107 n., 108 n., 153 n., 154 n., 185 n., 204, 218, 221, 260, 280 n., 305
  Administration of Budgets and Estimates, 60 n.
  Administration of Financial Supervision, 66 n.
  auditing, 271
  budget control, 35–8, 38 n., 54, 60, 60 n., 61, 61 n., 63, 66, 66 n., 73, 133, 185–6, 204, 241–2, 267, 269–74
  communists in, 66–7 n.
  compilation of plans, 183–6
  control, 233, 238, 242
  expenditure inspection, 208, 253, 271
  financial plan, 99, 184
  investment plan, 162 n., 208, 209
  loans, 69–70, 72
  material budget, 40 n., 41, 44–5
  private concerns, 110, 233
  profits of enterprises, 71, 162
  republics, 79, 302
  staff reduction, 57 n., 202
  Supervision administration or department, 66 n., 241–2, 271–2, 273
  taxation, 69, 69 n., 201, 202, 211, 212 n., 215, 217, 275, 283, 284, 309
financial congress 1919, 20 n., 32–3 n.
financial departments (*finotdely*), 19, 20, 32 n., 56 n., 110, 215, 263, 270, 273, 274, 275, 280, 304, 309
  Congress of Heads, 20 n., 32–3 n.

359

financial norms, 190, 190 n.
financial plan, 97–100, 133, 136, 145, 150, 152–4, 158, 173, 176–9, 183–4, 186, 189, 195–7, 204, 209, 210, 221, 231, 240, 278, 285 n., 327
financial planning, 97–9, 147–50, 152, 155, 165, 178–9
financial policy, 3, 11–13, 18, 53–4 n., 66, 78, 86, 97–8, 109, 136, 194
   'balancing', 87, 177
   Lenin on, 14–16, 18–25
   on price reduction, 93–4, 248
financial system, 97, 100, 101, 139, 155, 195, 196, 201, 228–9, 235, 248
   behind plan, 141–3, 193, 195, 341
   collective farm, 168, 172–3
   interrelations, 177
   limitations, 322–6
   local, 15, 18–20, 29, 33, 34, 40, 56, 75, 78, 182, 214, 303
   mixed, 150–1
   reconstruction, 196 n.
   supervision, 200 n., 235
financing
   agriculture, 134–5
   double, 77 n.
   economy, 70, 72, 72 n., 107, 128, 133, 136, 148, 155, 213
   industry, q.v.
   investment, q.v.
   machine-tractor stations, 262–4
   regulation of, 133–4
   social services, 264–72
   transport and posts, 135–6, 239–40
Florence, P. Sargant, 96 n.
food
   army, 131, 249, 291
   cattle, 281
   compulsory purchase, 28, 38, 246
   dictatorship, 14
   free, 39 n.
   industry, 274, 278, 292, 317 n.
   per patient, 190
   People's Commissariat of, 23 n., 32 n., 42, 80, 286
   prices, 143, 171, 228, 249, 251, 315, 321, 321 n.
   supplies, 49, 51, 86–7, 91, 92 n., 172, 194, 197, 227, 238, 341
   taxation, 123, 218, 219, 274, 285–6, 291–3
foreign affairs, 80
   NK of, 132 n., 268
foreign capital, 3, 8, 21, 21 n., 101, 124
foreign exchange, 90
foreign-financed firms, 72 n.
foreign hostility, 21
foreign trade, 79, 80, 302

Frumkin, 108 n., 196 n.
fuel, 7, 39 n., 188, 192, 249, 291 n.
   costs, 143, 247, 319
   machine-tractor stations, 262, 263 n., 264, 291 n.
   norms, 105
   oil, 173, 174, 176, 291 n.
   prices, 105, 228, 249
   stocks, 157, 231
Fulfilment, Commission of, 242, 242 n.
Fund for Improving Workers' Welfare (FUBR), 71, 106, 119, 120, 163, 220, 221, 277
   see also Director's Fund

Galenson, W., 197 n.
Gatovskii, L., 219 n.
Gedvilas, M. A., 330 n.
Georgian S.S.R., 79, 298, 307
Germany, 14, 245
Gindin, I. F., 7 n.
Gladkov, I. A., 19 n., 21 n., 22 n., 23 n., 32 n.
glass industry, 235 n., 291 n.
glavk, 157, 160, 161, 163, 165–6, 167, 170, 183, 184, 186, 212, 213, 232, 236, 256, 257, 273, 275, 276, 283, 324, 325, 325 n., 335
   see also combine
Glavvoenstroi (Chief Military Building Administration), 250
Glukser, B., 330 n.
Gobza, N., 79 n.
gold, 3, 16, 28, 40 n., 52, 58, 90
Golovanov, S. G., 36 n., 80 n.
Gordin, A., 275 n., 277 n.
Gorky, M., 7 n., 9 n.
Gosplan, 60, 61 n., 62, 63, 100 n., 108 n., 145, 178, 182–6
grain, 21 n., 26, 50 n., 68, 69, 69 n., 73 n., 109, 246
   reluctance to supply, 89, 90, 92, 341
   tax, 281 n., 283, 285–6, 292 n., 293
   see also compulsory deliveries
Granick, D., 181 n., 319 n., 323 n., 328 n.
grants to mothers, 296, 302
grants to students, 264–5, 268
Grigoriev, A. A., 240 n.
Grin′ko, G. F., xxi, 154 n., 161 n., 223 n., 249 n., 259 n., 274 n., 280 n., 281 n., 283 n., 291 n., 304 n.
Gukovskii, I. E., xxi, 16 n., 18 n., 19 n., 21 n., 22 n., 23 n.

Haensel, P., 9, 59 n., 108 n., 126, 128 n.
health, 42, 55 n., 83, 106, 265 n.
   army, 249
   backwards areas, 304, 306

health (cont.)
  construction, 299
  hospitals, 189, 203
  local budget, 56, 75, 182, 264, 297, 301, 302, 313
  People's Commissariat of, 39 n.
  state budget, 7, 56–7, 130 n., 132 n., 148, 254, 265, 296, 301, 337
  see also doctors
Hoeffding, O., 129 n.
Holzman, F. D., 294 n.
household, tax assessment (peasants), 114–17, 222–3, 282
household utensils, 287, 288, 324
housing, 83, 119 n., 130, 142, 153, 163, 175, 182, 225, 233 n., 234, 254, 264, 265, 265 n., 295, 296, 299, 302, 313 n., 334

Ikonnikov, V. V., 208 n., 210 n., 230 n.
incentives and disincentives, 96, 118, 147 n., 148, 159, 164, 221, 225, 337
  bonus, 159
  Director's Fund, 323, 324–5
  effectiveness of, 323–5, 325 n., 337
  efficiency, 205, 220, 243, 255–6
  enterprise and trust, 95, 160, 238, 272
  financial, 106, 162, 162 n., 239, 253, 264, 277, 317, 322–4, 341, 343
  investor, 259
  management, 248
  profit as, 276, 278, 279, 324
  supervision, 273–4
  tax assessment, 117 n., 215
  wage, 175, 245
income
  differing levels, 142
  farmers, 170–3, 223
Incomes and Expenditures of the Population, Balance of Money, 177–9, 183, 191
income tax, 6, 7, 9, 11, 11 n., 17 n., 18, 20–1, 21 n., 22 n., 26–7, 27 n., 42, 59, 61 n., 67, 69, 70, 71, 74, 74 n., 76, 82, 110, 113, 118, 170, 175–6, 193, 225, 252, 309, 321, 338
  accumulation and, 109–10
  collective farms, 169, 173, 281
  discrimination, 175
  on enterprises, 71, 220
  estimates, 60–1 n., 190, 295
  limits of planning, 118
  loans, 70, 124–5
  local revenue from, 182, 306, 308, 309, 311 n.
  reform, 13, 13 n., 110–11, 224–5
  surtax on, 17 n., 20, 316
  on trusts, 119–20
index of prices, 89, 108 n., 187, 187 n., 228

Industrial Bank (Prombank), 71 n., 119, 120, 134, 166, 208, 209, 233, 240, 261 n.
Long-term Credits, 208, 208 n., 209, 233
industrialisation, 106, 129, 174 n., 235, 242, 327, 329, 337, 338, 340, 341
  agriculture and, 172
  defence and, 131, 315
  early stages of, 3, 130 n., 205
  financing of, 102, 106, 125, 127, 145, 243, 253
  inflation and, 174, 195–7, 340
  loans for, 125, 127 n., 128 n.
  policy, 85–6, 94, 99, 197, 206
  rate of, 91, 131, 145, 151, 326
  regime of economy and, 104
  savings and, 145, 194
  social services and, 240
  strain of, 108, 179, 244
  subsidies, 238
  v. other uses of revenue, 124
industry, 9, 11, 14, 26, 50–2, 54, 55, 61, 64 n., 88 n., 89, 120, 132, 139, 140, 187, 206
  accumulation, 106, 124, 145, 147–8, 150, 152, 193, 195, 198, 221, 244, 256, 278–9
  allocations to, 28, 32, 54, 97, 108, 130, 140, 199, 205–9, 239
  banks, 134, 233–4
  budget, 24 n., 30–3, 106, 296–7
  capacity of, 85
  capital repair, 160–1, 333–5
  combines, 214, 214 n.
  consumer goods, q.v.
  costs, 147, 165–6, 187, 251 n., 255, 323, 329
  costs reduction, 105, 150, 228–9, 246 n., 248, 253, 261, 319, 323
  credits, 63 n., 145–6
  efficiency, 141, 143, 143 n., 147, 162–3, 165, 192, 193, 209, 220, 228, 244, 255, 332, 338, 342
  expansion, 3, 7, 63, 105–6, 146
  financing, 72–4, 83, 94, 102–4, 106–7, 120–1, 124, 125, 129, 143 n., 145–9, 196, 199, 209, 220, 255, 262
  financial plans, 152–3, 155, 177–9, 183–4
  financial system, 209, 228–33, 255–6
  heavy, 86, 90, 95, 101, 103, 103 n., 120, 124, 140, 141 n., 146–7, 149, 150, 151, 159, 164, 181 n., 194, 197, 205, 212, 226, 235, 246, 255, 274–9, 292, 299, 312, 315, 317, 317 n., 323, 324, 341; NK of, 300–1
  incentives, 162–4
  investment, 85–7, 88, 90–2, 94, 97, 101–4, 120, 130 n., 147, 150, 163, 166, 187, 194, 198, 205, 228, 255, 258–9, 334

361

industry (cont.)
  light, 86, 91, 95, 101, 103, 141 n., 149, 164, 173, 185 n., 235, 274, 278, 292, 317 n., 324; NK of, 300–1
  loans from, 126–7, 225
  local, 56 n., 75, 182, 207
  location, 336
  norms, 255
  planning, 95–6, 104, 134, 139, 152, 207, 322–3
  prices, 50, 51, 55–6, 87, 88 n., 89, 91–3 n., 95, 101, 140, 228, 247, 253, 278, 315
  private, 95, 98, 109, 113, 139, 224
  production, 26, 29, 49, 54, 85, 87, 91, 93, 100, 101, 105, 106, 132, 140, 207
  productivity, 87
  profit motive, 71, 71 n., 97 n., 206, 207, 209, 276–7, 279, 324
  profits, 119–20, 136, 147, 150, 165–7, 198, 206, 208, 228, 243, 255, 278, 321, 321 n.
  régime of economy, 104–5
  self-financing, 3, 102, 104, 106, 124, 145, 147, 195, 255–6, 278–9
  Stalin's view of, 247
  subsidies, 102, 165–6, 237, 237 n., 238, 243, 317
  supervision by tax inspectors, 274–5, 317
  taxation, 6, 55 n., 68, 74, 74 n., 101, 110, 111, 113, 113 n., 118, 211–13, 214, 274–5, 292, 317
  transfer prices, 90, 119, 247, 255
  varying rates of profit, 277–8, 317, 320 n., 323–4
  wages, 251
  working capital, 157; *see also* capital, working
inflation, 51–4, 101, 174, 194–8, 217, 225, 227, 242, 248, 251, 279, 337, 340
  control of, 26–7, 90, 145, 227, 251, 273
  of credits, 230
  of estimates, 24, 31, 53
  of industrial costs, 237
  excises under, 122
  investment, 87–9, 94, 97, 130 n., 136, 150, 194, 208, 340
  issues, 89, 104
  loan repayment, 125 n.
  and moneyless system, 40
  problem, 16, 36–7, 89–90, 323, 340
  savings and, 90, 100, 145
  shortages and, 236, 273
  suppression of, 90–1, 93–4, 197, 227, 244, 317–18
  wages, 159, 227, 315, 322, 343
  war, 7, 10, 16, 22, 25, 28–9, 227, 315–16
innovation, 180, 323, 325–9, 332–5

inspection, 242, 261, 271–2, 273
  NK of Workers' and Peasants' (NK RKI), 35, 55 n., 60, 66 n., 80, 200, 200 n., 201–2, 208, 242
  see also control
insurance, 153
  cattle, 252
  farm, 170–1
  see also social insurance
interest, rate of, 44, 141, 146, 161, 333
  agriculture, 134–5, 172
  loans, 69–70, 125–7, 134, 146–7, 261, 281–2
  savings, 128, 144–5
interest, tax on, 4, 42
Internal Affairs, NK of (NKVD), 17 n., 19, 19 n., 33, 33 n., 34 n., 42, 249–51
invalids, 56, 57, 169, 302
investment, 3, 86–7, 90, 92, 98, 100, 106, 132, 148–9, 155, 163, 182, 184–5, 189, 194
  above-limit, 207, 235–6, 256–7, 326, 330
  accumulation, 87, 106, 144, 150, 178
  agriculture, 171–4, 178
  below-limit, 256, 334
  budget, 107, 118, 136, 150, 160, 191, 268
  centralisation, 207, 330
  choice between projects, 140, 206, 206 n., 235
  compilation of estimates, 234–7, 255, 332
  control, 134, 146–7, 149, 155, 205–8, 229, 233, 243, 255, 261, 301, 302, 315, 317, 326, 338, 341
  costs, 321
  decentralised, 163, 172, 179, 188, 256, 326, 326 n., 330, 332, 334
  defence, 251
  financing, 136, 146, 147 n., 147–50, 209, 244, 255–6, 261 n., 277, 278–9, 335
  fixed, 194
  in industry, 85, 90–3, 102–3, 130 n., 148–9, 187, 197–8, 205, 226, 228, 247, 253, 299, 341
  industries, 151, 198, 258–9
  inflation, 340
  illegal, 181
  loans, 69–70, 125–6, 134, 145–7, 209
  'methods 1 and 2', 147–52, 162, 195, 278, 337–8
  per capita, 305
  plans and programmes, 88–9, 96–7, 100, 120, 147–9, 150, 152, 155, 160–3, 167, 172, 177–9, 188–9, 193, 198, 199, 206–7, 216, 220–1, 232, 236–7, 256, 267, 269, 278, 299, 326, 327, 330, 336–8, 340
  prices, 140, 320
  private, 100
  private savings and, 144, 340

investment (*cont.*)
  profits as source for, 134, 147–8, 162, 277, 324, 331
  sources of, 101–3, 133, 146–7, 208–9, 234, 255–6
  transport and posts, 135–6, 239
  in West, 95 n., 340–1
  working capital, 209–10, 232
  see also building; capital; capital goods; contract; construction
iron and steel, 3, 228, 317 n., 329, 332 n.

Kaktyn', A., 88 n., 89, 105
Kalinin, M. I., 115 n.
Kaluga, compulsory to read *Pravda* in, 18 n.
Kaplan, N. M., 163 n., 279 n.
Kaser, M. C., 318, 319 n.
Katsenelenbaum, Z. S., 103 n., 107 n., 145, 145 n.
Katzenellenbaum, S. S., 29 n., 31
Kazakh S.S.R., 298, 305, 307, 310, 329
kerosene, tax on, 4, 6, 51 n., 58 n., 64 n., 122, 122 n., 123, 218, 246, 287, 288, 290, 291, 291 n.
Kharlamov, I., 319 n.
khozraschot, 73, 79, 93, 132, 154 n., 159, 180, 184, 185, 214, 215, 230, 234, 239, 261 n., 262–4, 267, 303, 304, 335 n., 338
  administration, 132, 143 n.
  budget, 185, 252, 297
  construction, 233, 258
  control, 154, 208, 272–80
  investment, 95, 251
  legal definition, 71, 71 n., 97
  profits and the budget, 119, 119 n., 120, 220
  subsidies and, 160, 238
Khrushchev, N. S., 320 n., 330 n.
Kiparisov, M., 162 n., 257 n., 261 n.
Kirghiz S.S.R., 79, 185 n., 298, 307, 310
Kirzhner, A., 323 n.
Kisman, N., 331 n.
Kistenev, S. T., 196 n.
Klepikov, S., 44 n.
Kondrashev, D., 331 n.
Kondratiev, 91
Kozlitin, I. P., 35 n.
Kozlov, G. A., 15 n., 16 n., 114 n., 115 n., 116, 126, 127 n., 161 n., 165 n., 242 n., 270 n., 271 n., 312 n.
Krestinskii, N., xxi, 19, 19 n., 23 n., 27 n., 32 n., 33 n., 34 n., 35 n., 36 n., 53 n., 280 n.
Kreve, 44
Kritsman, L., 59 n.
Kronrod, Ya., 144 n., 161 n., 164 n., 333 n.
Krylov, P., 330 n.

kulaks, 86, 100, 114, 116, 222, 223, 223 n.
  see also collective farms; peasants
Kutler, P. N., 118 n.
Kuznetsov, 100 n.

labour
  allocation of, 96, 139, 144, 146, 180, 227, 248
  bidding for, 181, 337
  construction, 206, 234, 257
  control of, 49
  costs, 237, 277, 333
  -days, 170, 171
  discipline, 104, 320
  force, 197, 214, 327, 338
  -intensive products, 164 n., 324, 336
  norms, 255, 260
  People's Commissariat of (NK Trud), 60, 78–80, 264, 265
  plan, 99, 139, 141, 184, 197, 248, 330
  priorities, 227
  productivity, 14, 91, 92, 104, 105, 158–9, 195–7 n., 227, 244, 319, 320, 327, 339 n., 339–40
  safety, 266 n., 296
  shortage of, 95, 159, 227, 248, 327
  skilled, 159, 227
  -statistics index, 53
  tax, 52 n., 68, 76, 110
  transfer of, 144, 146, 198, 209, 226, 315, 323
  units, 40 n., 44, 53 n., 141
  unskilled, 327, 329, 338
Labour and Defence, Council of (STO), 45, 71, 207, 236
land, 5, 14, 17 n., 21, 27 n., 42, 86, 114, 167, 263, 311, 311 n., 312
landowners, 6, 12 n., 86
Lange, O., 140 n.
Larin, Yu., 66 n., 110 n.
leather goods, tax on, 22 n., 202, 288, 289, 292
Left oppositions, 40 n., 91, 114
Lenin, V. I., 11, 12 n., 13 n., 14–16, 17 n., 18–20, 21 n., 22 n., 23 n., 40 n., 41 n., 50
levy, 18, 20 n., 29, 33, 52 n., 55 n., 67, 82, 120, 201, 295
  agricultural tax, 293–4
  capital, 112, 222
  collective farm markets, 311, 312
  cultural and housing, 175, 182, 222, 225, 295
  equalising, 6, 66, 214
  local, 56 n., 76, 182, 216 n.
Liberman, M., 319 n., 325 n., 328 n. 333 n., 335 n.
licence fee, 6, 66, 111, 121, 202, 311
Lifits, M. M., 251 n.

363

loan(s), 42, 69–70, 72 n., 90–1, 119, 124–8, 176, 225, 253, 295, 311 n., 334
    agriculture, 134–5, 170, 172–4
    amounts, 82, 83, 109, 124, 225, 282, 295
    bank, 99, 101, 102, 104, 147, 148, 154, 154 n., 155, 208, 209, 253
    budget, 125, 130, 295, 296, 316
    commissions, 127–8
    compulsory, 9, 70, 70 n., 127
    conversion, 225–6, 281
    of economic restoration, 103–4, 126
    to finance economy, 72–3, 102–3, 145–7, 205
    foreign, 21, 21 n., 101, 124–5
    industrialisation, 16, 127 n., 128 n., 145
    investment, 87
    Liberty Loan, 9, 12 n.
    local, 33 n., 34 n., 56, 76, 309, 311 n., 313
    long-term, 134, 155
    lottery, 127, 127 n., 226
    propaganda for, 127–8
    raising, 175, 226, 281, 282
    rate of interest, 69–70, 125, 126–7, 134, 145–7, 261, 281–2
    repayment, 134, 145–7, 148, 198, 280–1, 282
    uses of, 8, 9, 16, 19, 70, 125, 129, 134
    see also credits
local budget and finance, 7, 7 n., 17, 17 n., 18–20, 30, 33–6, 42, 55, 56, 70, 74–7, 81, 83, 84, 130, 135, 153, 164, 177, 182–3, 233 n., 275, 297 ff., 330, 336
    control by centre, 77, 242, 266, 297–8, 326
    decentralisation, 329, 330, 336
    district (*raion*) finance, 299 n., 312
    district (*uyezd*) finance, 77, 117, 117 n.
    education expenditure, 7, 56, 77, 77 n., 182, 264, 298–9, 301, 302, 313
    health expenditure, 7, 56–7, 130 n., 132 n., 148, 254, 264–5, 296, 301, 337
    province (*gubernia*) finance, 7, 27, 77, 115 n.
    regional (*oblast'*) finance, 222, 299 n., 300
    relations with central budget, 34–5, 42, 54–5, 56, 74–9, 81, 152, 154, 182, 186, 297–8, 303, 304, 317, 329, 330, 336, 338
    social and cultural expenditure, 240
    town finance, 7, 77, 299 n., 312
    village finance, 7, 84, 91, 225, 225 n., 299, 312
    volost' finance, 7, 77, 77 n., 84, 117, 298–9, 299 n.
    see also taxation, local; soviets, local
Lokshin, E. Yu., 187 n.
Lomako, 330 n.
Long-term Credit Bank, *see* Industrial Bank

Lorimer, F., 307
lorry, price of, 228
lottery, 69–70, 127, 127 n., 175, 226, 226 n.
Lozovskii, 23 n.
luxury goods, tax on, 12 n., 13, 21, 111, 111 n., 121, 121 n., 122–3, 290
Lyashchenko, P., 9

Machine-Tractor Stations (MTS), 143 n., 167, 168, 172–4 n., 176 n., 239, 239 n., 262–4, 281, 291, 295, 302, 313 n., 332
machinery, 22 n., 227, 237, 257, 258
    shift-norms, 255, 260
    see also equipment
Magidovich, I., 69 n.
Maizenberg, 331 n., 332 n.
management, 162–4, 197, 227, 248, 257, 323, 333
Margolin, N. S., 178 n.
market, 28, 41, 50–2 n., 54, 69, 87–8, 94, 98, 139–41, 187, 230
    abolition of, 29, 30, 39, 40, 49, 140
    black, 30, 198 n., 219, 237
    collective farm, 139, 168–73, 177, 181, 251, 251 n., 283, 294, 311, 312, 315
    determination of investment by, 85, 86, 140–1, 186
    free, 142, 168, 172, 177, 245, 293, 314, 315, 341
    illegal, 89, 139–40, 328
    interest rates on, 126, 134
    prices, 32, 89, 93, 140, 141, 282
    reappearance of, 50, 50 n., 55, 56, 140 n., 336
mark-up, *see* price
Marx, K., 10, 10 n., 11, 11 n., 13, 40, 50, 333 n.
matches, tax on, 4, 42, 51 n., 123, 218, 248 n., 287, 288, 289 n., 292
material bank, 41 n.
material budget, 40 n., 41, 53 n.
material plan, 98, 183, 199
materials, 28–9, 51, 56 n., 118, 183, 192, 329
    agricultural raw, 86, 139, 143 n., 172, 238, 290
    allocation of, 28–32, 96, 97, 144, 146, 151, 164, 180, 181, 209, 226, 227, 315, 323, 326, 331
    construction, 206, 234
    costs, 165, 166, 247, 260, 319, 321
    norms, 105, 255, 260
    plans, 98, 99, 141, 183, 188, 199, 239–40
    pricing, 95, 105, 143, 149, 322
    scramble for, 181, 236, 273, 323, 337
    stocks, 157, 231
meat, 246, 286, 293
Mensheviks, 9

Menzhinskii, V. P., xxi, 15 n., 16 n.
metal, price of, 237
    tax on, 288
metallurgical industry, 201, 329
Michelson, A. M., 7 n., 9 n., 123
Mikoyan, A., 94 n., 318 n., 339 n.
Military Affairs, NK of, 23 n., 79, 131
Military Health, Administration of, 131
milk, price of, 228
Milyutin, V. P., 33 n.
Ministers, Council of, 317, 326, 330, 335 n.
Mitlyanskii, Yu., 56 n.
Molotov, V. M., 7 n., 257 n., 274
money, 10–12, 12 n., 13 n., 18 n., 20 n., 39, 49, 51, 52, 58, 86, 87, 94, 98, 101, 144, 147, 176, 180, 198, 207
    abolition, 40, 41, 41 n., 53
    decline in use of, 30, 35, 38, 39, 141, 141 n.
    essentialness of, 41, 55, 142–4, 342
    revival, 50–5
    wages, 51, 52, 142, 147, 342
Moscow, 23 n., 27 n., 79, 81
municipal economy, 75, 153, 233 n., 234, 296, 297, 302, 311

national debt, 3, 8, 15, 15 n., 70, 125, 126, 128, 128 n.
National Economic Accounts (Reports), Central Administration of (TsUNKhU), 236 n.
    see also statistics, Administration
national economic plan, 136, 153, 153 n., 177–8, 183, 185–8, 190–2, 206, 234, 267, 269, 299, 302, 313, 326, 330
    and the budget, 186–90, 191–2, 299, 302, 306
    compilation of, 183–9
    control figures, 97, 99, 100, 131, 152, 153
National Economy, Council of (VSNKh), 16 n., 17, 21 n., 23, 23 n., 30 n., 32 n., 37 n., 38, 42, 44, 59, 71, 73, 79, 80, 102, 108 n., 132, 207–9, 211, 212 n., 219, 236, 300
national income, 3, 6, 6 n., 118, 125, 130, 153, 153 n., 343
    amount, 107, 152
    and budget, 99, 107, 121, 225
    investment and, 86, 194
    rise in, 108 n., 129, 129 n., 131, 321
nationalities, policy towards, 78
Nationalities, Soviet of, 186
navy, 5, 249, 250, 291
    NK of, 23 n., 131, 131 n.
Neiman, G., 219 n.
Nekrasov, N., 333 n.
nepmen, 67, 100, 109, 112, 122

Neusypin, A. A., 99 n., 107 n.
New Economic Policy (N.E.P.), 20, 25, 35, 50–1, 53, 67 n., 90, 98, 100, 110, 141, 225, 226, 338
    banking under, 71–2, 72 n.
    budget and, 54, 60, 60 n., 61, 79, 193, 199
    inflation, 90
    private sector, 109-10, 122
    state industry, 70–4
    tax apparatus, 51, 51 n., 199, 200
Nikitskii, A. A., 61 n., 99 n., 132 n.
Nodel', V., 219 n.
non-commodity operations, tax on, 218, 219–20, 295, 313 n.
norms, 39 n., 44, 57, 61, 68 n., 105, 114, 190, 190 n., 192, 192 n., 223, 231, 232, 241, 248, 255, 259, 260, 264, 266, 270, 282–3, 283 n., 303, 304, 312, 317, 319, 326, 331, 333, 339

Obolenskii, L., 20 n.
obsolescence, 151, 160, 161, 333, 333 n.
oil, 122, 228, 235 n., 246, 291, 292, 329, 332
    see also kerosene; fuel
Orlov, A., 80 n., 336 n.
Ostrovityanov, K., 11 n.
Ovcharenko, 114 n.
'over-all budget', defined, 84 n.
overall financial plan, 152, 178–9, 182
    see also financial plan
overheads, 93, 105, 119, 133, 165, 166, 187, 208, 237, 238, 319, 334
overtime, 159
Oxley, V. J., 190 n.

Padeiskii, N. A., 107 n.
Paevskii, V., 335 n.
paper, 22 n., 235 n., 290 n.
parish, see *volost'*
payments, abolition of, 39, 41
    reintroduction of, 52, 52 n., 55–6
pay offices (*kassy*), 6, 66, 203, 205, 269
peasants, 14, 26, 49, 50, 86, 109, 124, 134–5, 193, 198 n., 315, 340
    better-off, 114–16, 134, 135
    budget, 77 n., 84
    Committees of Poor, 26, 28
    compulsory deliveries, q.v.
    discrimination by state against different groups, 109, 113–14, 134, 175, 222
    food supplies by, 86, 87, 89, 90–1, 194, 197
    grain loans, 69
    hoards, 28, 29 n., 315
    income assessment, 68, 115 n., 116, 117, 117 n., 223

peasants (cont.)
  loans from, 127 n., 128, 128 n., 134–5, 226, 282
  opposition of, 49, 91, 92
  poorer, 109, 114, 115, 115 n., 116, 134, 135
  purchasing power, 88–94, 97, 294, 320–1
  and régime of economy, 104–5
  scissors crisis, 63 n.
  taxation, q.v.
  see also agriculture; collective farms
Pegov, N. M., 330 n.
pensions, 56, 130 n., 165, 249, 252, 254, 264, 265, 265 n., 266, 301, 302, 339
People's Bank (temporary name of State Bank, 1917–18), 15, 24
Pergament, I., 61 n.
Petrograd, 12 n., 17 n., 23 n., 27 n.
petrol, see fuel; kerosene; oil
plan(s), 96, 141, 181, 181 n., 184, 206, 277, 329, 342
  1941, 187, 187 n., 202–3
  accumulation, 152–4, 177, 200
  aims of, 97, 141
  bank loan, 154
  capital repair, 160
  cash, 177, 184
  circulation, 231
  compilation of, 182–6, 196, 210, 235, 328
  construction, 260, 299
  co-ordination with budget, 98 n., 136, 152
  costs, 96, 97, 105, 147, 149, 150, 162–3, 186–7, 197, 220, 227, 230, 248, 275, 277, 330
  credit, 99, 134, 145, 152, 167, 176, 177, 184, 191 n., 229, 230
  currency issue, 154
  economic, 98 n., 99, 100, 136, 158, 179, 186, 189, 204, 336
  financial, 97–100, 133, 136, 145, 150, 152–4, 158, 173, 176, 177–9, 183–4, 186, 189, 195, 196–7, 204, 209, 210, 221, 231, 240, 278, 285 n., 327
  five-year plans, 181 n., 193: first, 86, 90, 97, 99, 106, 139, 141, 145, 150, 159, 161 n. 174, 178, 194–200, 203–4, 210, 211, 222, 226–7, 242, 244, 248, 251, 256 n., 257, 300, 304, 312, 340; second, 174, 178, 242–3, 244, 245 n., 246, 246 n., 248, 257, 264; fifth, 328
  illegalities, 181
  industrial, 104
  investment, 96–7, 147–9, 155, 160, 162, 167, 172, 177–9, 188, 193, 198–9, 206–7, 216, 220–1, 232, 236–7, 256, 267, 269, 299, 326, 327, 330, 336–8, 340
  labour, 99, 139, 141, 184, 197, 248, 330
  livestock, 328
  material, 98, 99, 141, 183, 188, 199, 239–40
  national economic, q.v.
  operative, 179, 183–4, 186
  overall financial, 152, 178–9, 182
  in physical terms, 98–100, 133, 141, 147, 204
  production, 96–8, 108, 127, 134, 141, 158–9, 162, 164, 171, 178, 181, 184, 187, 188, 192, 197, 199, 207, 209, 216, 220–1, 227, 229, 231, 248, 263, 273, 275, 277, 285 n., 322–3, 327, 333, 337
  profit, 120, 141, 158, 163, 164, 178, 200, 275
  régime of economy, 104–5
  revenue, 100
  supply, 184, 187, 187 n., 229, 231, 331
  tax, 274
  trading, 177, 179, 231
  unified financial, 152–4, 155, 177–9
  wage, 158–9, 174–5, 179, 188, 248, 267, 269, 275, 337
planned economy, 10, 11, 13, 25, 50, 87, 117, 125, 136, 140, 144, 145, 148–9, 153, 159, 179, 230, 243, 247, 342
planners, 96, 140, 153, 178, 181, 191, 196, 206, 206 n., 235, 284–5, 285 n., 315, 322, 327, 332 n., 333, 336
planners' plans, 179
planning, 11, 229, 329
  agriculture, 167, 171, 172–4, 181, 181 n., 193, 328
  balance, 179, 179 n., 183
  bodies, 87, 117
  decentralisation, 180–1, 328
  decisions, 140–1, 180–1
  direct, 95–6, 96 n., 98, 98 n., 139, 141, 145–6, 151, 153, 171, 178–9, 181–2, 193, 314, 322, 326–7, 331, 336, 338–43
  financial, q.v.
  indirect, 167
  industry, 11, 97, 165, 172, 181 n., 193, 207
  investment, 207, 209
  limitations, 322–6, 327–35
  local finance, 182, 302
  powers, 327
  and price mechanism, 94–5, 95 n., 118, 140, 142–3, 147, 158, 178, 181, 215
  private sector, 95
  profitability, 141
  revenue, 174–6
  savings, 145
  stages in, 182–6, 207, 207 n.
  State Planning Commission, see Gosplan
  synthetic, 179, 179 n., 183, 236, 266
  system, 140 n., 181, 206, 299
  tax, 200–1, 214–15

366

planning (*cont.*)
  transport, 135–6
  Western, 94–5, 95 n., 327
  and wishes of people, 180 n.
platinum, monopolised by state, 16
Plotnikov, K. N., 107, 212 n., 215 n., 223, 266 n., 277 n., 280, 282 n., 295, 300, 318
ploughland as unit of taxation, 68, 117
Polanyi, M., 96 n.
Polyudov, 77 n.
Pomanskii, M., 331 n.
Pontovich, E. E., 35 n.
Popova, O., 55 n.
posts and postage, 4, 6, 12 n., 17 n., 39 n., 42, 55, 55 n., 65, 70, 73, 79, 80, 82, 83, 129, 130, 133, 135–6, 204, 240 n., 302, 329
  and telegraphs, NK of, 107, 132
potatoes, 286 n., 288, 289, 290, 339 n.
Potyaev, 34 n.
Preobrazhenskii, E. A., 53 n., 66 n.
price, 10, 56, 93, 108 n., 141, 228, 231, 339
  agricultural, *see* agriculture
  agricultural cf. industrial, 89, 92, 93, 95, 101, 143, 178, 205
  artificial, 95, 140 n., 142, 150, 227
  bureaux of checks, 260
  capital repair, 160–1, 333
  commercial, 219, 245
  compulsory deliveries, *see* 'procurement prices'
  consumer goods, 122, 189, 224, 228, 238, 244, 246, 248, 251, 314, 321, 331, 332, 335–6
  control, 197, 328, 339, 340
  costs and, 104, 105, 140, 142, 150, 237
  determination of, 87, 140–1, 142–3, 144, 243, 245, 277, 331, 331 n., 332 n., 339
  dual, 160, 324
  increases, 159, 175, 198, 227–8, 245, 314, 337
  indices, 9, 24, 29 n., 31, 53, 89, 187
  industrial, 71, 89, 92, 95, 101, 178, 218
  internal subsidies and, 160, 218
  labour units as, 44
  limits of planning, 322–6
  market, q.v.
  mark-ups, 22, 22 n., 115 n., 118, 124, 142, 150, 173, 211, 212, 212 n., 213, 218, 219 n., 283, 286, 288, 321, 342
  mechanism, 41, 87, 140, 200, 243, 245
  planning, 94–5, 95 n., 118, 140, 142–3, 147, 158, 178, 187, 215
  profits and, 164, 277
  ration, 219, 244, 245
  reduction, 93, 93 n., 94, 195, 195 n., 196, 247, 285 n., 318, 318 n., 319, 321, 321 n., 322, 339, 340, 340 n.

  reform, 245–6, 253, 316
  retail prices, q.v.
  stabilisation, 12 n., 93–4, 280
  state fixed, 28–9, 36–7, 56, 64 n., 93, 95, 117, 139, 141–4, 168, 191, 255, 281, 293, 303, 342
  subsidies, 160, 213, 238
  taxation and, *see* taxation
  transfer prices, q.v.
  wage cost, 143–4, 158–9
  wholesale prices, q.v.
priorities, 16, 38, 51, 86, 100, 156, 163, 164, 164 n., 227, 237, 240, 285
private ownership, 11, 50, 51, 90, 168, 239
private plots, 167, 170, 173, 223, 282
private sector, 51, 55, 55 n., 64, 65, 67–9, 71 n., 74, 75, 88, 95, 98, 100, 101, 109, 113, 121, 141, 144, 147, 199, 200, 201, 282–3, 342
  elimination of, 109–11, 139, 155, 224
procurement of agricultural products by state, 26, 28, 56, 91, 92, 109, 281, 286, 296, 302
  see also compulsory deliveries; peasants, food supplies by; requisitioning
'procurement prices' (compulsory delivery prices), 168–73, 224, 237–8, 244, 246, 248, 251, 286, 293, 314, 320, 320 n., 321, 341
producer goods, *see* capital goods
production, 26, 29, 32, 49, 58, 63, 85–6, 88–9, 91, 93, 100, 111, 132, 158, 197 n., 210
  agricultural, 139, 167–8, 172
  capacity, 85, 333 n.
  and consumer choice, 327, 336
  consumer goods, 88, 90, 91, 94, 140, 143, 144, 146, 173, 191, 195, 197, 198, 227, 245, 247, 285, 320, 320 n., 322, 335, 336, 337, 339
  control of, 11, 14, 127, 207, 272–4
  meetings, 105
  plan, 96–8, 108, 127, 134, 141, 158, 159, 162, 164, 171, 178, 181, 184, 187, 188, 192, 197, 199, 207, 209, 216, 220, 221, 227, 231, 263, 273, 275, 277, 285 n., 322, 327, 333, 337
productivity of labour, 14, 44, 91, 92, 94, 104, 105, 158–9, 188, 195, 196, 197, 197 n., 226–7, 236, 244, 265, 319, 320 n., 327, 339–40
  need to raise, 54, 93, 104
product-mix, 277, 323–4
profits, 64 n., 66 n., 71, 74, 102, 112, 119–20, 134, 141, 154, 158, 188, 208, 246, 277–8, 337
  accumulation via, 147, 152, 178, 193, 209, 213, 278

profits (*cont.*)
   on by-products from waste, 256
   capital replacement, 160–1
   control by, 180, 275–9, 338
   deductions from, 74, 74 n., 82, 109, 118, 119, 120, 124, 150, 155, 157, 165, 166, 167, 185, 190, 198, 200, 200 n., 211–13, 220–2, 277–8, 280, 295
   excess, 92, 93, 110, 111, 113
   glavk, 160, 212–13
   increasing, 119, 136, 192, 228, 277, 279, 321
   inflation and, 90
   and investment, 134, 147, 150, 155, 161, 189, 195, 205, 244, 255, 277, 279, 324, 335, 337
   less than planned, 162, 164, 189, 198
   motive, 141, 207, 209, 276–7, 269, 324
   'normal' level in private industry, 110
   plan, 120, 141, 158, 163, 164, 178, 187–9, 200, 275, 277–9
   rate of, 164, 164 n., 280, 321 n., 324
   retained, 134, 152, 163 n., 280
   'single tax' on, 211, 212 n., 295
   society's long-term, 141
   taxation of, 6, 7, 9, 20 n., 66 n., 71, 101, 103, 110–11, 113, 117, 119, 120, 149, 150, 163 n., 174, 189, 192, 211–13, 220–2, 226, 232, 242, 275, 277–80, 291, 311, 317, 318, 321, 331, 333, 342
   trading, 93, 94
   transport and posts, 135–6, 240
   variation in levels, 212–13, 274, 277–9, 317, 320 n., 323–4
   working capital met from, 157, 163 n., 189, 209, 220–1, 323
   see also Director's Fund; Fund for Improving the Workers' Welfare
Prokopovich, S. N., 6 n., 7 n., 24 n., 27 n., 33 n., 310, 335, 337
Prombank, *see* Industrial Bank
Promtax, 4, 6, 7, 27 n., 34 n., 42, 51, 55 n., 56 n., 58, 60 n., 64–6, 71, 74 n., 76, 83, 108, 110, 111, 113, 118–19, 119 n., 121, 122, 124, 150, 195, 199, 200, 200 n., 201–3, 211, 213, 214, 214 n., 216 n., 224 n., 297–8, 308 n., 309, 309 n.
property, 6, 11, 12, 12 n., 14, 17 n., 18, 21, 27, 28, 40, 75, 82, 280
   tax on, 13, 18, 22, 22 n., 26–7, 27 n., 42, 59, 67 n., 109–10, 342
provinces (*gubernii*), 7, 27, 77, 115 n.
purchasing power, 86, 88, 89, 89 n., 91, 92, 92 n., 93, 94, 97, 124, 125, 128 n., 142, 143, 145, 175, 177, 191, 194, 197, 200, 217, 244, 245, 251, 293–4
Pyatakov, 32 n., 56 n.

railways, 4, 6 n., 30, 45 n., 65, 70, 78, 80 n., 161, 205, 239, 240 n., 302, 322 n.
rationalisation, 106, 132, 163, 230 n.
rationing, 29, 57, 149, 198 n., 217, 219, 224, 227, 242–6, 261, 285, 286, 314, 316, 337
   abolition of, 50, 175, 236, 244–6, 247, 253, 264, 270, 280, 283, 284, 285
   replacing price system, 39, 44, 90, 141, 197
Red Cross Societies, 220 n.
Reingold, I., 123
rent, 6, 76, 112, 311, 311 n., 312
repair
   capital, q.v.
   Machine-Tractor Stations, 263 n., 267 n., 268
   machinery, 258
reparations, 321 n.
republics, 117, 128, 133, 133 n., 183–6, 207, 215, 223, 233 n., 242 n., 265
   budgets of, 60, 70, 78–81, 81 n., 84, 107, 135, 182, 185, 271, 297–315, 317, 326, 329–30, 336, 338
requisitioning, 26, 28–30, 38, 49, 50, 68, 69
research, 135–6, 165, 239, 266 n., 267 n.
Resettlement Committee, 134
retail distribution, 139, 141, 144, 147
retail market, 92, 94, 97, 151, 155, 159, 173, 176–82, 198, 227, 237, 238, 242, 247, 284, 318, 339
retail prices, 88, 89, 91, 93, 94, 118, 122, 142, 143, 146, 148, 168, 173, 175, 177, 191, 194, 195, 200, 215, 217, 219, 228, 244–6, 277, 292, 314, 318, 318 n., 321, 343
   reform of, 253, 316
retail trade, 50, 121, 142, 149, 251 n., 253, 292, 310, 335, 337
rich, limitations of taxing the, 12 n., 13, 18, 21, 33, 109, 110, 115
Right opposition, 91, 108, 116, 196
roads, 220, 302
Robinson, E. A. G., 95 n.
Rovinskii, N. N., 161 n., 162 n., 163 n., 164 n., 187 n., 192 n., 234 n., 249 n., 254 n., 261 n., 262 n., 263 n., 265 n., 269 n., 272 n., 301, 302 n., 312 n., 313 n.
rubber, 123, 291 n., 292
Russian Soviet Federative Socialist Republic (R.S.F.S.R.), 79, 298, 305, 307, 310
Ryazanov, 17 n., 123 n.
Rykov, 71 n., 118 n., 280 n.

Safronov, A., 330 n.

sales tax, *see* turnover tax
salt, tax on, 58 n., 64 n., 67 n., 122, 122 n., 123, 218, 288, 289 n., 290 n.
savings, 86, 90, 101, 102, 106, 127, 127 n., 128 n., 136, 144, 175, 196, 340
  and investment, 144, 145, 147
  see also accumulation
savings banks, 126, 128, 128 n.
scissors crisis, 63, 63 n., 73, 91, 92, 93, 113
'self-taxation', *see* taxation
sel'khozbank, *see* agriculture, bank
Senin, I. S., 330 n.
Serkov, 21 n.
sewing machines, 22 n., 218, 288
Shakhnovskaya, S., 212 n.
Shavrin, V. A., 312 n.
Shefler, 40 n.
Shenger, Yu. E., 178 n., 185 n., 187 n., 248 n., 279 n., 285 n.
shipbuilding, 250
Shmelev, K., 38 n., 39 n., 44, 49 n., 77 n.
shoes, price of, 228
shops, 18 n., 171, 217, 219, 318
shortages, 123, 198 n., 236, 248, 286, 318, 322, 338, 339
  goods, 88, 89, 91–4, 108, 112, 159, 178, 191, 196, 197 n., 217, 227, 242, 246, 337, 339–40
  labour, 95, 159, 227
  materials, 227
sickness benefits, 56, 165, 252, 254, 264, 266
Simkin, 276 n.
Sirinov, N., 77 n., 80 n.
Sitnin, 276 n.
Skvortsov, I. I., xxi, 115 n.
Smilga, I., 154 n.
Smirnov, 18 n., 40 n.
Smit, M., 44 n.
Smit, O., 64 n., 99 n.
SNK, *see* Commissars, Council of People's
social and cultural expenditure, *see* culture; social services
social insurance, 57 n., 129, 130 n., 152, 153, 154, 165–7, 176, 177, 252, 295, 296, 300, 301, 302
  budget, 264–72, 300, 302
social security, 39 n., 42, 56–7, 129, 130 n., 296
social services, 54, 75, 88, 107, 129, 130–2, 191, 228, 239–41, 264–72, 296, 299, 305–6, 312, 316, 342
Sokol'nikov, G. Ya., xxi, 7 n., 15 n., 16 n., 17 n., 21 n., 23 n., 38 n., 53 n., 55 n., 56 n., 57 n., 59 n., 61 n., 62, 63 n., 64 n., 66 n., 69 n., 72 n., 73 n., 77 n., 99, 99 n., 114 n., 280 n.
Sokolov, A. A., 196 n.
Sosnovskii, V., 326 n., 331 n.

Soviet, Supreme, 183, 186, 267, 272 n.
Soviets, Central Executive Committee (TsIK or VTsIK), 16 n., 19, 21 n., 25, 34 n., 42, 59 n., 62, 75 n., 77 n., 78 n., 80 n., 81 n., 83, 99 n., 111, 111 n., 113, 115 n., 116, 118 n., 121 n., 122 n., 123 n., 124 n., 125 n., 126, 128 n., 131 n., 132 n., 133 n., 152 n., 153 n., 154 n., 161 n., 184 n., 204 n., 208 n., 223 n., 226 n., 237 n., 239 n., 240 n., 242 n., 249, 274 n., 282 n., 285 n., 304 n.
  budgets adopted by, 35, 36 n., 60, 124, 132 n., 152, 153, 153 n., 154, 186 n., 204, 297
  excises, attitude to, 122–3
  and financial planning, 152–3
  prohibition, views on, 124
  tax collection policy, 113
  'turnover' allocations, view of, 39 n.
Soviets, Congress of, 19, 25, 56 n., 57 n., 64 n., 67 n., 78, 106, 107, 109, 114, 117 n.
soviets, local
  executive committee, 20, 57, 271
  powers of, 14, 17 n., 56, 222–3, 297–8, 303, 313 n., 330, 336
  property of, 75
  revenues, 75–7, 306, 310–11
  services to Union bodies, 216
  supervision of industry, 274
  tax collection, 17, 21 n., 27, 75, 113, 190, 215
  see also local budget and finance
sovznak, 58, 63, 63 n.
sown area as tax unit, 68, 117, 223, 224, 281
Stalin, J. V., 27 n., 53 n., 92 n., 93 n., 99 n., 101 n., 104, 106, 108 n., 114 n., 118 n., 124 n., 128 n., 140, 141, 141 n., 196, 197 n., 230 n., 247, 249, 280 n.
State Bank
  bank machinery, 3, 12 n., 15, 71–2, 134, 205, 234, 272–3
  Bolshevik policy, 12 n., 15, 16
  budget and, 5, 73, 83, 272–3
  capital repair and, 166, 256, 334
  cash plan, 177
  control, 154 n., 229–30, 230 n., 241, 251, 260, 272–3, 275–6
  credit, 229–30, 230 n., 232, 276, 276 n., 316
  currency, 58
  efficiency control, 232, 234
  financing the economy, 16, 30, 134, 157, 158, 166, 176, 209, 229–30, 230 n., 232, 239 n., 256, 260, 262, 275–6, 276 n., 316, 334
  personnel, 57 n.

State Bank (*cont.*)
  planning, 154 n., 205
  taxation, 216
State Control Department, 6–8
State Expenditure, Committee for the Reduction of, 17
state ownership, 40, 50, 70, 139, 144, 167, 168, 205
State Security, NK of, 250 n.
statistics, 96, 113, 190
  Administration (TsSU), 44–5, 69 n., 100 n.
stocks, 56 n., 157, 159, 188, 189, 231, 233, 276, 302
  army, 249
  capital, 160–1, 324, 325, 332–5, 338
  construction, 258
  economic manœuvring, 86
  machine-tractor stations, 263 n., 264
  norms, 231, 317
Strumilin, S. G., 41 n., 44, 45 n.
Studenikin, S., 250 n.
subsidies, 17 n., 51, 76, 77 n., 81, 95, 167, 185, 189, 232, 238, 239, 251, 263, 263 n., 267, 273, 298
  abolition, 246, 246 n., 248, 253, 274, 278, 317
  backward areas, 306–10
  hidden, 102, 249
  internal, 160, 213, 324
  losses, 159, 164, 165–6, 237, 238, 243, 315
  new products, 159, 238
  policy, 237–8
Suchkov, A. K., 283 n., 291 n.
sugar, 4, 6, 42, 51 n., 58 n., 69 n., 122, 123, 157, 202, 218, 228, 235 n., 291, 292
Supervision, NK of State, 35, 242 n.
supplies
  cash issues to obtain, 26, 28, 29
  centrally distributed, 32, 55
  compulsion to get, 28–9
  foodstuffs, 49, 50, 51, 85–7, 90–2, 94, 102, 194, 197, 244
  in kind, 51
  number in receipt of, 57
  see also materials
supply and demand equalisation, 91, 92, 151, 177–8, 191, 217, 245, 247, 284, 285–6, 286 n., 288–90, 292–4, 322, 327, 335, 336, 338, 342
surtax, 17 n., 20, 74 n., 306, 316
Sverdlov, 33 n.
synthetic balances, 179, 179 n., 183, 191
Syromolotov, 17 n., 41 n.

Tadjik S.S.R., 298, 307, 308, 308 n., 310
Tatarinov, 6, 6 n.

taxation and taxes, 6, 17 n., 18 n., 64, 67, 67 n., 68, 74, 108, 124, 136, 142, 147, 195, 198, 199, 225 n., 317
  agricultural, 58 n., 60 n., 67–70, 74, 82, 91, 108, 113–17, 124, 170, 171, 173, 174, 190, 222–4, 225, 281, 282, 295, 297–8, 306, 308, 309, 313, 316, 321 n.
  apartment, 111, 112, 112 n.
  assessment, 68, 113, 117, 117 n., 221, 223
  on bachelors, 316
  cinemas, 218, 219–20, 287 n., 311
  civil tax, 52 n.
  collection, 7, 17, 20, 27, 27 n., 51, 75, 81, 112–13, 215, 274, 280
  collective farms, 142, 190, 222–3, 223 n., 281–2, 294–5
  control, 154, 274–5, 317
  co-operatives, 111, 221 n.
  defaulters, 280
  direct, 6, 9, 10, 12 n., 20, 20 n., 21, 22 n., 27, 42, 59, 64 n., 65, 67, 68, 70, 75, 81, 109, 110, 112–13, 115, 117, 118, 121, 147 n., 174, 175, 191, 200, 223, 224, 224 n., 252, 280, 297–8, 308, 309, 316, 318
  discrimination by, 68–9, 70, 110–12, 175, 199, 222, 223, 285 n., 289
  double, 202, 214 n.
  employers, 110–12
  enterprises, 68, 113, 200–1, 201 n., 202–3, 211–13, 214, 214 n., 215, 218, 220, 309
  equalising, 66, 111, 112, 214
  exemptions, 114, 115, 115 n., 176, 223, 274, 280
  Extraordinary Revolutionary, q.v.
  glavk and, 212–13, 275
  in ideal economy, 118
  in kind, 21 n., 22 n., 28, 28 n., 41 n., 49, 52, 58, 60 n., 67 n., 68–9, 69 n., 198 n., 224, 246, 293, 341
  income tax, q.v.
  indirect, 4, 6, 7, 9, 11 n., 12 n., 13, 20, 21, 22, 22 n., 28, 42, 64, 64 n., 65, 68, 121, 200, 309
  inheritance, 112
  limits of planning, 118, 144, 322
  local, 17, 17 n., 18, 19, 19 n., 20, 33, 35, 55 n., 56, 56 n., 75, 75 n., 76, 110, 182, 201, 216, 295, 304, 306–11, 312
  of luxuries, 12 n., 13, 21, 121; *see also* turnover tax
  of necessities, 21, 64 n.; *see also* turnover tax
  peasantry, 21 n., 22 n., 27, 27 n., 58, 60 n., 64 n., 67 n., 68–9, 74, 77, 84, 91, 109, 113–17, 173, 175, 222, 281, 293

taxation and taxes (*cont.*)
  planning, 118, 144, 274, 322
  policy, 12, 13, 40, 109, 145, 148, 200–3
  poll-tax, 52
  prices and, 21 n., 22, 142, 145, 200–2, 212–13, 215, 217, 281, 294
  of private sector, 109–13
  progressive, 7, 22 n., 67 n., 69, 109, 110, 113, 115 n.
  of property, 13, 18, 22, 22 n., 26–7, 27 n., 42, 59, 67 n., 109–10, 342
  rates of, 112–15, 122, 124, 284–9, 292–4
  reform, 84, 110, 200–3, 211-13, 220, 229, 242, 309
  republican, 81, 304–11
  revenue, 28, 51–2, 58–60, 74, 82, 87, 90, 94, 102, 103, 108, 118, 136, 146, 147, 216, 216 n., 295, 306
  RKI report on, 200–1
  'self-taxation' in villages, 91, 225, 225 n., 266 n., 312
  single tax on profits, 211, 212 n., 295
  skims off purchasing power, 92, 93, 94, 101, 118, 198, 219, 227
  soul-, 6
  stamp-, 199, 308, 308 n., 311
  super-, 113
  supplementary, 68, 68 n., 110
  turnover tax, q.v.
  vehicles, 311
  war, 7–8, 10, 110 n., 316
tea, tax on, 42, 51, 122, 123
teachers, 16 n., 56 n., 77 n., 175, 176, 190
technical crops, 224, 281, 282
telegraphs, *see* posts and postage
telephone, 55 n., 56 n., 204
textiles
  industry, 120, 277, 277 n.
  prices, 248, 248 n.
  tax on, 58 n., 123, 203, 214, 248, 292
timber
  cost of, 188
  grants to industry, 16 n., 185 n.
  tax on, 42, 65, 76, 81, 82, 216 n., 292, 311, 322, 332
title-list (*titul'nyi spisok*), 207, 234, 235, 326, 330
tobacco, tax on, 4, 6, 17 n., 42, 51 n., 58 n., 122, 200, 200 n., 202, 218, 246, 287, 287 n., 288, 292
Tolstomyatov, 45 n.
Torgulov, N., 33 n.
town, 3, 7, 194
  discontent, 49
  food, 49, 91, 197
  loans, 69–70
  price ratio, 92, 93

private trade in, 109–13, 139
purchasing power of, 88, 91, 94, 142, 175, 197
taxes, 27, 59, 67, 77, 109–13, 115; *see also* taxation
trade, 52, 58, 88, 316, 336
  Bank, 71 n., 119, 120, 134, 166, 208, 209
  budget allocation, 83, 130, 296, 302
  co-operative, 50, 88, 93, 109, 139, 251 n., 318, 318 n.
  costs, 93, 94, 187, 188
  foreign, 79, 80, 302
  illegal, 30
  NK of Internal, 218, 219
  levy, 20 n., 56 n.
  Ministry of, 4, 335
  money, 49, 50, 58
  plan, 153, 177, 179, 215
  prices, 89, 93, 94
  private, 67, 90, 95, 98, 109, 112, 113, 139–40, 224
  republican control of, 79
  state agencies, 93, 139, 142, 173, 198 n., 202, 219, 233 n., 247, 251 n., 292, 318, 318 n., 335
  taxation of, 6, 55 n., 110, 113, 274, 292
  terms of, 89
  see also market; retail; wholesale
Trade Union, 24, 49, 71, 91, 119 n., 127, 165, 252, 265–6, 265 n., 266 n.
transactions in kind, 38–45, 52–5, 73, 168, 172, 174, 262
Transcaucasus, 7, 80, 80 n., 289 n., 298, 305, 307, 308 n., 309, 310
  see also Armenian; Azerbaijan; Georgian S.S.R.'s
transfer prices, 90, 119, 147, 148–9, 159, 164, 166, 167, 177, 187, 189, 195, 198, 209, 212, 213, 218, 220, 237, 238, 243, 247, 255, 262, 278 n., 287, 290, 293, 321
  gap between t.p. and costs used for accumulation, 158, 166, 195, 198, 220, 244, 277–9
  see also wholesale prices
transport, 4, 7, 38–9, 53, 55, 55 n., 56 n., 131, 153, 247, 250, 274, 305, 332
  army, 249
  budget, 73, 73 n., 80, 82, 83, 129, 130, 135 n., 239–40, 247 n., 297
  costs, 143, 160, 240, 260, 291, 292
  deficit, 73, 73 n., 74
  expenditure, 42, 65, 70, 75, 296, 302
  investment, 135–6, 233 n., 239–40
  NK of, 42, 45, 73, 73 n., 79, 107, 132, 305
  norms, 61
  priorities in, 237, 240
  road, 220, 302

371

Tsar, budgetary powers, 6, 9
Tsekombank, 234
Tsyurupa, 62
Tugan-Baranovskii, 9
Turetskii, Sh., 29 n., 105, 161 n., 237 n., 238 n., 275 n.
Turkmen S.S.R., 298, 305, 306, 307, 308, 308 n., 310
turnover tax, 64 n., 111, 113, 118, 121, 121 n., 150, 155, 173, 174, 174 n., 176 n., 177, 185, 189, 190, 192, 193, 202–3, 211, 211 n., 212, 212 n., 213–20, 238, 242, 243, 245–9, 252, 253, 274, 275, 278–80, 283 ff., 304, 309–10, 313, 316, 321, 331–2, 337–9, 341–2
   control, 274, 275, 275 n., 317
   control percentage, 274–5, 278, 317
   discrimination by, 286–7, 288, 289–90, 292–4, 336
   rates, 214–15, 216–20, 284–90, 290–2, 320, 321, 336
   reform, 213–20, 283–4
   revenue, 32, 167, 216, 216 n., 295, 316, 318, 321, 331
   supply and demand equalisation, 91, 92, 285–6, 286 n., 288–90, 292–4, 322, 336, 338

Ukraine, 55 n., 61 n., 66 n., 77, 78, 79, 80, 80 n., 117 n., 289 n., 298, 305, 307, 308 n., 310, 326, 329
unemployment, 88
   benefit, 56, 57 n., 254
Unified commissariat, 78, 79, 80, 80 n., 81, 297–8
   see also Union authorities
'unified state budget of the U.S.S.R.' defined, 84 n.
unified financial plan, 152–4, 154 n., 155, 177–9
   see also financial plan
Union authorities, 80, 81, 84, 84 n., 184–6, 207, 214, 215, 265 n., 271, 275, 297–8, 298 n., 329–30
Union, Soviet of, 186
United Nations, 90, 90 n., 251 n.
United States, 3, 190 n.
Uspenskii, V., 335 n.
Uzbek S.S.R., 298, 305, 306, 307, 308 n., 310

Varga, E., 45 n.
village, 7, 49, 77, 86, 109, 134–5, 281
   budgets, 84, 299
   'face to the village' campaign, 115
   soviet, 225, 299, 311
   see also agriculture; collective farms; taxation

Vladimirov, 67 n.
vodka, tax on, 64, 91, 121, 122, 123–4, 200, 200 n., 203, 246, 246 n., 287, 288, 292
volost', 7, 12 n., 77, 77 n., 84, 117, 298–9, 299 n.
Voronoff, 7 n.
Voroshilov, K., 131 n.
Voznesensky, N., 251 n., 292, 315 n.
Vsekobank, 234
Vul'ff, G., 125 n.

wage(s), 21, 26, 29, 32, 38 n., 44, 60, 71, 87, 101, 151, 192, 197, 198 n., 216, 227, 267 n., 368
   budget and, 57, 176, 198
   construction workers, 234, 255, 260, 261 n., 269
   control, 158–9, 197, 247, 251, 267, 269, 269 n., 270, 275, 315, 319, 322, 329
   costs, 57, 57 n., 90, 93, 143–4, 148, 159, 165, 166, 319
   differentials, 245
   earners, 88, 97, 144, 175, 294
   fund, 88, 95, 152, 165, 173, 178, 184, 187, 188, 190, 191, 227, 234, 244, 245, 245 n., 248, 249, 251, 251 n., 254, 264, 270, 276 n., 277, 281, 282, 319
   incentive, 162 n., 175, 227, 248
   increase in, 132, 225, 225 n., 315–16, 319 n.
   labour units, 44
   limits of planning, 118, 322
   Machine–Tractor Stations, 262, 263 n., 323
   money, 51, 52, 142, 147, 342
   norms, 61, 190, 248, 319, 339
   and output, 164, 247
   piece-rates, 319, 321 n., 323, 340
   plan, 118, 142, 147, 158–9, 174–5, 179, 188, 248, 248 n., 267, 269, 270, 275, 322
   policy, 91, 92, 95, 101, 118, 143, 323
   productivity, 101, 105, 158–9, 195, 319, 320 n., 339–40
   ratio to profit, 277
   railway, 240
   social insurance and, 165, 264
   state fixed, 20–2, 117, 142, 147, 255, 260, 270, 303, 342
   taxation, q.v.
   teachers, 77 n.
Weber, M., 328 n.
welfare, 170, 234, 265, 268, 326
   fund, *see* Fund for Improving the Workers' Welfare
wholesale prices, 119, 188, 200, 219, 228, 246, 283, 285, 286, 287, 316, 320, 321, 331 n., 332, 336

wholesale trade, 50, 89, 93, 94, 97, 148, 149
Wiles, P. J. D., 318 n.
wine, tax on, 122 n., 123, 288, 290
Witte, S., 3
workers, 51, 90, 104, 112, 130 n., 143, 165, 198, 245
  control, 11, 14, 49
  incentive to, 162 n.
  industrial, 21, 49, 50, 89, 92, 198
  loans to state by, 127, 226, 281, 282
  norms, q.v.

shock, 245
wages, q.v.

Yevreinov, 27 n.
Yurovskii, L. N., 9, 15 n., 29 n., 31, 45 n., 50 n., 52 n., 53, 58 n., 93 n., 196 n.

Zangvil', 107 n.
Zverev, A., xxi, 279 n., 318, 319 n., 326 n., 330 n., 334 n.
Zvorykin, A., 323 n.